MICHAEL COLLINS: DU

Michael Collins: Dublin 1916–22

Joseph E.A. Connell Jnr

Wordwell

To Pam

First published in 2017
Wordwell Ltd
Unit 9, 78 Furze Road, Sandyford Industrial Estate, Dublin 18
www.wordwellbooks.com

Cover image—Michael Collins and the Gresham Hotel, O'Connell Street (NLI).
Back cover—Michael Collins at Arthur Griffith's funeral (NLI).
Frontispiece: Michael Collins by Jim FitzPatrick.

ISBN 978-0-9933518-8-4

British Library Cataloguing-in-Publication Data.
A catalogue record for this book is available from the British Library.

All images © National Library of Ireland except where indicated.

Typeset in Ireland by Wordwell Ltd
Copy-editor: Emer Condit
Cover design and artwork: Ger Garland
Printed by Gráficas Castuera, Pamplona

Contents

Acknowledgements

I always thank my parents for everything; without them I would have had no such love for Ireland. And, of course, my brothers and sister and their families supported me at all times.

I am most grateful to Wordwell Ltd, and it has been a pleasure to work with Nick Maxwell, Dr Una MacConville, Helen Dunne and everyone at the publishing house. Emer Condit is a wonderful editor, and I cannot thank her enough. Tomás Ó Brogáin has produced beautiful maps. Everyone at Wordwell has added polish to my efforts and all their assistance is most appreciated.

Tommy Graham of *History Ireland* has been encouraging and helpful at all times. I am indebted to him for allowing me to write a 'Countdown' column in *History Ireland*.

Tom Duffy has been unstinting with his time and support, and his knowledge of Dublin, its history and its people is unequalled.

Clare Cowley has been indispensable for me in Ireland. Her care and advice are always most welcome.

Áine Broy, daughter of Ned Broy, has been an immense help to me and I thank her unreservedly.

My thanks to Anthony Tierney for his continuing advice and suggestions.

Dr Patrick Geoghegan and Susan Cahill have given me the privilege of a recurring spot on their NewsTalk radio show, *Talking History*. It has been a joy to work with them over the years and I am most grateful.

Mícheál Ó Doibhilín, the editor of www.kilmainhamtales.ie, has let me submit articles for his site and has published small books of mine under his imprint. His editing and guidance are much appreciated.

I greatly appreciate the advice and corrections of Revd Paul Connell, a fine author and historian.

I am especially grateful to Pól Ó Murchú, James Langton, Diarmuid O'Connor, Simon Draper and Terry Fagan for their assistance with the photographs.

I have always been welcomed throughout Ireland with the greatest kindness and hospitality, and I thank everyone with whom I've spoken. Those individuals who have helped and encouraged me are too numerous to mention and I thank them all. Everyone I asked always gave me assistance, reassurance and direction. All heartened me when I needed that most, and from time to time most fed me when I needed that most, too. At the risk of offending someone I omit, I must especially mention Ray Bateson, Catherine Bligh, Christy Burke, Lorcan Clancy, Bob Clarke, Dr Marie Coleman, Lorcan Collins, C.B. Connell, Briny M. Connell, Constance Cowley, Carla Cowley-Ralph, Críona Ní Dhálaigh, Carol Dooley, Myles Dungan, Kerry Edwards,

Bob Fuquea, Col. David Fuquea, Liz Gillis, Conor Goodman, Kevin Hannaway, James Connolly Heron, Barbara Hollandsworth, Grainne Áine Hollandsworth, Marcus Howard, Lar Joye, Peggy Keating, David Kilmartin, Dr Mary McAuliffe, Sinéad McCoole, Francie McGuigan, Jim McIlmurray, Mary Mackey, Brenda Malone, Barbara and Dominic Montaldi, Msgr Raymond Murray, Gregory O'Connor, Kevin O'Sullivan, Donal Ó hUallachain, Yetti Redmond, Nial Ring, Michael Smyth, Detta and Seán Spellissy, Arminta Wallace, John and Judy Wohlford, and Padraig Yeates.

And, always, Pam Brewster for all things.

Abbreviations

Ancient Order of Hibernians	AOH
Baronet	Bt
Criminal Investigation Division	CID
Defence of the Realm Act	DORA
Dublin Metropolitan Police. An unarmed force, its jurisdiction included the city of Dublin, Blackrock, Dalkey, Kingstown, Pembroke and Rathmines. The 'A' to 'F' Divisions were geographical. 'G' Division dealt with serious crime, including surveillance of political suspects and subversive movements.	DMP
Gaelic Athletic Association	GAA
General Post Office	GPO
Headquarters	HQ
Honourable	Hon.
Irish Citizen Army	ICA
Irish Trade Union Congress	ITUC
Irish National Aid and Volunteers' Dependants' Fund	INAVDF
Irish Republican Army. It is difficult to pinpoint when the Irish Volunteers became the Irish Republican Army. Under the direction of IRB men like Collins and Richard Mulcahy, as well as Cathal Brugha, who left the IRB, the Volunteers had been reorganised throughout the country after the Rising. The Volunteer newspaper *An tÓglach* ('The Young Warrior/ Soldier') stated that 'the Irish Volunteers are the Army of the Irish Republic' in December 1918. About this time the term 'Irish Republican Army' came into widespread use. The IRA was always distinct from the IRB, a secret society. In Irish it is *Óglaigh na hÉireann*. An individual member was usually called a 'Volunteer'. During the War of Independence they were referred to as the IRA/Volunteers. During the Civil War, those who were pro-Treaty fought in the Free State Army. The anti-Treaty forces took on the mantle of the IRA and were called the IRA/Republicans. Some sources refer to them as the 'Irregulars'.	IRA
Irish Republican Brotherhood	IRB
Irish Transport and General Workers Union	ITGWU
Irish Women's Workers' Union	IWWU
King's Counsel	KC
Member of Parliament	MP
Queen's Counsel	QC
Reverend	Revd
Royal Irish Constabulary. An armed, semi-military force, its jurisdiction extended to the entire country, except Dublin.	RIC
Teachta Dála	TD
Trinity College Dublin	TCD
University College Dublin (formerly the National University)	UCD

Military/rank abbreviations

Adjutant	Adj.
Aide-de-camp	ADC
Brigadier	Brig.
Captain	Capt.
Chief of Staff	C/S
Colonel	Col.
Commandant	Cmdt
First Lieutenant	1Lt
General	Gen.
General Officer Commanding	GOC
General Headquarters	GHQ
Headquarters	HQ
His Majesty's Ship	HMS
Lieutenant	Lt
Lieutenant Colonel	Lt Col.
Lieutenant General	Lt Gen.
Major-General	Major-Gen.
Officer Commanding	O/C
Quartermaster	QM
Second Lieutenant	2Lt
Sergeant	Sgt

British award/decoration abbreviations

Companion of the Most Honourable Order of the Bath	CB
Companion of the Most Eminent Order of the Indian Empire	CIE
Companion of the Most Distinguished Order of St Michael and St George	CMG
Distinguished Service Order	DSO
Grand Cross of the Bath	GCB
Grand Cross of the Most Distinguished Order of St Michael and St George	GCMG
Grand Cross of the Royal Victorian Order	GCVO
Knight Commander of the Most Excellent Order of the British Empire	KBE
Knight Commander of the Most Honourable Order of the Bath	KCB
Knight of the Most Noble Order of the Garter	KG
Knight Commander of the Most Distinguished Order of St Michael and St George	KCMG
Member of the Most Excellent Order of the British Empire	MBE
Military Cross	MC
Order of Merit	OM

Street name changes/area alterations

Following the revolutionary period, 1913–23, many streets, barracks, bridges and other areas were renamed, often in honour of those who had been leaders or served in the Rising, the War of Independence or the Civil War.

For street names containing 'Upper', 'Middle' or 'Lower', the name may be determined as follows: the 'Lower' part of a street is that part nearest to the mouth of the Liffey.

The following is a list of street/area names in italics, with their contemporary names in non-italics.

Amiens Street: Eastern end of Seán MacDermott Street.

Amiens Street Railway Station: Connolly Station.

Barrack Street—Tighe Street: Benburb Street.

Clarence Street (Great Clarence Street): Macken Street.

Clarence Street South: Macken Street.

Constabulary Barracks: Garda Síochána HQ in Phoenix Park.

Corporation Street: James Joyce Street.

Densil or *Denzille Street*: Fenian Street.

Drogheda Street: First name of the street that became *Sackville Street* and then O'Connell Street.

Drumcondra Lane: Dorset and Bolton Street.

Findlater Place: Cathal Brugha Street (the first block off O'Connell Street).

Gloucester Street: Cathal Brugha Street (the continuation east from O'Connell Street).

Gloucester Street North (see *Great Martin's Lane*): Upper Seán MacDermott → Lower Seán MacDermott Street.

Grangegorman Road Upper: Rathdown Road Upper.

Great Britain Street: Parnell Street.

Great Brunswick Street: Pearse Street.

Great Clarence Street: Macken Street.

Great Martin's Lane (until 1733): *Mecklenburgh Street* (until 1887), then named *Tyrone Street*, until it was named *Railway Street* for its proximity to *Amiens Street Railway Station*. Now Waterford Street.

Islandbridge Barracks: Partially demolished, it was renamed Peadar Clancy Barracks. It was sold to developers in early 2004.

King George V Hospital: St Bricin's Military Hospital.

King's County: County Offaly.

Kingsbridge Railway Station: Seán Heuston Station.

Kingstown Harbour: Dún Laoghaire Harbour (seven miles south-east of Dublin).

Marlborough Barracks: McKee Barracks in Phoenix Park.

Mecklenburgh Street (see *Great Martin's Lane*): in 1887 it was named *Tyrone Street*, then
    Railway Street for its proximity to *Amiens Street Station*; now Waterford Street.

North Dublin Union: St Lawrence's Hospital.

Portobello Barracks: Cathal Brugha Barracks.

Queen's County: County Laois.

Queenstown: Cobh, Co. Cork.

Richmond Barracks: Originally on Bulfin Road, Inchicore, it became Keogh Barracks,
    then was taken over by the Christian Brothers and became St Michael's
    Primary School, then Keogh Square.

Royal Barracks: Collins Barracks, part of the National Museum of Ireland.

Royal University: National University.

Rutland Square: Parnell Square. The surrounding streets were once known as
    Charlemont Row (Parnell Square West), *Cavendish Row* (Parnell Square East),
    Palace Row (Parnell Square North) and *Great Britain Street* (Parnell Street).

Sackville Street: O'Connell Street (before *Sackville Street* it was *Drogheda Street*).

Ship Street Barracks: Government Buildings next to Dublin Castle.

Clarence Street South: Macken Street.

South Dublin Union: St James's Hospital.

Stafford Street: Wolfe Tone Street.

Wellington Barracks: Griffith Barracks (now a college).

Westland Row Railway Station: Pearse Station.

Profile

The story of Michael Collins in Dublin is the story of Irish nationalism and separatism in Dublin from 1916 until 1922. When Collins left Cork in 1906 on a boat bound for London to work in the British Post Office Savings Bank he had never been to Dublin, but his influence there was ubiquitous from 1916 until 1922. He is widely remembered today for the significant part he played during the 'Tan War' of 1919–21. His undertakings then as adjutant-general of the IRA, director of intelligence, director of operations, president of the Irish Republican Brotherhood (IRB) and minister for finance had him establish several offices and safe houses throughout the city. It was said that he never slept in the same house two nights in a row after he went on the run in April 1918 until the Truce in July 1921. Truly, he made Dublin his own until his untimely death in 1922. He once famously said that 'Whoever controls Dublin controls Ireland'. He was right.

One cannot talk about the German Plot and the follow-on imprisonments, the election of November 1918, the establishment of Dáil Éireann, the War of Independence, Bloody Sunday, the Treaty negotiations and debates, the Civil War or almost any other event in those years without talking about Michael Collins and his role in them all, particularly in Dublin. And yet, for many, discussion of Collins is often limited to the Anglo-Irish Treaty—just for or against.

I freely admit to beginning this work as a means of getting to know the participants in those events better. I wanted to know where they worked and dreamt, whether they were successful or not, and where they lived and where many died. What began as a study of their surroundings evolved into a complete account of the locations of that time and as much as I could of Collins and his associates. To paraphrase German historian Theodor Mommsen, 'History is neither made nor written without passion'. I am no historian, but it was easy to see the passion of those who participated in the events of the time.

Born on 16 October 1890 near Clonakilty, Co. Cork, Collins was the third son and youngest of eight children. His father, Michael Sr, who was 75 when Michael was born, was a member of the Fenians as well as the IRB, and a brilliantly self-educated man. On his deathbed, Collins's father told the family to take care of Michael, because 'one day he'll be a great man. He'll do great work for Ireland.' Like his father, Michael was gifted with mathematical ability, and like him he enjoyed philosophy, economics and the use of words. He first

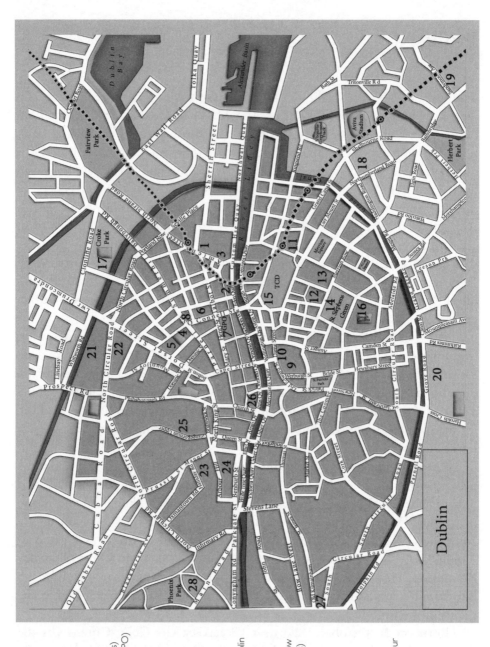

Dublin

went to school at Lisavaird at the age of five, and then at the age of thirteen he attended Clonakilty National School. During the week he stayed with his sister Margaret and her husband, Patrick O'Driscoll, while at weekends he returned to the family farm. O'Driscoll founded the *West Cork People* newspaper, and Collins helped out with general reporting jobs and in preparing the forthcoming issues. While at primary school, Collins came to idolise his teacher, Denis Lyons, who was a member of the IRB and who imbued all his students with a desire for Ireland's separation from Britain. Collins later said of him:

> In Denis Lyons, especially his manner, although seemingly hiding what meant most to him, had this pride of Irishness which has always meant most to me.[1]

Lyons's influence on the impressionable Collins was immense. James Santry, the local blacksmith and also a member of the IRB, was another major influence on the young Collins. By the time he left school, thanks to the tutelage of his father, Lyons and Santry the teenage Michael was well versed in Irish history and tragedy.

After leaving school at fifteen, Collins took a British Civil Service examination in Cork in February 1906, and was thereafter employed by the Royal Mail office in Cork and then in the Post Office Savings Bank in Hammersmith, London. His time in the post office, learning how it worked, served him well back in Dublin, where he used many postal employees in his intelligence operations. He moved to London in 1906, staying in the London home of his elder sister Hannie (Johanna). After his mother died in April 1907, Hannie took on a 'motherly' role and tried to steer the young Collins on the straight and narrow path of life, as she felt that he was doing too many wild things in London. Their sister Mary wrote that after their mother's death Hannie was Michael's 'mother, sister and friend'. But when Hannie found that Ireland was the passion of his life, she warned him that Irishmen would let him down and betray him. Mary said that he refused to believe her.[2]

In 1910 Collins became a messenger at the London stock brokerage firm of Horne and Company in Moorgate, and studied law and creative writing at King's College. He also took classes in public speaking, and was able to use the lessons learned there to his advantage upon his return to Ireland. He had one serious fault in public speaking, however: he was always driven more by emotion than by circumspection. In late 1914 he went to work for the London Board of Trade in Whitehall. He joined the London GAA and the Geraldines football and hurling club. Through the GAA he continued on the path forecast for him by his father, Lyons and Santry, and his interest in all things Irish led him to join the Gaelic League and Sinn Féin. Sam Maguire, a republican from Collins's native County Cork, swore the nineteen-year-old Collins into the IRB in 1909. Maguire became head of the IRB in London and remained close to Collins all his life. Whenever Collins needed things done in England, he called on Maguire first. On 25 April 1914 he enrolled in the London unit of the Irish Volunteers along with his cousin, Seán Hurley. Hurley, a fellow west Cork man, and Joe O'Reilly, who would become Collins's closest assistant in Dublin, all became fast friends at this time. (Hurley was killed in the Rising, fighting at a barricade in Church Street on 26 April 1916.) Many of those he met while living in London would play major roles in Collins's life when he returned to Ireland. For example, Frank Thornton, whom he met when they played a hurling match in Liverpool on the day World War I was declared, became one of his most important intelligence operatives.

Collins later read a paper at an IRB meeting:

> ... with the decline of the pro-IRB movement so did ours come into prominence.
>
> But, by comparison, this revitalised IRB is a vastly different proposition to former movements. In, for example, organisation. Organisation—a lack of it—was chiefly responsible for the failure of several risings of recent times. It is, therefore, of greater significance—and of some urgency also—that, if and when the occasion should demand it, the IRB should be even better organised, and so better prepared to meet such an emergency.[3]

While still under the age of 25, Collins was exhibiting the qualities and thinking that would serve him so well. He became a skilled debater and liked to enter into any discussion. His personal organisation was an example, as from his time in London he kept a daily pocket diary. Throughout his life, his actions were governed by a shrewd—some would say calculating—brain, reinforced by an indomitable will. He was able to stand back in judgement of himself, and made himself a professional in all that he attempted.

At this time he considered going to America to live with his older brother Patrick, who wrote: 'Ten years ago [1915] I had a job all fixed for Mike with the First National Bank here in Chicago. He bought his passage and was all ready to leave for America when at the last moment he changed his mind. I think he was at the dock, ready to embark, when he backed out. I was sorely disappointed when I got a letter from him telling me that he couldn't come to America. There was important work for him at home, and succeeding events bear testimony to this.' Collins decided to visit Tom Clarke and Seán MacDermott in Dublin and they advised him to stay in London, as 'within a year there would be something doing in Ireland'.[4] In August 1915 he was recalled to Dublin to meet with Clarke, and the IRB gave him instructions. He was told to be ready for the call, and to return to London with plans to energise the London IRB circle.

In 1915 Collins took a job with the Guaranty Trust Company of New York, where he honed his financial acumen and where he was employed until his return to Ireland the following year.

After his return to Dublin in January 1916, Collins went to work for the accountancy firm of Craig, Gardner and Co. He also worked for Count George Plunkett, and was assigned to go to Kimmage to liaise with the Volunteer garrison there. What is often overlooked is that Collins was in the GPO during the Easter Rising, though he played a minor role. Later stories overshadow his part in the Rising because he did not make his mark on events until after his release from Frongoch Prison Camp at the end of 1916. After that, Collins never did anything without understanding exactly what he was doing, nor without a clear purpose in view. 'Method, but unorthodox, has them beaten the whole time.' Throughout his life, he was never in doubt as to what to do next, no matter what motivations or suspicions he had. He was always in control, and from this time forward he carefully and methodically built his organisation so that it controlled what he wanted it to control.

There are a number of anecdotal explanations for the origin of his nickname, 'the Big Fellow'. It's known that it was not because of his size. A well-built man, Collins's file in Dublin Castle listed him as '5' 7" or 8"', though his true height was 5' 11",[5] so he probably would not have stuck out because of his size. The name might have originated within his family, who stated that he was so called by them while still a child: it had been a term of endearment for their youngest brother, who was always keen to take on tasks beyond his years. It was certainly already established by his teens, long before he emerged as a political or military leader.[6] Many others, however, point to his time at Frongoch, when he was deemed 'too big for his britches', and claim that it was a term of derision. Half-mocking and half-reverential, whatever the origin, the nickname stuck absolutely.

Oliver St John Gogarty said that Collins 'moved with the natural grace of a ballet dancer, holding himself erect and striding purposely, with a jaunty slightly swaggering air'. Gogarty described Collins as 'Napoleonic. But a bigger and more manly specimen of manhood than Napoleon … His skin was like undiscoloured ivory. You could see it in the unlined face and small, womanly hands.'[7] Gogarty was among the many who gave Collins a key to his house to be used as a safe house if he needed it, and that key was found in his uniform pocket when Gogarty embalmed Collins's body. Collins would have been delighted with the comparison; Napoleon was one of his heroes and in some ways his role model. But Collins was no Napoleon when it came to decision-making. In military matters, for example, he often collaborated with Richard Mulcahy or Dick McKee, preferring the safety and comfort of a group whenever possible and accepting their verdict even if it went against him.

Collins was a man of many gifts, but his outstanding quality was his ability to penetrate quickly to the heart of a complex problem. He had a clear, incisive intelligence, a disciplined mind and an unerring grasp of the essentials in any situation. He was a 'realistic idealist' and always eminently pragmatic. Éamon Broy, Collins's spy in the 'G' Division of the DMP, said of him: 'I shall never forget seeing the way Collins' mind worked. It was like putting information into a computer.' He went straight to the heart of a matter and sought to have it dealt with by the most direct means. He had the ability to achieve simplicity and success even in the most complicated situations and the most complex of problems. Like all good administrative politicians, he bypassed the formal hierarchy, such as it was, and had his own extensive networks. He lacked finesse and could be ungracious at times, but the work was done speedily and efficiently. Collins's flair for organisation enabled him to control a highly effective force of selected lieutenants. Besides conducting daily operations in Dublin, he kept in touch with IRA men and Cumann na mBan women throughout the country. He was compulsively organised, and no detail was too trifling to add to the general picture. His genius was this ability to grasp detail. He had the capacity to look reality hard in the face, search for a solution and, when he had found it, put it into action.

His natural intelligence, organisational capability and sheer drive galvanised those who came in contact with him. Like his nickname, however, Collins was a mass of contradictions, for he had a protean personality, with a knack of making himself all things to all men and of leaving people with the view of him that he wanted them to have. Even Lloyd George struggled to describe him: 'Vivacious, buoyant, highly strung, gay, impulsive, but passing from gaiety to grimness and back again, full of fascination and charm—but also of dangerous fire'.[8] Collins said neither 'Good morning' nor 'Good night', and he avoided handshakes as he avoided anything savouring in the least of formality. He laughed easily, but flew into rages and out of them just as suddenly. Anecdotes preserve the living man, but they can distort or exaggerate him as well. There is no need to exaggerate or glorify Collins. Still, the descriptions do give us a sense of his common humanity. There were three personal qualities that defined Collins all his life: humour, passionate tenderness and a fiery temper. How one viewed him depended on the relationship one had with him, and there were many. He was described variously as a 'man's man', brave, a bully, noisy, athletic, intensely hard-working, handsome, abrasive, demanding, tireless, methodical, charismatic, courageous, witty, a born improviser, sometimes inconsiderate, a man who calculatingly ordered the death of other men, 'laughing boy', brutal, generous, charming, vain, cruel, audacious, a childish practical joker, ruthless, anti-clerical, a lover of the elderly and children, prideful, keen to take command, a perfectionist, intimidating, interfering, dismissive, loyal, sarcastic, arrogant, critical, sometimes religious, quick-tempered, curious and harsh. People meant a lot to him and he was not ashamed to laugh or cry with them. One thing that was said by many was that 'in all things in life, *Michael had to win!*' One cannot imagine him doing anything half-heartedly, but another added that 'he was not only a bad loser, he was a bad winner!' Certainly he was an individualist, and may have been driven by the vanity that is so often at the core of such a person. Most agreed that one of his worst faults was baiting people. Collins had the capacity to arouse not only devotion but also jealousy. He was a caring boss and a fine comrade, but he could be an offensively assertive colleague.

Richard Mulcahy, chief of staff of the IRA/Volunteers, described Collins as

... intensely interested in contact with persons—for a purpose—his purpose carried his concentration into these contacts as zealously as his concentration was carried into office work ... he couldn't slow down, he was entirely geared for action.[9]

His friend Batt O'Connor said of him:

I have described an occasion when he praised me. There was another when he gave me a sharp rebuke. In business hours he was abrupt and stern in his manner. He had no patience for excuses for failure to carry out an order, and would waste no time listening to explanations. ... I went to Michael and began explaining the situation to him but I had hardly uttered half a sentence before he snapped out, 'Have you got it, or have you not got it? If you haven't got it, don't mind the excuses, but go and get it'.

... But with all Michael Collins's superficial sternness, he was of a tender and generous nature. He found time to help all who were in trouble or affliction. He was very thoughtful of the prisoners. He found means to get letters of encouragement and other more material consolations smuggled into them. How he accomplished such things, and got warders and wardresses in helping him to risk not only their livelihood, but their freedom, was another proof of his power which made him rise to such a height in our regard. Although it was so dangerous for him to go near the homes of those who were engaged actively in the fight, he never failed to do so if a visit from him would give support or consolation.[10]

Collins remembered every weakness of everyone who was a prisoner, and went far to find their favourite brand of tobacco or cigarettes. And he knew which sweets his other operatives liked. 'I know you don't smoke, but I remember you saying you liked candies', he wrote to Kathleen Clarke when he sent her a package in Holloway Prison. He had an understanding of the minor ridiculous necessities of men and women, as well as the headaches that money or attention could mend. Whenever there were difficulties about money and others were shocked or annoyed, Collins understood and sympathised. During his employment with the Irish National Aid and Volunteers' Dependants' Fund he always treated recipients with genuine respect, and that was apparent to all. Part of the loyalty that he attracted stemmed from the fact that he was really concerned about individuals and would go to any lengths to help them. No matter how dire the circumstances, despair had no place in his philosophy, and he had little patience when he detected it in others.

Yet Collins undoubtedly ordered many men killed in cold blood. (He is not known to have ever killed anyone himself.) Were these assassinations or murders? Even biographers on the same side do not agree. He was ruthless but not bloodthirsty. Collins gave orders to the Squad that no one was to be shot except under orders or in self-defence while on active service. Almost all revolutions are born in spilled blood, and the Irish fight was no different. With our 21st-century mentality and sensibilities it is difficult to comprehend the tenor of the times. Clearly there is a need to have some understanding of the value systems and mind-sets through which people in different periods organise their lives. Understanding the past is always conditioned by our view of the present and context. Historical interpretation is always in flux.

As time progressed, Collins gathered round him a group of ruthless guerrilla fighters. It was not the least of his gifts that he knew how to select efficient operators. But Paddy Daly, leader of Collins's Squad, remembered:

Michael Collins then gave me a lecture on revenge and told me that the man who had revenge in his heart was not fit to be a Volunteer. I had to convince him that I never thought of shooting Winters, but I passed the remark that if Winters was on our list I would like to carry out the job.

That lecture shows clearly that Collins or any of the headquarters staff would not shoot merely for revenge.[11]

Throughout the period, all sides continued with their tit-for-tat killings, equally convinced of the necessity and righteousness of their actions.

Collins deliberately provoked the British authorities into over-reacting throughout the War of Independence in such a way as to alienate the overwhelming majority of the Irish people. He was certainly the prototype of the modern urban guerrilla, and it could be said that he was the architect of the Black and Tan War. Political realities always weigh more heavily in guerrilla wars than in conventional ones. The Irish had no armies to imitate in the pursuit of guerrilla war—the Boer War was their only example. Others modelled their wars after the Irish tactics. Revolutionaries from Lenin to Mao Zedong and Zhou Enlai studied Collins's methods. Yitzhak Shamir sought to emulate the anti-British struggle of the IRA and used the nickname 'Michael' in Israel.

Collins's plans worked well through the early months of 1920. The IRA would ambush a patrol, and a few hours later the Crown forces would arrive in strength and shoot, burn and loot. They acted as if all the Irish were against them, so they did not bother to differentiate: to be Irish was to be guilty. Nothing could have brought the Irish over to the nationalist side more completely. In essence, the people were driven into the arms of the IRA—which was exactly what Collins had envisaged when he set out to provoke the confrontation. Dublin, being the headquarters of both the British and the Irish, developed into a bloody battleground. During the day, the IRA/Volunteers kept up the pressure by attacking patrols, raiding post offices and shooting key men in the British intelligence services. After dark, the midnight murder squads of the British went out in the comparative safety of curfew to shoot at will. Collins was deeply conscious of the sufferings of the Irish, but he clearly realised that these tactics must go on. With few men and little ammunition, he knew he could not beat the British by force, but he could and would defeat them through their conduct.

What set Collins apart from other guerrilla fighters was that he was always thinking not just of war but also of peace and how to achieve it as quickly and advantageously as possible. His views on violence were carefully considered. He said that he had 'strong fighting ideas, or I should say I suppose ideas of the utility of fighting'. Above all, though, Collins was a rationalist. He was always concerned about shaping public opinion and about the political impact of violence. (That's not to say that there were no plans to assassinate British politicians, for example, which would have inflamed public opinion: there were. Plans were mooted to assassinate the prince of Wales, Lloyd George and his cabinet ministers, Lord Fitzalan, the last lord lieutenant of Ireland, Sir Basil Thompson, the head of the Special Branch of Scotland Yard, various Unionist MPs and Sir Henry Wilson.[12] For the most part, however, Collins did not agree with those plans. He said, 'Do you think the British can have only one cabinet'?) He regularly stressed using the minimum force necessary to achieve the objective in a politically acceptable and productive way. Nevertheless, he was a believer in the military principle of getting his retaliation in first. He was said to be discriminating when he determined that killing was necessary, but mistakes were made, particularly on Bloody Sunday.

No one knew him as a soldier—as a fighter and military planner, certainly, but not as a soldier. Perhaps he saw himself as such; in his speeches he said that he was a soldier, not a politician. No one wanted to be viewed as a politician. In fact, he was neither a soldier nor a politician: he was an administrative genius, able to compartmentalise all matters and keep them separate. He ran the whole revolution as though it were a business concern. Like any modern CEO, Collins had a risk-averse style and always wanted to keep his options open, not wanting to force a decision before he had to. Just managing the Departments of Finance and Intelligence, as well as handling arms importation and distribution and the needs of all his operatives, would have taxed several lesser individuals. He did not believe in 'red tape' and cut through it as quickly as possible. He had an orderly, trained mind—that of the natural civil servant— but he was consistently looking to take on additional challenges. ('Exceeding his brief', some of his cabinet colleagues would have termed it. Collins was blandly indifferent to what constituted another's preserves. The way he crossed the bounds of his portfolio to express views on other matters might have been more palatable if he had not been so resentful of similar interference in his own areas. In his myriad administrative capacities, though, he was capable of double-dealing that certainly justifies the charge levelled at him by his critics that he put expediency before principle.) One should always look for the photo of Collins behind his desk ticking off mundane administrative matters, not just the ones of him in uniform with a gun ordering some new action. Those photos with a pen in his hand rather than a gun at his side are hard to find! To examine Collins's life in those years is to look into a secret—and, above all, a contradictory—revolutionary career.

Collins was a demanding taskmaster—especially of himself. Never resting, he never allowed anyone else to rest either. He was always pushing to get things done. 'There was no burden too big to put on Mick's shoulders, and there was no job too small for him to do', according to Dan Breen. 'Whenever anyone wanted anything done, they were told to go to Michael Collins', said Tom Barry.

> The outstanding figure in all GHQ was Michael Collins. This man was without a shadow of a doubt, the effective driving force and the backbone of GHQ of the armed action of the nation … A tireless, ruthless, dominating man of great capacity, he worked like a Trojan in innumerable capacities to defeat the enemy.

Barry also remembered Collins's audacity, shown when Barry visited him in Dublin. One evening, making their way across the city on a jarvey car, they were stopped for questioning. Barry, aware that he was in the company of one of the most wanted men in the country, was alarmed. Collins muttered from the side of his mouth: 'Act drunk!' As they were being searched, Collins entertained the military with bawdy jokes and bad language, which soon had them all laughing. He and his 'drunken' companion were waved on their way.[13] But Barry also felt that, though Collins was good-hearted, he was 'a man who could be easily disliked. He was very domineering.'[14]

Collins was brazenly foolhardy at times.

> One morning I met Michael Collins. He told me, laughing, that he had just been held up. He was returning from a week-end in the country where he had been attending to military matters. When he reached Ballsbridge he found a cordon of military who were stopping and searching all incoming cars. Without waiting to be questioned, he stepped out of his car and walked up to the officer in charge and began to converse with him. They became quite friendly as Michael sympathized with him on the unpleasantness of his job. From a silver cigarette case he offered the officer a cigarette. While this little comedy was being played, the soldiers were searching the car, and questioning the other men who were in it. Coming back to the officer they saluted: 'Car and passengers all right, Sir.' They did not think of searching the man who was talking and laughing with their officer. The papers were in his pockets, documents and maps which would have led to his discovery. 'I was the only one of us who had anything on him,' he said, 'but thinking I must be a friend of their officer, they never touched me.' With a final word of chaff with his new acquaintance he stepped back into the car and continued on his way.[15]

To this day there is no satisfactory explanation as to how Collins avoided arrest. He walked and cycled openly about the city. At that time the central business area of Dublin was smaller than today, and he seldom moved far from the centre of it, yet he was never arrested. While some believed that Collins moved about the city in disguise, highly armed and well protected, he usually went alone, unarmed, often on a bicycle, and undisguised. It was said that some of the detectives recognised him but that he had so terrorised the police that they were afraid to apprehend him. Collins himself said: 'I do not allow myself to feel I am on the run. That is my safeguard. It prevents me from acting in a manner that would arouse suspicion.' Ormonde Winter, head of the British secret operations in Dublin Castle, once wrote that 'his many narrow escapes, when he managed to elude almost certain arrest, shrouded him in a cloak of historical romance'. Dublin's Scarlet Pimpernel, indeed.

Collins was not a blind bureaucrat but he hated time-wasting and inefficiency. John Regan notes very clearly the enigma that was Collins—and the difficulty in understanding how he should be assessed:

> While the exploits of Collins and his hand-picked assassins, the Squad, are repeatedly treated in minute detail by biographers, the much better documented war against the anti-Treaty IRA during the civil war (his role as a civil war commander is arguably the best documented aspect of his public life) is continually treated with decidedly less vigour.
>
> Collins was an administrator first and foremost. With unprecedented success he organised the campaign against the British intelligence system, and while undeniably a brilliant soldier, he was a paper-shuffling soldier and not the gunman implicit in some of the more martial representations of him.[16]

Still, the romantic/militarist portrayal of Collins remains the dominant and popular image of the man, and his contributions to the foundation of the Free State administration are often given short shrift or forgotten.

Collins's natural impatience and impulsiveness were recognised by some who worked closely with him. His rashness contrasted with his methodical approach. Both Richard Mulcahy and Dick McKee agreed that Collins should not be chosen as the chief of staff in March 1919. Mulcahy noted:

> McKee, as he came away from the meeting with me, expressed satisfaction and relief that Collins was not being recommended. The main reason for that was that in the light of what he knew about Collins' temperament, and the short period and the circumstances in which my information about him had been outlined, McKee—like others—was a little bit wary of entrusting him with anything like complete control. In fact he did want time to disclose himself and his qualities.[17]

One of Collins's blind spots was taking action too hastily. Some colleagues thought that his enthusiasm got the better of his judgement. As a man of action, he was so anxious to get things done that he sometimes acted before the dust had settled so that his agents could get away or cover their tracks. He also kept documents smuggled from the British for far too long, which led to the arrest of many of his best sources. Further, in his desire for action Collins often failed to realise the significance of symbolic events, such as the reading of the 1916 Proclamation or the keeping of Eoin MacNeill in the movement. There is no doubt that Collins could not have united Sinn Féin as Éamon de Valera was able to do in 1917–19.

In judging Collins as a leader, it should be noted that the formative role played by the many strong, competent, loving women around him in his family produced a man who deeply respected women and thrived on female company of all ages; yet others described him as a 'womaniser'. Collins was not what would be called a feminist today: he shared with Winston Churchill somewhat unenthusiastic feelings for the role of women in politics. Nevertheless, Collins was influenced by women and receptive to their influence: he had been under the wing of his older sister, Hannie, while living in London as a post office clerk. He was also very attached to his sister Helen, who became a nun (as Sister Mary Celestine), and he wrote to her on 16 October 1921 that he was touched that she was the only one who had remembered his birthday—which would be his last.[18] In all capacities in Dublin, many women helped and supported him. It was even thought after the publication in 1927 of Piaras Béaslaí's first biography of Collins, in which he was described as a man who loved to wrestle and take a 'piece of ear', and in which no mention was made of female relationships, that Collins was gay.[19] The tales about Michael Collins are as complex as the man himself![20]

I always want to include all the women and their stories that I can find. The commitment of women before, during and after the Rising helped to bring the Irish nation to support the separatist movement. The widows of those executed in Kilmainham Gaol after the Rising did more to bring attention to the independence movement than any other group. The widows and female relatives of the captives filled the voids in leadership and ensured that Irish independence did not die with their loved ones. They began their own War of Independence while many of the men were still imprisoned.

Collins simply wouldn't have been able to operate without the aid of his women spies and couriers. He had grown up in a family dominated by strong and resourceful women, and throughout his life he respected such women. He was usually more comfortable in the company of slightly older women—Moya Llewelyn Davies and Lady Hazel Lavery, for example. He had a small army of women working for him as secretaries, typists and couriers, and all were devoted to him. Once a woman began to work for him, he forbade her to become openly involved in Cumann na mBan or any other nationalist organisation. He did not want them to attract attention to themselves by going to parades or meetings. In particular, he did not want them wearing their uniforms in public: Collins had a special aversion to women in uniforms. Lily Mernin, Nancy O'Brien, Molly O'Reilly, Máire Comerford, Eileen McGrane, Madeline 'Dilly' Dicker, Sister Eithne Lawless, Moya (O'Connor) Davies, Anna Fitzsimmons, Susan (Sinéad) Mason and so many others were invaluable to him. And he was one of the few orators of the time who used gender-inclusive language in his speeches and explicitly acknowledged women's contributions and concerns on a regular basis.

After 1918 Collins was 'on the run' and slept all over Dublin. Most of those safe houses were run by women and Collins could not have survived without them. Mrs Bridget O'Connor, Mrs Julia O'Donovan, Mrs Doyle, Mrs Nora O'Keefe, Mrs Maurice Collins, Mrs Mary Woods—all opened their homes to him and adjusted the family routine to his presence. They were all hospitable women with nerves of steel and, above all, the same fortitude that women all over Ireland possessed. These women tended the men, treated their wounds, fed them, hid them, and faced interrogation or the ransacking of their homes by the British. They did it day after day, and brought up their young families as if this were the normal way of life.

Though Collins worked there, the Irish National Aid and Volunteers' Dependants' Fund was run primarily by Kathleen Clarke, widow of Tom, and Sorcha MacMahon, who was in the GPO during the Rising. Clarke was left access to the IRB's funds after the Rising, and she used those funds to begin the support of the dependants. She also had the list of IRB members, and through the efforts of Clarke and Collins that organisation and its hold on Irish policy was re-established. Members of Cumann na mBan were the Fund's foremost activists, collecting and disbursing its funds. And its women operatives were the principal means used to contact men and to pass along messages from the IRB throughout the country. Collins recognised this, and some of his favourite and most successful agents were women.[21]

Subsequently, in the Irish Civil War the role of women was paramount. Particularly on the anti-Treaty side, Republican women used every means at their disposal to get across their message about the fate and conditions of Republican prisoners, despite the harassment and imprisonment that became their lot. Women imprisoned in Kilmainham Gaol, Mountjoy Prison or the other prisons throughout the country left a history of hunger strikes and escapes. Those who were not imprisoned led innumerable demonstrations that attacked the censorship of the press. Many of those who had worked so closely with Collins took the anti-Treaty side, and they used the lessons they had learned while working for him against the Free State government.

Always looking ahead, Collins was asked after the Treaty by a visiting American senator: 'Now that you've secured military freedom for your country, how can you possibly survive economically?' Collins replied: 'We will survive economically if we export to the growing sophisticated markets of the world, goods of quality which they're entitled to demand at a price beyond which they will not pay and on the day they rightly demand delivery. To meet this there is only one criteria: the pursuit of excellence.' And so it works for Ireland today.

This is the story of Michael Collins's Dublin—the town he 'controlled'.

Overview

On 15 January 1916, the night prior to the introduction of the Conscription Act in England, Michael Collins, along with other members of the IRB, left London after being summoned by Seán MacDiarmada to return to Ireland. Before he departed, Collins secured a release from his employer, the Guaranty Trust Company of New York, by telling his manager that he wished to go to Dublin to 'sign up' in an Irish regiment. The manager, Robert Mackey, assumed that Collins was seeking leave to join the British army. After warmly congratulating him on his decision, his boss allowed him to leave immediately, paying him an extra month's salary to enable him to take a holiday before he went away. Collins later exchanged the cheque for gold in the Bank of England, and on arriving in Dublin he handed it over to MacDiarmada.

Collins then reported to the Dublin Irish Volunteers, became one of the ADCs to Joseph Plunkett and served in the GPO during the Easter Rising. Arrested after the Rising, he was taken to Stafford Jail and then sent to Frongoch Prison Camp in Wales, where he became known as one of the leaders of the IRB. Life in prison was difficult for all the men initially: for the first three weeks at Stafford they were in solitary confinement, and their attempts to come to terms with prison life were amateurish. Yet Collins and the rest soon efficiently mastered the ways to make that life more bearable and open lines of communication with the outside world.

By the end of 1916 the British authorities had determined to release most of the rebels, and many were home in Ireland by Christmas. They returned to a riotous welcome, a complete turn-round from the send-off they had been given by the populace eight months earlier on the way to prison. The second time Collins 'returned' to Ireland was upon his release from Frongoch on 23 December 1916. Having furthered his contacts in the IRB and enhanced his reputation among the imprisoned revolutionary nationalists, he became heavily involved in every aspect of Irish nationalism from then until his death.

In the Treaty debates of December 1921, Collins was described by Arthur Griffith as 'the man who won the War [of Independence]'. No one man or woman ever won a war; in fact, Collins, alone, did not plan, start, direct or control every aspect of the war. He would be the first to deny any suggestion that he alone won that dour struggle; he realised that it was one of teamwork. But Collins participated in every phase of the war and had remarkable successes in intelligence, organisation and finance; he was the one person without whom the War of Independence would not have succeeded. Then, between the end of the Treaty debates in January 1922 and June 1922, he divided his time between trying to get the Free State government up and running and trying to avoid the Civil War. Ultimately he failed to prevent that conflict, but much of its pursuit, strategy, direction and further attempts to stop the Civil War in Dublin up to his death in August 1922 must be attributed to his actions.

Collins ran the intelligence operations during the period, as well as finance. But he was also president of the IRB and commanded his 'Squad' and the Active Service Units. Through his agents he controlled all activities on the docks, and on the ships he sent and received information from across the oceans. He had his finger on the importation of almost every weapon or piece of ammunition that came into Ireland. He looked after the defence of court-martial prisoners, and the needs of their relatives. If they were imprisoned, he kept in touch with them through his network of warders. He went to the home of Batt O'Connor and sat up with him when he was ill, and he went to the home of Sinéad de Valera and played with her children while Éamon was imprisoned or in America. All the while, he probably infringed on every other ministry and stepped on the toes of every other minister.

The Irish War of Independence between 1919 and 1921 would not have occurred without the conversion of the Irish people from supporters of Home Rule to advocates of an open and, shortly, a violent revolution. The Rising should have been an adequate warning that events and forces in Irish society were moving out of the grasp of the Castle administration and its police. There was very little public support for the rebels during the Easter Rising.[22] For the most part the Irish supported the British war effort. Moreover, many civilians were killed or lost their property in the fires that occurred in Dublin. When the rebels were marched off to boats bound for prisons in Britain, many were pelted with vegetables, bottles and even the contents of chamber-pots. Nothing these men and women had done during the week led the public to take their side, though the bitterness was tinged with a little admiration—the Irish had fought well against the regular British troops.

Soon, however, the admiration of the people for the rebels who fought well and honourably against the British began to move closer to approval. Shortly after the Rising, one woman wrote in her diary:

Of course this is not Ireland's rebellion—only a Sinn Féin rising … The Sinn Féin leaders were such good men. They died like saints. Oh! the pity of it! And Ireland wanted them so much. They were men of such beautiful character, such high literary power and attainments—mystics who kept the light burning … But as sure as God's sun rises in the east, if England does not get things right ... if there's not immediately conciliation and love and mercy poured out on Ireland—all the Sinn Féin leaders will be canonized ... Already the tone is changing.[23]

Britain, still engaged in World War I, determined that the Rising was an act of 'treason' and that the participants and leaders should suffer the fate of traitors in wartime. Moreover, the rebels had enlisted German support, a move that prompted outright vilification.[24] When General Sir John Grenville Maxwell ordained that all seven signatories of the Proclamation be executed in Kilmainham Gaol, he was going against the British Imperial Staff policy that executing rebels just made martyrs of them. Those men and several other prominent commanders of rebel positions were executed—a total of fourteen men in Dublin, as well as Thomas Kent in Cork and Sir Roger Casement in London.

Later, when Maxwell refused to hand over the bodies for burial, he wrote that

Irish sentimentality will turn these graves into martyr's shrines to which annual processions, etc. will be made which will cause constant irritation in this country.[25]

The executions created a wave of protest and outrage in Ireland.[26]

The Rising had hardly been the work of a massive conspiracy, but the British acted as if it were.[27] Over 3,000 men and women were imprisoned, many in jails in England and Wales. Most, like Collins, were never charged, and there were certainly many who had not participated at all. These mass arrests and the increased British military presence throughout Ireland demonstrated bluntly that Ireland was under the control of an oppressive and alien government that could only rule the country by force. Though it was never enforced outside Dublin, Maxwell's declaration of martial law throughout the country showed the people that they were being treated as second-class citizens by a British government no longer in touch with Ireland.

When the Irish learned of the British army murders of fifteen innocent men and boys in North King Street on Saturday 29 April and the murder of Francis Sheehy-Skeffington and two newspaper editors, Thomas Dickson and Patrick MacIntyre, by British Capt. J.C. Bowen-Colthurst—and that he was only given a minimal sentence even after another British officer, Sir Francis Fletcher Vane, put his career on the line to bring Bowen-Colthurst to justice— they began to change their view of the Rising and its participants. Furthermore, the same influences that had inspired many of the rebels—the

GAA, the Gaelic League and Irish nationalism/separatism—also appealed to the younger members of the clergy. As the dying words of the executed leaders were reported in a religious vein, the attitudes of the clergy, too, began a very slow change.[28] Later some support for the nationalist ideals appeared in the younger priests who came forward at nationalist rallies and on Sinn Féin platforms. The conversion of some priests into more outspoken nationalists was vital to the growth of the movement after the Rising. A police report noted of the priests: 'They exercise an immense influence over the youth in their parishes and unless some means can be used to make them abstain from interference in politics I fear that disaffection will be dangerously spread'.[29] No one body contributed more than the Christian Brothers to the making of the new Ireland that we know today. It could well be said that the insurrection of 1916 was a Christian Brothers Easter Week. 'Almost all the leaders of that heroic uprising, and the glorious years that followed, had been pupils of the Christian Brothers … from the Brothers the 1916 leaders learned their love of freedom, their desire for nationhood and the Gaelic way of life'.[30] Many Irishmen in the years 1919–21 died in the belief expressed by Liam Mellows, a prominent IRA tactician and fighter, in his last letter to his mother: 'I believe that those who die for Ireland have no need for prayer'.[31]

Some in Ireland began to feel a communion with past fighting generations, and the words of James Fintan Lalor were often quoted: 'Somewhere, somehow, and by someone, a beginning must be made'. Patrick Pearse, the idealist, and James Connolly, the Lalor disciple, had begun the rebellion in Lalor's words: 'even if [it was] called premature, imprudent or dangerous—if made so soon as tomorrow—even if offered by ten men only—even if offered by men armed only with stones take their side'.

In 1917–18 there were parliamentary by-elections in Roscommon, Kilkenny and Longford. Count George Plunkett, father of the executed Joseph Plunkett, was elected under the Sinn Féin banner in North Roscommon in 1917 in what was termed the 'Election in the snows'. Collins came late to campaign for Plunkett, only getting to Roscommon on the day of the election because of the inclement weather, but he was credited with a masterly propaganda speech:

> Because he will not associate with the Irishmen who cheered when his son was shot against a wall for loving Ireland, will you insult him in North Roscommon, as the Royal Dublin Society did, and tell the British Government that he is not the man you want?
>
> No—There are Irishmen in North Roscommon yet!

Joseph McGuinness, who was in Lewes Jail in England, won the by-election in Longford in 1918 using the campaign slogan 'Put him in to get him out'. Collins was involved in the organisation and campaigning for these by-election candidates, and it was he who convinced the prisoners in England that Irish opinion had undergone such a change that McGuinness's election to parliament was possible.

The death in 1917 of Thomas Ashe from being forcibly fed while on hunger strike aroused tremendous passion. His funeral led to massive defiance of the orders against uniformed marches. Volunteers from all over Ireland gathered in Dublin to pay their last respects. Collins's funeral oration gave some hint of things to come: 'Nothing additional remains to be said—the volley we have just heard is the only speech it is proper to make above the grave of a dead Fenian'.[32]

These, then, were the major antecedents of the War of Independence: an increasingly inefficient British administration faced by Irish men and women fired with revolutionary zeal and convinced that they could attain their ends by war. A set of contingent events was to provide the final catalyst, as there was yet to come another imperious decision that would harden Irish attitudes against the British.

Though about 210,000 men from Ireland served in the British army during World War I, of whom some 35,000 died, not one was conscripted.[33] Most entered the army for financial reasons, because they were poverty-stricken and employment opportunities were so few in Ireland. Others, particularly the Irish National Volunteers who heeded the call of John Redmond, followed the recruiting promises of the British and believed that enlisting 'to fight for small nations' would lead to Home Rule for Ireland. By the spring of 1918, reinforcements had become such an urgent necessity for the British army that the government decided to apply military conscription to Ireland. The British military situation that spring in France was critical, but the government fatally underestimated the depth of feeling against conscription in Ireland. (As it turned out, the extension of conscription to Ireland was not needed.) At the time, Collins was in jail in Sligo for a seditious speech he had made, and he wrote to his sister Hannie on 10 April, anxious to know 'what Lloyd George has done about conscription for this country. If he goes for it—well, he's ended.'

In April 1918 Westminster passed a compulsory Conscription Act, a move that greatly solidified Irish public opinion against Britain. The conscription issue had united in spirit, if temporarily, the two strands of nationalism, militant and moderate. Thousands of people now joined the Irish Volunteers to resist any forcible call-up. Though no Irishman was in fact conscripted during the war, the threat of conscription was such that a multi-party Irish Conference was convened as a protest against its possibility and issued the following pronouncement: 'The attempt to enforce conscription will be unwarrantable aggression which we call upon all true Irishmen to resist by the most effective means at their disposal'.[34] The Catholic hierarchy concurred with this sentiment at their annual meeting in Maynooth, declaring in their own manifesto:

> An attempt is being made to force Conscription on Ireland against the will of the Irish nation and in defiance of the protests of its leaders. In view especially of the historic relations between the two countries from the very beginning up to this moment, we consider that Conscription forced in this way upon Ireland is an oppressive and inhuman law, which the Irish people have a right to resist by every means that are consonant with God.[35]

By now even the opinion of the Church had shifted and was more in tune with the emerging spirit of nationalism. In this fashion the plan to introduce conscription in Ireland led to widespread support for independence, and it greatly fuelled support for the Republican separatist movement and Sinn Féin.

In a further heavy-handed attempt to quell this reaction to conscription, the British viceroy, Lord John French, claimed that there was evidence of a treasonable 'German Plot' between Sinn Féin and the German military. Collins was informed that arrests of Sinn Féin leaders were to take place, but Éamon de Valera decided to ignore Collins's warning that the leaders should not sleep in their homes and should try to avoid arrest. Those arrested on 17–18 May 1918 included 73 Sinn Féin leaders, among them Arthur Griffith, Seán Milroy, Kathleen Clarke, Desmond FitzGerald, Joe McGrath, Maud Gonne MacBride, Darrell Figgis and de Valera. This had severe unintended effects: many of those arrested were among the more moderate nationalist leaders, while those left free included the most strident separatists, such as Collins, Cathal Brugha, Richard Mulcahy and Harry Boland.

So it was that within two years of the Easter Rising Ireland had abandoned the Irish Parliamentary Party and its goal of Home Rule and was marching forward resolutely under what was then described as the Sinn Féin banner but was in reality Collins's IRB standard. For the first time in Irish nationalist history, the advocates of physical force and those of political agitation would work together rather than against each other.

The failure of the Rising and the execution or internment of so many of the senior personnel of both the Volunteers and the IRB made it appear, on the surface at least, as if the Irish underground had been virtually destroyed.

Nevertheless, the work of two men in particular—Collins, operating amongst his IRB contacts, and Cathal Brugha, working through the Volunteers—began quickly and effectively to reconstitute the Irish underground. Brugha, very seriously wounded in the 1916 fighting, escaped execution and when discharged from medical care in late 1916 immediately began recruiting for the Volunteers. He made contact with senior Volunteer officers still in Ireland, and a group of some 50 men assembled under his chairmanship at Fleming's Hotel in Dublin in October 1916. It was at this meeting that a provisional executive of the Volunteers was formed.

There was, then, a gradual change of political allegiance on the part of the Irish in the period between the end of the 1916 Rising and the onset of the War of Independence in 1919. The legitimacy of the incumbent British administration dwindled in almost inverse proportion to the growing support in favour of the underground government of the Irish Republic proclaimed in front of the GPO at Easter 1916 and endorsed through a series of elections, culminating in the Dáil Éireann elections of 1918.

In 1917, following the Sinn Féin annual convention in October, national coordination of the IRA began in earnest. The convention elected a National Executive with Brugha as its chairman, Collins as director of army organisation, Richard Mulcahy in charge of training, Rory O'Connor in charge of engineering, Diarmuid Lynch supervising communications and Michael Staines in charge of supply. Although the National Executive functioned in name at least through to 1920, real power over the army had passed by March 1918 to the GHQ staff and then to the Ministry for Defence when Dáil Éireann, the Republican underground government, was proclaimed in January 1919. Nevertheless, Collins and Mulcahy remained in effective command of the army as well as intelligence throughout the war.

The most tangible change that occurred in Ireland after the Rising was this power shift in Irish politics from the Irish Parliamentary Party to the newly unified Sinn Féin. Immediately following the Armistice in November 1918, the British government called for a general election, in which Sinn Féin comprehensively defeated the Redmondite parliamentarians. That led in turn to the formation of the first Dáil Éireann, which convened on 21 January 1919. One must acknowledge the central place of the December 1918 election in determining the future course of Irish history: as one looks down the names of successful candidates, the governments of Ireland for the next 30 or 40 years emerge.

The election of 1918

... declared to the British that they had no claim to Ireland that was not rendered null and void by the Irish people's repudiation of such claim, and that the only just and constitutional government in Ireland was the Government of Dáil Éireann, which was elected by the people and represented the people. There is no gesture in Irish history quite so magnificent, quite so proud as that; and nothing that has happened can take away from it ... It brought the people to the point that they gave their allegiance to Dáil Éireann, obeyed it and recognized it, and helped it, suffered British government but did not recognize it and did not help it.[36]

Present with the foreign press at the first meeting of the Dáil was the French journalist Yves-Marie Goblet. He was one of the few, it seemed, who realised what was to come:

Those who knew it, partisans or adversaries, divined that a new epoch was beginning, and one that would be terrible.[37]

An echo of W.B. Yeats and his 'A terrible beauty is born', perhaps.

Collins was one of the members of that first Dáil (a member was known as a *teachta dála* or TD), representing the Cork South constituency. He would represent that same constituency until his death in 1922. Collins and his partner Harry Boland did not, however, attend the first session of the Dáil, though they were marked as present. A great many TDs were in British jails, and those two were in Britain arranging the escape of Éamon de Valera, who remained in jail after the 'German Plot'. Following his dramatic escape from Lincoln Prison on 3 February 1919, de Valera was elected *priomh aire* (prime minister) of the Dáil on 1 April and went to the United States to highlight British injustices in Ireland and to drum up support for an Irish Republic. He was most successful in raising funds for the Dáil Loan but failed in his efforts to get either of the US political parties to officially recognise the Irish Republic in their 1920 election programmes. He remained in the US until December 1920.

From 1919 to the end of 1921, the Irish waged the War of Independence with strong reliance on intelligence, propaganda, politics and guerrilla tactics, coordinated by Collins to make up a fully orchestrated plan of campaign. British forces, on the other hand, at no time fought their campaign in all these arenas. Their approach was piecemeal. They had no overall strategy and no conception of a coordinated counter-insurgency. During the summer and autumn of 1920 they began to reorganise and develop in the intelligence, political and military arenas, but by this time it was perhaps too late to put down the revolt. Primarily the war was between the British Secret Service and the Collins network in Dublin, a war of harassment and reprisal in the country, and a war of propaganda. Collins's intelligence ring and his ruthlessly used killers were the linch-pin of the war effort in Dublin, and he sent directives across the country coordinating efforts in almost every field.[38] The IRA won the battle for the hearts and minds of the Irish people. The IRA/Volunteers became the fighting arm of an underground, alternative government.[39]

In the early years of the War of Independence, Collins, as director of organisation, set about reorganising the Volunteer movement. At first the British ridiculed the Irish and their attempts at warfare, but during this period Collins developed the morale and discipline of his fighting men to the very high degree that characterised it for the next four years. He recognised that guerrilla warfare was the only way forward, both in Dublin and in the countryside. In fact, it was the sheer efficiency of Collins's planning which was its most valuable asset. (Physical fighting against the British was of a rather different character in rural areas from what it was in Dublin. In the country, attacks on RIC barracks were first undertaken by men who assembled at night and who, after carrying out the operation, resumed their ordinary civilian life. Later, small bodies of men in flying columns remained on full-time active service in the countryside, receiving shelter and food from the country people, obtaining assistance from local IRA men and civilians in their activities, and operating on the hit-and-run method. Leadership of these columns required certain qualities. The column leader had to be fearless, as well as resourceful, alert and responsible.) Collins, through the dual areas of intelligence and operations, ruled the active side of the IRA/Volunteers with the same concentration that he expected of all who worked for him. He knew that the fundamentals of intelligence were acquisition, analysis, counter-intelligence and implementation. His intelligence department, under Liam Tobin, Tom Cullen and Frank Thornton, handled the first three, and he delegated the fourth to his Squad.

As the Volunteer director of intelligence from January 1920 to July 1921, Collins became the mastermind of an Irish intelligence network that successfully countered British intelligence in Ireland. It did so by making a mirror image of the British intelligence system and then improving on it. Collins was the first to understand the necessity for an intelligence service that would penetrate the British military and civil administration in Dublin Castle. The success of the revolutionary movement was largely due to this effort. Inexperienced personnel, who had no rigid ideas about the kind of organisation needed, helped build up his intelligence organisation from nothing. But he was entirely clear about the results he wanted from any organisation set up. In this sphere, success or failure depended largely on his vision and energy, as well as his efficient operatives. Slackness and inertia, the failure to put weapons to good use and failure to file reports produced harsh rebukes.

Though Collins often walked and cycled throughout Dublin after the Dáil met in January 1919, he was never arrested, despite the fact that the head of the British army in Ireland, Gen. Nevil Macready, wrote to his superiors in London in March 1921 to recommend that the British government offer £10,000 for his capture.[40] (The average worker's wage at the time was £2.2s per week, yet no one seriously thought of betraying Collins. The story of a £10,000 price on his head is not strictly true. After Detective Inspector W.C. Forbes Redmond was killed on 21 January 1920, a £10,000 reward was offered by Dublin Castle for information leading to the arrest and conviction of the person(s) responsible for his death, 'especially to the man who issued the order'. This is where the story of the Collins reward probably originated, as he was the one who ordered Redmond's killing. Rewards of £5,000 had previously been offered in regard to the deaths of other DMP detectives, Smith, Hoey and Barton, and these rewards were now doubled, but there was never a specific reward offered for Collins's capture.)

Collins recognised at an early stage that his twin enemies were the spy and the informer, the enemies of any revolutionary movement, and he systematically removed both. Thus the removal of informers and spies was a crucial element of IRA tactics. As late as the spring of 1921 they were still being shot. Between January and April 1921, 73 bodies with placards round their necks announcing the removal of an informer or spy were taken from the Irish streets. The secrecy of IRA operations was rigorously maintained, and Collins's intelligence agency could act with a considerable feeling of security.

Once this internal sanction of eliminating British agents had been institutionalised, the weapon was turned, with great effect, on the special branches of both the Dublin Metropolitan Police (DMP) and the Royal Irish Constabulary (RIC) outside of Dublin. (The DMP had always been an unarmed force; the RIC had always been armed but its command structure had never been designed to deal with a war situation.) Collins's view in 1920 was simple:

> a man might have been murdered in broad daylight (and many were) in the Dublin streets, and not one policeman have lifted a finger. The uniformed men on point duty would have gone on waving traffic this way and that ... the attitude of the police was reasonable—while they stayed neutral they were safe; as soon as they interfered they became marked men.[41]

The intelligence network was organised on two distinct levels: the civil and the military. The military side, the more important of the two, operated mainly through the underground cells of the IRB that Collins commanded. Formally, the IRA/Volunteers were organised along British military lines. Each company and battalion had an intelligence officer whose reports were passed through a brigade intelligence officer to the central office in Dublin. This, however, was an adjunct to Collins's own network of IRB spies operating separately in most Irish communities. On the civil side Collins had men and women in post offices, and the Irish Post Office was certainly one of his most useful sources. In addition, he had men on the railways, on channel ferries, in every prison in Ireland and many in England. The trade unions were mobilised to hamper police and military movements by road, rail and sea. Collins had many operatives who worked in all the various telephone exchanges, whether military or civilian, as in hotels, for example. Men and women in hotels and restaurants throughout Ireland were especially helpful sources. Similarly, dockers in all parts of Europe and the USA served in what Collins called his 'Q' Division.

Collins studied previous Irish risings and recognised the extent to which espionage had been responsible for their failure. Throughout the centuries, spies had infiltrated every revolutionary organisation, a relatively easy task in a small country like Ireland, where a careless word spoken at a fair or in a pub travelled quickly to the headquarters of the British spy network, Dublin Castle. The eyes and ears of this network, especially in villages and the countryside, were the members of the RIC, who reported all snippets of information to the DMP's political section, 'G' Division, based at Great Brunswick police station. Some 'G' Division detectives roamed freely around the city, following those suspected of disloyalty to the Crown or meeting informants and taking notes. Other 'G-men' were positioned at railway stations or docks to watch the arrivals and departures. At the end of each working shift, all the G-men would transfer their notes and reports into a large ledger-type book held at the police station, so that all members of the division would have access to the same information. This served as a communal cross-reference and also avoided unintentional encroachment on the work of a colleague, which might jeopardise months of intelligence-gathering. All important reports were dispatched to Dublin Castle for sifting and correlation. The system was simple, even crude, but very effective.

By far the most important amongst Collins's agents were the men and women working for him in military intelligence and the civilian special branches. They were at the heart of the British administration, with access to restricted information, all British military and government codes and the like.

In particular, three Dublin policemen, Ned Broy, Joseph Kavanagh and James McNamara, as well as Dave Neligan in Dublin Castle, helped to turn what had been Britain's greatest security asset in Ireland against itself. Broy gave Collins a detailed inside knowledge of the British police system in Ireland. Collins learned how the system worked and how the police were trained; Broy turned him into an intelligence master. On the military side, Lily Mernin worked in the military intelligence offices in Ship Street Barracks. She was one of Collins's most important sources within the British military and would always make an extra carbon copy of relevant information for Collins.

> Before the 21st November 1920, it was part of my normal duty to type the names and addresses of British agents who were accommodated at private addresses and living as ordinary citizens of the city ... The typing of the lists ceased after the 21st November 1920 [Bloody Sunday].[42]

Although he had knowingly embarked upon his ruthless path, Collins was also aware of a possible public backlash. Republican newspapers and those sympathetic to the ideals of Sinn Féin were fed with appropriate propaganda. This policy of killing G-men led in turn to suppression and censorship by Dublin Castle. Such a knee-jerk reaction, together with the obvious alarm caused by the killings of the G-men, confirmed to Collins that he was hurting the British intelligence system, but he realised that London and Dublin would increase their efforts to smash his organisation. The first killings had been carried out by Volunteers, but he reasoned that a specialist unit was needed, a killing unit, who would react to orders efficiently and, most importantly, without qualms of conscience.

Collins needed a dedicated band of men to carry out the killings that he ordered. The 'Squad' was formally initiated on 19 September 1919, though by that time it had been in operation for four months and had already carried out two killings. Collins and Mulcahy presided at a meeting at which the unit was officially formed. Its original meeting had been on 1 May 1919.[43] Ben Barrett, Paddy Daly, Seán Doyle, Tom Keogh, Joe Leonard, Mick McDonnell[44] and Jim Slattery[45] attended. Barrett, Daly, Doyle and Leonard were told to leave their jobs, as they would become full-time employees. Daly was named the O/C.[46]

> We met Michael Collins and Dick Mulcahy at the meeting and they told us that it was proposed to form a squad. This Squad would take orders directly from Michael Collins, and, in the absence of Collins, the orders would be given through either Dick McKee or Dick Mulcahy. Dick [Mulcahy] told us that we were not to discuss our movements or actions

with Volunteer officers or with anybody else. Collins told us that we were being formed to deal with spies and informers and that he had authority from the Government to have this order carried out. He gave us a short talk, the gist of which was that any of us who had read Irish history would know that no organisation in the past had an intelligence system through which spies and informers could be dealt with, but that now the position was going to be rectified by the formation of an Intelligence Branch, an Active Service Unit or whatever else it is called.

Michael Collins only picked four of us for the Squad that night, Joe Leonard, Seán Doyle, Ben Barrett and myself in charge. He told the others that he had special work to do, but he told the four of us that we were to leave our employment and that we would be compensated for lose [sic] of work.[47]

William Stapleton was soon chosen to be a member, and he described the method of working in the Squad:

[Bill] Tobin or [Tom] Cullen [from Collins's intelligence staff] would come down and tell us who we were to get. It might be one of the Igoe Gang or a British spy sent over to shoot Collins. Two or three of us would go out with an intelligence officer in front of us, maybe about 10 or 15 yards. His job was to identify the man we were to shoot. Often we would be walking in the streets all day without meeting our man. It meant going without lunch. But other times the intelligence staff would have their information dead on and we could see our quarry immediately we came to the place we had been told he would be at. The intelligence officer would then signal us in the following way. He would take off his hat and greet the marked man. Of course, he didn't know him. As soon as he did this we would shoot. We knew that very great care was taken that this was so. As a result we didn't feel we had to worry. We were, after all, only soldiers doing our duty. I often went in and said a little prayer for the people we'd shot afterwards.[48]

The Squad was on the streets every day observing movements. They had a list of agents who were to be shot on sight, including certain 'G' Division detectives.

The Catholic Church in Ireland was split on the issue of the morality of the killings. While bishops condemned the gunmen, many of their priests were nationalists and supported the objectives and activities of the IRA. Squad member Vinnie Byrne said: 'I went to confession one day and told the priest I had shot dead a man. He asked me why and I told him, "Because he was a spy". The priest then asked me: "Did you believe you were right to do this?", and I said, "Yes, Father, because I was a soldier and the man was one of the enemy". The priest smiled and said, "Good man yourself".'

Collins's intelligence system was a crucial asset in the Irish War of Independence. In all the important military centres throughout the country, on the railroads, and on the docks and ferries Collins succeeded in planting someone who kept him well supplied with information. Nevertheless, he decried the need for it: 'This damn spying business plays hell with a man. It kills the soul and the heart in him. It leaves him without pity or mercy. I am fed up with the whole rotten business … Look how the poor girls are ruined by us. There is no softness in them anymore!'[49]

There was one serious drawback in Collins's intelligence organisation: he never did know what was happening in the inner circles of power in Westminster. Although he had a first-rate military intelligence system, he had no political intelligence organisation whatsoever. Ultimately this was a major flaw, particularly since there is strong evidence to suggest that the British had a fairly good idea of the thinking within the Dublin cabinet, and it became a grave defect as the Treaty negotiations ensued in late 1921. Still, the British intelligence war was widely acknowledged as being disastrous, with Collins and his men and women operatives consistently out-spying his majesty's secret services.[50]

The streets of Dublin were the front line in the conflict between the police and the IRA. The G-men who specialised in political work proved particularly vulnerable to IRA attacks. Collins's decision to assassinate these men was partly pragmatic. Their elimination would remove a vital source of intelligence from the British administration in Ireland, allowing the IRA vital breathing space. Collins believed that

> England could always reinforce her Army. She could replace every soldier that she lost … But there were others indispensable for her purposes that were not so easily replaced … To paralyse the British machine it was necessary to strike at individuals. Without her spies, England was helpless. It was only by their accumulated and accumulating knowledge that the British machine could operate.

But there were also political and symbolic motives. The G-men were the most hated symbols of the British regime, particularly despised for their role in picking out the leaders of the rebellion for execution in 1916. Their killings could be depicted as justifiable, while the British response to them would escalate the conflict. Between July 1919 and May 1920, a dozen DMP men were assassinated. By the end of Collins's brutal but effective campaign, the DMP's intelligence-gathering capabilities had been destroyed and the force was on the verge of collapse. The DMP was compelled to withdraw from direct involvement in the conflict, its members refusing to carry arms or to assume any responsibility for political crime.[51] When the new Secret Service men were assigned to Dublin, there were few policemen of the old persuasion who could or would help them. Collins forced each man to start from scratch, and the British intelligence system was never the same.

The leading edge of the terror campaign of Collins's Squad was selective assassination, involving groups of three to ten men. Collins set out to undermine the morale and effectiveness of the police in order to knock out the eyes and ears of the British administration. Police, magistrates, informers and men prominent in public life were shot. Assassinations ran the whole gamut from police killings to military killings (such as that of an officer in the British army, Capt. Percival Lea-Wilson, who had severely mistreated Tom Clarke and other combatants of the Rising), to necessity. W.C. Forbes Redmond, chief inspector of the DMP, had to be removed because he was pressing Collins too hard. Similarly, the magistrate Alan Bell, taken in daylight from a Dublin tram and shot without anyone interfering, was assassinated because he was carrying on a most successful investigation into the origin and whereabouts of the Dáil Loan deposits.[52] Collins regarded assassinations such as these, and particularly the removal of spies, as essential to the success of the IRA campaign. Police intelligence reported in 1919 that 'according to information received from various sources the Irish Volunteer HQ has directed all county commanders to hold a certain number of men armed and in readiness to execute orders to attack barracks and assassinate police'.[53]

In 1919 the already busy Collins received yet another responsibility when Éamon de Valera appointed him as minister for finance. From then on, and concurrently with his intelligence and military activities, Collins acted as a civil administrator leading a central ministry charged with keeping the Irish government afloat financially. He was brilliant in the position: he devised and oversaw the Dáil Loan that raised millions for the cause of Irish independence and to sustain the revolutionary government. The Loan provided the funds necessary for all departments, as well as the purchase of weapons to make possible the IRA's campaign. Raising money and hiding it from government agents was an old Irish custom. The Fenians did it with their 'Fenian Loan' in the 1860s and the Land League did it in the 1880s. Collins was following in their footsteps and was even more successful. He established an elaborate mechanism to secure the funds from British seizure, including converting some of the funds into gold bullion, which was hidden in numerous places around Dublin. And when the British did discover one of his hiding places he reacted ruthlessly, using his intelligence sources to protect the funds and to eliminate those who would confiscate them for the British. The final Loan total, subscribed by over 135,000 Irish people, was £378,858 in Ireland alone. A further $5,123,640 was raised separately in the United States. Both were immense sums for the time.

The War of Independence was a guerrilla campaign mounted against the British government in Ireland by the IRA/Volunteers from January 1919 until the truce in July 1921, under the proclaimed legitimacy of the First Dáil. Military operations remained limited during 1919, although raids for arms became a regular occurrence. Even though the Irish had abandoned the idea of Home Rule and embraced separatism, the violence was at first deeply unpopular with the broader Irish population. But attitudes gradually changed in the face of the terror of the British government's campaign of widespread brutality, destruction of property, random arrests, reprisals and unprovoked shootings. The small groups of IRA/Volunteers on the run were extremely vulnerable. Their success could make or break the activity of the IRA in a particular district; losing them often meant the end of operations. The local populaces provided more than just moral support: in many cases they provided logistics, intelligence, and men and women for local actions. In September 1919 the Dáil was banned by the British, which served to make it easier for the IRA/Volunteers to carry out attacks, because their more moderate politicians no longer had a public platform from which to restrain them.

For the remainder of 1919 and into 1920 the level of violence throughout Ireland increased. The British had to exert effective control over much of the countryside or lose the war. Nearly all the Irish lived in the country, on farms or in villages, and various quasi-official bodies like the Dáil/Republican Courts or the IRA effectively neutralised loyalists found throughout Ireland. The IRA benefited from the widespread support given to them by the general population, which regularly refused to pass information to the British. Much of the IRA's popularity was due to the excessive reaction of British forces to insurgent activity. An unofficial government policy of reprisals began in September 1919 in Fermoy, Co. Cork, when 200 British soldiers looted and burned the main businesses of the town after a soldier was killed when he refused to surrender his weapon to the local IRA. Actions such as these increased local support for the IRA and international support for Irish independence.

The British government was unwilling ever to admit that a rebellion existed which had to be countered with military methods. The conflict was never defined, and the issue was obscured by attempting to distinguish between war and insurrection, summed up by British Prime Minister David Lloyd George's comment, 'You don't declare war against rebels'. The struggle was never a conventional war; it was rarely more than a police action. The British army was used only sparingly, and greatly resented the blame that became attached to them by the actions of the police, the Black and Tans and the Auxiliaries. In fact, with some exceptions, the military enjoyed a more civil relationship with the civilian population.

The arrival of the Black and Tans in March 1920 changed the entire complexion of the war. The 'Tans' were established as a section of the RIC and first appeared in the village of Upperchurch, Co. Tipperary. The Tans were not all prisoners released from English jails, as has been claimed, but they were too ignorant of the law to be useful at police work, and too undisciplined to have any military value. The British government needed more troops in Ireland to maintain its position, and turned to unemployed demobilised soldiers from World War I. The name came from their uniforms, which consisted of black tunics and dark tan or khaki trousers, some with civilian hats but most with the green caps and black leather belts of the RIC.[54] Collins viewed the Black and Tans and the terror that came with them (and with the Auxiliaries who followed shortly) as a sort of mixed blessing. Clearly it drove any doubting nationalists into the arms of Sinn Féin. 'Apart from the loss which these attacks entail, good is done as it makes clear and clearer to people what both sides stand for.'[55] The Tans were a force calculated to inspire terror in a population less timid and law-abiding than the Irish. There was no question of discipline: they robbed and killed on a daily basis. Collins took advantage of the public's reaction and knew that the terror backfired on the British. By late 1920, Gen. F.P. Crozier, the O/C of the Black and Tans, had dismissed or imprisoned more than 50 for indiscipline or criminal acts.[56]

Their appearance in Dublin altered the whole view of the city. Kathleen Napoli McKenna, who worked on the *Irish Bulletin* and saw Collins almost daily, wrote of what a Sunday morning in Dublin looked like. Instead of empty streets with only Mass-goers about,

> … citizens were thronging to hear Mass through the streets filled with British Regulars carrying rifles with fixed bayonets, Auxiliary Cadets, Black and Tans and here and there, broad-shouldered plainclothesmen distinguishable as members of the 'G' Division of the Dublin Metropolitan Police engaged in political espionage. A tank was ambling along Bachelor's Walk, military lorries, filled with armed-to-the-teeth troops, their rifles at the ready, were racing through O'Connell St., and military cordons were

drawn with barbed wire around entrances from Grafton St. from Nassau St. and College Green.[57]

That was the Dublin that resulted from Collins's plans and actions from March 1920 onwards.

Between November 1920 and the Truce in July 1921 the pace of the war intensified. Bitterness increased on both sides. No description of guerrilla warfare can fully convey the horror of a situation in which soldier and civilian occupy the same area and are turned with hatred on each other. In Ireland, the sole purpose of the police and the military was to subjugate the IRA/Volunteers by whatever means they could. The sole purpose of the civilians was to support the Irish forces arrayed against the British. The civilian population inevitably suffered the most, emotionally as well as physically, living in a constant state of trauma.[58] The British were clearly out of touch with the temper of the Irish people, as was evident from some of the ideas proposed in the British cabinet. In 1920 the GOC of the British army in Ireland, General Sir Nevil Macready, proposed to take on the IRA with more mobile forces, but Field Marshal Sir Henry Wilson said that Macready's plan was useless. Wilson pressed the British 'to collect the names of Sinn Féiners by districts; proclaim them on church doors all over the country; and shoot them whenever a policeman is murdered; pick 5 by lot and shoot them!'[59]

And so rebellion continued in Ireland, not with a great take-over of Dublin or with pitched battles but with brutal city and country ambushes designed to demoralise representatives of the British government and the British people themselves. Primarily the war was between the British Secret Service, the DMP and the RIC and Collins's network in Dublin, as well as a war of harassment and reprisal in the country, and a war of propaganda. Collins's plans for urban and rural guerrilla warfare kept the British from exerting control over the country, and inexorably turned the tide of opinion against British rule in Ireland.

General Macready refused to take responsibility for the RIC, the Black and Tans or the Auxiliaries and openly condemned their acts of indiscipline. This friction between the military and the police was a major factor in Britain's failure to implement an effective security policy during 1920. By October 1920 the 'King's Writ' no longer ran in the countryside. The Irish strategy of making Ireland ungovernable by Britain was beginning to work. British rule in Ireland had virtually collapsed, and the Dáil made astonishing strides in setting up the counter-state. People dutifully paid their rates to local republican authorities and ignored the tax demands of the British. The wholesale destruction of tax offices made the British tax-gathering system unworkable.

In addition, the Dáil/Republican Courts proved far more effective and prompt than the old system ever was. All British forces were now being concentrated in the towns, or, at least, in very strong barracks, obviously with a view to shortening the front. The IRA/Volunteer forces opposing them were becoming stronger and more highly organised, albeit with little overall coordination from Dublin. Collins had begun to exert some control over matters outside Dublin but still concentrated his efforts within the city.[60]

Further complicating matters for the British, there was usually little coordination between the Royal Irish Constabulary, the Black and Tans, the Auxiliary Cadets and the regular British army. As a result of the lack of control over the Tans and Auxiliaries there was widespread hostility throughout Ireland, often directed at any British official. Consequently, the British military and civil administration was torn between those who thought it best to ride out the storm, letting politicians negotiate a settlement, and those who advocated sterner measures to stamp out the IRA/Volunteers completely.

Neither the Tans nor the Auxiliaries exhibited much in the way of military discipline and the levels of their violence and reprisals mounted daily. Their arrival and the brutality of their tactics drove more and more Irish to support the IRA. The Irish, ruled by the British for so long, now began to think of their resistance as patriotism. By late 1920 public opinion had swung wildly against the British presence in Ireland. The Dublin execution of an eighteen-year-old medical student, Kevin Barry, for killing a British soldier, the shooting of the lord mayor of Cork, Thomas MacCurtain, in front of his wife, and the arrest and death on hunger strike of the succeeding lord mayor of Cork, Terence MacSwiney, were events that made the British position in Ireland ever more untenable.[61]

Terence MacSwiney's death on 25 October 1920 seemed the most important event that occurred in the country at that time. Ireland went into mourning when he died on the 74th day of his fast. He had become a symbol of a new nation—disciplined, hard, clear, unsentimental, uncompromising, a conscious using of vigour to build up strength.[62] The only really new weapon used by the War of Independence prisoners was the audacious and formidable one of hunger strike. This desperate form of protest was not an official policy of any of the national organisations; nobody was ever ordered to adopt it. Prisoners were free to decide to hunger strike, either individually or in combination, but Volunteers were instructed that, once embarked upon, it should not be abandoned until victory was won or death intervened. It was an elemental conflict between the individual prisoner and the power that held him or her captive. The early British reaction to hunger strike was the application of the Prisoners (Temporary Discharge for Ill-Health) Act 1913, usually known as the Cat and Mouse Act. This permitted the release of hunger strikers and their re-arrest for completion of their sentences after the lapse of such time as the authorities assumed had enabled them to recover from the effects of their fasting. But when Irish political prisoners so released disappeared and could not be re-arrested, or when, as was usual, they refused to give the required undertaking to return to prison at the end of a specified period, use of the Act was discontinued. Collins disliked such strikes, however, and had hated to see his friend Tom Ashe die as a result of a hunger strike in 1917. Once he told MacSwiney that 'I'd rather take one peelers' barracks than all your moral victories'. Collins was a veteran of hunger strikes in Frongoch and was at that time a believer in their effectiveness. He always stood faithfully by the protesters, but he had changed his mind about the strikes and became opposed to them in principal. Along with MacSwiney's wife, Muriel, he tried to persuade MacSwiney to stop the strike; they failed, and he disapproved of all hunger strikes thereafter. Collins wanted men who would work for a cause, not die for it. Immediately after MacSwiney's death, Collins and Griffith ordered the remaining IRA prisoners to end their protest. He was instrumental in getting Sinn Féin to forbid the strikes, though some individuals continued down that path.[63]

The IRA had shot 182 policemen and 50 soldiers by the end of 1920. In response to the growing violence, the British government introduced the Restoration of Order in Ireland Act. This act, passed in August 1920, allowed for the internment and court-martial of civilians and led to the arrest of a large number of IRA officers. The level of public support for the IRA, however, continued to rise. The British government initially asserted that it was dealing with civil disorder rather than with war, but by this stage it realised otherwise. The struggle was embittered by successive acts of violence and terror, and by the reprisals and counter-reprisals that followed. In December 1920 the British sanctioned official reprisals, raising the level of violence to new heights and further alienating the local populations.

The condemnation of British reprisals was not limited to the Irish, nor expressed only in quiet British government communications. General Sir Hubert Gough wrote to the *Manchester Guardian* in early October:

> In Ireland at the moment murder and destruction are condoned and winked at, if not actively encouraged. The murder of policemen and others by the 'Irish republicans' have been inexcusable. As you say, the leaders of Sinn Féin and the Irish priesthood are very greatly to be condemned for not having taken a far more active part against such methods, but that is no excuse for any government, and especially a

government of the great British empire, adopting such methods.[64]

In an effort to placate those in the North who were still opposed to any movement in the direction of Home Rule in Ireland, on 11 November 1920 the Government of Ireland Bill was passed in the British House of Commons and was enacted on 23 December. It proposed separate Home Rule parliaments for southern Ireland and for northern Ireland. A Council of Ireland was to be set up, with members from each parliament, in the hope of one day removing partition and reuniting the two entities. Both parliaments would be subject to Westminster.

The Parliament of Northern Ireland came into being in 1921. At its inauguration in Belfast City Hall on 22 June 1921, King George V made his famous appeal for Anglo-Irish and north–south reconciliation. The speech, drafted by David Lloyd George's government on recommendations from Jan Smuts, prime minister of the Union of South Africa, with the enthusiastic backing of the king, opened the door for formal contact between the British government and the Republican administration of de Valera.

The Parliament of Southern Ireland never became a reality. Both it and the Parliament of Northern Ireland were to be bicameral legislatures as part of 'Home Rule'. The Second Dáil was elected on 19 May 1921 in the 26 counties of the south and on 24 May in the six counties of the north. This election became known as the 'partition election' because it was the first time that an election was held at different times in the six counties and in the 26 counties. All 128 MPs elected to the House of Commons of southern Ireland were returned unopposed, and 124 of them, representing Sinn Féin, declared themselves TDs and assembled as the Second Dáil of the Irish Republic. When only the lord lieutenant, the four Unionist MPs (all representing graduates of the Irish universities) and fifteen appointed senators turned up for the state opening of the southern parliament in the Council Room of the Department of Agriculture and Technical Instruction in Dublin (now Government Buildings) in June 1921, the new southern House of Commons was suspended.

The Senate of Southern Ireland was to consist of the lord chancellor of Ireland as its chairman; fifteen peers of the realm, resident in southern Ireland, elected by their peers; eight privy councillors, elected by the privy council; two representatives of the Church of Ireland; two representatives of the Catholic Church (which declined to nominate); sixteen individuals nominated by the lord lieutenant, including two who were to be nominated after consultation with the Labour movement (which declined to be involved); and seventeen elected by the members of the county councils in different territorial constituencies. By this point local government was completely under the control of Sinn Féin and no nominations were received for the seventeen places. After a few attempts at meeting, neither southern house met again.

James Connolly had predicted that a partition previously proposed in 1914 by British Prime Minister H.H. Asquith and agreed upon by John Redmond, leader of the Irish Parliamentary Party, would be a disaster for Ireland. In the *Irish Worker* he wrote of partition:

> It is the trusted leaders of Ireland that in secret conclave with the enemies of Ireland have agreed to see Ireland as a nation disrupted politically and her children divided under separate political governments ... Such a scheme as that agreed by Redmond and Devlin—the betrayal of the national democracy of industrial Ulster—would mean a carnival of reaction both north and south, would set back the wheels of progress, would destroy the oncoming unity of the Irish Labour Movement and paralyse all advanced movements while it endured. To it Labour should give the bitterest opposition, against it Labour in Ulster should fight even to the death if necessary.[65]

These 1920/21 partition actions again backfired on the British government because they infuriated the IRA/Volunteers, but they did establish the partition that exists to this day.[66] As Connolly had foreseen, however, the British had agreed with the North on partition long before 1920. On 29 May 1916 (just a month after the Rising), David Lloyd George, Britain's minister for munitions, wrote to Edward Carson:

> My Dear Carson
> I enclose Greer's draft resolutions.
> We must make it clear that at the end of the provisional period Ulster does not, whether she wills it or not, merge in the rest of Ireland.
> Ever sincerely
> D. Lloyd George
> P.S. Will you show it to Craig?[67]

In 1920 the British had organised a special intelligence unit whose sole purpose was to break Collins's organisation. The men charged to carry out this policy became known as the 'Cairo Gang'. For six months Collins had watched the British get closer and closer. From their first appearance in Dublin he had been gathering information on them: he set his own spies to open their correspondence, had the contents of their wastepaper baskets taken by the housemaids, and had duplicate keys made for their rooms. Collins had clearly become a prime goal of the British intelligence organisations, and they were getting close.

In November 1920, the single most damaging event in relation to the British intelligence organisation in Ireland occurred. On Sunday morning, 21 November 1920, Collins's Squad executed fourteen British intelligence agents, most of them members of that Cairo Gang, who had been poised to eliminate him and other important leaders. In response, Auxiliaries, Black and Tans and RIC units drove in armoured cars to Croke Park during a football match between Dublin and Tipperary, shooting into the crowd at random.[68] Fourteen unarmed people were killed and 65 wounded. Later that day three republican prisoners, Dick McKee, Peadar Clancy and Conor Clune (an innocent young man from County Clare who had simply come to Dublin to meet and talk about Gaelic language studies), were 'shot while trying to escape' in Dublin Castle.[69] This day became known as Bloody Sunday.

Dave Neligan, a Collins spy in Dublin Castle, reported that the killing of the intelligence personnel 'caused complete panic in the Castle'.[70] Later, when asked how he felt about the episode, Collins stated: 'For myself, my conscience is clear. There is no crime in detecting and destroying, in wartime, the spy and the informer. They have destroyed without trial. I have paid them back in their own coin.'[71]

The executions of the British agents had a shattering effect on the morale of the British in Ireland, as well as in England. The British public and government were shocked and stunned and could not believe that with all their mighty resources they could be so humiliated. Though Lloyd George fumed about 'murderers' in public, it was this event as much as any other that led him to begin sending emissaries to Ireland seeking peace.

By spring 1921 the IRA/Volunteers had become a force in Dublin and its 'flying columns' had become feared throughout the counties of Cork, Kerry and Clare. The columns were mobile units of from ten to 100 men, who could strike in devastating ambushes and then melt into a hinterland that they knew far better than the British military units who were deployed to fight them. Nevertheless, most IRA units were chronically short of both weapons and ammunition.

> At this particular time things were so bad with all the units that it was a question of how long they could last, would we last a month, a fortnight? The only reason was we had little left to fight with. We had no ammunition; we had a few guns. So bad was it that they cut down Winchester ammunition to fit .45 and several members of the ASU and

other units met with serious accidents as a result.[72]

Earlier in the war, Collins had said that 'without guns you might as well be dead'. Now the emphasis was on a lack of ammunition. By the end of spring 1921, though a formidable opponent, the IRA had not been able to dislodge the British forces, and it became clear to Collins that the Irish could not defeat those forces in the field.

Éamon de Valera returned to Ireland from the United States in December 1920, and the continued British and US newspaper references to the IRA/Volunteers as 'murderers' led him to press for a full-scale engagement with the British as opposed to the guerrilla tactics used by the IRA. Soon after he returned from America de Valera told Richard Mulcahy: 'You are going too fast. This odd shooting of a policeman here and there is having a very bad effect, from the propaganda point of view, on us in America. What we want is one good battle about once a month with about 500 men on each side.'[73] De Valera overruled Collins's objections to the strategic error of attacking the British in large numbers in a single battle, and plans were discussed for a large-scale attack. At first de Valera wanted an attack on Beggar's Bush Barracks, but Oscar Traynor, O/C of the Dublin Brigade of the IRA, refused. Finally it was decided to attack and set fire to the Custom House in Dublin. The attack was calamitous for the IRA/Volunteers in Dublin. On 25 May 1921 the IRA burned down the Custom House, the centre of British administrative rule in Ireland. As a military operation it was a disaster for the IRA, with over 80 men captured and five killed. The venture into conventional warfare was a setback, and Collins knew it. As worldwide propaganda, though, it was a huge success, demonstrating to the wider world how strong the IRA was and how weak the British position now was in Ireland. That 'strength' was illusory, however, and most IRA leaders, and especially Collins, recognised that the organisation's desperate shortage of weapons and ammunition would soon allow the British to wear it down.

Throughout the War, IRA propaganda, like its intelligence, was highly efficient. It reached and was planned to reach all the major European capitals and the USA. The department had been established in April 1918 under Robert Brennan. Its function had initially been to supply Sinn Féin leaders with data on which to base their movements, but it soon dropped this information work and became an aggressive arm of the campaign. The *Irish Bulletin* was its main organ and was distributed free to press correspondents and liberal-minded men of political influence in England. By 1921, £4,000 a year was being spent for the 'general routine work' in the London office alone.[74]

Of the intelligence and propaganda war, Collins himself wrote:

Ireland's story from 1918 to 1921 may be summed up as the story of a struggle between our determination to govern ourselves and to get rid of British government and the British determination to prevent us from doing either. It was a struggle between two rival Governments, the one an Irish Government resting on the will of the people and the other an alien Government depending for its existence upon military force—the one gathering more and more authority, the other steadily losing ground.[75]

As British hopes of controlling the country faded, they began to wonder whether Ireland was worth the price. It now cost more to defend and control than it was worth. On the Irish side, morale was deteriorating with the escalating British reprisals and raids. The IRA/Volunteer numbers had been greatly reduced by imprisonments and internment. In the rural areas the need for intelligence had not really been understood, and Collins did not have the same sources throughout the countryside as he had in Dublin.[76] Although their positions were greatly different, both sides began to realise their own shortcomings. Later Collins would write:

We took as much of the government of Ireland out of the hands of the enemy as we could, but we could not grasp all of it because he used the whole of his forces to prevent us doing so, and we were unable to beat him out of the country by force of arms. But neither had he beaten us. We had made Ireland too uncomfortable for him. There were too many ambush areas in country areas, and too many gloomy street corners in Cork and Dublin. The British had not surrendered and had no need to agree to humiliating terms any more than we would have done. It was a time for settlement that would secure for us their withdrawal and evacuation. There was duress, of course. On their side, the pressure of world opinion to conform their practice to their professions, to make an honourable peace with us. On our side, the duress the weaker nation suffers against the stronger, the duress to accept really substantial terms.[77]

At that time, as president of Dáil Éireann, de Valera authorised members of the government to open negotiations with Britain. 'Peace feelers' were extended progressively throughout the first half of 1921, and in July 1921 a truce was negotiated. On 9 July terms were agreed upon, and the Truce came into effect at noon on 11 July 1921. Frank Thornton, one of Collins's most important lieutenants, wrote that the Truce came with dramatic suddenness.

Whether the truce was a good thing or not remains for historians to record, but, in my humble opinion, had it not taken place we would have found ourselves very hard set to continue the fight with any degree of intensity, owing to that very serious shortage of ammunition, because men, no matter how determined they may be or how courageous, cannot fight with their bare hands.[78]

Collins, too, emphasised that suddenness of the Truce. 'When we were told of the offer of a truce, we were astounded. We thought you [the British] must have gone mad.' But there was trepidation as well. Mulcahy agreed that to drive the British from anything more substantial than a police barracks was beyond them,[79] and Collins said that 'once a Truce is agreed, and we come out into the open, it is extermination for us if the Truce should fail ... We shall be ... like rabbits coming out from their holes.'[80] It has been said that Collins was an extremist, but the evidence of history shows that he was really more moderate than de Valera.

> Unlike the President [de Valera], who tended to portray a moderate public image while advocating a more hardline approach, Collins tended to do the opposite. Privately he was much more moderate than generally believed.[81]

Following the Truce, de Valera and British Prime Minister David Lloyd George engaged in meetings in London to determine how negotiations should proceed. Both had reputations as skilled negotiators, and they probably possessed the shrewdest political minds in Europe at the time. De Valera continually pressed his interpretation of the meetings in correspondence through the next few months. Lloyd George, however, just as firmly made it clear that Britain would not enter negotiations on the basis that Ireland was 'an independent sovereign state'.[82]

The basis of the conference was the 'Gairloch Formula' proposed by Prime Minister Lloyd George (named after his country house in Scotland, where Harry Boland went on behalf of de Valera to deliver messages to Lloyd George while he was on holiday). According to this formula, the status of a republic, previously demanded by de Valera, was not acceptable, and instead the purpose of the Irish delegation was to ascertain 'how the association of Ireland with the community of nations known as the British Empire may best be reconciled with Irish national aspirations'. It was said that de Valera's difficulty was that Lloyd George 'offered the Irish what they don't want [a dominion], and the one thing they do want—unity with Ulster—he had no power to give them'.[83]

On 18 September 1920 Lloyd George wrote:

> From the very outset of our conversation I told you that we looked to Ireland to own allegiance to the Throne, and to make her future as a member of the British Commonwealth. That was the basis of our proposals, and we cannot alter it. The status which you now claim for your delegates is, in effect, a repudiation of that status.

Finally, after more correspondence between the two over the next two weeks, on 30 September de Valera chose to write:

> Our respective positions have been stated and are understood and we agree that conference, not correspondence, is the most practical and hopeful way to an understanding. We accept the invitation, and our Delegates will meet you in London on the date mentioned 'to explore every possibility of settlement by personal discussion'.[84]

The 'date mentioned' was 11 October, and on that date treaty negotiations began in London. Arthur Griffith, Collins, George Gavan Duffy, Robert Barton and Éamonn Duggan represented the Irish, as plenipotentiaries.

The day before he left for London, Collins wrote presciently:

> At this moment there is more ill-will within a victorious assembly than ever could be anywhere except in the devil's assembly. It cannot be fought against. The issue, and persons, are mixed up to such an extent as to make discernability [sic] an impossibility except for a few. ... the trusted ones, far from being in accord, are disunited ... This is a time when jealousy and personal gain count for more than country.[85]

Although Griffith was the top-ranking delegate, Collins was recognised as the *de facto* leader. Collins was extremely uncomfortable with being chosen as a delegate. It was not his field of expertise but it was his duty and he accepted it grudgingly.[86] Batt O'Connor, a close friend, described how Collins bitterly complained that 'It was an unheard of thing that a soldier who had fought in the field should be elected to carry out negotiations. It was de Valera's job, not his.'[87]

The War of Independence, while bringing the British to the bargaining table for the first time, was not a clear military victory and certainly did not produce a social revolution, as so many had hoped. Nor was there a progressive administration in place to take over the operation of a new state, whatever form that state was to take. There were many forces opposing one another in Ireland—liberalism vs conservatism; socialism vs capitalism; dominion (or even monarchy) vs republic. During the whole period there were short-term goals, but no long-term solutions to all the problems facing the Irish had been developed, least of all what form the new government was to take. There must have been many in the Dáil who realised that, as unified and homogeneous as it had seemed during the war, there were now apparently irreconcilable differences. In fact, during the whole period little thought was given to a new government for Ireland. Florence O'Donoghue wrote:

> I do not think that in 1917, or indeed during the following years of struggle, any of us thought very much about forms of government. I had no clearer definition of national freedom than that envisaged by the ejection of British troops and British machinery of government out of the country. Republicanism was no more than a convenient term of expression, not a faith or a belief in a particular form of government.[88]

Since 1916, and really since 1913, there had been tremendous changes in thought and expectation in Ireland, but the very rapidity of that change fostered confusion. Freedom from Britain seems to have been considered the sole end in itself, with little or no thought—and certainly no preparation—for what was to come afterward. This, however, didn't really seem to matter until the Truce came into effect in July.

One thing was absolutely clear from the London meetings in July 1921 and the follow-on correspondence between de Valera and Lloyd George: there was no question of a Republic. Both the cabinet in Dublin and the cabinet in London were aware of that. De Valera clearly grasped what was on offer: an acceptance of partition, an Irish Free State with the same Dominion status as Canada or Australia, an oath of allegiance to the Crown and the installation of a governor-general.[89] The Republic had been shelved before the negotiations began, and everyone concerned, particularly de Valera, recognised it.[90] In July 1921 he had told Prime Minister Smuts: 'If the status of a Dominion is offered to me, I will use all our machinery to get the Irish people to accept it'.[91] When asked to be a member of the delegation, Arthur Griffith agreed but told de Valera, 'You are my chief, and if you tell me to go, I'll go. But I know, and you know, that I can't bring back a Republic.'[92] De Valera explained to the Dáil why he insisted that Collins go to London: 'It was from the personal touch and contact I had with the Minister for Finance that I knew he was vital to the delegation'. Collins disagreed; he was to say: 'if we all stood on the recognition of the Irish Republic as a prelude to any conference we could very easily have said so, and there would have been no conference … It was the acceptance of the invitation that formed the compromise.'[93]

On 6 December 1921 the negotiating team for the British and the Irish plenipotentiaries signed the Articles of Agreement for a treaty, and the Irish delegation returned to Ireland for ratification. De Valera was much opposed to the Treaty, though it has been said that he was more affronted that he had not been consulted on the final day before signature in disregard of his 'instructions'. On learning of the details of the Treaty, de Valera announced that it was a matter for the cabinet. At an acrimonious cabinet meeting, the Treaty was approved by a majority of four to three. When the cabinet approved the agreement, he said it was a matter for the Dáil. It was then presented to the Dáil for ratification, where the divisions of ideology and personality that had always existed were put on public display.

The 'Treaty Debates' in the Dáil took place between 14 December 1921 and 7 January 1922, when the Dáil voted 64–57 in favour of the Treaty. Those Treaty Debates were considered by some the most vituperative in Irish history. Invective was hurled at and by both sides, personality conflicts that had simmered for many years degenerated into name-calling and *ad hominem* insults, and the vote was considered a 'betrayal of the ideals of 1916' by those who felt that the only acceptable treaty would be one unequivocally recognising an Irish Republic. Accusations of bad faith filled the air. Most importantly, the Treaty called for an oath of allegiance to the British Crown, and Republicans considered that traitorous. Finally, the Treaty called for partition of the North, and, although partition was an established fact after 1920, the conflict in the south only served to further undermine any possibility of reunification. Partition, however, was hardly mentioned in the Treaty Debates.

Terence deVere White described the Debates and their descent into eccentricity amidst

> … much latent hysteria; the calm, courteous, but unsound reasoning of Childers; the restless, sometimes effeminate emotionalism of de Valera; the moderation of Collins; the firm manliness of Griffith; the withering blight of Mary MacSwiney; the naivety of the other women; the weakness and candour of Barton; the sterile bitterness of Brugha; the incorrigible idealism of Mellows; the cynicism of J.J. Walsh; and the intelligence of two young men, Kevin O'Higgins and Patrick Hogan.[94]

Finally, that democratically elected body of Irish men and women had spoken, but de Valera led the anti-Treaty contingent from the assembly. De

Valera claimed to know 'in his heart' the wishes of his Irish countrymen, and refused to accept the Dáil vote as binding. Collins led the fight for Treaty ratification in the Dáil and in the country, and was vilified by the most hard-case republicans for selling out to the British. When the Dáil approved the Treaty in a close vote, de Valera raised the bar and contended that only the Irish people could ratify the Treaty, and so an election was scheduled for 16 June 1922.

Collins established an 'army reunification committee' to reunite the IRA and organised an election pact with de Valera's anti-Treaty political followers to campaign jointly in the June election and form a coalition government afterwards. He also tried to reach a compromise with anti-Treaty IRA leaders by agreeing to a republican-type constitution (with no mention of the British monarchy) for the new state.

In early March, de Valera formed the 'Cumann na Poblachta' (Republican Association) party while remaining a member of Sinn Féin, and commenced a speaking tour of the more republican province of Munster on 17 March 1922. During the tour he made controversial speeches, saying at one point: 'If the Treaty were accepted, the fight for freedom would still go on, and the Irish people, instead of fighting foreign soldiers, will have to fight the Irish soldiers of an Irish government set up by Irishmen'. More seriously, many IRA officers were also against the Treaty, and in March 1922 an *ad hoc* Army Convention repudiated the authority of the Dáil to accept the Treaty.

Collins's proposal for a republican constitution was vetoed by the British as being contrary to the terms of the Treaty, and they threatened military intervention in the Free State unless the Treaty were fully implemented. Collins reluctantly agreed. This completely undermined the electoral pact between the pro- and anti-Treaty factions. Meanwhile, under the leadership of Collins and Griffith the pro-Treaty Provisional Government set about establishing the Irish Free State, and organised the National Army—to replace the IRA—and a new police force.

The Treaty was ratified in that June 1922 election and the Irish Free State was established. There could no longer be any argument about which side spoke for the Irish people. Collins's words—'in my opinion, it gives us freedom. Not the ultimate freedom that all nations desire and develop to, but the freedom to achieve it'—resonated with the people. Upon the Treaty's ratification, de Valera resigned as president of the Republic and failed to be re-elected by an even closer vote of 60–58.

The June 1922 election did not represent a vote of confidence in the Provisional Government, and still less an expression of resistance to Republican ideals. It represented a popular realisation of the need for stable government and the acceptance of a realistic compromise with regard to Anglo-Irish relations. The desire for settled conditions was more important to the electorate than the endless debate over constitutional authority. Thus the election played an important role in legitimising the Treaty and the status of the Provisional Government. Although it did not prevent the Civil War that was shortly to follow, it greatly helped to facilitate the establishment of the Free State government during and after the war.

The most 'Republican' members of the IRA, the Dáil and the public still refused to accept the Treaty or the establishment of the Free State; they initiated an insurrection against the new Free State government, which they accused of betraying the Irish Republic. On 13 April 1922, Dublin's Four Courts was occupied by IRA/Republican troops led by Rory O'Connor. Upon taking it over, they issued the following proclamation:

> Fellow citizens of the Irish Republic. The fateful hour has come. At the direction of the hereditary enemy our rightful cause is being treacherously assailed by recreant Irishmen. Gallant soldiers of the Irish Republic stand rigorously firm in its defence. The sacred spirits of the Illustrious Dead are with us in this great struggle. 'Death Before Dishonour'. We especially appeal to our former comrades of the Irish Republic to return to that allegiance and thus guard the Nation's honour.

Griffith was in favour of using force against these men immediately, but Collins, who wanted at all costs to avoid civil war, left the Four Courts garrison alone until late June 1922. Collins was coming under increasing pressure from London to assert his government's authority in his capital. Finally, at 3.40am on 28 June 1922, the insurgents in the Four Courts were given an ultimatum to surrender by troops of the Free State under the command of Collins; when they refused, firing commenced twenty minutes later and the Irish Civil War had begun.

The outbreak of the Civil War forced pro- and anti-Treaty supporters to choose sides and split the IRA. The IRA/Republican/Irregulars who fought against the Free State were many of the same men who had fought in the IRA/Volunteers during the War of Independence, and thus used the same organisational structure, ranks and tactics as during the preceding conflict. When the War broke out, the anti-Treaty IRA (concentrated in the south and west) outnumbered the pro-Free State forces by roughly 15,000 men to 7,000. The paper strength of the IRA in early 1922 was over 72,000 men, but most of them were recruited during the truce with the British and fought in neither the War of Independence nor the Civil War. Moreover, the anti-Treaty

IRA lacked an effective command structure, a clear strategy and sufficient arms. As a result, they were forced to adopt a defensive stance throughout the war. By contrast, the Free State government managed to expand its forces dramatically after the start of the war. Collins and his commanders were able to build up an army that was able to overwhelm their opponents in the field. British supplies of artillery, aircraft, armoured cars, machine-guns, small arms and ammunition greatly assisted the pro-Treaty forces. The National Army amounted to 14,000 men by August 1922, and ultimately numbered 55,000 troops and 3,500 officers by the end of the war in May 1923. The most effective unit in the National Army was the élite Dublin Guard, which was recruited from the Dublin Active Service Unit that Collins had commanded in the War of Independence, and in particular from his Squad. It was this Dublin Guard which was implicated in the most brutal atrocities of the war.

The IRA/Republicans had three major problems in the Civil War, and they were unable to overcome any of them.

- They were fighting against an army most of whose leaders knew as much, if not more, about guerrilla fighting as they did.

- They had no Michael Collins to organise a vital intelligence system.

- The ordinary people of Ireland were suffering greatly economically and wanted peace—they simply were not with the Republicans.

With Dublin in pro-Treaty hands, conflict spread throughout the country. The war started with the anti-Treaty forces holding the towns of Cork, Limerick and Waterford as the so-called 'Munster Republic'. Since the anti-Treaty side was not equipped to wage conventional war, however, anti-Treaty O/C Liam Lynch was unable to take advantage of the Republicans' initial advantage in numbers and territory held. He hoped simply to retain control of the Munster Republic long enough to force Britain to renegotiate the Treaty. The large towns in Ireland had all been taken relatively easily by the Free State by August 1922. After the fall of Cork, Liam Lynch ordered anti-Treaty IRA units to disperse and form flying columns as they had when fighting the British, but they did not have the support of the people in the countryside that they had enjoyed during the War of Independence, and they were forced further and further south and west. Lynch was not only stubborn but also unrealistic.

When Collins was killed in an ambush by anti-Treaty Republicans at Béal na mBláth, near his home in County Cork, on 22 August 1922, he was on a mission to recover Free State funds in Cork City and to continue his attempts to bring the war to an end. To all intents and purposes it looked as if the war was drawing to a close, for there had been little indication since the fall of Cork on 12 August that the anti-Treaty forces could continue any programme of organised military opposition. To this end, Collins had instructed Frank Thornton to try and make contact with officers on the other side in order to arrange some meetings or negotiations. Collins's death increased the bitterness of the Free State leadership towards the Republicans and probably contributed to the subsequent descent of the conflict into a cycle of atrocities and reprisals.

The Civil War lasted until mid-1923 and cost an estimated 3,000 lives, including some of the leaders of the independence movement—notably Free State President Arthur Griffith, who died of a cerebral haemorrhage on 12 August 1922 that was attributed to the stresses of his office, and Collins, who was killed just ten days later. Well-known anti-Treaty Republicans Cathal Brugha, Harry Boland, Liam Mellows, Liam Lynch, Joe McKelvey, Dick Barrett, Erskine Childers and Rory O'Connor all died during the war. Intransigence and inflexibility were attributes of both sides in the conflict, and certainly impeded progress towards peace.

When Collins was killed on 22 August he was 31 years old. He was killed in a freakish ambush that even those opposing him said had gone wrong. His rise to Irish and world prominence had been meteoric, and his loss was devastating to the nascent Irish Free State government. His ascent had been spectacular, but his future could have made that pale into insignificance. He was killed just when he was needed most—even more than during the War of Independence.

The *London Daily Sketch* editorialised thus:

> The hand that struck down Collins, guided by a blinded patriotism, has aimed a blow at the unity of Ireland for which every one of her sons is fighting. Collins was probably the most skilled artisan of the fabric of a happier Ireland. Certainly he was the most picturesque figure in the struggle; and in the rearing of a new State a popular ideal serves as the rallying point to draw the contending elements. The death of Collins leaves the ship of the Free State without a helmsman.[95]

Collins's body was taken to St Vincent's Hospital in Dublin, where Dr Oliver St John Gogarty embalmed it and had Sir John Lavery paint Collins's portrait. Albert Power sculpted the death mask.

Collins's remains were taken to the chapel in St Vincent's on Thursday 24

August 1922, then late that evening to Dublin City Hall for the public lying-in-state. On Sunday evening his body was taken to the pro-cathedral, where it remained under guard overnight. His funeral Mass was celebrated there by several bishops on Monday 28 August.

Ironically, the gun-carriage on which the casket was transported to Glasnevin Cemetery had been borrowed from the British and had been used in the bombardment of the Four Courts in June. The Free State government specially purchased four black artillery horses from the British to pull the caisson to Glasnevin. Over 100,000 people lined the streets of Dublin to bid Collins farewell.

Richard Mulcahy, who would take Collins's place as commander in chief of the army, delivered the oration:

> ... Tom Ashe, Tomás MacCurtain, Traolach MacSuibhne, Dick McKee, Mícheál O'Coileain, and all you who lie buried here, disciples of our great chief, those of us you leave behind are all, too, grain from the same handful, scattered by the hand of the Great Sower over the fruitful Soil of Ireland. We, too, will bring forth our own fruit.
>
> Men and women of Ireland, we are all mariners on the deep, bound for a port still seen only through storm and spray, sailing still on a sea full 'of dangers and hardships, and bitter toil'. But the Great Sleeper lies smiling in the stern of the boat, and we shall be filled with that spirit which will walk bravely upon the waters.[96]

The Civil War was a tragic and passionate break between those who had fought side by side against the British, a break made more disastrous by the clear sincerity of those on both sides. What Ireland lost by Collins's death can never be known. It may be that his greatest accomplishments were behind him. But why Collins died is more important than how, where or at whose hand. If Collins's adult life embraced the struggle of independence, the cross at Béal na mBláth stands as a reminder of the wasting disease of civil war.[97] Like many who die young, Collins's death sealed his immortality.

Notes

1   Letter from Collins to Kevin O'Brien, 16 October 1916.
2   Mary Collins Powell, 'Living history' (undated).
3   Neeson 1968, 152.
4   Talbot 1923, 6.
5   McGuigan 2011.
6   The memoirs of Mary Collins Powell and of Sister Celestine (Helena Collins); family correspondence to cousin Michael O'Brien, 1922.
7   Gogarty 1937, 171. It is known that Collins had a stomach ulcer, and Gogarty speculated when he embalmed his body that it was a bleeding ulcer, hence the colour of Collins's skin. Collins wrote to Austin Stack about his stomach trouble on 1 July 1919. Later he told the Laverys that he suspected appendicitis (Lavery 1940, 216).
8   'Mr Lloyd George tells first story from within', NLI MS 498.
9   Richard Mulcahy, Notes on Béaslaí's *Michael Collins*, vol. I, 135.
10 O'Connor 1929, 155–6.
11 Daly, Gen. P.: Witness Statement 387.
12 Hart 2003, 198ff.
13 Barry 1981, 164–6.
14 Griffith and O'Grady 1982, 169–70.
15 O'Connor 1929, 144–7.
16 Regan 1995.
17 O'Connor 1996, 127.
18 Kenny 2007.
19 Béaslaí 1926b; 'The society of girls had apparently no attraction for him. He preferred the company of young men, and never paid any attention to the girls belonging to the Branch, not even to the sisters and friends of his male companions'. But see Dwyer 2015; see also Norris 2012.
20 See also Ryan 2007; McCoole 1996; Osborne 2003.
21 For a contrasting view see Ferriter 2014b: 'As for his feminist credentials, it is true that Collins relied on numerous women to assist in the fight against the Crown ... though mostly as secretaries, couriers and covers for his safe houses'. He quotes Hart (2006, 256) that Collins likely saw female republican activists as 'the servant class of the revolution, rarely as colleagues or comrades, more often as landladies, maids or cooks'.
22 Ironically, Patrick Pearse's play *The Singer*, written in autumn 1915, foretold this 'quietness' in the country (Pearse 1922):
    'Cuimin: We've no one to lead us.
    Colm: Didn't you elect me your captain?
    Cuimin: We did; but not to bid us rise out when the whole country is quiet.'
23 20 MS II,016, Bryce Papers 1915/16 (i). Letter from Margaret Ashton, 16 July 1916, National Library of Ireland, Dublin.
24 Curran 1966, 22.
25 Hally 1967, 53.
26 See Toby 1997.
27 Falls 1967, 203f.
28 One prayer-card for the executed leaders read: 'O Gentlest Heart of Jesus, have mercy on the souls of Thy servants, our Irish heroes; bring them from the shadows of exile to the bright home of Heaven, where, we trust, Thou and Thy Blessed Mother have woven for them a crown of unending bliss'. Prayer-cards for the repose of the souls of the following Irishmen who were executed by English law, 1916, TCD MS 2074.
29 Public Records Office (PRO), CO 904/102, January 1917.

30 Myles 1960.
31 Coogan 2000, 33.
32 O'Donoghue 1967.
33 There is no agreement on the total number of Irish soldiers who served in the British army and navy in the First World War. There appears to be a consensus on the figure of 210,000, of whom at least 35,000 died, though the figure on the National War Memorial is 49,400.
34 *Manchester Guardian*, 13 May 1918.
35 Kee 1972, 619.
36 O'Hegarty 1924 [1998], 23, 25.
37 Y.-M. Goblet, *Irlande dans la crise universelle* (Paris, 1921), quoted in Macardle 1937 [1965], 276.
38 Younger 1968, 93.
39 Bowden 1973.
40 Coogan 1992, 209.
41 See Nankivell and Loch 1922.
42 Mernin, Lily: Witness Statement 441.
43 Leonard, Joseph: Witness Statement 547.
44 McDonnell, Michael: Witness Statement 225.
45 Slattery, James: Witness Statement 445.
46 Leonard, Joseph: Witness Statement 547.
47 Daly, Gen. P.: Witness Statement 387.
48 O'Connor 1996, 143.
49 Malone 1996, 155.
50 McGuigan 2011.
51 McGarry 2006.
52 PRO, CO 904/177/1.
53 Collins 1996, 69–70. At first the Squad numbered only four, but it was later expanded to include some twenty men. There is some confusion over the O/C. Some claim that it was Paddy Daly (O'Daly) from the start, whereas others claim that Mick McDonnell led the Squad until medical issues forced him to emigrate to the US. See Donal O'Kelly, 'The Dublin scene', in Nolan 1946. See also PRO, CO 904/109 (3), Inspector General's Monthly Report, September 1919.
54 'This day, 25 March, Feast of the Annunciation, 1920, marked the arrival of the first Black and Tan in Limerick, *en route* to Newcastle West. To the late Christopher O'Sullivan, a local journalist/editor/proprietor of the old *Limerick Echo*, goes the credit of having given the new police force their colourful name, due to their manner of dress: a black tunic, as worn by the Royal Irish Constabulary, and khaki or tan trousers of the British soldier.' *Limerick Leader*, 25 March 1980; Bennett 1964.
55 Letter from Collins to Donal Hales, 13 August 1920.
56 *Daily News*, 18 October 1920.
57 McKenna 1970.
58 Neeson 1968, 42.
59 Diary of Thomas Jones, Lloyd George's personal secretary, 31 May 1920.
60 Dublin GHQ recognised that a 'war zone' existed in counties Kerry, Limerick, Tipperary and especially Cork. Other than some activities under Seán MacEoin in County Longford, those were the areas in which most fighting occurred. Townsend 1979b, quoting Richard Mulcahy papers.
61 Mac Eoin 2001.
62 O'Malley 1936 [1979], 203.
63 Collins was not alone in disliking the strikes. During the Civil War, when he went on a hunger strike, Ernie O'Malley wrote that 'we had since the death of Terence MacSwiney regarded it as an obsolete weapon'; O'Malley 1978, 250.

64 *Manchester Guardian*, 10 October 1920.

65 *Irish Worker*, 14 March 1914.

66 See D. Gwynn 1950.

67 Coogan 1992, 67.

68 Foley 2014, 155f.

69 Henderson 1945.

70 Neligan, David: Witness Statement 380.

71 Gleeson 1962, 191.

72 McDonnell, Dan: Witness Statement 486.

73 Coogan 1995, 215f.

74 PRO, CO 904/162/1, Sinn Féin Propaganda; DE 2/10, Correspondence with Publicity
    Department, 14 February 1920, with a report on the department dated April 1922, Dáil
    Éireann Reports, NLI.

75 Coogan 1995, 65.

76 Collins was involved in all aspects of the war throughout the country, though he did not visit
    those other commands often. For example, when the Cork No. 3 Brigade was formed at
    Caheragh, Drimoleague, on 16 August 1919, Collins presided at the meeting, but that was the
    last time he visited that particular brigade until mid-1921.

77 O Broin 1980, 83–4.

78 Thornton, Frank: Witness Statement 615.

79 Commanders in the field mostly disagreed. They thought that the IRA was 'winning' and soon
    would have a military victory. See Deasy 1998, 11f.; O'Malley 1978, 13.

80 Taylor 1970, 110.

81 Dwyer 1981, 31.

82 Pakenham 1935 [1972], 77.

83 Younger 1968, 162.

84 Pakenham (1935 [1972], 77–9) details at length the correspondence between de Valera and
    Lloyd George leading up to the Treaty negotiations. He takes pains to note that there were two
    separate 'debates' entangled in the correspondence: (1) whether England had any right to
    restrict Ireland's form of government and (2) on what basis a Conference could be held in the
    light of the first issue. He opines that discussion on the first issue favoured Ireland and that on
    the second issue favoured England. He further points out that in de Valera's eyes the position of
    a Republic 'had been preserved', but the British position was clearly that Ireland would remain
    a member of the Empire. He concludes: 'On abstract rights De Valera had secured an agreeable
    academic triumph. On the question of status at the Conference he had, formally at least, held
    his own. But in the race to secure opinion favourable to the settlements that they respectively
    contemplated, De Valera was still waiting for the pistol while Lloyd George was half-way
    home'. For a contrasting view see FitzGerald 1935. FitzGerald contends that de Valera's
    correspondence with Lloyd George was coloured by his need to placate Cathal Brugha (and to
    a lesser extent Austin Stack), who was 'a convinced irreconcilable' to whom the Truce was only
    a period in which to re-arm. As a result, in de Valera's correspondence 'it will be seen that the
    word "Republic" is never used, while nothing is said that directly implies a readiness to accept
    the Crown'. FitzGerald asserts that 'Mr Pakenham has failed to understand the situation at the
    time. This is probably due to the fact that documents were not available to him. Indeed, there is
    no documentation of that time.' FitzGerald concludes: 'Mr Pakenham's book reveals much that
    was not known to the public, and it is a valuable contribution to the history of our time. But
    the author omits vital facts and wrongly interprets others. In the absence of documents this
    may have been more or less inevitable. There are questions to which no answer perhaps can be
    given … His narrative, however, is eminently readable.'

85 Neeson 1968, 50.

86 Pakenham 1935 [1972], 266.

87 O'Connor 1929, 171.

88 Borgonovo 2006a, 32.
89 Coogan and Morrison 1998, 20.
90 O'Hegarty 1924 [1998], 46–8.
91 Kee 1972, 721.
92 O'Hegarty 1924 [1998], 87.
93 Collins, Dáil Éireann Treaty Debates, Dáil Reports, GSO, p. 32.
94 White 1948 [1986], 69.
95 Editorial, 'The helmsman gone', *London Daily Sketch*, 24 August 1922.
96 Statement by General Richard Mulcahy at Collins's graveside, *Irish Independent*, 29 August 1922.
97 Yeates and Wren 1989, 1.

Dublin 1

Dublin I

1 26 Abbey St. Lower: Abbey Theatre
2 35–37 Abbey St. Lower: Wynn's Hotel
3 10 Abbey St. Upper: 'the Squad' HQ
4 36 Amiens St.: J. & M. Cleary's pub
5 Marlborough St. (at corner of
   Cathedral St.): pro-cathedral
6 32 Bachelor's Walk: INAVDF office,
   Finance office
7 18 Beresford Place (at Eden Quay):
   Liberty Hall
8 44 Mountjoy St.: Munster Private Hotel
9 1–2 Denmark St. Great: Barry's Hotel
10 Rutland Sq. (now Parnell Sq.)
11 Great Britain St. (now Parnell St.); the
   Rotunda Hospital
12 25 Rutland Sq.: Gaelic League building
13 41 Rutland Sq. (now Parnell Sq.): Irish
   National Foresters' Hall
14 46 Rutland Sq. (now Parnell Sq.):
   Gaelic League HQ
15 29–30 Rutland Sq.: Vaughan's Hotel
16 49 Great Britain St. (now Parnell St.):
   Jim (Séamus) Kirwan's pub
17 68–69 Great Britain St.: Devlin's pub
18 6 Gardiner Row: Engineers' Hall, HQ
   of the IRA/Volunteers
19 35 Gardiner St. Lower: Typographical
   Union Hall
20 Sackville St. Lower: GPO
21 11–22 Sackville St. Upper: the 'Block';
   included the Crown, Granville,
   Gresham, and Hammam hotels
22 21–22 Sackville St. Upper: Gresham
   Hotel
23 94 Talbot St.: Republican Outfitters
24 45 Henry St.: Ministry for Home
   Affairs office; Finance Ministry offices
25 22 Mary St.: Primary Dept. of Finance
   office

Dublin I

Key locations

Abbey Street
Bachelor's Walk
Custom House Quay
Gardiner Row
Gardiner Street

Mary Street
Mountjoy Square
Rutland Square (Parnell Square)
Sackville Street (O'Connell Street)

O n any given day in 1917–21, Michael Collins was up and about long before the DMP detectives, the RIC, the Auxiliaries or the Black and Tans were on the streets of Dublin. He might walk from his rooms in Mountjoy Square or one of his safe houses to Phil Sheerin's Coolevin Dairy on Amiens Street. He often had breakfast there and met railwaymen carrying messages throughout the country. Collins established a fine communications system using the railways: he could get a message from Dublin to Cork in thirteen hours.

> *'Whoever controls Dublin, controls Ireland'*
> Michael Collins

Or he might meet some sailors just off a ship that had docked at the North Wall: there could be gelignite from the coalfields of Scotland; possibly revolvers, hand grenades or ammunition in a sailor's hand luggage; rifles in boxes marked 'fragile'.

Then he might walk or cycle to his office at 22 Mary Street, where his assistant, Joe O'Reilly, would meet him with the morning's papers. Collins would go through the papers carefully, noting any developments of political or military interest. He was particularly interested in any British officials newly assigned to Dublin. Collins would compare the papers to any notes he had jotted down the night before. Meanwhile, O'Reilly would open the day's mail, stamp the letters with the day's date and pin the mail neatly to the envelopes. Collins would go through the letters with a coloured pencil, then dictate replies, and tot up the day's receipts for the Dáil Loan.

He'd meet with messengers carrying Loan funds in from the country, intelligence operatives with reports, officers from the country seeking men or weapons, or members of Sinn Féin who wanted to know what policies should be presented to the membership.

After lunch, Collins would walk to another of his haunts, maybe Jim (Séamus) Kirwan's pub on Great Britain Street. No matter where he went there was always someone to see, a note to be written or an assignment to make.

He remembered the usual routes of postmen and could always be there to pick up or mail an important packet.

His business was intelligence, and he pursued it wherever it might be found.

Collins's day in Dublin might seem to be that of a busy Dublin executive. Every day he received and reviewed as many as 50 letters, each of which usually required an answer. He would have a dozen or more interviews, and each of them was urgent to the person he met. He had funds coming in from all Ireland's counties, and several foreign countries, that could amount to several thousands of pounds and an accounting had to be made.

He carried a pocket notebook and a pen—never a pencil—and wrote countless notes to Joe O'Reilly and others, giving orders and life-or-death instructions.

All while not being caught—in the middle of a war. No wonder his relaxation—'getting a piece of ear'—has become legendary.

There would always be a crowd waiting for him at Vaughan's Hotel on Rutland Square, or one of the other hotels on the square. Or he might go to Phil Shanahan's pub on Foley Street. Shanahan was originally from County Tipperary and his pub was 'home' to Volunteers from 'the country'. Collins used this as a meeting place for those new to Dublin. Shanahan and Collins often advanced them money and found them shelter.

Collins's day had no clock. At the end of one day he would arrive at one of his regular safe houses or rendezvous to continue discussing, organising and planning the next day.

Every day was a working day for Collins—and every night, too. From teatime until he dragged himself to bed, it was the same hurried schedule, unless Collins decided to go to the theatre. Some evenings, when he was finished at Vaughan's, he walked or cycled to Liam Devlin's pub, just off Rutland Square. Devlin and his wife had given Collins a neatly furnished room and it was one of his safest places to spend the night. Within a month, Collins and his comrades had destroyed the room. There was scarcely a chair with a back to it, the delph was broken or had disappeared, and the bedclothes were ruined. When one of their other guests commented on this to the Devlins, they merely shrugged and said 'It eases his mind'.

Collins's footprint was on every street, laneway and alley in Dublin, but especially in Dublin 1.

And not just the steps of the 'businessman' Michael Collins.

On 21 November 1920 (Bloody Sunday), Capt. Patrick MacCormack was killed by mistake in the Gresham Hotel. Hugh Callaghan, the doorman who led the IRA to the rooms, erroneously took them to Room 22 instead of Room 24.

Later that same year, on Christmas Eve, Collins and a few of his close friends met at the Gresham to celebrate the holiday. The private dining room that Collins had arranged was not available, so they took a table in the public dining room. A raid by Auxiliaries took Collins to the cloakroom, where he was 'compared' with his 'official' photo. He was closely questioned and gave his name as 'John Grace', an alias he often used. Collins had an Ordnance Survey map in his pocket with the words '6 rifles' in the corner, but he convinced the officer it was 'refills' and was let go. It was his closest escape ever.

Almost as soon as the Truce came into effect, Collins moved his main office and residence to the Gresham. It had been one of his regular stopping places earlier, but after the Truce, until well into 1922, it became his headquarters. Still later, Collins often met his fiancée, Kitty Kiernan, in the Gresham.

The streets of Dublin are paved with stories, and a good way to build up one's knowledge of Michael Collins is to walk in his footsteps.

10 Abbey Street Lower: Offices of the Irish Engineering, Shipbuilding and Foundry Workers' Trade Union, which was established on 9 May 1920.

There has always been indirect evidence in Dáil Éireann and trade union archives of republican infiltration, and recently released Military Service Pension applications show that a number of IRA and IRB activists were engaged in precisely this exercise. The unit was given the cover name 'the Labour Board' and was established at an IRB meeting chaired by Collins's financial confidant, Joe McGrath TD.

One of the mysteries of the IES&FWTU in its early days was how it was funded. The deeds on the premises occupied by the union at 10 Lower Abbey Street were provided as collateral for a mortgage on the IES&FWTU's new offices at 6 Gardiner Place (where its successor, the TEEU, still resides). The only person who might have shed light on the subject was Joe McGrath, but he never divulged details of Collins's myriad financial transactions. By coincidence, another tenant in Abbey Street was George Moreland Cabinetmakers, a front for Collins's Squad. (See 10 Abbey Street Upper.)[1]

26 Abbey Street Lower (at Marlborough Street): **Abbey Theatre**. On the site of the former Mechanics' Institute Building, where there was a Mechanics' Institute Theatre. The name was changed in 1904, and the first performance as the Abbey was on 27 December 1904.

In 1921 Collins was attending a performance here when the theatre was surrounded by the Black and Tans. One of Collins's 'operatives', Nellie Bushell, worked at the Abbey as an usherette. She walked down the aisle and whispered in his ear that there was a raid, then led him to a backstage door through which he escaped. After the Tans searched the theatre and left, Collins slipped back in to watch the rest of the performance.

32 Abbey Street Lower: On 12 April 1920 a general strike was called here for the next day by Thomas Farren, chairman, and Thomas Johnson,[2] treasurer of the Irish Labour Party and Trades Union Council (a single body until 1930) and acting secretary of the National Executive of Trade Unions (in place of the interned William O'Brien).[3]

To the Workers of Ireland. You are called upon to act swiftly to save a hundred dauntless men. These men, our comrades, have been forcibly taken from their homes, imprisoned without charge or trial for alleged offences of a political character in outrageous defiance of every canon of justice. They are suspected of loving Ireland and hating her oppressors—a heinous crime in the sight of tyrants but one which hundreds of thousands of Irish working men and women proudly acclaim as their birthright.[4]

In combination with the hunger strike that had started about ten days earlier, this general strike resulted in the release of the striking prisoners at Mountjoy Prison, including Peadar Clancy, one of Collins's key men. (See North Circular Road, Mountjoy Prison, Dublin 7.)

35–37 Abbey Street Lower: Wynn's Hotel (often written 'Wynne's' but photos clearly show the name without an 'e'). Nationalists often used the hotel, which was the site of the founding meeting of the Volunteers in November 1913.

Abbey Street Lower and Sackville Street (O'Connell Street): The top floor of the building on the north-east corner over Mansfield's Boot Shop was an arms dump for Collins's Squad. They would get their weapons here as needed, and leave them here between 'jobs'. It is now a Clarke's shoe store.

64 Abbey Street Middle: Harry Boland's tailor's shop. When Thomas Gay received the information about the upcoming 'German Plot' arrests, he came directly here and gave the information to Boland. Boland passed the information to Collins, who tried to convince the Sinn Féin leaders to stay away from their homes, but de Valera overruled him and many were arrested. (See 'German Plot', 6 Harcourt Street, Dublin 2.) Following those arrests, Boland looked after Sinn Féin and Collins looked after the Volunteers, and neither did so with any moderation.

Though they were rivals for Kitty Kiernan's affections, Boland and Collins were fast friends and were together daily until Boland left for America in mid-1919. (See Granard, Co. Longford, Kitty Kiernan, Appendix VI.) Boland brought out the convivial side in Collins's character.[5]

When Boland left for America, Hanna Sheehy-Skeffington replaced him as the Sinn Féin national chairman. Collins was appalled, not only because she was a woman but also because she was much more moderate than Boland. Further, the party made the announcement, which greatly irritated Collins: '… our people give away in a moment what the Detective Division had been unable to find out in five weeks'.

84 Abbey Street Middle: The *Freeman's Journal* (main entrance) office. This was the most conservative, Catholic and anti–Parnellite of popular newspapers. It was said that the priests in the parishes read it to illiterates.[6] Originally owned by William Freeman, it was the only newspaper that seemed to accept that the responsibility for the riots associated with the Lockout of 1913 could not be laid primarily on the shoulders of Dublin's hooligan element or its socialists.

At the time, the newspaper one read defined the Irish population. The Anglo-Irish establishment read the Irish Unionist *Irish Times*. With the split in the Irish Parliamentary Party over Parnell's relationship with Katherine O'Shea, its readership also split. While the *Freeman's Journal* went with the majority in opposing Parnell, a minority moved to read the *Irish Independent*. The *Freeman's Journal* was considered the voice of the decidedly non-revolutionary United Irish League, and it was also the voice of John Redmond's Nationalist Party. It had opposed true Irish independence and accepted Home Rule as it was proposed in parliament. Redmond's party subsidised the paper at the time of the Rising, but it continued to incur losses and was sold off in 1919.

The proprietor in 1920 was Martin Fitzgerald. He was arrested, imprisoned and the paper fined £3,000 because of a report on ill treatment of a prisoner by the Black and Tans.

On 29 March 1922, the IRA/Republicans under the command of Rory O'Connor wrecked the office in retaliation for having published the names of the IRA Executive chosen on 26 March. The greatest loss was the very large collection of photographic plates, as the *Journal* was the first Irish newspaper to use photographs extensively.

10 Abbey Street Upper: The sign on the door read 'George Moreland, Cabinetmakers and Upholsterers'. Bill Stapleton chose the name 'George Moreland' because he said it sounded 'Protestant and Jewish'.[7] This was the primary meeting place for the Squad after they moved from the Antient Concert Rooms. (The Squad first assembled daily at 100 Seville Place, then at a schoolhouse on Oriel Street, then at the Antient Concert Rooms on Great Brunswick Street, but moved here because of the centrality of its location.) Paddy Daly and Vinnie Byrne were both carpenters. Some other members of the Squad were craftsmen and could answer callers' queries, but they always told callers that business was so good that it would be many months before they could deal with their orders, whereupon 'customers' would take their business to other shops.

Vinnie Byrne was a fifteen-year-old boy when he fought at Jacob's Biscuit Factory in the Rising. He went on to become one of Collins's most utilised members of the Squad.[8] He described life for the Squad:

It should be mentioned that while we were at Moreland's, the 'big fella', Mick Collins, visited us at least twice a week. Notwithstanding the enormous amount of work he undertook, he found time to visit his squad. The moral effect of his visits was wonderful. He would come in and say: 'Well, lads, how are ye getting on?', and pass a joke or two with us. He was loved and honoured by each and every one of us, and his death was felt very keenly by the squad. I am proud to say that Mick stood by us in our hard time, and that every single member of the squad stood by him in his hard times, without exception.

There is another a story worth relating, which also concerns Moreland's. One evening, early in 1920, all the boys, including myself, were playing cards. This was our usual pastime while awaiting instructions. Suddenly we heard the burst of grenades and revolver fire. It sounded as if it was outside our very gate. In fact, we thought the gates were being blown in. The lads made for the window in the glass roof. After a little while, Tom Keogh said: 'You had better go down, Vincie, and find out what all the row is about'. I threw off my jacket, tucked up my shirt sleeves and with my overalls on me, I looked the real hardworking fellow. I proceeded to the gate and opened the wicket. Standing outside was a British Tommy. I popped my head out and asked him what was all the shooting. He replied: 'Those bloody Shinners ambushed us'. I said to him: 'That's terrible' and then I remarked: 'I had better be getting back to my job, in case the boss is looking for me'. Closing the wicket, I went back to the lads and told them what had happened. Later, we learned that the ASU had attacked this lorry at the corner of Swift's Row and Ormond Quay.

Byrne was most graphic in painting how the Squad worked.

We'd be told to plug a particular man, but how we did it was up to us. If we'd no information about his habits or movements, we'd watch him for a couple of days to see where he went and at what times. Usually, we'd have eight men on a job. One man would do the pluggin', with another man close by in case anything went wrong. The other six men would be spread around to give cover and act as look-outs.[9]

Frank Thornton described the Squad's method:

The procedure adopted on all jobs, however, was this. The Intelligence Officer having carried out his investigations to the satisfaction of GHQ, the operation was then ordered by Mick Collins, but the Intelligence Officer or Officers who had carried out that investigation always accompanied the Squad for the carrying out of the operation to ensure correct identification of the individual.[10]

Thornton said that it was

amazing the number of [British] people who, when it was put up to them, eventually agreed to work for us—and did tremendous work afterwards, whilst at the same time keeping their connection with British forces.

41 Abbey Street Upper and Liffey Street: Bannon's pub, where Collins first met Dave Neligan in July 1920. This was an unfrequented pub, and Collins began to meet people in the upstairs room. The British never raided it, but after mid-1921 the Bannons asked Collins not to use the premises, as they were afraid for their lives.

Neligan did not join Collins's men until 1920, after he had resigned from the detective unit in Dublin Castle. Like Éamon Broy, he had offered his services to Sinn Féin but had been turned down. He hated his work in the Castle and, on the advice of family and friends, left the police force and returned to his native Kerry. Collins eventually heard about his original offer of help and asked him to come to Dublin to see him.

Neligan recalled that first meeting. 'I was brought upstairs by the bar owner to this room which smelled of stale beer, and there, sitting at a table with a dirty dust cover over it, was the famous Michael Collins. He asked me if I was still willing to help. I said, "Yes", and he said, "Good. We want you to go back to Dublin Castle". "Oh God", I said, "I'd do anything but go back to that bloody place". Collins said, "Look, Dave, the British trust you and we trust you. If you really want to serve the cause, go back". So back to the Castle I went'.[11]

It has been rebuilt and is now a Paddy Power shop.

Amiens Street: Phil Sheerin's Coolevin Dairy. Located under the Loopline Bridge, it was a most important intelligence and weapons clearing house for Collins's intelligence operations. Couriers from Belfast and other railway workers could drop messages unobtrusively, and it was conveniently near the docks for sailors or dockers who were bringing in arms. Collins had an office of sorts in one of the back rooms.

> He had a private room at the back of the shop. This room was often used by Mick Collins to meet one or other of our dispatch riders who were continually travelling up and down on the Great Northern Railway to Belfast. These dispatch riders were invariably members of the staff of the Great Northern Railway and as such were able to get through with the dispatches fairly easily. As well as that, Phil Sheerin's was used as a receiving station for sailors leaving in small parcels of firearms which they brought over on the boats. I often visited these premises with Tom Cullen and Mick Collins during the Black and Tan War. Although this premises was raided on one occasion, nothing was ever caught nor was Sheerin ever arrested.[12]

36 Amiens Street: J. & M. Cleary's pub. Directly across from Amiens Street Railway

Station (now Connolly Station), its proximity to the station made the pub a common meeting place for Collins and his operatives. Collins especially used it to meet railway workers on the Belfast run.[13] The interior was used for scenes in the motion picture *Michael Collins*.

32 Bachelor's Walk: Second office of the Irish National Aid and Volunteers' Dependants' Fund, primarily run by Kathleen Clarke and Sorcha MacMahon. For a short time Collins worked in the 10 Exchequer Street office (Dublin 2).[14]

> Constitution of the Irish National Aid Association Volunteers' and Dependants' Fund:
>
> The objects of the Association are to make adequate provision for the families and dependants of the men who were executed, of those who fell in action, of those who were sentenced to penal servitude, in connection with the Insurrection of Easter, 1916; and, in addition, to provide for the necessities of those others who suffered by reason of participation, or suspicion of participation, in the Insurrection.
>
> The Executive shall consist of the twenty-four members elected by the two Associations now amalgamated, together with five representatives to be elected by the Dublin Trades Council, and two representatives from each province to be elected by the branches of the Association and co-opted by the Executive.
>
> Weekly meetings shall be held on Tuesdays at 8 p.m.
>
> Seven members shall form a quorum.
>
> Any member who fails to attend at least six ordinary meetings of the Executive, in each half-year, without adequate reason, automatically ceases to be a member.
>
> The Executive shall have power to appoint sub-committees to deal with the departmental work of the Association, all such sub-committees to report to the Executive.

When Collins's name was put forward, Clarke said that 'he was just the man I was hoping for. He was IRB and a Volunteer, and in many ways reminded me of Seán MacDermott. If he's another Seán, he'll be all right. He also agreed that the fight for freedom must continue, the Rising to count as the first blow.'

Collins used the office and Mrs Clarke's contacts to further reorganise the IRB. Clarke gave Collins the names and contacts that Tom had entrusted to her. She said that she was 'never sorry for hiring him'. 'I gave all that information to Mick and that … gave him the leeway to get ahead … He had the ability and the force and the enthusiasm and drive that very few men had, to work on that.'[15] Collins went to work as secretary of the Fund on 19 February 1917, at a salary of £2.10s a week. He took his position quite seriously and it was never too late or too early for him to call on anyone who needed aid. He was to run the office and supervise the staff, keep track of the accounting, and monitor all inquiries regarding aid and make sure they were all resolved. He also assisted in raising money for the Fund. And when he had to, he dipped into his own pocket to help some of the down-and-outs of Dublin. The Fund and the IRB contacts gave Collins the perfect opportunity to influence the growth of the new republican movement—and to take his place at its fore.

Richard Mulcahy felt that Collins was very consciously pulling the threads of the IRB men together with 'a view to a situation which would develop politically and organisationally when all the prisoners, including those in Lewes Jail, were back home and political life was beginning again in Ireland'. Mulcahy wrote:

> There was little doubt that his position in the IRB and what he apparently wished to make of the IRB and its tradition gave him, in relation to those people that he was most responsibly and closely dealing with in matters of high secrecy, some kind of mystique which was a kind of cement in matters of loyalty and service; it probably helped particularly to penetrate, and make as effective as it was, the group of his associates inside the detective force and police.[16]

The IRB remained a secret organisation, however, and that caused friction over the years.

> Collins, de Valera, Cathal Brugha and some of the others were members of the IRB up to 1916. In Frongoch, Collins set up a new IRB. He and his adherents constituted the membership of it in Ireland. I believe de Valera and Brugha had severed their connection with the organisation sometime after the Rising. Collins—while he was Minister in the Dáil—and had sworn allegiance to it. Collins was in the closest contact and sympathy with the new IRB. In some places, through insidious whispering, people thought that the IRB was a more authoritative body than the Dáil as far as the national struggle was concerned, and Collins came to be generally regarded as the head of the organisation.
>
> In that capacity, he and some of his Frongoch associates made contact with as many of the leading men as they could reach as they came home from gaol … Thus, Collins had a secret organisation within the Army and even within the Dáil … I always felt it unfortunate that Collins or anybody else should have conflicting allegiances. His position in the IRB gave him and his followers an undue influence because unknown and unsuspected. I don't think it had any effect on the Dáil until the 'Treaty' debates came, but it had a great effect on elements in the Army. Without it, I don't think the Split would ever have reached the dimensions to which it grew. To my mind, its secret nature was its most

sinister aspect.

… I was present at a Dáil meeting after I came back from America the first time—June, 1922—and it was a pretty stormy meeting. I remained in Dublin a couple of months before returning to America. There was friction which we all deplored; Cathal Brugha and de Valera on one side, and Griffith and Collins on the other. It was Cathal stripped the whole thing to the bone, and I never heard anyone referring to the IRB in such scathing terms.[17]

Collins worked for the Fund until spring 1918. At that time he was heavily involved in the IRA/Volunteer GHQ, was adjutant-general of the Volunteers and had just been arrested. The Fund itself was winding down; most of the veterans and victims of the Rising had been helped, and income and expenditure were falling. Collins's political work was taking up so much of his time that the directors of the Fund decided to let him go, and with one month's severance pay he was dismissed on 1 July.

In the first two years of its operation, the Fund disbursed £134,520 to rebels' families.[18]

Joe O'Reilly went to work for Collins here. O'Reilly was from Bantry, Co. Cork, and they had met in London. He had been with Collins in Stafford and Frongoch prisons but couldn't find work when he returned to Dublin. In May 1917, O'Reilly gave up on finding a job and had just gone to work as a labourer when Collins asked him to go to work for him at the Fund. He was Collins's assistant, messenger, confidential courier and most devoted attaché from then until Collins's death. Innocent, ingenuous and intensely religious, his devotion to Collins was boundless, and others often berated Collins for treating him so poorly. He alone knew where Collins would be at any moment, and he had the one quality Collins valued most: he could keep his mouth shut. After Collins's death, O'Reilly became ADC to W.T. Cosgrave.

Collins, Tom Cullen, Bill Tobin and Frank Thornton used the office concurrently for intelligence work from 1917 to 1921. Members of the intelligence staff included Charlie Byrne, Paddy Caldwell, Charles Dalton, Joe Dolan, Joe Guilfoyle, Ned Kelliher, Patrick Kennedy, Dan McDonnell, Peter Magee, Frank Saurin and Thornton. (See 3 Crow Street, Dublin 2.) Collins used another office in the building as a Finance Office.

Collins was arrested outside this building on 2 April 1918, and he was taken to the DMP's Brunswick Street Station accompanied by Detectives Patrick Smith, John Barton and O'Brien. Later he was taken to the Bridewell, escorted by Detectives Smith, Thornton and Thomas Wharton. (O'Brien was later captured and tied to a railing. He was told that he would be shot if he continued his work; he took the hint and resigned. Wharton was shot, but survived and was pensioned off.[19] Smith and Barton were killed.) From there Collins was taken to the Longford Assizes, where he refused to recognise the court; since it was not Volunteer policy to accept bail, he was then imprisoned in Sligo on 10 April 1918. Ultimately he was set free on bail from Sligo and went on the run. (See Ballinamuck, Co. Longford, Appendix VI.)

The football match arranged at Croke Park on Bloody Sunday, 21 November 1920, was held as a benefit for this Fund; about £500 was raised.

56 Bachelor's Walk: Office of Kapp & Peterson, tobacconists.

Collins's intelligence team lured the British spy J.C. Byrne (Jameson) here. He told them that he brought revolvers and other handguns from England 'for the cause'. He left the heavy portmanteau with Frank Thornton, and it was transferred to the 32 Bachelor's Walk premises. When James McNamara tipped Collins off that there would be a raid on Kapp & Peterson's, it was more confirmation that Jameson was a spy.

> This was a very interesting individual. He came to Dublin with the highest recommendations from the late Seán McGrath and Art O'Brien in London.
>
> ... I am not fully aware of what the proposition was in detail that was put up, but it evidently impressed the London leaders because they contacted Mick Collins, who agreed to meet Jameson in Dublin. He actually met Mick Collins in Dublin. Following the meeting, at any rate, he was handed over to Tobin, Cullen and myself. It would appear that his chief activity as far as we were concerned was to procure arms and ammunition on this side of the water. It is rather a peculiar thing that sometimes the cleverest of men are caught out because somebody on the opposite side takes a dislike to them but that is actually what happened in the case of Jameson. Tom Cullen had forcibly expressed his dislike of the man from the beginning, and possibly this had reactions on myself. In any case there were none of us impressed. It was decided to start laying traps for him. He fell into the first trap laid. He arrived with Liam Tobin outside New Ireland Assurance Society's building at 56 Bachelor's Walk.
>
> ... Jameson handed over a portmanteau full of Webley revolvers to me in the hall of Kapp & Peterson's, which he stated he had smuggled into the country. His story was that he got them in through communistic channels. They were handed over to me in the hall door of Kapp & Peterson's, Bachelor's Walk ... When the coast was clear, I handed the portmanteau of revolvers over to Tom Cullen who was waiting at 32 Bachelor's Walk which was Quartermaster General's stores. Before all these things happened we had contacted Jim McNamara of the Detective Division, who was working for us, to keep his ears open for any unusual occurrence on that day, particularly if he heard of any raids to try and give us the information in advance. About mid-day I got a message from McNamara telling me that the New Ireland Assurance Society's premises at Bachelor's Walk would be raided at about 3 o'clock. I naturally had a good look around the premises to make sure that no papers or any documents or guns of

any description were left around.

... [F]ollowing other incidents which happened it was finally decided that Jameson was a spy and as such would have to be shot. He met Paddy Daly and Joe by appointment; making sure that no accomplice was shadowing the party he was brought out by tram to meet Mick Collins at Ballymun Road. Naturally Collins wasn't there but Jameson was told that he was going to be shot ... I think it is sufficient to say that Sir Basil Thompson clinched the matter when he described Jameson (alias Byrne) as one of the best and cleverest Secret Service men that [they] ever had.[20]

The second floor housed the New Ireland Insurance Company, run by Michael Staines, who was in the GPO during the Rising. Collins and others had discussed an insurance company in Frongoch. In April 1917 there was a meeting in Enniscorthy, Co. Wexford, and the original partners were brought together. Collins encouraged Staines, M.W. O'Reilly, Jim Ryan, Liam Tobin and Frank Thornton, all of whom had been in Frongoch, to form the company. Joe McGrath was brought in. Until the police figured out what was going on, both the Dáil Loan and Collins's intelligence department were being run under the cover of New Ireland Insurance:

... which resulted in the formation of the New Ireland Assurance Collecting Society. During an earlier period, before 1916, in preparation for things to come, Arthur Griffith had in his papers frequently urged that something should be done to stop the flow of insurance premiums out of this country as part of a campaign to deal with the economic situation. It always was the first plank of Sinn Féin that everything Irish should be supported and that every effort should be made to keep the monies of the country circulating around amongst the people and re-employ these funds to create further industry ... He was always very keen on trying to solve the problem of how to retain that £5,000,000 of insurance premiums which were being annually exported from the country. One of his biggest supporters in that direction was Mr M.W. O'Reilly, who became the founder of an Insurance Society at a later stage. As can be seen from the following history of events, Michael Collins, Doctor Jim Ryan, Liam Tobin, Éamon de Valera, the late Dick Coleman, Michael Staines and myself became the prime movers in bringing this idea to fruition.

... At a later stage, when it was decided to launch the Dáil Éireann Loan, our men played a very important part all over the country in collecting funds, and our Head Office at 56 Bachelor's Walk was one of the main calling stations for people coming to Dublin to deposit Dáil Loan money. It was during this period that I first met the late Tom Cullen, who was Acting Quartermaster General, Tom's office at the time being at 32 Bachelor's Walk, which was being used as a Quartermaster's Distributing Station. At the New Ireland offices, officials had often to remain late at night dealing with matters arising out of the Dáil Loan.[21]

On receiving notification that I was transferred to GHQ Intelligence, I informed Mr M.W. O'Reilly, then General Manager & Secretary of the New Ireland Assurance Company, that I required indefinite leave without pay from that society as I was going whole-time on Army work. This leave was readily granted and, although acting in a whole-time capacity in the Army I still kept in constant touch with the developments of the New Ireland Assurance Society.[22]

18 Beresford Place (at Eden Quay): Liberty Hall. In the early nineteenth century the building had been a chophouse. Later in the century it was the site of the Northumberland Commercial and Family Hotel, which had been the meeting place for members of the Young Ireland movement. Still later, the Northumberland became the meeting place for members of the Land League. By 1911 the hotel had become almost derelict.

In 1912 it became the headquarters of the Irish Transport and General Workers' Union (ITGWU). A decision to establish the Union had been taken at a meeting in Dublin in December 1908. The first members were enrolled, and union cards issued, on 20 January 1909 as the Irish Transport Workers' Union. (The name was quickly changed to the Irish Transport and General Workers' Union.[23]) The Union's first office was on Townsend Street, but it soon managed to rent a room at 10 Beresford Place. Later it secured affiliation to the Dublin Trades Council and, in May 1910, to the Irish Trade Union Congress. In March 1912 the rented room at 10 Beresford Place was vacated and the Northumberland Hotel was taken over in its entirety.

Following James Connolly's execution, the ITGWU's president, Thomas Foran, took over the acting general secretaryship. William O'Brien[24] and J.J. Hughes aided him. After the Rising, the Union leaders were uneasy about an 'Army'. Consequently, by December 1916 the Citizen Army was back in Liberty Hall but under the name of the 'Connolly/Mallin Social and Athletic Club'.

On 10 June 1917 a protest meeting was held in the hall on behalf of the prisoners still in English jails. Cathal Brugha and Count Plunkett addressed it. Inspector Miles of the DMP was hit on the head with a hurley during the protest and later died. (The Volunteers and ICA soldiers of the time used to refer to a hurley as a 'Tipperary rifle'.)

Beresford Place: Across from Liberty Hall stands the James Connolly statue. Sculpted by Éamonn O'Doherty, the work was unveiled by President Mary Robinson on 12 May 1996, the 80th anniversary of Connolly's execution. The flag that forms the background is the Starry Plough, the plough and the stars symbolising respectively the present and the future of the working classes.

4 Capel Street: Home of Seán and Noel Lemass.

Seán was a member of the Dublin Active Service Unit on Bloody Sunday, and fought for the IRA/Republicans in the Civil War. He was taoiseach from June 1959 to 1966. (See 119 Baggot Street Lower, Dublin 2; Bloody Sunday, Appendix IV.)

During the Civil War, Noel was captured in Glencullen but escaped and fled to the Isle of Man. He was suspected of tampering with Collins's mail and was also suspected of involvement in Seán Hales's murder. He was recaptured on 3 July 1923. Allegedly kidnapped by the CID and murdered, his body was found in the Dublin mountains on 12 October 1923.

106 Capel Street: Dublin Municipal Library. Thomas Gay was the librarian. Collins and his men used the premises as a 'drop'. It was Gay who told Harry Boland about the 17–18 May 1918 'German Plot' arrests; Boland passed the information along to Collins, who told the cabinet. Éamon de Valera advised, however, that they should all remain at home that night, and many of the cabinet members were arrested. (See 64 Abbey Street Middle; 6 Harcourt Street, Dublin 2; 8 Haddon Road, Dublin 3.)

Custom House Quay: The Custom House. Designed by James Gandon and completed in 1791. (It was once said of Gandon's buildings: 'Poor Gandon, all his sumptuous structures were either burned, bombed, or blasted in the cause of Irish freedom'.) It was the seat of nine British administrative departments, including two taxing departments and the Local Government Board.[25]

The Custom House was destroyed with the approval of the Dáil on Wednesday 25 May 1921.[26] (See 6 Gardiner Row; 40 Herbert Park, Dublin 4.) Collins thought the idea folly. Taking on the might of the British army in major battles was absurd in his eyes. If he had learned nothing else from the Rising, he learned that Ireland was militarily incapable of beating the British in an all-out war.[27]

The fire burned for days.

Everything went perfectly as per plan, except that just before all the floors had given the Officer Commanding the 'OK', someone blew two blasts on a whistle and all sections retired to the main hall. One officer reported that he had not completed his task of saturation. The Commandant sent him and his men back at once to finish the job. The few minutes loss here was the difference between the successful retirement of all the participants and the arrival of large numbers of enemy forces in lorries and armoured cars. These forces swept into Beresford Place at exactly 1.25 p.m., just five minutes after the time allotted in the plan for the completion of the operation. They were immediately engaged on entry to Beresford Place by the 1st Battalion units with volleys of revolver shots and the throwing of a number of hand-grenades.

... Everything within the four walls of the Customs House building was reduced to ashes. The fire was still burning ten days after the attack. The fire Brigades were unable to go into action for a considerable time. This delay, as well as the use of paraffin oil, played a decisive part in the total destruction of the inside of the building.

... Following the action at the Custom House and the capture of a large number of highly trained officers, NCOs and men, it was found necessary to carry out an almost complete re-organisation of the various units of the Dublin Battalion. This, of course, necessitated the appointment of a considerable number of new officers, and naturally while this re-organisation was taking place, actions as we had known them before almost ceased, with the exception of those carried out by the remaining members of the Active Service Unit. As time went on the Brigade units gradually assumed their old aggressiveness, and by the time the Truce was approaching a number of reasonably important operations were being planned.[28]

Tom Ennis was appointed O/C of the party ordered to seize the building, and was wounded. The operation was carried out by some 120 Volunteers, five of whom were killed: Tommy Dorrins, Seán Doyle, Dan Head, Capt. Paddy O'Reilly and sixteen-year-old Lt Stephen O'Reilly (brothers). Two civilians were killed: Francis Davis, caretaker of the building, who resisted the Volunteers, and Mahon Lawless, who was mistaken for a Volunteer by the Tans. About 80 IRA/Volunteers were arrested. Jimmy Slattery lost his arm in the attack. Paddy Daly described the operation:

The attack on the Custom House was organised by the OC of the Dublin Brigade, Oscar Traynor, on instructions from GHQ. To the 2nd Battalion was given the actual burning, in other words they were the inside men. The 2nd Battalion Commandant, Tom Ennis, was in command of the entire operation. Ennis was anxious to have all the men of the Squad and ASU who were members of the 2nd Battalion rejoin their unit for this operation, but he did not include the 1st, 3rd, and 4th Battalion men as he wanted it to be completely a 2nd Battalion job. I appealed to Michael Collins to have us all included as I was afraid it would cause dissension amongst the men if any of them were to be left out. After a conference with Oscar Traynor, the OC of the Brigade, this was accepted for the Squad only.

... Commandant Ennis detailed officers for every floor and every section of the building. Each officer had a number of men under him.

There was also an officer responsible for collecting all the staff.

... As I came out the door facing Liberty Hall I saw Oscar Traynor who beckoned me over ... He was very anxious at seeing no sign of smoke and said that the building should be on fire by now. As we were speaking a Tan lorry swung around from the quays and pulled right up beside us.

... The Tans were dismounting so I made my way around Marlboro [sic] Street.

... I received word that Tom Ennis had been badly wounded, so he was taken to his home in Marino.

... Mrs Ennis, with a month old baby, was wonderfully cool. She got water, towels and everything that was necessary. Oscar Traynor started to dress the wound and sent me to look for Batty Hyland. Batty Hyland was one of Mick Collins's drivers. While I was away, Oscar Traynor remained with Ennis, and I believe it was Traynor's skill in first-aid dressing that saved Ennis's life.

... [we brought him to] O'Donnell's [sic] Nursing Home in Eccles Street, one of the many places we could bring our wounded at any time.[29]

Piaras Béaslaí wrote in *An tÓglach*: 'The burning of the Custom House symbolised the final collapse of English civil administration in this country'.

A sculpture by Yann Renard-Goulet in the back yard of the Custom House commemorates the death of these five Volunteers, and all in the 2nd Battalion of the Dublin Brigade who gave their lives in the cause of freedom.

Denmark Street Great: Ossary Hotel. Seán Kavanagh, Collins's primary agent in Kildare, stayed here the night before Bloody Sunday after he was told to vacate Vaughan's Hotel.

1–2 Denmark Street Great: Barry's Hotel. The Tipperary football team stayed here the night before the match in Croke Park on Bloody Sunday. It is still a popular venue for visiting football and hurling teams. It was HQ of K Company, 2nd Battalion, during the War of Independence.

On 13–14 December 1920 a meeting of GHQ was held here to finalise plans to import arms from Italy. The IRA/Volunteers were in constant need of arms. Donal Hales, whose brothers Seán and Tom were both in the IRA, lived in Genoa and was the contact trying to buy the weapons. Cathal Brugha, Collins, Liam Mellows, Joe Vize, Liam Deasy and Florence O'Donoghue attended.

Michael Leahy, second-in-command of Cork No. 1 Brigade, and Seán O'Shea left Dublin for Italy on 2 January 1921.[30] Arms were to be distributed throughout the south-western counties of Kerry, Cork, Limerick and Tipperary. The project failed, and Leahy and O'Shea soon returned to Dublin.

About three or four months before the Truce a messenger came from Ireland to Italy for arms. We were requested by an Italian General to accompany him down to Rome to the military department. The man who came over first was a Mr O'Shea, I think. O'Shea had gone over to France to buy arms, being commissioned to do so by Collins. He failed to get them there. He was merely a messenger. I think he lives in Dublin but I do not know his Christian name. He was sent by Michael Collins to get in touch with me for the acquisition of arms in Italy ... Another man was also sent out from Cork called Leahy. They both came for arms ...

... I approached the Italian General who accompanied me to Rome for the arms. At that time contact would be difficult. In fact, through the good offices of the general we found we had no difficulty in getting the guns. We could get as many rifles as we wished—up to 100,000. These rifles were Italian rifles which had been used in the previous war; they were in good condition and only required cleaning. We could also get ammunition. There was some talk as to what ammunition would fit these rifles.

Things were in such a position in Ireland that we could not get quickly in touch with it.

O'Shea had returned to Ireland to report to Collins regarding the position and I did not hear anything further about sending the arms.

Just on his return to Dublin many raids and burnings, effected by the Black and Tans, took place in the city, which may have been the reason I could not have any news from him or from Michael Collins for some time after. I believe the truce came on shortly after this. These rifles were not removed. However, the British Consul-General must have been told by some one that I had hidden these arms in Genoa. He was informed probably by his Intelligence officer, that the guns were in Genoa awaiting shipment. That was not true because they were in Rome. They were not paid for and were never called for. My sister spoke to Collins then who said the money would present no difficulty at all. He mentioned the sum of £100,000 which she thought would be sent immediately. No money was sent and they were never removed.

My opinion is that the arrangements to procure the arms may have been to bluff England. If the Irish were fully armed they could hold out longer and kill most of the British soldiers here. The idea of getting the arms, I believe, would be to influence England to come to terms with Ireland. Collins may also have had the idea of trying to get in Ulster. Ulster would come in if there was a final settlement. There would have been some difficulty in shipping these arms to Ireland, how the British got the knowledge of them was extraordinary.[31]

(See Merchant's Quay, Dublin 8.)

Annie Farrington, previously of the Crown Hotel on Sackville Street Upper, purchased the hotel after the Truce in July 1921.

At the outbreak of the civil war the first place attacked in the North side was the Fowler Hall which was occupied by the Republicans and which they had to leave. The morning of the attack William, my porter, went down to the rere of the building and climbed some steps to see what was happening. He poked his head in the door at the top of the steps. We were watching him and we saw him suddenly withdraw his head from a flying bullet. He had a narrow escape. The people inside the building thought he was one of the attacking party. He hastened back to us and within an hour our own hotel was occupied by the Republicans and the Citizen Army.

Madame Markievicz was in charge of the Citizen Army and the leaders of the Republicans were there from time to time, including De Valera, Barton. I cannot remember the others. There were other women there too but I did not know them. This was on the Tuesday morning and the leaders were there till Wednesday night.

… They cleared out all the visitors—about forty—giving them barely time to pack their bags. They cleared out the staff, but I refused to go and Miss Keogh and William the Porter stayed with me. The Headquarters Staff left on Wednesday night and took over the Hammam but they left a garrison in Barry's.

The IRA brought in oceans of food but I thought it queer that they did not want to give us any of it. We were not allowed to pass through the rooms they occupied. I can't remember how we put in our time during the occupation. I was half out of my mind thinking of all the money I owed the bank which financed the purchase of the hotel and I now saw the possibility of the whole place going up in smoke. This was the reason I refused to leave although they pointed out the risk I was running by staying. I cannot remember anything about those days because I was so distraught.

… When Moran's hotel which was also occupied by the Republicans was being shelled the garrison in Barry's began boring holes in the walls of the houses at each side of the hotel to assure a way of escape in case of an attack. As I went up the stairs I saw them at this work but when I came down a short time afterwards they had got word to leave the hotel and they cleared out advising us to go with them as they were leaving land mines—one under the front door and another under the roof in the top storey. They left guns sticking out the window when they were going. However, the three of us stayed and I asked the man who was preparing the mines to cut the wires if that was humanly possible, but that if he had to do his duty, he could do it, but that we were staying. We knelt down to pray and I believe I said prayers that were never heard before or since. The man at the mines touched me on the shoulder and said 'It is all right, Miss, I have detached them'.

Before they left, they went very hard on us to throw in our lot with them and take our chance with the other women of Cumann na mBan who were with them. I said 'If the house is going up I will go up with it. We have nowhere else to go'.[32]

This was the first HQ of the Dublin Brigade of the IRA/Republicans during the Civil War until 19 June 1922, when Oscar Traynor moved HQ to 'the Block', and particularly the Hammam and Gresham hotels on Sackville Street Upper.

Eustace Street: Gearóid O'Sullivan, a member of the Volunteer GHQ, had his office here. He and Richard Mulcahy shared the quarters, beginning in 1920, but only stayed there for a few months. The office was raided early one Saturday morning; although copies of newspapers were found, no other incriminating papers were discovered. The men moved their offices to Jenny Wyse-Power's premises on Henry Street thereafter. Bridie O'Reilly worked as a secretary for both men.[33]

Findlater Place (now Cathal Brugha Street): Findlater Building, directly across from Thomas's Lane, which ran parallel to Lower Sackville Street and behind 'the Block'. The shot that killed Cathal Brugha was fired from this building, according to John Pinkman.[34] (See Granville Hotel, Sackville Street Upper.)

Foley Street (at corner of Corporation Street): Phil Shanahan's pub. Shanahan was originally from County Tipperary, and his pub was 'home' to Volunteers from 'the country'. Collins used this as a meeting place for those 'up from the country'. Shanahan and Collins often advanced them money and gave shelter. This was a haunt of Dan Breen, Seán Hogan, Séamus Robinson, Seán Treacy and others when in Dublin.

In the heart of Dublin's red-light district ('the Monto'), Shanahan's pub was often used as a place where prostitutes who relieved their British soldier clients of their guns could turn them over to the Volunteers.

Dick McKee and Peadar Clancy were here before their capture on the night before Bloody Sunday. They left the pub and went to a 'safe house' in Gloucester Street, where they were captured. (See 36 Gloucester Street Lower.)

14 Frederick Street North: Office of Countess Markievicz's Dáil Department of Labour. Joe McGrath, Dick Cotter and Eilís Ní Riain were on the staff of the department. RIC Constable Jeremiah Mee went to work here after he left the RIC in Listowel.[35] (See Molesworth Street, Dublin 2.)

18 Frederick Street North: Keating Branch of the Gaelic League. Prior to the Rising, Collins was active here. Cathal Brugha was branch president, and members included Conor Collins, Richard Mulcahy, Diarmuid O'Hegarty, Gearóid O'Sullivan and Rory O'Connor.

Gardiner Place: Fleming's Hotel, owned by Seán O'Mahony, who lived here.

In October 1916 Cathal Brugha organised a meeting attended by about 50 IRA/Volunteers. Brugha presided, though still on crutches. This was the start of the 'reorganisation' of the Volunteers. At this time they were known as 'Liberty Clubs' to escape the attention of the Castle authorities.

> I was elected a member of a provisional committee. Other members I recollect were Seán O'Murthuile, D. O'Hegarty, Father O'Daly, Liam Clarke, Luke Kennedy; Cathal Brugha, who was in hospital, was elected Chairman. When Brugha had recovered, we usually held the meetings in his home in Rathmines.
> In October, 1916 the first Convention was held in Fleming's Hotel, Dublin. An executive, of which I was a member, was elected to hold office for a year or less depending on circumstances. After the general release of prisoners another Convention was held in Barry's Hotel, Dublin, in March, 1917. I was again elected a member of the executive. After the release of the penal servitude prisoners another Convention was held in Croke Park in October, 1917. I retired from the executive to make way for younger men—Michael Collins, D. O'Hegarty, Eamon Price, E. De Valera, G. O'Sullivan were elected on this executive.[36]

O'Mahony was also a commercial traveller and used his travels and contacts to pass along messages for Collins.

Collins stayed here frequently. Nance Corcoran was some form of governess in England, and used to stay here on her way back from Cashel to England. Then the owners of the hotel asked her to work there as they regarded her as a safe member of staff to look after Collins. She mentioned to her family that 'he was uncouth, rough and did not have the manners or charm of the British gentlemen'.[37]

29 Gardiner Place: Home of Linda Kearns (MacWhinney), who was born in 1889 in Sligo. She also opened a nursing home here; though she did not take patients ordinarily, Kathleen Clarke stayed here after her 1918 imprisonment.

Kearns opened a first-aid station in an empty house in North Great Georges Street and treated both Volunteers and British casualties during the Rising.

Collins used the house for meetings. He and Diarmuid O'Hegarty came to Kearns in early 1917 and asked her to become a courier to County Sligo. On one of her missions to Sligo she met Billy Pilkington, O/C of the Sligo IRA/Volunteers. She was imprisoned in 1920 when she was caught smuggling a large consignment of arms in Sligo.

On one occasion Collins was eating dinner here when Auxiliaries raided the building. He grabbed his plate and cutlery and dived under the table, where he waited until the Auxiliaries left.

An opponent of the Treaty, Kearns joined the garrison in Barry's Hotel at the start of the Civil War, and treated the wounded in various garrisons in O'Connell Street. She was in the ambulance that took the wounded Cathal Brugha to the Mater Hospital and applied compression to his left femoral artery. She wrote:

> I had a conversation with Cathal about two hours before the end. I asked him was he acting wisely in going to his death. 'We have too many unnecessary deaths already', I said. He replied: 'Civil War is so serious that my death may bring home its seriousness to the Irish people. I feel that if it put a stop to the Civil War it would be a death worthwhile.' ... It was the most poignant moment of my life ... We went out into the lane. Cathal had a revolver in each hand and he kept shouting 'no surrender!' He was shot in the hip, the femoral artery being severed. I was beside him but was not hit. To give the Free Staters their due, I don't think they wanted to kill him and aimed low. But he was a small man, he was struck higher than they expected and in a vital part.[38]

(See Granville Hotel, Sackville Street Upper; Whitefriar Street, Dublin 2; Eccles Street, Dublin 7.)

4 Gardiner Row: Plaza Hotel. It was used as an IRA/Volunteer HQ for a short time in 1920. On 22 November, the day after Bloody Sunday, Oscar Traynor was appointed O/C of the Dublin Brigade to replace the murdered Dick McKee. At that time most of the 1,500 members of the brigade were in jail or in hiding and it was almost flat broke. He moved the HQ here because 35 Gardiner Street Lower was too well known by the British.

6 Gardiner Row: Engineers' Hall. This was the primary HQ of the IRA/Volunteers during the War of Independence.

In March 1918, the GHQ staff of the Volunteers was elected:

Chief of Staff: Richard Mulcahy
Deputy Chief of Staff: Eoin O'Duffy
Assistant Chief of Staff: J.J. (Ginger) O'Connell
Adjutant-General: Collins, followed by Gearóid O'Sullivan in summer 1919
Quartermaster General: Seán McMahon

Director of Chemicals: James (Séamus) L. O'Donovan

Director of Engineering: Rory O'Connor (also O/C Britain)

Director of Intelligence: Collins, replacing Éamon Duggan

Director of Munitions: Seán Russell

Director of Organisation: Éamon Price, followed by Collins, then by Diarmuid O'Hegarty[39]

Director of Purchases: Liam Mellows, until he went to the US with de Valera in 1919

Director of Training: Dick McKee

Editor of *An tÓglach*: Piaras Béaslaí, under the direction of Collins

Others closely involved with the initial GHQ staff included Diarmuid O'Hegarty and Michael Staines.

Both Collins and Mulcahy were considered for chief of staff. Dick McKee, director of training, who went on to be the O/C of the Dublin Brigade, agreed beforehand that Mulcahy, not Collins, should be chief of staff.[40] Mulcahy later noted:

> McKee, as he came away from the meeting with me, expressed satisfaction and relief that Collins was not being recommended. The main reason for that was that in the light of what he knew about Collins' temperament, and the short period and the circumstances in which my information about him had been outlined, McKee—like others—was a little bit wary of entrusting him with anything like complete control. In fact he did want time to disclose himself and his qualities.[41]

Mulcahy also felt that as chief of staff he could best protect Collins from his detractors 'from a flanking position'. Collins and Mulcahy tended to communicate with each other on a basis of understanding rather than through lengthy verbal encounters: 'We didn't exchange unnecessary information … Over main matters we exercised a constructive and Cistercian silence'.[42]

The military structure of the army can be divided into four different strands:

- GHQ staff;
- Collins, intelligence and the Irish Republican Brotherhood (IRB);
- the Dublin Brigade;
- the 'flying columns', located mainly in West Cork, Limerick, Cork, Tipperary, Longford and Dublin.

Both Collins and Mulcahy were committed to the army, its formal structures, ethical standards and military efficiency; both were committed to its subservience to the Dáil and the people of Ireland.[43]

Mulcahy was initially more conservative in his commitment to the war, being aware that many nationalists favoured peaceful non-cooperation with the British parliament and controlling local government, a view he shared with Cathal Brugha. A more active and brutal war was forced on GHQ at the end of 1919 because of the constant harassment of Sinn Féin deputies, speakers and supporters by the RIC, the suppression of the Dáil and mounting pressure from provincial volunteers.[44]

The first flying columns appeared in 1920. They consisted of IRA/Volunteers who had been forced on the run owing to knowledge of their other attacks. At a meeting at GHQ, this idea was discussed and the ideas were developed:

> Dick Mulcahy was not too keen on the idea, but Michael Collins was very keen on it: 'We'll have to get these bloody fellows doing something', said Collins referring to the men on the run. At that time and for some time later they were a bloody nuisance, for they lounged around, slept late, ate people's food and did not work for the Company or Battalion in which they happened to be.[45]

One of Collins's first tasks was to secure at least one individual in every government department who was prepared to work for GHQ.

Ultimately the members of GHQ met all over the city, though some had their own offices: Collins in Bachelor's Walk or Cullenswood House (Dublin 6), Gearóid O'Sullivan in Eustace Street. It could be said that the 'office' of GHQ was wherever its members happened to be.

In 1921 Collins summoned Tom Barry from County Cork to GHQ. Barry described him thus:

> The outstanding figure in all GHQ was Michael Collins, Director of Intelligence. This man was, without a shadow of a doubt, the effective driving force and backbone at GHQ of the armed action of the nation. A tireless, ruthless, dominating man of great capacities, he worked like a Trojan, in innumerable capacities to defeat the enemy.[46]

On 21 May 1921 a meeting was held here to finalise the plans to burn the Custom House. In attendance were Collins, Seán Dowling, Mulcahy, O'Connell and Oscar Traynor. As O/C of the Dublin Brigade, Traynor had a close view of Collins:

> … it was like a breath of fresh air to meet him or to talk to him. He was always full of ideas. His ideas were good, too. You got the impression of eventual success. This man wasn't beaten. This fellow didn't think we were finished nor did he give the impression of being finished himself. Mick Collins was very easy on men. He'd talk nicely to them, even if he didn't think much of them. After raging he'd

come back and apologise.[47]

While much of the insurgent action throughout the country was instigated at a local level in response to enemy activity, it is clear that GHQ as the central authority played an important and increasing role in guiding and organising the struggle. The more formal structure of the army achieved by the time of the Truce made it possible for Mulcahy and Eoin O'Duffy to organise a professional army during the frenetic few months between the Treaty ratification and the commencement of the Civil War, an army which would later deal effectively with the irregular/anti-Treaty forces.[48]

Gardiner Street: Home of Dr John Ryan TD. A friend to the IRA/Volunteers, and later the IRA/Republicans, he often treated them and 'patched them up' without notifying the police.

17 Gardiner Street Lower (and Talbot Street): Moran's Hotel. During Civil War hostilities in Dublin, Cumann na mBan used the basement as a large kitchen and several smaller rooms as an auxiliary hospital. (See Barry's Hotel, Denmark Street Great.)

Countess Markievicz took up sniper duty here at the start of the Civil War.

35 Gardiner Street Lower: Typographical Union Hall, HQ of the Dublin Printers' Union. Many of Dublin's printers were members of the IRB and their premises were centres of Dublin Brigade activities. Collins often attended meetings here. Dick McKee had his office as O/C of the Dublin Brigade here.

On 1 August 1919 Collins met with Terence MacSwiney and Liam Deasy as representatives of the Cork Brigade. Also present were Richard Mulcahy, Peadar Clancy and Dick McKee. They discussed the progress of the war in Cork and the need for more guerrilla actions in the countryside. Collins often had contact with commanders in the field throughout Ireland, although his extensive links with the country brigades were maintained chiefly by IRB contacts.

On 2 August representatives of the Cork, Kerry, Waterford and West Limerick Brigades met with Collins and the other members of GHQ staff in order to coordinate IRA activity in the countryside. The representatives were Terence MacSwiney (Cork No. 1 Brigade), Liam Lynch (Cork No. 2 Brigade), Liam Deasy (Cork No. 3 Brigade), Paddy Cahill (Kerry No. 1 Brigade), Dan O'Mahoney (Kerry No. 2 Brigade), Jeremiah O'Riordan (Kerry No. 3 Brigade), Pax Whelan (Waterford West) and Revd Dick McCarthy (West Limerick). Mulcahy outlined the GHQ policy with regard to ambushing: general ambushing was to be the principal form of attack against the British, but 'in all cases the enemy should first of all be called upon to surrender'.[49] Brugha supported Mulcahy, but all the men in the field objected that this was impractical. In the end, the principle of surprise as set forth by the brigade officers won the day.

On 20 November 1920 Collins met Brugha, Clancy, Paddy Daly, McKee, Mulcahy and Seán Russell here to finalise plans for Bloody Sunday. Frank Thornton argued strongly that each one of the agents on the list he had compiled with Charles Dalton was 'an accredited secret service man of the British Government'.[50] He proposed that over 40 should be killed, but the names of fifteen out of the 35 selected for assassination were turned down because of insufficient evidence.[51] Brugha set aside the dossier of any English civilian in Ireland who was not with certainty involved in activities harmful to the IRA.[52] Then Collins went to the bar at the Gaiety Theatre with Ned Broy, James McNamara, Liam Tobin, Tom Cullen, Thornton and Dave Neligan.[53]

Collins's Squad used this as a meeting place; most members of the Squad got their orders here for Bloody Sunday.[54] They all knew the gravity of the raids and were well prepared by Dick McKee's briefing. (See Gloucester Street Lower, 17 Richmond Street North; Bloody Sunday, Appendix IV.)

41 Gardiner Street Upper: Home of Joe and Kate McGuinness. Joe spent many years in the United States, where he worked with John Devoy and Joe McGarrity as a Clan na Gael organiser. On 9 May 1918 he was elected to the Dáil for South Longford. He was in Lewes Jail in England at the time.[55]

When the idea of standing for election was presented to him, McGuinness was against it: he was so uncompromising in his separatist principles that the idea of running in a pseudo-British election was repugnant to him. He chose not to run, and de Valera, who was also in Lewes Jail, agreed with him. De Valera said:

'Never allow yourselves to be beaten. Having started a fight, see that you win. Act then with caution. Carefully size up the consequences of a projected action. If you feel in the long run that you can be beaten, then don't begin.' He persuaded McGuinness to decline the invitation to run.[56]

Nevertheless, Collins convinced the leadership still in prison, and especially de Valera, that the temperament in Ireland had changed and that McGuinness would win. 'Put him IN to get him OUT' was the campaign slogan. McGuinness won, with 1,498 votes to the Irish Parliamentary Party candidate's 1,461.[57]

McGuinness caught pneumonia, took to his bed and died here on 31 May 1922. He was the uncle of Brigid Lyons (Thornton), and she often stayed with them when she visited Dublin during her time as a medical student at University College Galway.

Gloucester Street Lower (now Seán MacDermott Street): Pub owned by Thomas Hynes. John (Shankers) Ryan, the one who betrayed Clancy and McKee on the night before Bloody Sunday, was killed outside the pub on 5 February 1921. Ryan was the brother of Becky Cooper, one of Dublin's best-known madams.[58] Bill Stapleton led the squad that killed him, which included Paddy Kennedy[59] and Eddie Byrne.

> John Ryan was a British military policeman and was a brother of Mrs Becky Cooper of Corporation St. who ran a shebeen which was a favourite haunt of many of the British—Tans, Auxiliaries and Army. It was known through GHQ Intelligence that Ryan was responsible for the arrest and subsequent murder of Dick McKee, Peadar Clancy and Clune who, by the way, were in hiding from the enemy in the vicinity of the Gloucester Diamond very near to Becky Cooper's place. The Squad were told off to have this man executed and as usual an Intelligence Officer was appointed to identify him, in this case it was Paddy Kennedy. Before the two men were detailed to carry out the execution I asked to be allowed to take part in it as I felt very keenly about the murder of Dick McKee who was a great friend of mine with whom I fought in 1916 and served subsequently with him in the 2nd Battalion. My request was granted and the second man instructed to accompany me was Eddie Byrne, now deceased. About 10.30 o'clock on the morning of the 5th February, 1921, our Intelligence Officer located Ryan in Hynes's public house at the corner of Old Gloucester Place and Corporation St. We entered the public house with the Intelligence Officer and I saw Ryan standing facing the counter reading a newspaper and he was identified by the Intelligence Officer. Before doing the job we held him up and searched him but he had no guns or papers on him. I think we said, 'You are Ryan', and I think he rejoined, 'Yes, and what about it' or words to that effect. With that we shot him. I have an idea that the chap behind the counter was one of our Intelligence Officers' contacts as he made himself very scarce when we entered. We left the place then and proceeded towards the Gloucester Diamond and as usual the remainder of the Squad were following up to cover our retreat. We went back to the Squad dump which was in a stable off North Great Charles St. near Mountjoy Square and that concluded the operation as far as we were concerned.[60]

(See Railway Street; Bloody Sunday, Appendix IV.)

15 Gloucester Street Lower (now Seán MacDermott Street): Tara Hall. Printers' Union and **Painters' Hall**. It was the HQ of 'C' Company, 2nd Battalion, Dublin Brigade, under the command of Dick McKee from 1917. Joe Good was a member of 'C' Company.

35 Gloucester Street Lower (now Seán MacDermott Street): Home of Tom MacPartlin; on the upper floor of the HQ of the Builders' and Carpenters' Union. It was here that the National Executive agreed upon the general strike of 13 April 1920, notice of which was sent out from offices at 32 Abbey Street Lower. (See also Mountjoy Jail, North Circular Road, Dublin 7.)

36 Gloucester Street Lower (now Seán MacDermott Street): Home of Seán Fitzpatrick, often used as a safe house. Dick McKee and Peadar Clancy were captured here on the night of 20–21 November 1920. They had been delayed leaving the meeting in Gardiner Street, as they had to issue fresh instructions to one of the Bloody Sunday raiding parties: two of the British agents had changed residences and new orders were required. This delay caused them to be out just after curfew and they went directly to the Fitzpatrick house, where they were captured. The Fitzpatrick family delayed the raiders long enough for McKee and Clancy to burn their papers.[61] They were taken to Dublin Castle and were tortured and killed by a squad led by Captains King and Hardy. Fitzpatrick was arrested with McKee and Clancy. (See 16 Lower Railway Street; Dublin Castle, Dublin 2; Bloody Sunday, Appendix IV.)

72 Gloucester Street Lower (now Seán MacDermott Street): Convent of Our Lady of Refuge/Our Lady of Charity. Sr Eithne Lawless lived here after she joined the convent in the summer of 1920.[62] Previously she had been a secretary for Collins in Harcourt Street and Camden Street (see Dublin 2).

Great Britain Street (now Parnell Street): The Rotunda Hospital. Officially known as the Dublin Lying-in Hospital, it was founded in 1745 and moved to its present location in 1748. The hospital was totally dependent on charity and for this reason the buildings and environs were created with an eye to fund-raising. The 'social' rooms of the Rotunda existed to provide entertainment. The 'Round Room' became the 'Rotunda Picture House' and is now the Ambassador Cinema; the former 'Supper Rooms' became the Gate Theatre, and the 'Pillar Room' is used for concerts. The Roller Rink was in the basement.

On the Saturday night after the Rising the defeated Volunteers were marched here. In the early hours of Sunday morning, Capt. Percival Lea-Wilson took charge. Of Seán MacDermott, who because of polio walked with a limp and only with the aid of a cane, he said, 'So you've got cripples in your Army!' Lea-Wilson stripped Thomas Clarke and made him stand naked on the Rotunda steps in view of the nurses: 'That old bastard is Commander in Chief. He keeps a tobacco shop across the street. Nice general for your f—ing Army.'[63] Collins had Lea-Wilson killed in Gorey, Co. Wexford, on 15 June 1920.

Captain Lea-Wilson was not shot because he had ill-treated Seán MacDermott and other prisoners in 1916, because there were other British officers just as bad as he had been and no attempt was ever made to shoot them.

I believe he was shot because of the position he held at the time of his execution, and for no other reason.

I am satisfied from my long experience with the Squad that no man was shot merely for revenge and that any execution sanctioned by Michael Collins was perfectly justified.[64]

After the Rising, the Royal Mail was sorted in the basement of the Rotunda while the GPO was being rebuilt. Collins's intelligence agents often 'intercepted' the mail here, and the Dublin Brigade intercepted all the official correspondence for Dublin Castle on 15 July 1920. Oscar Traynor led the raiding party, which included Joe Dolan and Charlie Dalton. Collins had agents in the office—Pat Moynihan, Liam Archer and Dermot (Diarmuid) O'Sullivan—who 'set up' the raid. After the mail was opened and examined, it was delivered to the Castle marked 'Opened and censored by the Irish Republic'.

I remember one occasion when the Director of Intelligence, Michael Collins, instructed me, through Frank Thornton, that a particular letter was going through the post from the British military headquarters in Parkgate Street, and that it was to be intercepted before it reached the Rink. I knew the number of the post office van going from Parkgate Street, and, accompanied by Pat McCrea, we held it up at the junction of Parnell Square and Parnell Street. We seized all the mails in the van. I was informed later that we had succeeded in our mission, as the wanted letter was amongst the many seized.[65]

Diarmuid O'Sullivan described how the men in the sorting room got the messages to Collins:

After we were officially appointed we did not go to Molloy's, although Mick said I could go there because sometimes I would find it hard to come down from the Rink and go down Parnell Square. We had to get places outside. We had McMahon's, the dairy in Parnell Street, we had Devlin's, and we had a public-house belonging to Séamus Kirwan. I used to go down to Vaughan's Hotel every Sunday and meet Dermot O'Hegarty, Gearóid O'Sullivan, Piaras Béaslaí, and sometimes Mick Collins would be there. We met together like a family. I used to go to see Mick in the Gresham Hotel. I was a personal friend of Mick Collins all the way through, and after the Treaty was passed he personally paid a tribute to the work Captain Moynihan and myself had done for him. His exact words were, 'Diarmuid, you and he have served me well. I shall never forget it for you'. Those words were said to me after Mick had arrived at Joint No. 2 [Liam Devlin's pub],

Left—Collins was the youngest of eight children. On his deathbed, Collins's father told the family to take care of Michael, because 'one day he'll be a great man. He'll do great work for Ireland'.

Below—'Woodfield' was the name given by Collins's mother to the new house that she built in 1908. The Essex Division, under the command of Major Arthur Emmett Percival, burned it on 16 April 1921 as a reprisal for a recent raid on an RIC barracks at Rosscarbery. The British forced the neighbours to bring straw into the house and then light it to burn it down. Collins said that 'they knew how to hurt me'.

Left—When conscription was to take effect in Britain in January 1916, Collins returned to Dublin. When he was appointed a Captain in the Volunteers, he bought a full uniform. This photo was taken in Clonakilty after his release from Frongoch in December—Collins is wearing the uniform that he wore in the GPO, and the shirt was placed on Thomas Ashe's body when Ashe was buried in September 1917.

Below—After the Rising, Collins was first taken to Stafford Prison. He is the fifth from the right. Also in the photo were Seán O'Briain, Fergus Kelly, Eunan McGinley, Desmond Ryan, Denis Daly, Brian Joyce, Eamon Dore, Joe Sweeney and J. Kilgallon.

Left—Upon his release from Frongoch, Collins went to work for the Volunteers' Dependants' Fund. From then on, he dressed as a successful Dublin businessman.

Below—Ned Broy worked in the DMP offices in Great Brunswick Street, and was one of Collins's most effective spies. Broy gave Collins a detailed, inside knowledge of the British police system in Ireland. Collins learned how the system worked and how the police were trained—Broy turned him into an intelligence master.

Boland and Collins with de Valera. Harry Boland and Collins were best friends and along with Desmond Lynch were the ones most responsible for choosing the men and women who were to form the First Dáil.

DAIL EIREANN, AN TARNA TIONOL, 10 ABRAN, 1919.

Sreath 1.—(i dtosach)—L. MacFhionnghail, M. O'Coileain, C. Brugha, A. O'Griobhtha, E. de Bhailera, S. Conte Pluingcéad, E. MacNéill, L. MacCosgair, E. de Blaghd.   Sreath 2.—P. O'Maoldhomhnaigh, T. MacSuibhne, R. O'Maolchatha, S. O'Dochartaigh, S. O'Mathghamhna, S. O'Deolain, S. MacAonghusa, P. O'Caoimh, M. MacStain, S. MacCraith, An Dr. B. O'Ciosog, L. de Roiste, L. Colibhet, An tA. M. O'Flannagain.   Sreath 3.—P. Mac an Bhaird, A. MacCaba, D. MacGearailt, S. MacSuibhne, An Dr. R. O hAodha, C. O'Coileain, P. O'Maille, S. O'Meadhra, B. O hUigin, S. de Burca, C. O hUigin.   Sreath 4.—S. MacDonnchadha, S. Mac an tSaoi.   Sreath 5.—P. Beaslaoi, R. Bartuin, P. O'Gallagain, Sreath 6.—P. O'Seanachain, S. Etchingham.

On 10 April 1919 the official photo of the First Dáil was taken. Many of the TDs were in prison at the first meeting on 21 January 1919, and both Collins and Harry Boland were in Britain arranging the escape of Éamon de Valera from Lincoln Prison.

Collins was persuaded to sit in the photo for the First Dáil for its historical value, but his expression indicated his dismay at having his photo taken at that time.

Collins grew a moustache, thinking that he needed a disguise. When his brother Johnny saw it he said, 'Next time you shave, don't forget your upper lip!'

Above—Both Collins and Harry Boland were keen sportsmen. Matches were held at Croke Park to raise money, and both often appeared and then stayed to enjoy the matches.

Left—A young-looking Collins dressed just like a successful businessman. His best disguise was that he was not in disguise.

Left—Collins's usual mode of transportation was a bicycle. It was considered normal and acceptable for a businessman and Collins constantly cultivated that image.

Below—When the Dáil Loan was passed, Collins used the opportunity to have a public signing of Loan documents and filmed the signing at St Enda's.

Above—From 1917 onwards, Collins and Arthur Griffith grew closer and were the leaders of the Treaty negotiations. Here, Collins is shown in the moustache he sometimes wore as a disguise.
Below—Collins at his desk, also with the newly grown moustache.

where Frank Thornton and others were waiting for him; I was immediately in Frank's company and Mick had a glass of sherry with us. I never met Mick or spoke to him after that.

... This correspondence was in many cases taken to Knocknagow Dairy if suitable, to Devlin's or Jim Kirwan's. Very often the correspondence would be at our Headquarters before the mails would leave the yard ... From the time we started, the correspondence was at the bottom of everything that was done. Paddy Daly told me that they often wondered why orders that had been given were suddenly countermanded. Of course, he or the rank and file did not know of the Intelligence Section's work in the post office. Our lips were sealed. In fact my own son, who was sentenced to be hanged, did not know I was in the IRB. I never told him, and he was very vexed with me because there were lots of things he could have done, but I could not open my lips and I could not say what way I was situated with Mick Collins. Even my wife did not know I was in the IRB and she was a member of Cumann na mBan and has her Service Medal.[66]

Charles McQuaile also worked in the Rotunda Rink, and he related a story of Collins's audacity and the lax British security:

One morning during the year 1920 or 1921, I am not clear which—as I was coming out the back door of the GPO at that time located in the Rink, two men met me. One was known to me as Peadar Breslin. They said to me 'Come along with us'. I went with them to, I think, No. 2 Dominick Street near Parnell Street. This was a tailor's shop and McMahon was the name. I was taken into a back-parlour in which about three men were seated at a table evidently awaiting our arrival. One of the men resembled Michael Collins. Breslin later confirmed that it was Collins.

This gentleman questioned me as to the procedure I adopted in the delivery of the packets at Dublin Castle and at GHQ. I explained the procedure in detail with the aid of a rough sketch of the Castle and the rooms through which I passed with the correspondence. He said 'Instead of you going this morning I am going. Do you think it will be a safe mission?' I confirmed that there was nothing to fear as the Castle Authorities were, in my opinion, rather lackadaisical. At this stage I handed him my pass and the packets and he told me to wait here until he came back. He returned in about an hour and a half and said everything went lovely. He returned the pass and told me I had nothing to worry about as he had met with no obstacles.

Some days later it was announced in the press that it was believed Michael Collins had entered Dublin Castle disguised as a coal porter but I knew otherwise.

It was noticed at this time that there was a certain laxity in the supervision of these offices at Dublin Castle and GHQ, and that the correspondence, although marked 'Secret' and 'Confidential', seemed to be there for anyone to handle. The cleaners could have access to them too.[67]

49 Great Britain Street (now Parnell Street): Jim (Séamus) Kirwan's pub. This was Seán MacDermott's 'local' and continued to be a republican meeting place after the Rising. It was known as '**Joint No. 3**'. Jim Kirwan was from County Tipperary and was a great friend of Dan Breen and Seán Treacy; when in Dublin they stayed here as often as once a week while 'on the run'. Collins hid some of the gold collected for the Dáil Loan in the basement here.

65 Great Britain Street (now Parnell Street): Home of Mr and Mrs Maurice Collins (no relation to Michael). *Who's who* claims that Bulmer Hobson was held here prior to the Rising.[68] Most commentators agree, however, that Hobson was held at Martin Conlon's home at Cabra Park and that Maurice was one of those guarding him on Holy Saturday.

Maurice opened a tobacconist and confectioner's shop here after he was released from Frongoch, and Batt O'Connor built a secret compartment in the wall to hide documents. Collins often stayed overnight, and it was raided on 31 January 1920.

68–69 Great Britain Street (now Parnell Street) (just off Rutland Square): **Liam Devlin's pub.** This was known as '**Joint No. 2**', Collins's 'unofficial HQ':

> ... from this period onwards Devlin's not alone became our meeting place but Mrs Devlin acted in the capacity of a very generous hostess. Visitors from the country never left without getting a meal and in quite a large number of instances a bed for the night. It can be readily understood that a headquarters of this kind in the heart of the city was valuable to the movement generally and particularly to the Intelligence end of things, for, being a public house, no notice was taken of people continually going in and out. I think the Devlin family deserve the very best thanks of the nation for their contribution to the fight for freedom.
>
> ... Mick Collins left this headquarters practically every night bordering on curfew on his old Raleigh bicycle and on many an occasion Tom Cullen, Liam Tobin and myself left about the same time and started on our journey across town to Rathmines where we had a flat in Grosvenor Road, but on numerous occasions it was found necessary to stay the night, sometimes because of enemy activity in the immediate vicinity or because it was necessary to remain in town for an early morning operation the following day.[69]

Collins waited here for Bloody Sunday reports. Joe O'Reilly cycled in and Collins first asked: 'Any casualties?' At that time O'Reilly reported that there had been none. Collins then said: 'There'll be no match today at Croke Park'. He knew that even if the match were cancelled a crowd would gather and it would be an obvious target for the British. 'Go down there and tell them to call it off.' It was too late, however, and the match went ahead. (See Bloody Sunday, Appendix IV.)

Finding that he could not stop the match at Croke Park, O'Reilly cycled back to Devlin's. On the way, a lad came up to him and told him that Dick McKee and Peadar Clancy had been captured the night before and that he was to take a message to Collins. O'Reilly was stunned and immediately went to Devlin's to tell Collins. When he heard, Collins screamed, 'Good God! We're finished now! It's all up!'

Collins then ordered James McNamara to find out where they were being held, and he thought it was at the Bridewell. Collins sent McNamara and Dave Neligan to search for them, but they found that McKee and Clancy were being held in Dublin Castle, where they were in fact killed, along with Conor Clune. Clune, a Gaelic Leaguer from County Clare, was taken in Vaughan's Hotel, a noted IRA meeting place. He had nothing to do with the Volunteers and only had come to Dublin to confer with journalist Piaras Béaslaí. (See Marlborough Street, Pro-Cathedral, Dublin 1.) McKee and Clancy were captured in Seán Fitzpatrick's house in Lower Gloucester Street, supposedly a safe house. John (Shankers) Ryan, the tout who turned them in, was later killed in Hyne's pub in Gloucester Place.

69 Great Britain Street (now Parnell Street): Home of Paddy Daly, usually considered to be the O/C of the Squad. He became a general in the Free State Army.[70]

70 Great Britain Street (now Parnell Street) (and Moore Lane) (formerly Patrick Conway's pub, now closed): Patrick Pearse surrendered to Gen. William Lowe outside this building at 3.30pm on 29 April 1916, ending the Rising. Lowe's son John, who was also an officer in the British army, accompanied the general. John Lowe later changed his name to 'John Loder' and became a successful actor and film producer in Hollywood.

74 Great Britain Street (now Parnell Street): Mooney's pub. Frequented by the British during the War of Independence.

75A Great Britain Street (now Parnell Street) (corner of Sackville Street): Tom Clarke's tobacconist's shop, opened in 1909. Clarke was arrested in London on 4 April 1883 and was imprisoned in Millbank, Portland and Chatham prisons as Henry Hammond Wilson. He was finally released on 21 September 1898. He was prisoner no. J464. Elizabeth O'Farrell was held prisoner here while waiting for Gen. Lowe.

Gregg Lane (now Cathal Brugha Street): During the War of Independence, Volunteer John O'Carroll and his wife, May Gahan, opened a milk bar here, called the Republican Bar, and painted the outside walls green, white and orange. British soldiers frequented it, and May often used the opportunity to buy guns from them. Her greatest success was to buy a machine-gun; she had it lowered over the wall of Ship Street Barracks and took it away in a pram.

21 Henry Street: Home of Jennie and Charles Wyse-Power.

Charles had been a member of the IRB and the Volunteers, but was told that he would be more valuable as a lawyer, free from these associations, and so did not take part in the Rising.[71]

The Proclamation was agreed upon here and six signed it: Thomas Clarke, Patrick Pearse, James Connolly, Thomas MacDonagh, Seán MacDermott and Éamonn Ceannt, probably on Tuesday 18 April. Joseph Plunkett signed on Easter Sunday morning.[72]

Jenny supported the Treaty and was appointed to the first Seanad of the Irish Free State, where she had an outstanding record as a champion of women's rights from 1922 to 1936.

Their daughter, Dr Nancy Wyse-Power, was an emissary to Germany during the War of Independence and was a close associate of John Chartres.[73] Both Wyse-Power and Chartres sent all their intelligence information directly to Collins.[74] She was later appointed to the Free State Department of Industry and Commerce and was a strong advocate for women's rights.[75]

21, 22 Henry Street: Jenny Wyse-Power ran a restaurant and grocer's shop under the name Irish Farm Produce Co. Collins used space here as a primary office and also as a Department of Intelligence office, but it was not in use for long.

After their office on Eustace Street was raided, Gearóid O'Sullivan and Richard Mulcahy also had temporary offices here above the restaurant, and Bridie O'Reilly worked as their secretary.[76]

45 Henry Street: Under the name of Murray & Quirke, Solicitors, this was Austin Stack's first Ministry of Home Affairs office, as well as one of Collins's Ministry of Finance offices. Patrick (Paddy) Sheehan worked here for Collins as a secretary and messenger. After Stack's office was raided in 1920, he moved his offices to the Clarence Hotel on Wellington Quay (Dublin 2).

Stack and Collins had been close friends since 1917. Collins was particularly impressed with Stack's effective leadership of the prisoners in Crumlin Road Jail, Belfast. It was through Stack that Collins secured the article on conscription in *An tÓglach* written by Ernest Blyth that impressed him so much. Collins had helped Stack to escape from Strangeways Prison in Manchester in October 1919, and had visited him there shortly before the jailbreak. Collins was keenly interested in the enterprise and sent a number of letters to Béaslaí and Stack about it. He sent these through the ordinary post and they contained information about affairs in Ireland, veiled in code. The letters were boldly signed 'Michael Collins', a name which then meant nothing to the prison censor. Collins brought the project before GHQ in Dublin, and Rory O'Connor was sent over to examine the plans on the spot. In the code used for communications between the prisoners and GHQ, Collins now became known as 'Angela' and Paddy O'Donoghue as 'Maud'. It happened that Austin Stack received a postcard from a convent school and signed 'Your loving cousin, Maud'. This contained the seemingly innocent information: 'We are all busy preparing for the examination. Professor Rory has arrived. He is a very nice man. I hope I shall pass.' The prison censor considered this message to be quite innocent. A few days later Collins arrived and, under a false name, paid a visit to Stack. Despite the presence of a warder throughout the visit, he contrived to give Stack a pretty good idea of the situation in Ireland and mentioned also that he was now living at his old address in Mountjoy Street, Dublin, as the G-men were afraid to interfere with him. Upon returning to Dublin, Stack was suffering from a septic leg that he had re-injured in his climb over the wall, and Collins had him placed in Batt O'Connor's home on Brendan Road for several months.[77]

> I knew Austin Stack very well. He stayed often at our house in Brendan Road and I got to like him very much. He was very gentle and kind. Afterwards when the unfortunate split came and many people became very bitter against their old friends he never did. I did not meet him for a long time but when I did—on the street—he greeted me as affectionately and warmly as ever.[78]

After Stack was appointed minister for home affairs with responsibility for establishing the Dáil/Republican courts and police systems, Collins wrote to him that he should not return to Kerry, as he was needed in Dublin:

> My own idea was that you'd be indispensable in Dublin and I don't think any consideration would change my mind in this regard.

Collins was looking forward to much cooperation between them, but things turned out differently because Stack was a poor administrator. He shirked difficult decisions and later admitted that he was out of his depth as minister, never mind that he was also the deputy chief of staff of the IRA.[79] Some saw a change in Stack after his imprisonment; he became morose and sensitive. As a minister for home affairs he was considered a failure,[80] and Collins was not the only one to note this. One of the reports from GHQ said: 'The Home Affairs and Judicial departments yielded to the first onset of the enemy … The plain fact is that our civil service have simply played at governing a republic.'[81] Collins found Stack to be an inefficient minister; at a cabinet meeting in 1920 he accused him of being a 'bloody incompetent', and their relationship was never mended. Collins abused him frequently and openly. 'Stack,' hissed Collins, loudly enough to be heard, 'your department is only a bloody joke.'[82] On another occasion, Collins referred to Stack's performance in Kerry when Stack was the O/C in the area prior to the Rising. He had gone to see Roger Casement in jail, and was himself arrested with many incriminating documents on him. Collins said of one of Stack's plans, 'I hope you won't make a mess of this the same as you did of the Casement landing'.[83] Stack was bitterly opposed to Collins thereafter and especially in the Treaty debates.

Stack's problems were not just with Collins. Padraic O'Keefe, who served with Stack as Joint National Secretary of Sinn Féin, noted that it was 'easy to work with him [Stack] … Of course he did no work!'[84] According to Richard Mulcahy, the IRA GHQ had twice established a republican police force and on both occasions it disintegrated when Stack took control of it as the minister for home affairs.[85] Mulcahy argued that Collins would have been content to let Stack alone if he had been working properly, but Stack had never been able to get on top of his job.[86] Understanding the growing rift between Collins and Stack is vital to understanding their disagreements in cabinet and at the Treaty debates. Mulcahy wrote further:

> … it is impossible to envisage what kind of a spirit, a heart or a mentality Stack could have had to have developed what would bring him so bitterly and so disastrously against Collins and drive the country into civil war.[87]

In contrast, J.J. O'Kelly disagreed:

> On one occasion—I think it was at a Dáil meeting—Michael Collins said something unbecoming about Austin Stack's department, one of those statements he was quite capable of making after a late night. It was something in the nature of a reproach. He seemed to think Stack was a timid type of man that he could overawe. But Stack promptly put him in his place, and showed himself a man not to be trifled with. He had great courage, as was proved in his fight in the Belfast prison. Yet he was very gentle, as was Cathal Brugha.[88]

Stack was remembered as a companionable man, but one whose capabilities did not match his responsibilities. In prison he had been an effective leader; he was placed in the cabinet on the basis of his performance there, but he did not possess the greatly different qualities needed in that office. Yet no one in the cabinet liked Collins's behaviour toward Stack, who was a courteous and decent man. Though Stack resented it, it was not until the meetings and debates about the Treaty that his antipathy was expressed publicly.

(See Wellington Quay, Dublin 2.)

Jervis Street (corner of York Street): The Swan Hotel. Collins often used it as a meeting place during the War of Independence.

14–20 Jervis Street: Jervis Street Hospital. Forty-five fatalities and 550 injured were treated here during the Rising.

Seán Hales and Padraig Ó Maille were taken here after being shot on 7 December 1922. Hales was dead on arrival but Ó Maille survived. (See Ormond Quay, Dublin 7.)

Marlborough Street (at corner of Cathedral Street): Pro-cathedral (St Mary's). Dublin's Catholic cathedral, begun in 1815 and opened in 1825. The portico is a copy of the Temple of Theseus in Athens. The three statues on it represent the Mother of God in the centre, with the two diocesan patrons, St Kevin and St Laurence O'Toole, on either side.

Seán Treacy was laid out here before being removed to Soloheadbeg for burial.

Collins sometimes served Mass here during the War of Independence years.

Peadar Clancy and Dick McKee were laid out here after Bloody Sunday, and Collins went to see their bodies. Despite pleas from his friends, Collins lovingly dressed his comrades, to whom he had been particularly close. Kathleen Clarke was there and saw him in the small mortuary chapel:

> While I was in the mortuary, Mick Collins came in: when he looked in the coffin of Peadar Clancy tears rushed down from his eyes and fell on Peadar. I did not wonder, all three men were terribly mutilated. One had a large hole in his forehead; it looked as if an explosive bullet had been used. All their faces had the looks of tortured men, which even death had not washed away the memory of. Mick Collins had no need to be ashamed of those tears. He took great risks of being captured in coming.[89]

The following morning Collins was even more distraught, but he insisted on going to the funeral. Just as the coffins came out of the church, he stepped out of the crowd and pinned a message to McKee's coffin: 'To the memory of two good friends, Dick and Peadar, two of Ireland's best soldiers. Miceal Ó Coilleann, 25/11/1920'. Then he shouldered the coffin with the other pallbearers and marched towards the funeral cortège.

When he was walking out of the church a woman in the crowd recognised him and shouted, 'Look, there is Michael Collins'. Collins turned and growled at her, 'Shut up, you bloody bitch'. (See Bloody Sunday, Appendix IV.)

Less than 24 months later, Arthur Griffith and Collins would both be buried from here.

Marlborough Street: Rabbiatti's Bar, frequented by British intelligence officers. Tom Cullen and Frank Thornton drank here in order to pick up information, and one day British spies asked them how they had learned the Irish brogue: 'we've been here for the last twelve months and can't get it'.[90]

5 Mary Street: Collins had an interim office here in 1919.

22 Mary Street: Collins's primary Department of Finance office.

> 22 Mary Street was the Finance Headquarters of Michael Collins and in his capacity as Minister for Finance of the Dáil he frequently visited that establishment. As in all other cases, of course, offices such as 22 Mary Street were used for other purposes as well, and on one occasion the premises were actually visited in mistake by the enemy, who left without carrying out any search. This was some time early in 1921.[91]

For a while in 1920 the Volunteer GHQ shared this space. Alice Lyons was his principal secretary here.

> We had rented new offices in Mary Street, a busy thoroughfare, with a constant stream of people passing continually along the pavement, and in and out of the building. He [Collins] liked such streets, where the presence of two or three fresh faces would pass unnoticed. He took me with him to look at the place, and to point out to me on the spot certain alterations he wanted made, and where new fittings were to be put in. As we were walking along the street we met two men of the DMP. He looked them straight in the face, and while they were still watching us, we went into a public-house. We remained there for about ten minutes. To behave in so casual a way was to disarm suspicion.
>
> 'Even if they recognized me, Batt, they would be afraid to report they saw me,' he said, 'and, supposing they did report it, it would take at least an hour before the necessary force to seize me could be mobilized. And, of course, all the time I would wait here until they were ready to come along! I will tell you something. I do not allow myself to feel I am on the run. That is my safeguard. It prevents me from acting in a manner likely to arouse suspicion.'

He had set up offices for the different departments of Dáil Éireann—Home Affairs, Finance, Trade and Commerce. They were all in busy streets like Henry Street, O'Connell Street, Bachelor's Walk, Frederick Street, and other frequented thoroughfares, and were situated in buildings where there would be a number of people constantly passing in and out, and where our men and messengers would not be likely to attract special attention. He usually entrusted me with the work of fitting up these offices with electric light, office furniture, new locks with a number of keys, and a brass plate with the name of solicitors who did not exist, so far as we knew, and other invented names of business firms carrying on all sorts of industries and wholesale trade.

We went once together on our bicycles to look at a vacant house at the junction of Upper Leeson Street and Sussex Terrace. I thought the position unsuitable. It stood on the V or junction of two streets, and was in an exposed position. When I pointed this out, he agreed with me, and abandoned the idea of taking it. We purchased instead a house in Wellington Road.[92]

It was raided on 26 May 1921 (the day after the Custom House fire). This raid was one of Collins's closest calls. Alice Lyons and Bob Conlan, the office messenger, were in the office when it was raided, but Collins had had a premonition and stayed away after his lunch with Gearóid O'Sullivan. Lying on his desk were the personal possessions of Major G.L. Compton-Smith, DSO, of the Royal Welch Fusiliers, who was taken hostage by the IRA in 1921 before being shot in retaliation for the execution of IRA prisoners.[93] Collins had actually tried to save him but was unable to do so.[94] Joe O'Reilly was near the door when the Auxiliaries entered, and cycled to intercept Collins. Collins always said that there was a traitor in the camp, and always claimed that he knew who it was and knew the details of the raid—including the fact that the tout had been paid £500 on condition that there would be no bloodshed. After the Treaty, Collins was drinking with a Dublin Castle official who said that there was an informer in Collins's camp, but Collins walked away, saying 'I don't want to hear of it'.

28–29 Mary Street: It was used as a small office and raided in June 1921. Batt O'Connor built a secret compartment in the draper's shop here.

Moore Lane (corner of Henry Place): Cogan's Greengrocer's. Volunteers from the GPO went through this shop to get to the home at 16 Moore Street, which was their last Rising HQ. The 'Provisional Government' spent Friday night here and ate breakfast here on Saturday morning, served by Mrs Cogan.

Moore Street: An area with many food-sellers, in 1916 and now; eleven buildings were burned here during the Rising. Rebel forces fleeing the GPO left there at 8pm on Friday 28 April, went into Henry Street, through Moore Street and Henry Place and into Moore Lane. As the escapees burrowed through the walls of houses in Moore Street on Friday night, they stopped and sheltered in many homes and shops.[95]

The following day Patrick and Willie Pearse, Tom Clarke, Joseph Plunkett and Seán MacDermott gathered around James Connolly's bedside in No. 16,[96] home of the Plunketts (no relation to Joseph Plunkett), to determine what course of negotiation to undertake. (Connolly, with some other wounded, had been taken to this house earlier.[97]) From here, Elizabeth O'Farrell and ultimately Pearse eventually approached British forces to declare the surrender.[98]

1 Mountjoy Square: Home of T.M. Healy before he became the first governor-general of the Irish Free State.

3 Mountjoy Square: Home of Alderman Walter Cole. The Dáil met here in 1919 and 1920. Collins sometimes stayed here.

> One such meeting was convened and held at Alderman Cole's house in Mountjoy Square, at which, I believe, important decisions were made regarding the progress of the war. Only those members who were not in jail or interned attended and, as most of these were Volunteer officers, and more particularly, because Michael Collins, Cathal Brugha and Dick McKee were attending, myself and a few other members of the Intelligence Department performed security guard duties at the house to deal with any attempted raid by Crown forces.[99]

Mountjoy Street: Home of Seán McGarry. He had been in charge of the security party on the pier at Howth when arms were landed from Erskine Childers's *Asgard* for the Volunteers in July 1914, and was editor of the *Literary Souvenir* for the O'Donovan Rossa funeral in August 1915.

McGarry was great friends with Tom Clarke:

> To him the Irish Nation was very real. He spoke of fighting for Ireland as casually as he did about any item of the day's news. To fight England was to him the most natural thing in the world for an Irishman.[100]

He accidentally shot Clarke in the elbow on 30 January 1916; the wound never completely healed.

On the night of 17–18 May 1918, when the Volunteer cabinet was seized in the 'German Plot' arrests, Collins stayed here after McGarry was taken. Collins thought it was the safest house in Dublin since the British would not come back a second time. (See 6 Harcourt Street, Dublin 2.)

McGarry escaped from Lincoln Prison with Éamon de Valera and Seán Milroy. Milroy was the prisoner who drew the cartoon Christmas card of a man with a key: the key was the shape of the one that Collins and Harry Boland made to open the doors for the escape. (See Lincoln Prison, Lincolnshire, England, Appendix VI.)

McGarry became an Irish Free State TD. During the Civil War, IRA/Republicans burned the McGarrys' Philipsburgh Avenue home on 10 December 1922, and their seven-year-old son, Emmet, died later from burns received. McGarry's electrical fittings shop was bombed the following month.

The family later moved to 25 Booterstown Avenue, Blackrock.

19 Mountjoy Street: Susan Killeen, a girlfriend of Collins before Kitty Kiernan, lived here with the family of her uncle, Patrick. Susan was from Doonbeg, Co. Clare, and Collins met her in London. She was a great friend of Collins's cousin, Nancy O'Brien, with whom she lived in London, and was described as his first real girlfriend. Around 1915 Susan lost her job in the Post Office because she refused to take the Oath of Allegiance, and moved back to Dublin. She went to work in P.S. O'Hegarty's bookshop in Dawson Street and became one of Collins's most valuable couriers. By 1917 their relationship had turned platonic, though she continued to work for him and undertook many dangerous missions. Their relationship soured in 1922, as she disagreed with him over the Treaty and was not happy about his engagement to Kitty Kiernan.

30 Mountjoy Street (across from the Munster Private Hotel): Home of Madeline Dicker, a girlfriend of Collins before Kitty Kiernan but after Susan Killeen. She lived here with her father, Edwin. Dilly (as Collins called her) was an ardent nationalist, and a member of Sinn Féin and Cumann na mBan. She undertook many risky tasks for Collins, frequently accompanying him as they posed as a couple. One of her most dangerous missions was to go on the mail-boat to London, disguised as a mail-sorter and hidden in one of the mail carts; in the sorting room, she would climb out of the mail basket, extract any post for Whitehall and bring it to Collins's men in England. On the return voyage she would do the same with the post for Dublin Castle and British agents, passing it on to Collins in Dublin.

Since this house was directly across from the Munster Private Hotel, whenever there was a raid on the street those in the house would signal the all-clear (by a particular arrangement of the window curtains) to anyone hiding in the rooms or on the roof of the hotel.

44 Mountjoy Street: Munster Private Hotel, also known as Áras na nGael or

Grianan na nGaedheal, owned by Myra T. McCarthy, a staunch republican from Kerry.

This was Collins's first residence after his release from Frongoch Prison, and it remained his primary residence until it was raided in December 1919. Even after Collins went 'on the run', he still left his laundry here and picked it up on Saturdays. Fionan Lynch (who was arrested with Austin Stack and Thomas Ashe for violations of the DORA) also lived here.

During 1918 the English spy Timothy Quinlisk stayed here. The Squad always suspected him; Seán Ó Muirthile was assigned to keep a watch on him, while another of the Squad called Dublin Castle to say that Quinlisk had vital information and would meet outside the offices of the *Evening Mail* that night. The Squad intended to shoot him when he turned up at the meeting, but he never came. He was later traced to Cork, and was killed there. (See Harcourt Street, Dublin 2, Appendix II; Winthrop Street, Co. Cork, Appendix VI.)

When Collins heard of Harry Boland's death on 2 August 1922, he burst into Fionan Lynch's room here and spent the evening crying helplessly.

Parnell Street: See **Great Britain Street**.

Parnell Square: See **Rutland Square**.

16 Lower Railway Street (now Waterford Street): Home of John (Shankers) Ryan, a corporal in Dublin's Military Foot Police. Collins believed that Ryan was a British spy who had betrayed his two top men, Dick McKee and Peadar Clancy, to Crown forces on the night before Bloody Sunday, so he gave the order for Ryan's execution.

> We shot a man on the following Thursday for that job. The unfortunate fellow was inside drinking in a public-house in Gloucester Diamond when he was executed. He was the gentleman who was alleged to have given Dick McKee away. He was living half-way between the two places. He could have stood at his door and seen Dick McKee going into the house. He probably saw him passing by. The evidence on which he was shot was conclusive there is no doubt whatever about that. Michael Collins gave the order to have him shot at once. I think the fellow was an ex-British soldier but I do not know his name. I think his execution took place less than a week after Bloody Sunday [*sic*; in fact, he was not killed until 5 February 1921].[101]

(See Gloucester Street Lower; Bloody Sunday, Appendix IV.)

Rutland Square (now Parnell Square): The first of Dublin's Georgian Squares, its four sides were originally known as Charlemont Row (west), Cavendish Row (east),

Palace Row (north) and Great Britain Street (south). The central park was named after the fourth duke of Rutland, who was lord lieutenant of Ireland in 1784–7. Now named for Home Rule leader Charles Stewart Parnell.

Rutland Square (now Parnell Square): Garden of Remembrance. The Rising prisoners were held in the open here overnight on 29 April 1916. The current garden, opened in 1966 on the 50th anniversary of the Rising, was designed by architect Daithi Hanly and features a sunken pool with mosaics depicting discarded weapons. The statue by Oisin Kelly represents the Children of Lir, an ancient Irish legend about four children who were turned into swans and condemned to live for 900 years; the spell was finally broken by St Patrick, who restored them to their human form and baptised them before they died.

Rutland Square (now Parnell Square): Geraghty's Hotel; Neary's Hotel; Meath Hotel; Minerva Hotel. All were located around the square, a few doors from Vaughan's Hotel. The IRA/Volunteers from the country during the War of Independence used all of them.

10 Rutland Square (now Parnell Square): Orange Hall and Fowler Memorial Hall. In March 1922 the Orange Hall was seized during a social function by IRA/Republicans, who announced that they were taking the buildings in the name of Catholic workers expelled from the Belfast shipyards. They converted it into a dormitory[102] and used the Fowler Memorial Hall to the rear of the building as a Centre of Direction for the seizure of private property. In the following days, fifteen families from Belfast, totalling 83 individuals, were put up in the buildings, and 70 single men from Belfast were given meals there.[103]

11 Rutland Square (now Parnell Square): Kevin O'Higgins's office. Also in this building were the offices of Dublin County Council, which were raided on 25 November 1920. The British were looking for Collins and some specific evidence in the County Council offices, and though they 'lined up' O'Higgins and his staff they ignored their offices. O'Higgins was an assistant minister for local government in the First and Second Dáil, and became minister after the Treaty.

20 Rutland Square (now Parnell Square): Banba Hall. Collins used the Grocers and Vintners' offices here for meetings.

25 Rutland Square (now Parnell Square): Gaelic League Building (Coisde Gnotha Branch). This was the usual parade hall of 'C' Company, 2nd Battalion, prior to the Rising. The 1st Battalion of the Dublin Brigade drilled here weekly after the Rising.

It was also the Central Branch (the original branch) of Cumann na mBan. There were 43 affiliated branches before the Rising. The officers of the Central Branch at the time of the Rising were Kathleen Clarke, president, and Sorcha MacMahon, secretary; branch members included Áine Ceannt,[104] Louise Gavan Duffy, Niamh Plunkett and Jennie Wyse-Power.

Cumann na mBan played a more public role during the Civil War than during the Rising or the War of Independence. It held its own convention on the Treaty on 5 February 1922, voting 419 to 63 against it. Countess Markievicz was elected president at that time. Pro-Treaty members were asked to resign, and they formed their own group, called Cumann na Saoirse (Society of Freedom), which was not militarily active during the Civil War.

P.S. O'Hegarty wrote:

As the war lengthened, it became more brutal and more savage and more hysterical and more unrelievedly black. But the worst effect was on the women. They were the first to be thrown off their base, and as the war lengthened they steadily deteriorated. They took to their hearts every catch-cry and every narrowness and every bitterness, and steadily eliminated from themselves every womanly feeling ... War, and the things war breeds—intolerance, swagger, unwomanness—captured the women, turned them into unlovely, destructive-minded, arid begetters of violence.[105]

The IRA/Republicans used it as HQ from March 1922.

29–30 Rutland Square (now Parnell Square): Vaughan's Hotel; owned by Mrs Vaughan of Clare, who sold it to Tom McGuire, formerly of Limerick. It was Collins's **'Joint No. 1'**, but after mid-1920 was considered unsafe for the Volunteers.

Christy Harte was the usual night porter. It was said that he was offered many thousands of pounds by the British to turn in Collins and others; he was promised money, protection, transportation out of Ireland and a new name. Irish wags said that he'd have to change his name to 'Christy Eleison'.

He was arrested shortly before midnight on the night of 31st December, 1920, and detained in Dublin Castle where he was ill-treated. The time was fixed in his memory by the fact that church bells were ringing in the 'New Year' as he was entering Dublin Castle under arrest. A few days later, the exact date he cannot remember, while still in custody in the Castle he was questioned in a dark room as to his knowledge of Collins. He denied all knowledge of him, but was confronted with the statement that he had frequently been seen carrying Michael Collins's bicycle down the steps of Vaughan's Hotel from the hall into the street.

It was suggested to him by his unseen questioner that he was a poor man and that he would like to earn some money. He was informed that the authorities would be prepared to pay a large sum, perhaps up to even £10,000 for information leading to the capture of Collins.

The scheme suggested to him was that on some occasion when Collins would be in Vaughan's Hotel, he, Christopher Harte, should ring up the Castle, Extension 28, and give the following message: — Brennan: The portmanteau is now ready.[106]

On 14 October 1919 Liam Deasy came to Dublin to meet the men of GHQ for the first time. He wrote of his meeting Collins in Vaughan's:

My recollection of that night in Vaughan's is of a very informal meeting where GHQ staff were constantly coming and going, and it was a surprise to me to see how nonchalantly they seemed to accept the constant risk that was theirs.[107]

Conor Clune was arrested here on 20 November 1920, the night before Bloody Sunday. He was an Irish scholar from the west who had nothing to do with the IRA/Volunteers but who had come to see Piaras Béaslaí about Irish-language projects. Harte warned all the members of the IRA/Volunteers, and most headed for the back of the hotel. Béaslaí and Seán O'Connell escaped out the back on that night. (See Dublin Castle, Dublin 2; Bloody Sunday, Appendix IV.)

Though the hotel became very dangerous as the war went on, Collins still called there. Following the Truce in July 1921, there was a celebratory gathering.

Shortly after the Truce there was a great gathering in Vaughan's Hotel of all the men who were 'round Mick Collins. It was a farewell party given to Harry Boland before proceeding to America. Apart from Mick Collins and Harry Boland there were also present Gearóid O'Sullivan, Diarmuid O'Hegarty, Liam Mellows, Liam Tobin, Rory O'Connor, Frank Thornton, Colonel Broy, the late Detective-Sergeant McNamara who was working for Mick Collins, Seán Etchingham of Wexford and many others. It was a joyous occasion and Mick Collins recited 'Kelly, Burke and Shea', and Liam Mellows sang 'McDonnell of the Glens'—an old Scottish song. Little did we think that night of the events that were in store before another year had passed. It is well for mortal man that he cannot see into the future.[108]

39 Rutland Square (now Parnell Square): Home of Dr Paddy Browne of Maynooth College (later president of University College Galway), from where Collins watched the raid on Vaughan's on 20 November 1920 (during which Conor Clune was arrested). Earlier that evening, Collins had a meeting at the Gaiety Theatre bar.

41 Rutland Square (now Parnell Square): Irish National Foresters' Hall. On Bloody Sunday an active service unit met here, but their mission was aborted.

> On the night before Bloody Sunday, 21st November 1920, Paddy Holohan, our Coy. O/C, instructed us to be present the following morning at 41 Parnell Square at ten minutes past eight. He told us that we were to carry our guns. Six of us were detailed and we reported next morning at the appointed time. Paddy Holohan arrived and told us to go home as the job had been called off. The only information he gave me was that 'we were to have gone to some house in Phibsboro'. He just mentioned this in casual conversation afterwards when the results of Bloody Sunday were known.[109]

In 1922 the IRB held conferences here for the express purpose of endeavouring to save the organisation from disruption on the Treaty issue. Collins and Liam Lynch were the principal protagonists of the opposing views. On 10 January 1922 those in favour of the Treaty argued that to accept would be in line with well-accepted IRB policy, that it was a matter of expedience and not of principle.

Collins was very explicit on the matter:

> I have been sent to London to do a thing which those who sent me had to be done but had not the courage to do it themselves. We had not, when the terms were offered, an average of one round of ammunition for each weapon we had. The fighting area in Cork … was becoming daily more circumcised [*sic*] and they could not have carried on much longer.[110]

> If we all stood on the recognition of the Irish Republic as a prelude to any conference we could very easily have said so, and there would have been no conference … it was the acceptance of the invitation that formed the compromise. I was sent there to form that adaption, to bear the brunt of it.[111]

Those opposed to the Treaty argued that the Republic was 'established' and that acceptance of the Treaty would disestablish it. On 18 March (postponed from 12 March) Collins determined to accept the Treaty and to do whatever was necessary to operate it, and tried to convince all of the necessity for it. Lynch decided that even if the people voted for the Treaty the Army could not be committed to it. On 19 April Collins and Lynch squared off once again, but neither side was able to convince the other. Attendees included Collins, Harry Boland, Eoin O'Duffy, Diarmuid O'Hegarty, Michael Staines,[112] Seán Ó Murthile, Gearóid O'Sullivan, Martin Conlon,[113] Seán

McKeown, Lynch, Humphrey Murphy, Pax Whelan, Florence O'Donoghue,[114] Joe McKelvey, Seán Boylan,[115] Michael Sheehan, Larry Brady, Patrick Mullaney, Seán O'Hegarty, Tom Hales, Seán Moylan and Tom Larkin. On 1 May, after long discussion, an agreement was reached on a certain basis of settlement and entitled the 'Army Document':

> We, the undersigned officers of the IRA, realise the gravity of the position in Ireland, and appreciate the fact that, if the present drift is maintained, a conflict of comrades is inevitable; we hereby declare that this would be the greatest calamity in Irish history and would leave Ireland broken for generations.
>
> To avert this catastrophe, we believe that a closing of ranks is necessary.
>
> We suggest to all leaders, army and political, and to all citizens and soldiers of Ireland, the advisability of a union of forces on the basis of the acceptance and utilisation of our present national position in the best interests of Ireland; we require that nothing shall be done that prejudice our position or dissipate our forces.
>
> We feel that on this basis alone can the situation be faced, viz.:
> 1. The acceptance of the fact, admitted by all sides, that the majority of the people of Ireland are willing to accept the Treaty.
> 2. An agreed election with a view to
> 3. Forming a government which will have the confidence of the whole country.
> 4. Army unification on the above basis.[116]

Seán Moylan was the only one who refused to sign.

Later, the Supreme Council of the IRB held a conference at which it was decided to endorse the Treaty. Liam Lynch cast the only dissenting vote but stated, 'Thank God all parties can agree to differ'.[117]

Collins had been elected president of the Supreme Council in 1919 and would remain in the post until his death. This fact may explain his activities following the Treaty, which seemed inexplicable to both the Irish and the British. As president, he sought to maintain unity at least until the full possibilities of the Treaty could be explored in the constitution that he was in charge of preparing and that he hoped would be more expressive of Irish will than the bare language of the Treaty.

All IRB TDs were allowed to vote according to their consciences on the Treaty.

46 Rutland Square (now Parnell Square): Gaelic League HQ (Conradh na Gaeilge). The League was founded here on 31 July 1893.

In October 1917 a meeting was held here to establish a National Executive of Óglaigh na hÉireann (IRA). It was decided to have the meeting at the same time as the Sinn Féin Ard-Fheis, which met on 25 October 1917. Present were Thomas Ashe, Cathal Brugha, Collins, Éamon de Valera, Diarmuid Lynch,[118] Richard Mulcahy, Diarmuid O'Hegarty and Michael Staines,[119] among the leaders. The IRB was well represented, with Collins, Diarmuid Lynch, Diarmuid O'Hegarty and Seán Ó Muirthile. Collins and the others planned a 'take-over' of Sinn Féin, but their plan failed miserably. (See the Tenth Sinn Féin Ard-Fheis, 25–6 October 1917, Mansion House, Dawson Street, Dublin 2.)

Joe Good wrote that in April 1918 Brugha and Mulcahy chaired a meeting here at which it was decided to send IRA/Volunteers to London to attempt to assassinate the British cabinet.[120] Brugha led the team to London in May and it stayed there until August, but he never received approval for the assassinations. Those on the team included Tom Craven, Good, Matt Furlong, Martin Gleeson, James 'Ginger' McNamara, James Mooney, Peter Murtagh, Sam Reilly and William (Bill) Whelan.[121] Collins disagreed with this plan, along with several of Brugha's later similar schemes. Collins said: 'Do you think the British can have only one cabinet?'

Brugha, the minister for defence, was responsible for some of the most bloodthirsty proposals and pursued them ardently and independently. Once he proposed the bombing and machine-gunning of crowds in theatres and cinemas. At a cabinet meeting Collins threw up his hands in horror and said, 'Ye'll get none of my men for that'. Brugha answered, 'I want none of your men, Mr Collins'. The cabinet rejected the plans without question, but afterwards Brugha pursued Collins with unrelenting hatred, and Austin Stack usually seconded him. The cabinet meetings began to degenerate into quarrels between Brugha and Stack on one side and Collins on the other.[122]

At times it seemed that Brugha's panacea for everything was a campaign against the British cabinet. In 1918 he had moved to London to oversee the massacre of the government's front bench by members of the Dublin IRA should conscription be enforced in Ireland, playing billiards and looking after his baby daughter while he waited. This phony war had two sides, as British police forces and intelligence services worked to ward off the attacks that never came. Reports and rumours of assassins being sent from Ireland frequently reached the British cabinet and individual MPs, often through Basil Thomson, assistant commissioner of London's Metropolitan Police. Bodyguards were assigned to 50 people in London, and policemen were stationed behind newly erected barricades in Westminster and Whitehall. Collins thought it an embarrassment and a waste of resources.[123] (See Brixton Prison, south London, Appendix VI.) Brugha continued to advocate sending men to Britain, and even sent several in November 1921 to raid for arms. As the Treaty negotiations were already under way at that time, their arrest and imprisonment created a delicate atmosphere for the negotiators.

'The Squad' was initiated here on 19 September 1919 (although by that time it had been in operation for two months and had already carried out two killings). The

Squad and the Active Service Unit went on to kill several members of the DMP. De Valera had wanted to block the killing of policemen, but in his absence in the US Collins authorised many such operations.

- Detective 'Dog' Smyth was shot at his home in Drumcondra on 30 July.
- Detective Daniel Hoey was shot in Townsend Street on 12 September.
- Detective John Barton was shot in College Green on 30 November.
- Constable John Walsh from Enniscorthy was killed in Dublin on 20 February 1920.
- Detective Constable Henry Kells was killed on Upper Camden Street on 14 April 1920.
- Detective Constable Laurence Dalton was killed at Broadstone Station on 20 April 1920.
- Detective Constable Robert Spencer was walking with Dalton and was also shot by mistake. Dave Neligan said that 'it was one of the tragedies of the time'.[124]
- Detective Sergeant Revell was killed on Connaught Street in May 1920.
- Detective Thomas Wharton was shot on the western side of St Stephen's Green but survived.
- Detective Walsh was shot in Drumcondra on 14 December but survived.

Collins and Mulcahy presided at the meeting at which the unit was officially formed. (Its original meeting had been on 1 May 1919.[125]) Ben Barrett, Paddy Daly, Seán Doyle, Tom Keogh, Joe Leonard, Mick McDonnell, Vinnie Byrne[126] and Jim Slattery[127] attended. Barrett, Daly, Doyle and Leonard were told to leave their jobs, as they would become full-time employees. Daly was named the O/C.[128] Squad members were paid £4.10s per week, a tradesman's average wage but substantially well over what they had previously made.

> Dick McKee bid Joe Leonard and myself to report to 46 Parnell Square—the meeting place of the Keating branch of the Gaelic League—on 19th September 1919.
>
> I did not know who would be at the meeting. I only knew that Joe Leonard would be there, and I think I suggested to Dick McKee that Ben Barrett should be asked to it. When I went to the meeting there were Joe Leonard, Ben Barrett, Seán Doyle, who was afterwards killed at the Custom House, Tom Keogh, who was killed during the Civil War, Jim Slattery, Vin Byrne, and Mick McDonnell.
>
> We met Michael Collins and Dick Mulcahy at the meeting and they told us that it was proposed to form a squad. This Squad would take orders directly from Michael Collins, and, in the absence of Collins, the orders would be given through either Dick McKee or Dick Mulcahy. Dick [Mulcahy] told us that we

were not to discuss our movements or actions with Volunteer officers or with anybody else. Collins told us that we were being formed to deal with spies and informers and that he had authority from the Government to have this order carried out. He gave us a short talk, the gist of which was that any of us who had read Irish history would know that no organisation in the past had an intelligence system through which spies and informers could be dealt with, but that now the position was going to be rectified by the formation of an Intelligence Branch, an Active Service Unit or whatever else it is called.

Michael Collins only picked four of us for the Squad that night, Joe Leonard, Seán Doyle, Ben Barrett and myself in charge. He told the others that he had special work to do, but he told the four of us that we were to leave our employment and that we would be compensated for lose [sic] of work. We were to have a fixed point where we could be mobilised, and I gave him 10 Beseboro Avenue, North Strand, where I had relations and where I practically lived at the time.

Michael Collins emphasised to us that under no circumstances whatever were we to take it on ourselves to shoot anybody, even if we knew he was a spy, unless we had to do it in self-defence while on active service. He also told us to remember that all members of 'G' Division and the police were not our enemies, and that indiscriminate shooting might result in the death of friends. We discovered afterwards that many of them were our friends.

We had a list of enemy agents who were to be eliminated. The first person we were to look [sic] was Detective Officer Hoey, but before we had time to do so he was shot. The Squad did not shoot him; he was shot by Mick McDonnell. Mick and Hoey were alone together and it was either Mick or Hoey so Mick shot him. Mick McDonnell was one of the best men in Dublin but he had one fault. He was always butting in, and on account of that he often did damage because he was too eager. He was not a member of the Squad [at that time].[129]

The first four members were Ben Barrett, Paddy Daly, Seán Doyle and Joe Leonard (who came right behind Daly in the chain of command).

In his witness statement Daly says that he was the first leader, though some have McDonnell as the first leader. Frank Thornton wrote: 'Mick McDonnell was the first O/C of the Dublin Squad and remained O/C until some time after Bloody Sunday, when his health collapsed and he was sent to California by Mick Collins. About this period Paddy Daly took over control of the Squad.'[130] Joe Leonard said that Daly was the first leader and that McDonnell could not be leader because he couldn't leave his job.[131] Vinnie Byrne felt that Mick McDonnell was the leader. Charlie Dalton thought that the meeting was on Great George's Street (Dublin 2) and that Mick McDonnell was the leader.[132] Daly seems to have been resented, and in the spring of 1921 many did not want him as a leader when he got out of Ballykinlar.[133] In any case, Daly ultimately became the leader when McDonnell became ill. He later became a major-general in the Free State army.

Other 'original' members were McDonnell, James Conroy, Jim McGuinness, Jimmy Slattery (a Clareman with only one hand after being injured and losing part of his arm in the Custom House fire) and William 'Billy' Stapleton (a Dubliner). Attached for a time were the four Tipperary men, Seán Treacy, Dan Breen, J.J. Hogan and Séamus Robinson. Added to the 'original' nine in January 1920 to form the 'Twelve Apostles' (a name first applied, derisively, by Austin Stack) were Vinnie Byrne, Tom Kehoe (McDonnell's half-brother, from Wicklow, later killed in the Civil War) and Mick O'Reilly.[134]

Generally it was thought that those under Daly were full-time and had quit their jobs, whereas those under McDonnell were only part-time and had remained in their employment.[135] Most were in their twenties, though some were still in their teens. Most were single, though Daly was a 30-year-old widower. McDonnell was by far the oldest at 40. Collins never told members of the Squad what the others were doing. His organisations kept all agents and operations entirely separate.

Vinnie Byrne explained how the Squad came about:

So the 'big fella', Michael Collins, set up an Intelligence department to find out who were the men selected by the British Administration to do this work. It was well known that certain G-men were on this Work, which was called political work, and three individuals, Smith, Hoey and Barton, made themselves very prominent. I believe these men were requested to cease their activities, but events proved that they became more zealous than ever. Instructions were received from the Director of Intelligence through his deputy, Liam Tobin, that these same men were a menace to the movement and would have to be got out of the way.

With this end in view, a selected number of men were picked and mobilised to attend a meeting, the majority of the men being members of the 2nd Battalion. When all had assembled, the object of the meeting was explained to them. There was no compulsion whatsoever on any man. He could volunteer or decline such work. In fact, one or two men conscientiously objected, one stating that he would have no hesitation in going out to face the enemy in open battle.

I believe that from this time onwards until the formation of the full-time squad, all operations of this nature were carried out by what was known as the 'unofficial' squad, which consisted of from six to eight men. As far as my memory serves me, I would say that, up to the time of the shooting of Barton, all operations were carried out by the unofficial squad. It was some time in the month of March 1920 that the whole-time squad was formed. The reason I make this statement is as follows:—I left my employment, together with Jimmy Slattery, and have in my possession a document which shows that I left my employment on 9th March 1920, and the reason for leaving my employment, with Slattery, was the formation of the first whole-time squad, which consisted of twelve men who were known as the twelve apostles. When this squad was formed, it came directly under the control of the Director of Intelligence or his deputy, and under no other authority. It was commanded by Mick McDonnell.[136]

Byrne recalled the following Squad personnel and organisation:

Squad Personnel. First part-time squad. Mick McDonnell, Tom Keogh, Jimmy Slattery, Paddy Daly, Joe Leonard, Ben Barrett, Vincent Byrne.

First full-time paid. Mick McDonnell, Tom Keogh, squad. Jimmy Slattery, Paddy Daly, Joe Leonard, Ben Barrett, Vincent Byrne, Seán Doyle, Paddy Griffin, Eddie Byrne, Mick Reilly, Jimmy Conroy.

After some time the squad was strengthened by the following members: Ben Byrne, Frank Bolster, Mick Keogh, Mick Kennedy, Bill Stapleton, Sam Robinson.

Owen Cullen (member of 2nd Battalion) was driver for a short time, and Paddy Kelly of Clare for a short time.

Intelligence Staff. Director of Intelligence: Michael Collins. Deputy Liam Tobin. 2nd Deputy Tom Cullen. 3rd Frank Thornton.

Members: Joe Dolan, Frank Saurin, Ned Kelleher, Joe Guilfoyle, Paddy Caldwell, Paddy Kennedy, Charlie Dalton, Dan McDonnell, Charlie Byrne.

Munitions Staff: As far as I can remember, the following were members: Matt Furlong, Seán Sullivan, Gay McGrath, Martin Kelly, Tom Younge, Chris Reilly.

Other men who were out on occasions with the squad. Dan Breen, Séamus Robinson, Seán Treacy, Seán Hogan, Members of the Tipperary Flying Column.

Mick Brennan of Clare.

Stapleton described the method of working in the Squad:

[Bill] Tobin or [Tom] Cullen [from Collins's intelligence staff] would come down and tell us who we were to get. It might be one of the Igoe Gang or a British spy sent over to shoot Collins. Two or three of us would go out with an intelligence officer in front of us, maybe about 10 or 15 yards. His job was to identify the man we were to shoot. Often we would be walking in the streets all day without meeting our man. It meant going without lunch. But other times the intelligence staff would have their information dead on and we could see our quarry immediately we came to the place we had been told he would be at. The intelligence officer would then signal us in the following way. He would take off his hat and greet the marked man. Of course, he didn't know him. As soon as he did this we would shoot. We knew that very great care was taken that this was so. As a result we didn't feel we had to worry. We were, after all, only soldiers doing our duty. I often went in and said a little prayer for the people we'd shot afterwards.[137]

The Squad was on the streets every day observing movements. They had a list of agents who were to be shot on sight, including certain 'G' Division detectives.

Daly remembered one Collins lecture in particular, after he asked about a certain RIC Inspector. Daly's small crippled daughter had been struck by RIC Superintendent Winters, who was accompanying a military search party to his house the year before. Daly's wife died the year the Squad was founded and during this raid Daly's daughter had called the RIC man a 'traitor'. The British soldiers had thrown Winters out of the house. Daly remembered:

Michael Collins then gave me a lecture on revenge and told me that the man who had revenge in his heart was not fit to be a Volunteer. I had to convince him that I never thought of shooting Winters, but I passed the remark that if Winters was on our list I would like to carry out the job.

That lecture shows clearly that Collins or any of the headquarters staff would not shoot merely for revenge.[138]

Other men were added later in January 1920 and thereafter, and were chosen for 'jobs' as needed. Not all did many 'jobs' for Collins, and many were members of various Dublin units who were picked by Collins to assist the 'regular' Squad members; this was particularly true on Bloody Sunday. Those sometimes chosen were Frank Bolster, J. Brennan, Ned Breslin, Ben Byrne, Bernard Byrne (brother of Ben), Charlie Byrne (a Dubliner called 'the Count' because of his cheerful mien in all situations), Eddie Byrne, Seán Caffrey, Paddy Colgan (from Maynooth, Co. Kildare), James Connolly, Jim Conway (the 'one-man column'), Andy Cooney, Tom Cullen (a teetotaller), Charlie Dalton (he wrote *With the Dublin Brigade* about his experiences as a member),[139] Jim Dempsey (a Dubliner and an old IRB man who had fought in the Rising), Joe Dolan (another Dubliner, always armed with a .45, who wore a British Army badge in his lapel), Joe Dowling, Pat Drury, John Dunne, Tom Ennis, Paddy Flanagan (the oldest one to work with the Squad), Paddy Griffin, Jack Hanlon, Seán Kavanagh (a Dubliner and later a prison governor), Ned Kelliher (a Dubliner), Mick Kennedy, Paddy Kennedy (from Tipperary), Martin Lavan, Paddy Lawson, Seán Lemass (the future taoiseach), Pat McCrea (Collins's primary driver), Pat McKeon, Peadar McMahon (later chief of staff of the Free State army), Diarmuid O'Hegarty (a Corkman, director of organisation of the Volunteers), Bob O'Neill (a Clareman), Albert Rutherford, Frank Saurin (a Dubliner, known as the best-dressed Volunteer), Frank Teeling, Liam Tobin, George White and Johnny Wilson. (See Bloody Sunday, Appendix IV.)

Sackville Street (formerly Drogheda Street, now O'Connell Street): Reputed to be Europe's widest street at 150ft, with a 50ft-wide central mall and two 50ft-wide roadways, it was designed in the 1700s by Henry Moore, earl of Drogheda, and named after his friend Lionel Sackville. In the early years of the twentieth century it was 'divided', with the west side being given over to the British military and their girls and the east side to the Dublin civilians. Its name was officially changed in 1924—a previous attempt to change it in 1885 was prevented by Hedges Eyre Chatterton, the vice-chancellor of Ireland, who obtained an injunction. The citizens started using the O'Connell name, though, and the old street name-plates disintegrated without replacement.

Sackville Street (now O'Connell Street): **Carlisle Bridge/Sackville Bridge/O'Connell Bridge**; 154ft wide, wider than it is long. In 1798 the captured United Irishmen were hung in the middle of it. The present concrete structure was started in 1879 and completed in 1882.

Sackville Street Lower (now O'Connell Street): **Nelson's Pillar**, between Henry Street and North Earl Street, distinguished Upper Sackville Street from Lower Sackville Street. The original stone was laid on 15 February 1808 and the monument was completed in 1809; it was the first such monument to Lord Nelson and cost £6,858, raised by public subscription. William Watkins of Norwich designed the pillar, but Nelson's 13ft-tall statue was the work of an Irish sculpter, Thomas Kirk. The pillar stood 134ft tall, carved out of white Portland stone, with 168 winding steps to the lookout balcony.

The pillar was blown up at 1.32am on 8 March 1966 by an IRA team led by Joe Christie and Seán Treacey. The Millennium Spire now occupies the spot.

Sackville Street Lower (now O'Connell Street): **General Post Office (GPO)**. Opened in 1818, it was 200ft long, 150ft wide and 50ft high in three storeys. Its architect was Francis Johnston. The site had been suggested for the new Catholic cathedral later opened on Marlborough Street, but the authorities did not think it appropriate for a Catholic cathedral to be built in this prime location. A major edifice of Dublin's eighteenth- and nineteenth-century classical architecture, it was built from mountain granite with a portico of Portland stone. The 50ft-long Ionic portico of six fluted columns has a pediment carrying statues by John Smyth of Hibernia, Fidelity and Mercury, and a tympanum decorated with the royal coat of arms.

On Holy Saturday 1916, Collins met his second cousin, Nancy O'Brien, and they talked briefly in Sackville Street before bidding farewell to each other on the bridge. (Later Nancy was to go to work for Sir James McMahon in the Posts and Telegraphs Office in Dublin Castle, decoding messages for the British. See Dublin Castle, Dublin 2.) Nancy had planned to go home to Sam's Cross for Easter, but her transfer to the GPO had come through and she was due to report there for work the following Tuesday. When she informed Michael of this, he simply quipped, 'You might have a rather long wait'. She would later recall that this thought was uppermost in her mind the following week as she followed the progress of the insurrection from her home on Howth Head. Other people who had met Collins during the week leading up to the Rising described him as being 'jocular and fooling about as usual'.

Collins had been working since January for the Plunkett family, and especially liaising with the men in Kimmage. Joseph Plunkett had been extremely sick, having just had surgery on his neck, and had slept every night in a nursing home until Good Friday. Collins had been assigned as one of Plunkett's ADCs, and on Friday brought him and his luggage to the Metropole Hotel just south of the GPO. On Easter Monday, Cmdt W.J. Brennan Whitmore was appointed to Plunkett's staff by Thomas MacDonagh to help Collins bring him from the nursing home to Liberty Hall. Before leaving, Collins helped Plunkett into his tunic and called a cab to take them to his previously rented room in the Metropole Hotel. When they arrived Plunkett had to rest again, and then he took maps, books and three revolvers from his trunk, and as they were leaving he said to Collins:

> You lead out and down the stairs, I and the Commandant will follow. We must not allow ourselves to be arrested under any circumstances. If necessary we must shoot our way out, but not unless it's necessary. There is an intelligence officer in the vestibule, a stout dark man. If he attempts to interfere he is to be shot at once.

As they arrived at the bottom of the stairs, however, the stout dark man simply bade them good day.

Just before noon the whole column of Citizen Army and Volunteers left Liberty Hall, with James Connolly at the head, Patrick Pearse on his right and Plunkett on his left. Although some departed to take up different positions around the city, the main body turned left up Abbey Street and on into Sackville Street, where they halted outside the GPO. Here, Collins stood alongside Plunkett, Pearse, Connolly, Clarke and MacDermott. Then Connolly gave the order to charge and the men rushed in and stormed the building. Once inside, Plunkett received a warm welcome from Pearse and Connolly.

Once the building was secured, the leaders went back outside. Collins stood immediately behind Plunkett, scanning the street carefully while Pearse read the Proclamation to the few bemused and curious bystanders looking on. When they went back inside the GPO, Collins carried out an intensive search of the building, checking provisions and stores that might come in useful for the siege ahead. When he discovered two tierces of porter, he had the alcohol poured down the drain, while explaining to those present, 'They said we were drunk in '98, but they won't be able to say that now'. Then he helped to tie up a captured British officer, Lieutenant A.D. Chalmers of the 14th Royal Fusiliers. 'Don't worry,' Collins reassured the terrified officer as he bundled him into one of the telephone kiosks, 'we don't shoot prisoners.'

Collins carried out his duties without drawing any further attention until Tuesday morning, when a squabble broke out in the GPO between the London Irish and Desmond FitzGerald, who was in charge of the commissary and refused them rations on the basis that they didn't have the requisite documentation. FitzGerald recalled what happened next:

> Michael Collins … strolled in one morning with some of his men who were covered with dust and had been demolishing walls and building barricades, and announced that these men were to be fed if it took the last food in the place. I did not attempt to argue with him, and these men sat down openly rejoicing that I had been crushed … but while they were eating, those of our most regular and assiduous customers who appeared at the door of the room were told to disappear or they would be dealt with.

FitzGerald added that Collins was the most efficient officer in the whole building. He alone, it seems, had the good sense to compile a list of the names and addresses of the Volunteers under siege in the GPO in case it would be difficult later on to identify casualties.[140]

During the week Collins frequently showed himself to be resourceful and resolute under fire. His courage was cool and calculating rather than reckless. He had a calming effect on his comrades and an inner strength that communicated itself to them. His cheerful good humour never once deserted him, even when the carnage and destruction seemed appalling, and he quipped to one Volunteer, 'Don't worry, ye old cod, we'll rebuild it, and the whole city, in ten years if necessary'.

Collins himself would later recall:

> Although I was never actually scared in the GPO, I was, and others also, witless enough to do the most stupid things. As the flames and heat increased, so apparently did the shelling. Machine-gun fire made escape more and more

impossible. Not that we wished to escape. No man wished to budge. In that building, the defiance of our men and the gallantry reached unimaginable proportions.

Collins led the main part of the garrison out of the GPO and into Moore Street on Friday night. Desmond Ryan remembered Collins under fire, and at the surrender:

> In the retreat from the burning post office through Moore Street, Michael Collins emerged, a truculent, dashing fighter in his green uniform who swore tremendously and shepherded men past a fire-swept barricade storming defiance at the flying bullets. Here, suddenly, Michael Collins grew into greatness, some spark in his soul blazed to splendour, and as the Easter Week leaders marched to their death, whatever fates guard Ireland reached out and quietly draped a mantle of leadership around the silent grim young man watching political detectives who would later pick out his comrades for the firing part [sic] at the prison cell.[141]

Collins's own description of the Rising was not complimentary:

> The actions of the leaders should not pass without comment. They have died nobly at the hands of firing squads. So much I grant. But I do not think the Rising week was an appropriate time for the issue of memoranda couched in poetic phrases, nor of actions worked out in a similar fashion.
>
> Looking at it from the inside ... it had the air of a Greek tragedy about it.
> These are sharp reflections.
> On the whole I think the Rising was bungled terribly, costing many a good life.
> It seemed at first to be well organised, but afterwards became subjected to panic decisions and a great lack of very essential organisation and co-operation.
> It was the greatest bloody fiasco that we ever engaged in. There was courage, there was patriotism, but there was bloody all else. There was no organisation! We were like lambs to the slaughter. 'Noble' they called it. 'Shameful' I'd call it.

His assessment of the leaders was typical of his bluntness:

> Connolly was a realist, Pearse the direct opposite. There was an air of earthy directness about Connolly. It impressed me. I would have followed him through hell had such an action been necessary. But I honestly doubt very much if I would have followed Pearse—not without some thought anyway.

Towards Clarke and MacDermott he was equally favourable:

> Both were built on the best foundations. Wherever he [MacDermott] walked there went with him all the shades of the great Irishmen of the past. He was God-given. He was humble in the knowledge of his own greatness and in the task he had chosen to do. He did not seek glory as a personal investment but as a National investment.[142]

In writing to friends, the only one of the leaders whom Collins did not mention was Joseph Plunkett.

Collins recognised early on, as one of the lessons of 1916, the futility of open warfare against a superior opponent, and had no time for the tradition of noble and chivalrous defeat.

Following the surrender, Collins was interned at Stafford Prison and then at Frongoch Camp in Wales. In Frongoch he wrote: 'Let us be judged by what we attempted rather than what we achieved'.

After the Rising, and before the GPO was reconstructed, a temporary 'GPO' was located at 14 Sackville Street, and Collins's men often intercepted mail there. (See Great Britain Street, the Rotunda Hospital.) The GPO was reopened in 1929 after renovation.

In 1966 a plaque was placed in the building's alcove near where Pearse read the Proclamation. It displays the following message in both English and Irish:

> Here on Easter Monday 1916, Patrick Pearse read the Proclamation of the Irish Republic. From this building he commanded the forces that asserted in arms Ireland's right to freedom. It is they who keep the fire alive.

(The last sentence was *not* translated into English.)

In the lobby there is a statue of Cúchulainn, sculpted by Oliver Sheppard, dedicated to the 1916 Rising.

Sackville Street Lower (now O'Connell Street): The Daniel O'Connell monument. O'Connell (1775–1847) was known as 'the Liberator'. His monument, designed by John Henry Foley, was unveiled in 1882. One of the higher female figures holds a copy of the Catholic Emancipation Act of 1829. Thomas Brock completed the work eight years after Foley died. He designed the lower figures of angels around the base, representing Patriotism, Fidelity, Courage and Eloquence. There are many bullet holes in the statue, relics of the Rising and the Civil War.

1 Sackville Street Lower (now O'Connell Street and Eden Quay): Hopkins and

Hopkins, jewellers and silversmiths. Hopkins and Hopkins made the Sam Maguire Trophy for the GAA in 1928, basing it on the design of the Ardagh Chalice.

Maguire was a Protestant, originally from Dunmanway, who moved to London, where he swore Collins into the IRB. Maguire joined and captained the successful London Hibernians Gaelic football team to several All-Ireland finals between 1900 and 1904. In 1907 he went into the administration of the London GAA, becoming the chairman of the London County Board. He later became a trustee of Croke Park. (See Barnsbury Hall and Eaton Square, Assassination of Sir Henry Wilson, Appendix VI.)

Sackville Street Upper (now O'Connell Street, at Great Britain Street): Charles Stewart Parnell monument. The obelisk was commissioned and the foundation stone laid in 1899; the monument was completed in 1910. Sculpted by Augustus Saint-Guadens, it bears Parnell's declaration, made in Cork City on 21 January 1885: 'No man shall have the right to fix the boundary to the march of a Nation'.

11–22 Sackville Street Upper (now O'Connell Street): The so-called 'Block' was the location that included the **Crown, Granville, Gresham** and **Hammam hotels.** During the Civil War it was taken by IRA/Republicans in late June 1922 and held until 5 July.

11 Sackville Street Upper (now O'Connell Street): Gleeson & Co., tailors and outfitters. The company advertisement stated: 'Irish goods only'. During the War of Independence it ran an advert with a man in a trench coat (the usual IRA 'uniform'): 'Don't Hesitate to Shoot—straight to Gleeson & Co.'

12–13 Sackville Street Upper (now O'Connell Street): The Hammam Hotel. The Civil War IRA/Republican HQ. Noted for its Turkish baths, it was part of 'the Block' of buildings held by IRA/Republicans. The IRA/Republicans under Oscar Traynor took it on 29 June 1922, and Cecil Malley, brother of Ernie O'Malley, commanded the garrison. (Only Ernie used the 'O' form.) Cecil was captured and imprisoned at Portlaoise and Mountjoy Prison. The billiard room became the IRA/Republican hospital. Éamon de Valera, Oscar Traynor and Austin Stack left on 3 July and went to a safe house, intending to start a guerrilla war; Seán M. Glynn led them to safety. Traynor was the O/C of the Dublin Brigade.[143] Seventeen men held the Hammam Hotel finally, and three women remained to nurse the wounded.

17 Sackville Street Upper (now O'Connell Street): Granville Hotel. John Charles (J.C.) Byrne, alias 'Jameson', was staying here in 1920. He attempted to meet with Collins many times, but the intelligence staff always thought that he was a spy.

Michael Collins then got Neligan or Broy to investigate the telephone messages, and the name given in those messages was Byrne. They discovered that the name he was using in the jewellery business was Jameson. He was stopping in the Granville Hotel in O'Connell Street. He made a third appointment with Collins, and when he went to meet him [Collins] Tom Cullen or some of the intelligence staff went into the Granville Hotel, into his room and through his belongings. Exactly what they got there I do not know, but they were perfectly satisfied he was a spy.[144]

Joe Leonard, one of the Squad, wrote:

This Mr Jameson carried jewels as a side line and was stopping at the Granville Hotel, and it was noticed that Mick Collins's office was raided immediately on the exit of our friend. Another meeting being satisfactorily arranged ... but he took the wrong tram to Ballymun and there was no more showing anyone.[145]

When his body was found, the *Freeman's Journal* reported:

The whole occurrence is a profound mystery. The arms of the corpse were covered in oriental-style tattoos, including a snake, a mermaid, flowers and a representation of what is said to be a woman with the name of 'Phyllis'.[146]

(See 56 Bachelor's Walk; Harcourt Street, Dublin 2; Brendan Road, Nutley Lane, Dublin 4; Ballymun Road, Dublin 11.)

Cathal Brugha was fatally shot here on 5 July 1922. He had been twice ordered to surrender by Oscar Traynor, O/C of the IRA/Republicans, but refused.[147] On 5 July Brugha ordered the others out and, after some reluctance, they left under a flag of truce and surrendered to the Free State soldiers who had sealed off the rear laneway, Thomas's Lane. Linda Kearns and Dr Joseph P. Brennan, Dublin county coroner, suspecting what Brugha was about to do, secured his permission to remain. Brugha ran out, and although the Free State soldiers were ordered to 'fire low' a bullet hit him in his left thigh.[148] Brennan and Dr Seán Geraghty treated him after he was shot. The bullet severed his femoral artery, and he was driven to the Mater Hospital with Linda Kearns holding the artery's end in her fingers. Finally, he died from loss of blood.

So it was that after eight eventful days the first chapter of the Civil War had ended with the death of one whose whole life had been devoted to the cause: a death which might be epitomised in two words—unrepentant—unyielding.[149]

(See Gardiner's Row; St Joseph's Church, Berkeley Road, 34–38 Eccles Street, Mater Hospital, Dublin 9.)

21–22 Sackville Street Upper (now O'Connell Street): Gresham Hotel. This was the surrender point for the 1st Battalion Volunteers under Cmdt Ned Daly's command during the Rising.

On 21 November 1920 (Bloody Sunday) Capt. Patrick McCormack in Room 22 was killed by mistake. The doorman, Hugh Callaghan, led the IRA/Volunteers erroneously to Room 22 instead of Room 24, as they had requested. McCormack, a member of the Royal Medical (Veterinary) Corps, was probably in Dublin to buy polo horses for the garrison in Egypt. Unlike the other British officers, McCormack, a Catholic from Castlebar, was buried in Ireland, at Glasnevin Cemetery. Also killed was L.E. Wilde (Room 14), who probably had no connection with the army or Intelligence.

Paddy Kennedy was one of the Squad:

> Seán Russell took charge for that night, and he gave us our instructions for the following morning. He explained that a big swoop was to be made simultaneously on all British agents residing in private houses throughout the city and that the operation was to be carried out at nine o'clock sharp. He detailed Paddy Moran to take his party to the Gresham Hotel and eliminate three British Intelligence Officers who were stopping there. Lieutenant-Colonel Wilde and Captain McCormack were two of the British agents; I cannot remember the name of the third man. I arranged with Paddy Moran to meet him next morning in North Earl Street. I met him as arranged and we proceeded to the Gresham Hotel. As we entered the hotel the other members of our party, who were in the vicinity, came in after us. Our first job was to disconnect the telephone. As we knew the rooms in which the Intelligence agents were located, our party split up, as pre-arranged, and proceeded to the rooms allotted to them by Paddy Moran. I remained with Paddy Moran while the shootings were taking place. There were people in the dining-room and we took up position at the door and held them there. Two British agents were eliminated that morning, the third man escaped. He was a Catholic, I believe, and had gone out to early Mass. The whole operation lasted less than ten minutes.[150]

James Doyle was manager of the Gresham at the time:

> At about 9 o'clock in the morning of 'Bloody Sunday' I was in bed in my room and was awakened by noise. It was a muffled sort of thing like the beating of a carpet. The porter called up to my room afterwards and I asked him what was the noise I had heard. He said that Captain McCormack, who was occupying a room

quite close to me, had been shot dead. I got out of bed and entered Captain McCormack's room and I saw that he was then dead.

The porter also told me that another man had been shot dead in a room on the next floor over Captain McCormack's. I went to this room also and saw the dead man. His surname was Wilde. I was totally ignorant of what took place or why these men were shot at the time.

I questioned the porter and he told me that a number of armed men had entered the hotel and asked to be shown to the rooms occupied by these two men.

McCormack had been staying here since September and had made purchases of race horses. He had booked his passage back to Egypt for December by the Holt Line. Although he had been a Veterinary Surgeon in the British Army there would appear to have been grave doubt as to his being associated with British Intelligence. While he was here I never saw him receiving any guests. He slept well into the afternoon and only got up early when a Race Meeting was on. When I found him shot in his room, 'Irish Field' was lying beside him.

I mentioned to Collins after the Truce that there was a grave doubt as to Captain McCormack being a British Agent. He said that he would make inquiries into the matter, but after this the matter was never referred to again.

Mr Wilde had been here for a considerable time before 'Bloody Sunday'. When Archbishop Clune visited this hotel again subsequently, I mentioned the shootings to him and he told me that Wilde had been put out of Spain; that he was well known there as a British Agent.[151]

The Volunteers were under the command of Patrick (Paddy) Moran.[152] He was hanged on 14 March 1921 in Mountjoy Prison for participation in the Bloody Sunday executions at Baggot Street Lower, although he was not actually there. While he was a prisoner at Kilmainham Gaol, he had an opportunity to escape but refused it, knowing that he was not guilty of the crime with which he was charged. (See Paddy Moran: North Circular Road/Mountjoy Prison, Dublin 7; South Circular Road/Kilmainham Gaol, Dublin 8.) (See Bloody Sunday, Appendix IV.)

On Christmas Eve 1920, Collins, Gearóid O'Sullivan, Rory O'Connor and Tom Cullen met here to celebrate (David Neligan was also invited but declined: Collins said, 'Dave's getting windy!'). The private dining room that Collins had arranged was not available, so they took a table in the public dining room. During a raid by Auxiliaries Collins was taken to the cloakroom, where he was 'compared' with his 'official' photo. He was closely questioned and gave his name as 'John Grace', an alias he often used. He had an Ordnance Survey map in his pocket with the words '6 rifles' in the corner, but he convinced the officer that it said 'Refills' and he was let go. It was his closest escape ever, and how he explained the map is unknown. After the raid they were released. They got drunk and went up to Rutland Square to Vaughan's and then to Devlin's pub. There Cullen and Piaras Béaslaí borrowed a car and drove them all to Julia O'Donovan's, where they slept until Christmas morning. It was the only occasion on which they ever saw Collins drunk.

> I never met Michael Collins until after the Truce. But I saw him coming into the hotel on Christmas Eve 1920 with three or four others who came in for a meal. While he was here the place was raided by military. I saw a military officer approach Collins and I heard him being asked questions in the front hall. His comrades at this time were in the dining room. I heard Collins mention the name of Grace. Presumably he had papers to identify him under this name. The raid did not take long and the military party left without arresting anybody. Collins and his party, I think, left immediately without partaking of the meal which they had ordered. When Collins and his party entered the hotel, information was evidently conveyed to the military by someone who had been in the hotel at the time. I suspected later that it was an Acting DI of the Royal Irish Constabulary. I cannot recall this man's name now but I believe an attempt was made to shoot him afterwards. I got to know Collins very well during the Truce period. A number of rooms in this hotel were taken over which were used by Collins and his staff as offices for liaison work. It was then that I recognised the man who had given his name as Grace on being searched by the British Military at the previous Christmas as being Collins.[153]

In April 1921 Lord Derby stayed here, ineffectively disguised by horn-rimmed glasses and using the name 'Edwards'. He also left his overcoat with his name embroidered into it to be found by a chambermaid in his room. He met with Éamon de Valera to begin negotiations for a truce but made little progress.

Almost as soon as the Truce came into effect, Collins moved his main office and residence here. It had been one of his regular stopping places earlier, but after the Truce, until well into 1922, it became his headquarters.

Sackville Street Upper (now O'Connell Street): Crown Hotel. Annie Farrington became the manageress of the hotel in 1919. (She bought Barry's Hotel on Denmark Street Great in 1921.)

> I became manageress of the Crown Hotel adjoining the Gresham in 1919. Before that I had been in the Spa Hotel, Lucan. Whenever Seán McKeon came to Dublin he stayed at the Crown under various names ... Collins came several times. ...
>
> ... Seán McKeon was staying in the Crown Hotel in April 1920. He was probably up to meet Collins and he had a visitor, a young girl from Westmeath

or Longford. He took her into the smoke room of the hotel and sat down at a large table that was there. She sat on the other side right opposite him. He told her that he had a message to send by her—I think to some member of his Company in Longford. He took a sheet of paper and started writing out the message and when he had finished he put it in an envelope which he closed and handed to her. He was not aware that she had followed every word as he wrote it and therefore knew the contents of the message.

She duly delivered the message to whoever it was for and the next morning early she went to an uncle of hers, a retired RIC man and told him the message that McKeon had sent. I don't know the name of either the girl or her uncle. I never saw her before or since. Probably Seán himself would be able to give the information. Evidently the uncle went to the Tans and told them about the message which gave the clue about the train he intended to travel by. As a result the train was met in Mullingar by the Tans who started to search for McKeon. He made a dash for the gate and drew his gun but was caught after being wounded, and sent to prison.

I did not see him again until he was let out of Mountjoy. The Crown was the first house he made for. I don't think he knew anyone as well as he knew us. We were always his friends.[154]

(See Mountjoy Prison, North Circular Road, Dublin 7.)

68 Sackville Street Upper (now O'Connell Street): The GAA held meetings here, often attended by Harry Boland. Dublin Castle held this to be the 'Central Council of the GAA' prior to the Rising.

On 20 July 1918, the GAA held a meeting here in response to the Dublin Castle edict banning GAA football and hurling matches without an official permit. After a short discussion, it was decided that 'no permits would be asked for under any conditions; and provisional councils, county committees, leagues and clubs were to be notified accordingly; and also that no member was to participate in any competition if any permit had already been obtained'. It was further decided 'to arrange for Sunday, 4 August, at 3pm a series of matches throughout each county to be localised as much as possible'.[155] In response, 1,500 hurling or football matches were held throughout the country on 4 August.

3 St Andrew Street: Batt O'Connor owned the building. Collins hid some gold here and also used the building to conduct some financial business.

100 Seville Place: The O'Toole Gaelic Football Club and Hall. The building was raided by the Black and Tans and one man was killed.

After 1919, the Squad met here daily. While awaiting Collins's orders, they read or played cards in what was a particularly secluded location. From here they conducted operations on orders from GHQ intelligence.

No. 100 Seville Place was the headquarters of the O'Toole Gaelic Football Club and a well-known meeting place for Gaels in that part of the city. One of our Intelligence Officers reported to us that an enemy agent was constantly watching this house. He was instructed to take no action in the matter, but just keep him under cover. We reported the matter to Mick Collins, who suggested that here was an opportunity of actually giving this particular agent something to work on and at the same time give us an opportunity of bringing off an operation against the enemy. The O'Toole's were asked to co-operate in one way and that was to arrange for a fairly continuous flow of people to and from the building over a couple of days. This was done and our Intelligence Officer reported that every now and again the enemy agent went to a telephone kiosk which was near the corner of Amiens Street and Seville Place, and rang up. In the meantime arrangements were made to mobilise every available man in the 2nd Battalion, the ASU and the Squad, and arrangements were made to take over Amiens Street Station, holding Portland Row and all the strategic positions around that area on 7th February, 1921. In the meantime we quietly arrested the agent, and without going into any details, we extracted from him certain information which was vulnerable [sic] to us and which included his number, his contact man inside and the telephone number he was using. At about 5 o'clock Tom Cullen and I rang the contact man in the Castle, and imitating as far as possible the enemy agent's voice, gave him the information that some very special meeting must be taking place in Seville Place as quite a number of men had gone in there inside the previous half-hour. In any event we told him a good story and in the meantime the 2nd Battalion had taken over Amiens Street Station, had occupied the telephone exchange there, the signal boxes, Portland Row, and went under cover. Cullen and I came down Talbot Street after ringing up and we were approaching Amiens Street when a large convoy of troops, at least ten lorries, passed us by. We continued on towards Seville Place but there was no sign of the enemy when we arrived there, it appears that when the head of the column arrived at the corner of Seville Place and Amiens Street it halted, stopped there for about five or ten minutes and then went on down the Strand, coming back again about half an hour afterwards and went back to Barracks. Whether they smelt a rat or not is something which is very hard to ascertain, but certainly it looked as if they left their own Headquarters with the definite intention of raiding 100 Seville Place. The only thing which may have upset the plan was the fact that their chief man inside may have been looking for his contact man, who was a prisoner of ours at the time, and not finding him, may have smelt a rat, but there it is, one of the biggest operations which would have taken place in Dublin fell through because the enemy just failed to come into the trap.[156]

(See 10 Abbey Street Upper, the final meeting place for the Squad.)

30 Summerhill Parade: Home of Frank Flood, 1Lt of the Dublin Brigade during the War of Independence. A student at UCD with Kevin Barry, Flood led an abortive ambush in Drumcondra and was hanged in Mountjoy Prison on 14 March 1921. (See Mountjoy Prison, North Circular Road, Dublin 7.)

42 Summerhill Road: Home of C.S. (Todd) Andrews, author of *Dublin made me*.[160] He was sent by IRA/Volunteers HQ to Donegal to organise during the War of Independence, but spent most of the time working for Collins in Dublin and was imprisoned in Mountjoy Prison, in Arbour Hill and finally in the Rath Internment Camp in the Curragh (he was prisoner no. 1569 in hut 32). He escaped from the camp after the Truce on 9 September 1921.

Andrews fought for the IRA/Republicans in the Civil War, and again was sent to Donegal to train the senior officers of the Donegal Brigade; he then became an ADC to Liam Lynch before Lynch was killed. He was captured in Cork and was imprisoned there, then was transferred to Newbridge, where he was again interned (he was prisoner no. 2571 in Newbridge and was in army hut no. 60 with many other Dubliners). In January 1924 he was transferred to an internment centre at the Curragh Camp, Tintown No. 2 (where he became prisoner no. 876 and was with Jack Plunkett).[161] He was one of the last IRA/Republicans to be released in April 1924.

82 Talbot Street: Home of Seán Milroy. He escaped from Lincoln Jail with Éamon de Valera and Seán McGarry. Milroy was the prisoner who drew the cartoon Christmas card of a man with a key—the key was the shape of the one that Collins and Harry Boland made to open the doors for the escape.[162] (See Lincoln Prison, Appendix VI.)

92 Talbot Street: Spiedel's pork shop, next door to Republican Outfitters. It was directly in front of this shop that Seán Treacy was shot and died. Jane Boyle, who worked in the shop, was killed in Croke Park on Bloody Sunday, only five days before her wedding. She knew all of Collins's men, and when there were soldiers on the street she would hide guns for the IRA/Volunteers. (See Bloody Sunday, Appendix IV.)

94 Talbot Street: Republican Outfitters, owned by Peadar Clancy, Maurice Brennan and Thomas Hunter.

When he was released from prison after the Rising, Clancy was selected as a Sinn

Féin candidate for an East Clare by-election, but the IRA GHQ did not ratify his candidacy. Éamon de Valera ran in his stead and won the seat, which he held until he left the Dáil.

Clancy became immersed in the underground movement and carried out a number of daring prison escapes. These ensured his rise to become the second-in-command of the Dublin Brigade, with the rank of vice-brigadier. He was also attached to GHQ, where he held the rank of director of munitions. His immediate superior was Dick McKee, with whom he was killed on Bloody Sunday.

Clancy was involved in the Republican breakout from Strangeways Prison in Manchester on 25 October 1919. Collins had taken a particular interest in the escape, and actually visited Austin Stack in the prison to finalise the arrangements. Six prisoners were to escape, among them Piaras Béaslaí, who had again been arrested after Clancy had arranged his escape earlier that year from Mountjoy.

Seán Treacy (Seán Ó Treasaigh) was killed in front of this shop on 14 October 1920. On that day the Squad, under the command of McKee and Clancy, planned to assassinate Hamar Greenwood and General Tudor. They met in the back of the shop in Talbot Street. When they received intelligence that neither of the officers would be present at the intended event, the operation was called off. As some of the Squad were leaving, they met Treacy and informed him of events. Treacy continued on towards the shop. The others had not moved much further away when they heard the shots ring out. A raid on the shop had been planned, and Treacy had arrived just before the soldiers.

Lt Price and 'G' Division Sgt Francis Christian were also killed. Two civilians, Patrick Carroll and Joseph Carrington, were killed, and indiscriminate Auxiliary firing wounded a DMP constable.

RIC Sgt Christian followed Treacy here after Treacy attended Professor John Carolan's funeral. (See Whitehall, 'Fernside', Drumcondra, Dublin 9.) RIC Sgt Roche was brought up from County Tipperary to identify Treacy, and gloated over his body in the street.

Treacy was in the process of planning the rescue of Dan Breen, who lay wounded in the Mater Hospital. He had learned that the hospital was to be raided and wanted to get Breen out in time. According to Breen, Treacy had been so intent on providing for his (Breen's) safety that he had neglected his own, failing to notice that he had been followed to the Republican Outfitters.[163] Treacy was the vice-brigadier of the Tipperary Brigade, of which Breen was a member, and was on his way to a meeting with Tom Cullen, Dick McKee, Joe Vize (a former British naval officer who was the Volunteer director of purchases and was arrested after the raid; he was succeeded by Liam Mellows), Frank and Leo Henderson, George and Jack Plunkett[164] and Liam Tobin.[165]

Volunteer Seán Brunswick went to 'help' Treacy and emptied his pockets of all documents before the RIC and DMP could get to him. Treacy was to have married May Quigley on 25 October 1920, within a fortnight of being killed.

Waterford Street: 'House' of Becky Cooper, a 'Monto' madam. British agents were alleged to use her as a front to pass on information. Collins also used the house and its residents to garner information. (See Gloucester Street Lower, Railway Street.)

Dublin 2

Key locations

Aungier Street
Baggot Street Lower
Camden Street
College Green
Dame Street (City Hall)
Dawson Street (Mansion House)
Dublin Castle
Earlsfort Terrace
Great Brunswick Street (Pearse Street)

Harcourt Street
Kildare Street
Mount Street
Pembroke Street
St Stephen's Green
Shelbourne Hotel
(Dublin 2 and Dublin 8 are the only postal codes to span the Liffey.)

No section of Dublin highlights the myriad roles played by Michael Collins as well as Dublin 2. His 'office' was more a state of mind than a location. Many of his safe houses were private homes, complete with residents and often with children. Almost all of his offices were above or behind shops, where visitors wouldn't be noticed.

> *'It gives us freedom—not the ultimate freedom that all nations desire and develop to, but the freedom to achieve it'*
> Michael Collins

Collins's workload was staggering. As well as his job with the National Aid Fund in the early years, he cycled around the city each day delivering instructions, receiving progress reports and meeting emissaries from out-of-town units.

Collins was a financier, creating and administering the Dáil Loan, but he was also a sales manager, charged with coordinating its agents throughout Ireland. He was a publisher of *An tÓglach* and wrote a column, 'Organisational Notes', for every issue.

He was a legislator, elected to the First Dáil in 1919, and a cabinet member thereafter.

As the IRA director of purchases, he was a smuggler, organising and managing his own gunrunning rings from Liverpool, Manchester, London and the United States.

As an IRB centre he was always engaged with others, and then in 1919 he was elected to be its president.

His first job on his return to Dublin from Frongoch was at 10 Exchequer Street, where he was the secretary of the Irish National Aid and Volunteers' Dependants' Fund. Collins used that position and Mrs Kathleen Clarke's contacts to further reorganise the IRB. Mrs Clarke gave Collins the names and contacts that Tom had entrusted to her, and said that she was never sorry for hiring him: 'I gave all that information to Mick and that … gave him the leeway to get ahead … He had the ability and the force and the enthusiasm and drive that very few men had, to work on that.' He was to run the office, keep track of all the accounting and deal with all

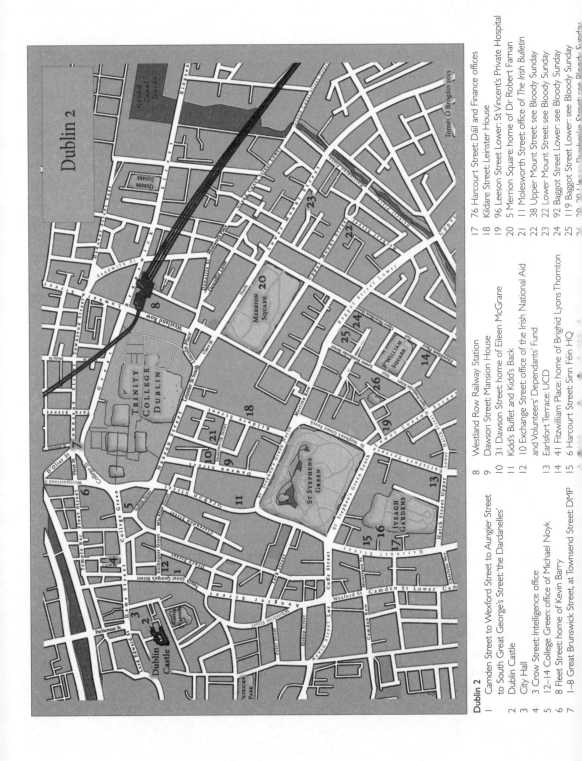

Dublin 2

Tomás Ó Brógáin 2015

Dublin 2

1 Camden Street to Wexford Street to Aungier Street to South Great George's Street: 'the Dardanelles'
2 Dublin Castle
3 City Hall
4 3 Crow Street: Intelligence office
5 12–14 College Green: office of Michael Noyk
6 8 Fleet Street: home of Kevin Barry
7 1–8 Great Brunswick Street, at Townsend Street: DMP

8 Westland Row Railway Station
9 Dawson Street: Mansion House
10 31 Dawson Street: home of Eileen McGrane
11 Kidd's Buffet and Kidd's Back
12 10 Exchange Street: office of the Irish National Aid and Volunteers' Dependants' Fund
13 Earlsfort Terrace: UCD
14 41 Fitzwilliam Place: home of Bríghid Lyons Thornton
15 6 Harcourt Street: Sinn Féin HQ

17 76 Harcourt Street: Dáil and Finance offices
18 Kildare Street: Leinster House
19 96 Leeson Street Lower: St Vincent's Private Hospital
20 5 Merrion Square: home of Dr Robert Farnan
21 11 Molesworth Street: office of The Irish Bulletin
22 38 Upper Mount Street: see Bloody Sunday
23 22 Lower Mount Street: see Bloody Sunday
24 92 Baggot Street Lower: see Bloody Sunday
25 119 Baggot Street Lower: see Bloody Sunday

inquiries regarding aid. He took his position quite seriously and it was never too late or too early for him to call on anyone who needed help.

In Dublin 2, Collins spent most of his time on his administrative duties for the Dáil, when it was in session (at the Mansion House on Dawson Street), or for his Sinn Féin offices (on Harcourt Street). He would stop most days at his Mespil Road offices to check on the Department of Finance, and usually in Camden Street to see to the day's Dáil Loan receipts.

He might call at the home of Eileen McGrane on Dawson Street, where he sometimes spent the night. He also had a partial office there, and foolishly left many papers there that were taken by the British when they raided the premises in December 1920.

One of the items the British took in that raid was the DMP day-book which he had taken from the DMP station at Great Brunswick Street and Townsend Street when Ned Broy let him in to view the files in April 1919. Collins was the first Irish revolutionary to have the entire *modus operandi* of the British police in Ireland laid out before him. It was on this foray that Collins read his own file, which indicated that he 'belongs to a family of "brainy" people and of advanced Sinn Féin sympathies. They are of the farming class.' That gave Collins such a good and loud laugh that Broy heard him and was concerned that Collins would be discovered.

Always mindful of the military side of his intelligence-gathering machine, in July 1919 Collins sent Dick McKee to Great George's Street to meet with a number of IRA/Volunteers to see whether they had any objections to shooting enemy agents. That was the genesis of Collins's 'Squad', though it wasn't officially formed until September.

Collins was one of the plenipotentiaries sent to London to negotiate the Anglo-Irish Treaty, but long before that he was involved in peace feelers extended by the British. Dr Robert Farnan was a prominent gynaecologist who lived at 5 Merrion Square. At Prime Minister David Lloyd George's behest, Collins met Archbishop Patrick Joseph Clune of Perth, Western Australia, there to discuss those early British peace overtures.

The Treaty Debates were held in the Mansion House on Dawson Street, and at the UCD campus on Earlsfort Terrace. Collins told the TDs that 'as one of the signatories of the document I naturally recommend its acceptance. I do not recommend it for more than it is. Equally I do not recommend it for less than it is. In my opinion it gives us freedom, not the ultimate freedom that all nations desire and develop to, but the freedom to achieve it.'

After the Dáil ratified the Treaty, the lord lieutenant of Ireland, Lord FitzAlan, formally handed over Dublin Castle to Collins and the Free State forces. Lord FitzAlan said, 'I am glad to see you, Mr Collins', to which Collins replied, 'Like hell ye are!' The handing over of Dublin Castle represented, physically and symbolically, the end of British domination in Ireland.

Just another day for Collins.

Aungier Street: *An tÓglach* ('The Young Warrior/Soldier'), 'the official newspaper of the Irish Volunteers'. Conceived by Collins in 1918 and edited by Piaras Béaslaí, it was published here. The primary printer was Joe Stanley, with whom Collins had become friendly in Frongoch. The newspaper was first a bimonthly and then became a weekly. Its office was here but it was printed by Mahon Printers on Yarnhall Street. (See Dublin 7.)

Collins played an active role in guiding editorial policy and finding writers. He also contributed 'Organisational Notes' until May 1919. In this column he laid out the official formula for unit organisation and the duties of officers.

It was a 'secret' internal journal printed in Dublin and distributed to the Volunteers throughout the country by the IRA, clandestinely circulated in flour sacks and other disguises. It was not only a 'military journal' but also contained much of the Sinn Féin ideology, and had a great influence on the IRA/Volunteers and, later, the IRA/Republicans. Instead of preaching the politics of a party or of any particular leader, it always emphasised that the Volunteer's allegiance was to the Irish nation.

The first issue appeared on 15 August 1918 and editorialised:

> Volunteers are not politicians; they were not created for the purposes of parades, demonstrations, or political activities; they follow no particular leader as such; their allegiance is to the Irish Nation. To their own chosen leaders they render the obedience that all soldiers render to their officers. Their obedience to their officers is not affected by personal considerations. It is the office, not the man, to whom deference is due.
>
> The Irish Volunteers have chosen in open Convention those leaders in whom they have confidence to control the public policy of the organisation. It is the duty of those leaders to conform that policy to the national will, by co-operating on the military side with those bodies and institutions which in other departments of the national life are striving to make our Irish Republic a tangible reality.[166]

In September, Lord Lieutenant French indicated that the English 'Government's policy toward Conscription for Ireland remains unchanged'. *An tÓglach* was the mouthpiece for the most violent opposition to conscription. In response to Lord French's statement, it editorialised:

> It is desired that we should eliminate all talk and all thought of passive resistance, because passive resistance means, in effect, no resistance at all.
>
> We must fight with ruthlessness and ferocity. …
>
> We must recognise that anyone, civilian or soldier, who assists directly or by connivance in this crime against us, merits no more consideration than a wild

beast, and should be killed without mercy or hesitation as opportunity offers.[167]

The article went on to quote George Bernard Shaw: 'Nothing is ever done in the world unless men are willing to kill each other if it is not done'. Collins liked the article, had many copies distributed and asked its author, Ernest Blyth, for more of the same.

54 Baggot Street Lower: Members of the Squad were dispatched here on Bloody Sunday, but it was a mistake. There were no British intelligence officers in residence.

> We all, Charlie Dalton, Frank Saurin, Jim Conroy, Barney Keogh and myself, met at the appointed time and proceeded to the house in question. We knocked on the door of the house concerned and it was immediately opened by a maid. We asked for the individual whose name we had, and the maid told us he did not sleep there that night. However, we did not take her word for it and searched every room in the house but without result. I think our instructions that morning were very precise, that we were to enter the house at 9.00 and that we were to be out of it by 9.10. There was some mistake about the retreat that morning following the operations. We had been directed that, when we finished at Baggot Street, we were to retreat to the South Quays where a boat would be in readiness to take us across the river to the north side. On arriving at the quayside, we found that there were about forty Volunteers assembled there. A boat was there alright but there was no man in it, or oarlocks. However, a docker was standing by the quayside and he asked us who were we. We said we were not Tans anyway. He said, 'Alright. I will get you across'. The forty of us scrambled into that small boat and he schulled it safely across. I think that this docker deserves a tribute because had a big number of us been left stranded, we would have been an easy capture for the British military immediately the results of that morning's operations became known. I don't know how the plans miscarried but the man who was detailed to row us across was not at the point we were directed to.[168]

92 Baggot Street Lower: A Mrs Stack owned this house. On Bloody Sunday Bill Stapleton[169] and Joe Leonard killed Capt. W.F. Newbury, Royal West Surrey Regiment, here. Leonard was in charge of Collins's men.

> There were fourteen engagements that morning, all the like results, and the English spy system was shattered, never to be of service in Ireland again.[170]

Newbury was killed in front of his wife, who was eight months pregnant, and she gave birth to a stillborn child two weeks later. Newbury tried to escape out the window but was shot as he straddled the sill.

(See Bloody Sunday, Appendix IV.)

119 Baggot Street Lower: On Bloody Sunday Capt. George T. Baggally, a one-legged barrister and courts-martial officer, formerly the army judge advocate, was killed here. He was known as a redoubtable prosecutor of the IRA, and was in charge of the detail that killed John Lynch in the Royal Exchange Hotel on 23 September 1920. (See Royal Exchange Hotel, Parliament Street.) He previously lived at 19 Eccles Street.

> The British agent in Baggot St. listed for elimination was, as far as I know, Captain Baggaly [*sic*], who was believed to have been one of Kevin Barry's torturers. On that Sunday morning I left home about 7.30 o'clock and made my way to the dump in North Great Charles St. I met the remainder of the men there—at least some of them. We collected our guns and got out the car. We timed ourselves to be in Baggot St. about five minutes to 9 o'clock. We arrived there up to time—I think it was two or three minutes to 9—and within three minutes another man, who was on the job, turned up. We parked the car a little to the rear of the house on the opposite side of the street. When our men arrived there was no delay, as arranged. Three or four men entered the house, leaving one man on each side of the building outside as a guard for the men who had actually gone into the house. They had particulars of the agent's bedroom. When the room was entered he tried to escape through the window, but before he reached the window he was put out of action. The job was completed in the space of a few minutes.
>
> We got away without incident. We left Baggot St. and we came down Merrion Square and Westland Row. When we came into Merrion Square we picked up a few men coming off the Mount St. job—one was Herbert Conroy. We arrived back at the dump without any interference from anybody. We replaced the car and dumped our guns.[171]

One of the Squad responsible for Baggally's death was Seán Lemass, future taoiseach.

Thomas Whelan and Patrick (Paddy) Moran were hanged in Mountjoy Prison on 14 March 1921 for this killing, despite both having solid alibis placing them away from this area on Bloody Sunday.[172] (See Bloody Sunday, Appendix IV.) (See also Sackville Street Upper/Gresham Hotel, Dublin 1; Paddy Moran: North Circular Road/Mountjoy Prison, Dublin 7; South Circular Road/Kilmainham Gaol, Dublin 8.)

134 Baggot Street Lower: Ferguson's Garage. This Ferguson location was a branch of a well-known Belfast firm. The garage was raided by a group of IRA/Republicans, led by Leo Henderson, who were intent on commandeering vehicles (valued at £9,000) on 26 June 1922.[173] The raid was in line with the so-called 'Belfast Boycott'. Henderson was acting as director of the Boycott, though the Free State government had (officially) abandoned it the previous March under an agreement between Collins, Griffith and Sir James Craig. (See the Craig–Collins Pact, London, Appendix VI.) The cars were intended for an expedition to the north headed by Peadar O'Donnell, but the raiders were stopped by Free State troops led by Frank Thornton on the orders of Collins, and Henderson and his men were taken prisoner.[174] Henderson was also a supporter of the minority, more militant wing of anti-Treatyites garrisoned in the Four Courts (as opposed to Liam Lynch's majority of those less militantly republican). Accordingly, Henderson was seen by the Free State forces as a suitable target for making a gesture to placate the British after the assassination of Sir Henry Wilson in London on 22 June 1922.[175] (See Eaton Square, Assassination of Sir Henry Wilson, Appendix VI.)

The capture of Henderson's group led to the retaliatory taking of Gen. J.J. 'Ginger' O'Connell (suggested by Ernie O'Malley) by the IRA/Republicans' Four Courts garrison, which led directly to Collins ordering the shelling of the Four Courts on 28–9 June.

Camden Street: Hartigan's Pub, a gathering place for those with republican sentiments.

Camden Street Lower: The area comprising this street together with **Wexford Street**, **Aungier Street** and **South Great George's Street** was nicknamed '**the Dardanelles**' during the War of Independence, because it was so dangerous for the British to travel in the area.

Camden Street Lower: The location of Nora (Mrs Padraig) O'Keefe's restaurant, known as 'The Farm Produce'. Collins often lunched here and used it as an interim office between his offices at 76 Harcourt Street and 22 Mary Street. There was a room above the shop where Collins stayed for a few weeks in 1919 until he moved to 5 Mary Street.

Evelyn Lawless worked for Collins here as one of his secretaries. She usually worked alone until the summer of 1920, when she left to enter a convent.

> Joe O'Reilly was awaiting me outside 76 [Harcourt Street] with instructions from Mick to go to Mrs O'Keefe's house, the 'Farm Produce' in Camden Street, where I continued my work for Mick. The different departments split up again then and went underground. I was alone in Camden St. with a messenger. My

work was very varied in accordance with the various activities of Mick Collins who came irregularly to work there. Camden St. was a busy centre and it was easier to escape attention there than in residential quarters such as Mespil Road. Therefore, Mick made many appointments to meet people there for his purposes such as planning the escape of prisoners, &c. From there I went occasionally to Mespil Road to take notes or instructions from him about the work.

It was at that time that Harry Boland returned secretly from America for a few weeks. I'd say he came to report progress to Mick about the success of the Loan in America and to get the Cabinet sanction for continuing their activities in America. Correspondence would be liable to be censored or confiscated. The first intimation I had of Harry's return from America was an instruction I got from Mick to go to Mrs McGarry's in Fitzwilliam Square [Dublin 4] to take down and type Harry's report, which was duly accomplished. It was a long account of his entire mission up to that date for the benefit of the Dáil Cabinet. His departure for America was very secret and I did not see him again.

One day we got word that the office in Camden Street was to be raided and we transferred everything down to Corrigan's Undertakers' premises a little further down. We stayed there for a day or so and then we went back.

Shortly after that, in the first week of June 1920, I gave up the work to make preparations for entering a convent. Before I left, Mick—who did not feel secure in Camden St.—(I am not sure whether it was not even raided sometime we were not there)—was preparing offices in Mary St. over Robinson's, the Seed Merchants. It was a busy thoroughfare and therefore also likely to be free from observation by the military authorities. I never worked there, but I paid a couple of visits to it as I kept in touch with Mick Collins until the date of my entry into the convent. When I was leaving, he sent me a cheque for £25 and wrote me a letter expressing his good wishes and his appreciation of my work.[176]

5 Camden Street Lower: Corrigan and Sons Mortuary. 'K' Company (3rd Battalion) used the premises to make bombs. Collins secreted some £25,000 (figures vary) in gold here, sealed in tobacco tins and buried under the floor. He ordered a count of the funds during the Truce in 1921, and following the count the gold was secreted in butter boxes and a baby's coffin. Then it was all reinterred under Batt O'Connor's floorboards in 1 Brendan Road, Donnybrook (Dublin 4).[177] When Daithi O'Donoghue objected to moving the gold from a place where it had been secure for such a long time, Collins replied, 'There will be more gold coming in from the Second Dáil Loan and you can put that in Corrigans'.[178]

34 Camden Street Lower: Formerly housed the Irish National Theatre Society. The

Volunteers used these premises as a drill hall. It was the fourth meeting place of 'K' Company (3rd Battalion) after the Rising.[179]

In 1919 all IRA/Volunteers of the company took the oath to the Dáil here. After its suppression in 1919, this was one of the private premises where the Dáil met.

37 Charlemont Street: St Ultan's Children's Hospital, founded in 1919 (with £70 and two cots) by Dr Kathleen Lynn and Madeleine ffrench-Mullen. (See 7 Belgrave Road, Rathmines, Dublin 6.)

During the Rising, Dr Lynn was the O/C of the City Hall garrison after both Seán Connolly and Seán O'Reilly had been killed. Miss ffrench-Mullen was in charge of the Irish Citizen Army medical detachment in St Stephen's Green.

Dr Lynn was always a republican and often treated IRA/Volunteers without the police knowing. In 1918 she was one of those imprisoned during the 'German Plot', and was released later that year to treat patients in the influenza epidemic. (See 6 Harcourt Street.) Because of her republican activities she was considered 'on the run'. She always said that she 'evaded capture by dressing like a lady, in my Sunday clothes and feather boa, and by walking instead of cycling'.

In April 1921 she was called to one of Collins's offices because it had been raided. Collins's secretary, Patricia Hoey, and her mother lived upstairs in the house at 5 Mespil Road. Hoey had her mother fake a heart attack and called for Dr Lynn. Hoey then slipped Lynn a message to get to Collins. (See 5 Mespil Road, Dublin 4.)

Appalled by the fact that 16% of Dublin infants in 1919 were dying from preventable diseases, Dr Lynn and Miss ffrench-Mullen founded St Ultan's, a hospital 'for the medical treatment of infants under one year of age'. With due reference to her treatment by her medical masters while training at the Adelaide Hospital, they were 'adamant that the staff of St Ultan's would be confined to women medical staff only'. (Though she was the first woman to be elected a resident doctor at the Adelaide Hospital, prejudice prevented her from going into residence there.) St Ultan's became the front line in the battle against infant mortality and provided the opportunity for Dr Dorothy Price to continue her research on childhood tuberculosis, leading to the establishment of the research unit at the hospital. They introduced a Montessori ward in the hospital and made a significant contribution to the eradication of tuberculosis in Ireland. Louie Bennett, Kathleen Clarke, Charlotte Despard, Maud Gonne MacBride, Countess Markievicz and Helena Molony all greatly contributed.

Charlotte Despard, known as 'Madame Despard' (or, derisively, as 'Madame Desperate'), spent a great deal of time in Ireland, and in 1908 she joined with Hanna Sheehy-Skeffington and Margaret Cousins to form the Irish Women's Franchise League. (Ironically, her brother, General John French, was chief of staff of the British army and commander of the British force sent to Europe in August 1914. He became viceroy of Ireland in May 1918.) In 1920 Despard toured Ireland as a member of the

British Labour Party Commission of Inquiry, and together with Maud Gonne she collected first-hand evidence of British army and police atrocities in Cork and Kerry. In the early twentieth century, Charlotte Despard was imprisoned twice in England's Holloway Prison for demonstrating for women's suffrage, and learned at first hand the hardships and desolation of imprisonment.[180] In 1922 she was a founder (with Maud Gonne MacBride and Hanna Sheehy-Skeffington) and first president of the Women's Prisoners' Defence League to support republican prisoners. In January 1923 the Free State government declared the organisation illegal, and the police constantly broke up its meetings and demonstrations.

> … the Women's Movement is related also with the other great movements of the world. […] The awakened instinct which feels the call of the sub-human, which says:—'I am the voice of the voiceless. Through me the dumb shall speak,' is a modern phenomenon that cannot be denied.[181]

Despard died in 1939.

Louie Bennett fund-raised for the hospital on her trips to the US, as did Kathleen Clarke, who also sat on its board.

College Green: Bank of Ireland; former Irish parliament building, designed by Sir Edward Lovet Pearce in 1728, with later contributions by James Gandon. The bank took possession on 24 August 1803 following the Act of Union. The upper chamber remains as it was when the building housed the Irish parliament. The original buildings on the site were at various times a hospital (1603), a mansion (1612), the House of Commons (1730), the House of Lords (1787) and finally the bank.

The reviewing stand for the Volunteers' Parade on St Patrick's Day 1916 was here.

On 5 March 1922 Collins and Griffith addressed a massive rally in front of the Bank of Ireland building. Collins said: 'We could not have beaten the British by force, but when we have beaten them out by the Treaty, the republican ideal, which was surrendered in July, is restored'.[182]

On 20 April 1922 Collins spoke to another huge crowd here. He gave his view of the Treaty and said that it was a 'stepping-stone' that gave the 'freedom to achieve freedom'. He also assured his listeners that the boundary commission would give large parts of Northern Ireland to the Free State on the basis of demographics.[183]

College Green: Trinity College Dublin (TCD). Founded in 1592 by Queen Elizabeth I, it was built on land confiscated from the Priory of All Hallows. Its full name is the College of the Holy and Undivided Trinity. It was not until 1972, upon the death of Archbishop John Charles McQuaid, that it was no longer a 'mortal sin' for a Catholic to attend Trinity without written permission.

An 'Irish Convention', chaired by Horace Plunkett, sat in Trinity from 25 July 1917 to 5 April 1918 (there were also some sessions in Cork and Belfast). British Prime Minister David Lloyd George proposed the conference to the Irish Parliamentary Party chairman John Redmond in order to moderate nationalist opinion. The British thought that the Irish could debate the future government of Ireland, particularly with regard to Ulster. Its 95 members included mayors and chairmen of public bodies, together with almost every prominent Irishman outside politics, but its weakness was on the political side: Sinn Féin had five seats but declined to take part.[184] William O'Brien's All for Ireland Party also declined.[185] It reaffirmed the measure of disagreement between North and South. The membership was comprised of 52 Nationalists; 26 Ulster Unionists, headed by Hugh Barrie and George Clarke; nine Southern Unionists, headed by Lord Midleton; six Labour representatives; and two Liberals.[186]

College Green: Seán Treacy shot 'G' Division Detective Sergeant John Barton here on 29 November 1919. Barton's killing was a particularly galling blow for the DMP, as he was considered the finest detective in Ireland.

1 College Green (College Street): office of John R. Reynolds. Because of his Sinn Féin activities and sympathies, Reynolds was ordered by the English military officials to deport himself to Coventry, England, and remained there until 1917.

> The week following the surrender I went to John R. Reynolds who was acting for Mrs Clarke, who had a dependants' fund for the Volunteers. I assisted in collecting information about the dependants and distributing the monies.
> Diarmuid O'Hegarty was released early in May as a result of an error as to identification and I contacted him immediately. We started to get in contact with the men who had not been arrested and were prepared to carry on. We also contacted supporters in the country and in America.[187]

This was the first office used by Kathleen Clarke for the Irish Volunteers' Dependants' Fund. Clarke originally submitted the name 'Irish Republican Prisoners' Dependants' Fund', but that was not accepted by the censors and so no funds could be solicited in periodicals. The name was changed to the Irish Volunteers' Dependants' Fund and was accepted by censors for publication in newspapers. The Dependants' Fund combined with the Irish National Aid Association and moved to 10 Exchequer Street. Joseph McGrath was the first secretary of the combined fund. Collins began to work for the fund in February 1917. (See 10 Exchequer Street; 32 Bachelor's Walk, Dublin 1.)

12–14 College Green: Office of Michael Noyk, solicitor. He often appeared in

Dáil/Republican courts during the War of Independence, and gave advice to the Dáil.[188] Throughout the period, Noyk defended many members of the Volunteers/IRA. He was the solicitor for Éamon (Ned) Broy when Broy was imprisoned at Arbour Hill. In addition, he defended Seán MacEoin and Paddy Moran, though he was unable to get either released from prison, and was the solicitor for Arthur Griffith.

Noyk described the Collins he remembered in 1918:

I used to see Mick Collins every day. He was very young, handsome and full of personality, but I still did not think he possessed the depths which he later showed. He was full of fun and had a keen sense of humour which he exhibited in practical jokes. He had, in addition, a command of language that even a British Tommy might have envied … A great feature about Michael Collins … was that he did not like excuses when a project was suggested, but it was a different matter if the project could not be carried out … The word 'cannot' did not figure in his vocabulary.[189]

3, 4 College Street: Offices of the committee in favour of the Treaty, under the direction of Dan McCarthy. Brigid Lyons worked here in early 1922.[190]

5b College Street: Police station near Trinity College. Dave Neligan was posted here in 1918.

3 Crow Street: Collins's Department of Intelligence office was on the second floor, above J.F. Fowler, printers and binders. Along with his office at 32 Bachelor's Walk, this was technically Collins's main Department of Intelligence office but he came here only infrequently. Sometimes his operatives called this 'the Brain Centre'.

It was, as I say, early in 1919 that Collins began to create a regular Intelligence Department. He was fortunate in getting the services of Liam Tobin as Chief Intelligence Officer. Tobin had been previously doing Intelligence work for the Dublin Brigade. Later the Assistant Quartermaster General, the late Tom Cullen, was drafted into Intelligence. Next in command came Frank Thornton. The Intelligence Staff was built up slowly, as suitable men were not easily found. A good Intelligence Officer is born, not made, but even the man with a great deal of natural instinct for detective work requires to be taught a great deal of the technique of the business.[191]

Under the name of the Irish Products Company, Liam Tobin, Collins's chief of intelligence, had his office here,[192] and Tom Cullen and Frank Thornton assisted him.

The principal staff were Charlie Byrne, Paddy Caldwell, Charlie Dalton, Joe Dolan, Joe Guilfoyle, James Hughes, Ned Kelleher, Pat (Paddy) Kennedy, Dan McDonnell, Peter McGee, Con O'Neill, Frank Saurin and Jack Walsh. (See Bachelor's Walk, Dublin 1.)

I was very happy about this transfer to Intelligence as I liked Michael Collins. I was a great admirer of him. I recognised at an early stage, even as far back as my first contact with him in Liverpool, that he was a dynamic type of individual and, although at that period he was not in any directive position, still he was an outstanding individual on that famous day in Liverpool in 1915. Later on, working with him on organisation, I had a very quiet admiration for him which developed as the years went on. Michael Collins was a man with a determination to make a complete success of everything he put his hands to. He had a marvellous memory, and as I saw repeatedly happen in later years, he would deal with men from all parts of the country at night in our headquarters in Devlin's of Parnell Square, he would make a very casual note about the things which would have to be attended to on the following day or, as often as not, take no note of them at all, but never to my knowledge was anything left unattended to the next day. He was full of the exuberance of life and full of vitality. He had no time for half measures and expected from those who were serving under him the same amount of enthusiasm and constructive energy that he himself was putting into the job.

Michael Collins took a lively interest in the private affairs of each and every individual with whom he came in contact and was always ready to lend a helping hand to assist them to meet their private responsibilities. During the height of the War he travelled from post to post and office on his old Raleigh bicycle and, as often as not, did not leave Devlin's in Parnell Square until just on curfew. I think it is only right to say here, in view of the many and varied accounts given by various writers, who claim to have known Collins and his activities, that he never carried a gun during these journeys, neither was he accompanied by a bodyguard.

In the various activities carried out by the Dublin Squads, ASU and members of the Dublin Brigade, naturally from time to time men got either killed or wounded, but invariably Mick Collins was the first man to visit the relatives of these particular men, to either console them in their adversity or to see in what way he could help them to carry on their home affairs during the absence of their loved ones. Mick Collins was the ideal soldier to lead men during a revolution such as we were going through and I think all and sundry, whether they subsequently fought against him in the Civil War or not, who had close contact with him, must admit that he was: the one bright star that all the fighting men looked to for guidance and advice during those great days, particularly during 1920 and 1921. In some of the criticisms that have appeared from time to time about Mick Collins it has been suggested that he drank to excess. These statements are lies. As one who was very closely associated with him during those strenuous days, I can say that Collins rarely took anything and when he did it was a small sherry. Drinking was naturally discouraged everywhere those days because of the necessity of keeping a cool head under the very strenuous circumstances.

In singling out Collins I am doing so only because of the fact that I had such close association with him and knew what the officers and men of the Volunteers thought of him generally, but in singling him out in this fashion I am in no way taking away from the activities of the other members of the staff, Cathal Brugha, Dick Mulcahy or Gearóid O'Sullivan.[193]

Intelligence was divided into two areas: the gathering of information on British forces, and the gathering of information on British agents. Each company of IRA/Volunteers had its own intelligence officer (IO), and each of those was encouraged to recruit people in all walks of life who boasted of their British connections.

Dame Court: Stag's Head Pub, one of Dublin's most lavish Victorian pubs. Collins used it as a meeting place during the War of Independence.

Dame Street: Éamonn Duggan had his legal offices here, from which he also ran an intelligence office as the first IRA/Volunteer director of intelligence. He was primarily concerned with collecting and collating information that was available in the press but was mostly ineffective. Collins replaced him as the official GHQ director in spring 1918.

Dame Street: A Ministry for Labour office of Countess Markievicz after she was released from Aylesbury Jail in England in 1917. She wrote very unfavourably of her time in English jails: 'All they did was to teach you how to steal'.[194]

Dame Street (at Cork Hill): **Dublin City Hall**. The Church of St Mary del Dam was originally built here; it was demolished when the Royal Exchange building was built (completed in 1779). The building was taken over by Dublin Corporation as its City Hall in 1852. The city's motto is *Obedienta Civium Urbis Felicitas*, which can be roughly translated as 'Happy the city whose citizens obey'.

On 9 June 1918 Cumann na mBan organised an 'Ireland Women's Day' (*Lá na mBan*) as part of the anti-conscription campaign. Over 40,000 women signed this anti-conscription pledge at City Hall alone:

A Solemn Pledge for the Women of Ireland

Inaugurated on St Columcille's Day

Because the enforcement of conscription on any people without their consent is tyranny, we are resolved to resist the conscription of Irishmen;

We will not fill the places of men deprived of their work through enforced military service;

We will do all in our power to help the families of men who suffer through refusing enforced military service.[195]

On 3 May 1920, Dublin Corporation acknowledged the authority of Dáil Éireann as the duly elected government of Ireland, and undertook to give effect to all decrees promulgated by that body.

Collins's intelligence offices were in nearby Crow Street, and occasionally he came to the area:

I remember one morning early in January, 1921, when Volunteer Kerrigan and myself were on what we would term an Intelligence ramble. We were on the Castle side of Dame Street. The British had cordoned off several blocks of streets all round the Empire (now the Olympia) Theatre. On looking across, we saw a group of civilians being held up and searched. To our consternation, we saw Michael Collins was one of them. Knowing us, he winked at us. We reported the information immediately to our Company officer. Mick Collins, however, was not identified and was back at his headquarters in a short time.[196]

On 14 June 1921, Seán MacEoin was tried here in a special court martial, was condemned to death and was transported to Mountjoy Prison. Cathal Brugha, who wanted MacEoin to lead another foray to Britain to assassinate members of the cabinet, had summoned MacEoin to Dublin. When Collins found out that he was in town, he ordered him to see Richard Mulcahy, and Mulcahy promptly sent him back to County Longford. Dublin Castle discovered his location and MacEoin was arrested when he got to Mullingar. He was sent to Mountjoy Prison immediately after the trial and Collins made several abortive efforts to break him out. (See North Circular Road/Mountjoy Prison, Dublin 7.)

Immediately after the Treaty debates, the offices of the Provisional Government were moved here in January 1922.[197] On the mantelpiece of his office, Collins had a bronze plaque of Theodore Roosevelt's words:

I wish to preach, not the doctrine of ignoble ease, but the doctrine of the strenuous life, the life of toil and effort, of labor and strife; to preach that highest form of success which comes, not to the man who desires mere easy peace, but to the man who does not shrink from danger, from hardship, or from bitter toil, and who out of these wins the splendid ultimate triumph.[198]

On 2 February 1922 James Craig met Collins here to discuss Ulster, after their meeting with Winston Churchill in London on 21 January. Collins and Craig had been corresponding with regard to nationalist prisoners, three of whom were held under sentence of death in Derry, but Craig gave no assurances. They discussed the Boundary Commission, but British ministers had assured Craig that the commission would make only minor adjustments (if any) to the border, whereas Collins had been told that the commission would completely alter Ulster. They were both operating under the delusion that they knew what the British intended.[199] After the meeting, Collins issued a statement:

> Owing to the fact that Mr Collins stands on the Boundary Commission and the Irish Delegation agreements with Mr Lloyd George that large territories were involved in the Commission, and not merely a boundary line, as Sir James Craig was given to understand privately by several British Ministers and from statements by Mr Lloyd George in the House of Commons, no further agreement was reached, and a very serious situation has consequently arisen.[200]

This first Craig–Collins Pact lasted less than a week. (See London, Craig–Collins Pact, Appendix VI.)

On 7 December 1921, only hours before the cabinet split over the Treaty, the mayor of Derry, Hugh C. O'Doherty, indirectly accused Collins and his associates of having abandoned the Northern nationalists, without safeguards, to their 'hereditary enemies': 'Our representatives have given away what we have fought for over the last 750 years. It is camouflaged … We are no longer a united nation. You have nothing to give us for the sacrifice you call upon the people to make … We will be ostracised on account of our creed.' On 4 February Mayor O'Doherty met with Collins, Griffith, Kevin O'Higgins and Eoin MacNeill to discuss the transfer of Derry to the Irish Free State. Nevertheless, while he felt that the Boundary Commission would transform Ulster, Collins always contended that 'coercion of Ulster is unthinkable'.[201] He later reiterated: 'There can be no question of forcing Ulster into union with the twenty-six counties. I am absolutely against coercion of the kind. If Ulster is to join us it must be voluntarily. Union is our final goal, that is all.'[202] Those in the North, however, were convinced that 'all the evidence [was] that Michael Collins was totally committed to ending partition'.[203] It must be noted that de Valera's views on the North in the winter of 1921 seem to have been very similar to those of Collins. De Valera had argued for county option in the secret sessions of Dáil Éireann in August 1921.

Later, in 1922, National Army HQ was set up here. Also that year, the first director of medical services, Dr 'Stetto' Ahearne, opened his offices here. As her first assignment after passing her exams, Dr Brigid Lyons went to work here.[204]

7–10 Dame Street: Munster and Leinster Bank, Head Branch. This was the depository for much of the money collected for the Dáil Loan.

At the end of 1920 a chequebook from the bank was discovered during a raid, thereby alerting the British authorities to the possible location of some of the Loan funds. The bank itself was raided in February 1921 and about £18,000 was seized. These monies were under the name of Daithi Ó Donnchadha (O'Donoghue) and had been 'transferred from Mícheál Ó Coileáin' (Collins).[205] It was this raid that immediately precipitated the death of the bank auditor, Alan Bell.

Bell was particularly close to Lord French and had been specially assigned to this duty in order to cripple the Dáil Loan. He had been endeavouring to trace all the banks in which Collins had deposited the proceeds, and if he had succeeded the Loan would have been at risk. But Bell had also been an active police agent since the 1880s and had undertaken numerous spying missions in the west of Ireland, sending back reports on Land Leaguers and IRB members. Bell also reported directly to Sir Basil Thompson, head of British intelligence at Scotland Yard, and the committee on which Bell sat recommended that Sinn Féin 'be infiltrated with spies and some leaders assassinated'. Collins, according to Piaras Béaslaí, regarded Bell as one of the most important British intelligence agents in Ireland.[206] Unfortunately for Bell, his inquiry into the Sinn Féin accounts in March 1920 was much publicised in the newspapers, sealing his doom.

The British only managed to confiscate approximately £20,000 of all the money collected for the Loan.

(See Nutley Lane, Dublin 4.)

13 Dame Street: Messrs Callaghan & Son & Co., military tailors and gunsmiths. Many British officers were outfitted here. After 1922, Free Staters used this establishment for outfitting as well. Collins bought his military uniforms here. He was very fastidious about his appearance and often sent back items that he thought did not fit properly.

41 Dame Street: Craig, Gardner & Co., Chartered Accountants. Collins worked here before the Rising. His co-workers included Frank Henderson and Joe McGrath, who were also Volunteers. Collins and McGrath later worked for Kathleen Clarke at the Irish National Aid and Volunteers' Dependants' Fund.

McGrath was dismissed by the accountancy firm for his participation in the Rising. The Irish Transport and General Workers' Union recruited him as finance officer, an ideal position for laundering other funds. By 1923 he was the new state's minister for industry and commerce, as well as one of its leading businessmen.[207] He went on to found the Irish Hospital Sweepstakes.

Dawson Street: P.S. O'Hegarty's bookshop. It was used as a 'drop' for Collins.[208]

Dawson Street: The Mansion House, the official residence of the lord mayor of Dublin since 1713. Lord Mayor James Gallagher in 1916 called Dublin 'Louvain by the Liffey' after the destruction of the Rising.

On 20 April 1917 an auction was held here for the benefit of the Irish National Aid and Volunteers' Dependants' Fund. Items belonging to those executed after the Rising (as well as to survivors/imprisoned) were auctioned.

The Tenth Sinn Féin Ard-Fheis was held here on 25–26 October 1917. About 1,700 delegates attended, including members from 1,009 Sinn Féin Clubs.[209] The secretary stated that the total number of clubs was about 1,200, with a membership of almost 250,000.[210] De Valera was elected president of Sinn Féin and the Irish Volunteers. Vice-presidents: Arthur Griffith and Fr Michael O'Flanagan. Secretaries: Darrell Figgis (later Harry Boland) and Austin Stack (he remained hon. secretary until his death in 1929). Treasurers: Laurence Ginnell and William Cosgrave. Eoin MacNeill was elected to the 24-member Sinn Féin Executive Council. (There was controversy when MacNeill was proposed: Éamon de Valera, Arthur Griffith and Seán Milroy voted for him, but Kathleen Clarke, Helena Molony[211] and Countess Markievicz opposed him. Nevertheless, he received an outstanding majority of votes.)

The meeting began with Brugha (a former IRB member) barely consenting to sit in the same room as Griffith, and with Collins and Rory O'Connor walking out and being brought back by de Valera. Early cracks in 'Republicanism' were apparent even then and would widen until the Treaty split.

Collins took a hard line, supported by the IRB, to block-vote de Valera into the presidency. Though de Valera, too, was once a member, he had resigned after the Rising, and Collins's position was that in spite of this he should be leader of Sinn Féin, not Griffith, whom the IRB viewed as much too moderate. Griffith clung tenaciously to the notion that Ireland could achieve her ends by constitutional means. Collins viewed Sinn Féin with mixed feelings: on the one hand, he was entirely in agreement with its doctrine of self-reliance and separatism; on the other hand, he disagreed with achieving those goals by political efforts rather than by military force. At one stage Collins walked out of talks with Griffith, and eventually a compromise was reached. Griffith agreed to abandon his lifelong aim of restoring the sovereignty of Ireland under a dual monarchy, and in return the militants led by Collins agreed to accept Sinn Féin's economic policies and its strategy of abstention from parliament. Collins's hard line backfired badly for the IRB at the Ard-Fheis, as most of its delegates were not elected to the executive, although he himself was. Even Collins suffered, however, as he was only elected on the second ballot, held the next day. The other members elected to the executive were Piaras Béaslaí, Ernest Blythe,[212] Harry Boland, Cathal Brugha, Kathleen Clarke, Dr Thomas Dillon, Dr Richard Hayes, David Kent, Diarmuid Lynch, Fionan Lynch, Dr Kathleen Lynn, Seán MacEntee, Countess Markievicz, Joseph McDonagh, Joseph McGuinness, Seán Milroy, Seán T. O'Kelly, Count Plunkett, Grace Gifford Plunkett, Fr Matt Ryan, Fr Thomas Wall and James J. Walsh.

Cathal Brugha proposed the Sinn Féin Constitution, and Seán Milroy seconded it on 25 October. The constitution stated:

Whereas the people of Ireland never relinquished the claim to separate Nationhood; and

Whereas the Provisional Government of the Irish Republic, Easter 1916, in the name of the Irish people, and continuing the fight made by previous generations, reasserted the inalienable right of the Irish nation to Sovereign independence, and reaffirmed the determination of the Irish people to achieve it; and

Whereas the Proclamation of an Irish Republic, Easter 1916, and the supreme courage and glorious sacrifices of the men who gave their lives to maintain it, have united the people of Ireland under the flag of the Irish Republic, be it

Resolved that we, the delegated representatives of the Irish People, in convention assembled, hereby declare the following to be the Constitution of Sinn Féin.

The name of the organisation shall be Sinn Féin.

Sinn Féin aims at securing the international recognition of Ireland as an independent Irish Republic. Having achieved that status, the Irish people may by referendum freely choose their own form of government;

This object shall be attained through the Sinn Féin Organisation which shall, in the name of the Irish People:

Deny the right and oppose the will of the British Parliament and British Crown or any other foreign government to legislate for Ireland;

Make use of any and every means available to render impotent the power of England to hold Ireland in subjection by military force or otherwise.[213]

De Valera devised the following formula to open the Ard-Fheis: 'Sinn Féin aims at securing the international recognition of Ireland as an independent Irish Republic. Having achieved that status the Irish people may by referendum freely choose their own form of government.' He subsequently closed the Ard-Fheis by declaring, 'We are not doctrinaire Republicans'.[214]

On 18 April 1918 the Hon. Laurence O'Neill, lord mayor of Dublin, convened a national conference in the Mansion House. All sections of 'nationalist' opinion were to form the 'National Cabinet'. The Irish Parliamentary Party was represented by Joe

Devlin and John Dillon, Sinn Féin by de Valera and Griffith, the dissident element of the old Home Rule Party by F.J. Healy and William O'Brien, the Irish Labour Party by Michael J. Egan (Cork), Thomas Johnson (Belfast)[215] and William O'Brien (Dublin),[216] and the Independents by T.M. Healy.[217] The conference was convened primarily as a protest against the conscription measures passed by the British parliament on 16 April 1918. The declaration that it issued bore the indelible imprint of separatist thinking by basing the case against conscription on 'Ireland's separate and distinct nationhood' and 'denying the right of the British government or any external authority, to impose compulsory service in Ireland against the clearly expressed will of the Irish people':

> Taking our stand on Ireland's separate and distinct nationhood and affirming the principle of liberty that the Governments of nations derive their just powers from the consent of the governed, we deny the right of the British Government or any external authority to impose compulsory military service in Ireland against the clearly expressed will of the Irish people. The passing of the Conscription Bill by the British House of Commons must be regarded as a declaration of war on the Irish nation. The alternative to accepting it as such is to surrender our liberties and to acknowledge ourselves slaves. It is in direct violation of the rights of small nationalities to self-determination, which even the Prime Minister of England— now preparing to employ naked militarism and force his Act upon Ireland— himself officially announced as an essential condition for peace at the Peace Congress. The attempt to enforce it will be an unwarranted aggression, by which we call upon all Irishmen to resist by the most effective means at their disposal.[218]

The Catholic hierarchy concurred with this declaration at their annual meeting at Maynooth and declared in their own manifesto:

> An attempt is being made to force Conscription on Ireland against the will of the Irish nation and in defiance of the protests of its leaders. In view especially of the historic relations between the two countries from the very beginning up to this moment, we consider that Conscription forced in this way upon Ireland is an oppressive and inhuman law, which the Irish people have a right to resist by every means that are consonant with God.[219]

An anti-conscription pledge was set forth: 'Denying the right of the British Government to enforce compulsory service in this country, we pledge ourselves solemnly to one another to resist conscription by the most effective means at our disposal'.

Collins realised the implications: 'The conscription proposals are to my liking and

I think they will end well for Ireland. The controversy offers a tremendous opportunity for Sinn Féin to exploit public resentment.' Collins made sure that the conscription scare turned the Volunteers from a political minority into a national army. It was a blow from which the Sinn Féin moderates and the old-time parliamentarians would never recover.

On 17 May the British authorities decided not to implement conscription in Ireland, but by then the reaction had solidified support for Sinn Féin. (See the 'German Plot' arrests, which took place on the night of 17–18 May 1918, their effect on the British effort to enforce conscription, and the people's embrace of Sinn Féin throughout the country. For those arrested, see 'The German Plot', 6 Harcourt Street.)

On 7 January 1919, 26 Sinn Féin representatives met privately and made arrangements to convene the First Dáil Éireann.[220] Collins would be in Liverpool waiting to break de Valera out of jail and at first he opposed convening the Dáil. He thought that there would be so few TDs available that it would not have sufficient authority. He also saw it as a rallying point for the moderates, in contrast to the Volunteers in whom he placed his trust.[221] Nevertheless, when the decision was made, he threw himself into its organisation.

On 21 January 1919 the First Dáil met in the Mansion House. At 3.30pm, in the Round Room, Count Plunkett called the meeting to order and nominated Cathal Brugha to be Ceann Comhairle (speaker/chairman) for Dáil Éireann. Padraig Ó Maille seconded this. Brugha presided thereafter and, following the reading of the Declaration of Independence, he told the cheering assembly: 'Deputies, you understand from what is asserted in this Declaration that we are now done with England. Let the world know it and those who are concerned bear it in mind.' Fr Michael O'Flanagan read opening prayers. (See 6 Harcourt Street for a complete list of TDs elected.)

The Declaration of Independence was passed unanimously. Brugha read it in Irish, Éamonn Duggan in English and George Gavan Duffy in French. Piaras Béaslaí, Conor Collins, George Gavan Duffy, Seán T. O'Kelly, James O'Mara and James J. Walsh drafted the Provisional Constitution and the Declaration of Independence.

The 'Message to Free Nations' was read by Robert Barton in English and by J.J. O'Kelly in Irish.[222] (See Documents, Appendix VII.) When the documents were read in Irish, most of the delegates listened eagerly but few understood a word.

A Democratic Programme of Dáil Éireann was read and unanimously adopted, founded on the 1916 Proclamation. At the request of the Dáil, Thomas Johnson,[223] secretary of the Irish Labour Party, and William O'Brien[224] prepared and submitted a draft for a social and democratic programme. About half of their draft was included in the programme as finally written and submitted by Seán T. O'Kelly.[225] Many of the TDs, including Collins, were opposed to some of the socialist ideas in the Programme, and Collins was vocal in his opposition. It is not clear whether he was innately opposed to socialism or whether he feared that any ideology except nationalism would hinder the independence movement. He threatened (through the IRB) to suppress the Programme on the grounds that it was too radical.[226] Prior to its submission, O'Kelly amended the Programme to meet the objections of Collins and other senior IRB members, who wanted the removal of explicit affirmations of socialist principles such as the right of the nation 'to resume possession' of the nation's wealth 'wherever the trust is abused or the trustee fails to give faithful service'. O'Kelly also had to remove a reference that encouraged the 'organisation of people into trade unions and co-operative societies'.[227] Some think that if Collins had been present at the first sitting of the Dáil, rather than in England preparing for de Valera's escape, the Democratic Programme might not have been accepted.

Twenty-eight TDs attended this first session.[228] The answer to the roll-call for 34 absent deputies was 'imprisoned by the foreign enemy', and for three absent deputies 'deported by the foreign enemy'. Answering 'present' were 28 Sinn Féin TDs out of a total of 104 names called, including all other parties. Even Ulster's Edward Carson received an invitation—in Irish. Some TDs were elected for two constituencies, so there were only 69 persons elected. Two were ill, others had been deported, five were on missions abroad, but the majority were in jail in England. (Collins and Harry Boland were in England working on de Valera's escape from prison but were marked present to keep others from asking where they were.) Thirty-three per cent of Dáil members were under 35 years of age, and another 40% were between 35 and 40. There were only two Protestant members: Ernest Blythe and Robert Barton.

The press reaction in Britain was generally hostile, and in Ulster even more so:

> Thus Ireland is alleged to be a Celtic and Roman Catholic nation, and all who are not Celts and Romanists are regarded as foreigners. It is because Ulster knows that this is what Home Rule means that it will not have it.[229]

The officers elected were: Priomh Aire, Éamon de Valera; vice-presidents, Arthur Griffith and Fr O'Flanagan; secretaries, Austin Stack and Darrell Figgis; treasurers, William T. Cosgrave and Laurence Ginnell. The executive elected comprised Harry Boland, Collins, Seán T. O'Kelly,[230] Seán MacEntee, James J. Walsh and Kathleen Clarke. Clerks appointed were Risteard O'Fogladha (chief clerk), Seán Nunan,[231] Diarmuid O'Hegarty and Patrick Sheehan.[232] The photo taken that day showed 24 attendees.

No oath was administered to the TDs on 21 January. The elected deputies had signed a Republican pledge at their meeting on 7 January: 'I hereby pledge myself to work for the establishment of an independent Irish Republic; that I will accept nothing less than complete separation from England in settlement of Ireland's claims; and that I will abstain from attending the English Parliament'.[233]

On 1 April 1919 a private session of the First Dáil was held, with Seán T. O'Kelly as ceann comhairle. Éamon de Valera presided as priomh aire and named the cabinet as follows:

Minister for Home Affairs: Arthur Griffith (arrested); succeeded by Austin Stack

Minister for Defence: Cathal Brugha; Deputy: William Considine (Richard Mulcahy was Minister from January to April, when he became Assistant Minister under Brugha; he was the Volunteer chief of staff)

Minister for Fine Arts and for Foreign Affairs: Count George Noble Plunkett; Under-Secretary for Foreign Affairs: Robert Brennan

Minister for Labour: Countess Markievicz (first European female minister; when she was appointed, she was in Holloway Prison in England)

Minister for Industries: Eoin MacNeill

Minister for Finance: Michael Collins

Minister for Trade and Commerce: Ernest Blythe

Minister for Local Government: William T. Cosgrave; succeeded by Kevin O'Higgins, assisted by Rory O'Connor

Minister for Propaganda: Laurence Ginnell; succeeded by Desmond FitzGerald (arrested in February 1921); succeeded by Erskine Childers

Minister for Agriculture: Robert Barton; succeeded by Art O'Connor. [234]

At a meeting here just after the Dáil first met, Cathal Brugha forcefully told his subordinates in the Ministry for Defence that a new situation had arisen:

The Volunteers have become the army of a lawfully constituted government, elected by the people, and are entitled morally and legally when in the execution of their duty to slay the officials and agents of the foreign invader who is waging war upon our native government.[235]

Busy as he was, Collins wrote to his sister, Sister Celestine, about the election:

... it has been an historical one for very often we are actors in events that have very much more meaning and consequence than we realise ... The elected representatives of the people have definitely turned their backs on the old order and the developments are sure to be interesting ... We go from success to success in our guerrilla way. Escapes of prisoners, raids against the enemy, etc. ...[236]

On 4 April 1919 the second public session of the First Dáil was held. The photo taken on this day is the one most usually seen of the members of the First Dáil. (Collins was persuaded to sit for the photo for posterity, but it is obvious from his expression that he didn't want to be photographed.) That day, an Irish-American fact-finding mission was invited to attend—Frank P. Walsh, Edward F. Dunne and Michael J. Ryan, the first Americans to address an Irish parliament since Benjamin Franklin in 1782. The British decided on a raid primarily to capture Collins, but he slipped out the back and watched the raid from the roof next door. When the raid was over, Collins returned, dressed in full Volunteer uniform, to attend the formal social gathering hosted by the lord mayor. This was the first time that Collins had appeared in uniform since Thomas Ashe's funeral.

On 17 June 1919 the third public session of the First Dáil was convened. This established the consular service and the National Arbitration Courts, and set up the Dáil Loan. At first it was decided to obtain from the subscribers as much as possible of the previous Anti-Conscription Fund, which had been established in 1918, now that the threat of conscription had passed. The official name of that fund was the 'Self-Determination Fund', and the Irish had contributed £250,000 to it. Representatives of Sinn Féin cumainn were directed to be present outside churches on the Sundays on which the subscriptions were to be returned to solicit those funds for the Dáil Loan. Only about £17,000 passed to the Dáil Loan from the Anti-Conscription Fund but it was a straight contribution, not a loan. On 19 June the Dáil launched the National Loan prospectus, which it was hoped would raise £250,000. This money would enable the Dáil to function. The bonds were to be issued in denominations of £1, £5, £10, £20, £50 and £100, and the general population were invited to subscribe. The purpose of this range of certificates was to enable individuals on small incomes to subscribe. Each certificate would qualify for a 5% rate of interest, paid half-yearly. The National Loan was marketed as the means by which the general population could contribute to and have control of the future of Ireland. The appeal for subscriptions was published 'in national newspapers'. From the outset, the purpose of the Loan was to finance the operation of the government, not to finance the war effort.

De Valera delivered the Ministry of Finance proposal to the Dáil, and outlined Collins's role:

> It is obvious that the work of our government cannot be carried out without funds. The Minister of Finance [Collins] is accordingly preparing a prospectus which will shortly be published for the issue of a loan of one million pounds sterling—£500,000 to be offered to the public for immediate subscription ... in bonds and such amounts as to meet the needs of the small subscriber.[237]

(Raising money and hiding it from government agents was an old Irish custom. The Fenians did it with their 'Fenian Loan' in the 1860s, and the Land League did it in the 1880s. Collins was following in their footsteps and was very successful. And when the British did become aware of one of his hiding places he reacted ruthlessly. See Alan

Bell, Munster and Leinster Bank, Dame Street; Nutley Lane, Dublin 4.)

The Loan's official purpose was:

> To state Ireland's case to the world, to create an Irish Civil Service, to set up consuls abroad to aid Irish trade, to develop fisheries, forestry and industry, to prepare for a policy of land division, and to establish arbitration courts.[238]

Officially signed receipts in green, gold and black were issued in lieu of bonds; Colm Ó Lochlainn printed them. There were constituency organisers for each province, paid £30 per week each: Leinster, E. Flemming; Ulster, E. Donnelly; Munster, P.C. O'Mahoney; Connacht, P. Ryan. Accounts were opened in banks in many sympathisers' names throughout Ireland and Britain, and about half was converted to gold. (See Dame Street, Munster and Leinster Bank.) By September 1920 the following amounts had been subscribed: Leinster, £87,444; Ulster, £41,297; Munster, £171,177; Connacht, £57,797; England and France, £11,647; Cumann na mBan, £801. The final Loan total, subscribed by over 135,000 Irish people, was £378,858 in Ireland alone. $5,123,640 was raised separately in the US.[239] Both were huge sums for the time.

The Loan was Collins's greatest administrative accomplishment.[240] Many in the cabinet were sceptical at the outset, but later Griffith said that it was 'one of the most extraordinary feats in the country's history'. When Griffith found that Collins could back up his promise to 'raise a quarter of a million', he viewed Collins with new respect. The Loan was launched with great ceremony at St Enda's, and Collins had the event filmed. (See St Enda's, Rathfarnham, Dublin 14.) The appointed trustees of the Dáil Loan were Éamon de Valera, the Most Revd Dr Michael Fogarty (bishop of Killaloe)[241] and James O'Mara.[242] While de Valera was in the US, Arthur Griffith was acting trustee in his place. (O'Mara went to the US to help in selling the bonds for the Loan. In 1921 de Valera wanted to appoint O'Mara as ambassador to the US, but the latter was so displeased with de Valera that he refused, saying that he could no longer 'hold any official position under the government of the Irish Republic whose President claims such arbitrary executive authority, and in whose judgement of American affairs I no longer have any confidence'. He also resigned his post as a trustee of the Loan and as a TD. In lieu of just accepting O'Mara's resignation, de Valera sent him a telegram telling him that he had been fired.)

The fourth public session of the First Dáil, held on 19 August 1919, established the 'Dáil/Republican courts'.[243] They were set up under Austin Stack, minister for justice, and had civil and criminal jurisdiction.[244] Young barristers from the Law Library in Dublin's Four Courts drew up the Rules of Court under the direction of James Creed Meredith KC, a Protestant, who served as the president of the Dáil/Republican supreme court from 1920–2. These courts took advantage of the malaise within the British administration in Ireland. By directing their blows at the weak points of that structure, the IRA hastened its collapse. So effective was their campaign of terror and intimidation that in time the British courts, the police, the magistrates and the local authorities all abandoned their responsibilities and saw them assumed by the local officers and leading politicians of the underground government represented by Dáil Éireann. The British administration in Ireland thus failed to provide a modicum of internal law and order. Once a government can no longer guarantee public security it has abdicated its mandate. By 1919, with the result of the Dáil elections known, the British administration was thus doubly illegitimate.[245]

In the *Irish Times*, Irish landlord Lord Monteagle wrote of the courts:

> The Sinn Féin courts are steadily expanding their jurisdiction and dispensing justice even-handed between man and man, Catholic and Protestant, farmer and shopkeeper, grazier and cattle driver, landlord and tenant … sometimes with the acquiescence of the local military authorities, who thus show themselves wiser than either the Castle officials or the British government. And mark the double significance of this fact. It shows the powerlessness … of the 'government of the dissent of the governed'. It also shows the growing and remarkable capacity of the Irish people for self-government.[246]

The Dáil/Republican supreme court had three members who could sit as high court judges as well. Beneath this category were county/district and parish courts. Parish courts corresponded to the British petty sessions courts. The county courts corresponded to the British county courts and the judges were primarily women. There were five county/district judges, elected by those who presided at the parish courts. Within four days the parish court could appeal to the district court. The court decrees were enforced by the IRA/Volunteers and later by 'Republican Police' attached to companies. The mass of people, long deprived of tribunals with which they could identify, flocked to the Dáil/Republican courts. Attempts at suppression by the British were futile, and within a short while the courts were operating in 27 counties. In these courts the amateur judges endeavoured to give good and fair decisions, which may not always have been according to the letter of the law so much as according to the conscience and private knowledge of the judges themselves.[247] On 29 June 1920 the Dáil established courts of justice and equity,[248] appointing James Creed Meredith as president of the Dáil/Republican supreme court, with Arthur Clery and Diarmuid Crowley as the other members of that court. It appointed Cahir Davit (son of agrarian agitator and nationalist Michael Davit) as a high court justice.[249] These served as appellate courts for the Dáil/Republican courts previously established.

On 20 August 1919, in private session, certain Volunteers took an oath of allegiance to the Dáil. The oath, moved by Cathal Brugha and seconded by Terence

MacSwiney, was as follows:

> I _____ do solemnly swear (or affirm) that I do not, and shall not, yield a voluntary support to any pretended Government, Authority, or Power inside Ireland hostile or inimical thereto; and I do further swear (or affirm) that to the best of my knowledge and ability I shall support and defend the Irish Republic, which is Dáil Éireann, against all enemies foreign and domestic, and that I will bear true faith and allegiance to the same and that I take this obligation freely without any mental reservation or purpose of evasion. So help me God.

Ultimately, the oath was to be taken by all Dáil deputies, all IRA/Volunteers, all officials and clerks of the Dáil, and 'any other body or individual who, in the opinion of the Dáil, should take the same oath'. It was only in 1921 that Oscar Traynor, O/C of the Dublin Brigade, told his IRA/Volunteers that their 'activities would be directed by General Headquarters (GHQ), and the Government of the Republic will accept full responsibility for your operations against the enemy and for your future welfare'.[250] By October 1919 all deputies and officials had taken the Oath of Allegiance. Collins and the IRB opposed this because they still viewed the Dáil as a vehicle that the moderates would use to sell out the independence movement.

On 12 September 1919 the Dáil was officially suppressed as a 'Dangerous Association':

> Whereas, as by special proclamation dated July 3, 1918, in pursuance and by date thereof certain associations in Ireland known by the names of Sinn Féin organisation, Sinn Féin clubs, Irish Volunteers, Cumann na mBan and Gaelic League to be dangerous. And whereas the association known by the name of Dáil Éireann appears to us to be a dangerous association and to have been after the date of said special proclamation employed for all purposes of the association known by the names of Sinn Féin organisation, Sinn Féin clubs, Irish Volunteers, and Cumann na mBan, now we, the Lord-Lieutenant General and General Governor of Ireland, by and with the advice of the Privy Council in Ireland, by virtue of the Criminal Law and Procedure Act of Ireland of 1887, and of every power and authority in this behalf, do hereby, by this our order, prohibit and suppress within the several districts specified and named in the schedule the association known as Dáil Éireann. [251]

Collins and Mulcahy regarded this as a declaration of war, and it turned the passive resistance and defensive tactics of the IRA/Volunteers into an offensive war. According to Mulcahy, as a result of the suppression of the Dáil 'a formal decision was taken to let the Volunteers take an offensive initiation against the administration of the time'.[252]

In spite of this suppression, on 27 October 1919 the fifth public session of the First Dáil was held in the Oak Room. Nevertheless, the suppression had its effect: the Dáil met fourteen times in 1919, but that decreased to three meetings in 1920 and four in 1921. Because the Dáil acted as a moderating force, Collins was given a freer hand after it was forced underground.

On 11 March 1921 the Dáil agreed to the acceptance of a state of war with England, and that it would take full responsibility for the military operations of the Volunteers as the army of the Republic.[253]

The Second Dáil was elected on 19 May 1921 in the Twenty-Six Counties of the South and on 24 May in the Six Counties of the North. This election became known as the 'Partition Election' because it was the first time in which an election in the Six Counties was held at a different time from that for the Twenty-Six Counties. All 'nationalist' parties agreed not to run against Sinn Féin; the Six Counties were to elect thirteen representatives to the English parliament and the Twenty-Six Counties were to send 33. This was also the election in which proportional representation was introduced into Ireland on a national level. (It had been used on 15 January 1920 in urban and borough elections and on 15 June for county council elections.) In the Twenty-Six Counties, no elections were needed. All of the 124 seats filled by the popular election and the four seats allocated to the National University were given to men and women pledged to the Irish Republic. The entire elected opposition consisted of the four men returned by TCD unopposed. In Northern Ireland the total number of seats available was 52; Unionist candidates gained 40 seats, and the remaining twelve were divided between Sinn Féin candidates and other nationalists. Winston Churchill remarked that 'From that moment, the position of Ulster became unassailable'.[254]

On 8 July 1921 de Valera convened a consultation preparatory to a truce. Lord Mayor Laurence (Larry) O'Neill, Gen. Sir Nevil Macready, Lord Midleton (representing Southern Unionists), Arthur Griffith and Robert Barton attended the meeting; James Craig from Ulster refused to attend. The following day the terms of the Truce were agreed upon and settled at a 3pm meeting between Gen. Macready, Col. J. Brind and Alfred W. Cope for the British, and Robert C. Barton and Éamonn J. Duggan for the IRA/Volunteers. The terms went into effect at noon on 11 July 1921. Macready described Collins as

> the easiest to deal with … He had what few of his countrymen possess, a sense of humour and, above all, the gift during conversation of sticking to essentials … he would complete the discussion with the least possible waste of time.[255]

On behalf of the British, the Truce called for:

- No incoming troops, RIC and auxiliary police and munitions. No movements for military purposes of troops and munitions, except for maintenance drafts.

- No provocative display of force, armed or not armed.
- It is understood that all provisions of this Truce shall apply to the Martial Law area equally to the rest of Ireland.
- No pursuits of Irish officers, or men, or war material, or military stores.
- No secret agents, noting descriptions or movements, and no interference with the movements of Irish persons, military or civil, and no attempt to discover the haunts or habits of Irish officers and men.

  Note: there are other details concerning courts, motor transport etc. to be dealt with later.

On the Irish side it was agreed:

- Attacks on Crown Forces and civilians to cease.
- No provocative display of force, armed or not armed.
- No interference with British Government or private property.
- To discountenance [sic] and prevent any action likely to cause disturbance of the peace which might necessitate military interference.

Collins was not entirely pleased with the Truce. He wrote to Moya Llewellyn Davies that it was

> ... only the first step. The days ahead are going to be the truly trying ones and we can only face them with set faces and hearts full of hope and confidence.[256]

He wrote to Harry Boland, who was in the US:

> There's something about [it] which I don't like, and I have the impression that the whole thing is pressing on me. I find myself looking at friends as if they were enemies—looking at them twice just to make sure that they are really friends after all. I mention no names. After all it may be a wrong impression that's got into me. Frankly, though, I don't care for things as they are now.[257]

Collins's fears were well founded, as during the six months of the Truce the frustrations, antagonisms and personality clashes that had festered during the War of Independence contributed to many of the divisions that were to occur during the Treaty debates and after it was ratified. During the War of Independence the IRA/Volunteers showed a strong sense of responsibility and discipline, but the Truce led to many acts of bad public behaviour and to the intimidation of civilians. Many of those who 'joined' the IRA/Volunteers at that time were deemed 'Trucileers' and had not been involved in any action during the War. Their activities and the adverse influence of the circumstances created by the Truce that Collins had feared all had their effects on the genesis of the Civil War.[258]

At the time of the Truce more than 30 Dáil deputies were in prison or interned. The British agreed to release these in order to allow a full session of the Dáil. The only exception was Seán MacEoin, who was under a sentence of death, but Collins demanded that he be released and he was freed on 8 August. Next on Collins's list of prisoners to be released was Ned Broy, from Arbour Hill, and he was. The bulk of over 4,000 IRA/Volunteer prisoners, however, remained in jail.

On 14 July de Valera went to London to negotiate with Lloyd George. (See 10 Downing Street, London, Appendix VI.) Included in the delegation were Arthur Griffith, Count Plunkett, Austin Stack, Robert Barton and Erskine Childers. Collins wanted to go, and forcefully pressed to be included, but de Valera chose to leave him in Dublin. At first de Valera said that it was because he didn't want Collins to be photographed in case they returned to war, but later he indicated that he wanted to leave at least one senior politician in Dublin. This was an 'all-Sinn Féin' delegation, and it broke the unwritten rule that a Volunteer should be present at all negotiations. The talks quickly stalled when de Valera insisted on prior recognition of Irish sovereignty and Lloyd George refused, offering instead a limited form of dominion, with Northern Ireland remaining as it was, no military or fiscal autonomy for the south, and Home Rule government as part of the United Kingdom.

Upon his return to Dublin, de Valera called a cabinet meeting to persuade the members to agree to a settlement. He wanted to present a plan to the Irish people that would acknowledge Ireland's freedom and then accept the same *de facto* status as the dominions. Two days later he reconvened the meeting and presented his concept of 'External Association' with the British Commonwealth.[259] De Valera knew that the king had to be written into the agreement—but how could Ireland make the king utterly powerless? He came up with the idea of 'External Association', he said, while tying his shoes one morning:

- independence for Ireland re domestic affairs;
- alignment with the British Empire on foreign affairs;
- the king to be the head of the association.

In effect, it was what India got in 1948, but it was impractical politics in 1922.

Attending these cabinet meetings were:

- Cathal Brugha: 'I haven't much to add except to say how glad I am that it has been suggested that we circulate these documents and consider them fully before we meet again, if for no other reason than to give you and the great masters of English you keep at your elbow an opportunity of extricating us from the morass in which ye have landed us'. 'We have proclaimed a Republic in arms … it has been ratified by the votes of the people, and we have sworn to defend it with our lives.'

- Arthur Griffith: '… the British offer is better than expected'.
- J.J. O'Kelly (Sceilg): '… elements of friction were already present'. He said that the relevant documents should be circulated for more consideration.
- Collins: arrived late. He said 'you all know my opinion', and described the proposals as 'a step forward'. De Valera's notes on Collins indicated that he said: 'Step on road … Free Dominion a step'.
- Countess Markievicz: agreed with O'Kelly.
- Kevin O'Higgins.
- Austin Stack: very critical. 'Cathal was bluntly opposed to anything less than the recognition of the Republic, and I supported him as well as I was able.'
- Robert Barton.
- Erskine Childers: very hostile.
- Joe McDonagh.
- Ernest Blyth.
- Eoin MacNeill: welcomed the British offer.
- W.T. Cosgrave: agreed with Griffith that the British offer was better than expected.
- Count Plunkett.
- Diarmuid O'Hegarty.[260]

The debate on the forthcoming negotiations had already begun, even though it had not been agreed to hold negotiations.

The First Session of the Second Dáil was held on 16 August 1921 in the Round Room. There were 130 Republican TDs, six Nationalist TDs and 44 Unionist TDs (who absented themselves as usual). All TDs present took the oath to the Dáil. The Dáil was to consider de Valera's correspondence and negotiations with London, and the British offer of dominion status for Ireland. Among those listening in the public gallery was Brigid Lyons:

> I was shattered to hear de Valera say his oath to the Republic was the best measure of freedom he could get. For me, I didn't think that was enough, or for him either. When I look back on it, of course, it was a sensible statement, and the only one anyone could make, but at the time I thought it was the Republic or nothing for me—still, like a lot of others not knowing exactly what a Republic was. The Dáil rejected the British offer and a stalemate followed.[261]

On 17 August the Dáil's foreign representatives were named as follows: John Chartres (Germany), Harry Boland (USA), Seán T. O'Kelly (Paris),[262] George Gavan

Duffy (Rome),[263] Art O'Brien (London), Dr Patrick McCartan (Russia),[264] Éamon Bulfin (Argentina)[265] and Frank W. Egan (Chile). De Valera addressed the Dáil: 'I would be willing to suggest to the Irish people to give up a good deal in order to have an Ireland that could look to the future without anticipating distracting internal problems'.

In a private session on 22 August, de Valera told the TDs that if they were determined to make peace only on the basis of recognition of the Republic then they were going to be faced with war, only this time it would be a real war of British reconquest, not just a continuation of limited military coercive measures 'in support of the civil police' to force people to obey the law. He clearly indicated his willingness to compromise, even on partition: 'I do not consider myself bound to consider anything, I feel myself open to consider anything'.

On 26 August the cabinet and ministers for the Second Dáil were appointed as follows:

> Minister for Foreign Affairs: Arthur Griffith
> Minister for Home Affairs: Austin Stack
> Minister for Defence: Cathal Brugha
> Minister for Finance: Michael Collins
> Minister for Local Government: William T. Cosgrave
> Minister for Economic Affairs: Robert Barton

The following were appointed ministers outside the cabinet:

> Minister for Fine Arts: Count Plunkett
> Minister for Propaganda: Desmond FitzGerald
> Minister for Education: J.J. O'Kelly
> Minister for Labour: Countess Markievicz
> Minister for Trade and Commerce: Ernest Blythe
> Minister for Agriculture: Art O'Connor
> Minister for Fisheries: Seán Etchingham
> Kevin O'Higgins was appointed as a minister to assist William T. Cosgrave in Local Government
> Director for Publicity: Desmond FitzGerald

On 7 September Lloyd George wrote to de Valera requesting a 'definite reply as to whether you are prepared to enter a conference to ascertain how the association of Ireland with the community of nations known as the British Empire can best be reconciled with Irish national aspirations'. He proposed that the conference should begin at Inverness, Scotland, on 20 September (he was then in his holiday home in Gairloch, Scotland). De Valera could delay no longer. A reading of the Official Correspondence

Relating to the Peace Negotiations, June–September 1921, makes it clear that Lloyd George was offering dominion status for the 26 counties and nothing else. De Valera was committed to an imaginative and far-sighted scheme of his own creation, that of an external association between Ireland and Britain, but he failed to communicate to his colleagues the strength of his feelings on this subject. What is not in doubt is that de Valera knew before the delegation left Ireland that the offer of an Irish Republic was not on the table for discussion. He had told the cabinet earlier that he was not going to the negotiations. In the last analysis, his decision to stay in Dublin was based on solid grounds. He knew that those who went were likely to become scapegoats—with the radicals if they compromised, and with the moderates if they did not. 'We must have scapegoats', de Valera told the cabinet.[266] In essence he was following the well-established diplomatic maxim that principals should not engage in negotiations but remain in reserve as the ultimate arbiters. Where that broke down in this case was that Lloyd George was fully engaged in the negotiations, and de Valera's absence undoubtedly left the Irish delegation at a disadvantage. There were other motives. By staying away he hoped to protect his status as president of the Irish Republic, and thus the Republic itself, rather than be involved in invidious negotiations about it, in which he might be accused of a conflict of interest. De Valera's other concern, a very natural one for any political leader, was to preserve the unity of the movement. He thought that he could keep the more republican wing on board by staying at home. He may have contemplated joining the delegation at the very end but, if so, he left it too late. De Valera was a devoted admirer of Machiavelli, and especially of *The prince*.

> If the Prince's advisors tell him he is not going to get what he desires, he shouldn't go to the negotiations.

He had also seen how President Woodrow Wilson lost touch with the American public while in Versailles, and he didn't want to fall into that trap. Collins was determined that de Valera should go. A vote was taken in the cabinet, with each member being asked whether he should go. Griffith, Cosgrave and Collins voted 'yes', while Brugha, Stack and Barton voted 'no'. With the vote tied, de Valera voted not to go.

Collins addressed the Dáil after a very heated debate:

> To me the task is a loathsome one. If I go, I go in the spirit of a soldier who acts against his judgment at the orders of a superior officer.[267]

Later he was more explicit to the IRB:

> I have been sent to London to do a thing which those who sent me had to be done but had not the courage to do it themselves. We had not, when the terms

were offered, an average of one round of ammunition for each weapon we had. The fighting area in Cork ... was becoming daily more circumcised [*sic*] and they could not have carried on much longer.[268]

On 14 September 1921 the plenipotentiaries were chosen for the treaty negotiations: Arthur Griffith, Robert Barton, Collins, George Gavan Duffy and Éamonn Duggan. Gavan Duffy objected to the term 'plenipotentiaries' but de Valera insisted. He wished to use the term 'to give the world the impression that they are sent over with full powers—to do the best they could do to reconcile the Irish position with the British position. They should have full powers because if they go over they needed the moral feeling of support of the position to do the best for Ireland.' Neither Stack nor Brugha was chosen. Stack said that 'it consoles me to feel that from the outset I instinctively and openly set my face against negotiations in London; so did Cathal'.[269] There was the tragic dissent: no matter what compromises the plenipotentiaries brought back, Brugha and Stack were bound to raise objections.

On 15 September de Valera proposed that the army (IRA/Volunteers) 'be put on a regular basis'. The cabinet, in late November, affirmed: 'The supreme body directing the Army is the Cabinet. The immediate executive representative of the Government is the Minister for Defence who is, therefore, Administrative Head of the Army. The Minister for Defence is a civilian. All Army appointments are to be sanctioned by the Minister for Defence, who is to have the power of nomination and veto.' (See Ailesbury Road, Dublin 4.)

On 18 September Lloyd George wrote to de Valera:

From the very outset of our conversation I told you that we looked to Ireland to own allegiance to the Throne, and to make her future as a member of the British Commonwealth. That was the basis of our proposals, and we cannot alter it. The status which you now claim in advance for your delegates is, in effect, a repudiation of that basis.

On 30 September 1921 de Valera issued a final 'acceptance' of the treaty conference 'terms':

We have received your letter of invitation to a Conference in London on October 11th 'with a view to ascertaining how the association of Ireland with the community of nations known as the British Empire may best be reconciled with Irish national aspirations'.

Our respective positions have been stated and are understood and we agree that conference, not correspondence, is the most practical and hopeful way to an understanding. We accept the invitation, and our Delegates will meet you in

London on the date mentioned 'to explore every possibility of settlement by personal discussion'.[270]

De Valera authorised members of the government to open negotiations with Britain in October. Previously, he had had talks with Prime Minister Jan Smuts of the Union of South Africa, who came to Ireland at the behest of Lloyd George to mediate. In their conversations, Smuts indicated that Britain would never give the Irish a 'republic' and, in fact, the South Africans had never asked for one. Smuts said, 'Ask what you want, but not a republic'. 'If the status of a dominion is offered,' de Valera replied, 'I will use all our machinery to get the Irish people to accept it.'[271] Smuts reported on his Irish visit to the British cabinet the next day.

The basis of the conference in London was the 'Gairloch Formula' proposed by British Prime Minister Lloyd George. According to this formula, the status of a republic, as previously demanded by de Valera, was not acceptable, and instead the Irish delegation was to ascertain 'how the association of Ireland with the community of nations known as the British Empire may best be reconciled with Irish national aspirations'. Although Griffith was the top-ranking delegate, Collins was recognised as the *de facto* leader. Collins was extremely uncomfortable with being chosen as a delegate. It was not his field of expertise but it was his duty and he accepted it grudgingly.[272] Batt O'Connor, a close friend, described how Collins bitterly complained that 'It was an unheard of thing that a soldier who had fought in the field should be elected to carry out negotiations. It was de Valera's job, not his.'[273] Nevertheless, Collins was also aware that the IRA was exhausted and that an agreement, even a compromise, was preferable to fighting a ruinous war. Later he argued that the restrictions of the 'Gairloch Formula' eliminated any pretence of sustaining the republic:

> If we all stood on the recognition of the Irish Republic as a prelude to any conference we could very easily have said so, and there would have been no conference . . . it was the acceptance of the invitation that formed the compromise. I was sent there to form that adaption, to bear the brunt of it.[274]

It has often been charged that as a military man Collins was too prone to interpret political rhetoric literally. Yet Robert Barton, who disagreed with the Treaty, also came to the same conclusion:

> The English refused to recognise us as acting on behalf of the Irish Republic and the fact we agreed to negotiate at all on any other basis was possibly the primary cause of our downfall. Certainly [it was] the first milestone on the road to disaster.[275]

Collins was therefore committed to advancing Irish nationalism rather than to establishing a republic.

On 7 October letters were issued to the plenipotentiaries.

TO ALL WHOM THESE PRESENTS COME, GREETING:

In virtue of the authority vested in me by Dáil Éireann, I hereby appoint

    Arthur Griffith, TD, Minister for Foreign Affairs, Chairm.

    Michael Collins, TD, Minister for Finance

    Robert C. Barton, TD, Minister for Economic Affairs

    Edmund J. Duggan, TD

    George Gavan-Duffy, TD

As Envoys Plenipotentiary from the Elected Government of the REPUBLIC OF IRELAND to negotiate and conclude on behalf of Ireland with the representatives of his Britannic Majesty, GEORGE V, a Treaty or Treaties of Settlement, Association, and Accommodation between Ireland and the community of nations known as the British Commonwealth.

IN WITNESS WHEREOF I hereunto subscribe my name as President.

      [signed] Éamon de Valera

Done in the City of Dublin this 7th day of October in the year of our Lord 1921 in five identical originals.

While de Valera was not prepared to lead the delegation in London, this did not prevent him from attempting to direct events from Dublin. Accordingly, he drew up the following document of *instructions* that he circulated to the plenipotentiaries:

(1) The Plenipotentiaries have full powers as defined in their credentials.

(2) It is understood before decisions are finally reached on a main question, that a dispatch notifying the intention to make these decisions will be sent to members of the Cabinet in Dublin, and that a reply will be awaited by the Plenipotentiaries before final decision is made.

(3) It is also understood that the complete text of the draft treaty about to be signed will be similarly submitted to Dublin and a reply awaited.

(4) In case of a break the text of final proposals from our side will be similarly submitted.

(5) It is understood that the Cabinet in Dublin will be kept regularly informed of the progress of the negotiations. [276]

De Valera clearly intended that these instructions, particularly clauses 2 and 3, would enable him to veto any draft document that he considered unacceptable. It is also accepted that these instructions were formulated in order to placate Cathal Brugha and

Austin Stack, who were much more doctrinaire and ideological than the Irish people, who were desperately anxious for a settlement. Griffith and Collins, however, were unhappy with the limitations, and they chose to ignore these further instructions, which had not been approved by the cabinet, considering them only as guiding principles, not mandatory. There are contrasting views of these 'instructions'. A rigid interpretation is not reconcilable with the 'plenipotentiary' credentials, defined as one who is invested with the full power of independent action on behalf of the government. Since the Dáil had already conferred full plenipotentiary powers, the instructions from the cabinet, an inferior body, were not legally binding in any instance in which they limited the powers of the delegation. Brugha and Stack, however, viewed the 'instructions' as requiring the delegation in London to keep the cabinet in Dublin duly informed at every step, and not to sign the final draft without submitting it to the cabinet and awaiting a reply.[277]

There was an implicit contradiction overhanging the negotiations. Were the delegates plenipotentiaries or were they acting on instructions to report back to the cabinet? The plenipotentiary status conferred by the Dáil was superior to instructions from the cabinet. The delegates in London were not pleased with what they deemed to be interference from de Valera. In October Griffith sent a letter to de Valera saying that they were plenipotentiaries and that they were not to be instructed on all the minutiae of the negotiations.

Griffith's health being far from robust, in London he asked Collins to act as the unofficial leader of the delegation. This Collins did, and carried as much of the burden of the conference as he could. It was an unhappy delegation from the start, containing within itself the elements of unresolved tension that existed within the cabinet. From the outset, that tension worried Griffith and Collins greatly, and the fact that they had been given additional 'instructions' only added to the confusion. Griffith once said, 'We are, after all, to be plenipotentiaries'.

Harry Boland was to go to London as a secretary to the delegation along with Childers, Diarmuid O'Hegarty and Fionan Lynch, but de Valera sent him back to the US instead. He told Joe McGrath: 'I have a nice job to prepare Irish-America for a compromise'. He was 'going back to America on the President's instructions to prepare the American people for something less than a Republic'.

During the weeks leading up to the signing of the Anglo-Irish Treaty in December 1921, and the Treaty debates that followed, the precise form that a government should take was imagined and debated by different wings in Sinn Féin— from Arthur Griffith's vision for a monarchy or de Valera's concept of 'External Association' to those who were adamant that only a republic would be acceptable. All of the women TDs in the Dáil were ready to reject anything less than a republic with full independence from Britain. Tensions mounted as the delegates returned with the agreement.

De Valera continued to press his plan for External Association, but no one really knew what he wanted. 'External Association' was an impossible concept in the minds of the British negotiators. Extremist Republicans, and most TDs, saw no virtue in any kind of association with Britain. Collins simply could not see the point of it, and Griffith, though he argued strenuously for it in London, was unconvinced.[278]

At the outset of negotiations both sides were ready to compromise. The British were demoralised and under pressure at home and from international opinion. Collins knew that the Irish were out of arms, especially ammunition. Mulcahy agreed that to drive the British from anything more substantial than a police barracks was beyond them.

Lloyd George was the head of a coalition government and partially reliant on Conservatives to remain in power, as they outnumbered his Liberals both in cabinet and in the parliament. He lost his prime ministership in October 1922, and he placed much blame for that on the compromises that led to the Treaty.

After the July meetings, de Valera knew that he was not going to get a republic or 'External Association'. The best that the Irish could hope for was a self-governing dominion within the British Commonwealth. Several times he said 'We are not doctrinaire Republicans', and the Irish delegation never looked for a republic in the negotiations—their purpose was to eliminate the king from the equation.

There were three cabinet members who were delegates (Griffith, Collins and Barton) and four who remained in Dublin (de Valera, Stack, Brugha and Cosgrave). The Republican faction dominated the cabinet members in Dublin, while moderates dominated those in London.

The Irish contended that there were three main issues in the negotiations:

- Military and naval strategic interests and facilities, especially in what became known as the Treaty Ports.
- Ulster: the Irish wanted 'essential unity'.
  Partition was already in force from the Government of Ireland Act in 1920. The Treaty only confirmed it and accepted existing realities. The British had determined that Ulster would not be consulted in the negotiations.
- The Crown.
  The British felt that the Empire would 'crack' if there were no king.
  Allegiance to the Crown was a sticking point for the Irish.
  The British view was that Ireland would be inside the Commonwealth, not outside.

It was intended that if there was to be a 'break' it would be on Ulster. Sovereignty, status and the role of the king were most important to the leaders; Ulster and partition were most important to the people.

The chief mistake the Irish delegation made was to allow the two all-important issues of the Crown and Ulster to become confused. They did not sufficiently single out Ulster as the issue on which to challenge the British. This was largely because, though the unity of Ireland was more important than the issue of allegiance to most Irish citizens, the issue of allegiance was of equal importance to the minority of Republican dogmatists whom the delegates also represented.[279]

During the Treaty negotiations Collins had argued that the six-county state represented an artificial partition:

South and east Down, south Armagh, Fermanagh and Tyrone, will not come in Northern Ireland and it is unfair to ask them to come in it. We are prepared to face the problem itself—not your definition of it.

In later comments he would regret the clause which surrendered the north-east to British rule, and there is evidence that his government was certainly implicated in cross-border hostilities.[280] (See King's Inns Quay, Four Courts, Dublin 7, notes on Collins and O'Connor trading weapons to go to the North; Eaton Square, London, Assassination of Henry Wilson, Appendix VI.)

Griffith's agreement with Lloyd George in early November prevented that break on Ulster.[281] Griffith was asked in a private meeting to 'help' Lloyd George against a Conservative revolt. Griffith said that if Lloyd George would agree to a boundary commission, the Irish would not break on Ulster. None of the other delegates knew this. Griffith did not sign or initial any agreement, but he honoured his word when Lloyd George showed him the minutes of that earlier meeting near the end of the negotiations. From that point partition ceased to be a main point of contention.

In London the plenipotentiaries had seven plenary sessions, 22 sub-conferences and nine meetings of special committees. Lloyd George adapted these traditional manoeuvres of splitting the Irish delegation to suit the circumstances, realising the difficulty of coping with a united Irish delegation. He also proposed that he and Churchill meet Griffith and Collins in private conferences. Collins later gave a very unflattering impression of Lloyd George:

Lloyd George … I find to be particularly obnoxious. He is all comradely, all craft and wiliness—all arm around the shoulder … not long ago he would have had me joyfully at the rope end.

The Irish delegation was so divided that after the last cabinet meeting in Dublin on 3 December it returned to London in two groups by two different routes. Clearly it was not a delegation in which the cabinet could have confidence that it would conclude a Treaty on grounds discussed in cabinet. The intention to negotiate further is implicit in the circumstances and was explicit in the cabinet minutes. At this last cabinet meeting de Valera rejected the proposed treaty mainly on the grounds that the oath was unacceptable. Brugha said that as Collins and Griffith had been doing 'most of the negotiating' the British had selected 'their men'. Griffith was outraged, but Collins just considered that it was Brugha who said it. During a break in the meeting Collins met with Seán Ó Muirthile, who passed along the IRB's reservations, which basically concerned the oath (Collins passed along the one he had previously given to the British) and the positions that had been presented on defence and partition. When the cabinet meeting resumed, Griffith indicated that he would never break on the issue of the Crown. He said that he would not sign a Treaty but would bring it back to the Dáil. Although the discussion took several hours and many issues were discussed, the oath was the single item that aroused the most criticism. Prior to adjourning the meeting, it was decided that the delegation should return to London with the same powers and instructions. Griffith, Collins and Duggan went back to London on one boat, while Gavan Duffy, Barton and Childers travelled on another boat.

Collins said that he was confused, because de Valera had proposed an oath that was consistent with dominion status. Collins said that the proposals had been discussed again and again with the British and had been rejected, and he was not going to go over the same issues again. On their return to London the British again flatly rejected 'External Association', as Collins had predicted. Thereafter, in meetings with the British Collins attacked hard on defence and trade issues. Griffith wanted further discussion on the oath and insisted that the law and practice of the Crown in Canada should govern the action of the British in Ireland. All the arguments had been presented before and the British rejected them again.

On 5 December Lloyd George said that he had two envelopes, one of which was to be delivered to a destroyer taking it to James Craig that night. In one there was news that there would be a treaty, and the other indicated that there was no treaty. Collins said that Lloyd George threatened the Irish delegates with a renewal of 'terrible and immediate war' if the Treaty were not signed at once. Lloyd George's secretary, Geoffrey Shakespeare, said that he knew that Lloyd George was bluffing on the 'war', but that he was not bluffing that he had gone as far as he could. Referring the Treaty back to Dublin that night was not an issue: Collins, Barton and Gavan Duffy all said that they had not thought of it, and Childers wrote that he had not thought of it either. Griffith reasoned: 'I like what I see; I can accept this Treaty'. He got what he always wanted: a single king over two countries, going back to his famous articles on 'The resurrection of Hungary'. He first channelled this idea in a series of 27 articles in his newspaper *The United Irishman* in 1904.[282] Collins came around; it was a stepping-stone for him. Collins, Griffith and Barton thought that they had fulfilled their duty and signed around 2.30am that night. Gavan Duffy and Duggan signed the next morning. (It should be noted that Collins's celebrated stepping-stone argument—his admission that the Treaty conferred not freedom but the freedom to achieve freedom—also contributed to the corrosion of his revolutionary reputation in the eyes of those who opposed the Treaty because it offered not so much an inducement to recognise how much had already been achieved as a calculus for future progress.)

On 6 December 1921, 'Articles of Agreement for a Treaty'[283] were formally signed in London, and two days later the Irish cabinet met. (See Documents, Appendix VII, for full Agreement.) It has been written that Barton and Gavan Duffy signed under pressure from the other three plenipotentiaries. Duggan signed because Collins did, and Collins followed Griffith.[284] Griffith's decision to sign forced the others to their decisions. Only Griffith was absolutely sure that he was doing the right thing, and he was not a man to swerve from what he deemed to be the right course. Collins was acutely aware of the weakened military position of the IRA/Volunteers. Moreover, he was 'convinced that Ireland could not get substantially better terms and that the alternative to settlement was war and defeat'. He agonised over his decision, but in the taxi that night he announced that he was going to sign.[285] He was under no illusion about what the Treaty meant, but it was really no more or less than he had expected from the start.

On the way back from London, Collins heard that the press welcomed the Treaty.

The Treaty had been welcomed with acclaim on both sides of the Irish channel. The peace brought by the truce was secured forever. The future was bright … until de Valera repudiated the Treaty the day after it was signed and the inevitability of disharmony among their leaders occurred to the bewildered populace.[286]

The Treaty was generally welcomed by the people. The 'establishment' was massively in favour—the Catholic Church, the press, business interests, the Supreme Council of the IRB (only Liam Lynch was opposed) and the majority of the GHQ staff. The IRA rank-and-file, however, were mostly opposed. Many of those who were the most effective and active commanders in the War of Independence were opposed. The position of the IRA was: 'We are Ireland—not the people. Going back to the Rising, we represent Ireland; the people don't.'

No one defended the Treaty as the best settlement. Everyone agreed that the British had sold the Irish a pup; the question was whether the pup should be reared until it could grow teeth and take on the British.

Those in attendance at the cabinet meeting of 8 December were Barton, Brugha, Collins, Cosgrave, de Valera, Griffith, Stack, Childers and Gavan Duffy. Collins and Griffith returned from London thinking that there could be dissatisfaction over the Treaty but that de Valera would believe that the delegation had acted as he would have wanted. They were quickly disillusioned.[287] De Valera was furious and felt that the delegates had folded under pressure. Moreover, he felt personally betrayed.[288] At the end of an extremely angry six-hour meeting, Brugha, de Valera and Stack voted against the Treaty. Barton (angry, opposed in principle but honour-bound to stick to his signature), Collins, Cosgrave and Griffith voted for it. De Valera denounced the delegates for their breach of faith in failing to consult him before signing, but Barton countered by insisting that the real problem had been caused by de Valera's refusal to attend the conference.[289] De Valera said that he would resign if the Dáil accepted the Treaty, while both Griffith and Collins said that they would do the same if it were rejected. Later, de Valera told the Dáil:

> ... now I would like everybody clearly to understand that the plenipotentiaries went over to negotiate a Treaty, that they could differ from the Cabinet if they wanted to, and that in anything of consequence they could take their decision against the decision of the Cabinet.[290]

That evening de Valera issued a press statement, which he called a 'Proclamation to the Irish People', indicating that he could not recommend acceptance of the Treaty:

> The terms of this agreement are in violent conflict with the wishes of the majority of this nation, as expressed freely in successive elections during the past three years. I feel it my duty to inform you immediately that I cannot recommend the acceptance of this treaty either to Dáil Éireann or to the country. In this attitude I am supported by the Ministers of Home Affairs and Defence ... The greatest test of our people has come. Let us face it worthily without bitterness, and above all, without recrimination. There is a definite constitutional way of resolving our political differences—let us not depart from it, and let the conduct of the Cabinet in this matter be an example to the whole nation.[291]

The normal difference of opinion that was bound to result from the signing of the Treaty was immensely complicated by the fact that instead of two parties there were three: republican die-hards, moderates and de Valera.[292] The issues of the Treaty might have appeared simple enough—peace or a resumption of the war; a conceptual republic or a positive dominion status—but there were no simple questions for deputies with little political experience who were easily swayed by emotional attachments or other considerations.

On 14 December 1921 the Dáil assembled, but there was no 'debate' on the Treaty—just a discussion of the actions of the plenipotentiaries in signing the Treaty without 'permission' from the cabinet. At the start of the debates, de Valera admitted that the plenipotentiaries had *not* exceeded their powers by signing the Treaty without consulting Dublin first.[293] Immediately upon mention of the 'Treaty', Collins pointed out that no 'Treaty' had been signed but rather 'Articles of Agreement', and that the signing implied referral to their respective legislatures, not acceptance. Both the Dáil and the English House of Commons had to ratify the Articles before they would take effect.[294] He pointed out that the Irish plenipotentiaries had done nothing irrevocable: the Treaty still had to be ratified by the Dáil. (The English wasted no time in ratification, as the Articles were approved quickly by both the House of Commons and the House of Lords and received the assent of the king on 31 March 1922.)

Just as in the cabinet, the key questions in the Dáil debates were the issues of oath/republic/Crown, not partition.[295] The lack of importance attached to discussion of partition can be seen in the records of the debates: only nine pages of the public Dáil debates dealt with partition, and over 300 pages did not. Likewise, in the private debates, only three of 181 pages were devoted to partition.

The next day the Dáil assembled in private session and de Valera proposed his 'External Association'/'Document Number Two' (Collins dubbed it that, and the name stuck). It was rejected and de Valera 'withdrew' it, asking that it be held as confidential. With regard to partition, Document Number Two included the six partition clauses of the Treaty verbatim. The only difference was a declaration to the effect that 'the right of any part of Ireland to be excluded from the supreme authority of the national parliament and government' was not being recognised, but for the sake of internal peace and in order to divorce the Ulster question from the overall Anglo-Irish dispute de Valera said that he was prepared to accept the partition clauses of the Treaty, even though they provided 'an explicit recognition of the right on the part of Irishmen to secede from Ireland'.[296] When he read the document, Griffith challenged de Valera regarding 'recognition': 'Obviously, any form of association necessitates discussion of recognition in some form or another of the head of the association'. Some form of recognition of the Crown was inevitable.

On 19 December the debates continued, and de Valera and Collins stated their positions on the Treaty. Collins said:

> What I want to make clear is that it was the acceptance of the invitation that formed the compromise. I was sent there to form that adaptation, to bear the brunt of it. Now as one of the signatories of the document I naturally recommend its acceptance. I do not recommend it for more than it is. Equally I do not recommend it for less than it is. In my opinion it gives us freedom, not the ultimate freedom that all nations desire and develop to, but the freedom to achieve it.[297]

(See Documents, Appendix VII, for complete Collins speech.)

On 22 December the Dáil adjourned on the motion of Collins to reassemble on 3 January 1922. At adjournment, de Valera reiterated to the Dáil, 'There is a definite constitutional way of resolving our differences'.[298]

After the debate on 22 December, Kathleen Clarke came to visit Collins. She had spoken against the agreement and explained that if her husband Tom were alive he would not vote for it. Collins responded: 'I wouldn't ask you to vote for it. All I ask is that, if it's passed, you give us a chance to work it.'

Thereafter the debates were continued in the Convocation Hall of the National University in Earlsfort Terrace. (See Earlsfort Terrace for the progress of the Treaty debates from 3 January to 8 January 1922, including the vote of the TDs on 7 January 1922.)

On 12 January 1922 the Dáil delegates again assembled in the Oak Room of the Mansion House following the Treaty debates and vote at Earlsfort Terrace.

On 14 January only pro-Treaty TDs met to formally ratify the Treaty and to select a provisional government. Officers and ministers of the provisional government were elected as follows:

> Arthur Griffith: President.
> Michael Collins: Minister for Finance.
> William Cosgrave: Minister for Local Government.
> Éamonn Duggan: Minister for Home Affairs (replaced Austin Stack).
> Richard Mulcahy: Minister for Defence (replaced Cathal Brugha).
> Kevin O'Higgins: Minister for Economic Affairs.
> Patrick J. Hogan: Minister for Fisheries and Agriculture (replaced Art O'Connor).
> Joseph McGrath: Minister for Labour (replaced Countess Markievicz).
> Michael Hayes: Minister for Education (replaced J.J. O'Kelly).
> Desmond FitzGerald: Minister for Publicity.
> Ernest Blythe: Minister for Trade and Commerce.
> Fionan Lynch and Eoin MacNeill were added to the provisional government.
> The ministers of the Dáil became ministers of the provisional government.

On 21 February the Civic Guard, An Garda Síochána, was established. (See Merrion Road, Dublin 4.)

The draft constitution with Collins's republican ethos was ready to be examined by T.H. Healy and George O'Brien by 15 March 1922.[299] Collins chaired the committee that was established to draft the constitution, but Darrell Figgis wrote most of it. (Figgis was the deputy chairman of the committee, and he and Hugh Kennedy were the greatest contributors to it.[300]) The committee members were Collins, James Douglas, Figgis, C.P. France, Kennedy (the new Free State attorney general), James Murnahan, John O'Byrne, James O'Neill, Alfred O'Reilly and Kevin O'Shiel.[301] (See Shelbourne Hotel, St Stephen's Green North.)

On 26 March 1922 an IRA convention was held in the Mansion House.[302] Over

230 delegates attended, representing 49 brigades of the IRA and claiming to represent approximately 95,000 members of the organisation (about 80% of its membership, almost all of whom had joined after the July Truce and had never participated in the War of Independence). The meeting went forward despite the fact that Richard Mulcahy, as minister for defence, tried to avoid convening a body that was clearly anti-Treaty. Only anti-Treaty men attended the convention. It was adjourned until 9 April, when Liam Lynch was elected chairman.[303] The control of the IRA was turned over to a sixteen-man 'executive' and Liam Lynch was named chief of staff.[304] The executive also included Frank Barrett, Liam Deasy, Tom Hales, Michael Kilroy, Joe McKelvey, Liam Mellows, Seán Moylan, Joseph O'Connor, Rory O'Connor, Peadar O'Donnell, Florence O'Donoghue, Seán O'Hegarty, Ernie O'Malley, Séamus Robinson and P.J. Rutledge.[305] Working closely with the executive were Stan Dardise, Tom McGuire and Liam Pilkington. (See *Freeman's Journal*, Abbey Street, Dublin 1.) (Twelve members of the executive were in the Four Courts when it was attacked on 28 June, starting the Civil War; Liam Lynch and Liam Deasy left the building shortly before the attack and were arrested but then released because Mulcahy hoped that they would be an influence for peace.) The executive demanded that the recruitment for the Civic Guard and the Free State army, both headquartered at Beggar's Bush Barracks in Ballsbridge, cease immediately. On 9 April this convention of the IRA narrowly rejected a proposal for a Republican military dictatorship. The executive then appointed an army council: Liam Lynch (chief of staff), Joseph McKelvey (deputy chief of staff), Florence O'Donoghue (adjutant-general), Ernie O'Malley (director of organisation), Joseph Griffin (director of intelligence), Liam Mellows (quartermaster general), Rory O'Connor (director of engineering), Séamus O'Donovan (director of chemicals) and Seán Russell (director of ammunition).

On 26 April a Labour Party conference was held here, convened by Dr Edward Joseph Byrne, archbishop of Dublin, Lord Mayor O'Neill and Stephen O'Mara of Limerick. William O'Brien,[306] Tom Johnson[307] and Cathal O'Shannon were among those who attended. The conference made proposals to all parties for a return to the Dáil's sovereignty, the unification of the army, the establishment of a police force under civilian control and a revised electoral register. It proposed a meeting between Arthur Griffith and Collins, de Valera and Brugha and the Republican Army executive, but Collins refused to attend. As soon as the conference began, Griffith advocated a prompt general election, but de Valera demurred in order to have more time.[308] The conference broke down on 29 April because of de Valera's refusal to consider anything less than a further postponement of the election for six months, 'to allow a fresh register and the cooling down of the people's panic'.

On 4 May 1922 a conference was held between the Free State army leaders and the IRA/Republicans. The two factions declared a truce to last while the conference continued, and then an open-ended truce was agreed upon. The objective was to try to reunify the army and avert a civil war. Collins, Seán MacEoin, Richard Mulcahy, Eoin O'Duffy, Diarmuid O'Hegarty and Gearóid O'Sullivan represented the Free State army. Liam Lynch, Liam Mellows, Seán Moylan, Rory O'Connor and Séamus Robinson represented the IRA/Republicans. The parties presented conflicting reports to the Dáil on 16 May.

On 20 May 1920 there was a meeting (proposed by Seán T. O'Kelly the night before) between Collins and de Valera to discuss the election. O'Kelly, Rich Mulcahy, Harry Boland and John Chartres joined the meeting later, and the group agreed on a united panel of candidates in the ratio of their existing strength, and that they would form a coalition government in which there would be an election for president and a cabinet elected in the normal fashion. Harry Boland must be given credit for pushing the parties to an agreement. In short, the Treaty would not be an election issue at all between the members of Sinn Féin.[309]

On 20 May 1922 the Collins–de Valera Election Pact was agreed;[310] it was ratified by the Dáil on 23 May and provided:

(1) That a National Coalition panel for this Third Dáil, representing both parties in the Dáil and in the Sinn Féin Organization, be sent forward, on the ground that the national position requires the entrusting of the Government of the country into the joint hands of those who have been the strength of the national situation during the last few years, without prejudice to their present respective positions.

(2) That this Coalition panel be sent forward as from the Sinn Féin Organization, the number for each party being their present strength in the Dáil.

(3) That the candidates be nominated through each of the existing party executives.

(4) That every and any interest is free to go up and contest the election equally with the National Sinn Féin panel.

(5) That the constituencies where an election is not held shall continue to be represented by their present Deputies.

(6) That after the election the Executive shall consist of the President, elected as formerly; the Minister for Defence, representing the Army; and nine other Ministers—five from the majority party and four from the minority, each party to choose its own nominees. The allocation will be at the hands of the President.

(7) That in the event of the Coalition government finding it necessary to dissolve, a General Election will be held as soon as possible on adult suffrage.[311]

The Pact in essence provided for an election that would take the Treaty out of consideration and elect the third Dáil in succession to the first two rather than to the provisional government. John Regan argues:

The agreement suited de Valera in that it afforded him an opportunity to regroup and campaign and it postponed a looming and potentially devastating electoral defeat. The agreement was crucial for the Provisional Government in that it gave them breathing space to produce a constitution that if sufficiently republican in tone could draw the teeth of militant republicanism and avoid civil war. Deferral of the vote also afforded time to publicise the benefits of the Treaty, not least of which was the very public departure of British troops, and above all it gave them a chance to rebuild the machinery of state, including the new Civic Guard and the new Free State Army.[312]

According to this agreement, both strands of Sinn Féin would contest the election as one party and not oppose each other. In an attempt to portray some semblance of democracy, other parties were not excluded from contesting the election, although it was hoped that other parties, such as Labour, would not put candidates forward. Thomas Johnson, leader of the Labour Party, alluded to this in a letter to his son:

> there was a pact between De Valera and Collins by which a free election was guaranteed but the two parties were not to oppose each other. There was a clause inserted however which said that all parties were free to act if they so chose, but it was evidently hoped by De Valera, and perhaps by Collins, that no one would enter the ring [...] However we [the Labour Party] concluded that we had stood down long enough, and we nominated eighteen men.[313]

Griffith was shaken by the Pact. He believed that by signing the agreement Collins had sold out to de Valera. The warm friendship that had developed between Griffith and Collins ended. From then on, Griffith addressed him as 'Mr Collins', not as 'Mick'.

> The only clear recollection I have of any feeling shown by Griffith was when Collins agreed to the Pact election. Griffith was totally against it and I was present when he tried to prevail on Michael Collins to abandon the idea. But Collins had given his word and believed the arrangement would be successful and would bring about a reconciliation between the parties. Therefore, in spite of his eloquent pleading Griffith failed to divert Collins from his purposes. I was not present at any other discussion on the question of the Pact election so I do not know what other influence, if any, was brought to bear on Michael Collins.[314]

It wasn't just Griffith who was dismayed—most of the cabinet disagreed with the Pact. Ernest Blythe related how the meeting ended:

We all realized if Griffith said 'no', a split, the consequences of which could hardly be foreseen, would almost be upon us. On the other hand, I think the majority of us almost wished that he would say no, in the hope that Collins would be forced to reconsider his support of the Pact. Ultimately, however, Griffith said 'I agree' and made no further comment.[315]

On 14 June, in Cork, Collins repudiated the Pact, saying 'I am not hampered now by being on a platform where there are Coalitionists. I can make a straight appeal to you—to the citizens of Cork, vote for the candidates you think best. The country must have the representatives it wants. You understand fully what you have to do and I call on you to do it.'[316] This statement ripped the Pact apart, producing political turmoil just before polling day. Collins's clear breach of the Pact so enraged some anti-Treatyites in the crowd that they started shooting revolvers in the air.[317] Liam Deasy wrote that the speech 'blighted all hope of unity'.[318] Why Collins broke the Pact as he did is a subject of debate. One theory is that it was a politically astute move from the first, and that Collins only associated himself with the Pact because he needed its support and apparent unity to further his own image. Another theory is that he had come to the conclusion (fostered by the British) that the Pact would not work in any case and decided to disassociate himself from it. Churchill had summoned him to London regarding the Pact, and Collins may have repudiated it to placate British concerns about the draft constitution.[319]

On 15 June 1922 the Constitution was published. The next day a general election was held. The turnout was just less than 60%, as 620,283 votes were cast, and the results were announced on 24 June. The pro-Treaty party received 239,193 votes and 58 of its members were elected to the Dáil as TDs. The anti-Treaty party (Cumann na Poblachta) received 133,864 votes and a representation of only 36 TDs. Seventeen TDs were elected for the Labour Party, seven for the Farmers Party, six Independents and four TDs for Trinity College. Anti-Treatyites won only five of 44 seats in Leinster and did poorly in Ulster and in Cork city. Connacht produced a small anti-Treaty majority and Munster a small pro-Treaty majority. A total of 466,419 electors voted for the Treaty and 133,864 against.[320] The anti-Treaty candidates would have done considerably worse had there not been an election panel, pursuant to the Collins–de Valera Pact. A more open election would undoubtedly have caused further losses to the anti-Treatyites, yet it would have hurt the pro-Treaty candidates as well: there is evidence that anti-Treatyites voted for the pact more consistently than did Treaty supporters.

The election was notable for the large anti-Sinn Féin vote. It was not an example of perfect democracy: the election was held against a backdrop of the British threat to return to war. Nor did it entirely represent a vote of confidence in the provisional government, and still less an expression of resistance to republican ideals. It represented a popular realisation of the need for stable government, and the acceptance of realistic compromise with regard to Anglo-Irish relations. Settled conditions were more important to the electorate than the endless debate over constitutional authority.[321] In essence, the election played an important role in legitimising the Treaty and the status of the provisional government. Although it did not prevent the Civil War, it greatly helped to facilitate the establishment of the Free State government during and after the war.

Prominent anti-Treaty TDs who were defeated included Constance Markievicz, Seán Etchingham, Art O'Connor, Erskine Childers, Liam Mellows, Séamus Robinson, Kathleen Clarke, Margaret Pearse, Domhnall Ó Buachalla[322] (later the last governor-general—*seánaschal*—of the Irish Free State) and Dr James Ryan.

On 18 June 1922 an Extraordinary Convention of the Irish Republican Army was held. Tom Barry suggested an immediate attack on the British.[323] A majority of the executive was in favour of this. Cathal Brugha opposed the suggestion, as did Liam Lynch, Liam Deasy, Frank Barrett and Seán Moylan. The twelve who favoured the action were subsequently in the Four Courts as the Civil War began, repudiated the authority of Liam Lynch and appointed Joe McKelvey chief of staff.

On 12 July a 'War Council' was appointed, composed of Collins, Mulcahy and Eoin O'Duffy, to command the Free State army. Collins resigned as head of the provisional government, and thereafter acted as army O/C only. The cabinet did not force Collins into this. In fact, he believed that the top priority of the provisional government was to conclude the war as quickly as possible, and he felt that he was the best man to accomplish this.

The first session of the Third Dáil was convened on 9 September 1922. It met in Leinster House in Kildare Street, where the Dáil meets to this day. The Third Dáil was never 'accepted' by the Republicans, and the Second Dáil remains the 'provisional government' of Ireland according to strict Republican doctrine.

2 Dawson Street: Briefly Irish Volunteer HQ in 1914, but prior to the Rising their HQ moved to Great Brunswick Street.

The *Irish Volunteer* was printed here, edited by Eoin MacNeill. It was a very successful recruiting and propaganda tool used by separatists, and its philosophy carried over after the Rising. In an early issue Patrick Pearse wrote: 'We want recruits because we are absolutely determined to take action, the moment action becomes a duty ...'.[324] P.S. O'Hegarty was a member of the supreme council of the IRB from 1908 until he was deported to Wales in August 1914. He wrote: 'The Insurrection of 1916 came because the Supreme Council of the Irish Republican Brotherhood decided that it would come ... It was the Supreme Council of the IRB which decided the Insurrection, planned it, organized it, led it and financed it.'[325]

The *Irish Volunteer* was suppressed and subsequently reissued by a pro-Unionist printer in Belfast. The last issue was dated 22 April 1916, two days before the Rising.

It was said that the Orangemen of Belfast were 'not loyal to the Crown so much as to the half-crown' and they would always print whatever was sent to them with payment.

21 Dawson Street: Home of Eileen McGrane, a lecturer at the National University (now UCD). Collins, Arthur Griffith and others came here from time to time for meetings at a small room in the centre of the flat. It was a part-time office for Collins and Ernie O'Malley during the War of Independence.

> Shortly after I took my flat at 21, Dawson St. which was shared by Mary McCarthy and Margot Trench, the Republican government headquarters seemed to have great difficulty in getting suitable rooms for their work. I offered to Michael Collins the use of a small room in the centre of the flat which he was very glad to accept. Of course there was no question of rent. He put into it some office furniture and files of various kinds were deposited in the office. No official personnel were located there. Mick Collins, Tom Cullen, Arthur Griffith and others came from time to time for conferences or to collect or deposit papers. The principals had a key to the door of the flat and access to the key to the office which was in my custody. The only servant we employed was a cleaner, Mrs McCluskey, whose husband was caretaker in the National Land Bank. He often did guard on the Street outside when Mick Collins came to the office and on one occasion at least gave warning of a raid in the neighbourhood.[326]

The house was raided on 31 December 1920. McGrane was imprisoned in Mountjoy Prison, then sent to Walton Prison in Liverpool and subsequently returned to Mountjoy.

A whole bundle of Collins's documents was found in that raid, after he foolishly left them here. These included many of the documents taken from Dublin Castle and those of the 'G' Division, as well as the DMP headquarters daybook that he had carried away from his raid on Great Brunswick Street. It demonstrated one of Collins's weaknesses: he hated to part with files, even when they ceased to be useful, and he never took sufficient precautions to ensure that the people referred to in the files could not be identified. This was the first intimation the Castle had received of the effectiveness of Collins's recruitment within their own ranks, and they began a long process of elimination that led them to Éamon (Ned) Broy. Some documents traced to Broy were found here, leading to his arrest. (See Arbour Hill Prison, Dublin 7.)

McGrane was taken to Dublin Castle, where she was interrogated by Ormond Winter. He was sure that she would talk to him but she spoke not a single word in one and a half hours.[327]

56–58 Dawson Street: Hodges & Figgis Books, associated with Darrell Figgis. Susan

Left—On 1 April 1919 a private session of the First Dáil was held. Richard Mulcahy (seen here on the left) was Minister for Defence from January to April, when he became Assistant Minister under Cathal Brugha. Collins was named Minister for Finance.

Right—Collins pictured at the Gresham Hotel. On Christmas Eve 1920, Collins, Gearóid O'Sullivan, Rory O'Connor and Tom Cullen met here to celebrate. The private dining room that Collins had arranged was not available, so they took a table in the public dining room. A raid by Auxiliaries took Collins to the cloakroom, where he was 'compared' with his 'official' photo. Collins had an Ordnance Survey map in his pocket with the words '6 rifles' in the corner, but he convinced the officer that it was 'Refills' and he was let go.

Left—While he was in London Collins met Frank Thornton (left). They first met when they both played in a hurling match in Liverpool on the day World War I was declared.

Left—Frank Thornton was one of Collins's most important intelligence contacts. He was an old friend, and Collins trusted him with the most dangerous and demanding assignments.

Left—Paddy Daly was one of the leaders of the Squad, along with Mick McDonnell. During the Civil War, Daly was the O/C in County Kerry and was responsible for one of the most reprehensible revenge killings of that war at Ballyseedy Cross. (Image from Military Archives.)

Below—(L–R) Joe Leonard, Paddy Daly, Charlie Dalton and Bill Stapleton. Collins's Squad was a group of ruthless guerrilla fighters. It was not the least of his gifts that he knew how to select efficient operators, and though they were on the run from mid-1919 they often dined together in Dublin's restaurants.

Above—Collins with two of his key men, Tom Cullen (L) and Liam Tobin (R). Cullen and Tobin were both members of Collins's intelligence staff, and he saw them almost daily.

Left—Emmet Dalton and his younger brother Charlie became trusted confidants and operatives for Collins. Charlie (R) was a member of the Squad, and Emmet, who had served in World War I as a member of the British Army, became a member of Collins's protection detail in London and a general in the Free State army.

DUBLIN: SATURDAY, FEBRUARY 5, 1921

M.F.P. CORPORAL SHOT

Killed in Dublin Publichouse
This Morning

SEARCHES FOLLOW TRAGEDY

Above—The Cairo Gang. These British intelligence agents were recruited and had but one mission: find and eliminate Collins. They were not to go near the Castle but to report to Colonel Ormonde Winter daily at either the Cairo Café or Kidd's Buffet restaurant. They called themselves the Cairo group; the Squad called them the 'Cairo gang'.

Left—Pub owned by Thomas Hynes. John (Shankers) Ryan, the one who betrayed Peadar Clancy and Dick McKee on the night before Bloody Sunday, was killed outside the pub on 5 February 1921. Ryan was the brother of Becky Cooper, one of Dublin's best-known madams.

Above—Black and Tans outside the pub after Shankers Ryan was killed. Bill Stapleton described the killing: 'About 10.30 o'clock on the morning of the 5th February, 1921, our Intelligence Officer located Ryan in Hynes's public house … Before doing the job we held him up and searched him but he had no guns or papers on him. I think we said, "You are Ryan", and I think he rejoined, "Yes, and what about it" or words to that effect. With that we shot him.'

Left—Dan Breen (seated, front row) and Seán Hogan were involved in the Soloheadbeg ambush on 21 January 1919, considered the 'start' of the War of Independence. After he was wounded in an ambush at Ashtown in December 1919, Breen was taken to the Malone home, where he met Brighid (seated, front row). He married her on 12 June 1921, with Collins and many of the IRA/Volunteers in attendance.

In the Custom House fire, five Volunteers were killed: Tommy Dorrins, Seán Doyle, Dan Head, Capt. Paddy O'Reilly and sixteen-year-old Lt Stephen O'Reilly (brothers). Two civilians were killed: Francis Davis, caretaker of the building, who resisted the Volunteers, and Mahon Lawless, who was mistaken for a Volunteer by the Tans.

Piaras Béaslaí wrote in *An tÓglach*: 'The burning of the Custom House symbolised the final collapse of English civil administration in this country'.

Above—After the Truce, Collins attended matches at Croke Park with Paddy Daly (beside Collins), who was a member of the Free State Army, and his friend Harry Boland (behind Daly). Following the Treaty, Boland took the anti-Treaty side, and since he was also a suitor for Kitty Kiernan their friendship was broken.

Left—Collins and Kitty Kiernan (pictured) got engaged on 8 October 1921, just before Collins went to London for the Treaty negotiations. On 14 October, Kitty wrote: 'you are everything to me and surely you know it'.

Killeen worked here; she was one of Collins's most valuable couriers and 'the Bookshop' became a veritable post office for messages to and from Collins.

Denzille Lane: Batty Hyland's garage. Batty and his brother Joe were among Collins's regular drivers.

I joined the Volunteers sometime in 1917, when they were being reorganised following the release of prisoners from English Jails and Internment Camps. I was not attached to any Battalion. At the time I was running a hackney business in the city and it was on that account that I first became attached to the Transport Section of GHQ. It was through the late Joseph O'Reilly that both myself and my brother Batty came to know Michael Collins. From the time that I got to know Collins my car was extensively used by the Headquarters staff for various jobs. I garaged my car at the Southern Garage in Denzille Lane. Whenever I was wanted for any particular job I was notified by Joe O'Reilly, Tom Cullen or Tom Keogh.

... At the time that there was a heavy price on the head of Michael Collins I drove him one night from Palmerstown Park, from the house of Phil Sayers, who was at that time in the Motion Picture Line. I was taking Collins to Mountjoy Street. He told me to drive him through the back streets. This I refused to do, as I always held it was best to keep to the main streets. Going up Capel Street a British Military patrol turned out of Britain Street and ran down towards the car with their rifles at the 'ready'. When I saw the patrol approaching me I slowed down and the next thing I heard was the rear door of my car opening and closing quickly. I thought at the time that Collins had jumped out of the car and ran up Mary's Lane. The officer in charge of the patrol asked me who my passenger was. I told him I didn't know. He was an ordinary passenger as far as I was concerned. While the officer was questioning me I saw to my amazement that Michael Collins was standing by the car. The officer ordered the two of us to be searched and as he found nothing on us we were let go. I said to Collins when I reached my destination that it was a very narrow escape. He said 'little does that officer know what he has let slip through his fingers'.

... On many nights on which I drove Michael Collins to different places in the city I was the last to know where he would be stopping for that night. I have heard him tell Seán Ó Muirthuille and others of his colleagues that he intended to stay in a certain place and when I parted with him it would be at a totally different address that he would put up for the night. At that particular time it must be remembered that there was a price of £10,000 on the head of Michael Collins. Once I became associated with Michael Collins I was used extensively by him to be at his command whenever he wanted me or wanted anything done.[328]

The IRA/Volunteers had a 'munitions factory' here in which they manufactured 'bombs'—mostly hand grenades. The Squad used 'littlers' (young boys) to deliver these to them so that they wouldn't be caught carrying them. They were most effectively used when thrown into Black and Tan lorries.

Dublin Castle: Construction began in 1204 by order of King John. The entrance used to be on Castle Street, but the main route is now on Lord Edward Street. The statue of 'Justice' is above the old Castle Gate; small holes are drilled in her scales to drain water so that they don't become 'unbalanced' in the rain. An old Irish rhyme runs:

> The Statue of Justice
> Mark well her station,
> Her face to the Castle
> And her arse to the Nation.

Sir James McMahon was director of the Posts and Telegraphs Office here in 1918–19. He called in Nancy O'Brien, Collins's second cousin, who worked in the Post Office. He told her that the management knew of her dedication and work and wanted to promote her within the department. He explained that they knew that Collins had information even before the officers to whom it was sent received it. Because of her abilities he was going to hire her to decode messages in his office. When he heard that she had been given the job, Collins said, 'Well, Christ, I don't know how they've held their empire for so long. What a bloody intelligence service they have.' Nancy had moved to London at the same time as Collins in 1906, and they were always very close. As a spy she was invaluable to him, and she would often spend her lunchtime in the ladies' toilet copying papers to give to him later. Once, when Collins berated her for not finding a message that he was particularly interested in, she turned on him angrily. Later that night he went to her home in Glasnevin and apologised, leaving a present of her favourite 'bull's-eye' candies for her. On one occasion, when she was going to Cork because her father had passed away, Collins asked her to complete a mission for him: to carry in her luggage a load of guns that had just come in from England. Nancy had a policeman help her with the very heavy case. She married Johnny Collins (Michael's brother) after Johnny's first wife died in January 1921, leaving eight children.

One of Collins's best sources was Head Constable Peter Folan, who worked in the Castle.

I got acquainted with Michael Collins when he was home on holidays from London. My brother-in-law, Michael Barrett, was a constable stationed at Clonakilty and was very friendly with the Collins family, especially with Mrs

Collins O'Driscoll and her husband, who was a free-lance reporter on one of the Cork papers. I used to visit them and thus met Michael Collins.

... Some time in 1918 a Galway friend of mine, Michael McHugh, who was a compositor in the *Freeman's Journal*, and Seán Ó Muirthile, whom I had not known before, sent for me to come to McHugh's house in Manor Street. Some years previously—in 1915—I had been discussing with McHugh my position in Dublin Castle which I was anxious to resign, although there was no other employment open to me. McHugh, who described himself as being in the 'inner circle' of the national movement, advised me to stay in the job, as I could be useful to them if I kept my mouth shut and did not discuss anything with anybody in the Castle ... He said they had others working for them there, but did not tell me who they were. They asked me what I could do for them in the way of getting information, copies of documents, etc. Of course I promised and did ...

... I took out copies of secret documents. My method was to take shorthand notes of the documents on the files, translate them into longhand and pass the translations to them. I had various friends through whom I sent them. On one occasion, I cannot remember the date, the military had collected the names of all the IRA on the North side of the city. The list ran into several pages. The military were to arrest everyone on the list that night between 12 o'clock and dawn. Knowing that I would not be able to give a complete list, I brought the file home with me inside my shirt. I then communicated with Father Paddy Flanagan in Aughrim Street. He gave us the loan of his room and we got a few typewriters and copied the whole list. Father Flanagan had a couple of girls to type it. In the meantime a number of friends were summoned and they went around to every address warning the Volunteers to be out of their houses that night. The next morning I left the file back in its place. There was hell to pay in the Castle. The military had gone out in their lorries; they visited the nests but the birds had flown. Of course General Tudor and the higher ranking officers could not understand how it had happened that they found no one and they concluded that there must be a leakage.

I was never suspected. I was very cautious and knew how far I could go.

... One night there was a raid on Michael Collins's place in Mountjoy Square. The Auxiliaries had surrounded the place even before he knew it and while they were knocking at the door he went upstairs and out on the roof. That was easy because there were skylights. Apparently going along the roofs he escaped down to the street. I heard he was out on the street among the spectators watching the Auxiliaries raid the house. Next morning, as I was going in to my work in the Castle, I was overtaken by my friend Michael McHugh, who told me the incident of the night before, and said that Michael Collins would be ever so grateful if I could recover for him the five parabellum revolvers (Automatics) that had been taken. I went into the office where all the stuff that was seized during the night was left on the tables. ... I located the sack containing the parabellums, mixed with a lot of documents, etc. I took out the five parabellums, put them into my pockets, I put back the label on the sack and came down to the RIC department where there was a room, seldom or never used, containing old papers. I put the revolvers under a heap of the loose papers. I went back to the room with an innocent face and sat down to my work translating documents. When the Staff Officers, Colonels and Majors, came in after ten o'clock they began to examine the contents of the sacks. Soon there was a furore when it was found that the captured guns were missing. They came to the conclusion that it was the Black and Tans who had been in the raiding party that had pinched them.[329]

Captains William Lorraine King and Jocelyn Lee Hardy led the intelligence officers in the Castle during the War of Independence.[330] (Hardy had lost a leg in France and his gait earned him the nickname of 'Hoppy' Hardy.) They beat Christopher Carbury and made him drink his own blood. They beat Ernie O'Malley unconscious; he gave them the name Bernard Stewart but yielded no other information. Their mock threats of summary execution happened regularly and sometimes went so far as to ask the prisoner for a last statement.

It was King and Hardy who interrogated Peadar Clancy, Dick McKee and Conor Clune on Bloody Sunday and murdered them while 'trying to escape'.[331] The director of British Intelligence, Sir Ormonde Winter, interrogated each prisoner separately, and they were then turned over to King and Hardy. (Hardy and King were on the IRA hit list for the following morning but escaped because they were still in the Castle interrogating prisoners. See 91 Lower Leeson Street: Eastwood Hotel.) On Saturday night a large number of Volunteers were arrested in British army raids. When news arrived at the Castle the next morning of the deaths of the intelligence officers, Winter ordered all the prisoners off to different barracks, but McKee, Clancy and Clune were held back for further 'questioning'. At 11am the three men were executed. The official Dublin Castle communique stated that they had been shot while attempting to escape, producing staged photographs as 'proof'. The extent of the torture to which McKee and Clancy had been subjected was evident later, when their bodies were identified in the King George V Hospital by Molly O'Reilly, who swore that they both had bayonet wounds.[332] William Pearson, an ex-colonel in the British army and a doctor, accompanied Edward McLysaght to the King George V Hospital to identify Clune's body. On examination of the thirteen wounds on the corpse, Pearson believed that these 'could not have been inflicted if Clune had been trying to escape'.[333]

Of the killings in the Castle, Gen. F.P. Crozier, O/C of the Auxiliaries, wrote:

The evidence before the military inquiry, which enquired into these deaths, was faked from beginning to end, evidence being given by the police that the unarmed and closely guarded men attempted to 'overpower' the guard (in a guard room inside 'The Castle' which was itself closely guarded) in an attempt to 'escape'. Anything 'did' for a paper acquittal then because Parliament accepted anything willingly as an explanation.[334]

In January 1921, another group of British intelligence officers—the Igoe Gang— arrived in Dublin; headquartered in the Castle, they were tasked with getting Collins. Named after their leader, Head Constable Eugene Igoe from Galway, they gradually began to play a very significant role. Following Bloody Sunday, the greatest threat to Collins was this 'Gang'.

Dublin at this time was anything but a peaceful city. The Dublin Brigade were carrying out ambushes practically every day, despite the fact that the British military were patrolling the streets in armoured cars, Lancia cars and also a foot patrol extended across the roads. To add to this concentration of forces a new menace appeared on the scene. These were grange [sic] of RIC drawn from different parts of the country under the leadership of Chief Constable Igoe. They wore civilian clothes, were heavily armed and moved along the footpaths on both sides of the road looking out for either city men whom they might know or Volunteers up from the country. They were not easy to deal with because they suddenly appeared at most unexpected places and, despite several attempts, our men never got really into action against the gang proper.[335]

The 'Gang' walked around the city heavily armed, often tailing IRA/Volunteers, unexpectedly dropping into pubs and shops and generally making a nuisance of themselves.

Igoe was an RIC man who hailed from the west of Ireland. Around him, the Castle authorities formed a group of RIC men who were selected from different parts of the country—especially those who had a good knowledge of the active officers of the IRA, wanted by the British. Their routine was to visit different railway termini as trains were arriving or departing, and to see if any wanted men were travelling. If they happened to capture any such men, well, it was a gamble whether they ever lived to tell what had happened to them. The usual report would appear—'shot while trying to escape'.

This gang adopted the same procedure as did the squad. They moved along in pairs, on each side of the street or road, with a distance of a yard or two between each pair. So you will understand that it was going to be a very heavy operation to get the lot of them. Igoe and his gang had been moving around for a little while, when one day they picked up a Volunteer, named Newell, who was from the west, and who, before being picked up, was in touch with the Intelligence staff and hoped to be able to point out Igoe. Up to this time, we had no description of what he looked like.

... Igoe, himself, or the remainder of the gang, were never got.[336]

Despite some assertions to the contrary, the Squad never did 'get' Igoe or any of his men. After the Truce, Igoe seems to have left Ireland and never returned for fear of reprisal.

The Castle was formally handed over to Collins and the Free State forces on 16 January 1922 by Edmund Bernard FitzAlan-Howard, 1st Viscount FitzAlan of Derwent, KG, PC, lord lieutenant of Ireland, who said, 'I am glad to see you, Mr Collins'. Collins is reported to have replied, 'Like hell ye are!' The British O/C was Gen. Nevil Macready. Collins arrived late for his meeting with him. To Macready's comment that he was 'seven minutes late', Collins supposedly replied, 'You've been here seven centuries, what bloody difference does seven minutes make now that you're leaving?'

The handing over of Dublin Castle represented, physically and symbolically, the end of British domination in Ireland. For many nationalists it was the epoch-marking event in the long struggle against British rule. Batt O'Connor, a pro-Treaty close personal friend of Collins, wrote a letter to his sister describing the day:

I witnessed the greatest event in all my life the day I stood amongst a crowd of sightseers at Dublin Castle and beheld Michael Collins accompanied by his other Ministers drive in to the Upper Castle Yard in their swell Autos to take the surrender of Dublin Castle. I wonder can you picture my feelings, joy and gratification in seeing the man above all others who laid the plans to break the power of this same castle, politely walk in and take over its power and all it stood for. No matter what ever may become of me now and no matter what I have mislaid and suffered . . . I am repaid a thousand times over to witness what I saw taking place that never to-be-forgotten day at Dublin Castle. As Michael stepped out of the door of the Castle after finishing the job he stepped into his car with three more ministers. He beheld me in the crowd and beckoned me over to the car, opened the door, shook my hand and insisted that I should sit beside him and amongst thunders of cheers our cars drove out through the multitude.[337]

2 Duke Street: The Bailey pub; upstairs was the smoking room, where Parnell and his followers were wont to meet. A haunt for barristers and solicitors from the Four Courts and surrounding area, it was a particular favourite of Oliver St John Gogarty.

It was also a meeting place for the IRA/Volunteers during the War of Independence.

Arthur Griffith frequented this pub and in 1922, when the ministers of the Free State were virtual prisoners in the Castle, he had food imported from the Bailey.

21 Duke Street: Davy Byrne's pub; frequented by Collins and Arthur Griffith, and later by Brendan Behan and Padraic O'Connor.

Earlsfort Terrace (at corner of Hatch Street): University College Dublin (UCD). Founded in 1851 as the Catholic University of Ireland on St Stephen's Green, it became a constituent college of the National University of Ireland. UCD is now located at Belfield, Dublin 4.

Kevin Barry enrolled at UCD in the autumn of 1919 to study medicine. He joined a UCD Volunteer contingent that included Frank Flood, Tom Kissane and Mark Robinson. They were all involved in the Church Street ambush. Flood was hanged on 14 March 1921 for 'high treason'. (See Church Street, Monk's Dairy, North Circular Road/Mountjoy Prison, Dublin 7.)

The 'Treaty Debates' began in the Mansion House in Dawson Street on 19 December 1921. (See Dawson Street/Mansion House.) The Dáil assembled and Éamon de Valera's 'Document No. Two' was derided by Arthur Griffith and Seán Milroy. Griffith moved that the Treaty be ratified and Seán MacEoin seconded the motion. The next day the debate continued; de Valera remarked that 'Something else besides the Treaty came from Downing Street'.[338] (See Dawson Street.)

On 21 December 1921 the Dáil adjourned on the motion of Collins to reassemble on 3 January 1922. The debates resumed on that date and continued for five days here in the Convocation Hall of the National University of Ireland.[339] Prior to the close of the last Mansion House session, de Valera addressed the Dáil and said:

> I would like my last word here to be this: we have had a glorious record for four years; it has been four years of magnificent discipline in our nation. The world is looking at us now.[340]

The Christmas break was crucial to the debates; the TDs went home and encountered pressures for peace. But tempers worsened after the break.

Though there was disagreement over the lack of a named 'Republic', dominion status versus 'External Association' and Ulster partition, the primary disagreement was over the oath required in the Treaty:

> I ... do solemnly swear true faith and allegiance to the Constitution of the Irish Free State as by law established and that I will be faithful to HM George V, his heirs and successors by law, in virtue of the common citizenship of Ireland and

Great Britain and her adherence to and membership of the group of nations forming the British Commonwealth of Nations.[341]

De Valera proposed an oath along the following lines in 'Document No. 2':

I ... swear true faith and allegiance to the Constitution of Ireland and to the Treaty of Association of Ireland with the British Commonwealth of Nations and to recognise the King of Great Britain as head of the Association.[342]

(However, Colm Ó Murchada, the acting secretary to the cabinet, made this official note of the oath that de Valera had proposed earlier:

I ... do solemnly swear true faith and allegiance to the constitution of the Irish Free State, to the Treaty of Association and to recognise the King of Great Britain as head of the Associated States.[343])

In London on 30 November Collins had proposed the following oath:

I ... do solemnly swear to bear true faith and allegiance to the Constitution of the Irish Free State as by law established and that I will be faithful to His Majesty King George V in acknowledgment of the Association of Ireland in a common citizenship with Great Britain and the group of nations known as the British commonwealth.[344]

That oath was not acceptable to either de Valera or the British.

On 7 January 1922 the Dáil voted 64–57 to ratify the Treaty. A total of 122 TDs answered the roll for the day, but Eoin MacNeill (who would have voted in favour), as chairman, did not vote. Frank Drohan resigned, as he was unwilling to vote for the Treaty but did not want to flout the will of his constituents and vote against it. Tom Kelly (who would have voted in favour) was too ill to attend. Laurence Ginnell (who would have voted against) did not attend, as he was in Argentina. Five TDs represented more than one constituency (Collins, de Valera, Griffith, Liam Mellows, Milroy) but all cast only one ballot, even though Griffith objected strenuously to such multiple constituencies being 'disenfranchised'.

It was an afternoon meeting, beginning at 4.00pm, and voting began at 8.35pm, with Diarmuid O'Hegarty calling the roll, continuing until 9.00pm. Those who voted for the Treaty were:

Robert Barton, Piaras Béaslaí, Ernest Blythe, Patrick Brennan, Éamon (Frank) Bulfin, Séamus Burke, C.M. Byrne, Thomas Carter, Michael Collins, Richard

Corish, Philip B. Cosgrave, William T. Cosgrave, John Crowley, Liam De Roiste, James Derham, James N. Dolan, George Gavan Duffy, Éamonn J. Duggan, Desmond FitzGerald, Paul Galligan, Arthur Griffith, Seán Hales, Dr Richard Hayes, Michael Hayes, Seán Hayes, William Hayes, P.J. Hogan, Peter Hughes, Andrew Lavin, Frank Lawless, Seán Leddy, Fionan Lynch, Joseph Lynch, Joseph MacBride, Alex McCabe, Dr Patrick McCartan, Daniel McCarthy, Seán MacEoin, Seán McGarry, Dr J.P. McGinley, P.J. McGoldrick, Joseph McGrath, Joseph McGuinness, Justin McKenna, Seán Milroy, Richard Mulcahy, James Murphy, George Nicolls, Thomas O'Donnell, Eoin O'Duffy, John O'Dwyer, Kevin O'Higgins, Padraig O'Keefe, Padraig Ó Maille, Daniel O'Rourke, Gearóid O'Sullivan, Lorcan Robbins, William Sears, Michael Staines, Joseph Sweeney, James J. Walsh, Peter Ward, J.B. Whelehan, Dr Vincent White.

Those who voted against the Treaty were:

E. Aylward, Harry Boland, Cathal Brugha, Daniel Buckley, Frank Carty, Erskine Childers, Kathleen Clarke, M.P. Colivet, Conor Collins, Daniel Corkery, Dr Seán Crowley, Dr Brian Cusack, Éamon Dee, Thomas Derrigg, Éamon de Valera, James Devins, Séamus Doyle, Dr Ada English, Seán Etchingham, Frank Fahy, Dr Frank Ferran, James Fitzgerald Jr, Thomas Hunter, David Kent, James Lennon, Joseph MacDonagh, Seán MacEntee, Thomas McGuire, Mary MacSwiney, Seán MacSwiney, Countess Constance Markievicz, Liam Mellows, P.J. Moloney, Seán Moylan, Charles Murphy, Seán Nolan, Count P.J. O'Byrne, P.S. O'Cahill, Kate O'Callaghan, Daniel O'Callaghan, Art O'Connor, Joseph O'Doherty, Thomas O'Donoghue, Samuel O'Flaherty, Brian O'Higgins, J.J. O'Kelly ('Sceilg'), Seán T. O'Kelly, Seán O'Mahoney, Margaret Pearse, George Noble Count Plunkett, Séamus Robinson, Éamon Roche, P.J. Rutledge, Dr James Ryan, Philip Shanahan, Austin Stack, W.F.P. Stockley.[345]

There were six women TDs, and the Oath of Allegiance was anathema to their socialist and republican beliefs. They felt that, as well as betraying their dead comrades' convictions, it would continue to subject Ireland to the British government and its class-ridden political system. The women were opposed to compromise, and all voted against the Treaty.[346] Four★ of the six (known as the 'Black Widows') had lost male relatives in the Rising or the War of Independence: Kathleen (Mrs Thomas) Clarke★ (who was also the sister of the executed Ned Daly), Dr Ada English, Mary MacSwiney★ (elder sister of Terence), Countess Markievicz, Kate (Mrs Michael) O'Callaghan★ (widow of the former lord mayor of Limerick) and Margaret Pearse★ (mother of Patrick and Willie). Expressing the views of all of the women, and many of the male members of the Dáil, Dr Kathleen Lynn wrote:

Peace Terms, but what a peace! Not what Connolly and Mallin and countless died for. Please God the Country won't agree to what Griffith, Barton, Gavan-Duffy, Duggan, and Mick Collins had put their names to, more shame to them, better war than with such a peace. It is terrible how many who should know better seem quite pleased with the terms.[347]

The HQ staff of the IRA was split on the issue. Those opposed to the Treaty were:

Cathal Brugha, Minister for Defence
Austin Stack, formerly Deputy Chief of Staff
Liam Mellows, Director of Purchases
Rory O'Connor, Director of Engineering
Seán Russell, Director of Munitions
Séamus O'Donovan, Director of Chemicals
Oscar Traynor, O/C of the Dublin Brigade

Those in favour of the Treaty were:

Richard Mulcahy, Chief of Staff
J.J. O'Connell, Assistant Chief of Staff
Eoin O'Duffy, Deputy Chief of Staff
Michael Collins, Director of Intelligence
Diarmuid O'Hegarty, Director of Organisation
Piaras Béaslaí, Director of Publicity[348]

Collins's friend Batt O'Connor summed up his feelings about the close vote and the results that followed:

The Treaty was ratified. But it was ratified only by a majority of seven. If there had been a more decisive verdict our subsequent history would certainly have been different. The opponents of the Treaty took heart from the smallness of the majority, a totally inadequate one as expressing the opinions of the people, who were not consulted. If their wishes had been ascertained and their true verdict on the Treaty expressed by an ample majority in the Dáil, there is little doubt that there would have been no Civil War, and consequently no Boundary. Had the opponents of the Treaty relied upon 'a constitutional way of settling our differences' [as said by de Valera], opposition and fair criticism in the Dáil would have not weakened but strengthened our power to use the Treaty for the fulfilment of those national aspirations upon the promotion of which we had hitherto all been united. It was not the wish of Michael Collins to see all the Irish people, through their representatives, supporting the Treaty as the last word in Irish Independence. A left wing in the Dáil, in constitutional opposition, would have strengthened his hands.[349]

On 9 January de Valera resigned and put himself forward for re-election as president; he was defeated on 10 January (by 60 votes to 58). Griffith was elected; de Valera did not vote. De Valera's expressed view was that 'The Republic must exist until the people disestablish it'.[350] He also said: 'I hope that nobody will talk of fratricidal strife. That is all nonsense. We have a nation that knows how to conduct itself.'[351]

Richard Mulcahy recalled in some detail his views on the genesis of the Civil War, recording a number of factors that he considered as contributing to that tragic event. In his opinion, the biggest contributory factor was de Valera's immediate and violent reaction to the terms of the Treaty within a day or two of its signing, and his outspoken criticism of the people who took part in the negotiations. He makes the point that de Valera's vigorous reaction gathered force very quickly, set off shock waves that were widely felt and was contrary to his Dáil recommendation of September 1921, when the Plenipotentiaries were appointed, that the negotiators must be left a free hand and that their decisions would be subject only to the subsequent approval of the Dáil.

The effect of the proceedings since its first assembly on the 14th December 1921 to discuss the Treaty, following Mr de Valera's repudiation of them on the 8th December, had been to spread confusion and dismay through the country as a whole. The vast majority of the people were completely in favour of the Treaty. They were appalled by the fact that de Valera challenged it and by the way in which he did it in his statement to the people generally, before the Military met, and in the manner in which he did it in the Dáil. They were shocked and frightened by the obvious development of disorder and strife. There was nothing however that the great majority of the people could do about it—only talk and develop opinions and wait.

The Volunteers, the Army generally, were in a different position. They had heard from the highest possible level that the Plenipotentiaries had, as it were, behind the backs of de Valera, [and] the members of the Government, broken their word in London, and had done something which they should not have done; with the implication that they would not have been allowed to do it, if having obeyed what were alleged to be their instructions, they had consulted their colleagues at home before taking action; they were told that in future they would be the King's Army and that the King himself and his Governor General in Ireland would be the person who would permit and sign all their commissions;

and that while the British Army could go out now, it had every legal right to return where and whenever it pleased …

The binding and immobilising influence of the oath to the Republic was pressed home on them; and the inflexibility of any possible interpretation of that word in practice, except in accordance with some brainwave of Mr de Valera's or some aspect of de Valera's conscience, was pushed home. The eyes of their dead comrades were turned upon them, and the eyes of important people like Stack and Seán T. O'Kelly etc., who were ready to sacrifice their lives, either deliberately or in terms of a bet, against the idea of de Valera ever doing wrong …

As far as the general rank and file of the people were concerned with the challenge in all this, all they could do was think and pray and wait for the opportunity of saying what they thought, when they could go to the polls …

For the Army it was different. They were being challenged to stand to attention, and in the face of all this, to humiliate themselves by acquiescence or to take active steps to prevent, in one way or another, at the polls or otherwise, the bringing about of such a situation as would impose all these indignities on the country. With varied experience of the days in which they were struggling against the British, the situation offered and suggested very many varied types of opportunities to various types of people for obstruction, incitement and aggression …[352]

On 12 January the Dáil delegates again assembled in the Oak Room of the Mansion House. (See Dawson Street/Mansion House.)

28 Earlsfort Terrace: RIC Sgt John J. Fitzgerald was killed here on Bloody Sunday.[353] He had previously been kidnapped and the IRA/Volunteers had attempted to kill him in County Clare, but he had escaped with a dislocated arm and had been sent to Dublin for treatment. The Squad asked for 'Lt Col. Fitzpatrick'. Could it have been mistaken identity? Many documents were found in the house, recording the movements of senior IRA leaders. (See Bloody Sunday, Appendix IV.)

Ely Place, Ely House: House purchased by George Gavan Duffy for the Dáil, after receiving instructions from Collins. Collins, always the businessman and finance minister, only approved a transaction after making sure that purchases were economical.

Ely House.
A Chara,
Before bringing this matter before the Cabinet I should like if possible to have your consent to the proposal.

Through an old friend who was the confidential secretary to the late W.M. Murphy I have today had an opportunity of visiting Ely House in Ely Place, and was shown over it by Lady Aberdeen.

The house is to be let unfurnished, and I understand Lady Aberdeen has a lease of 30 years unexpired, for the whole of which or less if preferred she would be willing to let the house.

She pays an annual ground rent of £120

She claims to have spent £2,000 on the house interest

on which would be say £120

allowing her a profit rental of £60

the annual rent for the term would be £300…

The house is a beautiful Georgian house, thoroughly suitable for a Government Office at which foreigners have to be received, and it is central. Whether under a future change of Government it remains a Foreign Office or be used for some other Governmental purpose, it is, I think, a house which it would be eminently desirable to acquire for the Government, and it seems to me that it is offered cheap. It has four storeys and ample accommodation.

I should like to have your personal consent, before carrying the matter further, to taking up this proposal, and I should be grateful if you could let me hear from you as soon as possible.

You will remember at the last Cabinet meeting I was authorised to take the house No. 33 Stephen's Green, two doors from the Shelbourne, at £300 a year, including taxes, but the present offer seems to me altogether a very much more desirable one and I should like to be able to close with it.

Le meas,

George Gavan Duffy.[354]

15 Ely Place (now demolished): Home of Oliver St John Gogarty. The house was a Queen Anne house 'modernised' by Sir Thomas Dean, architect of the National Library and Museum. After the Treaty was signed, Collins often came here. Gogarty gave Collins a key to the house so that he could use it as a safe house. That key was found in Collins's uniform pocket when Gogarty embalmed his body.

On 12 January 1923 Senator Gogarty was kidnapped from here by the IRA/Republicans but escaped by diving into the Liffey.

10 Exchequer Street: The **Irish National Aid Association,** first under the direction of George Gavan Duffy and Alderman Patrick Corrigan, combined with Kathleen Clarke's Irish Volunteers' Dependants' Fund to form the Irish National Aid and Volunteers' Dependants' Fund. This was the first 'real' office. The Fund was administered by Kathleen Clarke, president; Áine Ceannt, vice-president; Máire Nic

Shiubhlaigh, treasurer; E. MacRaghaill, secretary; Margaret Pearse, Muriel MacDonagh, Eily O'Hanrahan,[355] Madge Daly[356] and Lila Colbert, directors.

The Fund was difficult to start.

> The work was then starting for the Volunteer Dependants' Fund. We found it very hard to get the necessary information. When we called at the houses sometimes the inhabitants denied all knowledge of the Volunteers in question, as they did not know us and they thought we might be setting traps for them. Gradually it became easier as the sympathy of the public had veered round to the victims of the Rebellion. Especially the Masses for the men of Easter Week did a good deal to give courage to all these people. They gave them the only opportunity they had of coming together and exchanging news from the various prisons.[357]

Nevertheless, it soon looked after its charges very well. Writing from Lewes Prison in December 1916, Patrick Fogarty told his mother: 'we know that all the men's wives, and those they supported are very well look [sic] after'.[358]

The first secretary was Joe McGrath. He took the job mostly to protect the interests of the prisoners (he evaded capture after the Rising) and of the IRB members, but by late 1916 he wanted out and Mrs Clarke searched for a new secretary. She hired Collins to work here after he was released from Frongoch, starting on 19 February 1917 at a salary of £2.10s per week, and he ensured that the work of the fund was meticulously recorded. Collins was also the IRB centre (leader) for the Dublin area, another paid position. These jobs gave him access to the people who were central within the complex network of parish committees throughout the country. He also had access to information and, as information represented power, he was now at the centre of intelligence regarding the fast-changing political arena in Ireland.

Batt O'Connor, who had been imprisoned with Collins in Frongoch, recalled that after the prisoners returned home they often gathered around the office to plead their cases:

> The place was packed with the Frongoch crowd and there was no sitting accommodation. When I entered Joe Gleeson came to me and said Michael Collins was the right man for the job but he was not known. He suggested that when names were proposed we should distribute ourselves throughout the room and call 'Michael Collins'. I got standing on a chair and Joe on another. People said some man was wanted who knew who was who. Joe shouted 'Collins' and others followed and that carried the crowd. The committee of women, Mrs Tom Clarke, etc., did not know Michael Collins but arranged the interview.[359]

Others noted Collins's early rise upon his return from Frongoch:

> It may be asked why these documents were given to Mick Collins at this early
> stage. He was only known to the small section with whom he had come in
> contact, but he was the official Secretary of the National Aid Association: a trusted
> friend of the Plunkett family and of Rory O'Connor. He was almost the only
> available enthusiast in the reorganising of the new army and he was always at
> hand. There was never any trouble in finding him at any time. Another trait in his
> character was that it did not matter about what one did in the past—'If you are
> prepared to do the right thing now, you are the man I want'. It was this attitude
> which raised him above suspicious men in the estimation of the men of the new
> army. We knew he was ambitious, but he was a man of action and that was what
> mattered.[360]

The committee was impressed by his ability but nettled by his apparent conceit.
Nevertheless, Mrs Clarke's views were definitive. (See also Bachelor's Walk, as the
Fund's offices moved there later in 1917.)

The football match arranged at Croke Park on Bloody Sunday, 21 November
1920, was held as a benefit for this Fund; about £500 was raised.

41 Fitzwilliam Place: Home of Dr Brigid Lyons Thornton.[361]

A niece of Joe McGuinness, she went to Longford to work for his election in the
by-election of 1917. After the first 'count', officials 'found a second' box of ballots,
giving him a 37-vote margin of victory. She was a very active campaigner and was
elated when he won.

In 1919–21 she was attending medical school in Galway, then was a doctor at
Mercer's Hospital, but was also a courier to Longford and Galway, carrying weapons
and ammunition as well as documents. Whenever confronted on a train or at a
roadblock, she wrote, 'I had recourse to a prayer and a piece of feminine guile'.

In 1921 she was sent to Mountjoy Prison several times to relay Collins's messages
to Seán MacEoin regarding his escape. As a woman and a doctor, she never aroused
any suspicion. It was also thought that she would be the best one to assess MacEoin's
physical condition. She recalled that she was summoned to 46 Rutland (Parnell)
Square to meet Collins. 'I took to the air,' she wrote. 'I was never so excited or thrilled
in my whole life.' She continued to see MacEoin until July, even though none of the
escape plans came to fruition. Just after the Truce, Collins sent her word that he would
like to see MacEoin, and she accompanied him to Mountjoy. Collins was named as
'James Gill' on the visitors' register.[362]

She was commissioned in the Medical Services of the National Army in 1922,
thus earning the distinction of being the only woman to serve in the Army at the

time.[363] Ironically, since she had been imprisoned there after the Rising, in December 1922 Dr Lyons was posted to Kilmainham Gaol as the Medical Officer to the republican women prisoners. The prisoners there were mainly members of Cumann na mBan, who now regarded their erstwhile colleagues as 'less than the lowest British Tommy'. Dr Lyons remembered well how she hated the assignment:

> Being sent as Medical Officer to Kilmainham was anything but a happy assignment for me. Many of those imprisoned there I had known in the Anglo-Irish War which made it sadder still for me and often extremely embarrassing.
>
> … But the crowning tragedy came one night when I was called to see a new prisoner. Of all people, it was Mrs Tom Clarke. 'We meet in strange places,' she said. She was hurt to meet me there, and I was hurt to meet her. In every way, it was all too, too cruel.
>
> She was already in poor health, and twice before she had been brought into these awful dungeons to say goodbye, first to her husband, and then to her only brother, Ned Daly, before they were executed. I did all I could to make things easier for her. We'd always been such great friends, with me and my aunt and my uncle …[364]

43 Fitzwilliam Place: James O'Mara's home. O'Mara was one of the trustees for the Dáil Loan, and went to the US in 1919–20 in order to guide the Loan past US financial regulators. (See Mansion House, Dawson Street.) Éamon de Valera often used the house for meetings with British emissaries prior to the Truce.

Fitzwilliam Square: Capt. Crawford of the Royal Army Service Corps was in bed with his wife here on Bloody Sunday when there was a knock at his door. The Irish came in and asked, 'Are you Major Callaghan?' Crawford indicated that there was a *Mister* Callaghan living upstairs but that he was not in the army and had no connection with the army. The Irish asked him many questions, searched the room, opened every drawer, and finally seemed satisfied that he was not the man they were looking for. When they left, they told Crawford and his wife to 'clear out of this country within twenty-four hours or we'll come back for you'. (See Bloody Sunday, Appendix IV.)

5 Fitzwilliam Square: In April 1919 the Irish-American fact-finding mission was invited to attend the Dáil, and they stayed here while in Dublin. Frank P. Walsh, Edward F. Dunne and Michael J. Ryan—the first Americans to address an Irish parliament since Benjamin Franklin—were very well received by the Dáil. Following their tour of Ireland, the Americans proceeded to Paris, where they were unsuccessful in getting Ireland's case in front of the peace talks.

There was a dinner for the delegation at Maeve McGarry's house at 31

Fitzwilliam Street Upper. (See 31 Fitzwilliam Square, below.)

The Dáil gave a reception in the Mansion House and a dinner at our house for the Delegates. We had a great big crowd in the house that night for the dinner which was supplied by Mitchell's. It was I did all the cooking for the rest of their stay. My mother and Frank P. Walsh used to stay up till three or four in the morning talking about Ireland. He was a noble character.

(See Mansion House, Dawson Street.)

64 Fitzwilliam Square: Home of Tommy O'Shaughnessy, Dublin recorder (judge). He worked in Dublin Castle and was often escorted by Dave Neligan, who used the opportunity to gather information to give to Collins.

31 Fitzwilliam Street Upper: House owned by Maeve McGarry. It was used to 'shelter' a Dáil department for Collins during the War of Independence. It was raided on 13 April 1921.

In 1919, when the Loan Bond campaign started, Daithí Ó Donnchadha had his office in the cottage which my mother had built on the site of the old stables at the back of No. 31 … The door leading into the rest of the cottage was kept locked. We had kept these two rooms for storage. We fixed up one of these rooms as a bedroom for Michael Collins and the other as an office where Daithi Ó Donnchadha worked all day. The only entrance to these two rooms was through the main hall door in Fitzwilliam Street. The main house was occupied by Dr Michael Burke who was friendly.

One day in 1921 there was a big raid on. Daithi Ó Donnchadha's office was raided by the Auxiliaries in full force with armoured cars and lorries. They broke in through the locked door in the back while Daithi was out at lunch. They took every paper and every bit of furniture out of it. They also searched every room and questioned everyone in the main house of No. 31, but found nothing there, although Fiona Plunkett and I and an engineering student called Harnett—a brother of Nellie Harnett's—had hidden some grenades and ammunition under the boards in the bathroom. I have one of the grenade cases still as a memento. I never heard that they got anything worthwhile among Daithi's papers either. He had the habit of taking everything important away with him.

My mother was in the Corporation and a Councillor for the Fitzwilliam ward since 1919. She had just come home from a meeting and was having a cup of tea, talking to the housekeeper, when the military broke in. She had an important paper in her bag and wondered where she would hide it. She stuck it down her blouse.

She concluded from the intensity of the raids on the Fitzwilliam Street and Square houses that the Castle had some reliable information. Fresh reinforcements of armoured cars, etc., kept coming along. So she uttered a fervent prayer, put on her hat and coat, walked coolly down the stairs, though the military and Auxiliaries were in every room and on the stairs—they had burst in the back and come up the garden—and she passed through the midst of them out the door. She could not make it out at all. They did not seem to see her. She said herself it was a miracle in answer to her prayer. She went by tram straight out to Loughnavale on the Strand Road, Merrion, where she found a meeting in progress. De Valera, Cathal Brugha, Seán McMahon, Collins, Dick Mulcahy were there. Mellows was in and out a good deal to Loughnavale and he must have been there too. When my mother went in and told about the raid, Collins turned to de Valera and said, 'It is time for you to leave here'. Countess Plunkett's maid also called a little later with the news of the raid. The meeting dispersed as rapidly as possible. Collins was the last to go because he remained to arrange about de Valera leaving that evening.

… There was a big raid a week afterwards at Loughnavale. De Valera had left the night he was warned and gone back to Dr Farnan's where he had been before. He was not able to do his work there, as he was stuck up in the top of the house and could see nobody. Kathleen O'Connell [de Valera's secretary] stayed on with us at Loughnavale. The raid was an awful one, even worse than any I had previously experienced in No. 5 [5 Merrion Square, Dublin 1]. The Black and Tans smashed in the door and the glass porch. They took possession of the house. Kathleen O'Connell had brought home quantities of presents from people in America to their friends here. The Tans took them all. I was in my room on the second floor in the back, sitting on the side of my bed preparing to get in, and I put out the light. They climbed up on each other's shoulders, pushed up the window and climbed in. I had heard nothing up to then and got a great shock. Then I heard the smashing in of the door. They asked me why I had put out the light. They lifted up the floorboards all through the house. They found a glove of de Valera's in a recess in one of the wardrobes. It had evidently been overlooked by Liam Mellows when he packed de Valera's things. The Tans stuck the glove—which had de Valera's name—up to my nose and asked me did I know anything about that. I said I didn't. All the important papers had been removed from the house after de Valera's departure. But quite a lot of papers—a couple of sackfuls—had been left behind, and Kathleen and my mother had spent the week burning them. Many of these were regretted afterwards as they had records of the American campaign. We felt great relief when they were all burned. There was only one man in khaki—the officer in charge, a drunken little brute who gave my father an awful time. He wanted me to sign a paper saying that they had done no harm, but I would not sign it.

He asked why. I said, 'You are taking my father away and I don't know what you are going to do with him!'

The raiders took my father away in a lorry and the Tans were singing as they went down the avenue. They were dragging a Sinn Féin flag along the ground. My father said, 'You have nothing against me. Take me to your commanding officer'. He was kept in the Castle that night.[365]

Mrs McGarry also wrote about Collins and de Valera visiting her before de Valera went to London:

… The night before he travelled to London, Collins came and the two of them spent hours walking up and down in the garden discussing things. De Valera and Collins were devoted to each other. Collins worshipped the ground that de Valera trod on and, while de Valera was in America, Collins went down to Greystones to Mrs de Valera every week to see that all was well there and to bring her her husband's salary. De Valera was equally fond of Collins. Some years later, when he came to 31 Fitzwilliam Street to look for consulting rooms for his son, he asked to see the room which Collins used to use.

Fleet Street at corner of D'Olier Street: In 1920 Kathleen Clarke opened a tobacconist's shop here. Though it was frequently raided by the Black and Tans, she often used to relay messages between IRA/Volunteers during the War of Independence. Later, Free State forces raided the shop, believing that it was used as a 'drop' to relay messages between IRA/Republicans.

8 Fleet Street: Home of Kevin Barry. He was born here on 20 January 1902, fourth of a family of two boys and five girls: Katherine, Mick, Monty, Kevin, Sheila, Elgin and Peggy. Katherine (known as Kathy) was a courier for the IRA/Republicans during the Civil War.[366] (See Church Street, North Circular Road/Mountjoy Prison, Dublin 7.)

Grafton Street: Mitchell's Café. Known as one of the most fashionable in the street, it was often used as a meeting place during the War of Independence, especially by women of Cumann na mBan.

Grafton Street: Kidd's Buffet (commonly known as 'Kidd's Back'), at the back of what was the Berni Inn in Nassau Street. A hangout for Castle 'touts' and Tom Cullen, Frank Thornton[367] and Frank Saurin.[368]

At that time most of the British Secret Service Agents and British Intelligence Officers and Auxiliary Intelligence Officers met at a place which was well known in Dublin as Kidd's Buffet. Kidd's Back it was known in Grafton Street, and presently Jammet's Back. Now here is where a lot of our information was picked up, and again it had to be picked up by taking a very big risk. Tom Cullen, Frank Saurin and myself were deputed to act with our two Secret Service friends who then frequented Kidd's Buffet with the Secret Service. We were introduced in the ordinary way as touts and eventually became great friends of men like Major Bennett, Colonel Aimes [sic] and a number of other prominent Secret Service Officers. Naturally Collins and all his staff and the whole activities of the organisation were discussed there daily. On one day, one of these officers turned suddenly to Tom Cullen and said, 'Surely you fellows know these men Liam Tobin, Tom Cullen and Frank Thornton, these are Collins' three officers and if you can get these fellows we would locate Collins himself'. Needless to remark, if the ground opened and swallowed us we could not have been more surprised, and for the moment we felt that we had walked into a trap, but that wasn't so at all. It was a genuine query to the three Irishmen, whom they believed should know all about the particular fellows they mentioned. The fact remains that although they knew of the existence of the three of us and they knew of the existence of Collins, they actually had no photograph of any of us, and had a very poor description of either Collins or the three of us.

However, the British at this time, realising that the terrorism of the Black and Tans burning and looting was not going to succeed unless they could actually put their finger on our Headquarters Staff and eliminate us in that way. With that end in view they aimed to set up a full time Secret Service outside of the army, working on proper continental lines with a Central Headquarters and other houses forming minor centres scattered all throughout the city in which they operated. In this way they built up quite a formidable organisation and were without doubt securing quite a lot of very valuable information.

Information was gleaned in a lot of instances through the carelessness or idle talk of individuals. But I am rather proud to say not from informers on our side, because there is one thing we can boast of in the movement from 1916 to 1921 and that is that we bred no informers.[369]

A raid was planned for the area later, but came to nothing.

At this time great numbers of Auxiliaries paraded up and down Grafton Street in civilian clothes and frequented Kidd's restaurant which was at the corner of Grafton Street. Michael Collins decided that there should be an attack on the Auxiliaries in this restaurant and in Grafton Street. The job was timed for the afternoon. This was the time the greatest numbers of enemy troops would be strolling in Grafton Street. The idea was to nail the whole lot in one blow. These were well known to the Intelligence Section and the Intelligence Section were on the job. The Active Service Unit were also on the job, but some of them did not arrive having been cut off by patrols. On the firing of a shot by me all were to shoot every Auxiliary seen in Grafton Street. Myself with six others were to go into Kidd's restaurant, but as I have already mentioned some of the Active Service Unit couldn't turn up to me as they were cut off by military patrols, and the same thing happened in certain parts of Grafton Street. We had arranged to have a Ford Van to take away our wounded and that couldn't turn up either. It was also cut off. Because all these things happened it was decided to call the whole thing off. Just as it was called off two members of the Active Service Unit shot two Auxiliaries called Appleby and Waring. We didn't do any shooting in Kidd's Restaurant at all.[370]

The building now houses Lillie's Bordello.

Grafton Street: Office of the Hon. Lord John Graham Hope de la Poer Beresford, Baron Decies, censor-in-chief during the War of Independence.[371]

1 Grafton Street: Home of the provost of Trinity College. During the Rising Trinity's provost was Dr J.P. Mahaffey, who memorably wrote on one occasion: 'In Ireland the inevitable never happens, the unexpected always'.

59 Grafton Street: **Cairo Café**; **Roberts' Café** (this was the second one, opened after the one in Suffolk Street). Both were often used as meeting places during the War of Independence for both the British and the IRA/Republicans.

94–95 Grafton Street: Edmund Johnson, jewellers—made the Liam McCarthy Cup, presented to the GAA in 1921. The cup, which is presented to the All-Ireland hurling champions, is named after Liam McCarthy, one-time chairman of the London GAA Board, where he served with both Sam Maguire and Collins.

An IRB member, McCarthy often counselled London Irish. When conscription was introduced he couldn't directly advise Irishmen to avoid it, as he was a county councillor, but in response to a question from Collins he said, 'If you come from Clonakilty it is obvious where you must go'.

In conjunction with his two sons, William and Eugene, McCarthy donated a sum of £50 for the purchase of ten certificates in the Dáil Loan set up by Collins. When the loan was redeemed, McCarthy used the money for the purchase of a silver cup based on the design of an ancient Gaelic meither (Irish loving cup). It is made from a 2.5kg single sheet of solid silver with only one seam and was panelled into four sections, to each of which a Celtic design was added, with the four handles soldered last. The whole process took four months. A replica replaced the original in 1988.

96 Grafton Street (at the corner of 1–3 Wicklow Street): Weir and Sons, jewellers, next door to the Wicklow Hotel. Collins bought Kitty Kiernan a watch, her 'unofficial' engagement present, at this store. When he gave it to her on 8 October 1921, he said that 'she could hear it tick and think of him 24 hours a day!'

Grand Canal Street: Sir Patrick Dun's Hospital. In June 1927 Countess Markievicz was admitted here to a ward filled with the poor. She had appendicitis and was operated on by Sir William Taylor. An infection set in following the operation and she developed peritonitis. She was very run down as a result of her many activities on behalf of the poor of Dublin and in support of Republicanism, and her health suffered badly. She was also heartsick, could not accept the Oath and could not enter the Dáil. At first she appeared to be getting better, but she died on 15 July 1927. Thousands of Dubliners followed her funeral to Glasnevin Cemetery.

13 Grantham Street: Home of Mrs Malone, mother of Michael Malone (who was killed at 25 Northumberland Road in the Rising), Brighid and Áine. Dan Breen was taken here to convalesce after the Ashtown raid of 19 December 1919. Breen married Brighid on 12 June 1921, with Collins and many of the IRA/Volunteers in attendance. (See Ashtown, Dublin 15.)

1–8 Great Brunswick Street (now Pearse Street) (corner of Townsend Street): Dublin Metropolitan Police ('G' Division) HQ. In order to monitor the political pulse of the capital, the DMP included within its structure a political section, the 'G' Division. This was a specially trained branch whose members thoroughly knew the city, its IRA/Volunteer officers and important separatists, and, guided by RIC information, followed all the marked men who came to Dublin from the country. Its primary role was to report and collate snippets of information picked up from the streets. At the end of every day, each member of the 'G' Division would copy and transfer notes to the records section in Pearse Street Station. Members of the station staff had free access to these records.

Officers' caps and constables' helmets over their respective doorways distinguished the entrances by class and can still be seen today, with the officers' peaked caps over the doors at the western end of the building, and bobbies' helmets over the doors at the eastern end.

Éamon (Ned) Broy, a Collins informant, let Collins and Seán Nunan into the file rooms here on the night of 7 April 1919 to look over the 'G' Division files on the Volunteers.[372] Nunan wrote:

Sometime during this period, I was sworn in as a member of the IRB, and used to meet Michael Collins and others at Vaughan's Hotel. One night, when I was there, Collins asked me to stay behind after the others had gone home and, at about 12.30 a.m., he suggested we go for a walk. After walking around the city for some time, we arrived at Brunswick Street (now Pearse Street) Police Station, where Sergeant Ned Broy was alone on night duty. Michael Collins had explained to me that his plan was to examine the files and reports of the G Division and ascertain precisely who, amongst them, was doing political work. Ned Broy took us up to Inspector McFeeley's office, and opened a large, steel safe in which the reports were kept. Collins and I stayed in the safe, listing the names and activities of the detectives on political work, until about 4 a.m., when we walked home—Collins to Mountjoy Street and I to Botanic Road.

As a result of the information thus obtained, warnings were issued to all those men engaged in spying to cease their activities, or else![373]

It was on this foray that Collins read his own file, which indicated that he 'belongs to a family of "brainy" people and of advanced Sinn Féin sympathies. They are of the farming class'.[374] That gave Collins such a good and loud laugh that Broy heard him and was concerned that Collins would be discovered. Upon leaving the next morning, Collins gave Broy another scare when he realised that he had left some papers behind and insisted on returning to retrieve them.

The reports that Collins studied that night had a great influence on his future actions. Despite their faulty judgements and inaccuracies, he realised that these secret files still constituted Britain's greatest hold on Ireland. A realist like Collins knew that it was necessary to shut down these resources of knowledge and blind the Dublin Castle administration. The information obtained enabled him to identify 'G' Division men, who then would be warned or killed by the IRA. Collins realised that in order to defeat the British they would have to take out their spies, as they would be unable to replace them. Collins stated to Broy: 'I am a builder, not a destroyer. I get rid of people only when they hinder my work.' He warned the detectives to look the other way or suffer the consequences. Those detectives who scoffed at the warnings paid the price.

Broy was a particularly good source, and he saw all the confidential information in the station. As a typist, he simply made an extra copy, and Collins had his information. Broy often gave copies of his typing to Patrick Tracy (who was married to Broy's cousin), a clerk at the Kingsbridge railway station, or to Thomas Gay, a librarian in Capel Street, for delivery to Collins.

Joseph Kavanagh, another Collins informant, was also stationed here. Broy, Kavanagh and Dave Neligan often met at Thomas Gay's house for weekly conferences with Collins. (See 8 Haddon Road, Dublin 3; 106 Capel Street, Dublin 7.) Collins's passion for secrecy was so intense that for many months none of these men knew of the existence of any of the others. On occasion they actually followed one another. Broy was godfather to Kavanagh's oldest son before he knew that they were both working for Collins.

> One evening, we were walking in St Stephen's Green, and we both made the discovery that we were in contact with Michael Collins. I told him about Mick's visit to No. 1 Great Brunswick St. He nearly fell, laughing, knowing the mentality in the G Division office and knowing Mick. He got me to tell it to him a second time, and he laughed so much that people looked at him as if he were drunk or mad. He asked me what did Mick look like in the office, and I said: 'He looked like a big plain-clothes man going out on duty, with a stick'. Shortly afterwards, when I met Mick, he apologised for not having told me about Kavanagh. I told him that that was what I had been preaching to him since I met him, not to tell anything, that the Irish people had paid too big a price for carelessness like that, in the past. Michael similarly apologised to Joe the next time he met him, but Michael was glad the two of us knew and understood each other.[375]

In 1916 Kavanagh was assigned to pick out the Rising's leaders when they were in Richmond Prison. Even then, however, his loyalty was clear, as he walked among the prisoners and asked 'Is there anything I can do for you' or 'Can I take a message for you'. Kavanagh was a key Collins spy for about a year until he succumbed to cancer, but by then he had recruited another valuable agent for Collins in James McNamara, who worked in Dublin Castle.

Collins encouraged his operatives to carefully recruit others who would help the cause. Consequently, several more constables became agents for Collins:

> We finally succeeded in enrolling the following DMP men: Two Culhane brothers of College Street, one of whom was a Station Sergeant there. Maurice Aherne, Constable at Donnybrook. Sergt. Mannix at Donnybrook. Sergt. Matt Byrne at Rathmines. Constable Neary at Kevin Street. Constable Peter Feely then Kingstown. Constable Paddy McEvoy at Donnybrook. Sergt. P. O'Sullivan at Fitzgibbon Street. Constable Mick O'Dea at Donnybrook.[376]

Collins, Broy and Richard Mulcahy agreed that the war had to be taken to the DMP detectives and that pre-emptive strikes were necessary.

> The authorities were apparently biding their time to have certain preparations made before the Dáil was suppressed. The work of men like Smyth, Hoey, and Barton, and the G Division generally, was being effectively snowballed to increase

the information regarding the persons who were particularly active and important both on the political and Volunteer side. To allow it to have developed any way effectively would have been disastrous. The initiative against the detectives was only begun in time.[377]

Daniel Hoey was killed outside 'G' Division HQ on 12–13 September 1919. He had led the raid on 6 Harcourt Street earlier that day, and Collins had him killed that very night. (See 6 Harcourt Street.) The Squad members were Mick McDonnell, Jim Slattery and Tom Ennis. They followed Hoey from the HQ to Hawkins Street, where he was shot. He was taken to Mercer's Hospital but was dead on arrival.[378]

> [Tom] Ennis, Mick McDonnell and I came down to Townsend Street. Mick said he thought that Detective Hoey would be going off duty at about ten o'clock, and he did go off. Hoey crossed over from College Street towards the police headquarters in Brunswick Street. I asked Mick if he was sure that this man was Hoey, and he said, 'I am not quite sure, but we will go after him'. ... We passed him by when he was looking at a window and Mick said, 'It is Hoey all right'. ... When we saw him approaching again, we crossed over to his side of the street, which was at the back of the barracks, and we shot him at the door of the garage. After shooting Hoey, Mick McDonnell said we had better go to Mick Collins and report to him direct that Hoey had been shot that night (12th September 1919) in Townsend Street.[379]

The British intelligence war was widely acknowledged as being disastrous, with Collins and his men and women consistently out-spying His Majesty's secret services. In the immediate post-war period the British made a detailed analysis of their intelligence failures in Ireland and, in a flurry of activity, papers were published, conferences held, reports commissioned and lectures given in which the failures were fully acknowledged. It is known that as late as May 1920 the chief of police had an intelligence staff consisting of one officer.[380] Its primary source of information, from the political detectives of 'G' Division of the DMP, had all but dried up, as Collins had ordered the assassination of most of those detectives. By late 1920 intelligence officers had been appointed to each divisional commissioner of the RIC to coordinate military and police intelligence. The military, then present throughout Ireland in force, together with Auxiliaries, had their own intelligence service with young officers, many of them noted for their zeal in intelligence matters.[381]

Even at the height of the IRA's campaign, the 'G' Division employed fewer than two dozen men exclusively dedicated to political work, while the RIC's Special Branch consisted not of a nationwide detective force along the lines of Scotland Yard but a confidential records office based in Dublin Castle, staffed by several clerks, a detective inspector and a chief inspector. The vast bulk of intelligence gathered by Special Branch was collected by ordinary RIC men throughout the country, and forwarded to Crimes Special Branch's small office in Dublin Castle. Until the final year of Dublin Castle's rule, there was no 'secret service' in Ireland; Special Branch did not run undercover agents, rarely recruited informers and made little effort to penetrate the organisations of its enemies. The documents gathered there demonstrated the old-fashioned methods employed by the police: republican premises were kept under observation, train stations and other public places were watched, suspects were shadowed from town to town, and their speeches were recorded by policemen.

Although some individuals in British service were dismissed on dubious or malicious grounds, the files indicate that the quality of evidence demanded for prosecution, or even dismissal, was generally high: no action was taken in many of these cases, despite the RIC's efforts to gather incriminating evidence. Consequently, the British administration in Ireland remained penetrated by republican sympathisers despite its periodic attempts to purge potentially subversive employees. (See Lily Mernin, Ship Street Barracks, Dublin 1; Clonliffe Road, Dublin 3; Mangerton Road, Parkgate Street, Dublin 8.)[382]

42e Great Brunswick Street (now Pearse Street): Antient Concert Rooms; home of the Dublin Orchestral Society.

This was an IRA/Volunteer Department of Intelligence office and an early HQ of the Squad, but Collins came here infrequently.

> For some months before Bloody Sunday our Intelligence Organisation underwent a change. We took on additional men, Ned Kellegher, Joe Kavanagh, Con O'Neill, Bob O'Neill and Joe Dolan. I took up my new Headquarters in the old Ancient [sic] Concert Rooms in Pearse Street with a sign on the outside of the hall-door 'O'Donoghue & Smith, Manufacturers Agents'. We actually had certain samples there if anybody called in to investigate. The main body of our Agents occupied the big room in the front as is well known, all the jobs carried out in Dublin at that time were carried out by the GHQ Squad which was, at the period of which I am speaking, under the control of Mick McDonnell.[383]

(See Abbey Street Lower, Dublin 1, where the Squad finally moved its HQ.)

The building now houses the Academy (a music venue).

144 Great Brunswick Street (now Pearse Street): St Andrew's Club. In 1921 it was the HQ of the IRA/Volunteers. Auxiliaries surrounded it on 14 March 1921, when it was thought that the Dáil was meeting here; a firefight ensued and there were casualties on both sides. The building is now part of Dublin City Library and Archive

(138–144 Pearse Street).

35 North Great George's Street: In July 1919, Collins sent Dick McKee to meet with a number of Volunteers to see whether they had any objections to shooting enemy agents. Among the men who agreed to do so were Jim Slattery, Tom Keogh, Tom Kilcoyne and Joe Leonard. Slattery wrote:

> Dick McKee addressed those of us who had been selected and asked if we had any objection to shooting enemy agents. The greater number of Volunteers objected for one reason or another. When I was asked the question I said I was prepared to obey orders.[384]

Most of the invited Volunteers objected, for various reasons. McKee was quite annoyed and asked why they had signalled their willingness to be involved in the first place. Along with Paddy Daly, these men were to form the nucleus of Collins's Squad. (Daly was still in Mountjoy Prison at this time, but was at the first 'official' meeting of the Squad at 46 Parnell Square on 19 September.)

Charlie Dalton thought that the meeting was at **42 North Great George's Street**:

> Regarding the formation of the squad, Mick [McDonnell] stated that a number of selected Volunteers were assembled at 42 North Great George's St. on the instructions of Dick McKee. These men, many of them with service in the 1916 insurrection, were informed by the Brigadier that a certain line of action would be necessary if the movement was to continue. In this connection he indicated that it would be necessary to shoot some members of the 'G' Division whose political activities had jeopardised the activities of the re-formed Volunteers. There were present three or four members of each of the five companies which then constituted the 2nd Battalion, and after the Brigadier's address, most of those present refused to give an affirmative answer to the request made by him. Some of the men advanced the reason that they could not do such work as it would be contrary to their consciences; others stated that they would think the matter over and get spiritual advice before giving an answer; and, finally, some of them stated that, while they were prepared to carry out acts of open warfare, they were not prepared to shoot a man down unwarned. (The 'G' men had received several warnings before action was taken.) Mick McDonnell told me that when the question was put to those present from 'E' Company, he stepped out of the ranks as also did Jim Slattery and, probably, Vincent Byrne and Tom Keogh. I was discussing this matter subsequently with Jim Slattery and he confirmed Mick McDonnell's story and stated that he said to the Brigadier: 'I am prepared to carry

out any and every order I receive from you'.

From my close association with the various members of the squad subsequently, I learned that in the initial stages a few jobs were carried out independently by Paddy Daly, Joe Leonard and Ben Barrett. At one period of the fighting Paddy Daly was imprisoned as was also Joe Leonard. This would suggest that two squads operated in the early stages. Later on, the squad consisted of about twelve members. Paddy Daly, after his release from Ballykinlar, took charge of the newly-formed active service unit, while Joe Leonard continued in the squad. During my association with the squad and previous to my joining the Intelligence Staff, Mick McDonnell was in charge of the operations I was concerned with, namely, the seizure of the mail van at Lower Dominick St. and the attempt to ambush 'G' men at SS Michael and John's Church. Later on, when the squad had reached its full strength of about a dozen men, they stood-to for hours at Seville Place and other centres and acted on the instructions of the Deputy Director of Intelligence [Liam Tobin].[385]

6 Harcourt Street: Home of John Cardinal Newman (1801–90). Known as St Mary's University House, it was the residence for students of the Catholic University in St Stephen's Green.

In 1910 Arthur Griffith acquired permanent rooms here and thereafter it was the headquarters of Sinn Féin and the Inghinidhe na hÉireann branch of Cumann na mBan. The Volunteers used it as a drill hall before and after the Rising. It was the first meeting place of K Company, 3rd Battalion of IRA/Volunteers, after the Rising: Capt. Tom Cullen, Adj. Laurence (Larry) Nugent[386] and Instructor Seán McClusky.

On 17–18 May 1918 Sinn Féin leaders and others were arrested because of the bogus 'German Plot', which put most of the Sinn Féin 'moderates' in prison.[387] The pretext for this 'Plot' was the capture of Joseph Dowling, a member of Roger Casement's ill-fated 'Irish Brigade', on an island off the coast of Galway on 12 April. (On the day of Dowling's capture, Collins was still in Sligo jail. He was incarcerated until 18 April, when he returned to Dublin.) The Germans landed Dowling from a submarine on their own initiative, but no one from Sinn Féin had ever contacted him, though Collins and some of the other GHQ staff were aware of the approach. Dowling, who was arrested immediately on landing, had been a lance-corporal in the Connaught Rangers. Captured by the Germans on the Western Front, he had joined Roger Casement's Irish Brigade in 1915 while a prisoner of war in Germany. Two years after Easter Week 1916, he was sent to Ireland by the German general staff to report on the prospects for another Irish rising. Since this was wholly a German idea, it was hardly evidence of a plot involving Sinn Féin and the Volunteers. Dowling was court-martialled, sentenced to penal servitude for life and held in jail in England until February 1924, despite resolutions by the Irish Free State.[388]

On 15 May Éamon Broy secured a list of prominent Sinn Féin members who were to be arrested. He passed the list to Patrick Tracy at Kingsbridge railway station, and Tracy passed the list to Harry O'Hanrahan (brother of Michael O'Hanrahan who was executed after the Rising).

In the case of the German Plot arrests in May, 1918, a large list of names and addresses of those to be arrested in Dublin came to my hands. There were continual additions to the list but, finally, in May, 1918, the list was complete, and several copies were made. Indirectly, it became obvious to me that the arrests would soon start. I gave Tracy a copy of the complete list on the Wednesday forty-eight hours before the arrests took place ... On the day of the proposed arrests as far as I recollect it was a Friday I met Tracy and told him: 'To-night's the night. Tell O'Hanrahan to tell the wanted men not to stay in their usual place of abode and to keep their heads'. Meanwhile, preparations were made for the raid. All the detectives, no matter what their usual duties were, several uniformed men and a military party with a lorry were ordered to stand-to. I had a talk with McNamara (a detective officer and one of Collins's men), and we deliberated on the question of refusing to carry out the arrests and calling on the others not to do so, but we finally decided that such a course of action would do no good whatever, and would probably lead to our dismissal from the service.

...To my astonishment, continual telephone messages arrived from the various police parties, saying that they had arrested the parties they were sent for. A telephone message came from a Detective Sergeant at Harcourt St. railway station, saying: 'That man has just left'. That was obviously de Valera. Superintendent Brien said to me: 'That man will get the suck-in of his life'.

... I did not know what to think of the whole raid, and what had gone wrong, but I thought that de Valera would surely get out at some intermediate station and not go home all the way to Greystones to be arrested there, as Superintendent Brien had immediately rung up the RIC headquarters in Dublin Castle, telling them that that man had just left Harcourt St. To my further astonishment, about an hour afterwards, a telephone message arrived from the RIC at Greystones to say: 'That man has been arrested'. As it turned out, the raid, from the British point of view, was as successful as any raid had previously been. I did not know what had gone wrong with my messages through O'Hanrahan. I wondered had someone got frightened.[389]

Another of Collins's operatives in Dublin Castle, Joe Kavanagh, also gave the list of those to be arrested to another Collins man, Thomas Gay, who passed the list to Collins. (It is an indication of Collins's inexperience at the time that he gave Gay £5 to give to Kavanagh for the information. Gay knew that Kavanagh would be insulted and so he never offered it to him. Collins had yet to learn that there were patriotic Irishmen even in the police and the Castle.) Collins notified de Valera and the other leaders of the forthcoming arrests, but de Valera chose to ignore the warnings. (See 5 Cabra Road, Dublin 7.) It was an example of the efficiency of Collins's network and how he seemed to have information even before the Castle had told the police. That series of raids on 17–18 May rounded up many, and these arrests were what brought Collins fully into the intelligence effort.

Seventy-three prisoners were deported to England immediately, followed by others later. Those first arrested were:

S. Barry, Tadgh Barry, G. Behane, Joseph Berrilla, W.J. Brennan-Whitmore, John J. Clancy, Kathleen Clarke, Alderman Walter Cole, Dick Coleman (he died of Spanish 'flu in Usk Prison),[390] Christopher Collins, William T. Cosgrave,[391] Brian Cusack,[392] Richard Davys, J. Defors, Peter de Loughrey (Parliament Street, Kilkeel), Éamon de Valera (he escaped from Lincoln Jail), Thomas Dillon, Brian Doherty, J. Dolan, Frank Drohan, Seán Etchingham, Frank Fahy,[393] Bernard Failbar, Raymond Fallon, Darrell Figgis, Desmond FitzGerald, Michael Fleming, Padraic Fleming, George Geraghty (he escaped from Usk Prison), Arthur Griffith, R. Haskins, Dr Richard Hayes,[394] Peter (Peadar) Hughes, Thomas Hunter, Stephen Jordan, Frank Lawless, George Lyons,[395] Countess Markievicz, Joseph MacBride, Maud Gonne MacBride,[396] Seán MacEntee,[397] Pierce McCann (he died in prison of Spanish 'flu), Seán McGarry (he escaped from Lincoln Jail), Denis McCullough,[398] Joe McGrath (he escaped from Usk Prison), Joseph McGuinness, Herbert (Barney) Mellows (he escaped from Usk Prison), J. Menahan, Seán Milroy (he escaped from Lincoln Jail), Philip Monaghan, Edward Moore (Moane), Charles Mullen, George Nichols, C. O'Connell, Jeremiah O'Connell, M.J. O'Connor, E. O'Driscoll, Coleman O'Gaoti, Brian O'Higgins, Peadar Ó Hourihane, John O'Hurley, Patrick (Padraig) O'Keefe,[399] G. O'Leary, John O'Mahoney, J.K. O'Reilly, P. O'Sullivan, Count Plunkett, G. Ready, T.M. Russell, Tom Ruane, Frank Shouldice (he escaped from Usk Prison), Michael Spillane, Patrick Sugrue and V. Travers.[400]

In October 1918 a Sinn Féin Ard Fheis (Convention) was held here. Even though many of the more conservative leaders were in English prisons, a respectable portion of the delegates still looked upon Boland and Collins with disfavour. They pushed for more moderate men and women, feeling that Boland and Collins were hotheads and not to be trusted. Boland and Collins remembered this during the nomination process for the election in November and ruthlessly went through each nomination, culling anyone they felt would disagree with them in the future. The candidates they chose were all staunch Republicans and had proved themselves unwilling to compromise.

Collins felt that it was vital that the bloc to be elected should be completely and unquestionably Republican to demonstrate a united front to the British. He left no room for political moderation or vascillation. The hotter they talked, the more Boland and Collins liked them. Ultimately, this was to Collins's disadvantage in the Treaty debates of 1922, when many were still not capable of seeing the value of compromise.[401]

Harry Boland worked here often, as did Frank Gallagher and Anna Fitzsimmons. It was raided on 20 November 1918, three weeks before the election. Robert Brennan, national director of elections and publicity, was arrested and imprisoned in Gloucester Jail.[402] James O'Mara took over this position.

The election was held on 14 December 1918, but the count was postponed until 28 December.[403] Sinn Féin won 73 seats, but with four candidates elected to two seats (de Valera, Griffith, Eoin MacNeill and Liam Mellows) the party returned 69 winning candidates. It should be noted that this was a 'first past the post' election. Sinn Féin polled 485,105 votes; the Irish Parliamentary Party received 297,393 votes and retained only six of their 80 seats. No votes were counted in 24 constituencies where Sinn Féin candidates ran unopposed. Unionists, with 315,394 votes, took 26 seats. Collins commented:

> Gone forever were policies which were a tacit admission that a foreign government could bestow freedom, or a measure of freedom, upon a nation that had never surrendered its national claim.

The franchise for the election had been greatly expanded by the Representation of the People Act of 1918. In 1910 there were 701,475 voters on the register; in 1918 there were 1,936,673. This increase enabled the Irish Parliamentary Party to retain its following in most constituencies but prevented it from securing its former seats, and its losses were widespread.[404]

Harry Boland announced the Sinn Féin winners of the most notable contests from a balcony of the building. Such was the extent of the management of the selection process by Collins, Boland and Diarmuid O'Hegarty that many of the candidates—especially those who were in jail—did not even know that their names had been put forward, and were no doubt surprised to receive messages of congratulations on their success at the polls.

The following are the Sinn Féin candidates who were elected to parliament and sat as the first Dáil Éireann:

Robert Barton	Wicklow West
Piaras Béaslaí	Kerry East
Ernest Blythe	Monaghan North

Harry Boland	Roscommon South
Cathal Brugha; President Pro Tem, then Ceann Comhairle	Waterford County
Séamus Burke	Tipperary Mid
Michael Colivet	Limerick City
Conor (Con) Collins	Limerick West
Michael Collins	Cork South
William T. Cosgrave	Kilkenny North
James Crowley	Kerry North
John Crowley	Mayo North
Brian Cusack	Galway North
Liam de Roiste	Cork City
Éamon de Valera	Clare East; won unopposed Mayo East; defeated John Dillon by 8,875 to 4,514 Lost in West Belfast to Joe Devlin by 8,438 to 3,045
James Dolan	Leitrim
Éamonn Duggan	Meath South
Seán Etchingham	Wicklow East
Frank Fahy	Galway South
Desmond FitzGerald	Dublin Pembroke
Peter Galligan	Cavan West
George Gavan Duffy	Dublin County South
Laurence Ginnell; he was one of two who sat in a 'parliament' previously, James O'Mara being the other	Westmeath
Arthur Griffith	Cavan East Tyrone North-West
Richard Hayes	Limerick East
Seán Hayes	Cork West
Thomas Hunter	Cork North-East
Thomas Kelly	Dublin St Stephen's Green
David Kent	Cork East
Frank Lawless	Dublin County North
James Lennon	Carlow
Diarmaid Lynch[405]	Cork South-East
Fionan Lynch	Kerry South
Seán MacEntee	Monaghan South

Eoin MacNeill	Londonderry City National University of Ireland
Terence MacSwiney. When he was sentenced to jail on 16 August 1920, he declared: 'I will put a limit to any term of imprisonment you may impose. I have decided the terms of my detention whatever your government may do. I shall be free, alive or dead, within a month.' He died on hunger strike in Brixton Prison, London, on 25 October 1920.	Cork Mid
Joseph McBride	Mayo West
Alex McCabe	Sligo South
Pierce McCann. He died on 6 March 1919 in Gloucester Prison from influenza. His death prompted the British to release many other prisoners on the orders of the prison doctor, Dr Bell. He was the brother of Alan Bell, an Examining Magistrate whom Collins later had executed in Dublin. (See Nutley Lane, Dublin 4.)	Tipperary East
Patrick McCartan	King's County (now County Offaly)
Joseph McDonagh	Tipperary North
Joseph McGrath	Dublin St James's
Joseph P. McGuinness	Longford
Countess Markievicz. She was the first woman to be elected to parliament. Her invitation to take her seat was sent to her at Holloway Prison.	Dublin St Patrick's
Liam Mellows	Galway East Meath North
P.J. Moloney	Tipperary South
Richard Mulcahy	Dublin Clontarf
Domhnall Ó Buachalla	Kildare North
Seán T. Ó Ceallaigh (O'Kelly)	Dublin College Green
A. O'Connell	Kildare South
Joseph O'Doherty	Donegal North
Brian O'Higgins	Clare West

Kevin O'Higgins	Queen's County (now County Laois)
Patrick O'Keefe	Cork North
John O'Mahoney	Fermanagh South
Pádraig Ó Máille	Galway Connemara
John J. O'Malley	Louth
James O'Meara (O'Mara); he was one of two who sat in a 'parliament' previously, Laurence Ginnell being the other	Kilkenny South
Count Plunkett	Roscommon North
James Ryan	Wexford South
William Sears	Mayo South
Austin Stack	Kerry South
Michael Staines	Dublin St Michan's
Joseph Sweeney; he was the youngest member	Donegal West
Roger Sweetman	Wexford North
James J. Walsh	Cork City
Peter Ward	Donegal South

The following were elected as MPs but refused their seats as members of the first Dáil Éireann:

Party	Name	Constituency
Irish Unionist Party (22)	William Allen	Armagh North
	Hugh Anderson	Londonderry North
	E.M. Archdale	Fermanagh North
	T.W. Brown	Down North
	Edward Carson	Belfast Duncairn
	W. Coote	Tyrone South
	Charles Craig	Antrim South
	Sir James Craig, Bt	Down Mid
	Herbert Dixon	Belfast Pottinger
	Sir Maurice Dockrell	Dublin Rathmines
	Denis S. Henry	Londonderry South
	W.A. Lindsay	Belfast Cromac
	J.R. Lonsdale	Armagh Mid
	R.J. Lynn	Belfast Woodvale
	Robert McCalmont	Antrim East
	Thomas Moles	Belfast Ormeau
	Hon. R.W. Hugh O'Neill	Antrim Mid

	D.D. Reid	Down East
	Arthur Warren Samuels	Dublin University
	Major P. Kerr Smiley	Antrim North
	Sir William Whitla	Queen's University Belfast
	Daniel M. Wilson	Down West
Irish Parliamentary Party (6)	J. Donnelly	Armagh South
	Joseph Devlin	Belfast Falls
	Thomas Harbison	Tyrone North-East
	E.J. Kelly	Donegal East
	Jeremiah McVeigh	Down South
	William Archer Redmond	Waterford City
Labour Unionist (3)	Thomas H. Burn	Belfast St Anne's
	T. Donald	Belfast Victoria
	S. McGuffin	Belfast Shankill
Independent Unionist (1)	Sir Robert Henry Woods	Dublin University

Lawrence Ginnell and Desmond FitzGerald used some of the premises for their first propaganda office.

Collins's Department of Finance office and some of his intelligence activities, involving Gearóid O'Sullivan, Diarmuid O'Hegarty and Joe O'Reilly, were situated here. On 12 September 1919 the 'G' Division of the DMP raided Collins's finance office. The raid was led by Det. Daniel Hoey, and Patrick (Padraig) O'Keefe told him, 'You're for it tonight'. Hoey was the detective who had picked out Collins's icon Seán MacDermott in Richmond Prison after the Rising. Hoey was killed that night outside DMP HQ. (See 1 Great Brunswick Street.) Another DMP Detective, Neil McFeely, was also on the raid. He did not think that Collins would be there and therefore wasn't looking for him.

Batt O'Connor had built a large mahogany wardrobe in the office, and Fintan Murphy had hidden the account books, Dick McKee's notebook and the gold and banknotes before the raiders could find them.

While we were in No. 6 the police and military made a raid on the premises, looking, I suppose, for wanted men. We had no warning of this raid at all. Mick Collins was in our room, also Fintan Murphy, Diarmuid Hegarty, Jenny Mason and myself and, possibly, Kitty O'Toole, who joined the staff with Fintan. Bob Conlon was there definitely. Ginger O'Connell had come in to see Mick and as he left the room he forgot to close the door, which Mick remarked on sarcastically. I was getting up to shut it when I saw a policeman standing on guard outside. I shut the door and told Mick it looked like a raid. At that stage we discussed what we were going to do. I think only Mick was armed. If any of the others were the girls took the arms from them. I stuck Mick's revolver down my stocking and anything else incriminating we girls took charge of. The police seemed to start the raid systematically from the bottom up thus giving us time to take these precautions. When they arrived, we had disposed of everything and they found nothing of any importance. They searched the men but not us. We had contemplated every possibility of escape for Mick whom we thought they were looking for, as it had been published that there was a large reward for anyone who helped to find him. There was no means of escape, however, as the military had occupied the narrow entrance in the back as well as the front. Mick said: 'We are caught like rats in a trap and there is no escape'. He remained seated at his desk, quite calm and collected until they came in. One of the police inspectors—I think Love was his name—had a special commission to capture Collins, but it was Inspector McFeely who came to our rooms, looking a little bit frightened. He went round searching the different desks and seemed desperately anxious to finish his task and get out. Mick sat very casually at his desk with one leg swinging and told him in no measured terms what sort of work he was engaged on. He was scathing in his remarks about it. 'What sort of a legacy will you leave to your family, looking for blood money. Could you not find some honest work to do, &c.?' The Inspector was writhing under the attack. At that stage they left the room, to our great relief, and passed on up to the caretaker's room overhead. Frank Gallagher's room on the same landing as ours was being examined the same time as ours. It was there that Ernest Blythe was arrested. He happened to be visiting Frank, probably on Dáil business. Frank, assisted by Michael Nunan, was engaged in propaganda work at the time. Blythe, when he heard a raid was on, hid in a small storeroom and was found there. If he had not done that, he might not have been arrested. The only other person arrested, as far as I remember, was Paidin O'Keefe. Seemingly it was Mick's coolness that saved him from being recognised. From time to time the girls would take a peep out at the corridor to see if the coast was clear and, as soon as we got word that the police had all left the caretaker's room, Mick managed to slip up the stairs, which were now empty. We suspected, however, that the police might come back. Sure enough, in a short time they came up again, this time Inspector Love, who seemed to be in charge of the raid, was with them instead of Inspector McFeely. They took a general survey of the room without questioning anybody and left again. After that, they cleared off finally, taking the two prisoners with them. Our relief this time was intense. Mick came down, sat at his desk and refused to leave in spite of our protestations. We all remained at our work until the normal time for our departure.[406]

On 25 November 1919 the Sinn Féin Party was officially suppressed along with the Dáil.

On 21–23 February 1922 a special Sinn Féin Ard Fheis was held to explore an attempted compromise with the Provisional Government. Its stated purpose was: 'To interpret the constitution of Sinn Féin with reference to the situation created by the signing at London of the Articles of Agreement for a Treaty, and the approval of Dáil Éireann by 64 votes to 57, and to decide the policy of Sinn Féin in view of possible forthcoming elections'. On the final day a draft agreement was prepared by Collins, Griffith and de Valera and passed without dissent.

> In order to avoid a division of the Sinn Féin Organisation, and to acquit an opportunity to the signatories of the London Agreement to draft a Constitution, so that when the people are asked to vote at elections to decide between the Republic and the Saorstát the Constitution of the latter may be definitely before them.
>
> It is hereby agreed: this Ard-Fheis shall stand adjourned for three months. In the meantime the Officer Board of the Organisation shall act as a Standing Committee. Dáil Éireann shall meet regularly and continue to function in all its departments as before the signing of the Articles of Agreement, and that no vote in Dáil Éireann shall be regarded as a Party vote requiring the resignation of the President and the Cabinet. That in the meantime no Parliamentary Election shall be held, and that when the Constitution of the Saorstát in its final form shall be presented at the same time as the Articles of Agreement. That this Agreement shall be submitted to the Ard-Fheis, and if approved, shall be binding.[407]

Dáil Éireann ratified this Agreement on 2 March. Griffith was strongly opposed to any compromise with anti-Treaty forces. He thought that a civil war was inevitable and that the sooner it started the sooner it would be over. The irony of this is that Collins was primarily responsible for compelling Sinn Féin to accept the IRB's doctrine of physical force, whereas Griffith had advocated a more non-violent means. Four hundred and fifty-five votes were cast for eleven pro-Treaty candidates, and 155 for the remaining four.

On 15 March 1922 de Valera founded a new party, Cumann na Poblachta, which he said should be translated as the 'Republican Party Organisation', and on 16 March he made an angry speech in Carrick-on-Suir, saying: 'They will have to march over the dead bodies of their own brothers. They will have to wade through Irish blood.

There are rights which may be maintained by force by an armed minority even against a majority.'[408] In Dungarvan on 16 March he said: 'The Treaty ... barred the way to independence with the blood of fellow Irishmen. It was only by Civil War after this that they could get their independence ... If you don't fight today, you will have to fight tomorrow; and I say, when you are in a good fighting position, then fight on.'[409]

He repeated this imagery in Thurles, and added that if the IRA 'accepted the Treaty and if the Volunteers of the future tried to complete the work the Volunteers of the last four years had been attempting, they would have to complete it, not over the bodies of foreign soldiers, but over the dead bodies of their own countrymen. They would have to wade through, perhaps, the blood of some of the members of the Government, in order to get Irish freedom.'[410] In Killarney on 18 March he went on: 'In order to achieve freedom, if our Volunteers continue, and I hope they continue until the goal is reached, if we continue on that movement which was begun when the Volunteers were started and we suppose this Treaty is ratified by your votes, then these men, in order to achieve freedom, will have, I said yesterday, to march over the dead bodies of their own brothers. They will have to wade through Irish blood ... The people never have a right to do wrong.'[411] (See Appendix VI: Carrick-on-Suir, Dungarvan, Killarney, Thurles. Later de Valera claimed that he was misunderstood, that he was merely warning of war rather than encouraging it, and that the *Irish Independent* misinterpreted his words on each occasion.) In Dublin on 25 April he addressed a crowd: 'Young men and young women of Ireland, the goal is at last in sight. Steady; all together, forward. Ireland is yours for the taking. Take it.'[412] (See particularly Killarney in Appendix VI.) (At the funeral of Liam Lynch in April 1923, de Valera said: 'You have to fling yourselves across the stampede of a nation ... It is better to die nobly as your Chief has died than like a slave.'[413])

Currently the HQ of Connradh na Gaeilge (the Gaelic League).

8 Harcourt Street: Ivanhoe Hotel; Collins hid on the roof here when No. 6 Harcourt Street was raided.

27 Harcourt Street: Collins had an office of sorts here for a short time in spring 1921. Liam Deasy came here on Easter Sunday to report to Collins on activities in Cork after the Crossbarry Ambush. He spent an hour going through reports and documents, and commented: 'Collins's immediate grasp of military detail, as was evidenced by his relevant and piercing questions, was astonishing and impressed me in a singular way'.[414]

74 Harcourt Street (at the corner of Clonmel Street): Standard Hotel. Collins escaped a raid on 76 Harcourt Street in November 1919 by going along the rooftops and swinging through the hotel skylight.

W.C. Forbes Redmond, Belfast RIC Assistant Commissioner of Police, stayed here before being killed on 21 January 1920.[415] Redmond was completely unfamiliar with Dublin, so he was assigned a 'minder' by Dublin Castle. As luck would have it, the minder was Collins's operative James McNamara. From then on, McNamara was able to follow Redmond's movements and report to Collins.

> Redmond was stopping in the Standard Hotel in Harcourt Street, and Tom Cullen … a man who was high up on the Intelligence staff and in the confidence of Michael Collins, was sent to stop in the same hotel in order to get all possible information regarding Redmond, particularly about his times of leaving and returning to the hotel, and what he did in the morning and at night.[416]

One of the British spies reporting to Redmond was John Charles (J.C.) Byrne, alias 'Jameson', who was assigned to capture or kill Collins. Redmond foolishly ridiculed 'G' Division detectives in front of McNamara, pointing out that he had an operative who made contact with Collins only a fortnight after arriving from London. One of Collins's agents in the Castle, David Neligan, informed Collins through Éamon Broy, and Redmond was killed a few days later.[417] 'Jameson' was killed on 2 March 1920.[418] (See 56 Bachelor's Walk, Granville Hotel, Sackville Street Upper, Dublin 1; Harcourt Street, Dublin 2; Brendan Road, Nutley Lane, Dublin 4; Ballymun Road, Dublin 11.)

Redmond led a raid on Batt O'Connor's home on 17 January and assured Mrs Bridget O'Connor that he 'wouldn't bother her again'. Collins's men made sure of it.

> One evening I saw Redmond coming down from the Castle but he turned back and went in again. Paddy Daly, Tom Keogh, Vinny Byrne and myself were waiting and Redmond came out again. Tom Keogh turned to Vinny Byrne and myself and told us to cover them off. Redmond went straight up Dame Street, Grafton Street and Harcourt Street, and we followed him. Just as he came as far as Montague Street Paddy Daly pulled out his revolver and shot him under the ear and Tom Keogh pulled out his revolver and shot him in the back. Daly and Keogh carried out the execution, and Byrne and myself acted as a covering party for them.[419]

The first shot shattered Redmond's jaw and he tried to draw a gun, but the second shot in the forehead killed him. Redmond was the highest-ranking casualty in DMP history.

The killing was carefully planned. Daly and Joe Dolan stayed in the hotel for two weeks beforehand to learn about Redmond's movements. The canteen manager of the King George V Military Hospital, a man named Houlihan, smuggled out the gun used in the killing. Mick McDonnell was in charge of the Squad.

76 Harcourt Street: Collins purchased the building for the Dáil for £1,130, and Batt O'Connor immediately set about building the secret compartments. The Dáil had an office here from June 1919 until it was raided on 11 November 1919. On that occasion Collins escaped through the skylight to the Standard Hotel.

> Mick Collins was in his own office upstairs and Diarmuid O'Hegarty, on hearing the raiders coming, had rushed up the stairs to warn him. What happened up there I don't know except that he got out through the roof by a pre-arranged method while we delayed them as long as possible downstairs. We afterwards heard he had succeeded in getting into the Standard Hotel over the roofs of the intervening houses. It did not seem as if the raid was directed against Mick Collins on this occasion, but rather for the purpose of enforcing the proclamation declaring the Dáil illegal. Hence the staff came in for attention and arrest as well as the TDs. There was nobody now left but Jenny Mason and myself. Mick returned about 5 o'clock and immediately set to work to reorganise the offices. He transferred the bulk of the work to No. 5 Mespil Road, where he already had an office. Miss Mason went with him and I stayed on in 76, working directly under the instructions which reached me daily through Joe O'Reilly. Mick used to write out in his methodical way a list of instructions regarding the correspondence or any other work he required to be done, as he did not come in regularly during working hours.[420]

In that raid Ernest Blythe, Seán Hayes, Frank Lawless, Michael Lynch, Dick McKee, Fintan Murphy, Dan O'Donovan, Diarmuid O'Hegarty, Paddy O'Keefe, Seán O'Mahoney and Patrick Sheehan were arrested, and then spent two months in jail.[421] Collins's agent Dave Neligan was one of the men designated to search the offices. Neligan said that he had no intention of finding anything: 'I went upstairs and counted the roses on the wallpaper until the raid was over!' Batt O'Connor had built secret hiding places in the offices, and many papers were hidden before the police could find them.

> … the British soldiers raided No. 6 Harcourt Street. Collins escaped to the roof, but I was arrested along with Paddy O'Keefe, the Secretary of Sinn Féin. After a day or two in the Bridewell, we were taken to Mountjoy where we were kept for a month or two before being tried. At that time the policy was that untried prisoners did not go on hunger-strike but that men went on hunger-strike when sentenced. A warder, who was very friendly and was in charge of prison repairs, came to me and said that Collins was prepared to make arrangements for my rescue. As, however, I knew that I had been arrested because of a letter for Dick Mulcahy which had been handed to me by James Kennedy of Nenagh, and which

had been found on me in a police search half-an-hour afterwards, and as I did not know what was in the letter or what propagandist use might be made of it, I said that I preferred to be court-martialled. When I was brought up for preliminary hearing I learned the contents of the letter for the first time. It advocated a system of attacks on the parents and relatives of RIC men, which was something of which I completely disapproved. I said at the court-martial that I had no knowledge of the contents of the letter until it was read for me at the preliminary hearing and that I disagreed with everything in it. As the policeman who first searched me had put the letter back in my pocket without re-inserting it in the envelope and as the District Inspector who followed him did not notice the empty envelope, Dick Mulcahy's name did not come into the case. The sentence of the Court was one year's imprisonment, and, as others were doing, I immediately went on hunger-strike. I was not more than four or five days on hunger-strike when I was released and transferred to the Mater Hospital, where I remained for a few days.

After I was released I was about to visit the Dáil Éireann offices which were in 76 Harcourt St., a house recently purchased, No. 6 having been left to Sinn Féin. As I arrived near the house I saw lorries around and realised that a raid was in progress. If I had been half an hour earlier I should have walked into a fresh arrest. Collins this time also escaped by the roof. As a matter of fact he owed his escape to the circumstance that a member of the staff, a Miss Lawless, looked out the window and saw the soldiers coming, rushed to the front door and slipped the Yale lock. The result was that the soldiers were sufficiently delayed in getting in to enable Collins to get on the roof and finally get down by a rather dangerous jump into the Standard Hotel. After that, 76 Harcourt St. was not used by any members of the Government.[422]

The British did take boxes of papers in the raid and among the most important were reams of Dáil Éireann stationery. Nothing was heard of the cache until March and April 1920, when a number of leading Republicans were murdered in their homes. Before their murder, each had received a death notice on that Dáil stationery. On 14–16 May 1920 every member of the Dáil who was not in prison received a threatening letter. Typed in capitals on the stationery was the threat:

AN EYE FOR AN EYE, A TOOTH FOR A TOOTH. THEREFORE A LIFE FOR A LIFE.

Arthur Griffith summoned the press on 18 May and told them that the letters were typed on the stationery stolen in the raid. He pointed out that all the death notices had been posted in Dublin, and he accused the British government of being a party to the assassinations of the elected representatives of the Irish people. W.E. Johnstone,

Chief Commissioner of the DMP, issued a statement on 27 May denying any involvement in the theft or the death notices. Neither the Irish nor the government made any further comment until September, when the *Irish Bulletin* dropped a bombshell and published copies of the official government correspondence indicating complete knowledge of the plans for assassination on the part of the British. (See *Irish Bulletin*, Molesworth Street.)[423]

The building was also used to house the Dáil Loan. (See Mansion House, Dawson Street; St Enda's, Rathfarnham, Dublin 14.) The British attempted to confiscate the funds and on 1 March a secret commission was established which summoned bank managers to appear and identify the funds held in their institutions. When Collins heard of it, he had the signatory of the summons, Alan Bell, shot. (See Dame Street, Munster and Leinster Bank, Dublin 2; Nutley Lane, Dublin 4.)

The building currently houses the corporate services division of the Department of Foreign Affairs.

17 Harcourt Terrace: Collins had a small office here that he used from the end of May until July 1921. This was a private home that Batt O'Connor rented for him, and then built secret compartments in the wall and floor.

Kevin Street: A major DMP barracks and training depot. At one time it was the palace of the archbishop of Dublin. Collins's spy Dave Neligan was first posted here. It was an 'A' Division post and was in the same yard as a detachment of mounted police. In 1917 it had Inspector Carey, Sgt Hurley and Constable Birmingham on its staff.

Kevin Street Cross: Fintan Murphy arranged for a shoemaker here to make special shoes for Harry Boland when he went to America, into which were placed copies of the Irish Declaration of Independence and a copy of the prospectus for the Dáil Loan. The copy of the Declaration bore the signatures of the Speaker of the Dáil and the holders of the ministries.

Kildare Street: Leinster House, where Dáil Éireann now meets, and did so after 1922. Lord Edward Fitzgerald was born here on 15 October 1763. He did not like the house, saying: 'It does not inspire the brightest ideas'.

The first session of the Third Dáil was held here on 9 September 1922. (The IRA/Republicans never recognised this Dáil. To this day, the strictest IRA supporters hold that the Second Dáil was never 'dissolved', is still in existence and is the basis for their Republican claims, because it was the successor in interest to the 'Republic' established by the Proclamation of 1916.) Only the elderly Laurence Ginnell attended as a Republican and he was rapidly ejected for his repeated enquiries as to its constitutionality. Because of the Republican abstention, the only source of criticism came from the Labour Party, especially Thomas Johnson[424] and Cathal O'Shannon.

This Third Dáil ratified the Constitution of the Irish Free State on 18 September 1922.[425] The document was drafted in the Shelbourne Hotel in the 'Constitution Room', which can now be seen by tourists. The committee appointed to draft the Constitution was chaired by Collins, but Darrell Figgis, the vice-chairman, and James Douglas, the new Free State attorney general, were responsible for most of its drafting.[426] (See Shelbourne Hotel, St Stephen's Green.)

William Cosgrave was elected president of the Executive Council of the Free State and minister for finance. Other cabinet members included:

Ernest Blythe, minister for local government

Desmond FitzGerald, publicity director and minister for external affairs

Patrick Hogan, minister for agriculture

Eoin MacNeill, Ceann Comhairle of the Dáil until 9 September, minister
without portfolio from January to August 1922 and minister for education
from August to the following September

Joe McGrath, minister for industry and commerce and economic affairs (labour)

Richard Mulcahy, minister for defence

Kevin O'Higgins, vice-president of the Executive Council and minister for home
affairs

James J. Walsh, postmaster general

Éamonn J. Duggan, minister without portfolio

Fionan Lynch, minister without portfolio, then took over the ministry for
fisheries

Michael Hayes was Ceann Comhairle of the Third Dáil,[427] and Padraic Ó Maille was Leas-Ceann Comhairle. Cosgrave replaced Collins in finance.

The Seanad na hÉireann (Senate) was established here and originally had 36 Catholic members and 24 non-Catholic members. In 1921 Arthur Griffith, as the leader of the Irish delegation at the Treaty negotiations, sought to ensure the status of the unionist and Protestant minority in a new Irish Free State. The day the Treaty was signed, Griffith met with southern unionist representatives and assured them of due representation in the Senate. Griffith did not live to realise his promise, but W.T. Cosgrave, president of the Executive Council, fulfilled Griffith's wishes.[428] Cosgrave appointed 30 senators to the Senate in December 1922 and the Dáil elected a further 30. In all, seven peers, a dowager countess, five baronets and several knights were represented. The Senate consisted of 36 Catholics, twenty Protestants, three Quakers and one Jew. Cosgrave's nominees numbered sixteen southern unionists. The members included a number of representatives from the landed gentry, as Griffith's policy had been to draw in all sections of the country and his offer to 'come and get the country under way' was well received by Protestant unionists. The earl of Dunraven and Mount-Earl, the earl of Granard, the earl of Mayo, the earl of Wicklow, Sir Hutchinson Poe, Sir Thomas Esmonde, Sir Nugent Everard, Sir John Purser Griffith, H.S. Guinness, Andrew Jameson, W.B. Yeats and Oliver St John Gogarty were among those who became Free State senators. The first presiding officer of the Seanad (Cathaoirleach Seanad na hÉireann) was Lord Glenavy, who had been an ally of Carson in 1912.[429]

Anti-Treaty forces believed, however, that the Senate was designed primarily for the purpose of upholding the interests of the pro-British element in the Irish Free State. The execution of Erskine Childers in November 1922 introduced a new dimension into the ongoing Civil War. Anti-Treaty forces under the command of Liam Lynch gave notice that senators were legitimate targets unless they resigned their office, but the new senators rejected this request. By the end of March 1923, 37 senators' homes had been burnt to the ground.[430] (See 'Orders of Frightfulness', Beggar's Bush Barracks, Shelbourne Road, Dublin 4.)

On 27 September 1922 the Public Safety Act was passed; it set up military courts, which were given powers, including that of execution, for various offences. This ushered in a harsher period of the Civil War. Ernest Blythe pointed out that the reluctance to take life had weakened their cause previously.[431] Mulcahy was convinced that compromise was impossible. The Labour TDs were the only dissenters, pointing out the dangers of a military dictatorship.

In early October an amnesty for surrendering IRA/Republicans was agreed. On 7 December Seán Hales was killed outside the Dáil and Padraic Ó Maille, Leas-Ceann Comhairle of the Dáil, was wounded by IRA/Republicans of the Dublin No. 1 Brigade in reprisal for the passage of the Public Safety Act. This was the only time when the reprisal orders of Liam Lynch (called 'Orders of Frightfulness'), which were to kill any TD who voted for the bill, were carried out. Dick Barrett, Joe McKelvey, Liam Mellows and Rory O'Connor were executed in Mountjoy Prison on 8 December 1922 in reprisal for the shooting. This is such an infamous event in the Civil War that it has long been questioned who was 'responsible'. It appears that Mulcahy took the initiative, and that Kevin O'Higgins and Joe McGrath were the last cabinet members to give their consent. (See North Circular Road/Mountjoy Prison.)

In the general election of 27 August 1923 Cumann na nGaedheal won 63 seats (415,000 votes for the former pro-Treatyites), Sinn Féin (abstentionists) won 44 seats (286,000 for 'Republicans'), Independents won sixteen seats, the Farmers won fifteen seats, Labour won fourteen seats and Independent Labour won one seat.

1–3 Kildare Street: Kildare Street Club (fronted the grounds of TCD and extended into Kildare Street). The IRA/Republicans in the Civil War used it as a major position, and it housed many refugees from the North who were fleeing the pogroms in Belfast.

King Street South: Gaiety Theatre. On Saturday night, 20 November 1920, Collins went to the bar here for a further meeting after the 'final' Bloody Sunday meeting had been held. He often met people in this bar: 'It had a respectable air of legal and loyal comfort, no one would expect a Republican to pollute its atmosphere'.

Leeson Lane (on St Stephen's Green): St Vincent's Hospital (located in St Stephen's Green in 1834 and relocated to its present site in Elm Park in 1970).

Harry Boland died in St Vincent's on 2 August and his body was removed to the Church of Our Lady of Mount Carmel in Whitefriar Street. (See Skerries, Grand Hotel, Appendix VI.) Hearing of his death, Collins wrote to Kitty Kiernan:

> Last night I passed by St Vincent's Hospital and saw a small crowd outside. My mind went in to him lying dead there and I thought of the times together, and, whatever good there is in any wish of mine he certainly had it. Although the gap of 8 or 9 months was not forgotten—of course no one can ever forget it—I only thought of him with the friendship of the days of 1918 and 1919 … I'd send a wreath but I suppose they'd return it torn up.[432]

Less than three weeks later, Collins himself was 'laid out' in the mortuary chapel before his body was removed to the pro-cathedral for burial. Oliver St John Gogarty and Desmond FitzGerald supervised Collins's embalming. Gogarty sent Seán Kavanagh for sculptor Albert Power to fashion Collins's death-mask.

Leeson Street: Home of the MacGilligan family. IRA/Volunteers and IRA/Republicans often stayed here. Ernie O'Malley stayed here and often used the house for meetings with Collins during the War of Independence. O'Malley also used the house during the Civil War.

91 Lower Leeson Street: Eastwood Hotel. On Bloody Sunday, the IRA failed to find Capt. Thomas Jennings here. Other targets who escaped were Capt. Jocelyn Hardy and Major William Lorraine King, both of whom were in Dublin Castle at the time and were the ones who tortured and killed Peadar Clancy, Dick McKee and Conor Clune. (See Bloody Sunday, Appendix IV.)

96 Leeson Street Lower: St Vincent's Private Hospital, run by the Sisters of Mercy. (This was a private hospital, not to be confused with the St Vincent's Hospital in Leeson Lane.)

Oliver St John Gogarty admitted Arthur Griffith here, and Griffith died of a cerebral haemorrhage on 12 August 1922 at the age of 51. The worries and anxieties of the past few years had taken their toll.[433]

P.S. O'Hegarty wrote of Griffith: 'He forced England to take her right hand from Ireland's throat and her left hand out of Ireland's pocket'.[434]

William Cosgrave said: 'Though he was only 51, the worries and anxieties of the past two years had taken a terrible toll on him. The hard bargaining with the British and all the travelling back and forth during the Treaty negotiations had broken his health. Finally the eruption of the Civil War was a blow from which he never recovered.'[435]

Griffith loathed Erskine Childers, calling him 'that damned Englishman' in the Dáil. At the time of Griffith's death, Childers was the editor of the anti-Treaty newspaper *Poblacht na hÉireann*, and he sincerely and graciously wrote of Griffith that 'he was the greatest intellectual force at stimulating the tremendous national revival'.[436]

Collins said that 'only those who have worked with him know what Arthur Griffith has done for Ireland; only they can realise how he has spent himself in his country's cause'. At the graveside in Glasnevin Cemetery, Collins said: 'In memory of Arthur Griffith let us resolve now to give fresh play to the impulse of unity, to join together one and all in continuing his constructive work, in building up the country which he loved'.[437]

Standing next to Collins was Revd Dr Michael Fogarty, bishop of Killaloe, who said: 'Michael, you should be prepared. You could be next.' Collins replied: 'I know. I hope to God nobody takes it into his head to die for another twelve months.' On 28 August Dr Fogarty was the principal celebrant at Michael Collins's funeral Mass.

Lombard Street: Peter Lanigan's timber yard. On St Patrick's Day 1858, James Stephens established the Irish *Revolutionary* Brotherhood here, but the name was soon changed to the Irish *Republican* Brotherhood.

Lord Edward Street: British 'Irish' Department of Labour. John Chartres was transferred here in 1920. He was an adviser to the Irish delegates, and particularly to Collins, during the Treaty negotiations in London in 1921.

5 Merrion Square: Home of Dr Robert Farnan, a prominent gynaecologist. Farnan was attending the wives of two Auxiliaries at the time, and he attributed to this circumstance the fact that his house was never raided or searched.

Éamon de Valera stayed here on 26 March 1919—his first night home from England after his escape from Lincoln Prison on 3 February 1919. He also stayed here in December 1920 on his return from the US. (See 31 Fitzwilliam Street Upper.)

Collins met Archbishop Patrick Joseph Clune of Perth, Western Australia, here on 7 December 1920, at Prime Minister David Lloyd George's behest, to explore peace initiatives. (Archbishop Clune was an uncle of Conor Clune, who had just been tortured and killed on Bloody Sunday in November.) At this time the British were showing the first signs of negotiation in earnest. Lloyd George put out feelers for talks, but he did so in a fashion calculated to produce the maximum amount of distrust and obstinacy on the part of the Irish.

Archbishop Clune, born on 6 January 1864 in Ruan, Co. Clare, was first asked to mediate on behalf of his native land by the Hon. Lord Morris, T.P. O'Connor MP and Joe Devlin MP at a luncheon in London on 30 November. That night there were severe Black and Tan reprisals in Lahinch, Co. Clare, with several people killed and many homes burned. Lloyd George condemned all reprisals and asked the archbishop to go to Dublin, interview the Sinn Féin leaders, arrange a temporary truce and prepare an atmosphere for negotiations. These negotiations were opposed by Gen. Sir Nevil Macready but favoured by most of the British cabinet and government.[438]

Lloyd George could not guarantee the safety of the archbishop, however, and would not consent to a safe conduct for the Sinn Féin leaders to meet the archbishop. In order to remain incognito, Archbishop Clune travelled to Ireland on the mailboat as 'Revd Dr Walsh'. On arrival in Dublin on 6 December, he first stayed at All Hallows College, Drumcondra.

Joe O'Reilly, Collins's prime messenger, was assigned to bring the archbishop to Collins.

> My [O'Reilly's] next meeting with Dr Clune was the evening of the next day, Monday, 6th December, 1920, when about eight in the evening I called at the Gresham Hotel in O'Connell Street, met Dr Clune, and told him of the time and place where he would meet Michael Collins the next day. I again warned him to be very careful on leaving for the appointment, and to show no surprise if the driver of the car that I would send took a roundabout way. His Grace took me aside and expressed his uneasiness at the prospect of being followed by Dublin Castle. He then said to me: 'I will go to Dublin Castle and see if my movements have been watched. It were better drop the negotiations than risk the capture of Michael Collins'.

On 7 December, accompanied by Dr Michael Fogarty, bishop of Killaloe, Clune was driven here to meet Collins.

> The next day, Tuesday, 7th December, Dr Clune, accompanied by Dr Fogarty, Bishop of Killaloe, set out from All Hallows College, Drumcondra, for the first interview with Michael Collins. They were driving quite a time, not noticing where they were, too interested in their chat, when Dr Clune looked out as the car drew up before one of the fine residences in Merrion Square, a most unlikely

hide-out for a man with a price on his head. The driver knocked at the hall door and the two bishops were shown into the consulting room of Dr Robert Farnan, one of Dublin's leading gynaecologists. I called upon Dr Farnan in October 1935, and he told me that Dr Clune and 'Mick' Collins met in his house regularly during the negotiations. Mick usually came on a bike which he left at a tobacconist in Merrion Row, just round the corner. At that time, December 1920, Dr Farnan was attending the wives of two of the auxiliaries, and consequently his house was never suspected. He remembered the horrible feeling he had on one occasion as a lorry full of auxiliaries pulled up before the door while Mick and Archbishop Clune were upstairs. The doctor had a few bad minutes until the husband of one of the two patients handed him a message from his wife. Another day Mick came down the stairs arm-in-arm with the Archbishop. Both were laughing at some story as Mick opened the hall door, and stood behind it until Dr Farnan hailed a cab from across the street. As the Archbishop got into the cab a lorry full of 'Black-and-Tans' moved slowly past the house. Perhaps some one had recognised Mick on one of his many visits. Mick closed the door, drew his revolver and watched the lorry from a corner of the curtain. The lorry continued its beat up and down the street, so Mick decided to get out through the back garden. That his house was never once searched or suspected throughout the negotiations Dr Farnan attributes to his professional interest in the wives of the auxiliaries he was attending. Suspicion there undoubtedly was, probably through some policeman glimpsing Michael Collins on one of his visits, but, fortunately, the house escaped a search, luckily for all concerned.[439]

Following his meeting with Collins, Archbishop Clune assured the British cabinet that Collins 'was the one with whom effective business could be done'.[440] Collins was 'on the run' but Arthur Griffith was in Mountjoy Prison at this time, and on 8 December Dr Fogarty and Archbishop Clune met with Alfred W. Cope, the assistant under-secretary for Ireland, at Mountjoy, and then with Griffith. Cope had been appointed to his position with a brief to open covert lines of communication with the nationalist movement. Griffith enthusiastically welcomed the prospect of a truce. Then they met with Eoin MacNeill, who was not so enthusiastic but accepted it. The idea was presented to Michael Staines. Cope was told to present a draft of a truce agreement to Dublin Castle authorities, but this received a hostile reception from Chief Secretary for Ireland Sir Hamar Greenwood and the British military.[441]

Archbishop Clune returned to London and met Lloyd George on 10 December, had another meeting with him on 11 December and returned to Dublin that night. The British authorities in Dublin Castle agreed to meet with the Dáil, but Collins and Richard Mulcahy could not attend. Moreover, the proposed truce would require the IRA/Volunteers to surrender all their arms, and the Dáil could not meet publicly. Clune again returned to London on 18 December, and though meetings continued until 28 December the negotiations were at an end. (See St Stephen's Green, north.)

At the end of the negotiations, Archbishop Clune wrote to Bishop Fogarty, outlining the failure and his feelings:

Jermyn Court Hotel, London,
New Year's Day, 1921.

My Lord,

You have heard, I daresay, that I broke off negotiations on the morning of Christmas Eve and that in the afternoon the Prime Minister's secretary was here begging me not to leave town till the New Year, as Cabinet was to consider the whole question, and important developments might take place. He came again last Tuesday evening and took back with him a memo at the points of the truce. On Wednesday afternoon there was a long Cabinet meeting and another on Thursday, at which General Macready, Lord French and several others were present. The secretary rang me up on Thursday morning to inform me that he would call that night late or Friday (yesterday) morning. He came at 11.30 a.m. yesterday, and here is a summary of his oral communications.

That Cabinet etc. had given long and careful consideration to my proposals: that the proposed truce gave no effective guarantee for a permanent settlement: that consequently the Government had come to the conclusion that it was better to see the thing through as was done in the American and South African wars unless meanwhile the Sinn Féiners surrender their arms and publicly announce the abandonment of violent measures: that the Government felt sanguine that the new Home Rule Bill when studied and understood would be worked, in fact they felt sanguine that within six months all would be working in harmony for Ireland, etc., etc. He then added a few gracious personal compliments from the Prime Minister. My first comment was that I felt sure the Holy Ghost had nothing to do with such a decision which sent him off exploding with laughter.

What is the source of this strange optimism about all classes working the Home Rule Bill in harmony within a few months, I can't make out (Greenwood repeats it in a speech quoted in to-day's paper), unless it is a deduction from the whining [sic] across the water. This Government determination to carry on the policy of frightfulness to the bitter end may be bluff. I think it is not, and hence I believe that the position needs further reconsideration in the light of this considered declaration of policy on their part.

The secretary incidentally mentioned that from my conversations the Prime

Minister had a higher idea of the gunmen: that there could be no humiliation before the world in yielding to vastly superior forces: that the Home Rule Act can be worked for Ireland, not for England, and that through the working of it practically every English official could be sent out of Ireland in a few months, etc., etc.

The point I am coming to is: Ought our grand boys allow themselves to be butchered to make a Saxon holiday? Ought they not rely on passive resistan~ However, I suppose the advent of De Valera to Ireland will quickly solve these questions.

Though I am naturally sorry that my mission has not been successful, in another sense I am glad it has ended. I was beginning to feel the strain. It has done good, I think, indirectly. It has narrowed down the issues, and incidentally it has saved Your Lordship's life and All Hallows College from military occupation.

My programme is now to leave for the continent as soon as Father McMahon joins me, and to catch the boat at Naples on the 24th. I feel sure you need have no further apprehension about yourself. They have given me assurances that all necessary measures would be taken to safeguard your life.

Wishing Your Lordship a full measure of New Year graces and Joys.

I remain, with grateful memories of your kindness,

Yours very sincerely in Xt,

P. J. Clune Archbishop of Perth.

On 6 September 1922, less than a month after Collins had been killed, Msgr Ryan from San Francisco arranged a meeting here between Éamon de Valera and Richard Mulcahy. Previously the Free State cabinet had decided that further talks regarding the Civil War were futile, but Mulcahy, as leader of the army and minister for defence, agreed to meet and arranged a safe conduct for de Valera. Mulcahy felt that two things were imperative: (1) that the Free State government should be allowed to 'work' the Treaty, and (2) that if there was an army in Ireland it should be subject to the Dáil. De Valera then stated: 'Some men are led by faith and some men by reason, but as long as there are men like Rory O'Connor taking the stand that he is taking, I am a humble soldier following after them'.[442] As a result, Mulcahy decided on the drastic course of reprisal executions.[443] (See North Circular Road/Mountjoy Prison.)

The building is now the Dublin Institute for Advanced Studies.

85 Merrion Square: First HQ of the Free State Army Medical Services, under the command of Major-Gen. (Dr) Maurice Hayes. In September 1922 Dr Brigid Lyons went to work here as a 1Lt earning eight shillings per day.[444] (See Kilmainham Gaol, Dublin 8.) Following Dr Hayes as directors were Col. Tom O'Higgins and Frank Morrin.

Merrion Street: Provisional Government's departmental offices following the Treaty debates. Collins's offices moved here from their temporary quarters in City Hall (see Dame Street at Cork Hill, Dublin 2) after the Castle had been turned over by the British. Over time, he also moved some of his Department of Finance offices in Mary Street and his Harcourt Terrace functions here.

11 Molesworth Street: *The Irish Bulletin*. Desmond FitzGerald was the editor, succeeded by Erskine Childers. Piaras Béaslaí, a Dublin journalist, acted as Collins's liaison with IRA/Volunteer HQ.

An 'underground newspaper', it was by far the biggest journalistic bane of the British. The office, disguised as an Insurance Society, shared the building with the 'Church of Ireland Widows and Orphans Society'. Its journalists included Robert Brennan, Erskine Childers, Desmond FitzGerald and Frank Gallagher. Anna Fitzsimmons ('Miss Fitz') Kelly was the secretary, and the staff included Séamus Heaney, Séamus Hynes (messenger), Kathleen McGilligan, Kathleen McKenna, Honor Murphy, Sheila Murphy and Michael Nunan. It was published every day (except for Sundays and bank holidays) from 11 November 1919 until the Truce was declared.[445]

Mrs McKenna was a member of staff from the beginning and described the newspaper thus:

> The Bulletin was edited from its inception in November 1919 until his arrest on 11th February 1921 by Desmond FitzGerald, whose idea it was, and the information it contained was compiled by him and by Robert Brennan and Frank Gallagher. After Desmond FitzGerald's arrest Erskine Childers who had been appointed Substitute Director of Propaganda by the Dáil edited it for some months till after the Truce.
>
> ... All the statements made in the Bulletin were substantiated by proofs, and were of such a nature that, were it not for the Bulletin organisation, they would never have received Press publicity. The unmasking of British terrorist methods, the clear, truthful exposition of otherwise unknown aspects of the national struggle, the elaborate but futile attempts made by the British Intelligence service to suppress it, the publicity given in it to secret orders even prior to their being known in British Headquarters themselves, made of the Irish Bulletin a weapon which had a very considerable part in the breaking down of British morale in Ireland. After the Truce this fact was confirmed by statements made both from Dublin Castle and from Michael Collins.
>
> ... Each evening I crossed the city to a place known as 'The Dump' over Mansfield's Boot Shop in O'Connell Street and to the offices of Michael Collins first in Mary Street later in Maurice Collins's shop Parnell Street and Devlin's,

Parnell Square, to collect documents to be used in the compilation of the Bulletin.[446]

On 19 June 1920, the *Bulletin* reported the words of Lt Col. Gerald Brice Ferguson Smyth DSO, King's Own Scottish Borderers, and Divisional Commander for Munster, who addressed RIC members at their barracks in Listowel:

> Well, Men, I have something to tell you. Something I am sure you would not want your wives to hear. Sinn Féin has had all the sport up to the present, and we are going to have the sport now. The police have done splendid work, considering the odds against them. The police are not in sufficient strength to do anything but hold their barracks. This is not enough, for as long as we remain on the defensive, so long will Sinn Féin have the whip hand. We must take the offensive and beat Sinn Féin with its own tactics. Martial law, applying to all Ireland, is coming into operation shortly, and our scheme of amalgamation must be complete by June 21st. If a police barracks is burned or if the barracks already occupied is not suitable, then the best house in the locality is to be commandeered, the occupants thrown into the gutter. Let them die there, the more the better. Police and military will patrol the country at least five nights a week. They are not to confine themselves to the main roads, but make across the country, lie in ambush and, when civilians are seen approaching, shout 'Hands up!' Should the order not be immediately obeyed, shoot and shoot with effect. If the persons approaching carry their hands in their pockets, or are in any way suspicious looking, shoot them down. You may make mistakes occasionally and innocent persons may be shot, but that cannot be helped, and you are bound to get the right parties sometime. The more you shoot, the better I will like you, and I assure you that no policeman will get into trouble for shooting any man. In the past, policemen have got into trouble for giving evidence at coroners' inquests. As a matter of fact coroners' inquests are to be made illegal so that in future no policeman will be asked to give evidence at inquests. We want your assistance in carrying out this scheme and wiping out Sinn Féin. Are you men prepared to cooperate?

(Smyth denied giving this speech in this form.) There must have been some authorisation for the speech, as General Henry H. Tudor, chief of the police, was present.

A member of his audience, Constable Jeremiah Mee, replied: 'By your accent, I take it you are an Englishman, and in your ignorance you forget you are addressing Irishmen. These, too, are English [taking off his cap, belt and arms]. Take them, too.'[447] Collins introduced Mee to the editor of the *Freeman's Journal*, who questioned him at length. Thereafter both the *Freeman's Journal* and the *Irish Bulletin* covered the story comprehensively. Mee later worked in the Ministry for Labour for Countess Markievicz.[448] (See 14 Frederick Street North, Dublin 1.)

In its 21 June 1920 issue the *Bulletin* published lists of RIC men who had resigned. On 17 July 1920 it reported that Lt Col. Gerald Smyth had been killed in the Cork City and County Club.

On 10 September 1920 the *Bulletin* published its most memorable issue, in which it traced the story of the Dáil stationery stolen from 76 Harcourt Street in a raid on 11 November 1919, its use in death threats to Dáil members and leading Republicans, including Cork Lord Mayor Thomas MacCurtain in spring 1920, and the British government's knowledge of and involvement in their subsequent murders. It recounted Arthur Griffith's meeting with the press on 18 May 1920. Further, it repeated the denial of any knowledge of the theft or the death notices by the DMP Commissioner W.E. Johnstone on 27 May. Then the story continued: 'Certain official correspondence of high-placed British Government officials in Ireland is now in the hands of the Irish Republican Authorities'. That correspondence, which was photocopied and sent to American and British newspapers, consisted of four reports and letters.

- A report dated 16 January [*1920*] from Inspector Neil McFeely, who had been on the raid. The report was transmitted to W.C.F. Redmond, Assistant Commissioner, and initialled by him, indicating receipt.
- A letter from the North Dublin Union on 8 April *1920*, indicating the arrival of a 'Mr Hyam' and reporting about him to 'P. Atwood'.

These documents were important to the story, one because it was written by an Inspector of 'G' Division, McFeely, and initialled by Assistant Commissioner Johnstone, and the other because both 'Mr Hyam' and 'P. Atwood' were officers on the British General Staff, assigned to the North Dublin Union. And both documents were on Dáil Éireann stationery stolen from 76 Harcourt Steet in the 11 November 1919 raid. So, the heads of the police and the British General Staff knew, before the denial was issued, that the British had the notepaper and were using it.

- A third document was a letter from Capt. F. Harper-Shove of the British General Staff regarding a hunger strike in Mountjoy Jail that had just ended. The letter in itself had nothing to do with the notepaper, but *it was typed on the very same typewriter on which the death notices had been typed*.
- The final document was a letter from 'St Andrew's Hotel, Exchequer Street, Dublin', dated 22 March 1920. It was written by Capt. Harper-Shove to a 'Dear Hardy'. In this letter, Harper-Shove indicated that he had been given 'a free hand

to carry on, … Re our little stunt, I see no prospects until I have got things on a firmer basis, but still hope and believe there are possibilities'. The 'little stunt' was the assassinations, and they began on 22 March with the murder of Lord Mayor Thomas MacCurtain in Cork. Shortly thereafter, James McCarthy of Thurles and Thomas O'Dwyer of Bouladuff were also killed in County Cork. The method, even the hour, of killing was exactly the same for all three, and all had received a death notice on Dáil Éireann stationery.

The British continued to deny the theft and indicated that a 'complete refutation would follow', but that refutation never came.[449]

On 26–7 March 1921 (Holy Saturday night) 'C' Company of the Auxiliaries raided the paper, but all the office personnel escaped. From then on the paper went 'underground' and was published from various offices and homes throughout Dublin—but it never missed an issue until it was closed down after the Truce.

On Tuesday 29 March, Issue No. 56, Volume IV, was published from Maureen Power's front room in Harold's Cross. On the following day there were two issues, one of which, numbered as No. 56, Volume IV, was an 'official' forgery put out by Dublin Castle. The forgery collapsed after a month—it was often quoted by the real *Bulletin*. Collins was extremely concerned about this forgery; he worried that it would be taken to be authentic and might be a great propaganda tool for the British.

22 Lower Mount Street: On Bloody Sunday Tom Keogh killed Lt H.R. Angliss (generally known as, and referred to in most sources as, 'Patrick McMahon' or 'Mahon') here. Angliss and Lt Charles Peel were among the men recalled from Russia to organise the intelligence group in Dublin. Peel escaped by piling all the furniture against the door. Jim Slattery, Billy McClean and Jim Dempsey were in the Volunteer team.[450]

> I was assigned to 22 Lower Mount Street, where two enemy agents were located. One was Lieutenant McMahon, but I cannot remember the other man's name. Tom Keogh and myself from the Squad, with six others from 'E' Company of the 2nd Battalion, proceeded toward Mount Street. At the appointed hour on the following morning, 21st November, we knocked at the door and a maid admitted us. We left two men inside the door to see that nobody would enter or leave the house, and the remainder of us proceeded upstairs to two rooms, the numbers of which we had already ascertained. We had only just gone upstairs when we heard shooting downstairs. The housekeeper or some other lady in the house had seen a patrol of Tans passing by outside, and had started to scream. The Tans immediately surrounded the house and tried to gain admission. One of our young men, Billy McLean, fired at them through the door and eased the situation

for us for a little while, although he got wounded in the hand himself. I think the Tans fired first. We succeeded in shooting Lieutenant McMahon, but could not gain admission into the room where the other agent was sleeping. There was a second man in McMahon's bed, but we did not shoot him as we had no instructions to do so. We discovered afterwards that he was an undesirable character as far as we were concerned, and that we should have shot him. We went downstairs and tried to get out but found the British forces at the front of the house. We went to the back of the house, and a member of 'E' Company, Jim Dempsey, and myself got through by getting over a wall. We understood that the rest of our party were following us, but after going a little distance we found we were alone. What actually happened was that Teeling was the third man to scale the wall, and as he got up he was fired on from the house. We were all fired on, but Teeling was the only man who was hit. Teeling took cover in the garden. The other members of our party retired and got safely through the front door in the confusion. It was only hours afterwards that we discovered Teeling was wounded. Dempsey and myself went round by the South Circular Road, and got a wash-up in Golden's house, Victoria Street. We got home safely. Some time before the football match most of us met again, and it transpired that Teeling was on the missing list.[451]

Two Auxiliaries, Frank Garner and Cecil Morris, were killed outside. These were sent on foot to Beggar's Bush Barracks, but were intercepted and shot by IRA/Volunteer lookouts. A military motorcyclist saw the fight and drove to Beggar's Bush Barracks. Brig. Gen. Frank Crozier was inspecting the Auxiliaries in the Barracks and drove to the scene. He returned to Beggar's Bush with the first accurate reports. (See Bloody Sunday, Appendix IV.)

Frank Teeling was wounded by Auxiliaries and was taken to hospital. Collins arranged his escape from Kilmainham Gaol with Simon Donnelly and Ernie O'Malley. (See South Circular Road/Kilmainham Gaol.)

Keogh made a date with the housemaid here who opened the door, and when he was escaping he told the others, 'I've got to keep that date'.

22 Upper Mount Street: Home of Laurence (Larry) Nugent, an IRA/Volunteer adjutant, and his wife. The *Irish Bulletin* was housed here before moving to Molesworth Street.

Early in 1920, the Nugents agreed to lease the Dáil Propaganda Department a flat on the upper floor of their home. Nugent took the anti-Treaty side in the Civil War.

My place at 22 Upper Baggot Street was a small arsenal during these troubled times. Most of the stuff was under cover, but not all of it as it was changing hands from day to day.

... One of the best kept secrets of the IRA was the code word. It is doubtful if the inner working of this portion of the IRA activities was ever known by the British authorities in Ireland. My experience of this secret operation was that I happened to know personally an individual in the British Service who received this code word from London and sent it to various military and police posts in these areas. This person called to see me at the end of 1919. I did not know at the time of the call that the individual was such an important person and, in consequence, the reception was cool. The IRA intelligence department which, apparently, knew most things, knew of this particular visit, and in a few days I had a note from Mick Collins (with an enclosure) telling me to write to this individual asking that the enclosed request be carried out. Joe O'Reilly brought this note. For certain reasons I asked him to call back in an hour or so, and after a long consultation with Mrs Nugent I wrote as follows: 'Dear — This letter will be handed to you by — and if you are prepared to carry out the instructions conveyed to you in the enclosure, the contents of which I am aware, the only recompense you may expect will be the protection of the forces whom you are serving. Mise — L. Nugent'. Mick approved of my note and it was handed to the individual as arranged, and the instructions were faithfully carried out at a terrible risk but in a very safe way. Only three men in a Brigade area knew of the code word, the Brigade O/C, the Brigade Adj. and the Brigade I/O. I met the Brigade O/C of an area where my friend gave the code word, and he told me that on almost all occasions he had the code before the military or police in his district and he was able to tap the wires and get the orders intended to be carried out by the military or police, and so he was able to protect himself and his men. This arrangement was carried out in every Brigade area in the country.

... [In 1920] The railways were still almost idle, the railway men refusing to carry armed military or police or even army equipment. Food was getting scarcer and very dear in Dublin. The Belfast boycott was a success and the IRA were keeping a close watch on any attempts to import goods from that city.

... The military operation carried out by the IRA on what was often called Bloody Sunday was not decided upon in a hurry, nor was it carried out for any personal or collective motives. It was done for the purpose of saving the lives of the men and women constituting the IRA and Cumann na mBan and their various sympathisers and helpers and indeed their families. ... A number of people in Dublin referred to these executions as murders. As one who took a humble part in the preparation for the operation, I definitely repudiate any such suggestion. It was an act of war duly carried out under orders. True the IRA men did not like their job, but does any firing squad in any army like its job. That is a question which should be considered by critics.

... I have mentioned Mick Collins' dual personality. The 'two Mick Collins'.

Collins protested strongly against being named a Plenipotentiary for the Treaty negotiations. Nevertheless, while in London, he threw himself into the negotiations.

Collins was not camera-shy after the War of Independence, and during his time in London he often had his photo taken. Note that again he grew the moustache to look older and as a disguise.

Left—Another example of Collins photographed during the Treaty negotiations in London.

Below—At the Treaty debates in Earlsfort Terrace, Collins was habitually seen exiting his cab with a briefcase or sheaf of papers under his arm.

Left—Joe Leonard (L) and Charlie Dalton (R) with an unidentified officer after the Treaty. Like many of Collins's Squad, they joined the Free State Army.

Collins was described by Arthur Griffith as 'the man who won the War [of Independence]' in the Treaty debates of December 1921.

Above—After the Treaty was passed, Collins often appeared in public around Dublin, and here he is shown outside the pro-cathedral after attending Mass.

Left—Though he only wore a uniform a few times after he returned from Frongoch Prison, following the Treaty he was often seen in the uniform of a general in the Free State Army.

Left—In July 1922 Collins resigned as head of the Provisional Government, and thereafter acted as Army O/C only. The cabinet did not force Collins into this. In fact, he considered that the top priority of the Provisional Government was to conclude the war as quickly as possible, and he felt that he was the best man to accomplish this. Thereafter he was usually seen in uniform.

Left—Collins had his uniforms made at Callaghan & Sons. He was very fastidious about his appearance and often sent back items that he didn't think fitted properly.

In the background of the famous photograph of Collins in full dress uniform in the square of Portobello Barracks was Alphonsus Culliton. 'It was very hard to keep up with his stride….', said Culliton. 'He was a very strong, fit man, always moving…'. The boy was a street urchin who was virtually adopted by Michael Collins, signed into the army when he was fourteen, lived through the Civil War, and survived many ambushes as the mascot of the army.

Above—The front of the Bank of Ireland building in College Green provided a platform for speakers throughout the period. Here, Collins is waiting to speak at a rally for the Treaty in March 1922 with Joe McGrath and Seán McGarry.

Above—On 14 June 1922, in Cork, Collins repudiated the Collins–de Valera Election Pact, saying: 'I am not hampered now by being on a platform where there are Coalitionists. I can make a straight appeal to you—to the citizens of Cork, vote for the candidates you think better. The country must have the representatives it wants. You understand fully what you have to do and I call on you to do it.'

Above—Following the Treaty debates and prior to the June 1922 election, Collins spoke throughout Ireland. Here he is shown in one of his most typical poses, making his point that the Treaty was a 'stepping stone' to ultimate freedom.

Left—Collins on the speaking platform in Cork. Immense crowds came to hear him speak, but there were many hecklers in the crowd who were opposed to the Treaty—especially in Cork.

Further to this statement, when he visited Tralee on a tour of inspection during the Civil War he was in a hotel lounge there when his old friend, Brother Joachim of Dominick Street Priory who was in Tralee at the time, called to see him. Mick was dressed in the grand uniform of a General. He rose to meet and shake hands with Brother Joachim, but the saintly old man turned away and said, 'Ah, no, you are not my Mick'. Brother Joachim told me this story himself and I have no doubt as to the truth of the statement. Mick was drinking too much—he had 'turned on the tap'. ... When Mick was killed in action in Cork, accusations were widely circulated that he was murdered and men who have written of this event have tried to prove this statement, but in a very unconvincing way to anyone who would stop to study the situation. ... I was very sorry for Mick: we had been very good friends for a long time and I enquired from every possible angle in both Dublin and Cork as to the way in which he lost his life.[452]

38 Upper Mount Street: On Bloody Sunday Lt Peter Ashmunt Ames, Grenadier Guards, and Lt (Brevet Capt.) George Bennett (28), Royal Artillery, were killed here. Ames was the son of Mrs Eleanor Ames of Morristown, NJ. Bennett had been in British Intelligence in World War I, and was asked to rejoin to work in Ireland. Vinnie Byrne was in charge of the detail, which walked here after Mass and included Tom Ennis, Johnny McDonnell (who went on to play in goal in the GAA match at Croke Park that afternoon), Seán Daly, Michael Lawless, Tom Duffy, Seán Doyle, Herbie Conroy and Frank Saurin.[453]

I was detailed as IO to the Squad to execute Lieutenants Gerald Ames and Bennett at 38 Upper Mount Street. ... The only information I had as to their whereabouts at this address was a recently captured letter to Ames and in which Bennett was mentioned. At 10 o'clock on that night I went to Upper Mount Street to locate the house. Before leaving I arranged with the squad leader, Vincent Byrne, where to meet on the following morning. The time arranged for the 'jobs' throughout the city was to be 9 a.m. on the 21st. We gained access to Number 38 without any difficulty. I asked a maid where was Mr Bennett and Mr Ames. When she told me, we tried the door of Bennett's room, which was locked. Herbert Conroy, a member of the squad, had a sledge hammer under his coat and wanted to break in the door. I would not let him but instructed the maid to knock on the door, which was opened by Bennett. We took him to a return room where Ames was sleeping, and having asked the squad for as much time as possible, as I was interested principally in the papers these Intelligence Officers might have, they were then executed in Ames' room. In my anxiety to make a thorough search I was unaware that the squad had left and, hearing some shooting in the street, I walked to the door of Bennett's room. I heard a noise and looking down the hall I saw a British soldier outside the room where the two bodies were. I wheeled to shoot but the soldier jumped into the room. At the same time, Tom Ennis, who was shooting across the street from the doorstep of 38, called on me to 'come on'.[454]

Katherine Farrell was the maid who let the IRA into the house. (See Bloody Sunday, Appendix IV.)

11 Nassau Street: Home of Grace Gifford Plunkett for many years after the Civil War.

32 Nassau Street: British Department of Munitions Office, opened in 1917 to coordinate Ireland's World War I efforts. It was said that John Chartres was connected with this office.

45 Nassau Street: Frank Gallagher, cigar importer; later the Berni Inn. At the back of this was Kidd's Buffet on Grafton Street, known as 'Kidd's Back'. It was a very important meeting place for English touts. Collins's men Tom Cullen, Frank Thornton, Liam Tobin[455] and Frank Saurin[456] met their 'contacts' here and passed themselves off as friends of the English officers in order to get information.

At that time most of the British Secret Service Agents, and British Intelligence Officers and Auxiliary Intelligence Officers met at a place which was well known in Dublin as Kidd's Buffet—Kidd's Back it was known in Grafton Street, and presently Jammet's Back. Now here is where a lot of our information was picked up, and again it had to be picked up by taking a very big risk. Tom Cullen, Frank Saurin and myself were deputed to act with our two Secret Service friends who then frequented Kidd's Buffet with the Secret Service. We were introduced in the ordinary way as touts and eventually became great friends of men like Major Bennett, Colonel Aimes [*sic*] and a number of other prominent Secret Service Officers. Naturally Collins and all his staff and the whole activities of the organisation were discussed there daily. On one day, one of these officers turned suddenly to Tom Cullen and said, 'Surely you fellows know these men Liam Tobin, Tom Cullen and Frank Thornton, these are Collins's three officers and if you can get these fellows we would locate Collins himself'. Needless to remark, if the ground opened and swallowed us we could not have been more surprised, and for the moment we felt that we had walked into a trap, but that wasn't so at all. It was a genuine query to the three Irishmen, whom they believed should know all about the particular fellows they mentioned. The fact remains that although they knew of the existence of the three of us and they knew of the existence of Collins, they actually had no photograph of any of us, and had a very poor description of either Collins or the three of us. [457]

46 Nassau Street: Jammet's Restaurant (David Hogan wrote of 'Kidd's, which has since become Jammet's'); for some time previously it was located at St Andrew Street and Church Lane. It was the finest French restaurant in Dublin prior to and after the Rising. Yvonne Jammet, a sculptor and painter from Paris, came to Dublin with her restaurateur husband, Louis Jammet. Their restaurant was soon a meeting point for artists and writers.

Seán MacDermott took his closest friends here for a 'last meal' just prior to the Rising. Often used by Collins and Harry Boland, it was raided on 10 January 1921.

Harry Boland ate here with a former secretary of Collins, Anna Fitzsimmons (later Mrs Kelly), on 30 July 1922, and told her 'not to worry. Eat well, it may be your last meal with me.' Boland was shot on 31 July at the Grand Hotel, Skerries, and died on 2 August in St Vincent's Hospital. (See Skerries, Grand Hotel, Appendix VI.)

It subsequently moved to Grafton Street in 1928, and the building now houses Lillie's Bordello.

5–7 Parliament Street: Royal Exchange Hotel. It was a favourite of IRA/Volunteers from the country.

John Aloysius Lynch (a Dáil/Republican court judge and county councillor from Killmallock, Co. Limerick) was mistakenly killed here on 23 September 1920 by a detail led by Capt. G.T. Baggalley, who was subsequently killed on Bloody Sunday. Some feel that John was mistaken for Liam Lynch, but probably not,[458] as John was much older than Liam. Lynch had just delivered £23,000 to Collins for the Dáil Loan, but that was his only connection to the IRA/Volunteers. (See Bloody Sunday, Appendix IV.)

Collins said that 'there is not the slightest doubt that he was not in possession of a revolver', and knew that it was just a case of mistaken identity.

23 Lower Pembroke Street: Home of Frank and Cecelia Gallagher. A journalist who was the principal writer of the *Irish Bulletin*, Frank Gallagher wrote *The four glorious years* under the pseudonym of David Hogan. (See Molesworth Street.)

6 Upper Pembroke Street: Home of Desmond FitzGerald during the War of Independence.

28–29 Upper Pembroke Street: Boarding house run by Mrs Grey. She had many boarders, most of them British officers, and a staff of maids and porters to take care of their needs.

On Bloody Sunday, Major Charles M.C. Dowling, Grenadier Guards, Col. Hugh F. Montgomery, Lancashire Fusiliers, and Capt. Leonard Price MC, Middlesex Regiment, were killed here. (Montgomery was in hospital for three weeks before he died of his wounds.) Col. Wilfred James Woodcock DSO, Lancashire Fusiliers, Lt R.G. Murray, Royal Scots, and Capt. B.C.H. Keenlyside, Lancashire Fusiliers, were all wounded. Woodcock was not connected with intelligence and had walked into a confrontation on the first floor of the house as he was preparing to leave to command a regimental parade at army headquarters. He was in his military uniform, and when he shouted to warn the other five British officers living in the house, he was shot in the shoulder and back, but survived. As Keenlyside was about to be shot, a struggle ensued between his wife and Mick O'Hanlon. The leader of the unit, Mick Flanagan, arrived, pushed Mrs Keenlyside out of the way and shot her husband.

Caroline Woodcock, wife of Col. Woodcock, wrote prolifically about her period as a British army wife in Dublin in her book *Experiences of an officer's wife in Ireland*. Her diaries were published as a book in 1921.

The IRA/Volunteer Squad included Mick Flanagan (O/C), Martin Lavan, Albert Rutherford, George White, Charlie Dalton, Andy Cooney, Paddy Flanagan, Mick O'Hanlon, Leo Dunne and Ned Kelleher. Cooney removed a great many documents and took them to Collins. (See Bloody Sunday, Appendix IV.)

'Maudie' the maid had told her boyfriend about all the British who went out after curfew, and he passed the word to Collins. After the raid she said to her boyfriend, 'Oh, why did you do that to them? I thought you would only kidnap them and send them away.' James Green was the porter.[459]

I was instructed by the Deputy Director of Intelligence to contact a girl who had reported to a Volunteer about some strange residents who were occupying the block of flats in which she was a maid. I met her in this Volunteer's home over a shop in Talbot St. I think his name was Byrne. I questioned the girl, whose name was Maudie. She described the routine of the residents of the flats, and it would seem from her account that they followed no regular occupation but did a lot of office work in their flats. I arranged with her to bring me the contents of the waste-paper baskets. When these were examined we found torn up documents which referred to the movements of wanted Volunteers, and also photographs of wanted men. ... I last met Maudie on the Saturday evening, 20th November 1920, at our rendezvous, and she told me that all her 'boarders' were at home, with the exception of two who were changing their residence that night to Upper Mount Street. ... When I arrived at Upper Pembroke St. on the Sunday morning, I met Flanagan and a few other Volunteers. I explained to Flanagan that we had no keys for the hall doors in order to gain admission, so we went over our arrangements. Fortunately, at the zero hour of 9 a.m., the hall door was open and the porter was shaking mats on the steps. There were separate staircases in this double house and a party proceeded up either staircase to the rooms already indicated. I accompanied Flanagan and two other Volunteers to a room at the top of the house occupied by two officers, one of these being Lieut. Dowling. We knocked at the door and pushed it open. The two officers were awake in bed. They were told to stand up and were then shot. I told Flanagan that I wanted to search the room and he said: 'Search be damned! Get out of here'. We proceeded down the staircase to the hallway, where a number of other officers had been rounded up from their rooms and were lined up against the side of the staircase that led in the direction of the basement. Our reaching this level was the signal for a volley.[460]

Lavan, who went on to become a successful lawyer in Brighton, Michigan, recalled that he and Rutherford gathered after Mass at University Church in St Stephen's Green. Then they walked to 98 Pembroke Street, where they waited until the appointed time. They were all young: Lavan was eighteen, Rutherford was nineteen, Dalton seventeen, and Flanagan was the oldest at 25. They knocked on the door and Maudie the maid answered; then they crept up to the first floor and waited. Collins had told them not to start shooting until exactly 9.00, so they waited for the time. At 9.00 exactly they knocked on the doors of the men they had come to shoot.[461]

Dalton took a ferry across the Liffey to stay at his parents' house. Lavan and Rutherford went to Dolphin's Barn to play a football match for the 'Mickey Malones' team, thinking that this would aid their alibis.

Peter's Place: Home of Mr and Mrs Ely O'Carroll; meetings of the National Aid Association were held here.

3 St Andrew Street: After the office at 5 Mespil Road (Dublin 4) was raided twice within the month of May 1921, Collins moved his office here. He always thought that there was a 'traitor' who tipped off the British prior to the raids. This office was over the premises of Messrs Corrigan, solicitors, but wasn't used for very long.

26–27 St Andrew Street and Church Lane: Jammet's Restaurant was located here for some time. (See Nassau Street.)

St Stephen's Green: Covering about 60 acres and having eight gates, it was named after St Stephen's Church and Leper Hospital, sited from 1224 to 1639 in the vicinity of Mercer Street. In 1877 Sir Arthur Guinness paid for it to be refurbished.

There are monuments here to Countess Markievicz, the Fianna, Robert Emmet,

James Clarence Mangan, Tom Kettle, James Joyce, Jeremiah O'Donovan Rossa, Theobald Wolfe Tone, Oscar Wilde and W.B. Yeats; there is also a Famine memorial. The Fusilier's Arch is at the Grafton Street entrance (a Boer War monument to the Dublin Fusiliers); older Dubliners often called that entrance the 'Traitor's Gate'.

8 St Stephen's Green (north, next to Shelbourne Hotel): Hibernian United Services Club. Molly O'Reilly began working undercover in the United Services Club in 1918 and became an invaluable intelligence source for Collins.[462] She gathered information on British officers who frequented the Club, supplying Peadar Clancy with their names and private addresses. Things slackened off at the Club and Molly found out that the officers were now going to the Bonne Bouche in Dawson Street for dancing, and she subsequently transferred there. She gathered intelligence on officers and identified 30–35 secret service men, again supplying Clancy with names and addresses. It was a regular occurrence that officers hung up their guns in the gentlemen's room while dancing, and Molly passed that information to Clancy.[463]

11 St Stephen's Green (north): the Loreto Convent was originally here, then moved to 21 St Stephen's Green.

21 St Stephen's Green (north): Louise Gavan Duffy ran the school here. She formerly ran St Ita's. Collins used this school for meetings. Collins met Archbishop Patrick Joseph Clune of Perth, Western Australia, here in December 1920, at Lloyd George's behest, to discuss peace feelers. (See 5 Merrion Square).

27–32 St Stephen's Green (north, corner of Kildare Street): Shelbourne Hotel. Opened in 1824 by Martin Burke, originally of County Tipperary. The general manager from 1904 to 1930 was G.R.F. Olden.

In May 1916, 'the Commission to Inquire into the Rising' met here under the chairmanship of Lord Hardinge. The other members of the Commission were Mr Justice Montague Shearman and Sir Mackenzie Chalmers. Baron Hardinge of Penshurst had been viceroy of India for six years. Chalmers was a KCB and under-secretary of state, and had been on many royal commissions. Shearman seemed to have no qualifications at all and the papers of the time could only describe him as 'a jolly good sport who played rugby for Oxford'.[464]

A strike from April to June 1920 effectively closed the hotel, and only the assistant manager, Mr Powell, remained in residence.

For most of the period, the hotel telephonist was a Collins agent:

> The Shelbourne Hotel telephonist was one of my agents, and she tapped all calls going through the Shelbourne switchboard which might be of use. On one

occasion Mrs Walsh rang up Captain Walsh and told him that she had seen Austin Stack riding a bicycle. She said she was in a tram when she saw him; she got off the tram, but lost Stack. She asked Captain Walsh would she share the reward if they were successful in getting Stack. She was assured she would be rewarded and the figure of £2,000 was mentioned.[465]

On Bloody Sunday, 21 November 1920, a squad entered and tried to kill some British officers but they all escaped. The squad climbed a staircase, turned a corner and fired at armed men, only to find that they had fired at their reflection in a large mirror. The need for secrecy gone, the men ran to the room where they expected to find one British agent, but he had fled. The hotel was much too large to search quickly, so they grabbed what papers they could and ran out the front door.

From February to May 1922, the drafting of the Constitution of the Free State took place in Room 112, renamed the Constitution Room. (By the time this Constitution was replaced in 1937, 41 of its 83 Articles had been amended.) The drafting committee was composed of Collins (chairman), James Douglas, Darrell Figgis (vice-chairman, who actually did most of the drafting, along with Kennedy), Hugh Kennedy, C.P. France, James MacNeill, R.J.P. Mortished, James Murnaghan, John O'Byrne, Professor Alfred O'Rahilly, P.J. O'Toole and E.M. Stephens. Collins had selected the committee members, and while he only attended the first meeting, he did lay down the guidelines for the committee and all final decisions were his. He tried to get the British to agree to several drafts with more 'republican' language before one was accepted. In many senses 'Michael Collins was ultimately responsible for drafting the Constitution of the Irish Free State'.[466]

91 St Stephen's Green (south): Home of Seán T. O'Kelly. On 19 May 1922, O'Kelly suggested a meeting between Collins and de Valera with regard to the upcoming election. A meeting was scheduled for the next day. (See Collins–de Valera Pact, Dawson Street, Mansion House.)

113 St Stephen's Green (west): Home of Michael Donnelly. He approved the occupation of his home during the Rising. A lieutenant in the ICA, he pressed Collins for more involvement of the ICA in the War of Independence. In July 1920 Donnelly initiated a strike of railwaymen against the carrying of arms by the English soldiers. The strike lasted until December.[467] (See Westland Row Railway Station.)

123 St Stephen's Green (west): Royal College of Surgeons in Ireland. There are three statues atop the royal coat of arms: Athena, goddess of wisdom and war; Asklepios, god of medicine; and Hygeia, goddess of health. The College was opened to women in 1885.

Ship Street: Ship Street Barracks. Lily Mernin worked here for Major Stratford Burton, the garrison adjutant. Mernin was one of Collins's most important sources working within the British military. Major Burton was in charge of court-martial proceedings as well as the strength of various military posts throughout Dublin, and Mernin would always make an extra carbon copy of relevant documents for Collins.

> Before the 21st November 1920, it was part of my normal duty to type the names and addresses of British agents who were accommodated at private addresses and living as ordinary citizens of the city. These lists were typed weekly and amended whenever an address was changed. I passed them on each week to the address at Moynihan's, Clonliffe Rd, or to Piaras Béaslaí. The typing of the lists ceased after the 21 November 1920 [Bloody Sunday].[Mernin, Lily: Witness Statement 441.]

Mernin indicated that 'any information obtained was immediately passed to IRA intelligence'. (McGarry 2006)

Mernin reported to Frank Saurin, who described how she helped to identify Auxiliaries:

> In addition to Lily Mernin being one of our agents at Dublin Castle, she was also attached to me for visiting hotel lounges and the like for spotting and identification work of enemy personnel who used to frequent such places. She and my wife used to attend whist drives run by 'F' Company Auxiliaries in Dublin Castle. It was usual for one or two of the Auxiliaries to see the ladies to the tram. I followed from outside the Castle, all the time taking a mental description of the men—height, colour, features, clothes, etc. Subsequently I was given their names, rank and official position. In this way we got to know the identity of many Auxiliaries. So the identifying, watching and shadowing went on and on until such time as a job had to be carried out. The Squad were then notified for action and were generally accompanied by the particular IO [Intelligence Officer] who had been working on the case of the particular individual to be liquidated. [Saurin, Frank: Witness Statement 715.]

(See Clonliffe Road, Dublin 3; 167 Mangerton Road, Parkgate Street, Dublin 8.)

Suffolk Street: Quill's photoengraving shop; the family lived upstairs. It was close to Dublin Castle, and Collins used to have documents brought here from the Castle and 'copied' overnight, then returned before they were missed.

Suffolk Street: Robert's café; a second one was opened later on Grafton Street. An IRA/Volunteer meeting place during the War of Independence.

22–23 Suffolk Street: IRA/Republican HQ, Sinn Féin Party HQ during the Civil War. Éamon de Valera often used this as an office during the period between the Treaty debates and the outbreak of the Civil War. Joseph Clarke was the secretary of the post-Civil War Sinn Féin.

In June 1923 the Organising Committee of Sinn Féin decided to contest seats in the general election, and in August the party put up 87 candidates on an abstentionist policy. Their election manifesto stated: 'The Sinn Féin candidates in this election stand as they have stood in every election since 1917, for the unity and untrammelled independence of Ireland'. Of the 87 candidates, 64 were in prison or 'on the run'. Forty-three Sinn Féin candidates were elected, and two further seats were won in by-elections in November 1924: Dublin (Seán Lemass) and Mayo (Dr Madden).

Townsend Street (corner of Great Brunswick Street): DMP 'G' Division HQ. (See 1–8 Great Brunswick Street.)

Wellington Quay: An office of the Ministry for Home Affairs under Austin Stack. Madge Clifford managed the office. (See 45 Henry Street, Dublin 1.)

2–7 Wellington Quay: Clarence Hotel. Dave Neligan stayed here when he returned to Dublin to rejoin the DMP. (See Bannon's pub, 41 Abbey Street Upper, Dublin 1.)

Liam Lynch was sleeping here when the attack on the Four Courts commenced; he left to go to the south and was captured with Liam Deasy. They were taken for questioning by Eoin O'Duffy, who let them go, thinking that since they were moderates they might be amenable to further negotiations. They subsequently went to Kingsbridge Station and caught a train south with Séamus Robinson. From south-west Ireland Lynch and Deasy became the leaders of the anti-Treaty forces during the Civil War.

Wellington Quay: Dolphin Hotel. It was Emmet Dalton's forward HQ during the Civil War Four Courts bombardment.

Westland Row Railway Station: On 20 May 1920, Irish dockers embargoed British 'war materials' and railway workers followed suit. Frank Brooke was the chairman of the Dublin and Southeastern Railway, which had its terminus here. On 30 July Collins intervened in the embargo by making 'non-combatant' supporters of the British war effort in Ireland legitimate targets, and Brooke knew that he was in danger. That day Brooke chaired a meeting at the station, and Collins sent Jim Slattery to lead Squad members to kill him.

Frank Brooke was a Director of the Eastern Railway Company, and a member of the Advisory Committee to Lord French. I do not know much about him except that we received instructions to shoot him. In the forenoon of a day towards the end of July, 1920, Paddy Daly, Tom Keogh and myself proceeded to the offices of the railway company at Westland Row. Brooke was sitting at his table when we entered his office. We immediately opened fire on him and he fell. As we were going down the stairs again Daly said to me, 'Are you sure we got him?' I said I was not sure, and Daly said, 'What about going back and making sure?' Keogh and myself went back. When I went into the room I saw a man standing at the left of the door and I fired a shot in his direction, at the same time looking across at Brooke on the floor. I fired a couple of shots at Brooke and satisfied myself that he was dead. Although I did not wound the other man who was in the room [fellow director Arthur Cotton], I was informed afterwards that it would have been a good job if he had been shot, as he too was making himself a nuisance.[468]

36 Westland Row: Oriel House. HQ of Special Branch, a unit of the Irish Free State's detective section. It was under the command of Liam Tobin in the early years.[469] Of a semi-military character, it was the nucleus of a special detection and intelligence unit, and reached a strength of about 125 by the end of the Civil War.[470] It was primarily staffed by Collins's men who had worked in headquarters intelligence or in the 'Squad' during the War of Independence, together with a handful of DMP detectives who had taken pains to steer clear of any involvement in the investigation of political affairs during the War of Independence, or who had acted as informants for Collins and so had survived. It was run by officers personally loyal to Collins, although it adopted the form of a civilian detective bureau rather than a military organisation, its staff holding police ranks such as 'Detective Officer'.

In February 1923, all units of detectives and intelligence were merged under Joe McGrath, with a complement of about 350. In that same month the unit moved to 68 Merrion Square. Collins's operatives Dave Neligan,[471] Éamon (Ned) Broy, James McNamara and Tom Cullen worked in the unit after the Civil War.

The building now houses the Royal Irish Academy of Music.

Westmoreland Street: Kennedy and McSharry, outfitters. This was an upmarket store and Collins bought many of his clothes here.

5 Wexford Street: Shop of Richard Tynan. The shop was used by Collins as a clearing-house for literature, and especially for funds from the Dáil Loan.

Whitefriar Street: Church of Our Lady of Mount Carmel (Carmelite Church). Erected in 1825, this church occupies a site acquired by the Carmelites in 1280. It contains the statue of Our Lady of Dublin. In 1835 Pope Gregory XVI gave St Valentine's remains in a wine cask to Fr Spratt, and they are held here.

Harry Boland was buried from here; his remains arrived at the church from St Vincent's Hospital on 3 July 1922. Revd Michael Browne of Maynooth (later bishop of Galway) was the principal celebrant of the requiem Mass.[472] As the cortège proceeded up O'Connell Street to Glasnevin Cemetery, a Lancia armoured car containing Free State troops stopped; the troops disembarked, laid down their arms in the street, removed their caps and stood at attention until the hearse had passed. The government had allowed the funeral to proceed without interruption. Many thought that the armoured car incident was the only way Collins could pay his last respects. (See St Vincent's Hospital, Leeson Lane; Grand Hotel, Skerries, Appendix VI.)

Éamon de Valera was buried from here in 1975. As a member of the Carmelite Third Order, he was buried in a Carmelite habit.

Wicklow Street (corner of South William Street): Bryan Fergus Molloy was a British spy who offered to take Tom Cullen, Frank Thornton[473] and Liam Tobin[474] into Dublin Castle to obtain information, but they never took up the offer. His body was found here after Collins had him killed on 25 March 1920. (See Parkgate Street, Dublin 8.)

4 Wicklow Street: Wicklow Hotel, next to Weir's, one building away from Grafton Street. This was a usual meeting place for Tom Cullen, Dave Neligan, Liam Tobin and Collins. Paddy O'Shea, from Kerry, was the waiter and often passed messages.

> We used to go round to maids and boots in the different hotels and get information from them. Collins got information from Paddy O'Shea that Doran was giving information to the British. Collins used to dine in the Wicklow Hotel regularly and was satisfied that Doran was a British agent.[475]

William Doran, the porter, betrayed IRA/Volunteers and was killed outside the hotel on 29 January 1921 on Collins's order. Joe Dolan, a member of the Squad, arrived at the hotel in a taxi, and when Doran picked up the luggage he was shot. When Doran's wife put in a 'claim' on behalf of herself and her children, Collins arranged for her to be paid from Sinn Féin funds and they never knew the true circumstances of his betrayal. 'The poor little devils need the money,' Collins said.

Dublin 3

Key locations

Clontarf

Fairview

Jones's Road (Croke Park)

D ublin 3 was the location of one of the most outrageous and egregious acts perpetrated by the British forces during the War of Independence. But while Croke Park forms a central part of the Michael Collins story, other locations also played their part.

'Everywhere is relentless grief, everywhere panic, and everywhere countless shapes of death ...'
Msgr Maurice Browne, who was at Croke Park on Bloody Sunday, recalling Virgil from his seminary studies

Church Road, East Wall: Home of Tommy Dorrins, who was killed in the Custom House fire.

118 Clonliffe Road: Home of Capt. Pat Moynihan. Moynihan was a postal official in the sorting office when it was in the Rotunda Rink, and was the agent who gave Frank Saurin the information that led to the raids on the British mails.[476] (See the Rotunda, Great Britain Street, Dublin 1.)

Lily Mernin was one of Collins's most important sources on the military side. She would come to this house at night, when it was unoccupied, and type her reports for Collins, leave them in the typewriter and then depart. (See Ship Street Barracks, Dublin 1; 167 Mangerton Road, Parkgate Street, Dublin 8.)[477]

Clontarf (Marino): **Marino Casino**. There was a disused, wide, dry tunnel leading to Charlemont House, with interconnecting chambers and tunnels running underneath the grounds surrounding the Casino. James Caulfield, first earl of Charlemont, who built the Casino, originally excavated them. Some of the underground chambers were designed as bathing pools, but the purpose of others is still unclear. Collins, Harry Boland, Gearóid O'Sullivan, Tom Barry and others fired and practised with the Thompson machine-guns that Clan na Gael purchased in America for the IRA/Volunteers.[478] The tunnels are only a few feet below the ground, however, and the neighbouring Christian Brothers alerted the rebels that the supposedly secret target practice could be heard all over Marino and further afield.

The first small shipment of guns arrived in May 1920, and Collins ordered another 500 of the machine-guns but the ship carrying them was raided in New York harbour. The guns and a sizeable amount of money were lost.

> The Thompson guns were introduced in November or December 1920. The first introduction of these guns followed the arrival of two ex-officers of the American Army, one was Major Dineen and the other, whose rank I forget, was named Cronin. These two men were made available to the Brigade for the purpose of giving lectures and instructions in the use of the Thompson sub-machine guns. The lectures, which were given to selected men of the Dublin Brigade, consisted in the main of taking the gun asunder, becoming acquainted with the separate parts and securing a knowledge of the names of these parts, the clearance of stoppages, as well as the causes of these stoppages. In the early stages it was not possible to give practical demonstrations of the shooting powers of these weapons, but the handling of the guns, together with the methods of sighting, made the men reasonably proficient.[479]

The guns were used in several Dublin ambushes and had a psychological effect on both the Irish and the British, but there were too few to materially affect the war.

Nearby was an orphanage run by the Christian Brothers, who allowed Collins's men to use the grounds for drilling but warned Collins that the firing of guns would attract attention.

Haddon Road, Clontarf: The house known as 'Craigmillar' was the home of John P. Twohig. Collins often visited here, and Twohig was said to be his uncle.

8 Haddon Road, Clontarf: Home of Thomas Gay, the librarian at the Capel Street Municipal Library. (See Capel Street, Dublin 7.) Weekly conferences were held here for Collins's agents Broy, Kavanagh, McNamara and Neligan.

Jones's Road: Croke Park. The grounds were originally acquired by the GAA in 1913 and were named after Archbishop Thomas Croke of Cashel, patron of the Association.

On 19 November 1917 the Third Convention of the Irish Volunteers was held here. The officers elected were: President, Éamon de Valera; Chief of Staff, Cathal Brugha; Director of Organisation, Collins; Director of Communications, Diarmuid Lynch. The general secretary of the GAA at the time was Seán McGarry, who was also the president of the IRB.

On 6 April 1919 Tipperary played Wexford in Gaelic football to raise money for the Irish National Aid and Volunteers' Dependants' Fund. Collins and de Valera threw in the ball, and Harry Boland was the referee.

On 21 November 1920 Tipperary played Dublin in Gaelic football before a crowd estimated at 15,000. The Tans, Auxiliaries and RIC attacked the grounds at 3.45pm following Collins's attacks on the Cairo Gang throughout Dublin.[480] (See Bloody Sunday, Appendix IV.)

> GAA Challenge Match
> Tipperary (challengers) v. Dublin (Leinster champions)
> An All-Ireland test!
> At Croke Park tomorrow, 21st at 2.45 pm
> A thrilling game expected!

Jack Shouldice was on the committee and was in charge of the gate and collections that day.[481] Others on the committee with whom Shouldice discussed the possibility of cancelling the game were Alderman James J. Nowlan, Luke O'Toole, Andy Harty and Dan McCarthy. They decided to go forward with the game despite warnings of British reprisals. The game was played for the benefit of the Irish National Aid and Volunteers' Dependants' Fund and about £500 was raised. The referee was Mick Sammon from Kildare.

Tipperary player Mick Hogan was killed and is commemorated now by the Hogan Stand. Thomas Ryan was killed as he held Hogan and whispered the Act of Contrition in his ear. Ryan was from County Wexford, and soon Dublin's children were singing:

> Croke Park, Bloody Sunday
> As the dying goalman lay on the ground
> And as the British bullets went flying round
> Brave Thomas Ryan from Wexford fair
> Knelt by his side in dying prayer
> And as he aided the dying man
> Was brutally shot by a Black and Tan.
> God grant that both their souls
> Find rest in Heaven among the blessed.

An eyewitness, Frank Burke, who was playing for Dublin, gave an interview to Father Diarmuid Ó Peicin, recalling the events and the killing of Hogan.

> He remembered, 'Referee Mick Sammon threw in the ball at 2:45 p.m. Soon afterwards, an aeroplane flew over the ground and a red flare was shot from the cockpit. Black and Tans raided the ground and an officer on top of the wall fired a revolver shot and then the shooting started.'
> Hogan and Burke were contesting for the ball when the shooting started and

they, along with Dublin player Stephen Sinnott, were the last of 30 players left on the pitch.

'The players being so near the Hogan Stand entrance, most of them were over that end, they all got into the dressing room or got over through the gates, someplace, quickly, because they were over in that corner. There was nobody in the field at the time but myself, Hogan and Stephen Sinnott.'

They got down on their hands and knees and crawled towards the shelter of a small perimeter, but before they could get there Hogan was shot dead.

'We ran, we didn't know where we were going, but we ran to the centre of the field and we didn't realize we could see the bullets hitting the railway wall at the end.

'So we realized that they were shooting at somebody, into the crowd. And then the three of us threw ourselves onto the ground, Hogan was on the right hand side, I was in the centre, and Stephen Sinnott was on the left.

'And we started creeping, from the centre of the field up to a goalpost . . . I turned sideways and started rolling. And after making an Act of Contrition I was wondering what was going to happen at all.'

Eventually, through crawling and rolling, the men got up to a foot-high railing off the cycle track.

'We lay close to the edge of the field and all the time they were firing, and we were a bit away from it, four or five yards away.

'And then I heard, "I'm shot" from Hogan and the crowd running at the back of the goal post over towards Hill 16.'[482]

The Nally Stand is named after Pat Nally from Bally, Co. Mayo, an IRB and early GAA man.

Jones's Road: Home of Paddy and Stephen O'Reilly, both of whom were killed in the Custom House fire, 25 May 1921. Paddy was the quartermaster of the 2nd Battalion. Stephen was only sixteen, and a volume of his poetry, *Spirit flowers*, was published posthumously in 1923.

On the next evening I had the melancholy duty of going to St Agatha's Church, North William Street, to receive the remains of Paddy O'Reilly, Quartermaster, 2nd Battalion, who had been killed in the Custom House battle. After the majority of the relatives and friends were gone, his brother, Tom, opened the coffin for me and showed me where poor Paddy had, apparently, been finished by a bullet through the head. There was a small bullet entrance wound in the side of his nose, which plainly showed scorching, indicating that the gun, presumably an automatic, had been placed right at his head when fired. He told me also that there was another corpse in King George's (now St Bricin's) Hospital which he was sure was that of Stephen, his younger brother, who was Assistant Adjutant of the 2nd Battalion. Stephen was a brilliant young lad, only 16 years of age, who had already contributed profusely, in verse and prose, to Brian O'Higgins' 'Banba', a national paper for youths. Tom had been afraid to inform his mother but, unfortunately, it was too true, and the next evening I had to repeat my melancholy duty for Stephen.[483]

Jones's Road: Home of Denis Lynch, a chemist at the Dublin Whiskey Distillery (usually known as DWD). It was a frequent meeting place for IRA/Volunteers during the War of Independence, often including Collins.

15 Marino Crescent, Clontarf: Birthplace of Abraham (Bram) Stoker on 8 November 1847. He was the author of *Dracula*, though it was written after he left Dublin.

The Boland family moved here in about 1910. IRA/Volunteers from the country, including Seán Treacy, often stayed here.

31 Richmond Avenue, Fairview: Tom and Kathleen Clarke's home at the time of the Rising. She lived there afterwards with their sons.

Kathleen was one of the best-known women of the period and one of very few privy to the plans of the Rising. She served as a TD for the Dublin Mid constituency and was the first female lord mayor of Dublin. Born Kathleen Daly in Limerick, she preferred to be known as Caitlín Bean Uí Chléirigh (Mrs Tom Clarke) and has this inscription on her headstone. Tom Clarke met her uncle, John Daly, while in prison, and married Kathleen, 21 years his junior, on his release in 1898.

Kathleen was specifically given the responsibility to 'carry on' the IRB following the Rising, as Tom knew that many of its leaders would be killed or imprisoned. For her role, it was said that she was one of only two women (Una Brennan being the other) to be sworn into the IRB. 'On Holy Thursday, [I] was sent to Limerick with despatches. I took my three children with me to leave them with my mother, so that I could be free to take on the duty assigned to me in the Rising.'[484] After the Rising and her imprisonment, Kathleen was unwell and moved her sons to her uncle's home in Limerick until 1917. This house was let furnished to P.S. O'Hegarty during that time, and when she returned to Dublin she took a furnished house in Dundrum for a while. Following her imprisonment, she headed the Irish National Aid and Volunteers' Dependants' Fund, where she employed Collins. (See Bachelor's Walk, Dublin 1; Exchequer Street, Dublin 2.)

She was elected unopposed as a Sinn Féin TD to the Second Dáil in May 1921. Always adamantly against the Treaty, she failed to be re-elected in 1922 but was re-elected to the short-lived Fifth Dáil in June 1927; she again lost her seat in September 1927 and did not regain it. She contested the 1948 election on behalf of Clann na Poblachta. Following her failure to be elected to the Dáil in 1927, she was elected to the Seanad in 1928 and retained her seat in two subsequent elections until it was abolished in 1936. She was the first female lord mayor of Dublin (1939–41).

Upon her death, aged 94, in 1972 she received the rare honour of a state funeral.

122 St Lawrence Road, Clontarf: Home of Arthur Griffith; he moved here in 1910 after marrying the former Maud Sheehan.

The house was raided on the evening of 26/27 November 1920, and Griffith was arrested and imprisoned at Mountjoy Prison. He only occasionally stayed at his home at this time, but he was here that night because it was his wedding anniversary. Mrs Griffith was adamant that she and Arthur never discussed politics, and her comments indicate a common Irish aversion to family political discussions.[485]

I have no papers, notes or diaries belonging to my husband and he never talked to me about politics as I did not want to, having been brought up in a family in which my father was an ardent Parnellite and my mother a follower of William O'Brien, with consequent frequent disputes on political matters.

We had a lot of political publications but burnt them and all papers that might incriminate anybody from time to time for fear of raids. I never took part in any public functions or meetings, except one in Cootehill in the 1918 election where I went to stop people talking. Once when Mrs Sheehy-Skeffington wrote an article in 'The Irish World' saying that my husband always kept me at home and gave me a bad time, for the only time in my life I wanted to write an answer to it, but he said it was better not as that would only give her statement more publicity which was probably what she wanted.

Dublin 4

Key locations

Ailesbury Road
Ballsbridge
Brendan Road
Haddington Road
Herbert Park
Lansdowne Road
Merrion Road

Mespil Road
Morehampton Road
Nutley Lane
Sandymount
Shelbourne Road (Beggar's Bush Barracks)
Wellington Road

D ublin 4 shows the brutal side of Collins's organisation, in contrast with the humanity shown in his relationship with Batt O'Connor's family.

On 21 November 1920, in the quiet of a Dublin Sunday, groups of IRA gunmen began the systematic assassination of a group of specially trained and recruited secret servicemen. This British unit had been recruited in the summer of 1920 in London. In all, 60 agents were trained and despatched to Ireland.

Earlier that month, Prime Minister Lloyd George had confidently asserted that the IRA were defeated and that the British 'had murder on the run'. The attack, coming as it did when the British forces felt that they had the IRA at breaking point, was a momentous act of reassertion.

'The Cairo Gang' had been activated in Ireland by Col. Ormonde de L'Epee Winter, chief of the British Combined Intelligence Services in Ireland. The IRA/Volunteers knew him as the 'Holy Terror' because he was always prepared to descend to the most extreme methods to obtain information from prisoners. The Cairo Gang was ruthless and efficient, and each of its activities had as its ultimate goal to eliminate Collins and his Intelligence Department.

Collins, of course, was aware of the proposed intensification and knew that he would have to move to meet it. In the first two weeks of November, the Gang detained some of Collins's closest advisers. They held Frank Thornton for ten days but he managed to convince them that he had nothing to do with Sinn Féin. The Gang just missed capturing Richard Mulcahy. They raided Vaughan's Hotel and questioned Liam Tobin and Tom Cullen but let them go. Collins, Cathal Brugha, Mulcahy and the military and intelligence leadership felt that they had no choice but to attack.

> *'We have murder on the run'*
> David Lloyd George

> *'[Collins] was of a tender and generous nature'*
> Batt O'Connor

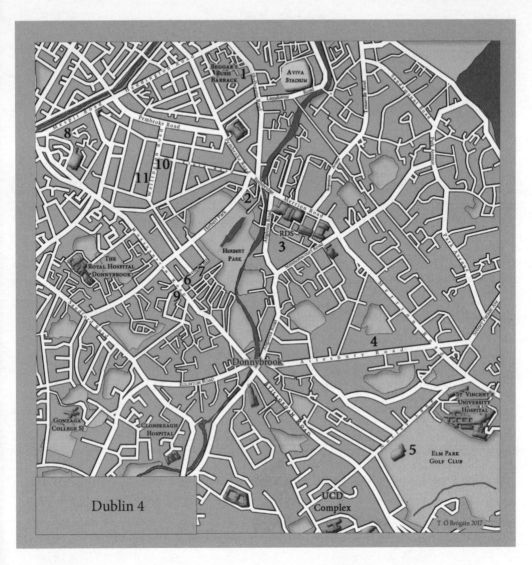

Dublin 4

1	Shelbourne Road: Beggar's Bush Barracks
2	40 Herbert Park, Ballsbridge: home of The O'Rahilly
3	Merrion Road, Ballsbridge: Royal Dublin Society grounds
4	36 Ailesbury Road: home of Nell Humphreys
5	Nutley Lane: Elm Park Golf Club
6	1 Brendan Road, Donnybrook: home of Batt and Bridget O'Connor
7	23 Brendan Road, Donnybrook: home of Sinéad Mason
8	5 Mespil Road: home of Patricia Hoey and Intelligence office
9	117 Morehampton Road: see Bloody Sunday
10	20 Wellington Road: home of Erskine Childers
11	55 Wellington Road: home of Seán T. O'Kelly

On the morning of 21 November, select groups of the Dublin Brigade received orders to mobilise in parts of the city. At exactly 9.00am the firing was to be started.

Just at 9.00, little Percival William Smith opened the door of his home at 117 Morehampton Road to Collins's men. Ten minutes later, his father, Thomas Herbert Smith, and Capt. Donald L. McLean of the Rifle Brigade lay dead.

Collins said:

> My one intention was the destruction of the undesirables who continued to make miserable the lives of ordinary decent citizens. If I had a second motive it was no more than a feeling I would have for a dangerous reptile. For myself, my conscience is clear. There is no crime in detecting and destroying, in wartime, the spy and the informer. They have destroyed without trial. I have paid them back in their own coin.

Some of the British who survived that morning escaped because bullets flew wildly from the guns of inexperienced Irish killers. Of the IRA/Volunteers who had taken part in that morning's raids, some would never completely recover from the nerve-shattering work. One must wonder about the life of young Percival William Smith.

Less than a mile away from the Smith home, also in Dublin 4, was the home of Batt O'Connor's family at 1 Brendan Road, Donnybrook. O'Connor was a builder and had 'built' Brendan Road. Collins visited the family regularly, often playing with the children. The five O'Connor children adored Collins, and always kept his secret. They gave up inviting other children home in order to protect him.

O'Connor was one of Collins's closest personal friends, and the one to whom Collins would confide his personal feelings more than to any other during the period. He wrote his impressions of Collins as a man, rather than as an administrator or soldier. Collins opened up to O'Connor as he did to no other.

O'Connor wrote of the man who planned the Bloody Sunday killings:

> But with all Michael Collins's superficial sternness, he was of a tender and generous nature. He found time to help all who were in trouble or affliction.
>
> … Although it was so dangerous for him to go near the homes of those who were engaged actively in the fight, he never failed to do so if a visit from him would give support or consolation. He went to see Mrs McKee after the tragic and terrible death of her splendid son [Dick] in Dublin Castle [on Bloody Sunday]. He went out regularly to Greystones to see Mrs de Valera and her children during the President's absence in America, and never failed to send him news of them in his official letters.

Michael Collins, the enigma.

36 Ailesbury Road: Home of Mrs Mary Ellen (Nell) Humphreys, sister of The O'Rahilly, and her family.[486] She and her husband David, a wealthy eye surgeon from Limerick, moved here in 1909, and she was involved in nationalist activities from her arrival in Dublin. She continued those activities after the Rising and was very opposed to the Treaty.

Nell's only daughter, Sighle, was raised at Quinsborough House, Co. Clare.[487] Dr Humphreys suffered from TB and died when she was four years old. When the family moved to Dublin, Sighle became a fluent Gaelic-speaker. Her two brothers, Emmet and Richard (Dick), attended St Enda's, and Dick served alongside The Ó Rahilly in the GPO in 1916. Sighle spent a year in Paris and on her return to Dublin joined Cumann na mBan when the organisation was reorganised in response to the very few women at the Sinn Féin Convention of October 1917. She served variously as secretary, director of publicity and national vice-president.[488] She was on the committee of the Irish Volunteers' Dependants' Fund after the Rising, where she met Collins and became one of his couriers.[489] During the War of Independence she was engaged in finding safe houses for those on the run, and the family home was used as an IRA safe house throughout the war. The Dáil cabinet had frequent meetings here and often used the big house on Ailesbury Road. Batt O'Connor built a false wall in the Humphreys' house, and it was often used to hide men and documents.

In September 1921 there was a meeting here between Richard Mulcahy and Cathal Brugha, with de Valera trying to act as mediator. Brugha wanted to curb the power of the army and bring it under his control, and Mulcahy and Collins resisted. There was an 'accommodation' but the bad feeling between them all continued.

During the Civil War, Ernie O'Malley stayed here and used it as an office from September 1922 until his capture on 4 November.[490] At the outset of the raid he went to a hidden room that had been built by Batt O'Connor during the War of Independence, but O'Connor, who was a Treaty supporter, had told the Free State troops about it and they went straight to it. O'Malley fled and was shot several times, but lived and was imprisoned in Mountjoy; sixteen bullets were removed from his body in hospital. Richard (Risteard MacAmhlaoibh) and Sighle were arrested and imprisoned after O'Malley's capture.

The 4 November raid resulted in a protracted shoot-out with Free State soldiers. At the time only Sighle, her mother and her aunt were staying in the house with O'Malley. Sighle is known to have played an active part in resisting the raid, though she always denied reports that she had been responsible for shooting a Free State soldier who died in the fighting.[491]

Beggar's Bush Barracks, Shelbourne Road: See Shelbourne Road.

1 Belmont Park, Donnybrook: Home of Mrs Áine (Annie) Heron, a judge of the

Dáil/Republican courts. She was pregnant with her third child when she was in the Four Courts during the Rising.

> I was selected by the Pembroke Combairle Ceanntair of Sinn Féin to act as Justice at the Sinn Féin Courts. The Pembroke and Rathmines Courts combined under the Chairmanship of Erskine Childers. Mrs Ceannt and I were co-trustees of the moneys of the Court. In fact, it was only a few years ago we handed over the last of the money to the Government when Seán MacEntee was Minister for Finance. It was about £11, I think, which was the sum left after paying all expenses of the Court. We felt it was time to bring the matter to a close in case either of us should die. During the whole of the Black and Tan period I continued being busily engaged at these activities, as well as being a member of the Committee of the IRPDP (Irish Republican Prisoners Dependents' Fund) [sic]. Fortunately I had a good maid who freed me from all domestic preoccupations and anxiety about the children, of which I had six.[492]

1 Brendan Road, Donnybrook: Home of Batt and Bridget O'Connor. O'Connor was in Frongoch with Collins, and on his return to Ireland he moved to Dublin, where he soon established himself as a 'speculative builder', constructing houses in Anglesea Road, Dolphins Barn, Eglington Road and Donnybrook. O'Connor also built the houses on Brendan Road and gave the street its name, eventually getting married and settling in No. 1 Brendan Road, named after the patron saint of his native Kerry. Collins often ate here, as Batt and Bridget were his very good friends, and he and others used the house for meetings. Collins used this as a 'safe house' and probably ate here more often than in any other. He rarely slept here, however, as it was too well known.

> As time went on meetings began to be held again in our house. Harry Boland, Cathal Brugha, Mick Collins, Austin Stack and several others used to come, and I knew them all intimately. Mick Collins was the one of those four that I knew the least because he was always too engrossed in his important occupations to take part in small talk. Women who worked for him and with him overlooked that characteristic in him and did not expect anything different from him because they knew how much he had on his mind.
>
> … Mick Collins slept at our house on only two or three occasions because it was too dangerous a place for him. On one of those occasions Mick, Harry Boland and Batt ate in the kitchen talking and enjoying a pleasant evening; I think it was after a meeting. They were discussing the life they had seen in various places. Mick Collins was describing the life he led in London and Batt was giving

his experiences in America. Harry Boland, who was very gay and lighthearted, said there was no place like Dublin. He asked me was there anything as enjoyable as getting on an outside car on a bank holiday with a few friends and driving to the strawberry beds or some such place, singing the good old Dublin songs like 'Cockles and Mussels'. When at last they decided to go to bed, Harry and Mick slept in the return room in the one bed, with the window open at the bottom so that if there was a raid they could slip out easily. I did not dare to go to bed, as I was always uneasy when any of the leaders was sleeping in the house. In the course of the night I opened the door of the bedroom gently and saw the two men sleeping quietly. Mick had his arm resting on the little table by the bed, with his revolver lying beside it.[493]

O'Connor and Collins first met in Kimmage prior to the Rising and remained fast friends. O'Connor was one of Collins's closest personal friends, and the one in whom Collins would confide more than any other during the period. O'Connor's view of Collins was unique inasmuch as it was more personal than as a nationalist. He wrote his impressions of Collins as a man, rather than as an administrator or soldier. Collins opened up to O'Connor as he did to no other, and O'Connor's personal views of Collins are invaluable. (See Death in Béal na mBláth for O'Connor's personal recollections, Appendix V.)

But with all Michael Collins's superficial sternness, he was of a tender and generous nature. He found time to help all who were in trouble or affliction. He was very thoughtful of the prisoners. He found means to get letters of encouragement and other more material consolations smuggled in to them. How he accomplished such things, and got warders and wardresses in helping him to risk not only their livelihood, but their freedom, was another proof of his power which made him rise to such a height in our regard. Although it was so dangerous for him to go near the homes of those who were engaged actively in the fight, he never failed to do so if a visit from him would give support or consolation. He went to see Mrs McKee after the tragic and terrible death of her splendid son [Dick] in Dublin Castle [on Bloody Sunday]. He went out regularly to Greystones to see Mrs de Valera and her children during the President's absence in America, and never failed to send him news of them in his official letters. He, himself, made all the arrangements for Mrs de Valera's secret visit to the United States to join her husband, arranged for a lady friend to travel with her, saw to procuring passports for them under other names and secured their tickets.[494]

O'Connor had a personal view of Collins during the Treaty negotiations as well:

Two later meetings with Michael Collins stand out in my memory. Perhaps because on both occasions he was in deep distress, and in my more familiar pictures I see him gay, laughing, self-reliant, sometimes stern and angry, but rarely downcast.

He came to see me on the day in September 1921 when he had been selected as one of the five plenipotentiaries to go to London to discuss terms of peace. He was greatly upset. He would not sit down, but kept pacing the floor, his face set in lines of pain and anxiety. 'I should not have been asked to go,' he said. 'I pleaded strongly against my selection.' 'But, Michael,' I urged, 'you are our big man. You will win better terms for us than anyone else.'

'It is a mistake to send me. De Valera should go. Who ever heard of the soldier who fought the enemy in the field being sent to negotiate the peace?' he cried. 'I am being put in an impossible position.'

'Sit down, man, and let us talk about it.' He did not seem to hear me, but continued to stride up and down the floor. 'I fought hard against my selection,' he burst out again. 'De Valera pressed me. For no other man living would I have consented.'

'Peace must mean of necessity some adjustment of the extreme demands on both sides—on ours as well as theirs. It is not the soldiers who fought on either side who should settle that adjustment. Who is to direct the fight if we have to go back to war, which is only too likely?'

But he did not shirk the odious duty, the one most uncongenial to him of all the services he rendered his country.

… He came back to Dublin on the 8th December with the Treaty, having fought the English as hard over the Conference table as ever he did in the field. He and his colleagues won for their country in two months a measure of Independence beyond the most sanguine hopes of the Fenians, and far in excess of the demands made by Parnell. They secured the recognition of Dáil Éireann as the de jure Parliament in Dublin; the IRA as the nucleus of a National Army, and complete fiscal freedom and the control of our own finances. The terms of the Treaty in regard to North-East Ulster were such that, while the six counties were not to be forced to come under the Dublin Parliament against their will, if we had remained united in the twenty-six counties behind the Treaty, and had not, by fighting amongst ourselves, seemed to show that we were unfit for self-government, the unity of Ireland in a short period was assured. It was in that belief that the clauses relating to North-East Ulster were agreed to by Michael Collins.

But de Valera refused to stand by the colleague who had undertaken, at his own urgent plea, the task which he himself had refused, and who had certainly 'done his best for Ireland in the circumstances' which arose.

It was late at night when I saw him on that day of his return home. I had read the Treaty terms in the newspaper that morning with profound thankfulness, both for what they gave in fact, and for what they held in promise for the future.

There was a knock at the door. I opened it myself. Michael Collins was on the doorstep. He did not walk in, but remained standing, looking at me with a strange expression. 'Come in. What are you waiting for? Ah, Michael! This is a day I never thought I would live to see.'

'I thought perhaps you would have no welcome for me, Batt,' he said.

Coming in, he told me at once that de Valera was going to repudiate the Treaty.

It is hard to describe his frame of mind. He was beside himself. Now at last I saw shaken to his depths that strong man on whom we had all leaned. He doubted his power to carry the Treaty against the opposition of de Valera.

He saw the Truce at an end, with no hope of a successful issue a second time. After the long truce the morale of the men was not what it was. Discipline had been relaxed. Everything was now known. Our men had appeared publicly. It was known where were all our secret meeting places. It would be impossible to carry on, on the old lines. 'I will leave Dublin at once,' he said, in a tone of extreme bitterness and distress. 'I will go down to Cork. If the fighting is going to be resumed, I will fight in the open, beside my own people down there. I am not going to be chivvied and hunted through Dublin as I have been for the last two years.'

I appealed to him not to desert the people who looked to him as their leader and saviour.

'Michael,' I said, 'I have never praised you. You would not have cared for that. But now I am going to tell you that you are such a man as we never had before in Ireland, so that we have grown to look to you to do what no one else can do for us. Do not fail us. You have brought back this Treaty. It is a wonderful achievement. The people want it. They must at least be given the chance to say what they think of it. Then if they reject it (only they will not reject it), you will have done your part, and will have no responsibility for the consequences.'

This appeal to stand by the people had an immediate effect on him. He had been, as on that former occasion, striding up and down the room, flinging out his arms, speaking words betraying passionate emotion. But now he grew calm, and sat down beside me at last. He did not leave till three o'clock in the morning. Before we parted he assured me that he would not leave Dublin. He would see the Treaty through the Dáil, and would see that its terms were fully discussed and put clearly before the people.

'I will accept their verdict,' he said.[495]

Collins hid £25,000 in gold in a baby's coffin under the floor of the house.

O'Connor built many 'secret rooms' and hiding places in buildings and houses throughout Dublin.

'Jameson' (John Charles Byrne) was lured here to see whether he was a spy. (See Nutley Lane; Bachelor's Walk, Granville Hotel, Sackville Street Upper, Dublin 1; Harcourt Street, Dublin 2; Ballymun Road, Dublin 11; Winthrop Street, Cork, Co. Cork, Appendix VI.)

6 Brendan Road, Donnybrook: This house was owned by the Dáil and was frequently used by Collins. Mrs Julia O'Donovan lived here. It was raided, but Collins was not staying here at the time. Nevertheless, the raid was an indication that the Castle knew of his safe houses and was one of the factors leading up to Bloody Sunday.

23 Brendan Road, Donnybrook: Susan (Jenny, Sinéad) Mason, Collins's secretary, moved into this house in 1918, along with her aunt. Batt O'Connor built a secret room, and Collins sometimes used it as a safe house. In addition, O'Connor built a secret compartment where Collins could hide gold, as he did in several houses and buildings.

Mason was Collins's personal and private secretary and bore an enormous workload, as well as dangerously carrying dispatches around Dublin and the country. For a while their friends, the Batt O'Connors and Collins's sister, Margaret Mary, thought they would marry.

Donnybrook Road: Dublin Metropolitan Police Station; Sgt Patrick Mannix, an undercover IRA/Volunteer agent, was stationed here. He obtained the names and addresses of the senior English secret service men sent from England, and he gave them to Frank Thornton. This comprised a great deal of the information that Collins used for the Squad's raids on Bloody Sunday.

> I was asked by Frank Thornton and Tom Cullen if I could get a few men at each Station who could give me any information that would help the IRA. I said yea, that I would. I introduced a number of men at each Station to Thornton and Cullen. I had two men at 'S' District, Donnybrook; one man named Keating in Irishtown, who is still there, and in Booterstown one man. In Dún Laoghaire I had two men. I secured some of the names and addresses of those who were to be shot on 'Bloody Sunday'. Keating, who was stationed in Irishtown, gave me the names of Secret Service Agents residing in Shelbourne Road and Upper Mount Street. I also learned of a Secret Service Agent named Captain McClean living in Morehampton Road. He used to report to the Commissioners whenever he was out at night if the police did not stop him and question him.

At this time I supplied information about Captain McClean and his associates. They were shot about five minutes to 9 o'clock on 'Bloody Sunday' morning. The owner of the house, named Smith, who was a Secret Service Agent, was also shot.[496]

(See Morehampton Road; Bloody Sunday, Appendix IV.)

Elgin Road: Home of Count and Countess Plunkett after 1916. George and Jack Plunkett also lived here upon returning from internment camps after the Rising.[497] The Free State government often raided the house during the Civil War.

Haddington Road: Home of the British provost marshal. In 1920 it was raided by members of 'K' Company, 3rd Battalion, for its collection of weapons. Under the command of Tom Cullen, they were disguised as DMP constables.

40 Herbert Park, Ballsbridge: Home of The Ó Rahilly. Michael Joseph Ó Rahilly was killed in the Rising while trying to find an escape route out of the GPO. His wife was Nancy Marie Browne Ó Rahilly (usually known as 'Nannie'), originally from Philadelphia; she was on the provisional committee of Cumann na mBan. Ó Rahilly was Eoin MacNeill's publisher.

On 2 March 1919 a meeting was held here about the establishment of Dáil/Republican courts in the Pembroke and south city areas; Margaret Buckley, Áine Ceannt,[498] Kathleen Clarke, Áine Heron,[499] Helena Molony[500] and Hanna Sheehy-Skeffington were among those chosen to sit as judges.

Margaret Buckley (née Goulding) was president of Sinn Féin from 1937 to 1950. Originally from County Cork, she joined Inghinidhe na hÉireann as a teenager. Arrested after the Rising, she was released in the amnesty of June 1917 and played a prominent role in the reorganisation of Sinn Féin. She opposed the Treaty and was interned in the North Dublin Union, Mountjoy and Kilmainham, where she went on a hunger strike; she was elected QM of the prisoners in the North Dublin Union, O/C in Mountjoy and O/C of 'B' Wing in Kilmainham. Her book *Jangle of the keys* is the classic history of the suffering of the imprisoned women.[501] She was an active member of the Women Prisoners' Defence League.

Early in 1921 a meeting was held here to finalise plans for the taking of the Custom House. Éamon de Valera's first choice was to capture Beggar's Bush Barracks, but Oscar Traynor deemed that impractical.

I arrived at Herbert Park at the appointed hour and found most of my colleagues already there. Those present, as far as my memory goes, were Cathal Brugha, Austin Stack, Richard Mulcahy, Dermot O'Hegarty, Michael Collins, Gearóid

O'Sullivan, Liam Mellows, Seán Russell, J.J. O'Connell, Seán McMahon, Piaras Béaslaí, and, I think, Eoin O'Duffy. There may have been one or two others but I cannot remember them at the moment.

...The meeting proceeded in a very normal way for some time, and then the President [de Valera] spoke, and he made it clear that something in the nature of a big action in Dublin was necessary in order to bring public opinion abroad to bear on the question of Ireland's case. He felt that such an action in the capital city, which was as well known abroad as London or Paris, would be certain to succeed. He suggested that the capture of the headquarters of the Black and Tans, which was situated in Beggar's Bush Barracks, would capture the imagination of those he had in mind, apart from the serious blow it would constitute to the enemy. As an alternative to this he suggested the destruction of the Custom House, which was the administrative heart of the British Civil Service machine in this country. It was finally decided that I, as the Officer Commanding the Dublin Brigade, should examine these propositions and report back to the Army Council in due course. I immediately set to work and was given the help of some members of the General Headquarters Intelligence service. Two weeks were spent on the investigation and examination of the possibilities of capturing Beggar's Bush Barracks. The experience of the men engaged on this work was such that they reported against such an operation. My activities were then turned to the alternative suggestion—the Custom House.

Immediately after my examination I took Commandant Tom Ennis of the 2nd Battalion into my confidence and asked him to make a similar examination and let me have his views. He carried out his task by methods similar to my own, and his report more or less confirmed my views.[502]

(See Custom House, Dublin 1.)

71 Heytesbury Street: Home of the Delaney family. Seán Treacy was a great friend and called here often, including on the morning of the day he was killed. Miss Delaney was engaged to Séamus Robinson. (See Talbot Street, Dublin 1.)

It was a meeting place for IRA/Republicans during the Civil War.

Lansdowne Road: W.T. Cosgrave's home after his return from Frongoch following the Rising. On the morning of 23 August 1922, Joe O'Reilly and Tom Cullen came here to give Cosgrave the news of Collins's death. They accompanied him to government buildings to break the news to the rest of the cabinet.

Merrion Road, Ballsbridge: Royal Dublin Society. The first enrolment of An Garda Síochána (the Civic Guard) took place here on 21 February 1922.[503] The first commandant was Michael Staines, former quartermaster of the Dublin Brigade and TD for Dublin (St Michan's, 1918–21; North West, 1921–23).[504] Staines soon retired and was succeeded by Eoin O'Duffy.

Some people complained that Collins was using former members of the DMP and RIC to help organise the new Garda Síochána, but he stressed that those were 'men who stood with us always'. 'Many of the greatest successes we gained were gained entirely by true men who stood for us in the enemy service,' Collins told a dinner in Naas on 16 April 1922. 'We are not one bit ashamed of it,' he added. 'Not only are we not going to apologise, but we are very proud to have them, and very glad to have them.'[505] District Inspector John A. Kearny of Boyle, Sgt Mattias McCarthy of Belfast, Constable Thomas Neary of Dublin and Sgt Éamon Broy of Dublin were all enrolled. Between six and seven per cent of the men enrolled were former members of the RIC. About half of those had resigned for patriotic reasons and the other half had been secretly involved in the IRA; however, Collins excluded those over 27 years old.[506]

9 Merrion Road, Sandymount: Home of Máire Comerford. Born in County Wicklow in 1892, she was in Dublin during the Rising. She volunteered to aid Countess Markievicz in St Stephen's Green, but was turned away and carried dispatches for the GPO garrison. Later she worked for the countess. She joined Cumann na mBan in 1918 and was an extremely valuable Collins courier and source. Collins knew her to be fearless.

She remembered what it was like to work for Collins:

> … [he was] a kind natured man, but foul mouthed, and on occasion very bad tempered. Mary Nelson once arrived from Glasgow with money for the Loan. In his office she found a girl all smeared with tears and ink. She was sitting before a very old typewriter. When Mary offered to help in the obvious trouble, the girl could only moan 'Oh, he is so angry' over and over again. Mary, now an indignant feminist, told her to wash her face and get ready to be on top of her job. When Mick stamped back into the room Mary had the machine and the work going. He asked her who the hell she was, and what she was doing there. She gave him back as good as she got, and he calmed down. He liked people with spunk and his anger passed quickly.[507]

She was active in the Civil War fighting in Dublin, and carried dispatches between the Four Courts and O'Connell Street. The most 'energetic' of Cumann na mBan members in the Civil War, she was passionately republican. She was shot in the leg while imprisoned in Mountjoy Prison but escaped. After recapture she was imprisoned in the North Dublin Union and Kilmainham, where she endured a hunger strike. She remained an avid republican her entire life—in 1976, aged 83, she was arrested for participation in a banned march to commemorate the Rising. She remained a member of what was generally seen as a committed group of republicans who would not compromise in terms of everyday politics on constitutional matters. She never married and died in 1982.

5 Mespil Road, Ballsbridge: The home of one of Collins's secretaries, Patricia Hoey, and her mother. They occupied the upper floor, while the lower floor was devoted to a Collins office.

Charlie Dalton described how Collins moved between offices:

During the daytime Michael Collins worked from an office of his own, and at no time did he visit the Crow St. or Brunswick St. offices. Inter-communication was maintained by his special messenger, Joe O'Reilly.

In the evening time Michael Collins used to meet Liam Tobin and Tom Cullen at one of his numerous rendezvous in the Parnell Square area—these were Jim Kirwan's, Vaughan's Hotel and Liam Devlin's. In the earlier years Michael Collins used to meet these men at 46 Parnell Square and at McCarthy's in Mountjoy St. They were all on the run and on many occasions they stayed together, sometimes at Joe O'Reilly's lodgings, Smith's of Lindsay Road, and on other occasions at Paddy O'Shea's house in Lindsay Road.

Michael Collins used as his personal office Miss Hoey's house in Mespil Road; also Mary St., and finally Harcourt Terrace. I was on duty at the Harcourt Terrace office, which was an ordinary dwelling-house, furnished as such, and in the front bedroom the DI had his papers. These were concealed in a secret cupboard on the landing, in which he himself could take refuge should the house be raided while he was in occupation.

It was from his personal office that Michael Collins dealt with all the Brigade and country Intelligence reports.[508]

When the office and home were raided, Miss Hoey was arrested when a revolver was found. She was released when she stuck to her story that the revolver must have been left by a former lodger. When she was taken home, the RIC hid in her house, waiting for Collins to appear. She had her mother fake a heart attack, and demanded that she be seen by a doctor. When Dr Kathleen Lynn arrived, Miss Hoey refused to allow her mother to be examined while the Black and Tans were in the room. She passed the word to Collins through Dr Lynn. On searching further, the RIC found a cache of documents and consequently sent Miss Hoey to prison for several months; she was not released until after the Truce.

5 Mespil Road, Ballsbridge: Close to Leeson Street Bridge, this was a portion of the Hoey home and was used as Collins's primary office and also as a Department of Intelligence office. Susan (Sinéad, Jenny) Mason was the secretary here. Collins used to come to this office almost every morning, a fact known only to Miss Mason, Liam Tobin and Frank Thornton.

It, too, was raided on 1 April 1921. Ellie Lyons worked here as a typist, and Tom Cullen came by every day. They were not in the office on the day of the raid and avoided arrest.[509] The British found some revolvers in a desk but, fortunately for Collins, they did not find his intelligence files. Batt O'Connor had built a secret compartment under a window, and the British never discovered it.

77 Mespil Road, Ballsbridge: Mrs Julia O'Donovan's dairy, the Pembroke Creamery. She was Gearóid O'Sullivan's aunt. Collins often used her homes here and in Rathgar as shelters, particularly for those coming from Cork. He also used her accounts to 'hide' Dáil Loan funds.[510] (See 77 Rathgar Road, Dublin 6.) Mrs O'Donovan had three dairies in south Dublin, and Collins often smuggled pistols in the butter boxes and rifles in the egg boxes. In July 1922, Mrs O'Donovan moved to a nearby house on Garville Road; as busy as Collins was during the period, he came here for dinner on several nights.

117 Morehampton Road: House owned by Thomas Herbert Smith. Capt. Donald L. McLean of the Rifle Brigade was killed here on Bloody Sunday (he was the British chief intelligence officer). John Caldow, McLean's brother-in-law and a former soldier with the Royal Scots Fusiliers, was wounded. The owner of the house, Thomas Smith, was a friend of McLean, but Smith, who was not in intelligence or the army, was also killed.[511] Smith, McLean and Caldow were taken into the hallway to be shot, when McLean asked that they not be killed in front of his wife. The three were taken to an unused bedroom and shot. Caldow survived his wounds and fled to his home in Scotland.

(See Bloody Sunday, Appendix IV.)

131 Morehampton Road: Home of Mary (Mrs Andrew) Woods. On 23 May 1921 Collins wrote to her, thanking her for letting him stay there. She also looked after other republicans 'on the run', including Liam Mellows, Austin Stack and Desmond FitzGerald.[512]

> One night my husband and I were in the hall on our way to bed when we heard a shuffling and noise outside. We opened the door. The night was very dark. We dare not put the hall light on [curfew regulations]. Some one or two men were at the gate. There was a muttering or whispering. My husband was in his slippers

and I in my stockinged feet. We went quickly to the gate; Collins was picking himself up, swearing softly as he picked up the bike.[513]

Liam Mellows had his office here. Una Daly, sister of Paddy Daly, was his secretary and often worked here.

Mrs Woods's house was an open house to everybody associated with the movement and there were people always coming in and out, sleeping and eating there at all hours. I don't know how she fed all the people that came. Officially I had digs, but I slept often at Woods's and I stayed up two whole nights typing work for Liam. At the time I started on this job things were not so dangerous as they had been previously and as they became afterwards during the Civil War.

My function was to enter in the ledger particulars of all transactions, receipts of arms, and to type correspondence for the O/Cs throughout Ireland and England. There was a good deal of correspondence with Seán MacMahon who was, I think QMG [Quartermaster General] at the time.

... I find it very hard to remember what happened between the beginning of the Truce and the Treaty, but I know that Liam had an office in Middle Abbey St. over the Clothing Company. Bob Briscoe used to come in there a good deal and a man called Charlie McGuinness. The latter had something to do with a boat about which there was an awful lot of trouble afterwards. I remember two detectives called long after at my flat in Hatch St. to ask me did I know anything about the boat or did I think McGuinness owned it. I could not enlighten them. [Robert Briscoe, later lord mayor of Dublin, was a major gunrunner for the IRA, and purchased boats in Germany to carry the guns to Ireland. Charles McGuinness was the captain of the vessels that Briscoe bought to run the guns from Germany to Ireland.]

I think it was during the Truce but before the Treaty that the Germans came over about arms and it must have been for this that the boat was bought. I can't say for certain that any arms were landed by the boat. Briscoe would know that as he was mixed up in the business as was also a man called Dick Kenny, a merchant in Ballinasloe. He used to travel a lot to Germany on his own business and I often saw him in Liam's office too. As far as I remember there were six of these Germans.

... I remained working with Liam all during the Truce and during the Civil War up to his arrest. He, with Rory O'Connor and the other leaders, took over a building in Parnell Square where we worked. Often it was quite late when we went home and on one occasion Rory [O'Connor] sent the two Plunketts [Jack and George] to see me home to Fleming's Hotel where I lived. We did not stay long in Parnell Square. Then we went into the Four Courts where we had a very posh office. We had to have passes to get in there. I still have mine. It is signed by Seán Lemass. I did not sleep in the building and, therefore, I was not there for the bombing. I was the first woman into the Four Courts. After that there was quite a big staff. Mrs Terry McSwiney used to be there. After the surrender of the Four Courts, Barry's Hotel was taken over, but I did not work there, although I went there often.[514]

Nutley Lane: at the corner of Simmonscourt Road—Elm Park Golf Club. Alan Bell was taken off a tram opposite here and shot on 27 March 1920. ('Come on, Mr Bell, your time has come.') Earlier that month he had signed an order requiring banks to disclose all details of clients' accounts. He had been working with Sir John Taylor, the under-secretary, and had recently seized about £20,000 from accounts in the Munster and Leinster Bank believed to belong to Sinn Féin depositors.

> Alan Bell was a Resident Magistrate who came from the North of Ireland to Dublin to locate the Dáil Funds, which were in the bank, and it was decided that he should be executed. He was carrying out his investigations in the Four Courts, and we often waited to get him when he would be passing between the Castle and the Four Courts. We had no possible means of identifying him until the 'Irish Independent' published his photograph. We discovered that he was living in Monkstown and that he travelled in to Dublin on the Dalkey tram.[515]

(See 7–10 Dame Street, Dublin 2.)
Bill Stapleton, Tom Keogh and Joe Dolan were the members of the Squad.[516]

> Tom Keogh and myself saw Bell on the tram that morning, and tried to follow it on our bicycles to give our men the word that he was coming. The tram was going very fast and we found it very hard to keep up with it. We saw our group of men at the corner of Anglesea Road and signalled to them that Bell was in the tram. We saw them signal the tram to stop and the whole group got into the tram. The next thing we saw was the tram being stopped and Bell being marched out by the group. Tom Keogh and I were just sightseers.
> Coming back we saw a policeman standing in the middle of the road. ... I was cycling along leisurely because I did not want to create any suspicion in the mind of the policeman. He put up his hand and I slowed down. The policeman asked me, 'Was there an accident up there?' I looked back and saw a crowd of people running in different directions. 'It looks like it', I said to the policeman. The policeman then said, 'I heard a shot, but if there is any shooting business there I am not going near it'.[517]

Previously Bell had been the English 'spymaster' handling 'Jameson', John C. Byrne. (See Brendan Road; Bachelor's Walk, Granville Hotel, Sackville Street Upper, Dublin 1; Harcourt Street, Dublin 2; Ballymun Road, Dublin 11.)

Shelbourne Road: Beggar's Bush[518] **Barracks.** This was the Dublin headquarters of the Auxiliaries (Auxies). (They had 'F' Company stationed at Dublin Castle, another at the North Wall, another at the North Dublin Union and the rest in the countryside.) The Irish considered them much more dangerous than the Black and Tans. Each of them carried two Webley .45 calibre pistols, a rifle and bandoliers of ammunition. Their transport was usually a Crossley tender, in which they sat in two rows, back to back. Their pay was £1 per day, twice that of the Tans, since they were formerly British Army officers. It must be noted that the Dublin Brigade did not inflict many casualties on the Auxiliaries, as they were too well armed and too mobile.

The barracks was turned over to the Provisional Government on 31 January 1922 and the Free State army set up its headquarters here. There was a high level of chronic unemployment at the time, so the appeal for recruits met with a large number of men wishing to serve, most for financial reasons. The 'Dublin Guards', mostly men who had fought in the War of Independence, were the first unit to be assigned here on 4 February. Cmdt (later Gen.) Paddy Daly (O'Daly) was their O/C.

On 10 March 1922, there was a meeting here between Collins, Mulcahy and Eoin O'Duffy, for the Free State, and Liam Lynch and Oscar Traynor, for the IRA, to divide up the Limerick RIC barracks. The crisis in Limerick was a major test of the Free State's will to enforce the Treaty and govern the country. Griffith urged that all barracks in the city should be taken and was, to some extent, supported by Collins. Collins, however, had always tried to maintain army unity and avoid civil war. Mulcahy vetoed proposals for open confrontation on the grounds of military logic, as he knew that the National Army was not ready for an all-out war at that time. Thus a peaceful settlement to this dangerous situation was sought. One was finally reached when both sides agreed to occupy several barracks each. The Free Staters would take the Williams Street Barracks, and the IRA would occupy the Limerick barracks. Both occupying forces would be of minimal size.

On 10 November 1922, Erskine Childers, the director of publicity for the anti-Treaty IRA/Republicans, was captured in County Wicklow. He had in his possession a .32 Spanish automatic pistol that had been given to him by Collins two years earlier.[519] In July 1914 Childers had run 900 rifles and 29,000 rounds of ammunition into Howth for the Irish Volunteers in his yacht *Asgard*. He was the darling of all Irish nationalists then and could never have imagined, after all his gunrunning hazards, that a 'toy' pistol would trigger his downfall. As unauthorised possession of a pistol was then punishable by death, Childers was taken to prison and tried by court martial in camera on 17 November. He was executed here on 24 November, although his case was still under appeal.[520] (See Annamoe, Co. Wicklow, Appendix VI.)

Jurists in Ireland and England generally regard this particular execution as judicial murder, for Childers was executed before his legitimate appeal, which had been granted, could be heard. As a result of this execution, the IRA/Republican executive decided on a policy of summary execution of prominent Free State figures, and Childers's death caused Liam Lynch to abandon all ideas of making peace.[521] It was immediately following this that Lynch issued his 'Orders of Frightfulness' that led to the shooting of Seán Hales. (See Ormond Quay, Dublin 7.) Lynch ordered that

All members of the Provisional Parliament who were present and voted for the Murder Bill should be shot on sight. Attached find list of names. Houses of members of Murder Bill, Murder Gang and active supporters of PG [Provisional Government] who are known to support Murder Bill decision are to be destroyed. All Free State Army officers who approve of Murder Bill and are aggressive and active against our forces will be shot at sight; also ex-British army officers and men who joined the Free State army since 6th of December 1921.[522]

(See Kildare Street, Dublin 2.) After this the Civil War entered an increasingly grim phase.

Sandymount: Lamb Doyle's; this well-known public house was used for Volunteer and IRA meetings.

Strand Road, Sandymount: House, known as Loughnavale, owned by Mrs Mary Woods. (See 31 Fitzwilliam Street Upper.)

25 Sydney Parade: Last home of Gen. Emmet Dalton; he died here on his 80th birthday, 4 March 1978.

Wellington Road: Home of Louise Murphy. Frank Gallagher stayed in this safe house. (He wrote *The four glorious years* under the pseudonym of David Hogan.)

20 Wellington Road: Erskine Childers lived here after he left the home of Mrs Green on St Stephen's Green and before he moved to 12 Bushy Park Road (Dublin 6W).

55 Wellington Road: Seán T. O'Kelly lived here with his family until he was elected president in 1945.

On 5 January 1922 a committee of five, from all sides of the Treaty question, met here. Proposals were made that if the Dáil voted in favour of the Treaty, Éamon de Valera should remain as president, the Dáil should retain ultimate authority and that only members of the Provisional Government would be called upon to declare allegiance to the Treaty. Collins and Arthur Griffith agreed, but de Valera turned them down and the recommendations were never forwarded to the Dáil. Eoin MacNeill and Liam Mellows dissented at the meeting.[523]

Seán T. O'Kelly became president of the Free State in 1945 and of the Republic of Ireland in 1949.[524]

Waterloo Road: Home of Erskine Childers. Collins often came here to discuss plans for propaganda during the War of Independence.

Dublin 6

Key locations

Belgrave Road

Rathgar

Rathmines

Ranelagh

D
ublin 6 is a primarily residential area in the south of County Dublin. Situated in the heart of that area, Rathmines has a long history, stretching back to the fourteenth century, when it and its hinterland were part of the ecclesiastical lands called *Cuallu* or *Cuallan*, later the vast parish of Cullenswood, which gave its name to a nearby area and to Cullenswood Road, on which Patrick Pearse first founded his school, St Enda's, in Cullenswood House. Rathmines was a popular suburb, attracting the wealthy and powerful, seeking refuge from the poor living conditions of the city, from the middle of the nineteenth century.

> *'... the Collins that stood by the grave of Ashe in September 1917 and the Collins of January to March 1920 were two figures of very different dimensions'*
> Richard Mulcahy

Early in the twentieth century Rathmines, and particularly Belgrave Road, became known as 'Rebel Road' on account of all the republicans living there, including Count and Countess Plunkett, Alderman Thomas Kelly, Robert and Una Brennan, Nora Connolly O'Brien, Count and Countess Markievicz, Dr Kathleen Lynn and Madeleine ffrench-Mullen.

Dr Kathleen Lynn was one of the most noted women of the period. During the Rising she served as a captain of the Citizen Army; as the medical officer in the City Hall, she surrendered the garrison after its ICA leaders were killed. Following her imprisonment, Dr Lynn continued her republican activities, saying that she 'evaded capture by dressing like a lady, in my Sunday clothes and feather boa, and by walking instead of cycling'.

Dublin 6 is also home to Portobello Barracks (now Cathal Brugha Barracks, named after the hero of the South Dublin Union). During the Rising it was the scene of one of the most infamous British atrocities: the murder of Francis Sheehy-Skeffington. It was from here that Collins left on his fatal trip to County Cork in August 1922.

At various times James Joyce, Éamon de Valera, Taoiseach Jack Lynch and Bram Stoker lived in Rathgar, always a most desirable residential area.

Collins and Richard Mulcahy shared space in Cullenswood House, the first location of Pearse's St Enda's school. Collins had a basement office here ('the Dug-

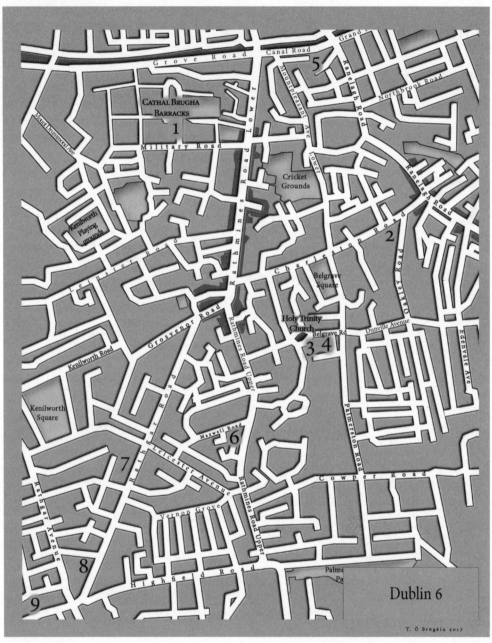

T. Ó Brógáin 2017

Dublin 6

1 Rathmines Road: Portobello Barracks (now Cathal Brugha Barracks)

2 Oakley Road, Ranelagh: Cullenswood House

3 7 Belgrave Road, Rathmines: home of Hanna Sheehy-Skeffington

4 9 Belgrave Road, Rathmines: home of Dr Kathleen Lynn and Madeleine ffrench-Mullen

5 7 Ranelagh Road: see Bloody Sunday

6 Fitzwilliam Terrace, Rathmines Road Upper, Rathmines: Ros na Ríogh, Home of Cathal Brugha

7 6 Airfield Road, Rathgar: Mrs Julia O'Donovan's home

8 77 Rathgar Road: Mrs Julia O'Donovan's dairy

9 12 Bushy Park Road, Terenure (Dublin 6W): home of Erskine and Molly Childers

Out'), while Mulcahy and his wife had the top-floor flat.

Following the publication of Piaras Béaslaí's book *Michael Collins and the making of a new Ireland* in 1927, many contested Béaslaí's views. In the 1950s Risteard Mulcahy, son of the general, asked General Mulcahy to read the book and to annotate it. General Mulcahy's descriptions of Collins show his development as a leader and how their relationship ripened.

In 1919 both Collins and Mulcahy were considered for the position of chief of staff of the Volunteer GHQ. Dick McKee, director of training, who went on to be the O/C of the Dublin Brigade, agreed beforehand that Mulcahy and not Collins should be chief of staff. Mulcahy later noted:

> McKee, as he came away from the meeting with me, expressed satisfaction and relief that Collins was not being recommended. The main reason for that was that in the light of what he knew about Collins' temperament, ... McKee—like others—was a little bit wary of entrusting him with anything like complete control. In fact he did want time to disclose himself and his qualities.

In one of his rare personal remarks about Collins in the annotation of Béaslaí's book, Mulcahy wrote:

> If, internally, he [Collins] had grown in power, strength of will and flexibility, as he had, he had done it by tireless, vigorous, almost turbulent hard work, applied to his office work as much as to his widespread and general personal contacts.

Both Collins and Mulcahy were committed to the army, its formal structures, ethical standards and military efficiency; both were committed to its subservience to the Dáil and the people of Ireland. Early in the campaign, Mulcahy was more conservative in his commitment to the war, being aware that many nationalists favoured peaceful non-cooperation with the British parliament and the control of local government, a view he shared with Cathal Brugha. A more active and brutal war was forced on GHQ at the end of 1919 because of the constant harassment of Sinn Féin deputies, speakers and supporters by the RIC, the suppression of the Dáil and mounting pressure from provincial Volunteers.

Collins evolved into the man to be sent to London to negotiate the peace.

16 Airfield Road, Rathgar: Home of Julia O'Donovan, aunt of Gearóid O'Sullivan and grandmother of Fionnuala Donovan. This was one of Collins's two main safe houses in south Dublin. (See Mrs Mary Woods's home, 31 Fitzwilliam Street Upper, Dublin 2.) O'Donovan also had a dairy in the area at 77 Rathgar Road, as well as another on Mespil Road. (See Dublin 4.) On the night of Bloody Sunday, Collins had dinner here. The famous wedding party photo, with Collins 'hiding' his face, was taken here after the wedding of Elizabeth Clancy and Michael J. O'Brien on 22 November 1920, the very next day.[525]

51 Lower Beechwood Avenue, Ranelagh: Home of Séamus Moore and his sisters, Bridie and Mary. It was used as a safe house and meeting place by the IRA/Volunteers, and then by the IRA/Republicans during the Civil War. Joe Aherne, Desmond FitzGerald, Frank Gallagher, Maureen McGavock and Ernie O'Malley often stayed here while on the run.

> I remember the morning of Bloody Sunday. Joe Aherne and myself walked down from Ranelagh where we lived, to University Church for, I think, 9 o'clock Mass. Everything was quiet and we noticed nothing unusual on the way. When we came out from Mass there seemed to be suppressed excitement and somebody spoke of shooting in Pembroke Street. Later in the day we heard of the raid on Desmond FitzGerald's flat in Pembroke Street, which was right opposite the service flats where the British Intelligence Officers were shot. In the evening we went to McGilligan's, Lower Leeson Street, where we found Desmond hiding. The McGilligan's got word that they were to be raided and we took Desmond home with us to 51 Lower Beechwood Avenue where we had rooms in the house of Séamus Moore, afterwards TD for Wicklow. Desmond stayed with us for three months. At that time he was Director of Propaganda. We insisted on his remaining indoors on the Monday, 21 November, 1920, as all the bridges were held by the British military, and I still remember his humiliation at the reproach—entirely undeserved—in a note from Mick Collins, 'What is all this digging in about?'[526]

7 Belgrave Road, Rathmines: Home of Hanna Sheehy-Skeffington. She lived here after her husband's murder and after being evicted from 11 (now 21) Grosvenor Place, Rathmines, where she had lived with Francis and their son Owen.

In mid-1919 she took Harry Boland's place as secretary of Sinn Féin when he went to the US with de Valera. (See 64 Abbey Street Middle, Dublin 1.) Later, she was a judge of the Dáil Éireann/Republican courts and was a member of the first Fianna Fáil Executive in 1926.

9 Belgrave Road, Rathmines: Home of Dr Kathleen Lynn and Madeleine ffrench-Mullen.

Born in Cong, Co. Mayo, and educated in Dublin, England and Germany, Dr Lynn qualified as a doctor in 1899. She saw a great deal of poverty as a child and recalled: 'The local doctor was a fount of help and hope so I decided to become a doctor'. Awarded degrees in surgery and medicine from the Royal University in 1899, having interned at Holles Street Hospital (1897–9), the Rotunda Hospital (1899), the Royal Victoria Eye and Ear Hospital (1899) and also the Richmond Lunatic Asylum, she became a Fellow of the Royal College of Surgeons in Ireland in 1909.[527] She fought in the Rising, was imprisoned and deported, but was released in 1918 to fight the influenza epidemic of that year.[528] She died in September 1955 and was given a military funeral, as she had been a commanding officer during the Rising.[529]

Madeleine ffrench-Mullen was a member of the Irish Women's Franchise League and a staunch supporter of James Connolly as a member of the Irish Citizen Army, serving in the Liberty Hall soup kitchens during the 1913 Lockout. During the Rising she commanded the medical detachment at St Stephen's Green, and was subsequently imprisoned in Richmond Barracks and Kilmainham Gaol. A frequent contributor to *Bean na hÉireann*, she had a lifelong commitment to the causes of labour and women's rights and the emancipation of the working class. She invested a significant portion of her life in building the Irish Women's Workers' Union, and was elected a vice-president in 1917 (as was Dr Lynn).

Helena Molony often lodged here.[530]

Dr Lynn and Miss ffrench-Mullen later founded St Ultan's Children's Hospital, and it became a locus for the eradication of tuberculosis in Dublin's children. (See 37 Charlemont Street, Dublin 2.)

10 Belgrave Road, Rathmines: Home of Robert and Una Brennan,[531] said to be one of only two women admitted into the IRB, as her husband would not join without her. Some sources name Maud Gonne as the other woman, but that seems unlikely; most cite Kathleen Clarke. It is accepted that Kathleen Clarke was given the responsibility to re-establish communications between surviving IRB members after the Rising, and Tom gave her access to the IRB funds. She was actually told by the IRB *not* to take part in the Rising so that she would be able to help the families of the men who were killed or imprisoned afterwards.

Charleston Road: Home of Margaret Foley. Frank Gallagher stayed here while on the run after the early summer of 1920. Gallagher was the editor of the *Irish Bulletin*, the Sinn Féin underground newspaper, and stayed in very close contact with Collins, coordinating stories for Sinn Féin advantage. (See Molesworth Street, Dublin 2.)

Fitzwilliam Terrace, Upper Rathmines Road, Rathmines: Ros na Ríogh, home of Cathal Brugha. (See Hammam Hotel, Sackville Street Upper, Dublin 1; St Joseph's Church, Berkeley Road, Mater Misericordiae Hospital, Eccles Street, Dublin 7.)

3 Mountpleasant Avenue, Ranelagh: Joe Leonard lived here. Members of Collins's Squad often met here, or returned here after actions.

Oakley Road, Ranelagh: Cullenswood House. The first location of Patrick Pearse's St Enda's school. Collins had a basement office here ('the Dug-Out'), and Richard Mulcahy and his wife had the top-floor flat.

When Piaras Béaslaí's *Michael Collins and the making of a new Ireland* was published in 1927, many contested Béaslaí's views. Risteard Mulcahy, son of General Mulcahy, asked his father to read the book and to annotate it; his annotation ran to several volumes.

His comments about Collins, de Valera, Griffith, MacNeill, Brugha, Stack, Dick McKee, Liam Lynch and many others are of considerable interest, not only because of his description of the important parts they played during the period but also because of the human touches added by his recording certain situations and conversations which he shared with them. Running right through the pages of the annotation, although it is hardly verbalised, is an impression of a deep sense of mutual trust, harmony and respect between himself and Collins. They shared a number of attributes. Both were trained in the British Civil Service and, despite the contrast in their personalities, they shared the same boundless energy and flair for organisation. In one of his rare personal remarks about Collins on page 134, Volume 2, of the annotation he states:

> From the point of view of public recognition and appreciation, the Collins that stood by the grave of Ashe in September 1917 and the Collins of January to March 1920 were two figures of very different dimensions. If, internally, he had grown in power, strength of will and flexibility, as he had, he had done it by tireless, vigorous, almost turbulent hard work, applied to his office work as much as to his widespread and general personal contacts. The impulse to make the necessary movement from place to place, and to meet an increasing number of different people to deal with various facets of work, added to his daring, gave him enormous momentum.[532]

Mulcahy's flat was raided on 31 January 1920 and many of his papers were found. They caused a sensation in Dublin Castle, as they 'gave evidence of a really big, determined and fairly well organised conspiracy'; there were plans describing Volunteers going abroad to put the electricity plant for Manchester out of action and for the destruction of the Liverpool docks.

44 Oakley Road, Ranelagh: In April 1917 a 'Conference of Women Delegates' met here to petition Sinn Féin for representation and to demand equality of status for women. The petition was for six members to represent women on the Sinn Féin executive: Áine Ceannt,[533] Kathleen Clarke, Alice Ginnell,[534] Dr Kathleen Lynn, Helena Molony[535] and Jennie Wyse-Power.

The conference was to protest that women had only one delegate (Countess Plunkett) on the Sinn Féin executive council. It noted that six members of the Irish Nation League had been seated on the executive and felt that women should have no less representation. Alice Ginnell, writing as the hon. secretary, noted that 'The claim of women to be represented is based mainly on the Republican Proclamation of Easter Week, 1916, which of course you are determined to uphold'.[536] The petition was presented to the Sinn Féin Convention of 1917 and was carried.[537]

Later in April 1917 the League of Women Delegates was founded. At a meeting on 16 October the name was Gaelicised to Cumann na dTeachaire. The primary focus was to promote the representation and participation of women in the reorganisation of Sinn Féin.

7 Ranelagh Road: Capt. Noble, a British intelligence agent, had rooms here. On Bloody Sunday, IRA/Volunteers led by Joe Dolan and Dan McDonnell[538] were assigned to kill him, but he wasn't home. Dolan was so angry that he wasn't there that he gave Noble's 'paramour' a 'right scourging with a sword scabbard. Then he set the room on fire.'[539]

> I was one of the organisers of that. I was in the Intelligence Section and was sent round all the hotels and boarding houses collecting information from waiters and footmen and others. I had supplied 75% of the information for this job. I got all the information I needed from the staff of the hotels I visited. There were 40 men to be executed that morning. I was also actively engaged in the operation. I was out in Ranelagh with Dan McDonnell at the house of Lieutenant [sic] Noble at 9 o'clock but he had left the house at 7 o'clock. The operations were carried out in all the areas as arranged except the 1st Battalion area. Of the 40 who should have been shot only about 17 were actually [shot]. Coming back from Ranelagh we met Tom Keogh. He was bringing along Bill McClean who had been wounded. They had been in Mount Street. I helped Tom Keogh to bring Bill back to North Richmond Street where he lived.[540]

Also in the Volunteer team were C.S. (Todd) Andrews, Francis X. Coghlan, Hubert Earle and James Kenny. (See Bloody Sunday, Appendix IV.) Coghlan was so incensed at Dolan's behaviour that he remained at the house to put out the flames and see the children to safety.

19 Ranelagh Road: Home of Richard Mulcahy after the raid on Cullenswood House in January 1920.

77 Rathgar Road: Mrs Julia O'Donovan's dairy. She was the aunt of Gearóid O'Sullivan and often lent her home for meetings, especially for Collins's men in the DMP.

> By this time the GHQ staff of the IRA had evidently recognised the assistance I was giving them, as the Constable Byrne I have referred to came to me one evening and asked me to attend a meeting at Mrs O'Donovan's house in an avenue off Rathgar Avenue. Byrne and myself went to the meeting together and on arriving at O'Donovan's house we met Constable Culhane who is now in America. I think there was a man named MacNamara [*sic*] of the 'G' Division there, but Colonel Broy was not present that night. From the IRA side there were Frank Thornton, Gearóid O'Sullivan and a man named O'Connell I think, or the name may have been Cullen. There were about five or six DMP men present. I cannot remember who presided at the meeting but I do recollect that we were all sitting around a table and the matter under discussion that night was the help that the DMP men, as a whole, could give. It was put to us that we should do our best to get at least one man whom we could rely on from each station in the Dublin Metropolitan Police area, to talk the thing over and to bring them along and introduce them at a future meeting.
>
> Following that meeting we got down to work and we had a discussion amongst ourselves as to the Stations and men of the Force that could be safely approached. I went to Fitzgibbon Street Station and there got in touch with Constable Terence O'Reilly (now Superintendent, Garda Síochána) who was a friend of mine. I put the matter to him as it had been represented to us at the meeting in O'Donovan's house, and he agreed to come in.
>
> I think some other members of our party approached Constable Mannix who was stationed in Donnybrook and who also agreed to give all the help he could. As a result of the first meeting we got about five or six men into our party. At the next meeting in O'Donovan's house we had three or four new members. There were others who could not come as they were on duty that particular night.
>
> Colonel Broy was at the next meeting. At this meeting a further appeal was made to enlist new men into our circle. I think it was Frank Thornton who expressed at that meeting his deep appreciation of our efforts to secure members and he added that no matter how hot things got none of us was to resign from the Force because if we did we would be of no use to him. Other meetings were held in O'Donovan's house. The subject discussed at these meetings was always the same. We were to get all the reliable DMP men we could to help us and any information that would come our way we were to pass on to the Intelligence staff as quickly as we possibly could.
>
> I remember at one of the meetings held in O'Donovan's house Michael

Collins was there. It was the first time I had seen him. Collins addressed us that night and told us he appreciated very much all we were doing, adding that he still felt that he could rely on us to get many more reliable men who were serving in the DMP to come over to our side.[541]

Collins often used Mrs O'Donovan's homes here and in Mespil Road as shelters, particularly for those coming from Cork. He also used her accounts to 'hide' Dáil Loan funds.

One night in the autumn of 1920 … I came home and a messenger called to ask my permission for a meeting to be held that evening in my house. [My daughter] gave permission and placed the usual refreshments in the drawing room. She was rather indignant to find that one of those at the meeting—Frank Thornton or Tom Cullen—sent out for more refreshments. She does not remember if Gearóid [O'Sullivan] or Mick were there yet as she only let in the first half-dozen and Thornton or Cullen let in the others. We heard afterwards that Broy was there … The meeting, which lasted a couple of hours, was over when I returned from the opera. We never knew what the meeting was about. We always refrained from showing any curiosity in such matters.[542]

(See 77 Mespil Road, Dublin 4.)

Rathmines Road: Portobello Barracks (now Cathal Brugha Barracks). This barracks was General Collins's office during the Civil War. He left Dublin from here on his fatal journey on 20 August 1922. (See Appendix V.)

The famous photo taken of Collins on that day had the fourteen-year-old Alphonsus Culliton in the background.

Cathal Brugha Barracks now houses the Irish Military Archives.

8 Victoria Terrace, Rathgar: Home owned by May Lanagan (later Mrs Kilbride); it was Erskine Childers's Ministry for Propaganda office. The staff included Lily O'Brennan and Moira O'Byrne.[543]

12 Villiers Road, Rathmines: Home of H.J. Tipping; he was the controller of the GPO and was in charge of opening accounts and funding after the Rising.

Dublin 6W

Key locations

Kimmage
Terenure

L arkfield, in Kimmage, south–west Dublin, has the postal code Dublin 6W. (Take Harold's Cross Road to Kimmage Road to reach it.) The estate was on the boundary of Rathmines and Kimmage, and lies between what were then the rural villages of Crumlin, Kimmage and Terenure.

'... he [Collins] was not well liked ...'
Joe Good

In 1913 Countess Josephine Plunkett took a lease on Larkfield House and Mill and set about making some changes. According to Geraldine Plunkett Dillon, her mother dismantled the internal structure of the mill's boiler house and created two four-roomed cottages. Within the mill there were now two businesses in operation.

Geraldine moved to Larkfield in 1914 and became the main carer for her brother Joseph, who was suffering from advanced glandular tuberculosis. Joseph continued with his writings and planning for the Rising and was able to make use of the printing press that had been set up here. By the autumn of 1915 he was a member of the Irish Republican Brotherhood Military Council and the primary planner of military operations for the Irish Volunteers. He spent much of 1915 travelling to and from Germany, having medical treatment while meeting with Roger Casement and seeking German support for the IRB's plans for a rising. When he was in Dublin he stayed at Larkfield and it became his headquarters. By early 1916 the activity at Larkfield Mill had become more intense, as it was transformed into an armed camp with about 90 men living on the premises. Commandant Éamonn Ceannt's 4th Volunteer Battalion trained and billeted here before the Rising.

When conscription was imposed in England in January 1916, Collins returned to Ireland from his home in London. He was made one of Joseph Plunkett's aides-de-camp and went to Kimmage almost daily, though he was not listed as a member of the Kimmage Garrison. It seems that the Volunteer military staff had given him specific responsibility for the garrison. Joe Good said that he was 'impressed with the hurry and earnestness in Collins, but had little sympathy for his drastic methods ... since he was abusive to us. He was not well liked.'

12 Bushy Park Road, Terenure: Home of Erskine and Molly Childers. When they first came to Dublin they lived at the St Stephen's Green home of Alice Stopford Green, then moved to 20 Wellington Road. This was their last Dublin home. During the Treaty negotiations in London, Erskine Childers had been the chief secretary to the Irish delegation. He took the anti-Treaty side in the Civil War and was captured at the home of his cousin, Robert Barton, in Annamoe, Co. Wicklow. Before his execution in Beggar's Bush Barracks, he shook the hand of each man in the firing squad and said, 'Come closer, boys, it will be easier for you'. (See Beggar's Bush Barracks, Dublin 4; Annamoe, Co. Wicklow, Appendix VI.)

Kimmage, Larkfield: Home of Count and Countess Plunkett.

The 4th Battalion of the Dublin Brigade trained and billeted here before the Rising.[544] Nearly all the men in the 'Kimmage Garrison' were born in or came from England, or were Irishmen who were 'on the run'. Men from this garrison, along with men from the ICA, formed the core of the GPO garrison.[545]

Almost all the men were members of the Gaelic League and the GAA, and most believed that those organisations were 'hijacked' by the IRB for recruiting purposes.[546] Arthur Agnew,[547] Joseph Gleeson,[548] Joe Good,[549] John (Blimey) O'Connor and Séamus Robinson[550] were among those who came from England and who lived and worked here prior to the Rising. Peadar Bracken,[551] Séamus Brennan, Denis Daly[552] and Francis and Michael Flanagan were among those Irishmen who were 'on the run'.

Geraldine Plunkett thought that Collins was still very much a country boy when he first came to Kimmage:

> He was crude socially, his business manner was his best, he had crude ideas which offended others and [a] coarse point of view which made them think he was a materialist, they even thought he was an adventurer and not a nationalist at all. He was a clever peasant with a peasant's virtues and vices, he was shrewd and plain but he drank a great deal too much … He was a very rough diamond.[553]

Collins was employed by the Plunkett family to try to sort out their financial records. When he returned to Dublin from London in January 1916, he also went to work for the accountancy firm of Craig, Gardiner & Co. on Dame Street. His salary at the time was 30 shillings a week, which was comparable with London commercial rates but quite high for Dublin. When he was appointed a captain in the Volunteers, he bought a full uniform. His less fortunate comrades in Larkfield resented his new-found affluence, and whenever he appeared in his Volunteer captain's uniform they would chant 'Who killed Michael Collins?', which always aggravated him.

Terenure: First home of Mr and Mrs Kevin O'Higgins after their marriage. The IRA/Republicans attacked it during the Civil War, and Mrs O'Higgins moved into the safety of Government Buildings.

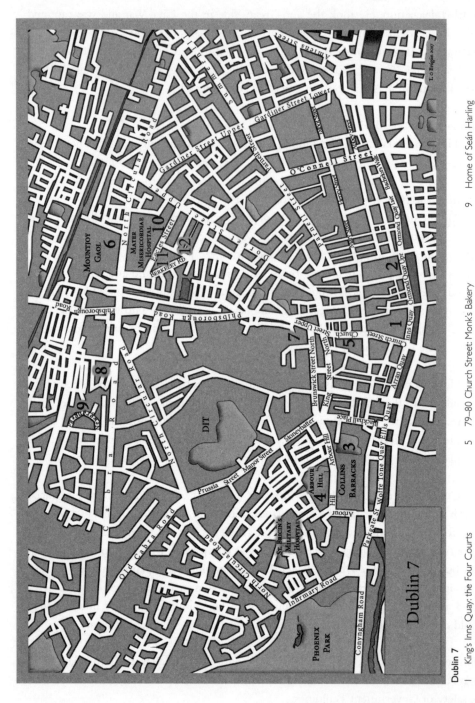

Dublin 7

1 King's Inns Quay: the Four Courts
2 Ormond Quay: Ormond Hotel
3 Royal Barracks: Collins Barracks, now part of the
   National Museum of Ireland
4 Arbour Hill
5 79–80 Church Street: Monk's Bakery
6 North Circular Road, Cowley Place: Mountjoy
   Prison
7 North Dublin Union
8 Home of Michael Foley
9 Home of Seán Harling
10 Mater Misericordiae Hospital
11 O'Donel's Private Nursing Home
12 St Joseph's Church

Dublin 7

Key locations

Arbour Hill

Cabra Road

Church Street

North Circular Road (Mountjoy Prison)

Eccles Street (Mater Misericordiae Hospital)

Infirmary Road

King's Inns Quay (Four Courts)

Newgrange Road

Ormond Quay

Phibsborough Road

When Collins returned from London in 1916, his first residence was 16 Rathdown Road. He lived here until the Rising, and it was the address he listed when he was sent to prison in Wales.

Fionan Lynch cried out to Thomas Ashe,
'Stick it, Tom'
Ashe replied:
'I'll stick it, Fin'

From that time onwards, Dublin 7 was a pivotal area in Collins's life. He first met Ned Broy here; one of his Irish nemeses, Cathal Brugha, worked and died here; Collins's operatives were often sent to Mountjoy Prison; and the Four Courts were where the Civil War effectively started.

Ned Broy became one of Collins's most important sources within the DMP, and their first meeting was at the Foley home at 5 Cabra Road. Since the Rising Broy had been trying to pass information along to Sinn Féin, but until he met Collins his information was mostly disregarded.

From his role in the Rising onwards, Cathal Brugha gained a reputation for courage, single-mindedness and incorruptibility, and he remains one of the most admired men of the period. Yet he and Collins never saw eye to eye as cabinet members. Brugha distrusted the IRB and left the organisation, whereas Collins became its president. During his entire time in cabinet, Brugha was the managing director of Lalor's Ltd on Ormond Quay and worked there daily. After being wounded in the Civil War fighting on O'Connell Street he was brought to the Mater Hospital on Eccles Street, where he passed away. Collins said of him: 'I would forgive him anything … When many of us are forgotten, Cathal Brugha will be remembered.'

The Mater Hospital was also where Thomas Ashe died on 25 September 1917, following force-feeding in Mountjoy Jail.

Collins remembered every weakness of everyone who was a prisoner in Mountjoy or any other jail, and went far to find their favourite brand of tobacco or cigarettes. And he knew which sweets his other operatives liked: 'I know you don't smoke, but I remember you saying you liked candies', he wrote to Kathleen Clarke when he sent her a package in Holloway Prison. The loyalty that Collins inspired was in part due to the fact that he was really concerned about individuals and would go to any lengths to help them. Most especially, he was always ready to try to break them out of jail. He knew how important jail-breaking was to the republican tradition.

Collins was involved in the escape of Éamon de Valera from Lincoln Jail in February 1919, and throughout the period he was always trying to free his friends and operatives. He arranged Robert Barton's escape from Mountjoy in March 1919, managing to smuggle in a file and a rope. Barton filed through the bars, and when ' went over the wall Collins was waiting to take him to Batt O'Connor's home on Brendan Road.

Just two weeks later there was another, much larger, jail-break. Peadar Clancy, along with Richard Mulcahy, was instrumental in the escape of leading Republican prisoners from Mountjoy on 29 March. In all, nineteen prisoners escaped; it was considered a major coup by Republicans and was a boost to morale. Collins waited for news of the jail-break at the Wicklow Hotel and Joe O'Reilly cycled there to give him the news. When Collins asked 'Is Fleming out?', O'Reilly answered, 'The whole jail is out!'

Following his capture and trial, Kevin Barry was taken to Mountjoy, where he was hanged on 1 November 1919. Collins proposed several plans for his escape but, tragically, Barry's mother was opposed, as she felt sure until the last minute that his sentence would be commuted because of his youth.

Seán MacEoin was imprisoned in Mountjoy in March 1921 and Collins devised several attempts to free him. The first was when Collins had a friendly priest see MacEoin, and in the middle of an anti-IRA tirade the priest told MacEoin that he was from Collins. A plan was passed to have MacEoin escape with help from IRA men dressed as British warders, but MacEoin was transferred before the plan could be carried out. Next, Collins sent a female doctor to see MacEoin, and she passed him plans of the prison's layout. This plan did not come to fruition either, and MacEoin remained in prison. The most ambitious of these attempts took place on 14 May, utilising a commandeered armoured car commanded by Emmet Dalton, dressed in his British Army uniform. Once again the attempt failed, and MacEoin remained in Mountjoy until the Truce in July.

If there was one thing a prisoner could rely on it was that Michael Collins would not forget him or her.

In April 1922 the Four Courts were occupied by IRA/Republican troops, led by Rory O'Connor. That threw down a challenge to the Free State, and at 3.40 on the morning of 28 June 1922 the occupying force was given an ultimatum to surrender. Collins ordered the artillery that had been lent to the Free State army by the British to begin firing twenty minutes later.

The Civil War had begun.

Arbour Hill: Arbour Hill Detention Centre. Built in 1835 and redesigned in 1845, it was the smallest of Dublin's Victorian prisons. Its chapel has stained-glass windows by Earley Studios. The bodies of the executed 1916 leaders are buried here in a pit of quicklime; some DMP and British soldiers reported that they were buried in the order in which they were executed.[554]

During the War of Independence C.S. Andrews was a prisoner here, as was Éamon (Ned) Broy. Broy's papers had been found in a raid on Eileen McGrane's home on 31 December 1920. (See 21 Dawson Street, Dublin 2.) In order to deflect suspicion, Collins threatened Broy's superior and told him to burn all papers relating to Broy. Then he arranged for it to appear that an associate of Broy's, ex-Sergeant Pat McCarthy, was the one to whom the papers belonged. Collins sent a man to London with a ticket for McCarthy to go to the USA, where he remained. Collins also found McCarthy a job there. This subterfuge saved Broy's life and he was never brought to trial. Although Collins had other agents in the DMP and Dublin Castle, Broy was really irreplaceable. He remained in Arbour Hill until the Truce and throughout his four months' imprisonment he was never allowed a change of clothes. When he was released after the Truce, Collins came to collect him and had had a suit made for him at Callaghan & Son on Dame Street.[555]

Broy went on to be a member of Collins's security detail in London during the Treaty negotiations. Following the establishment of the Free State, he joined the Free State Army and rose to the rank of colonel. He joined the Garda Síochána in 1925 and became the Garda Commissioner after Fianna Fáil took over for Cumann na nGaedheal in 1932.

Máire Comerford was imprisoned here during the Civil War. She escaped but was recaptured and imprisoned in Kilmainham Gaol and the North Dublin Union, where she went on hunger strike.

10–13 Berkeley Road, Phibsborough: St Joseph's Church, noted for its Volunteer Commemorative Masses. An annual Mass is celebrated on 22 August in memory of Collins.

Cathal Brugha passed away in the Mater Hospital on Eccles Street and was removed to St Joseph's Church on the evening of 9 July 1922. There was a Requiem High Mass at 10am on the following day, and the body was then taken to Glasnevin. He died faithful to the Republic, and to him the Republic and Ireland were inseparable.

Collins said of him: 'I would forgive him anything. Because of his sincerity, I would forgive him anything. At worst, he was a fanatic—though in a noble cause. At best I number him among the very few who have given their all that this country—now torn by the Civil War—should have its freedom. When many of us are forgotten, Cathal Brugha will be remembered.'[556]

Brugha was a small, sincere, resolute man, zealously dedicated to the cause of Ireland. His methods and ideas were always clear and simple; he would never back off from anything or anyone. While he worked unselfishly, seeking no glory for himself, he resented all the press attention given to Collins. Even Mulcahy, who disliked his attitude, never doubted his sincerity: 'He was naturally blunt and frank and was no more intending to intrigue than he was to diplomacy'. De Valera remarked to Mulcahy that 'I think Cathal is jealous of Mick. Isn't it a terrible thing to think that a man w⁻ the qualities Cathal undoubtedly has would fall a victim to a dirty little vice like jealousy'.[557] Brugha greatly resented Collins, and that became publicly apparent in the Treaty debates. He mistakenly believed that Collins only used his IRB position to acquire his influence, and that his influence and authority were not due to his administrative abilities.

Upon Brugha's death, his wife issued the following statement:

> Mrs Cathal Brugha requests that, apart from family relations and intimate friends, the chief mourners and the Guard of Honour should only include the women of the Republican Movement. She makes this request as a protest against the 'immediate and terrible' Civil War made by the so-called Provisional Government of the Irish Republican forces.
>
> She does not desire the presence of any of the representatives of the Free State or its officials at the funeral.
>
> NOTE—This does not exclude the general public from attending the funeral.[558]

The *Irish Times*, an implacable foe of Brugha's political ideas at the time, editorialised:

> The death of Cathal Brugha in the Mater Hospital removes a remarkable personality from Irish life. Of all Ireland's many extremists, he was the most extreme. The manner of his death was typical of his life. Cathal Brugha died, as he lived, in the last ditch. No other modern country save Ireland produces such types. They belong in point of time to the Middle Ages, when men would face the stake for an idea, whether it was right or wrong. Of such stuff was Cathal Brugha made. All his life he hated England with an intensity of feeling which is rarely found even in this country of painful memories. Whenever there was talk of a rebellion he was at the head of the insurgent movement. Whenever there was talk of a surrender he was found fighting to the last.[559]

The *Irish Times* also carried an anonymous letter:

> Cathal Brugha was as unforgiving as he was unflinching in his purpose; but he was broken by the forces against which he fought with all the strength of his

fragile body and all the wild zeal of an untameable spirit. ... Yet he was a fond husband and a devoted father. On such human contrasts Ireland's sorrows have been built.

From his role in the Rising onwards, Brugha gained a reputation for courage, single-mindedness and incorruptibility, and remains one of the most admired men of the period. He is commemorated in a memorial plaque on the building at the north-east corner of O'Connell Street and Cathedral Street, at first-floor level, over the Burger King restaurant.

(See Gardiner Place, Granville Hotel, Sackville Street Upper, Dublin 1; Mater Misericordiae Hospital, Eccles Street.)

4 Brunswick Street North: North Dublin Union. Members of the Volunteer 1st Battalion under Cmdt Ned Daly occupied the building during the Rising. Next door was St John's Convent of the Sisters of St Vincent de Paul. The nuns supported the Volunteers, prayed with them and pleaded with God for their safe return. Daly's men knew the nuns by name: Sisters Brigid, Agnes, Patrick, Monica and Louise.[560]

The building was used as a barracks by the Black and Tans during the War of Independence.

During the Civil War it was used as a women's prison.[561] On 6 May 1923, Máire Comerford, Maura Deegan and Aoife Taaffe escaped successfully. On the following night, 22 women escaped using the same route; most, however, were recaptured.

Now St Lawrence's Hospital.

5 Cabra Road: Home of Michael Foley.

The 'G' Division of the DMP, which at that time was stationed in College Street, had a mess account at Findlater's, and a mess man used to come every week to pay the bill. This mess man was changed every six months and in that way I got to know a number of the 'G' men, including Éamon Broy. I can't remember exactly when I met him first, but finding out that I was interested in the Gaelic League, he always talked Irish to me and always warned me when there was going to be a raid on the Volunteer houses.

One day in January 1919, he came in on some excuse to my cash office. He pretended to be settling up a bill and wrote in Irish on a piece of my blotting paper that some Volunteers had escaped from Usk. ... I telephoned the news immediately to Micheál who then had his office in 32 Bachelor's Walk that Broy had been giving me information for at least six months at that time.

When I was getting married on February 14, 1919, I left Findlater's a couple of days before that and from then on ... Broy used to come to our house in No.

5 Cabra Road, to meet Mick Collins who slept in our house for a couple of months at a time until it was no longer safe to do so, as the house became too well known. Piaras Béaslaí, Tomás McCurtain, Tomás Breathnach, Maurice Brennan used to sleep there. Later about 1921 Brennan and Breathnach took a flat in the top of the house and many Volunteers used to sleep there from time to time. At this time Mick Collins did not sleep there as raids were frequent.

Broy used to bring another 'G' man called McNamara sometimes to meet Collins. There was no one in the house that time but myself and Micheál and of course we never knew, nor did we inquire, what they were discussing.

Broy was a great athlete and so had Collins been, but the latter was getting rather soft for want of exercise and Broy used to take him out to give him running exercise at some Park in Sandymount. Broy was a member of the Amateur Athletic Association to whom the Park belonged.

He was very fond of Mick Collins and he even went as far as to bring him to the Headquarters of the 'G' Division. It was at our house that the plans for this venture were made. He showed him everything, letters that had been captured, notices offering rewards for the capture of prominent Sinn Féiners, etc. It was a very daring thing and should be remembered for Broy who risked his life in the undertaking. ... Broy was the official typist in the Castle and whenever he was typing anything that concerned the Volunteers, he always made a second copy and had it delivered to Mick Collins or someone else.[562]

Broy described his nationalism:

I come from Kildare. We were reared in a grimmer tradition than most. We remembered '98, the Yeomanry and what they did. There was a church once near where I was born and the Yeos rounded up the women and children, locked them in and set fire to the church. We remembered that, the pitch-capping and the flogging. And we talked about Wolfe Tone and the Fenians. The Fenians were riddled with informers. After 1916 I felt it was time we learned the lesson.

Since the Rising Broy had been passing information along to Sinn Féin through the Michael O'Hanrahan family. As O'Hanrahan had been one of those executed after the Rising, Broy felt that this was the best route to get information to the nationalists. Until he met Collins, however, Broy's information was mostly disregarded, as many of the Irish viewed him with reasonable suspicion since he worked in the 'G' Division.

I furnished Volunteer Headquarters with all secret and confidential G. Division reports from 1917 to 1921. From 1917 to 1919 these reports passed mainly through the O'Hanrahan shop, and where they were taken eventually I never ascertained. The main purpose was to have the reports in the Volunteer hands as soon as possible, and how these reports were eventually dealt with was a matter for the Volunteers. Subsequent to my first meeting with Michael Collins … all such reports went to him from me through his officers or I gave them directly to him myself.

Collins quickly recognised the potential benefit of having a spy within the DMP and Broy agreed to play a key role in the Collins spy network. He trusted Collins unreservedly and was fully aware of the risks involved in acting as a double agent. If discovered, he would be immediately arrested, tortured and eventually shot for treason. Broy wrote about his first meeting with Collins:

During the whole time of my association with Tracy [see Kingsbridge Railway Station, Dublin 8] and O'Hanrahan, I did not know who ultimately handled the documents I transmitted. I knew nothing about Michael Collins. I knew Miss Máire Smart (now Mrs Michael Foley). We had many talks about Sinn Féin, the insurrection and national activities, and we both solemnly agreed that violence was the only method. One day she said to me: 'you should meet Mick Collins' and I replied: 'Considering the things I have been doing, meeting anybody wouldn't be any more serious than what has already happened'. At the same time, I was very deeply intrigued, to know who or what this man Collins was like, because whoever was to handle the information I was giving directly would have to trust me, first of all; would have to understand the significance of the information; would need to have control of the Volunteers and be able to think and act quickly.

About the same time, at one of my meetings with Tracy, he said: 'The Volunteers want you to come to my house to-night'. I asked: 'What is it?' and he replied 'I believe it is a meeting'. Both of us had maintained that there would have to be a meeting. At Tracy's house, Millmount Avenue, Drumcondra, I met Greg Murphy.

He thanked me for all the information I had sent, said it was wonderful stuff, the like of which they never got before, and then, turning his mouth conspiratorially sideways, he said: 'Would you ever mind meeting Mick Collins?' I replied: 'In view of the things I have been doing, meeting anybody would be a small matter'. He asked me where I would like to meet him, and the only place I could think of was 5 Cabra Road, the residence of Mr and Mrs Micheál Ó Foghludha.

… I was filled with curiosity. Would this Michael Collins be the ideal man I had been dreaming about for a couple of years? … I had studied for so long the type of man that I would need to act efficiently, and the moment I saw Michael at the door … I knew he was the man. He thanked me for all the documents I had sent and all the information, and said it was of the utmost assistance and importance to them. We discussed why so many arrests took place and, particularly, the German Plot information—why that went wrong, especially the arrest of de Valera. He said a few minutes before train time de Valera looked at his watch and announced that, notwithstanding the threatened arrests, he was going home. They had dissuaded him but he insisted on going home and left the station. ... I asked Mick why he allowed de Valera to do that ... Mick shrugged his shoulders and looked at Greg Murphy, and Greg Murphy looked at him and they both smiled.[563]

Broy said that this was a place where every nationalist met at one time or another. He and Collins agreed that if the Volunteers did not resort to violence they would fail, but that they had to accept the risks of violence. Broy concurred with Collins that it was the only way, however difficult and dangerous. They also agreed that war had to be made on the RIC in their small stations in the countryside. With regard to the DMP, Broy recommended no attacks on the uniformed constables.

79–80 Church Street: Monk's Bakery. During the Rising, Commandant Ned Daly oversaw the distribution of bread from the bakery to the local residents, who depended on the bakery for their food.

Kevin Barry was captured here after an ambush on 20 September 1920 in which three British soldiers were killed. He stopped to reload his .38 calibre Luger (which the IRA always referred to as a 'Parabellum') and hid under a lorry. When it was about to be driven off, a bystander, Margaret Byrne, innocently shouted, 'There's a man under the lorry', and Barry was arrested. (Tragically, Byrne was killed in 1959 near the same spot on Church Street by a lorry sliding on the street in the rain.) The British troops engaged in this incident were from the 2nd Battalion of the Duke of Wellington's Regiment, commanded by Sgt Banks. The unit was on a thrice-weekly scheduled collection of the detachment's bread ration.

The IRA/Volunteers had mustered at the O'Flanagan Sinn Féin Club on Ryder's Row. 2Lt Tommy McGrane, John Joe Carroll, James Douglas, Dave McDonagh and Frank O'Flanagan had entered the bakery through the side entrance at 38 North King Street and were waiting for the British troops. Jim Moran and Paddy Young were to wait at the Brunswick Street corner. Maurice Higgins and Tom Kissane were to wait at the North King Street corner. Kevin Barry, 2Lt Bob O'Flanagan and Seán O'Neill were to follow the lorry into Church Street and hold up the troops for their weapons. Harry Murphy, Thomas (Tucker) Reilly and Christy Boy Robinson were to close in on the lorry from the Brunswick Street side. Séamus Kavanagh (the O/C), Frank Flood, Tommy O'Brien and Mick Robinson were to close in from a pub directly opposite. Eugene Fox, John Kenny, John O'Dwyer and Tom Staunton were to cover

Left—Upon his release from Frongoch Collins went to work for the Volunteers' Dependants' Fund. From then on he dressed as a successful Dublin businessman. Part of his 'businessman's uniform' was a dark fedora hat.

Below—The Castle was formally handed over to Collins and the Provisional Government Forces on 16 January 1922 by Edmund Bernard FitzAlan-Howard, 1st Viscount FitzAlan of Derwent, lord lieutenant of Ireland. After that, Collins was often seen in the Castle offices.

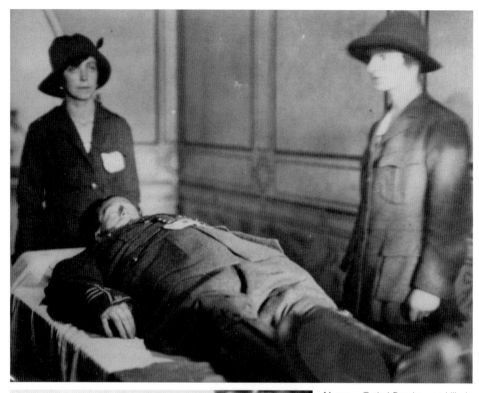

Above—Cathal Brugha was killed in the fighting on O'Connell Street at the beginning of the Civil War. He was one of the most courageous and resolute Republicans throughout the period.

Left—Arthur Griffith died suddenly of a cerebral haemorrhage on 12 August 1922, and was buried from the pro-cathedral on 16 August. Collins was one of the pall-bearers.

Left—At Arthur Griffith's funeral Collins met Revd Dr Michael Fogarty (bishop of Killaloe), who said: 'Michael, you should be prepared. You could be next.' Collins replied: 'I know. I hope to God nobody takes it into his head to die for another twelve months.' Two weeks later, on 28 August, Dr Fogarty was the principal celebrant at Collins's funeral Mass.

Below—Collins and Richard Mulcahy led the General Staff in the funeral procession for Arthur Griffith as it wound its way from the pro-cathedral to Glasnevin Cemetery.

This is the last known photo of Collins as he left Lee's Hotel (now the Munster Arms) in Bandon. His column was ambushed less than half an hour later.

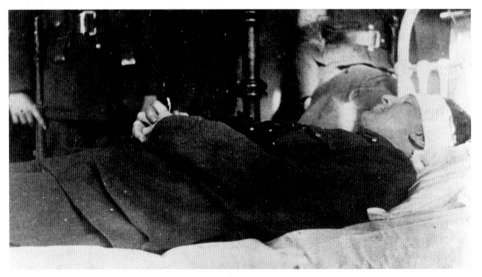

Dr Leo Ahearne examined Collins's body when it was brought to the Imperial Hotel, and then at Shanakiel Hospital. He was the first doctor to examine the body and pronounced Collins dead. His examination found a large, gaping wound 'to the right of the poll'. (Courtesy of Military Archives, IE-MA-ACPS-GRN-041.)

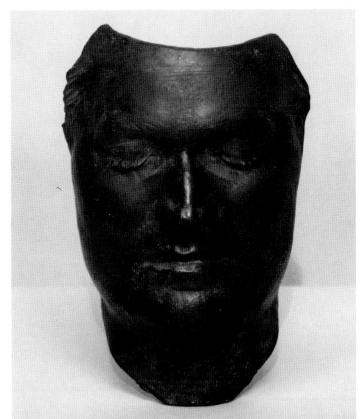

Left—Collins's body was embalmed in St Vincent's Hospital. His death-mask was sculpted by Albert Power.

Below—Oliver St John Gogarty supervised Collins's embalming. Here the staff of St Vincent's Hospital form a Guard of Honour as his casket is removed from the hospital to go to the City Hall, where it was to lie in state.

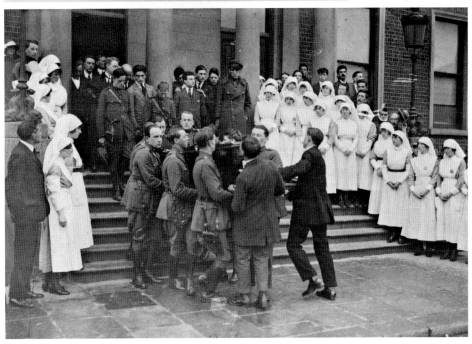

Above—Collins's body lay in state in City Hall from Friday 25 August until Sunday evening. Thousands of Dubliners passed by to pay their respects.

JESUS MERCY! MARY HELP!

O Merciful Jesus, give eternal rest to his soul, *7 years.*

Immaculate Heart of Mary pray for him, *100 days'*

In Undying Memory of
GENERAL
MICHAEL COLLINS
(Commander-in-Chief of Irish National Army)

Killed in Action at Bealnablath, near Bandon, Co. Cork,

On 22nd AUGUST, 1922
Aged 30 Years.

——✠——

Gone from us, but not forgotten
Never shall thy memory fade;
Sweetest thoughts shall ever linger
Round the grave where thou art laid

Left—There were many memorial cards for Collins. His death was a shock to the entire nation, and at his funeral, on 28 August 1922, 100,000 people lined the streets to see the cortège pass by.

Above—The gun-carriage on which Collins's casket was transported to Glasnevin Cemetery had been borrowed from the British and used in the bombardment of the Four Courts in June. The Provisional Government specially purchased four black artillery horses from the British to pull the caisson to Glasnevin.

Left—W.T. Cosgrave, who succeeded Collins as head of the Provisional Government, and Collins's brother Johnny (holding hat) at the grave in Glasnevin Cemetery.

Members of the General Staff of the Provisional Army give a final salute to Collins at his graveside.

Piaras Béaslaí laying a wreath on Michael Collins's grave in Glasnevin Cemetery at a commemorative service for Collins and Arthur Griffith in the 1940s.

the withdrawal up Constitution Hill, where an escape lorry was waiting on Coleraine Street, with drivers Davy Golden and Jimmy Carrigan.

Barry's .38 Parabellum jammed and he knelt down beside the lorry to clear it. He rose and it jammed again (on the fifth round) and he knelt under the lorry a second time. At that point the rest of the Volunteers withdrew owing to the returned fire and he was left isolated, hiding under the lorry.

Privates Harold Washington, Thomas Humphries and Marshall Whitehead were killed. Barry was tried for the murder of Marshall Whitehead, though Whitehead was killed with .45 calibre bullets. It is thought that Barry shot Pte Washington, but he was not charged with this killing.

Kevin Barry was the first IRA/Volunteer captured in action since 1916 and was the first person executed during the War of Independence.[564] When he was captured and sent to Mountjoy, Collins declared that 'there would be no more lonely scaffolds in our time'. Collins and his operatives contemplated several plans (none carried out) to get Barry out of prison.[565]

(See North Circular Road/Mountjoy Prison.)

138–142 Church Street: Capuchin Franciscan Friary and **131–137 Church Street: Fr Mathew Hall**, also known as **Capuchin Hall**.

North Circular Road (near Jones's Road): MacDermott Sinn Féin Club. This became one of the most active clubs and many Collins operatives joined, including Molly O'Reilly.

North Circular Road, Cowley Place: Mountjoy Prison ('the Joy'). Collins's intelligence apparatus had four warders here who passed on information: Frawley, Daly, Breslin and Patrick Joseph Berry.[566]

Prisoners started a hunger strike here in September 1917, demanding political status and to be treated as prisoners of war. The three leaders of the strike were Austin Stack, Fionan Lynch and Thomas Ashe. Ashe was subjected to force-feeding, and his lung was pierced during feeding by Dr Lowe on 23 September; he was taken to the Mater Hospital, where he died on 25 September 1917 of 'heart failure and congestion of the lungs'. Ashe had been arrested on 20 August, just before he was to travel to Skibbereen with Collins. Upon hearing of his arrest, Collins wrote to his sister Hannie: 'Tom Ashe has been arrested so that fixes him'.

Tomas Ashe, of whom my husband always had a great opinion, came to stay with us for a week and he was coming back here after some meeting in the country where he expressed himself very strongly against the government, when he was arrested. He was walking along the street with Micheál Ó Foghludha on the

Saturday when the detectives—Hoey and Smith—walked up beside him and said they would have to arrest him. It was during that week that he sang for us the song he had composed and set to music himself, 'Let me carry your cross for Ireland, Lord'. He never sang it for anyone else; he said he never had an opportunity. His death was the greatest tragedy of all. On the morning before his arrest he apologised for the trouble he was giving me. That day I stood on the doorstep and watched him go down the road till he got on the tram. I shall always remember him as I saw him then. He was a beautiful man with his tall noble figure and lovely wavy hair. I still have a letter that he wrote me from Mountjoy a short time before his death.[567]

In Mountjoy, as Ashe was carried away to be force-fed, Fionan Lynch cried out, 'Stick it, Tom'. Ashe replied, 'I'll stick it, Fin'.

The verdict of the jury in the inquest on Ashe's death was as follows:

We find that the deceased, Thomas Ashe … died from heart failure and congestion of the lungs on the 25th September, 1917; that his death was caused by the punishment of taking away from the cell bed, bedding and boots, and allowing him to be on the cold floor for 50 hours, and then subjecting him to forcible feeding in his weak condition after hunger striking for five or six days.

We censure the Castle Authorities for not acting more promptly, especially when the grave condition of the deceased and other prisoners was brought to their notice …

That the hunger strike was adopted against the inhuman punishment inflicted and a refusal to their demand to be treated as political prisoners …[568]

As Collins had predicted, the British authorities quickly granted the strikers' demands after Ashe's death.[569]

Collins was always devoted to his friends, and Tom Ashe was the first of many whose death plunged him into a savage gloom and despair. 'I grieve perhaps as no one else grieves,' he said.

Thomas Ashe's funeral procession from the Mater Hospital to the Pro-Cathedral was enormous as was the procession to the City Hall for the lying-in-state, where Volunteers in uniform kept guard. Over 30,000 viewed the remains and all festivities were called off. The funeral of Thomas Ashe was of very large dimensions. Volunteers marched in uniform and carried rifles with bayonets fixed. The public houses were closed. The British military were confined to barracks and the police were not to be seen on the streets. A firing party at the graveside in Glasnevin fired the usual salute, the Last Post was sounded and an oration was delivered by Mick Collins as follows:—

'Nothing additional remains to be said. The volleys which we have just heard is the only speech which is proper to make over the grave of a dead Fenian.'

Most Reverend Dr Walsh, Archbishop of Dublin, sent his carriage officially to the funeral. The Fire Brigade was also in attendance; in fact, everything possible in the city took part in the procession. But the IPP [Irish Parliamentary Party] and the AOH [Ancient Order of Hibernians] ignored the whole proceedings. [570]

Collins arranged Robert Barton's escape from Mountjoy on 16 March 1919.[571] Collins always admired anyone who had qualities he lacked, and Barton was of the landowning class that Collins respected, as were Erskine Childers, the Laverys and the Davies. Collins succeeded in smuggling in a file and a rope, and Barton filed through the window bars. When he went over the wall, Collins was waiting to take him to Batt O'Connor's home on Brendan Road.[572] (See Dublin 4.)

Just two weeks later there was another, much larger jail-break. Peadar Clancy and Richard Mulcahy were instrumental in the escape of leading Republican prisoners on 29 March 1919. Among those to escape were Piaras Béaslaí, J.J. Walsh, Paddy Fleming and Thomas Malone. The original plan had been devised especially for the benefit of Fleming and the four prisoners who were being treated as criminals. It envisaged the use of explosives to breach the wall near the canal bank at a time when the prisoners were exercising in the field immediately inside the wall. It also included provision for transport to a safe place once they had got out. The objection to this plan was that the explosion was certain to bring the guard of soldiers and armed policemen hurrying to the scene, and it was decided to try a less noisy method. Clancy and Mulcahy were in charge of those who were to help the escape from outside the prison, while Collins and his intelligence squad were to look after the plans within the prison. In all, nineteen prisoners escaped. This was considered a major coup by Republicans and was a boost to morale. Collins waited for news of the jail-break at the Wicklow Hotel, and Joe O'Reilly cycled there to give him the news. When Collins asked 'Is Fleming out?', O'Reilly answered 'The whole jail is out!'[573] Later that day, Collins would burst out laughing every so often at their success and impudence.

Another hunger strike for POW status began on 5 April 1920 and continued until 15 April 1920. The prisoners had served the following demand on the governor on 1 April: 'The undersigned, acting on behalf of all untried and uncharged prisoners, hereby demand that on or before the morning of April 5th all such prisoners be released or given prisoner-of-war treatment'.[574] Among those on strike were Frank Gallagher and Peter Starkey.

Mountjoy Prison under strike. The Prisons Board report that the condition of all the prisoners on hunger strike in Mountjoy Prison this morning was weak and some were nearing the danger zone. The number on hunger strike at present is 89. The total of the so-called political prisoners at present in Mountjoy Prison, including those excluded from the ameliorative treatment, is 151. The number of those under sentence is 70, and the number under detention, including those for trial, is 81.[575]

Kevin Barry was hanged in Mountjoy Prison on Monday 1 November 1920. The hangman, John Ellis, was brought over from England for the execution, which took place one day after Terence MacSwiney was buried in St Finbarr's Cemetery in Cork (he died on 25 October in Brixton Prison). Acting Judge Myles Keogh signed Barry's death warrant, and it was in this warrant that the details of Barry's torture were outlined. Barry was attended and accompanied onto the scaffold by Fr Waters and Fr MacMahon from Clonliffe College. Later Fr Waters would write to Barry's mother:

> You are the mother, my dear Mrs Barry, of one of the bravest and best boys I have ever known. His death was one of the most holy, and your dear boy is waiting for you now, beyond the reach of sorrow or trial.

While in prison, Barry was tortured and was specifically urged to inform on Collins. His torturers asked him: 'What can your leaders do for you now?' Barry responded: 'They can do nothing for me, but I can die for them'.

On the eve of Barry's execution a large crowd gathered outside Mountjoy. People held lighted candles and recited the rosary right through the hours of darkness. Barry's mother was there; she was invited inside the prison but refused and remained with the crowd, although in a very distressed state. Those gathered continued to pray that he would be shot as a patriot rather than hanged, as he had been arrested in uniform. Barry was buried in Mountjoy in a plain, roughly painted coffin at 1.30pm on 1 November, All Saints' Day. (Either through indifference or ignorance, the British chose 1 November as the date of execution. All Saints' Day was a Holy Day of Obligation for all Catholics, and thus Catholic churches throughout Ireland were filled with those who prayed for Barry's soul.) The grave was in a small laurel plot near the women's prison.

Collins mooted several plans for Barry's escape but, tragically, Barry's mother was opposed, as she felt sure until the last minute that his sentence would be commuted on account of his youth.

On the Sunday morning prior to Kevin Barry's execution a meeting was called at the house of, I think, John O'Mahony of Gardiner's Place. I am not certain of the persons who were present at the meeting, except for the fact that the Brigadier, Dick McKee, Peadar Clancy and Rory O'Connor were there. I think the following were also present—Michael Collins and Dick Mulcahy. Several suggestions as to ways in which it might be possible to rescue Kevin Barry were put forwards. Eventually one plan was agreed upon. The plan was that two members of the Volunteer force disguised as clergymen should enter the prison during the visiting hours and an effort would be made by these men to disarm the Black and Tan who was in charge of Kevin Barry in the visiting room. From that they were to make their way to the front gate where it was also planned the Volunteers would have taken possession, by a ruse of handing in a parcel. When the front gate was opened to receive the parcel the warder was to be held up and the gate was to be ready for the exit of the party from the visiting room. It was known that Mrs Barry was to have a visit on that day. It was decided at the meeting that she should be informed of the attempt at rescue, and a courier was sent with this message to Mrs Barry. He later returned to say that Mrs Barry was very perturbed about this effort, that unless some kind of guarantee as to its success could be given no extra lives should be endangered, and that she very much feared that there would be such extra loss of life. I was sitting in the room of the house mentioned when this message was delivered to the Brigade OC. Having heard the message the OC informed the meeting that the attempt was off, giving the reasons which I have just stated.[576]

Also hanged in Mountjoy and then buried there during the War of Independence were Thomas Bryan, Edmond Foley, Patrick Maher, Thomas Traynor, Patrick Doyle, Frank Flood, Patrick (Paddy) Moran, Bernard Ryan and Thomas Whelan. On 14 October 2001, the bodies of nine of the 'Forgotten Ten' were reinterred in the Republican Plot in Glasnevin. (Patrick Maher was not reburied with the others. In accordance with his wishes, and those of his family, he was reinterred in Ballylanders, Co. Limerick.) There was a huge funeral parade through the streets of Dublin, and they were buried with the honours, respect and dignity they deserved.

Moran and Whelan were hanged in Mountjoy on 14 March 1921 for their 'participation' in the Bloody Sunday killings, though both had clear alibis placing them outside Dublin at the time. Nevertheless, the Volunteers at the Gresham Hotel on Bloody Sunday were actually under the command of Paddy Moran.[577]

(Paddy Moran was imprisoned in Kilmainham Gaol when the escape of Simon Donnelly,[578] Ernie O'Malley and Frank Teeling was planned. Moran was one of those whom Collins wanted to 'break out', but Moran was so sure of acquittal owing to his alibi that he absolutely refused to leave, saying that his flight would be interpreted as guilt if he were captured.)

John Ellis was employed as the British hangman in all these cases. Collins sent his Squad to try to intercept Ellis and his assistant Thomas Pierrepoint, but the attempts were unsuccessful.

On three or four occasions a number of Volunteers had been hanged in Mountjoy jail by the public hangman, who crossed from England to carry out the executions. On each occasion an effort was made to intercept the hangman before he reached the jail, but in no instance was this successful. On one such occasion I was instructed to proceed to Kingstown, as a report had been received that Ellis, the hangman, and his assistant were to arrive there some days before the date fixed for the executions.

We had a description of the hangman, but no passenger thus alighting resembled him. The information which we had received was of the most meagre character, and subsequently it was ascertained that the hangman always arrived in Dublin several days before the executions, was taken to Mountjoy in an armoured car and left there under special protection.[579]

While imprisoned here in December 1920, Arthur Griffith and Michael Staines met with Archbishop Patrick Joseph Clune. (See Dr Robert Farnan, 5 Merrion Square, Dublin 4.)

Seán MacEoin was imprisoned here in March 1921 and Collins made several attempts to free him. Cathal Brugha, who wanted MacEoin to lead another foray to Britain to assassinate members of the cabinet, had summoned MacEoin to Dublin. When Collins found out that he was in town, he ordered him to see Richard Mulcahy, and Mulcahy promptly sent him back to the countryside. The British discovered his location and MacEoin was arrested when he got to Mullingar. The first escape attempt was when Collins had a friendly priest see MacEoin, and in the middle of an anti-IRA tirade the priest surreptitiously told MacEoin that he was from Collins. A plan was passed to have MacEoin escape with help from IRA men dressed as British warders, but he was transferred before the plan could be carried out. Next, Collins sent a female doctor, Brighid Lyons, to see MacEoin, and she passed him plans of the prison's layout.

I knew Mick Collins was planning another attempt at Seán's rescue. At any cost, he wasn't going to lose his warrior friend, Seán MacEoin.

… A warder—sometimes an armed Auxiliary—was present all during the meeting. We had to talk double-talk or pass the odd vital word very quietly. I usually had a handwritten note between my fingers and I managed to slip that to him, and collect his note, when I first went in or was about to leave. Once while he was in the prison hospital, I failed to get that note to him. As usual, it was ready, hidden between my fingers. When it was time to go, Seán, in desperation, said 'Brigid, have you nothing to say to me?'

'I have,' said I, putting a break in my voice. 'But I can't say it with that fella looking on.' Turning his back, the Auxiliary said 'Get on with it, Missie, and be quick'. In a flash, I slipped the note under Seán MacEoin's pillow.[580]

Again the plan did not come to fruition, and MacEoin remained in prison.

The most ambitious of these attempts took place on 14 May, when a commandeered armoured car, commanded by Emmet Dalton dressed in his British Army uniform, and with a 'crew' of Joe Leonard (also dressed in a British officer's uniform),[581] Pat McCrea (as the driver),[582] Tom Keogh, Bill Stapleton[583] and Paddy McCaffrey, attempted to break MacEoin out. The 'schedule' at Mountjoy had MacEoin in the warden's office at the appointed time on a daily basis, but on that day the schedule was changed and he was in the infirmary. Paddy Daly outlined the plan:

> Some time in April 1921 word came to us from Mick Lynch, OC of the Fingal Brigade and superintendent of the Corporation abattoir on the North Circular Road, that an armoured car called at the abattoir every morning to escort a lorry carrying the meat supplied to Portobello Barracks and he saw many chances of the car being captured. Michael Collins immediately requested a report from intelligence and Charlie Dalton was put on the job. From a window … [in a house across the street] … Charlie had a splendid view of the car and was able to observe the movements of the driver and crew.
>
> … Michael Collins was endeavouring to get Seán MacEoin out of Mountjoy, and probably held up the capture of the car until plans were complete to bring off the double.
>
> Michael Collins outlined the plan at a meeting in a private room in Kirwan's public house. Emmet Dalton and myself were to be dressed as British officers and would be in possession of a release or transfer order for Seán MacEoin. Emmet Dalton was to do all the talking as he had good experience, being an ex-British army officer. We were to present our credentials to the governor of the prison asking him to hand over John MacEoin. We were to make sure not to use the word 'Seán'.
>
> … Arrangements were made for MacEoin to find some cause to have an interview with the governor every morning at ten o'clock and to delay over the interview and in the passage as much as possible. We hoped MacEoin would actually be in the office when the car would arrive.
>
> … The British crew of the car were armed with revolvers. One of the crew who resisted was shot and died the next day. The others were rounded up and held prisoner. The new crew immediately got into the car and drove off. I, seeing that everything was allright in the abbatoir, even to the destruction of the telephone, cycled after the armoured car.
>
> … When I arrived at Mountjoy, the car had got in.
>
> … Seán Doyle, who was in charge of the group at the door, and his men force [sic] his way in, holding up the warders, taking the keys from warder Condron and pushing him into his duty-room. … Seán's instructions were to

make sure that the phone that would be in the duty-room be dismantled immediately they entered. This was done. The men proceeded to open the main gate and Pat McCrea drove the car in and got the nose right in the second gate.

... Time seemed to be hanging on our hands ... I saw Joe Leonard and Emmet Dalton coming out of the prison into the yard and Joe Leonard picked up a rifle. I then saw Joe going down on one knee ... Then he stood up quite coolly and vaulted into the back of the armoured car and the car drove out of Mountjoy, Joe shouting to me 'No luck'.[584]

As was usual, Pat McCrea was a driver on the mission, and he described how Collins demonstrated his concern for his men:

On Tuesday morning I reported to Squad headquarters in Abbey St. about 10 or 11 o'clock. Michael Collins was there. He saw me coming and let me in. He shook hands with me and complimented me on my part in what had happened. I inquired who brought away the uniforms, if any member of the Squad had done so, as I was worried about my collar which bore a laundry mark that could be identified. During the day a message came through from one of the Christian Brothers in the O'Brien Institute [in Clontarf] that the Tans and military had searched their grounds the previous day with a bloodhound. The hound got the clothes and the party picked up some uniforms and took them away. When this was reported to Collins he was worried about my collar. He sent for me and asked me the name of the laundry and what was the mark. I told him it was the Phoenix Laundry in Russell St. and that the mark was 'M.C. 17'. He just laughed and said: 'They will think it was me was on this job'. However, he told me that he would send two men down to see the manager of the laundry and warn him not to give any information concerning laundry marks or he would have to send another message to him, &c. which he would understand. He [Collins] advised me to go out the country for a week or two until it had blown over.

All attempts to rescue MacEoin failed.[585] When the Truce was agreed in July 1921 he was still a prisoner. On the night of 13 July, two days after the Truce came into effect, Collins visited MacEoin with Dr Lyons. She requested a visit for herself and 'James Gill'. At that time Collins told MacEoin that he would be out before the Irish would proceed with any negotiations. Collins demanded that he be released, and he was released the next day. Although MacEoin was not rescued, the attempt was not without very valuable results from the point of view of the IRA. It was a great shock to public opinion in Britain to find that an armoured car could be captured from the regular British army, could be driven straight into a prison and that the raiders could escape unscathed in broad daylight in Dublin. Answers in the House of Commons by Sir

Hamar Greenwood, the chief secretary for Ireland, constantly repeated that 'outrages' in Ireland were the work of a small band of 'murderers'. Here, in the attempted rescue of MacEoin, was proof positive of the existence of an armed force, widespread in its membership, well led, disciplined and daring. MacEoin, who had been elected a member of Dáil Éireann while a prisoner in Mountjoy, was released in August following a threat that negotiations with the British would be discontinued unless he was freed at once. Thirty-seven other TDs who had been held by the British had already been released.

Women arrested and imprisoned here during the War of Independence included May Burke, Eithne Coyle, Moya Llewelyn Davies, Patricia Hoey, Linda Kearns, Aileen Keogh and Eileen McGrane.[586] On 31 October 1921, Oliver St John Gogarty helped Eithne (Ni Chumhaill) Coyle,[587] Linda Kearns (MacWhinney), May Burke and Aileen Keogh to escape. They scaled a 25ft wall with a rope ladder and got away in Gogarty's motorcar to County Wexford, and then to County Kildare.[588]

During the Civil War, the governor of the prison was Patrick (Padraig) O'Keefe.[589]

Among the IRA/Republicans captured in the Four Courts at the start of the Civil War were Dick Barrett, Joe McKelvey, Liam Mellows and Rory O'Connor. Mellows was a socialist and was one of the few leaders on either side who had tried to articulate what an Irish Workers' Republic might actually look like. They were executed in Mountjoy on 8 December 1922 in reprisal for the shooting of Seán Hales and wounding of Padraic Ó Maille on 7 December.[590] This was such an infamous event during the Civil War that the question of who was 'responsible' has long been debated. It appears that Richard Mulcahy took the initiative and that Kevin O'Higgins and Joseph McGrath were the last cabinet members to give their consent. (Rory O'Connor was best man at O'Higgins's wedding in late 1921.) Terence de Vere White notes: 'O'Higgins was appalled, and argued against it in Cabinet at great length, only agreeing after Eoin MacNeill, whom he greatly respected, acquiesced. Kevin was the second to last to agree, followed by Joseph McGrath, who was utterly opposed and gave in for the sake of unanimity.'[591] Ernest Blythe thought that O'Higgins had been 'over-sensitive about the executions'.[592] Tim Pat Coogan has written that 'a certain awfulness hung about his [O'Higgins's] name'.[593] Besides being members of the IRA executive, the four represented all of Ireland's four provinces: O'Connor was from Leinster, Barrett from Munster, McKelvey from Ulster and Mellows from Connacht. The executions of these four was officially expressed: 'As a reprisal for the assassination of Brigadier Seán Hales, TD, as a solemn warning to those associated with them who are engaged in the conspiracy of assassination against the Representatives of the Irish People'.[594]

(The execution of Erskine Childers was another case that caused great hatred among the anti-Treatyites: see Beggar's Bush Barracks, Shelbourne Road.)

The executions of these four, coming so soon after that of Childers on 24 November, made it plain that a campaign of authoritative terror had begun. Following the death of Collins in August 1922, there was a hardening of the cabinet's attitudes towards the IRA/Republicans. Collins had helped to moderate this mood, but without his restraint a more severe attitude emerged, mostly through the influence of Mulcahy and O'Higgins.[595] Free State forces executed a total of 77 men during the Civil War. These executions embittered the anti-Treatyites even more than the outrages of the Black and Tans. The measures probably extended the duration of the fighting, as attitudes hardened on both sides and left the people of Ireland divided for generations.

Máire Comerford was imprisoned here during the Civil War, after being arrested for attempting to kidnap William T. Cosgrave. She was wounded in the leg during an escape attempt and was taken to the North Dublin Union, from where she escaped. She was rearrested and imprisoned in Kilmainham, where she went on hunger strike, and was finally released. Among other women imprisoned in Mountjoy during the Civil War, many of whom went on one or more hunger strikes, were Rita Bermingham, Moira Broderick, Margaret Buckley, Gretta Coffey, May Coghlan, Kathleen Devaney, Lily Dunn, Peg Flanagan, Cecelia Gallagher, Bridie Halpin, Sheila Hartnett, Mary Ellen (Nell) Humphreys, Sheila (Sighle) Humphreys, Maud Gonne MacBride, Annie MacSwiney, Mary MacSwiney, Florence McDermott, Annie McKeown, Lily McClean, Dorothy Macardle, Countess Markievicz, Kathleen Molony, Nora Connolly O'Brien, Lily O'Brennan, Kathleen O'Carroll, Teresa O'Connell, Lena O'Doherty, Kathleen O'Farrell, Annie O'Farrelly, Rita O'Farrelly, Bridie O'Mullane,[596] Áine (Anna) O'Rahilly, Molly O'Reilly, May O'Toole, Melina Phelin, Grace Gifford Plunkett and Roisin Ryan.[597]

147 North Circular Road: Home of Michael Collins's eldest sister, Margaret, and her husband, Patrick O'Driscoll. Michael often visited here. Margaret was elected to the Dáil, and served as a TD from 1923 until 1933.

6 Dalymount Terrace, Phibsborough: Harry Boland's family home. James and Catherine Boland moved here from Phibsborough Road. Harry was born here in 1887. Nellie was the oldest child in the family, followed by Gerald, Harry, Kathleen and Ned.

The Boland family moved to 15 Marino Crescent, Clontarf (Dublin 3), about 1910.

13, 14 Dominick Street Lower: During the Civil War, IRA/Republican forces held these houses until driven out.

24 Eccles Street: O'Donel's Private Nursing Home, owned by Geraldine O'Donel.

Her sister Lil looked after the home and patients. Collins often sent IRA/Volunteers here to be treated without being reported to the police. Whenever wounded men needed time to recover, they were cared for here rather than in a hospital. The IRA/Republicans continued to use the home to nurse their wounded during the Civil War.

> Another patient we had after the Custom House affair was Tom Ennis. His hip was shattered. I believe he was in charge of the operation and was the last to leave the Custom House. Mr McAuley [surgeon] threw up his hands in the operation theatre when he saw the condition he was in. But he made a remarkable recovery. We always attended ourselves to the IRA patients. All the other nurses except Miss Macken were unaware of the fact that these wounded were IRA men. They were visited by members of their units. Headquarters paid the expenses of these wounded whom, of course, we kept at a very reduced rate. The military looked everywhere except in our house for Tom Ennis. They knew he came that way. He must have been at least two months with us. He went into a convalescent home then. The two doctors thought of the idea of bringing in the British officer as a patient, as it would serve as a good blind for the seven Republican wounded we had. He was Dr Ryan's patient and had appendicitis. Dr Ryan asked Mr McAuley to operate on him. After a while this man got quite friendly and told us he had been in France, India and other countries. He described the system of espionage the British had in India. They would employ the crossing-sweepers and people like that, who passed on information to each other. He said he had no difficulty in getting on in those countries, but he was only a fortnight in Ireland and he was terrified. One of my nurses, Miss Macken, who was also trained in the Mater, was very good about looking after the IRA wounded. She was the only one of the nurses who was in the secret.[598]

32–38 Eccles Street (and Berkeley Road): Mater Misericordiae Hospital. Originally established in the 1820s by Catherine McAuley's Congregation of Sisters of Mercy as the House of Mercy for Women on Baggot Street. During the whole period the authorities in Dublin Castle believed many of the nuns at the hospital to be Volunteers or sympathisers.[599] In fact, many IRA/Volunteers were treated here 'off the books' during the War of Independence. Collins often had men sent here, with no fear that a report of them would appear on any hospital record.

Thomas Ashe died here on 25 September 1917, after being force-fed while on hunger strike in Mountjoy Prison. (See North Circular Road/Mountjoy Prison.)

Dan Breen was taken here to recover from the wounds received in the raid on Professor John Carolan's home on 11 October 1920. (See Whitehall, Dublin 9.)

Cathal Brugha died here on 7 July 1922, at the age of 48. Upon his admission on

5 July, Dr Patrick Smyth, Dr David Cotter and Dr Alexander Blayney operated on him and tried to repair the damage to his left thigh, but his sciatic nerve and femoral artery had been severed and he died from 'shock and haemorrhage'. Brugha died on a 'First Friday'; he received the Blessed Sacrament from Fr Young, a hospital chaplain, and Fr Francis Ryan administered the Last Rites. His body lay in the chapel here on 8 and 9 July, and was removed to St Joseph's Church on Berkeley Road on the evening of 9 July. (See Berkeley Road.)

Infirmary Road (Montpelier Gardens): King George V Hospital (now St Bricin's Military Hospital). Seán MacEoin was brought here after he was wounded in Mullingar, and he was visited by Brigid Lyons when she was studying at Mercer's Hospital.

Seán Treacy's body was brought here and was identified by Nora O'Keefe and Mollie Gleason.

Following their murder in Dublin Castle on Bloody Sunday, the bodies of Dick McKee and Peadar Clancy were brought here. Molly O'Reilly identified them.[600]

> Dick McKee and Peadar Clancy were great personalities and were idolised next to Michael Collins by all men of the Dublin Brigade.
>
> The worst came shortly after that when we were informed they had been murdered. Volunteer [sic] Clune was also with them. The bodies were removed to Bricin's hospital, and Michael Collins sent a note to the O/C of the Dublin Brigade that a number of Volunteers, not prominent in the Movement, were to be sent to Bricin's hospital to carry out the bodies from the mortuary to a waiting hearse, as he did not wish to have the remains handled by the Tans. Oscar Traynor detailed me to find suitable men for this mission, but not to go on it myself, nor any member of the Squad. I found it difficult in the short time at my disposal to procure Volunteers readily available. After picking up a couple (one was Tommy Gay), I made up three including myself. As I had only got two Volunteers I thought it better to accompany them. When we got to Bricin's hospital we walked up to the front entrance. There were several Tans walking around the hospital grounds as we approached it. When they saw us going towards the mortuary they turned their backs to us in what I thought to be a spirit of decency. They entered the hospital and I did not see them again. Some relatives of the deceased were present. The coffins were uncovered and I had an opportunity of examining the bodies very closely while waiting for the hearse to arrive. While noting that the remains were properly laid out and prepared for burial, I observed that Peadar Clancy had a large hole in the temple between the eye and the ear which had been plugged with cotton wool and that he was also badly wounded about the throat. As his throat was also covered with cotton wool,

it was obvious to me that it was badly marked. Although he gave me the impression that he was maltreated, he still wore his characteristically pleasant smile, even in death.

Dick McKee's remains also bore evidence of maltreatment, as the face and head were badly marked. After paying our last respects to the remains, we covered the coffins. In order to make a fourth to carry the coffins to the hearse, we had to call on the services of Dick McKee's fiancée. The funeral cortège was small as we wended our way to Marlboro' St. Church on a wet, gloomy evening and there appeared to be a sadness over the city. I cannot remember who met us at Marlboro' St. Church.

Although it was a great blow to Collins to have lost Dick McKee, he still carried on as actively as ever.[601]

38 King Street North: Private entrance of Monk's bakery. Three IRA/Volunteers entered here to take over the office during the raid in which Kevin Barry was captured. (See Church Street Upper.)

King's Inns Quay (between Richmond and Whitworth Bridges): **The Four Courts**. These are: Exchequer (presided over by the chief baron of the exchequer); Chancellory (presided over by the lord chancellor); King's Bench (presided over by a chief justice); and Common Pleas (presided over by a chief justice). The site was once a priory of the Friars Preachers, confiscated during the Dissolution of the Monasteries in the reign of Henry VIII. The King's Inns is the governing body of Irish barristers. The full title is the Benchers of the Honourable Society of the King's Inns.

On 1 June 1921, members of the Squad were involved in a daylight raid in which it was hoped to recover the arms of between 25 and 30 British soldiers. Joe Dolan, Tom Keogh and Jim Slattery attacked the gate and subdued the guards. Jimmy Kavanagh and David Golden drove up with a car and the Squad took off with thirteen rifles, as well as a Lewis machine-gun. Kevin Barry was a member of the raiding party and led a confused section into the building. His quick thinking saved the raid. He was seen coming out of the guardroom with the Lewis machine-gun in his arms.

On 13 April 1922 the buildings were occupied by IRA/Republican troops, led by Rory O'Connor, although Joe McKelvey was chief of staff. Liam Mellows, Seán Moylan and Ernie O'Malley were also present. Other positions occupied included the Masonic Hall, Fowler Hall, Kilmainham Gaol, Moran's Hotel and the Ballast Office. The takeover of the Four Courts was intended as a symbolic signal to the country of the Free State's failed authority and their inability to govern. In addition, the anti-Treaty executive of O'Connor, Mellows and O'Malley in the Four Courts hoped that by openly challenging the Free State government they could provoke the British into re-intervening in Ireland, ultimately forcing both factions of the IRA together in a renewed war against the British.

> We of the Four Courts were the centre of the armed Republican resistance. We
> had to defend the independence of our country, and whether we made mistakes
> or not, we were going to make a last attempt to prevent the stampede of the
> nation.[602]

Upon taking their positions, they issued their proclamation:

> Fellow citizens of the Irish Republic. The fateful hour has come. At the direction
> of the hereditary enemy our rightful cause is being treacherously assailed by
> recreant Irishmen. Gallant soldiers of the Irish Republic stand rigorously firm in
> its defence. The sacred spirits of the Illustrious Dead are with us in this great
> struggle. 'Death Before Dishonour.' We especially appeal to our former comrades
> of the Irish Republic to return to that allegiance and thus guard the Nation's
> honour.

Collins and O'Connor were engaged in 'weapons trading' while the
IRA/Republicans held the Four Courts. During the first six months of 1922 Collins
had been actively engaged in channelling weapons to the IRA in the North in order
to counter the loyalist threat in the six counties,[603] but he had to ensure that the
military hardware that the British provided for the Free State army was not found in
the North lest the British government discover his involvement. This policy ran
contrary to the terms of the Treaty, hence the secrecy.[604] Collins therefore made a
secret deal with O'Connor in which some of the guns that the British had given to
the Free State army were swapped with similar weaponry in the possession of the anti-
Treaty forces and transported to the North. In order for the plan to run efficiently,
Collins delayed taking action against the anti-Treaty men in the Four Courts for as
long as possible. In one of the anomalies of the pre-Civil War period, on 18 May
Collins arranged with O'Connor to give his men inside the Four Courts a further
supply of new weapons that Collins had secured from the British in exchange for the
older, non-traceable weapons held by the IRA/Republicans. These non-traceable
weapons were then sent north.[605] (See Eaton Square, London, Assassination of Henry
Wilson, Appendix VI.)

At 3.40 on the morning of 28 June 1922, the occupying force was given an
ultimatum to surrender.[606] Collins ordered the artillery that had been lent to the Free
State army by the British to begin firing twenty minutes later. There were cordons
around the city centre, so many residents were unaware of what was happening. Joe
Considine, Seán Cusack and Thomas Wall were killed in the Four Courts
bombardment and attack.[607]

'Twas England gave the orders,
'Twas England gave the guns,
'Twas Collins dressed the boys in green
To shoot our darling sons.

England blew the bugle
And threw the gauntlet down,
And Michael sent the boys in green
To level Dublin town.

On 1 July, J.F. Homan of the St John's Ambulance Brigade tried to arrange a cease-fire following the surrender of the Four Courts garrison. He met Collins, who said:

Tell these men that neither I, nor any other member of the government, nor any officer in the army (and I learned the feeling of every officer in Dublin on my rounds yesterday), not one of us wishes to hurt a single one of them in any way that can be avoided. They, and their leaders, are at liberty to march out and go to their homes unmolested if only they will—I do not use the word surrender—if only they will deposit their weapons in the National Armoury, there to remain until and unless in the whirl of politics these men become a majority in the country, in which case they will have control of them.[608]

Homan also went to Fr Aloysius and de Valera, but no accommodation could be reached regarding the turning over of weapons.

The IRA/Republicans had deliberately mined the Records Office, a free-standing building within the walls of the Four Courts, which the garrison used as a munitions block. Prior to their surrender on 30 June, they detonated the mines they had planted there.[609] Ernie O'Malley wrote that it had been decided that the Four Courts would be blown up or burnt rather than surrendered: 'These are records of British oppression, so let's destroy them'. Irish records going back to the twelfth century were lost.

We did not fire a mine. It was the spirit of freedom lighting a torch. I'm glad she played her part.[610]

The garrison surrendered on 30 June 1922. One hundred prisoners were taken and sent to Mountjoy Prison, among them Rory O'Connor, Liam Mellows, Joe McKelvey and Dick Barrett. These four were executed in Mountjoy on 8 December 1922 in reprisal for the killing of Seán Hales on 7 December. (See Kildare

Street/Leinster House, Dublin 2; North Circular Road/Mountjoy Prison.) Ernie O'Malley and Seán Lemass were among a group who escaped on the way to Mountjoy.

Éamon de Valera quickly described the members of the Four Courts garrison as the 'best and bravest of our nation', and joined the IRA/Republicans as an unranked soldier after the bombardment of the Four Courts.

174 James's Street: Early home of Phil and William Cosgrave. Phil became quartermaster of the Dublin Battalion during the War of Independence, and was later governor of Mountjoy Prison. William succeeded Collins as president of the Provisional Government (upon Collins's resignation) in July 1922 and then Griffith (on Griffith's death) as president of the Dáil cabinet in August 1922, merging the two posts from September 1922 as president of the Executive Council of the Irish Free State.

112 Newgrange Road, Cabra: Home of Seán Harling. He worked as a secretary for de Valera upon the latter's return from America in December 1920.

From then on I was completely with the President and that ended my former type of work. There was only Kathleen O'Connell [de Valera's secretary], himself and myself then and everything had to be attended to for him. We left Dr Farnan's [5 Merrion Square, Dublin 2] after about a fortnight and went to 'Loughnavale', Strand Road, Sandymount. Miss McGarry bought this house from Dáil Éireann funds in her own name. My duties then were to keep daily in touch with each of the Ministers, bring all communications from them to the President, and bring back the replies to them. This was the general work which went on daily. I continued to supervise the communications office in Church Street. From the time the President came home to the Truce a lot of people were seeking interviews such as newspaper people etc. In this respect very special precautions had to be taken to ensure that these people would not be followed by British Agents. The method I used was I came into town in the mornings and got in touch with Collins. For example—he'd tell me the Hearst Press in America wanted an interview with the President. I would see the President and find out if he would grant the interview. Once the President 'okayed' it I would arrange for a 'safe' house where the interview would take place. I had a list of these— some in Leinster Road, Pembroke Road, Fitzwilliam Street, etc. I would then go to the hotel where the newspaper correspondent was staying, inform him that the President had agreed to see him and to be ready at the hour which I would arrange to pick him up. I'd use two cars. I'd send one for the President and I'd go in the other myself for the correspondent. I always made sure the President had arrived in front of us. This was done by the President's driver remaining until he saw us coming along the street. Then he would drive off. This method was used in the interview with Lord Derby, Sir James Craig and General Smuts.

... After spending about four months at 'Loughnavale' we moved to 'Glenvar', Mount Merrion Avenue, Blackrock. The work at 'Glenvar' was much the same as at 'Loughnavale'. It was looking after correspondence with the Ministers and conveying it. This continued every day. Before we occupied 'Glenvar', the late Mr Batt O'Connor, a building contractor, constructed a secret dump in a rockery in the garden. It had a secret system of opening and closing. Each night before curfew all documents and correspondence were placed in a deed box which was then put in the rockery, and removed in the morning.

... On the night of 28th June, 1921, I was in the study with the President. I saw a detachment of British soldiers extended across the meadow advancing in the direction of the house. I told the President: we had not any time to dump the deed box which was always on the study floor. The President instructed me to get away. So I crossed the back meadow to the grounds of Professor MacNeill's house and on to Nutley Avenue. It was then after 10 o'clock. Curfew was in force between 10 p.m. and 5 a.m. I made for the tram depot in Blackrock and I slept in a tram until 5 o'clock next morning when curfew was over. Then I returned to 'Glenvar'. Miss McGarry was in the house and informed me that Kathleen O'Connell and the President had been arrested the night before. I asked her for the particulars. She told me that the officer in charge of the raiding party and the President were speaking in the study while the soldiers were searching the house. They found nothing. But when the Sergeant returned to report to his officer the deed box was discovered on the floor. The first document in the box was one emanating from the Department of Defence from Cathal Brugha stating that he was about to intensify the campaign. Mr de Valera was then known as Captain Hayden, a retired British Army officer, and had papers to that effect. The officer informed him that the contents of the deed box were of a very seditious nature and he would have to take him to Dublin Castle. Miss O'Connell then said the deed box and its contents were hers. But the President said they were his. The officer said, 'We won't argue; the two of you had better come along'. I then left for Brendan Road, Donnybrook, to report to Mick Collins.

I met him at 6 o'clock in the morning. Collins told me he had already been notified by his agents in the Castle of these arrests. He added that the President was not now at the Castle but was in Portobello Barracks. He instructed me to proceed to a house on Rathmines Road and to remain there until I got information as to what was happening. I went immediately to this house and later that morning, the 29th (the arrest was on the 28th), a workman in civilian clothes from Portobello Barracks came to this house. He asked me if I had been sent there by Mick Collins. And when I said yes, he said, "Well, the 'long fellow' is having a posh time in officers' quarters". He added that if I hung on he might have news for me later on. About 12 o'clock this same man returned and told me that the 'long fellow' would be shortly coming out. Roughly, about ten minutes later the President and a staff officer walked down the military road of Portobello to the corner. After a few minutes, approximately, they parted and the President walked towards Portobello Bridge.[611]

Ormond Quay: Office of *The Republic*. The editor was Darrell Figgis. It was suppressed in September 1919, following publication of an advertisement for the Dáil Loan.

Figgis was a novelist before the Rising, and helped raise money for the *Asgard*'s gunrunning to Howth.[612] He wrote *Recollections of the Irish war*, and was elected to the Third Dáil as an independent pro-Treaty TD. Later, Figgis was deputy chairman to Collins of the committee that wrote the Irish Constitution in 1922, and he was the greatest contributor to it. That same year he wrote a book, *The Irish Constitution explained*.[613] At the time many disliked Figgis; he was thought too vain.[614] He committed suicide in London in 1925 after his lover, Rita North, died following an abortion. His wife had shot herself in a Dublin taxi a year earlier.[615]

7–11 Ormond Quay: **Ormond Hotel**. Seán Hales stayed here the night before he was shot.

30 Ormond Quay, over the Reliance Tailors: Offices of Gearóid O'Sullivan. He moved his offices here after raids on Harcourt Street and Eustace Street. His secretary, Bridie O'Reilly, rented the rooms in early 1921.[616]

14 Ormond Quay Lower: Lalor Ltd, ecclesiastical candlemakers. Cathal Brugha was the managing director. (See Eccles Street, Mater Misericordiae Hospital, Dublin 7.)

On 15 October 1919 Liam Deasy met Brugha, Richard Mulcahy and Collins. Deasy wrote of this meeting:

> The informality of the previous night [at Vaughan's Hotel with the GHQ staff] was gone. In an atmosphere of military efficiency the discussion opened with Dick McKee's report … It was clear that in the view of this meeting military efficiency was the target to be aimed at in all Volunteer units; and it was no less clear that the inculcation of all the principles of guerrilla warfare was to be an essential part of all training.[617]

Phibsborough Road (formerly Avenue): Home of Mrs Toomey; Dan Breen was first brought here after the attack on Gen. French on 19 December 1919. Dr James M. Ryan treated his wounds.[618] Breen then went to Mrs Malone's house on Grantham Street (Dublin 2).[619]

16 Rathdown Road: The Belton family home. Seán Hurley found Collins a room here on Collins's return from London in January 1916. This was the address he gave to the British after the Rising when he was sent to Frongoch. From the time the prisoners returned from Frongoch the British were tracking them, and the DMP detective notes of 18 January 1917 indicated that 'Collins had not returned to his lodgings' here.[620]

Yarnhall Street (just off Bolton Street): *An tÓglach* ('The Young Warrior/Soldier'), 'The official newspaper of the Irish Volunteers', was printed here. (See Aungier Street, Dublin 2.)

Dublin 8

Key locations

Kilmainham Gaol
Parkgate Street
South Circular Road
(*Dublin 8 and Dublin 2 are the only
postal codes to span the Liffey.*)

C ollins grew up surrounded by women, his
mother, Marianne, running the family after his
father died when Michael was seven. His early
life accustomed him to strong, resourceful women. He
found it natural that women should care for him, and
he, in turn, appreciated, admired and respected them.

*'Lt G is aware of things.
He suggests the 21st. A
most suitable day, I
think '*
Collins to McKee

He was usually more comfortable in the company of slightly older women—Moya
Llewelyn Davies and Lady Hazel Lavery, for example.

Collins simply wouldn't have been able to operate without the help of his female
spies and couriers. He had a small army of women working for him as secretaries,
typists and couriers and all were devoted to him, though many considered him difficult
to work with because he always concentrated on his work above all else. Lily Mernin,
Nancy O'Brien, Molly O'Reilly, Máire Comerford, Eileen McGrane, 'Dilly' Dicker,
Sister Eithne Lawless, Moya Davies, Anna Fitzsimmons, Susan Mason and many others
were invaluable to him.

The women working in clubs, post offices, railway stations, British military and
civilian offices, boarding houses, hotels, Dublin Castle and elsewhere were in positions
to monitor the activities of British agents. All reported to Collins directly or through
intermediaries, and he co-ordinated all these disparate data. His detailed and
methodical handling of the information meant that no piece of it, no matter how small
or seemingly tangential, did not fill in a piece of the puzzle for him.

Like the others in his intelligence department, Collins often used the ploy of
walking down a street linked arm in arm with 'a likely young girl' who would squeeze
his arm to identify a British officer.

Lily Mernin, who was one of those likely young girls, lived on Mangerton Road.
She would walk up and down the streets of Dublin on the arm of Tom Cullen or
Frank Saurin, pointing out British agents who worked in Dublin Castle. In her witness
statement, she outlined her activities and noted that Collins referred to her as the 'little
gentleman'. She was supplying information to Collins on the British military as

Éamon Broy was supplying information on the DMP, and, like Broy, she was able to recommend and recruit other clerical personnel in British offices throughout Dublin.

Collins couldn't have run his intelligence organisation without the women but he was aware of the strains it imposed on everyone, especially the women, and decried the need for it: 'This damn spying business plays hell with a man. It kills the soul and the heart in him. It leaves him without pity or mercy. I am fed up with the whole rotten business … Look how the poor girls are ruined by us. There is no softness in them anymore!'

Bridgefort Street (at the corner of Usher's Quay): Location of the eighteen-pounder guns, under the command of Emmet Dalton, used to shell the Four Courts at the start of the Civil War. The British would not trust the Irish with high-explosive shells, so they used shrapnel shells.[621] Dalton said that 'it was like hitting the building with peaches'. The Free State soldiers were completely inexperienced in the use of the artillery pieces, and many of the shells fired at the Four Courts missed the building, while others barely scratched the surface of the stone structure. Some they undershot, hitting the quay walls, and often they overshot the Four Courts building, with the shells landing in Smithfield. Finally, Dalton himself had to take control and operate the field guns in order to ensure that the shells hit their intended targets. A total of 375 rounds were fired. The other eighteen-pounder was set up on the quays at Winetavern Street. (See King's Inns Quay, Four Courts, Dublin 7.)

Kingsbridge Station (now Seán Heuston Station): Éamon (Ned) Broy's relation, Pat Tracy, worked here and was a major contact between Broy and Collins. Tracy also collected messages from the railwaymen who passed through the station and forwarded them to Collins.

167 Mangerton Road: Home of Lily Mernin.[622] Mernin was identified as one of Collins's most important sources, 'Lt G'.[623] (See Parkgate Street; Ship Street Barracks, Dublin 1; Clonliffe Road, Dublin 3.)[624]

17 Merchant's Quay: Seán O'Shea, who worked here, was sent to Italy with Michael Leahy to purchase arms. (See 1–2 Denmark Street Great, Dublin 1.)

> As far as I can recall, the order to go to Italy came from Cathal Brugha who asked Micheál Ó Coileán to go down and see me at 17 Merchants Quay. Sometime during the day before Micheál called, I noticed considerable activity on the part of the DMP and the CID around my place, and I recall distinctly a big 'bleachtaire' [detective] outside near the forge as Micheál Ó Coileán came up the

gateway and both made the same signal simultaneously, that is, they put their thumbs into their eyes. Micheál came in and gave me instructions to see Cathal Brugha, which I did subsequently. As Micheál went out, I accompanied him down to the gate, to find leaning up against the Liffey wall another big 'bleachtaire' and, to my surprise but to my great pleasure, the same signals were exchanged, that is, the thumbs to the eyes, which to me indicated that Micheál had got his friends inside the Castle working for him.[625]

Parkgate Street: Phoenix Park Works. In 1918 the British used part of the building as a shellworks.

Joe Good worked here as an electrician, along with Matt Furlong, Joe Leonard[626] and Sam Reilly. Good described his knowledge as dangerous:

Richard Walsh of Balls, Co. Mayo, brought many of his officers to the house where I lived. I instructed them in the elementary use of explosives. My knowledge was very elementary. I used and demonstrated only with batteries, that is, accumulators. I had not the necessary technical knowledge to make exploders, and I believe at that period we lacked technical knowledge from those who were competent to give instructions. In retrospect I dread to think of the possible consequences of my ignorance.[627]

Parkgate Street: British Army Pay Corps HQ. At the end of the Rising, Patrick Pearse was taken here to meet Gen. Maxwell. Ironically, the office where Pearse was held captive after signing the surrender became the office of the Irish minister for defence.

During the War of Independence, the Pay Corps employed dozens of civilian clerks, many of whom were IRA/Volunteers or IRB members. Martin Hoare, a Volunteer, was arrested here while armed. Seán Tumbleton, another Volunteer, used to throw bombs at the British in 'the Dardenelles'. He finally had to go on the run when Hoare was arrested.

Bryan Fergus Molloy was stationed here.[628] He worked for the chief intelligence officer at Parkgate, Col. Hill Dillon. Through a Sinn Féin TD, Dr Frank Ferran (who voted against the Treaty in 1922 and died during the Civil War in the Curragh internment camp), Molloy was introduced to Batt O'Connor; he told O'Connor that his superiors wanted him to join the British Secret Service, but he would do so only if he could pass information to Collins. Thereafter Liam Tobin,[629] Tom Cullen or Frank Thornton[630] would meet Molloy in the Café Cairo or Kidd's, but they never trusted him. His true identity was known almost from the start, having been revealed by Piaras Béaslaí's cousin, Lily Mernin, who was a typist for Col. Dillon.[631] Molloy was killed on 25 March 1920 outside the Wicklow Hotel by a team led by Mick

McDonnell.[632] (See Wicklow Street, Dublin 2.)

Mernin was 'identified' as one of Collins's most important sources, 'Lt G'.[633] She was able to recommend and recruit other typists in British military offices throughout Dublin, including Sally McAsey, who married Frank Saurin. She was supplying information to Collins on the British military as Broy was supplying information on the DMP. She also worked for Major Stratford Burton, the garrison adjutant at Ship Street Barracks. Mernin would walk up and down the streets of Dublin on the arm of Cullen or Saurin, pointing out British agents who worked in Dublin Castle. She also went to matches at Lansdowne Road with Cullen and pointed out agents.

> One of the contacts referred to, who was invaluable to us, was a girl named Miss Lillie [*sic*] Mernin. She was employed as Typist in Command Headquarters of Dublin District, the intelligence branch of which was under the control of Colonel Hill Dillon, Chief Intelligence Officer. This girl put us in touch with other members of the different staffs working for the British Military in Dublin. This girl worked mainly with Frank Saurin and is one to whom a large amount of the credit for the success of Intelligence must go. She is at present employed at GHQ, Irish Army, Parkgate Street.[634]

(See Mangerton Road; Ship Street Barracks, Dublin 1; Clonliffe Road, Dublin 3.)[635]

40 Parkgate Street: Margaret O'Callaghan's restaurant. Collins used the restaurant often, and Mrs O'Callaghan's statement indicates how widespread his network was:

> It was on the advice of Michael Collins that I took over a restaurant called the West End at 40 Parkgate Street, a few months after the arrival of the Black and Tans. He thought it would put me in a position to be of great use to the Volunteers as it was just beside Kingsbridge [railway station] and on the direct road in from Kildare, and he knew that it was frequented by the British forces. Mick Collins asked me did I need any financial help but I said I did not. I got money from home and had saved some myself. I had been on the look out for a place of the kind for some time. I installed myself there and things turned out as expected.
>
> I had a Cumann na mBan assistant, Máire [Molly] Gleeson, who is now dead, and another girl, Katie Tracy. They were both very reliable.
>
> ... I was able to get a lot of information from these men for the Volunteers. I also got quite a lot of guns (revolvers) and ammunition. They sometimes had no money and would leave their guns, which I handed over to the Volunteers, P.J. Ryan, Baby Duggan. Ted Ryan who had a sister of [*sic*] Mrs O'Conaill (Eilís Ní Riain) and a student in Maguire's College, used to come for the guns. ... We were

often able to get information from the soldiers on guard at the Military Barracks, Arbour Hill and the Royal—about where Volunteer prisoners were located and passed it on to Mick Collins's men.

... Frank Thornton and Liam Tobin used to meet the British Intelligence Officers at my place. The appointments were made by me.

Seán Ó Conaill who used sometimes to be on duty in the Post Office at Kingsbridge Railway Station used to bring me messages from Mick Collins's Intelligence Department.

The people who came to our restaurant were the rank and file of the Black and Tans; the Auxiliaries, who were the officers, were in Beggar's Bush, and never came to us.[636]

Because it was frequented by the Black and Tans, raiding the restaurant was once considered. The adjutant-general, Gearóid O'Sullivan, called the raid off because the restaurant was such a fine source of information on the Black and Tans.[637]

Rutledge Terrace: The McGrath family lived here. The two eldest sons, George and Joseph, were active in the Volunteers in the Rising and afterwards. George, the eldest son, became controller-general of finances in the Free State government. Joe, the second eldest, first worked with Collins at the Irish National Aid and Volunteers' Dependants' Fund, then was elected to the Dáil in 1918, became substitute minister for labour in 1920–1 and after the Treaty became minister for labour. In September 1922 he was appointed minister for industry and commerce, including the former ministry for labour. He left politics in 1924 and went into business, founding the Irish Sweepstakes.

South Circular Road: Home of Professor Michael Hayes, raided on 10 November 1920. Richard Mulcahy was almost captured in this raid but escaped. The raid did, however, provide the British with many crucial files, which included almost 200 names and addresses of Volunteers.

South Circular Road: Kilmainham Gaol. There has been a prison on this site since the twelfth century, originally known as the 'Dismal House of Little Ease'. By the eighteenth century the extant building was in deplorable condition and had to be replaced. The current gaol was opened in 1796 on a site known as Gallows Hill, altered in 1857 and reopened in 1863. Over the main door is a bronze relief of five entangled snakes. These were known as the 'Demons of Crime' and were twisted and chained together to present a warning to all who passed through the gates. Henry Joy McCracken was a prisoner here after the 1798 Rebellion, as was Robert Emmet in 1803. The Invincibles were held and executed here in 1882. John J. O'Leary, John

Devoy, Jeremiah O'Donovan Rossa and Charles Stewart Parnell were all imprisoned here.

On 14 February 1921, Simon Donnelly, Ernie O'Malley and Frank Teeling escaped from here. A sympathetic British soldier provided the bolt-cutters and weapons. Patrick (Paddy) Moran, Frank Flood, Thomas Bryan, Pat Doyle, Thomas Whelan and Bernard Ryan were also prisoners at the time but did not escape. They were all hanged in Mountjoy Prison. (The Volunteers at the Gresham Hotel on Bloody Sunday were under the command of Paddy Moran. Collins and the others pleaded with him to escape, but he refused because he would not betray those who placed him in Blackrock at his home or at Mass that morning.[638] Moran was hanged on 14 March 1921 in Mountjoy Prison for participation in the Bloody Sunday executions at Baggot Street Lower.[639] See Sackville Street Upper/Gresham Hotel, Dublin 1; North Circular Road/Mountjoy Prison, Dublin 7.)

The gaol was occupied by IRA/Republican troops on 13 April 1922, but was quickly retaken by the Free State.

During the Civil War Kathleen Clarke, Máire Comerford, Mary Coyle (Mrs Todd Andrews), Sheila (Sighle) Humphreys, Dr Kathleen Lynn, Maud Gonne MacBride,[640] Dorothy Macardle,[641] Annie MacSwiney, Mary MacSwiney, Nora Connolly O'Brien, Lily O'Brennan, Kate O'Callaghan,[642] Áine (Anna) O'Rahilly, Molly O'Reilly, Grace Gifford Plunkett and Nell Ryan (among other women) were held prisoner here.[643]

Dorothy Macardle wrote one of the earliest histories of the period, *The Irish Republic*. During the Civil War Macardle sided with Éamon de Valera, was very anti-Treaty, was imprisoned by the Free State in 1922, and served time in the North Dublin Union, Mountjoy and Kilmainham. She recounted her Civil War experiences in *Earthbound: nine stories of Ireland* (1924), and wrote a pamphlet, *The tragedies of Kerry* (1924). She also meticulously researched her book *The Irish Republic*, which was first published in 1937. Her political opponents consider her to be a hagiographer for Éamon de Valera. Though she was somewhat disillusioned with the new Irish state, in particular with its treatment of women and especially in the Constitution of 1937, she left the royalties from *The Irish Republic* to her close friend de Valera, who wrote the foreword to the book. She died in 1958.

Upon hearing of the death of Collins, the anti-Treaty prisoners in Kilmainham showed their respect and grief:

I was talking with some other prisoners on the night of August 22nd, 1922, when the news came in that Michael Collins had been shot dead in west Cork. There was a heavy silence throughout the jail, and ten minutes later from the corridor outside the top tier of cells I looked down on the extraordinary spectacle of about a thousand kneeling Republican prisoners spontaneously reciting the Rosary aloud for the repose of the soul of the dead Michael Collins, President of the Free State Executive Council and Commander-in-Chief of the Free State forces. There was, of course, little logic in such action, but I have yet to learn of a better tribute to the part played by any man in the struggle with the English in the War of Independence. Through all the hates and bitterness of Civil War, those Republican prisoners remembered that the dead leader, latterly their enemy, was once an inspiration and driving force in their struggle with the alien army of occupation.[644]

The first executions of the Civil War were carried out on 17 November 1922. Peter Cassidy, James Fisher, John Gaffney and Richard Twohig were all executed here for illegally possessing arms.

During the Civil War the mail censor was Peadar Kearney. Kearney, a well-known poet and writer, composed the words to *A Soldier's Song/Amhrán na bhFiann.*

The gaol was closed in 1924. Éamon de Valera was the last prisoner.

28 South Circular Road: Home of Patrick Dowling, Kevin Barry's uncle, his mother Mary's brother. Barry often stayed here and had been staying here for several nights before the raid on Monk's bakery. After that incident the home was itself raided and pulled asunder.

Sarsfield Road, Inchicore (3 St Michael's): Home of Timothy Donovan. Collins often visited here, and Donovan was said to be his uncle.

Winetavern Street (at intersection of Merchant's Quay): Location of eighteen-pounder gun, under the command of Emmet Dalton, used to shell the Four Courts at the start of the Civil War. A total of 375 rounds were fired. The other eighteen-pounder was set up at Bridgefort Street.

Dublin 9

Key location

Drumcondra

C ollins studied previous Irish risings and recognised the extent to which espionage had been responsible for their failure. The eyes and ears of the British network in Dublin were the members of the Dublin Metropolitan Police's political section, 'G' Division, based at Great Brunswick police station. Some 'G' Division detectives roamed freely around the city, following those suspected of disloyalty to the Crown, or meeting informants and taking notes. Other G-men were positioned at railway stations or docks to watch the arrivals and departures. The system was simple, crude even, but very effective.

> *'We had .38 guns and they were too small ...'*
> James Slattery

Although he had knowingly embarked on the ruthless path of having 'G' Division detectives killed if they would not take themselves 'off the job', Collins was also aware of a possible public backlash. Republican newspapers and those sympathetic to the ideals of Sinn Féin were fed with appropriate propaganda. But Collins's policy, in turn, led to suppression and censorship by Dublin Castle. Such a knee-jerk reaction, together with the obvious alarm caused by the killings of the G-men, confirmed to Collins that he was hurting the British intelligence system, and he realised that London and Dublin would increase their efforts to smash his organisation—leading to further resentment on the part of Dubliners.

The first of those detectives to be killed was Patrick 'Dog' Smyth, shot here in Drumcondra by the Squad.

Drumcondra: Archbishop Dr William Walsh's palace. His feelings were always nationalist but he thought the Rising 'madness'. Count Plunkett went to inform him of the Rising, as the pope had requested. Walsh was ill and Plunkett was giving the message to Walsh's secretary, Revd Michael Curran, when word came of the fighting at the GPO.[645]

Sometimes Walsh expressed his attitude in subtle ways. When Thomas Ashe was buried in Glasnevin Cemetery, 'Most Reverend Dr Walsh, Archbishop of Dublin, sent his carriage officially to the funeral'.[646]

Éamon de Valera stayed in the gate lodge here in 1919 prior to leaving for New York, and the archbishop was unaware of his presence. After leaving Dr Farnan's house in Merrion Square (Dublin 4), however, de Valera was in constant contact with Walsh's secretary, Fr Curran.

Drumcondra: Home of Police Detective Captain Patrick Smyth. Known as 'Dog' Smyth, he was shot here on 30 July 1919 and was the first member of the 'G' Division to be killed. The members of the Squad were Jim Slattery, Tom Keogh, Tom Ennis and Mick Kennedy.

Smyth arrested Piaras Béaslaí, who was carrying many incriminating documents. Collins sent word to Smyth not to testify, but Smyth ignored the warning. 'I'm not going to let any young scuts tell me how to do my duty.' Béaslaí was sentenced to two years in jail instead of the two months he expected. Though Collins preferred moral persuasion or ostracism, it was obvious that these tactics were not going to work on Smyth.

Smyth was shot four times. The Squad used .38 calibre weapons, which they found were not powerful enough. Although Smyth was mortally wounded, he lived for five weeks before finally dying of an abscess of the lung caused by his wounds.

> We had .38 guns and they were too small. I thought the minute we would fire at him he would fall, but after we hit him he ran. ... I met Mick McDonnell the following morning and he said we had made a right mess of the job the night before, but I can assure you that I was more worried about it until Smith [*sic*] died than Mick was.[647]

Afterwards, they always used .45 calibre weapons.

Following Smyth's shooting, Dublin Castle banned Sinn Féin, and Collins used this to outmanoeuvre the more moderate Sinn Féin members—they would not have the ability to temper the more aggressive tactics that Collins favoured.

(Note: Eugene Smyth was a telegrapher in Dublin Castle in 1916. His witness statement listed his last name as 'Smith' and that is how he is always identified. His last name was actually spelled 'Smyth', however, and that is how he *signed* his statement. In early April 1916 Eugene Smyth gave Patrick J. Little a signed and witnessed statement that he recognised what became known as 'the Castle Document', indicating that the British planned a swoop on the individuals and premises of the Volunteers in Dublin. It was one of the primary pieces of propaganda that Joseph Plunkett used to try to bring Eoin MacNeill on board with a Rising. Smyth swore that the document was genuine and abstracted from the Castle files.[648] Eugene Smyth and 'Dog' Smyth were brothers, on opposite sides even then.)

82 Lower Drumcondra Road: Home of Piaras Béaslaí, writer of the first biography of Collins in 1927, *Michael Collins and the making of a new Ireland*. Following the publication of Béaslaí's book, many contested his views. In his later life, Gen. Richard Mulcahy was asked by his son, Risteard, to read the book and to annotate it. Mulcahy did so and his annotation ran to several volumes.

Millmount Avenue, Drumcondra: Home of Patrick Tracy. Tracy was a cousin of Éamon Broy's wife and worked at Kingsbridge Railway Station. Broy often passed messages to Collins through him.

> About the same time, at one of my meetings with Tracy, he said: 'The Volunteers want you to come to my house to-night'. I asked: 'What is it?' and he replied 'I believe it is a meeting'. Both of us had maintained that there would have to be a meeting. At Tracy's house, Millmount Avenue, Drumcondra, I met Greg Murphy.
>
> He thanked me for all the information I had sent, said it was wonderful stuff, the like of which they never got before, and then, turning his mouth conspiratorially sideways, he said: 'Would you ever mind meeting Mick Collins?' I replied: 'In view of the things I have been doing, meeting anybody would be a small matter'. He asked me where I would like to meet him, and the only place I could think of was 5 Cabra Road, the residence of Mr and Mrs Micheál Ó Foghludha.[649]

109 Richmond Road, Drumcondra: Home of Michael Lynch. Collins sometimes stayed here. Joe Good lived here from 1918 onwards.

> I lived in a house exactly opposite Liam Lynch's house, where Collins was frequently harboured. The name of the house was Walter House. The house where I lived was No. 109 Richmond Road. During the period from 1919 to 1921 I would say there were always at least half a dozen Volunteers living in my house. At no time during the whole period were we raided.[650]

Other IRA/Volunteers often stayed here. Opposite, and beyond the home of Michael Lynch, vice-brigadier to Dick McKee, at the Walter House across the street, were the grounds of Croke Park.

8 St Columba's Road Upper, Drumcondra: Home of Emmet Dalton. During World War I he fought with the Royal Dublin Fusiliers, winning the Military Cross at Ginchy; at the time, he believed he was fighting for Ireland. He joined the Volunteers in 1914, and rejoined after his World War I service in 1919. He was with Collins on the fateful journey to Cork when Collins was killed. (See 25 Sydney Parade, Dublin 4; Appendix V.)

Whitehall, Drumcondra: 'Fernside', Professor John Carolan's house. On 11 October 1920 the Cairo Gang surprised Dan Breen and Seán Treacy (Seán Ó Treasaigh) here.[651] Breen and Treacy escaped but killed two of the Gang, including Major George O.S. Smyth. Smyth was the brother of Lt Col. Gerald Brice Smyth, who had been killed for his address to the RIC at Listowel. (See *The Irish Bulletin*, Molesworth Street, Dublin 2.) Upon Lt Col. Smyth's death, Major Smyth requested a transfer from Egypt to Ireland to go after Breen and Treacy, whom he mistakenly blamed for his brother's death. Breen was wounded several times and cut himself badly on a broken windowpane in making his escape.[652]

Professor Carolan was put up against a wall and shot. Before he died, he was able to give a full account of what happened. (See 92 and 94 Talbot Street, Dublin 1.)

Dublin 11

Key location

Glasnevin

Ballymun Road: British spy 'Jameson' (John Charles Byrne) was shot dead here on 2 March 1920. His identity was only confirmed after his body was claimed by his wife, of 34 Laurel Bank, Romford, England. (See Bachelor's Walk, Granville Hotel, Sackville Street Upper, Dublin 1; Harcourt Street, Dublin 2; Brendan Road, Nutley Lane, Dublin 4.)

> *'This Mr Jameson showed jewels as a side line and was stopping at the Granville Hotel, ... but he took the wrong tram to Ballymun and there was no more showing anyone'*
> Joe Leonard

89 Botanic Road, Glasnevin: Home of Seán (Johnny) Collins when he settled his brother, Michael's, estate. Michael died intestate, leaving an estate of £1,950.9s.11d.

Nancy O'Brien, Michael's second cousin, lived here while employed in Dublin Castle, and later married Johnny Collins.

Glasnevin: Bon Secour Hospital. Sister Angela from the hospital smuggled food and comforts to Mountjoy Gaol prisoners, particularly the women, during the Civil War.

Iona Road, Glasnevin: Ernie O'Malley's family home. O'Malley was the only one in the family to use the 'O' in his name. His brother, Cecil, was in the IRA/Republican garrison on O'Connell Street during the Civil War, and his younger brother, Charles, was killed in the O'Connell Street fighting. His two youngest brothers were members of the Fianna.

O'Malley left home in 1918 during the War of Independence and didn't return to see any of his family until September 1922, when he was on the run after the capture of the Four Courts.[653]

Iona Road, Glasnevin: Nancy O'Brien, Collins's second cousin, lived here for a short time while she was working as a Collins spy in Dublin Castle. (See Dublin Castle, Dublin 2.)

Dublin 13

Key location
Howth

The Baily, Howth: The Stella Maris Convent. On 14 May 1921, the members of Collins's Squad who had attempted to break Seán MacEoin out of Mountjoy called on the convent, still in their British army uniforms. Joe Leonard, Emmet Dalton and Pat McCrea fled Mountjoy Prison with a wounded man, and they brought him here, knowing that the nuns would care for him.

Church Street, Howth: 'Foil-tra'; Collins's relations named Butterley lived here in 1914. Collins often stayed here and some say that he was here during the landing of the Howth guns.[654] The four-storey house faced onto Harbour Road in the front and Church Street and Dunbo Hill at the rear.

Evoura Terrace: Home of the O'Rourke family. Collins used to stay here, and if there were British troops in the area he would climb from the roof of No. 6 to escape to the roof of No. 1.

Harbour Road, 1 Island View House, Howth: Home of Mrs Quick. She rented rooms to many young women, and Collins often enquired after them in letters. From 1914 to 1917, Collins's cousin Nancy O'Brien, Susan Killeen (a London Collins 'girlfriend') and Dolly Brennan, among others, had lodgings here, and Collins often visited them.

After all those women had left, Collins still used the house as an office where he used to steam open some of the mail that his agents had intercepted.

Dublin 14

Key location

Rathfarnham—St Enda's

Dublin 14 is the location of St Enda's School, or *Scoil Éanna*, the secondary school for boys founded by Patrick Pearse. Originally opened in 1908 in Cullenswood House on Oakley Road in Ranelagh, Dublin 6, it moved to its present site on Grange Road in Rathfarnham in 1910. Pearse named the school for St Enda of Aran, who abandoned the heroic life of a warrior to teach a devoted band of scholars in the remote seclusion of the Aran Islands. St Enda's offered an education through the Irish language which also sought to inspire and nurture its pupils. Formerly known as 'The Hermitage', it was an eighteenth-century house set in 50 acres of woods and parklands, enhanced by a lake and river near its boundary. It boasts a wide variety of flora and fauna, currently interpreted in a specially dedicated nature study centre. In the centre of the park is the Pearse Museum, which is housed in Pearse's home and the school.

'That film brought tears to me eyes. Gee, Boy! You are some movie actor. Nobody could resist buying a bond and us having such a handsome Minister for Finance'
Harry Boland

The current exhibitions give visitors a sense of the spirit of the house during Pearse's time. His study and the family sitting room are preserved and allow very personal glimpses into the private life of Pearse and his family. Side by side with these rooms are the more public spaces in which Pearse's pupils lived and worked, rooms such as the school dormitory, study hall and chapel.

Collins famously filmed a sales-promotion film for the Dáil Loan at St Enda's.

Grange Road, Rathfarnham: 'The Hermitage'. St Enda's (*Scoil Éanna*) was situated here from 1910 until the British army occupied it after the Rising.[655] (See Cullenswood House, 21 Oakley Road, Ranelagh, Dublin 6.)

In spring 1919 Collins used the grounds to make a short film advertising the Dáil Loan. He knew that adverts in newspapers would be censored, so he decided to use the 'new' medium of film. John MacDonagh, brother of the executed Thomas, produced the film at a cost of £600. Collins invited many notables to St Enda's to buy bonds, including Kathleen Clarke, Margaret Pearse, Grace Plunkett and Arthur Griffith. Collins and Diarmuid O'Hegarty sat in front of the steps of St Enda's and their bond certificate was signed on the block on which Robert Emmet had been beheaded. Collins had two copies of the film made, then his men took the film out to theatres and forced the cinema operators to show it—and carefully took it away with them before it could be confiscated. The film was also very effectively shown in the US.[656] The film brought Collins's name and image before the public as never before. His appearance in the film is even more remarkable, since as late as the Treaty negotiations in London in 1921 he would deliberately look away from a camera in order to blur his image. He was always conscious of a camera, however, and all photographs show him well-groomed, and in most cases posing for the photo.[657]

Among the handbill adverts for the Loan were:

'Pearse gave all. Won't you give a little? Buy Dáil Éireann Bonds today!'

'Ireland has been SOLD often enough. Subscribe to the Dáil Éireann Loan and help to BUY Ireland for the Irish. Act today!'

'Leave Ireland better than you found it. Buy Dáil Éireann Bonds today!'

'Won't it be grand—the day we see them clearing out bag and baggage? You can hasten the day. Buy Dáil Éireann Bonds and lose no time about it!'

'England fears the loan.'

'Put your money on Ireland.'

St Enda's was raided on 20 January 1920.

Dublin 15

Key location
Ashtown

Ashtown, Co. Dublin: An ambush of Viceroy Lord French (formerly Field Marshal Sir John Denton Pinkstone French, GCB, OM, GCVO, KCMG, PC) took place here on 19 December 1919. This was the latest of several attempts on French. Dan Breen

'We don't shoot our prisoners'
Paddy Daly

calculated that, in all, twelve attempts were made. Tomás MacCurtain took part in one attempt and told Treacy and Robinson that the only good thing about it was that he (MacCurtain) had been able to retain a revolver that he hadn't had before.

The IRA/Volunteers were Ben Barrett, Dan Breen,[658] Vinnie Byrne,[659] Paddy Daly (O/C of the operation and of one section),[660] Seán (J.J.) Hogan, Tom Keogh, Tom Kilcoyne, Joe Leonard, Mick McDonnell (O/C of the other section),[661] Séamus Robinson, Seán Treacy, Jim Slattery[662] and Martin Savage.

The Volunteers were to mill about near 'Kelly's Inn' (the Halfway House) and to let the first car go by, as their information was that French would be in the second car. In fact, French was in the first car and escaped. The plan went awry, the road was not barricaded, Breen was wounded and Savage was killed.[663]

> The final attack took place on 19 December when the Honourable Lord French was returning from Boyle [Co. Roscommon], and there were only thirteen in the attacking party.
>
> Michael Collins gave me instructions to take command and to bring the members of my squad, as well as Mick McDonnell, Tom Keogh, Jim Slattery, Vincent Byrne and the four Tipperary men [Seán Hogan, Seán Treacy, Dan Breen and Séamus Robinson].
>
> When we were going out that morning Martin Savage came to me and told me he was going. I was in a quandary and did not know if I should take him or not, because the men were more or less picked by Collins. Martin Savage was assistant QM of the 2nd Battalion. I told him to get a bicycle and come with us. I said to him, 'you should not have known where we were going' but he did know. Either Tom Keogh or Mick McDonnell must have told him.
>
> Before the final arrangements were made for the final attempt on Lord French, two Volunteers, Bob Holland and Joe Leonard, were sent up to the Phoenix Park to see if a machine gun could be fired, but there was no suitable cover, and the men who would be firing the gun would be easy targets.

I got definite information from Michael Collins that Lord French would be returning from Boyle on such a train on 19th December.

… The night before we went to Ashtown I arranged that Ben Barrett would go off ahead to the Ashtown station and that he would be unarmed. Then when the train came into the station he was to stand facing it as if he was waiting to meet somebody. He was to find out which car Lord French got into. If Lord French got into the first car Ben Barrett would, without attracting attention, rub his nose with his left hand; if he got into the second car, he would do it with his right hand, and if there was a third car and French got into it Barrett would fiddle with his hat or scratch his head.

Before we left the city for Ashtown we planned that the Squad, plus the additional men with us, would divide into two groups. Three men and myself would take up a position on the railway station road, and we were to attack with bombs and revolvers the car which Lord French was travelling in. The second group, under Mick McDonnell, were to wheel out a heavy dung-cart and block the road, or cause sufficient obstacle to slow down the cars. We knew that Detective Officer Halley always rode in front on a motor-cycle.

We set off for Ashtown about 11 a.m., travelling in groups of two, well separated. When we reached Kelly's public house, at the corner of the road, we decided to go in so that we would not attract so much attention. Every man knew exactly what his job was, as he had been detailed the night before. I was to take No. 1 group, which meant that we would open fire, and Mick McDonnell's group knew they had to block the road at the last minute with a big dung-cart, if possible to time it to cause a crash.

At noon [when] we heard the whistle of the train we left the public house. I went through the back door into a yard with Joe Leonard, Seán Hogan and, I think, Seán Doyle. … Mick McDonnell left by the front door with his men to put the dung-cart into position. I saw the dung-cart at the gate leading into Kelly's field, ready to go into position.

… When the train came in I saw our scout, Barrett, on the platform of the railway station. … There was no delay, they made straight for the cars after alighting from the train. I saw Lord French going towards one of the cars, I thought it was the second car but was not sure. Ben Barrett then gave the signal that Lord French was in the second car which confirmed my impression. … Hogan and myself had grenades and I think the others had revolvers only. I saw the flash of uniforms in the first car as it passed, and I threw a bomb through the glass of the second car and heard a loud crash. The military lorry was advancing and I stooped down to pull out my revolver, but just as I did I heard Hogan shout 'Look out'. When I looked down I saw that Hogan had dropped a bomb right between us and the pin was out of it. I said 'Dive flat on the ground' and did the same myself. The bomb went off. It did not give either of us a scratch but covered us with clay which we were able to brush off. The military lorry had passed by this time. Probably the bomb incident saved our lives, because we would have been very much exposed to the military lorry. I got up full of abuse for Hogan, but he was sitting on the ground grinning and saying 'That was a near miss'! His laughing attitude took away my anger and I could not abuse him.

... We made for the main road to assist the other party because there was heavy fighting going on at the corner. ... When we got to the corner we saw Martin Savage lying on the footpath mortally wounded; he had been shot through the jaw. Dan Breen was sitting down with blood flowing from his leg. There was no sign of Lord French or his escort. He had gone right through.

... The military driver of the car that was wrecked came round the corner with his hands up. I think Martin Savage was dead by this time. ... The driver of the wrecked car said 'I did not fire', and I told him 'whether you did or not makes no difference. We don't shoot our prisoners'.

... I told the Volunteers that we would take Martin Savage into the public house and I knew we could not possibly take him with us. One of the men had whispered an Act of Contrition into Martin's ear before he died. When Kelly, the publican, saw us coming he banged the door in our faces, and pushed over the bolt, and although we kicked the door he would not admit us. We then decided we would have to leave the body of Martin Savage there, and get the rest of the crowd away, particularly Dan Breen. Breen was a very heavy man and we did not know how to manage him. I had a big, strong bicycle and ... told Breen to put the foot of his uninjured leg on the backstop to relieve some of his weight.

... We decided to bring Dan Breen to Toomeys on Phibsboro' Road [sic]. I think it was No. 88, it is past Doyle's Corner. ... Mrs Toomey quietly walked out with a cloth and wiped the blood up.

I left the Tipperary men there, as they wanted to form a guard over Breen, but I told the other men to go away and not come back to the house. I went home myself then because I needed a change of clothes. Between lifting Martin Savage and carrying Dan Breen my clothes were covered with blood.

I came home from Ashtown convinced we had got Lord French, and, whether it was the excitement or soldier's talk, I think we were all of that opinion. I discussed the affair with Ben Barrett who had given the signal. We agreed that the signal was given correctly, but that the second car, in which French was travelling, actually started first and became the first car, so that the wrong car was attacked.

The failure to get Lord French was mainly due to the road not being blocked, but had the road been blocked I think none of us would have come back alive from Ashtown, because we were outnumbered by at least three to one, rifles against revolvers. All our bombs would have gone and we would not have had a chance with revolvers. Had we stopped Lord French's car we would have stopped the military lorry, and although the element of surprise would have been in our favour, we were outnumbered.[664]

After this attempt, Lord French was particularly critical of the British intelligence services, and especially the 'G' Division.

Our Secret Service is simply non-existent. What masquerades for such a service is nothing but a delusion and a snare. The DMP are absolutely demoralised and the RIC will be in the same case very soon if we do not quickly set our house in order.[665]

Appendix I

Principal homes and safe houses

Until he refused to appear in court after being released from Sligo Jail in April 1918, Collins's usual residence was the Munster Hotel in Mountjoy Street. After that he went on the run. Throughout his time on the run, Collins had keys to, and stayed at, several homes throughout Dublin. He had rooms in many hotels, as well as staying in private homes. He usually never stayed in the same place more than a few nights in succession.

16 Airfield Road (Dublin 6): Home of Mrs Julia O'Donovan.

1 Brendan Road (Dublin 4): Home of Mr and Mrs Batt O'Connor. Although he ate here often and used it for meetings, he rarely slept here, as it was too well known.

23 Brendan Road (Dublin 4): Home of Susan Mason. She was one of his secretaries.

Camden Street (Dublin 2): Home of Mr and Mrs Paddy O'Keefe.

Church Street, Howth (Dublin 13): The Butterley home.

15 Ely Place (Dublin 2): Home of Oliver St John Gogarty.

31 Fitzwilliam Street Upper: House owned by Maeve McGarry.

Gardiner Place (Dublin 1): Fleming's Hotel.

29 Gardiner Place (Dublin 1): Linda Kearns's Nurses' Home.

65 Great Britain Street (now Parnell Street) (Dublin 1): Home of Mr and Mrs Maurice Collins.

5 Mespil Road (Dublin 4): Home of Miss Patricia Hoey and her mother.

131 Morehampton Road (Dublin 4): Home of Mrs Andrew (Mary) Woods.

1 Mountjoy Square (Dublin 1): Home of Walter Cole.

Principal offices and meeting places

32 Bachelor's Walk (Dublin 1): Collins had several offices here: his office for the Irish National Aid and Volunteers' Dependants' Fund, a finance office and an intelligence office. It was never raided but he was arrested outside the office on 2 April 1918.

Camden Street (Dublin 2): The location of Nora (Mrs Padraig) O'Keefe's restaurant, known as 'the Farm Produce'. Collins often lunched here and used it as an interim office between the ones he had at 76 Harcourt Street and 22 Mary Street.

6 Harcourt Street (Dublin 2): Ministry of Finance office, raided on 12 September 1919.

76 Harcourt Street (Dublin 2): Ministry of Finance office, raided on 20 November 1918 and 12 September 1919.

17 Harcourt Terrace (Dublin 2): Used from the end of May to July 1921.

21, 22 Henry Street (Dublin 1): Used as a primary office and also a Department of Intelligence office. It was not in use for long.

5 Mary Street (Dublin 1): Collins used this as an intelligence office for a short while in 1919.

22 Mary Street (Dublin 1): Collins's primary Department of Finance office at the time, until it was raided on 26 May 1921 (the day after the Custom House fire). This raid was one of Collins's closest calls.

28–29 Mary Street (Dublin 1): Raided in June 1921. Batt O'Connor built a secret compartment in the draper's shop here, big enough for people to hide in, as well as hiding documents.

5 Mespil Road, Ballsbridge (Dublin 4): Close to Leeson Street Bridge, it was used as a primary office and also as a Department of Intelligence office. It was raided on 1 April 1921.

Other meeting places

Collins had many 'joints' around Dublin where he used to meet and conduct his intelligence operations on an almost daily basis. He met brigade officers at Vaughan's, men from the country in Devlin's pub or Shanahan's pub, sailors in Devlin's pub or Kirwan's pub (Dublin 1), and detectives in Thomas Gay's house in Clontarf (Dublin 3).

Joint No. 1: 29 Rutland Square (now Parnell Square), Vaughan's Hotel. This was a kind of clearing house for him.

Joint No. 2: 69 Great Britain Street (now Parnell Street), Liam Devlin's pub. Collins met select people here, including members of the Dublin Brigade.

Joint No. 3: 49 Great Britain Street (now Parnell Street), Jim (Séamus) Kirwan's pub. Jim Kirwan was from County Tipperary and was a great friend of Dan Breen and Seán Treacy; when in Dublin they stayed here about once a week while 'on the run'.

16 Airfield Road, Rathgar (Dublin 6): Home of Julia O'Donovan, aunt of Gearóid O'Sullivan and grandmother of Fionnuala Donovan. This was one of Collins's main safe houses in south Dublin, where he met his DMP and Castle contacts after Sunday dinner.

Amiens Street: Phil Sheerin's Coolevin Dairies (Dublin 1). Collins often had breakfast here and met railwaymen carrying messages throughout the country.

1–2 Denmark Street Great: Barry's Hotel (Dublin 1).

Foley Street (at corner of Corporation Street) (Dublin 1): Phil Shanahan's pub. Shanahan was originally from County Tipperary and his pub was 'home' to Volunteers from 'the country'.

Gardiner Row: Fleming's Hotel (Dublin 1).

20 Rutland Square (now Parnell Square): Banba Hall (Dublin 1).

41 Rutland Square (now Parnell Square): Irish National Foresters' Hall (Dublin 1).

46 Rutland Square (now Parnell Square): Gaelic League HQ (Conradh na Gaeilge) (Dublin 1).

Appendix II

Major individual British spies to seek Collins

Alan Bell: See Dame Street, Harcourt Street, Dublin 2; Nutley Lane, Dublin 4.

John Charles (J.C.) Byrne ('Jameson'): See Bachelor's Walk, Granville Hotel, Sackville Street Upper, Dublin 1; Harcourt Street, Dublin 2; Brendan Road, Nutley Lane, Dublin 4; Ballymun Road, Dublin 11.

Bryan Fergus Molloy: See Wicklow Street, Dublin 2; Parkgate Street, Dublin 8.

Timothy Quinlisk: See Mountjoy Street, Dublin 1; Harcourt Street, Dublin 2; Brendan Road, Dublin 4; Winthrop Street, Co. Cork, Appendix VI.

Appendix III

Primary women who worked for Collins as secretaries, spies and couriers

Dell Barrett (Clare)

Josephine Barrett (Clare)

Peg Barrett (Clare)

Mary Collins-Powell (Collins's sister; he asked her to liaise with Emmet Dalton in Cork)

Máire Comerford (one of Collins's primary couriers in Dublin and down to the countryside)

Siobhán Creedon (Mallow post office in Cork City)

Agnes Daly (a sister of Kathleen Clarke from Limerick)

Madge Daly (a sister of Kathleen Clarke from Limerick)[666]

Moya Llewelyn (O'Connor) Davies (a very good driver, she often used her car to smuggle guns and was one of Collins's most important couriers to Cork)

Madeline 'Dilly' Dicker (a girlfriend, she was one of Collins's primary spies going back and forth to England)

Anna (Miss Fitz) Fitzsimmons (Kelly) (she worked at the *Irish Bulletin* and was a frequent courier for Collins)

Louise Gavan Duffy (Collins used her school on St Stephen's Green for meetings)

Madge Hales (she was a link between Collins and the Volunteers in Cork; she also travelled to Italy, as her brother, Donal, was trying to buy arms there)

Patricia Hoey (one of Collins's secretaries in the office on Mespil Road)

Sighle (Sheila) Humphreys (she met Collins at the National Aid Fund and became one of his couriers)

Linda Kearns (MacWhinney) (she was caught smuggling a large consignment of weapons to her native Sligo and was imprisoned; she made one of the most famous escapes from Mountjoy Prison)

Susan Killeen (a girlfriend, she was one of Collins's couriers and became devoted to 'the cause' in 1917 and thereafter)

Siobhán Lankford (while working for the Mallow post office, she had been involved in setting up a Gaelic League club as a cover for IRA activity and she became an integral part of the intelligence network for the Cork No. 2 Brigade, IRA; when any telegram reached a post office it was always written out in duplicate—one for the customer and a copy for filing in the post office—and Lankford would slip a third piece of paper underneath the two sheets of paper, and then slip it into her pocket and pass it on to her IRA contact)

Lady Hazel Lavery (wife of the painter Sir John Lavery, she acted as a go-between to the British during the Treaty negotiations and afterwards, passing information along to Collins)

Sister Eithne Lawless (she worked in Harcourt Street and then in Camden Street Lower, where most of the Dáil Loan money was counted)[667]

Kathleen Lynn (a doctor, she treated Mrs Hoey's mother and carried messages for Collins)[668]

Brigid Lyons (Thornton) (as a medical student, then as a doctor, Collins used her often to carry messages when she was acting in her medical capacity)[669]

Eileen McGrane (she kept papers for Collins and let him use her house as a safe house until it was raided on 31 December 1920)

Kathleen (Napoli) McKenna (she was on the staff of the *Irish Bulletin* and became a courier, coming to one of Collins's offices daily)[670]

Josephine Marchmont (Cork Military Barracks) (she married Florence O'Donoghue)

Susan (Sinéad, Jenny) Mason (Collins's primary secretary; they were so close that many friends thought they would marry)

Lily Mernin ('Lt G.', one of Collins's primary military spies)[671]

Nancy O'Brien (Collins's second cousin, she decoded messages in Dublin Castle)

Molly O'Reilly (Corcoran) (she worked at the Hibernian United Services Club and was one of Collins's most effective spies in gathering information and weapons from British officers)

Leslie Price (a courier to Cork, she later married Tom Barry)

Nora Wallace (Cork Military Barracks)

Nancy Wyse-Power (she gathered intelligence on the Continent and worked as a courier for Collins)[672]

Appendix IV

Bloody Sunday, 21 November 1920

92 Baggot Street Lower (Dublin 2)
119 Baggot Street Lower (Dublin 2)
Croke Park/Jones's Road (Dublin 3)
28 Earlsfort Terrace (Dublin 2)
117 Morehampton Road (Dublin 4)
22 Mount Street Lower (Dublin 2)
38 Mount Street Upper (Dublin 2)
28 Pembroke Street Upper (Dublin 2)
Gresham Hotel, Sackville Street Upper (Dublin 1)

On 21 November 1920, in the quiet of a Dublin Sunday, groups of IRA gunmen began the systematic assassination of a group of specially trained and recruited secret servicemen, mostly MI5 and SIS specialists.[673] This British unit had been recruited in London in the summer of 1920 and placed in the charge of Major C.A. Cameron. In all, 60 agents were trained and dispatched to Ireland. It now seems certain that the majority of the men assassinated were members of this group, although the Irish made some mistakes in identification and some civilians were killed in error.

Earlier that month, Prime Minister Lloyd George had confidently stated that the IRA were defeated and that the British 'had murder on the run'.[674] The attack, coming just when the British forces felt that they had the IRA at breaking point, was a momentous act of reassertion. Its timing was also crucial for the Irish, since it had become apparent to the police—and certainly to Collins—that the IRA boycott of the police was faltering and that general allegiance to the Republican cause could be weakening. Hence Bloody Sunday not only removed a major threat to the IRA but also warned the Irish people that any weakening of their resolve to continue the struggle and support the guerrillas would not be tolerated.[675]

Intelligence chiefs in London were pragmatic: their goal was to locate Michael Collins, thus severing the head from the body of the IRA. Collins was aware of the intensification and knew that he would have to move soon to meet it. He received information from a contact in Scotland Yard that this group of men was coming to Dublin with the avowed intent to smash the IRA/Volunteers, and particularly Collins's intelligence operation. He could not defeat the British in pitched battles but he could 'put out the eyes and ears' of the intelligence service upon which the military relied.

In 1920, that special intelligence unit was organised by the British into one whose ultimate purpose was to break Collins's organisation. Their strategy was simple:

they intended to assassinate the political members of Sinn Féin who were moving openly in public or who were involved in the military struggle. After this, they felt, the IRA would be bound to make some moves that would flush its leaders to the surface. After September 1920 the number of raids increased and intense searches were carried out nightly in the city. The men effecting this policy became known as the 'Cairo Gang'.[676]

For months Collins had watched the British getting closer and closer. From their first appearance in Dublin he began gathering information on them, and found that they were usually living as private citizens in respectable rooming houses. He set his own spies to open their correspondence, had the contents of their wastepaper baskets taken by the housemaids and had duplicate keys made for their rooms. In addition, the IRA had co-opted most of the Irish servants who worked in the rooming houses where the officers lived, and all of their comings and goings were meticulously recorded by servants and reported to Collins's staff. He waited and accumulated evidence before going to the cabinet to seek authorisation for his operation.[677] Lily Mernin, who worked at Ship Street Barracks for Major Stratford Burton, the garrison adjutant, was one of Collins's most important sources on the British military. Major Burton was in charge of court-martial proceedings as well as the strength of various military posts throughout Dublin, and Mernin would always make an extra carbon copy of all reports and documents for Collins.

> Before the 21st November 1920, it was part of my normal duty to type the names and addresses of British agents who were accommodated at private addresses and living as ordinary citizens of the city. These lists were typed weekly and amended whenever an address was changed. I passed them on each week to the address at Moynihan's, Clonliffe Rd, or to Piaras Béaslaí. The typing of the lists ceased after the 21st November 1920 [Bloody Sunday].[678]

Locating Collins had become a prime goal of the British intelligence organisations, and they were getting close. In a meeting in a café on Grafton Street, a member of the Cairo Gang joined Tom Cullen, Frank Thornton and Charlie Saurin as they were pretending to be British spies. The real British officer said to them: 'Surely you fellows know Liam Tobin, Tom Cullen and Frank Thornton—these are Collins's three officers and if you can get them we can locate Collins'.[679] If they knew the names of his lieutenants (though not what they looked like), the British were getting uncomfortably close. It boded ill for any of Collins's men who fell into their hands now.

The Cairo Gang had been activated in Ireland by Col. Ormonde de L'Epee Winter, chief of the British Combined Intelligence Services in Ireland from the spring of 1920 until the Truce. The IRA/Volunteers knew him as the 'Holy Terror' because he was always prepared to descend to the most extreme methods to obtain information from prisoners. In October Winter organised the Central Raid Bureau to coordinate the activities of his agents and the Auxiliaries. Soon they began to make their presence felt. The Cairo Gang were ruthless and efficient, and intended to eliminate Collins and his Intelligence Department operatives. They had been primarily responsible for tracking down Dan Breen and Seán Treacy, and had killed Treacy in Talbot Street (Dublin 1).

In the first two weeks of November the Gang detained some of Collins's closest advisers. They held Frank Thornton for ten days but he managed to convince them that he had nothing to do with Sinn Féin. On 10 November they just missed capturing Richard Mulcahy, who had to escape out the skylight of Professor Michael Hayes's house on South Circular Road. On 13 November they raided Vaughan's Hotel and questioned Liam Tobin and Tom Cullen but let them go. Collins, Cathal Brugha, Mulcahy and the military and intelligence leadership felt that they had no choice but to attack.

Mulcahy, who had almost been captured in that November raid, commented: 'We were being made to feel that they were very close on the heels of some of us'. He was quite clear about the guilt of those against whom the IRA directed their operations on Bloody Sunday:

> They were members of a spy organisation that was a murder organisation. Their murderous intent was directed against the effective members of the Government as well as against GHQ and staff at the Dublin Brigade.[680]

Collins, Brugha, Mulcahy, Dick McKee, Peadar Clancy and others sentenced over twenty officers at their meeting on 20 November in 35 Lower Gardiner Street (Dublin 1). The names of fifteen out of the 35 selected for assassination were turned down because of insufficient evidence.[681]

The operation was to start at 9.00am sharp. Collins told them all that 'it's to be done exactly at nine. Neither before nor after. These whores, the British, have got to learn that Irishmen can turn up on time.'[682]

Paddy Daly, leader of Collins's squad, was not one of the men assigned to carry out the attacks on Bloody Sunday, but he was intimately involved in the organisation and planning. He recalled:

> The four Battalions of the Brigade were engaged, and the OC of each Battalion was responsible for a certain area, not his own area because most of the spies were grouped in certain districts. If the 2nd Battalion Volunteers had been confined to their own area, they would not have done anything but the Gresham Hotel job. All other operations allotted to the 2nd Battalion were outside their Battalion

area, in fact they were in the 3rd Battalion area.

Seán Russell picked the men for the various operations, and in every case he appointed a member of the Squad in charge of the various groups.

There were five operations allotted to the 2nd Battalion and five different groups were appointed to carry them out. In other words, the 2nd Battalion had 13 spies to deal with. One operation, on the east end, did not come off as the spies had left that address the previous day and there was nobody in the home when the Volunteers went there. The other eleven were all accounted for.

Joe Leonard was in charge of Baggot Street; Tom Keogh was in charge of 22 Lower Mount Street; I cannot remember who was in charge of Upper Mount Street, it was probably Seán Doyle; Paddy Moran was in charge in the Gresham Hotel. Paddy Moran was not a member of the Squad but he volunteered for the work. He was Captain of 'D' Company of the 2nd Battalion, and on that account Seán Russell did not put a member of the Squad in charge of the Gresham Hotel operation, knowing that he could not improve on Paddy Moran. Paddy Moran was not in Mount Street on Bloody Sunday. The evidence that was sworn against him was that he was in Mount Street and was sentenced to death for the Mount St. job.

The arrangements for the Bloody Sunday operations were made by Dick McKee.

About a fortnight or three weeks before Bloody Sunday, we had a meeting, which I am positive was held in the Printers' Hall in Gardiner Street, but Joe Leonard is equally positive it was at the Brigade Headquarters in the Engineers' Hall in Gardiner Row. I personally think I am right because Brigade headquarters was very much shunned after the death of Seán Treacy, and Dick McKee, since Seán's death, was using the Printers' Hall in Gardiner Street more often than the hall in Gardiner Row. ... The four Battalions were represented at this meeting in the Printers' Hall, and I was there as OC of the Squad. Details were given to us about the various houses that were to be raided and we got detailed descriptions of the individuals who were to be eliminated.

On the Saturday afternoon there was a 2nd Battalion meeting, definitely at the Printers' Hall in Gardiner Steet. All the men taking part in the 2nd Battalion operations were at this meeting. Dick McKee and Peadar Clancy were there.

At this meeting Dick McKee questioned every officer in charge of operations as to their reconnoitring of their positions and the arrangements they had for getting their men back to the North side of the city, because the operations were taking place on the South side. He impressed on them that they were to be careful of the bridges on the way back. The 2nd Battalion had arranged to commandeer a ferry-boat to take the men across the Liffey to get back to the North side.

At this meeting Seán Russell put me in charge of all the operations, instructing me to have some first-aid people at No. 17 North Richmond Street, the house of Mrs Byrne. He also told me that I was to take up my position there and make any arrangements I could to go to the assistance of anyone who might be wounded during the operations. I did not like this because it would be the first time since the Squad was formed that the men would be going into action without me, but I was told that I was not going because I had other business to do. Dick McKee turned and said 'Paddy, I'm not going either. Have you not full confidence in the men appointed?' Of course I told him I had. He explained to me that Seán Russell got instructions to appoint all the officers for all their various operations in the city, and he paid the Squad the great compliment of putting them in charge of the various groups even outside their own Battalion area.

Operations were timed for nine o'clock on Bloody Sunday, and at about 8.15 a.m. I saw each group leave for its objective.

The first to return to North Richmond Street was Tom Keogh, bringing with him Billy McClean who had been wounded in the hand. They told me that when they were coming out of 22 Mount Street on the completion of their task, a lorryload of Tans, who had heard the shooting, pulled up and started to dismount. Tom Keogh immediately gathered his men in the hall and told them they might not get time to attack. 'We must attack first', said Tom. He swung open the hall door, absolutely charged the Tans, and succeeded in wounding or killing one of them. The lorry then drove off and left some Tans on the ground, but the party did not wait to see whether they were alive or dead. Tom Keogh also reported that the task, as far as he was concerned, had been completed.

All the Volunteers had been told to report back, if possible, to 17 North Richmond Street. Joe Leonard and some of the men living in the South side were told not to report back if they did not think it advisable, but to send word that all were safe or otherwise. As the various reports came in we discovered that Frank Teeling was missing. Tom Keogh said that Teeling had not been shot coming out from the house in Mount Street. He also said that all the men left the house but that Teeling may have gone out the back way. A few hours afterwards, toward mid-day, we heard that Frank Teeling had been wounded and captured. This was a big disappointment to everybody. Teeling and McClean were the only two casualties we had in the four operations.

There was an all–Ireland match in Croke Park that Sunday and all Volunteers who had taken part in the operations spoke about going to it. I advised them to keep away from Croke Park because I knew there were bound to be spotters and spies round the turn-stiles. There were servant girls and landladies in the houses our men had visited that morning and we had no guarantee that they were friendly. The obvious place to find anybody of an Irish-Ireland outlook that day would be Croke Park.

Tom Keogh jokingly remarked that it was a good-looking maid who opened the door for him and that he made a date with her. That was Tom's attitude.

I did not go to Croke Park so I cannot describe what happened there, but most of the Volunteers went.[683]

(See 35 Lower Gardiner Street, 17 Richmond Street North, Dublin 1; Croke Park, Dublin 3.)

On the morning of 21 November the operation began at 9am, exactly as planned. Some of the men targeted refused to come out of their rooms and were shot in bed. Others came to the door and were shot as they opened it. Of the IRA/Volunteers who had taken part, some would never recover completely from the nerve-shattering work of that morning.[684] By 9.30 the killings were finished.

The military were slow to realise what had happened. About 9.20am General F.P. Crozier was passing 22 Mount Street with a group of Auxiliaries when they heard the shooting. Crozier and the Auxiliaries jumped out and ran to the house. Tom Keogh, who burst through the soldiers as they surrounded him, shot two Auxiliaries who were in the back of the house. After Crozier saw what had happened upstairs, he went to the garden and found an Auxiliary about to shoot Frank Teeling, a Squad member who had been wounded. Crozier stopped the Auxiliary and saw that Teeling was taken to hospital, then headed to Dublin Castle. Throughout the city, panicked British officers packed their belongings and moved into the Castle.

Collins's men had gone out to kill twenty that morning, but some of them could not be found. The publicised and 'official' figures stated that eleven officers were killed and four escaped.

(Frank Thornton's memoirs listed fifteen killed, at eight different addresses in Dublin:

List of Secret Service Men killed or wounded on Bloody Sunday, 21st November, 1920.
2 Earlsfort Terrace. Captain Fitzpatrick Defence Officer, Co. Clare. **K.**
117 Morehampton Road. Mr Smith **K.** Captain McClean **K.** Mr Caldron **W**
22 Lr Mount Street. Mr Mahon **K.** Mr Peel escaped. A. Morris Auxiliary **K.** Frank Furniss Auxiliary **K.**
92 Lr Baggot Street. Captain Newbury Court Martial Officer. **K.**
38 Upper Mount Street. Lt. Aimes Grenadier Guards **K.** Lt. Bennett Motor Transport **K.**
28 Upper Pembroke Street. Major Dowling Grenadier Guards **K.** Capt. Price

Royal Engineers **K**. Capt. Keenlyside Lancashire Fusiliers **W**. Colonel Woodcock **W**. Colonel Montgomery died of wounds **K**. Lt. Murray Royal Scots **W**. Gresham Hotel. Capt. McCormack **K**. Lt. Wilde **K**.

119 Lower Baggot Street. Capt. Baggally Court Martial Officer **K**.

Admitted by British: **K**. 2 Court Martial Officers. **K**. 2 Auxiliaries. **K**. 11 Other Officers.

4 Wounded

13 Officers Killed, 2 Auxiliaries killed.[685])

In fact, eleven British officers, two Auxiliary cadets and two civilians (T.H. Smith and L.E. Wilde) were killed in eight locations, as follows:

92 Baggot Street Lower: Capt. W.F. Newbury (a courts-martial officer).

119 Baggot Street Lower: Capt. George (Geoffrey) T. Baggallay (a one-legged courts-martial officer).

28 Earlsfort Terrace: Sgt John Fitzgerald (he was in the RIC and was probably killed for that alone, as the Squad asked for 'Col. Fitzpatrick').

117–119 Morehampton Road: Capt. Donald L. McLean (an intelligence officer at Dublin Castle) and T.H. Smith (a civilian landlord not engaged in intelligence at all).

22 Lower Mount Street: Lt H.R. Angliss (alias Patrick 'Paddy' McMahon, a British intelligence agent); Auxiliary Cadets Garner and Morris.

38 Upper Mount Street: Lt Peter Ashmunt Ames, Capt. George Bennett (Ames and Bennett were leaders of the intelligence unit).

28–29 Pembroke Street Upper: Major C.M.G. Dowling (a British intelligence officer), Col. Hugh F. Montgomery (a staff officer and 'in the wrong place', who took three weeks to die from his wounds) and Capt. Leonard Price (a British intelligence officer).

Upper Sackville Street, Gresham Hotel: Capt. Patrick MacCormack (almost certainly buying horses for the Alexandria Turf Club and not engaged in intelligence activity at all) and L.E. Wilde (a civilian).

Ames, Angliss, Baggallay, Bennett, Dowling, Fitzgerald, MacCormack, McLean, Montgomery, Newberry, Price, Wilde, Smith, Morris and Garner were killed. Keenlyside, Woodcock, Murray and Caldow were wounded. Peel, amongst others, escaped unscathed.

The dead included British Intelligence officers, British Army courts-martial officers, two Auxiliaries, an RIC officer, a number of soldiers in the wrong place at the wrong time and two civilians. Of those killed by the IRA, Ames, Angliss, Bennett, Dowling, McLean and Price were intelligence officers. Baggallay and Newberry were court-martial officers not involved with intelligence. McCormack and Wilde appear to have been incorrectly targeted or were innocent ex-officers. Fitzgerald was a policeman who was probably mistaken for someone else. Smith was the landlord of a house where some of the army men were staying and was killed by mistake. Morris and Garner were Auxiliaries on their way to warn the barracks, as was Montgomery, who happened to be in the wrong place at the wrong time.

Services for six of the Protestant officers were held at Westminster Abbey, and services for the Catholic men, Peter Ames, George Bennett and H. R. Angliss, were held at Westminster Cathedral.

Some of the targets had escaped death by not being home, and Collins's men were able to recover only a few papers of import. But if every spy or agent in Ireland had been killed it could not have had a greater effect on Dublin Castle. Dave Neligan stated that the incident 'caused complete panic in Dublin Castle. ... The attack was so well organized, so unexpected, and so ruthlessly executed that the effect was paralyzing. It can be said that the enemy never recovered from the blow. While some of the worst killers escaped, they were thoroughly frightened.'[686]

Prime Minister David Lloyd George said: 'They got what they deserved—beaten by counter-jumpers!' 'Ask Griffith for God's sake to keep his head and not to break off the slender link that had been established. Tragic as the events in Dublin were, they were of no importance. These men were soldiers, and took a soldier's risk.'[687]

Collins said:

My one intention was the destruction of the undesirables who continued to make miserable the lives of ordinary decent citizens. I have proof enough to assure myself of the atrocities, which this gang of spies and informers have committed. Perjury and torture are words too easily known to them. If I had a second motive it was no more than a feeling I would have for a dangerous reptile. By their destruction the very air is made sweeter. For myself, my conscience is clear. There is no crime in detecting and destroying, in wartime, the spy and the informer. They have destroyed without trial. I have paid them back in their own coin.[688]

Later he said:

I found out those fellows we put on the spot were going to put a lot of us on the spot, so I got there first. ... When will it all end? When can a man get down to a book and peace?

It was this incident, more than any other, that gained Collins the reputation as a gunman and a 'murderer'. The British press made much of the fact that the men were

British spies in civilian clothes and, under assumed names, playing a game of 'kill or be killed'. That same press, for the most part, ignored the activities of the Black and Tans and Auxiliaries at Croke Park.

The extent of the killing of the British officers even stunned some of the Irish. Desmond FitzGerald and William Cosgrave were shocked. Arthur Griffith was horrified: 'In front of their wives on a Sunday in their own homes'. Some of those on the raids were even chastised by members of their own family:

> I was told that the British had raided the Tipperary Football team where they were staying in Gardiner's Row. We, therefore, decided that there would be no football match for us that day; that we would not attend it, as we thought there would possibly be trouble there. I returned home about 2 o'clock and lunched. After lunch I had been in the habit of going to football matches on a Sunday, and my family asked me was I not going to the match. I said no, that I was feeling tired and would lie down and have a rest. I lay on the couch in the room and fell asleep. I was awakened that evening about 4 o'clock. My wife came into the room crying, with a 'Stop Press' in her hand. I woke up and asked her what was the matter. Before speaking she handed me the 'Stop Press' and wanted to know was this the fishing expedition I had been on [he had told her he was fishing that morning]. Seeing that there was no use in concealing things any longer from her, I said: 'Yes, and don't you see we had a good catch', or words to that effect. She then said: 'I don't care what you think about it, I think it is murder'. I said: 'No, that is nonsense; I'd feel like going to the altar after that job this morning', and thus I tried to calm her. I don't think she put out any lights in the house during the following winter. I did not stay at home then for about a week. That Sunday night I slept in a grove in the demesne known as St Anne's, which was nearby.[689]

Collins waited for the reports in Devlin's pub just off Rutland Square (Dublin 1). Joe O'Reilly cycled in and Collins first asked: 'Any casualties?' At that time O'Reilly reported that there had been none. Collins then said, 'There'll be no match today at Croke Park'. He knew that even if the match were cancelled a crowd would gather and would be obvious targets for the British. 'Go down there and tell them to call it off.' It was too late, and the match went ahead.

Following the morning raids, a combined group of British Army, Black and Tans and Auxiliaries raided Croke Park. (See Jones's Road, Dublin 3.)

Jones's Road/Croke Park:[690] According to the police, the 'official plan' was that fifteen minutes before the final whistle there would be an announcement by megaphone. Instead of the usual 'stewards to end of match positions', the crowd would hear someone telling them to leave by official exits and that all men would be searched for weapons. In the event, however, no sooner had the police, Black and Tans and Auxiliaries arrived at the Park than they started shooting. The exact events that led to the shooting have never been determined, with each side contradicting the other. The only public and official statement was one by Dublin Castle, blaming the IRA for starting the shooting.[691]

Central to all inquiries and still in dispute is the question of who fired first. All that is agreed upon is that the firing started at the south-west corner of the pitch, where Jones's Road crosses the Royal Canal. Some witnesses at the inquiries said that the firing started within the Park, presumably by armed spectators, before the British troops had entered the grounds.

Those killed were:

Jane Boyle (26)
James Burke (44)
Daniel Carroll (30)
Michael Feery (40)
Mick Hogan (24) (Tipperary football player, for whom the Hogan Stand is
    named)
Thomas Hogan (19)
James Matthews (48)
Patrick O'Dowd (57)
Jeremiah (Jerry) O'Leary (10)
William (Willie) Robinson (11)
Thomas Ryan (27) (shot dead while whispering the Act of Contrition in Mick
    Hogan's ear)
John William Scott (14)
James Teehan (26)
Joseph Traynor (21)

Sixty-two people were injured in Croke Park during the raid, and another twelve were injured in the stampede to get out.

Major E.L. Mills, who commanded the Regular Army back-up troops, reported adversely on the actions of the Black and Tans, Auxiliaries and RIC. He blamed the 'excited and out of control RIC constables for the deaths', and said: 'I did not see any need for any firing at all and the indiscriminate firing absolutely spoilt any chance of getting hold of people with arms'.

Gen. Crozier, O/C of the Black and Tans and Auxiliaries and who would shortly resign in protest over the British administration's condoning of misconduct by his troops, publicly stated that one of his officers told him that the Auxiliaries started the shooting. 'It was the most disgraceful show I have ever seen,' the officer said. 'Black and

Tans fired into the crowd without any provocation whatever.'[692]

Crozier interviewed Major Mills, who was furious. 'A rotten bloody show ... the worst I've ever seen,' Mills said.

'The military surrounded the hurley ground according to plan and were to warn the crowd by megaphone to file out of the gates where they were to be searched for arms. A rotten idea anyhow, as, of course, if anyone had a gun on him he'd drop it like a hot poker! Well, would you believe it, suddenly the Regular RIC from Phoenix Park—Black and Tans from England, arrived up in lorries, opened fire into the crowd, over the fence, without reason and killed about a dozen and wounded many more! I eventually stopped the firing. What do you think of it?'

'Rotten' I [Crozier] replied, 'sit down here now, write a report to me and I'll forward it to the Castle at once.'[693]

Mills's report, though incomplete and with some inaccuracies, was damning.

At 1.30 pm 21st inst. I was detailed to take charge of a mixed force of RIC and Auxiliary Division to hold up and search people at CROKE PARK.

I arranged with Major Dudley, DSO, MC, who was in charge of a party of 100 RIC, to split up the two forces so that there would be an equal number posted on the 4 gates of the ground to search people as they came out.

... I was in a car in a rear of the RIC leading the Auxiliaries. As we approached the railway bridge ... I saw men in the tender in front of me trying to get out of their car and heard some of them shouting about an ambush. ... At this moment I heard a considerable amount of rifle fire. As no shots were coming from the football field and all along the RIC constables seemed excited and out of hand, I rushed and stopped the firing with the assistance of Major Fillery. There was still firing going on in the football ground. I ran down into the ground and shouted to all the armed men to stop firing at once and eventually the firing ceased.

The crowd by this time was in a state of panic.

... I went round the ground and found two children being carried out apparently dead. I found one female who had been trampled to death, also a man who had apparently died the same way. I saw a few wounded men and I got some sense into the crowd. I got the DMP to get ambulances for the wounded. We found no arms on any of the people attending the match.

... I did not see any need for any firing at all and all the indiscriminate firing absolutely spoilt any chance of getting hold of any people in possession of arms.

The men of the Auxiliary Division did not fire [sic].

The casualties I personally saw were 6 dead, and 4 wounded, 2 of the dead were apparently trampled to death.

The Auxiliaries fired a total of 238 rounds of small-arms ammunition, in addition to a single drum of 50 rounds fired from the Lewis machine-gun in the armoured car.

A secret court of inquiry found that the shooting was unauthorised and excessive, even if some members of the crowd fired on the Auxiliaries. Major-Gen. G.F. Boyd, O/C of the British soldiers in Dublin, concluded that the firing on the crowd, which began without orders, was both indiscriminate and unjustifiable.

Finding that he could not stop the match at Croke Park, Joe O'Reilly cycled back to Devlin's. On the way, a lad came up to him and told him that Dick McKee and Peadar Clancy had been captured the night before, and that he was to take a message to Collins. O'Reilly was stunned and immediately went to Devlin's to tell Collins about McKee and Clancy, who had planned the operation. When he heard, Collins screamed, 'Good God. We're finished now. It's all up.'

Collins then ordered his police agent James McNamara to find out where they were being held, and he thought it was at the Bridewell. Collins sent McNamara and Dave Neligan to search for them at the Bridewell, but they discovered that McKee and Clancy were being held in Dublin Castle. McKee and Clancy had been captured in Seán Fitzpatrick's house in Lower Gloucester Street—supposedly a 'safe house'. (John [Shankers] Ryan, the tout who turned them in, was later killed in Hyne's pub in Gloucester Place.) Conor Clune, a Gaelic Leaguer from County Clare, was taken in Vaughan's Hotel. Clune had nothing to do with the Volunteers and had only come to Dublin to confer with journalist Piaras Béaslaí, but he was staying in Vaughan's, which was a noted IRA meeting place, and so he was taken to Dublin Castle, where he was killed with McKee and Clancy. (See Gloucester Street, Marlborough Street, Pro-Cathedral, Dublin 1; Dublin Castle, Dublin 2.)

McKee, Clancy and Clune were killed in the Castle at 11.00am on Sunday morning. Mulcahy realised what a blow their deaths were to Collins personally, as well as to their operations.

In McKee and Clancy he [Collins] had two men who fully understood the inside of Collins's work and who were ready and able to link up the Dublin resources of the Dublin Brigade to any work that Collins had in hand and to do so promptly, effectively and sympathetically.[694]

Of the killings in the Castle, General Crozier wrote:

The evidence before the military inquiry, which enquired into these deaths, was faked from beginning to end, evidence being given by the police that the unarmed and closely guarded men attempted to 'overpower' the guard (in a guard room inside 'The Castle' which was itself closely guarded) in an attempt to 'escape'. Anything 'did' for a paper acquittal then because Parliament accepted anything willingly as an explanation.[695]

A court of inquiry was convened at Dublin Castle and at Jervis Street Hospital. On 8 December 1920 it issued its verdict. The court concluded that during a raid on Croke Park on 21 November 1920 by a mixed force of RIC, auxiliary police and military, firing was started by unknown civilians, either as a warning of the raid or else to create a panic, and that the injuries to dead civilians were inflicted by rifle or revolver fire from the canal bridge by the RIC, some of whom fired over the crowd's heads, others of whom fired into the crowd at persons believed to be trying to evade arrest. It also found that the RIC firing was carried out without orders and in excess of what was required but that no firing came from the auxiliary police or the military, except that soldiers in an armoured car (at the St James's Avenue exit) fired a burst into the air to stop the crowd from breaking through and out of the ground.

Appended to the inquiry report is a copy (marked 'Secret and V. Urgent!') dated 21 November 1920 of the (unsigned) order given by a brigade major, Infantry Brigade, to the RIC and containing details of the operation planned to take place that day at Croke Park. The ground was to be surrounded and pickets placed at specified points, e.g. on the railway and at the three known exits. One infantry platoon was to be kept in reserve and at 3.15pm two (army) armoured cars would meet the mixed RIC and auxiliary police at Fitzroy Avenue (opposite the main entrance). A quarter of an hour before the end of the match a special intelligence officer would warn the crowd by megaphone that anybody trying to leave other than by the exits would be shot, and that all males would be stopped and searched.

The opinion of the competent military authority which convened the court of inquiry on 11 December 1920 was:

(i) that it agreed with the court findings (summarised above);
(ii) that the first shots were fired by the crowd and led to the panic;
(iii) that the firing on the crowd was carried out without orders and was indiscriminate and unjustifiable, with the exception of any shooting which took place inside the enclosure.

Major-Gen. Boyd, commanding officer, Dublin, certified this opinion.[696]

Appendix V

Collins's death at Béal na mBláth

Béal na mBláth, Co. Cork (usually translated as 'the Mouth of Flowers/Blossoms'):

GENERAL MICHAEL COLLINS,
COMMANDER-IN-CHIEF OF THE IRISH ARMY,
WAS KILLED IN AN AMBUSH BY IRREGULARS
AT BEAL NA MBLATH
BETWEEN MACROOM AND BANDON,
ON LAST NIGHT (TUESDAY).
TOWARDS THE CLOSE OF THE ENGAGEMENT,
WHICH LASTED CLOSE TO AN HOUR,
THE COMMANDER-IN-CHIEF
WAS WOUNDED IN THE HEAD.[697]

Collins's fatal itinerary, 20–22 August 1922

Collins was ill and feverish before leaving Dublin and his doctor recommended that the journey be postponed. Had it been merely an inspection trip it could have been delayed, but it appears that Collins may have had something more in mind.[698]

Collins's convoy left Portobello Barracks, Dublin, at 5.15am on Sunday 20 August and made its first stop at Maryborough Jail (now Portlaoise Prison), where Collins discussed the transfer of some of the prisoners there to Gormanstown camp to relieve the overcrowded conditions. He also spoke with some of the prisoners, including Tom Malone, about ending the war. He asked whether Malone would attend a meeting to 'try to put an end to this damned thing'. As he left, he slapped his fist into his hand and said 'That fixes it—the three Toms [Malone, Tom Barry and Tom Hales] will fix it'.[699] The convoy then headed to Roscrea Barracks for an inspection and breakfast. At Limerick Barracks the O/C of the Southern Command, General Eoin O'Duffy, met Collins and discussed his belief that the Civil War would soon be over, and he understood that Collins wanted to avoid any rancour. The convoy then headed through Mallow and spent that night in Cork city, where Collins stayed at the military HQ in the Imperial Hotel. There he met his sister, Mary Collins-Powell, and his nephew, Seán Collins-Powell, who asked whether he could accompany his uncle the next day. Collins replied, 'You have your job to do and I have mine'.

The rest of the evening was spent in consultation with the O/C of the area,

General Emmet Dalton. Dalton felt that 'normality and law and order would not be too far off. We were in possession of the principal towns in County Cork. Michael Collins and I discussed this on the journey through West Cork.'[700] Most of the escort spent the first evening in the Victoria Hotel.

On Monday 21 August Collins again visited his sister, and then he and Gen. Dalton went to the *Cork Examiner* to discuss the general Free State position on publicity with the editor, Tom Crosbie. Collins also visited some local banks in an effort to trace and recover Republican funds lodged during their occupation of the city—first the Hibernian Bank, then the Bank of Ireland, then the Land Bank, and finally other smaller institutions. During July the IRA had collected £120,000 in customs revenue and had hidden this money in the accounts of sympathisers. At each bank Collins told the manager to close the doors; the banks would be permitted to reopen only if the managers cooperated fully. Collins had the bank directors identify the suspicious accounts, then he concluded that 'three first-class men will be necessary to conduct a forensic investigation of the banks and the Customs and Excise in Cork'. He asked William Cosgrave to consider three people but 'don't announce anything until I return'.[701] He and Dalton also travelled the 30 miles to Macroom, where Collins met Florence O'Donoghue, who was in the IRA but was neutral in the Civil War.[702] The first phase of the Civil War was over, O'Donoghue wrote. He and many others recognised at this point that the IRA/Republicans could not win and that Collins came south searching for peace.[703] Collins was desperately trying to bring the war to a close, as well as to offer some face-saving agreement to the leaders on the other side. It is thought that he asked O'Donoghue how to stop the war and to mediate for him. After lunch at the Imperial, they headed out to review the military in Cobh and then returned to Cork in the early evening.

Collins's party left the Imperial Hotel, Cork, at 6.15am on Tuesday 22 August. That day, the convoy included the following:

- A motorcyclist, Lt John 'Jeersey' Smyth (from Enniscorthy). He was shot in the neck while helping to move Collins's body, but continued with the column.

- A Crossley tender under the command of Cmdt Seán (Paddy) O'Connell (he said the Act of Contrition in Collins's ear), with Capt. Joe Dolan, Capt. Peter Conlon, Sgt Cooney, John O'Connell (the driver)[704] and eight riflemen.[705]

- Collins and Emmet Dalton in a yellow Leland Thomas Straight Eight touring car. The driver was English-born Pte Michael Smith Corry and the reserve driver was M. Quinn.

- A Rolls Royce Whippet armoured car (ARR 2), the *Slievenamon*. Jim Wolfe was the driver, Jimmy 'Wiggy' Fortune the co-driver. The Vickers machine-gunner on the armoured car was John (Jock) McPeak. (He deserted on 2 December 1922 with Billy Barry and Pat and Mick O'Sullivan and took the armoured car to the IRA; he said that he did it for a woman. He was arrested in Glasgow in July 1923 and was imprisoned in Portlaoise, where he went on an hunger strike.) Cooney and Monks were the other members of the armoured car crew.

About 8am the convoy went through Macroom towards Béal na mBláth, where it stopped to get directions, then through Crookstown and on to Bandon, where Collins briefly met in Lee's Hotel with Major-Gen. Seán Hales, O/C of the Free State forces in west Cork. It is thought that Gen. Hales was informed of a meeting that Collins intended to have with Civil War neutrals in Cork that evening, and of his meeting with O'Donoghue and others the day before, and they discussed how an end to the war could be achieved. The convoy stopped for lunch at Callinan's Pub in Clonakilty. (See Seán Hales, Ormond Quay, Dublin 7.)

In the afternoon the convoy went to Rosscarbery. Collins had a drink in the Four Alls pub (owned by his cousin Jeremiah) at Sam's Cross, where he declared: 'I'm going to settle this thing. I'm going to put an end to this bloody war.' But there is no sign that he was open to compromise. 'Clearly any hope he had of settling the Civil War would not be done at the expense of the Treaty.'[706]

(There is a sign over the pub door showing four pictures with the following inscriptions:

I rule all [king]
I pray for all [bishop]
I fight for all [croppy boy]
I pay for all [farmer].)

Collins told his brother Johnny that he would 'go further with the British government once there was peace here'. His principal aim was to end the Civil War. He said: 'The British have given up their claim on us. When we begin to work together we can help those in the northeast.'[707]

On the way back, the party passed by the burnt remains of Woodfield and Collins pointed to the rugged stone walls. 'There,' he said to Dalton, 'There is where I was born. That was my home.' Still, Collins was as happy as Dalton had seen him. 'He was able to let himself go, and also I think he felt things were now moving his way. He didn't say much as we travelled along the flat road towards Bandon.' He appeared lost in 'the myriad thoughts of a crowded and successful day'.[708]

The convoy left the Eldon Hotel in Skibbereen at 5pm and headed back to Cork. Collins met his great friend John L. Sullivan on this journey.[709] The convoy detoured around Clonakilty because of a roadblock and stopped at Lee's Hotel (now the Munster Arms) in Bandon for tea. (It has never been fully explained why they returned the same way they came out in the morning; when the anti-Treaty forces left Cork city, however, they blew up most of the bridges and cut most of the roads, so there were few passable ways to travel in County Cork.) There, again, he met Gen. Hales, who was the brother of Tom Hales, by coincidence a member of the ambush party. 'Keep up the good work! 'Twill soon be over,' was Collins's parting salute to Hales.[710] On the road out of Bandon, Collins said to Dalton: 'If we run into an ambush along the way, we'll stand and fight them'. Dalton said nothing.

In the early morning, the ambush party had met in Long's Pub (owned by Denis 'Denny the Dane' Long, who was the 'lookout' for Collins's party as it passed through Béal na mBláth). The men who assembled at Béal na mBláth were not a column but officers trained in guerrilla warfare who gathered to hold a pre-arranged important staff meeting. When Florence O'Donoghue met with the surviving members of the IRA/Republicans in 1964, they said that they were unaware that Collins was in the area until that morning.[711] The plan to ambush the party was decided on as part of the general policy of attacking *all* Free State convoys rather than the desire to ambush *this* convoy specifically. They saw the opportunity to overpower an enemy convoy on its return journey and they decided to take up the challenge.[712] The IRA/Republicans stopped a Clonakilty man, Jeremiah O'Brien, who was taking a cartload of empty mineral bottles to Bandon. They commandeered his cart and took off one of the wheels, blocking the road. They knew that this, in combination with the mine they were placing in the road, would cause the convoy to stop abruptly. The ambush party remained in place all day but there was no action. In the late afternoon they received a message that Collins's party was in Bandon; as it was thought unlikely that the convoy would come through Béal na mBláth a second time, they began to disassemble the mine and evacuate the position.

The ambush party originally numbered between 25 and 30, according to varying sources. Some men stayed all day; others came and went as the day wore on. Those there at one time or another included Dinny Brien, Pat Buttimer (after waiting all day, he left the ambush site and walked towards Newcestown, and was not there when shots were fired), John Callahan, Dan Corcoran, Tom Crofts, Jim Crowley, Seán Culhane, Liam Deasy, Bill Desmond, Bobs Doherty, Mike (O') Donoghue, Sonny Donovan, Charlie Foley, Tom Foley (he collected the gelignite which had been taken for the mine and was hidden in John Lordan's house), Shawno Galvin, Tom Hales (O/C of the original ambush party), Daniel Holland (O/C Cork 1st Battalion), Jim Hurley, Seán Hyde, Jim Kearney (an engineer, he helped set the mine), Pete Kearney (O/C Cork 3rd Battalion), Tom Kelleher (Cmdt Gen. 1st Southern Division, he fired the warning shot alerting the others that the convoy was approaching), John Lordan (the gelignite for the mine was taken from its hiding place in his house), Con Lucey,

Jeremiah Mahoney, Con Murphy, Joe Murphy, John O'Callahan (the Cork 1st Battalion Engineer, he was in control of the mine which was buried in the road and was also the only Republican casualty in the ambush), C. O'Donoghue, Denis (Sonny) O'Neill (from Maryborough, Co. Cork, who was to provide covering fire to retreating IRA ambush members), Jim Ormond, Tadhg O'Sullivan, Bill Powell, Tim Sullivan (an engineer, he helped set the mine) and Paddy Walsh.[713]

The ambush took place at Béal na mBláth (between Macroom and Crookstown, about ten miles outside Bandon) just before sunset, at 7.30pm.[714] When the first shots were fired, Dalton ordered 'Drive like hell'. Collins countermanded the order and yelled 'Stop, we'll fight them'.

Collins and Dalton first fired from behind the armoured car, and then Collins shouted 'There—they are running up the road'. The Lewis machine-gun in the armoured car jammed several times, and whenever it did the IRA/Republicans took advantage of the lull in firing to move their positions. Collins ran about fifteen yards up the road, dropped into a prone firing position and continued shooting at the IRA on the hill. Dalton said that he then heard the faint cry 'Emmet, I'm hit'. He and Cmdt Seán O'Connell ran over to where Collins was lying face down on the road, and found a

... fearful gaping wound at the base of his skull behind the right ear. We immediately saw that General Collins was almost beyond human aid. He could not speak to us. ... O'Connell now knelt beside the dying, but still conscious, Chief whose eyes were wide open and normal, and whispered into the ear of the fast sinking man the words of the Act of Contrition. For this he was rewarded with a light pressure of the hand. ... Very gently I raised his head on my knee and tried to bandage his wound, but owing to the awful size of it this proved very difficult. I had not completed this task when the big eyes quickly closed and the cold pallor of death overspread the General's face. How can I describe the feelings that were mine in that bleak hour, kneeling in the mud of a country road not twelve miles from Clonakilty, with the still bleeding head of the Idol of Ireland resting on my arm.[715]

Later Dalton said:

it was a very large wound, an open wound in the back of the head ... and it was difficult for me to get a 'First-Field-Aid' bandage to cover it, you know when I was binding it up. It was quite obvious to me, with the experience I had of a ricochet bullet, it could only have been a ricochet or a 'dum-dum'.[716]

The ambush was over in approximately 30 minutes; darkness had fallen before it ended, and so it was impossible to get off an aimed shot. No one in the IRA/Republican party was fully aware that Collins had been shot or that the convoy had suffered any losses. It was only when Shawno Galvin came back to Béal na mBláth that they got the first report of any casualties.

Who shot Michael Collins?

- Pete Kearney thought that he did.
- Shawno Galvin said that he did.
- Sonny O'Neill was reported to have said that he did.
- Mike Donovan said that he saw the man who did.
- Jimmy Ormond fired directly at him and said that he saw him fall.
- Bobs Doherty heard (or fired) a shot and said that he saw him fall.
- Joe Murphy thought that he might have.

The latest research indicates that Denis (Sonny) O'Neill apparently fired the fatal shot,[717] but that is not certain.[718]

Born in 1888 in Timoleague, Co. Cork, O'Neill was one of five brothers who were all active during the War of Independence and the Civil War. He had served as a mounted constable in the RIC and fought as a marksman for the British Army in France during World War I before being discharged after he was shot in the arm. Upon returning home he joined the IRA/Volunteers and was considered a prized intelligence asset, as he had free access to the RIC Depot, Dublin Castle and various British Army clubs. Another file written by an army intelligence officer in December 1924 described O'Neill as 'a first class shot and a strict disciplinarian'. A separate memo the same month described him as 'undoubtedly a dangerous man'. According to his pension application, O'Neill cited his presence at the Béal na mBláth ambush in west Cork, but he did not say that he was the one who actually shot Collins. He said that he was introduced to Collins in 1920 and was given over to a number of handlers close to Collins to pass on information. He also said that he met Collins on a second occasion in 1921 after being given a message to pass to him in connection with negotiations in London.[719] At the start of the Civil War, O'Neill took the anti-Treaty side and joined the IRA/Republicans.

Describing the day of the ambush, O'Neill said that they were about to abandon the ambush when they heard Collins's party approaching. In discussing the ambush with Jim Kearney, O'Neill said 'I used the wrong bullet'. 'What do you mean?' asked Kearney. 'It was a dum-dum,' said O'Neill. (O'Neill told Kearney the next day that 'I dropped him with one of these' [a dum-dum bullet he had captured from the Black and Tans].[720] O'Neill never admitted publicly that he had shot Collins.) After the Civil War he went on the run for years, never staying long in the same house, and then settled in Nenagh, Co. Tipperary. He became an election agent for de Valera in the

1932 election, and then a peace commissioner and a director of elections for Sinn Féin and Fianna Fáil. He died in 1950.

Many questions remain concerning the ambush, including whether Collins was hit by a ricochet bullet. There is agreement that the wound to Collins's head was 'large and gaping' but disagreement as to whether there was an entry wound and an exit wound. This has led to several different theories:

- that Collins was hit from behind by one of the IRA/Republicans who were just coming onto the scene;
- that a member of his own party killed Collins, either with a close-range bullet from a handgun or with a bullet from the armoured car;
- that the fatal wound was caused by a ricochet bullet;
- that a bullet fired by Sonny O'Neill (or another IRA/Republican) killed Collins.

The best evidence indicates the one IRA/Republican who said immediately after the ambush that he had shot Collins: 'I dropped one man'[721]—Sonny O'Neill.

The current monument at the roadside of Béal na mBláth is on the opposite side of the road to where Collins was hit and about 40 yards toward Bandon from where he fell.

On the way into Cork City, Dalton stopped the convoy at a church in Cloughduv. Obtaining directions to the priest's house, they knocked on the door and the curate, Fr Timothy Murphy, came to the railing. Seeing that Collins was beyond hope, he turned to get the sacred oils; Cmdt O'Connell mistook this for a refusal of his ministry and pointed a pistol at him, but Dalton knocked it away.

As they approached Cork City they stopped at the Sacred Heart Mission at Victoria Cross. Here Fr O'Brien administered the Last Rites to Collins. Then the convoy headed back to the Imperial Hotel, where Dalton, Cmdt O'Connell, Sgt Cooney and Lt Gough asked Major-Gen. Dr Leo Ahern to take charge of the body.

Dr Ahern first examined Collins's body when it was brought to the Imperial Hotel, and then at Shanakiel Hospital. He was the first doctor to examine the body and pronounced Collins dead. His examination found a large, gaping wound 'to the right of the poll. There was no other wound. There was definitely no wound in the forehead.'[722]

From the hotel Collins's body was taken to Shanakiel Hospital in Cork, escorted by Cmdt O'Connell and Cmdt O'Friel.[723] Dr Michael Riordan was detailed by Dr Ahern to examine and prepare the body, and they conducted the autopsy. Dr Christy Kelly was present during a thorough second examination later and confirmed a huge wound on the right side behind the ear, with no exit wound.[724] In contrast, Dr Patrick Cagney, a British surgeon in the British army during the war who had a wide knowledge of gunshot wounds and who examined the body still later, confirmed that there was an entry wound as well as a large exit wound.[725]

Eleanor Gordon, matron of Shanakiel Hospital, and nurse Nora O'Donoghue cleaned and attended to Collins's wounds and also later testified as to the nature of the wounds. His body was first taken to room 201 and then, after the autopsy, to room 121, where Free State soldiers guarded it until it was taken to the ship for transport to Dublin.

In the afternoon, undertakers from Cronin & Desmond Funeral Service performed their duties. Fr Joseph Scannell, army chaplain, and Fr Joe Ahern recited the funeral prayers.

A steamship, the SS *Classic* (later known as the SS *Kilbarry*), left Penrose Quay in Cork and brought Collins's body to Dublin. Gen. Dalton sent this telegram from the Cork GPO to the Dublin HQ:

CHIEF OF STAFF

DUBLIN

COMMANDER-IN-CHIEF SHOT DEAD IN AMBUSH AT BEALNABLATH NEAR BANDON 6.30 [*sic*] TUESDAY EVENING WITH ME, ALSO ONE MAN WOUNDED. REMAINS LEAVING BY CLASSIC FOR DUBLIN TODAY WEDNESDAY NOON. ARRANGE TO MEET. REPLY DALTON.[726]

Because of the downed telegraph lines, the message was transmitted via shortwave radio to Waterville, cabled from there to New York, and then back to Dublin via London.

As the vessel sailed down the channel from Cork it passed the assembled remaining British vessels, upon the decks of which the British sailors mustered and saluted while the *Last Post* was played.[727]

Although Éamon de Valera was within a few miles of Béal na mBláth on the day Collins was killed and had hoped to meet him, no plan had been made. De Valera had no involvement in the ambush; he had little political influence on the IRA at the time, and no military influence at all. Moreover, by this time he was trying to bring the Civil War to a halt. Liam Deasy had spoken with de Valera the night before, and de Valera's position was that, having made their protest in arms and as they could not now hope to achieve a military success, the honourable course was for the IRA/Republicans to withdraw. Deasy explained that there were over a thousand men in the area and they would not agree to an unconditional ceasefire. Next day de Valera went to Long's pub, where his efforts to achieve a ceasefire were rejected again. The most reliable evidence indicates that he also tried to prevent the ambush but was rebuffed by the

IRA/Republicans. Liam Lynch, O/C of the IRA in the south-west, had specifically given orders that de Valera's attempts to put a stop to hostilities should not be encouraged. Deasy met with de Valera again and explained to him that the men billeted in this area would consider Collins's convoy as a challenge that they could not refuse to meet.[728] Despite rumour and innuendo, there is no evidence that de Valera was involved in the planning or the ambush being laid for Collins. Later de Valera was quoted as saying 'A pity. What a pity I didn't meet him', and 'It would be bad if anything happens to Collins, his place will be taken by weaker men'.[729]

On the morning of 23 August Richard Mulcahy, as chief of staff, issued the following message to the army:

> Stand calmly by your posts. Bend bravely and undaunted to your task. Let no cruel act of reprisal blemish your bright honour.
>
> Every dark hour that Collins met since 1916 seemed but to steel that bright strength of his and temper his brave gaiety. You are left as inheritors of that strength and bravery.
>
> To each of you falls his unfinished work. No darkness in the hour: loss [sic] of comrades will daunt you in it.
>
> Ireland! The Army serves—strengthened by its sorrow.[730]

Hannie Collins, with whom Michael lived when he first went to London in 1906, had long been planning a holiday in Ireland in August. On the morning of 23 August she went to work at the post office in West Kensington. As she was about to enter her office she was stopped, taken into the superintendent's room and told that there was a rumour that her brother had been killed. She said that she was not surprised—during the night she had had a premonition that he had been killed. 'I know how unhappy he had been for so long—At the moment of death the load went … from his mind, so it went from mine.'[731]

She went to see her friends John and Hazel Lavery but they were not home, so she went to board the Irish boat-train at Euston Station. (The Laverys had already gone to Ireland, where Sir John was painting.) Winston Churchill, having been told of Hannie's distress by the Laverys' butler, reserved a compartment for her and paid her travelling expenses. A newspaper reporter at Euston recorded that 'Miss Collins, dressed from head to foot in black, was seen off by a lady friend. She was a calm but pathetic figure. She travelled alone.'[732]

George Bernard Shaw wrote to Hannie:

> Don't let them make you miserable about it: how could a born soldier die better than at the victorious end of a good fight, falling to the shot of another Irishman—a damned fool but all the same an Irishman who thought he was

fighting for Ireland—'a Roman to a Roman' ...

I met Michael for the first and last time on Saturday last, and I am very glad I did. I rejoice in his memory and will not be so disloyal to it as to snivel over his valiant death.

So tear up your mourning and hang up your brightest colours in his honour; and let us all praise God that he had not to die in a snuffy bed of a trumpery cough, weakened by age, and saddened by the disappointments that would have attended his work had he lived.

In Dublin, Collins's remains were taken to St Vincent's Hospital, where Dr Oliver St John Gogarty embalmed the body and had Sir John Lavery paint Collins's portrait. Albert Power sculpted the death-mask.

Collins's body was taken to the chapel in St Vincent's on Thursday 24 August, and then late that evening to Dublin City Hall for the public lying-in-state until Sunday evening.

Collins's great friend Batt O'Connor went to the City Hall to pay his last respects:

Early on the following morning I was standing beside his bier, alone; gazing fondly with a breaking heart upon all that was left of the grandest character I have ever known. I must draw a veil over the anguish of that morning.

If I were asked what I considered were the traits of character in Michael Collins which impressed me most, I would say, first, his amazing courage, and next, his close-mindedness. There was something in his manner which gave him the power or charm of imbuing those in close touch with him with a share of both those qualities. One could not feel fear in his company. His coolness was infectious. If it were suggested to him that he should not do a certain thing because of its dangerous nature, he would unhesitatingly start to carry it out. I believe he did so, not from any spirit of bravado, but to give us some of his own supreme confidence; to prove to us that nothing was too dangerous to do, if it was done with coolness, self-control, and steady resolution.

Perhaps the most remarkable thing about him was what I have called his close-mindedness, and I mean by that his power to keep his own counsel. He had very little to say about the things that happened. Striking, dramatic things were happening every day planned by him, or staged by the enemy for his capture. Yet nobody had less to say about them than Michael Collins. There were no notes of exclamation. He referred to them, if at all, in a word or two. It was not that he was not stirred by the events of the living drama of which he was the chief actor and hero, but that he had schooled himself to a habit of silence upon which not only his own life and the lives of others depended, but the success of the struggle in which we were engaged. But when he spoke, his words were plain, direct, and to the point. We could rely unquestioningly on their accuracy, whether he were describing something which had taken place, or were giving instructions how some action was to be carried out. Nothing could be more remote from the habit of mind of Michael Collins than to show any kind of brag or boasting in his speech. On the contrary, if he referred at all to what was being done and his own part in the fight, he did so with an air, as it were, of brushing it aside. Yet all the time, without thinking about it, we knew that he was the life and soul of the struggle. We knew that without him our fight would have been the fight of a handful of untrained and practically unarmed men against the enormous army of a mighty Empire. It was his brain and character—his indomitable will, his unerring judgment, his courage, and his matchless energy—in a word, the splendid genius of one young Irishman—which wiped out our inequalities, gave us strength of spirit for strength of numbers, the weapons of superior resourcefulness to make good the deficiency in our arms.

It was not that he practised any false modesty. He was too honest for that. He did not undervalue what was being done any more than he overvalued it. But it was not the time for gloating; nor for regretting. There was no time to weep, and the time had not yet come to rejoice. 'Get on with the work', was his watchword. Unconsciously, we modelled ourselves upon him. At least, so far as our lesser natures would allow. It was a proof of our admiration; one of the ways in which we expressed our worship of him. So there was very little loose talk.

We got on with the work.[733]

On Sunday evening Collins's body was taken to the pro-cathedral, where it remained under guard overnight. His funeral Mass was offered there on Monday by Dr Michael Fogarty, bishop of Killaloe, assisted by several other bishops.[734]

The gun-carriage on which the casket was transported to Glasnevin Cemetery had been borrowed from the British and had been used in the bombardment of the Four Courts in June. The Free State government specially purchased four black artillery horses from the British to pull the caisson to Glasnevin.

Collins's death was never officially registered; there was no inquest and no formal, independent autopsy. It was said that many papers relating to Collins's killing were taken from Portobello Barracks and burned by the order of Minister for Defence Desmond FitzGerald before the Fianna Fáil government took over in 1932. Collins died intestate, leaving an estate of £1,950.9s.11d, which passed to his brother Johnny.

At Collins's funeral in Glasnevin on Monday 28 August, Gen. Richard Mulcahy, who would take Collins's place as commander-in-chief of the army, delivered the oration:

Our country is today bent under a sorrow such as it has not been bent for many a year. Our minds are cold, empty, wordless, and without sound. But it is only our weaknesses that are bent under this great sorrow that we meet with today. All that is good in us, all that is strong in us, is strengthened by the memory of that great hero and that great legend who is now laid to rest.

We bend today over the grave of a man not more than thirty years of age, who took to himself the gospel of toil for Ireland, the gospel of working for the people of Ireland, and of sacrifice for their good, and who had made himself a hero and a legend that will stand in the pages of our history with any bright page that was ever written there.

Pages have been written by him in the hearts of our people that will never find a place in print. But we lived, some of us, with these intimate pages; and those pages that will reach history, meagre though they be, will do good to our country and will inspire us through many a dark hour. Our weaknesses cry out to us, 'Michael Collins was too brave'.

Michael Collins was not too brave. Every day and every hour he lived he lived it to the full extent of that bravery which God gave to him, and it is for us to be brave as he was—brave before danger, brave before those who die, brave even to that very great bravery that our weakness complained of in him.

When we look over the pages of his diary for 22nd August, 'Started 6.15am. Macroom to Ballineen, Bandon, Skibbereen, Rosscarbery, Clonakilty', our weakness says he tried to put too much into the day. Michael Collins did not try to put too much into the day. Standing on the little mantelpiece of his office was a bronze plaque of President Roosevelt of the United States, and the inscription on it ran, 'I wish to preach, not the doctrine of ignoble ease, but the doctrine of strenuous life, the life of toil and effort, of labour and strife; to preach that highest form of success that comes to the man who does not shrink from danger, hardship or bitter toil, and who, out of these, wins the splendid triumph'.

Unless the grain of corn that falls to the ground dies, there is nothing but itself in it, but if it dies it gives forth great fruit. Michael Collins' passing will give us forth great fruit, and Michael Collins' dying will give us forth great fruit. Every bit of his small grain of corn died, and it died night and day during the last four or five years.

We have seen him lying on a bed of sickness and struggling with infirmities, running from his bed to his work.

On Saturday, the day before he went on his last journey to Cork, he sat with me at breakfast writhing with pain from a cold all through his body, and yet he was facing his day's work for that Saturday, and facing his Sunday's journey and Monday's journey and his journey on Tuesday. So let us be brave, and let us not be afraid to do too much in the day. In all that great work, strenuous it was, comparatively it was intemperate, but it was the only thing that Michael Collins was intemperate in.

How often with a shout he used to get out of bed in the morning at 5 or 6 o'clock crying, 'All the time that is wasted in sleep', and would dash around the room, or into some neighbouring room where some of us lay in the hope of an hour or two's sleep, and he would clear all the blankets off us, or would pound vigorously at the door which prudence had locked.

Crossing the square of the barracks on the Saturday morning that I mention, he told of his visit to one of the barracks in the South on his first trip there, and of finding most of the garrison in bed at 10 o'clock; and thinking of all the lack of order, lack of cleanliness, lack of moral strength and efficiency that goes with this particular type of sloth, and of all the demoralisation following on the dissatisfaction that one has with one's self all the day that starts with an hour's disadvantage. 'Oh', he said, 'if our fellows would only get up at 6 o'clock in the morning'.

Yes, get up to read, to write, to think, to plan, to work, or like Ard Riogh hÉireann long ago, simply to greet the sun. The God-given long day fully felt and fully seen would bring its own work and its own construction. Let us be brave, then, and let us work.

'Prophecy', said Peter, who was the great rock, 'is a light shining in the darkness till the day dawn.' And surely 'our great rock' was our prophet and our prophecy, a light held aloft along the road of 'danger of hardship or bitter toil'. And if our light is gone out it is only as the paling of a candle in the dawn of its own prophecy.

The act of his, the word of his, the look of his was day by day a prophecy to us that loose lying in us lay capabilities for toil, for bravery, for regularity, for joy in life; and in slowness and in hesitancy and in weariness half yielded to, his prophecies came true in us.

And just as he as a person was a light and a prophecy to us individually, he looked to it and wished that this band of brothers, which is the Army, will be a prophecy to our own people. Our Army had been the people, is the people, and will be the people. Our green uniform does not make us less the people. It is a cloak of service, a curtailer of our weakness, and an amplifier of our strength.

We are jealous for his greatness. Words have been quoted as being his last words; Michael Collins is supposed to have said the fragile words, 'Forgive them'. Michael Collins never said these words, 'Forgive them', because his great big mind could not have entertained the obverse thought, and he knew those around and worked with him that they, too, were too big to harbour in their minds the obverse thought.

When Michael Collins met difficulties, met people who obstructed him, and worked against him, he did not turn aside to blame them, but facing steadily ahead, he worked bravely forward to the goal he intended. He had that faith in the intensity of his own work that in its development and in its construction he would absorb into one homogeneous whole in the nation, without the necessity for blame or for forgiveness, all those who differed from and those who fought against him.

He is supposed to have said, 'Let the Dublin Brigade bury me'. Michael Collins knows that we will never bury him. He lies here among the men of the Dublin Brigade. Around him there lie forty-eight comrades of his from our Dublin battalions. But Michael Collins never separated the men of Dublin from the men of Kerry, nor the men of Dublin from the men of Donegal, nor the men of Dublin from the men of Cork.

His great love embraced our whole people and our whole Army, and he was as close in spirit with our men in Kerry and Donegal as he was with our men in Dublin. Yes, even those men in different districts in the country who sent us home here our dead Dublin men—we are sure he felt nothing but pity and sorrow for them for the tragic circumstances in which they find themselves, knowing that in fundamentals and in ideals they were the same.

Michael Collins had only a few minutes to live and to speak after he received his death wound, and the only word he spoke in these few minutes was 'Emmet'. He called to the comrade alongside, the comrade of many fights and many plans, and I am sure that he felt in calling that one name that he was calling around him the whole men of Ireland that he might speak the last word of comradeship and love.

We last looked at him in the City Hall and in the small church in Vincent's Hospital. And, studying his face with an eager gaze, we found there the same old smile that met us always in our work. And seeing it there in the first dark hour of our blow, the mind could not help travelling back to the dark storm-tossed Sea of Galilee and the frail barque tossed upon the Waters there, and the strong, calm smile of the Great Sleeper in the stern of the boat.

Tom Ashe, Tomás MacCurtain, Traolach MacSuibhne, Dick McKee, Mícheál Ó Coileáin, and all you who lie buried here, disciples of our great chief, those of us you leave behind are all, too, grain from the same handful, scattered by the hand of the Great Sower over the fruitful Soil of Ireland. We, too, will bring forth our own fruit.

Men and women of Ireland, we are all mariners on the deep, bound for a port still seen only through storm and spray, sailing still on a sea full 'of dangers and hardships, and bitter toil'. But the Great Sleeper lies smiling in the stern of the boat, and we shall be filled with that spirit which will walk bravely upon the waters.[735]

The British press acknowledged Collins's part in the struggle for Irish freedom. The *Daily Chronicle* called him a 'young and brilliant leader'. The *Evening Press* described his death as a 'staggering blow'.[736] The *Daily Telegraph* wrote:

He was a bitter and implacable enemy of England while the English garrison remained in Ireland and Ireland was not free to govern itself in its own way. ... The dead man, without a doubt, was the stuff of which all great men are made.[737]

The *London Daily Sketch* editorialised thus:

The hand that struck down Collins, guided by a blinded patriotism, has aimed a blow at the unity of Ireland for which every one of her sons is fighting. Collins was probably the most skilled artisan of the fabric of a happier Ireland. Certainly he was the most picturesque figure in the struggle; and in the rearing of a new State a popular ideal serves as the rallying point to draw the contending elements. The death of Collins leaves the ship of the Free State without a helmsman.

Other sons of Ireland have risen from lowliness to eminence in the struggle, but Michael Collins, by his valour, his sufferings, his elusiveness during the more turbulent periods of the past, and by his own personal charm, bound a spell round the popular imagination and wove a romance which endeared him to his friends and inspired respect in his foes.

... Since the historic hour in the early morning of December 6 ... the progress of the new State has been dogged and delayed by a malignant Fate.

The next phase in the life of the Free State is veiled by the tragedy of the present. The helmsman has gone at a moment when no haven can yet be decried.

What is to happen now?[738]

Alice Stopford Green had been closely involved in the Howth gunrunning. In 1918 she moved to Dublin, where her house at 90 St Stephen's Green became an intellectual centre. She supported the pro-Treaty side in the Irish Civil War and was among the first nominees to the newly formed Seanad in 1922, serving as an independent member until her death in 1929. An admirer of Collins, she wrote:

No leader before him in Ireland has borne away so immense a love and eternal devotion as has been given to him. Their grief will know no consolation. ... All alike now strive together to carry on the work from which he was torn so piteously ...

Ireland has had many sorrows, but she has had no one like this. ... Our progress can be no longer along the hills of high adventure, but on the level ground where men less gifted must needs follow.

Dr Brigid Lyons Thornton, who often worked as a courier for Collins and was one of his most dependable agents within the 'establishment' in her role as a doctor, said of him:

There were many, many fine people but Michael Collins was like a colossus among them. He did so much for the country. He was so unselfish, so courageous, and at the grimmest moments, so cheerful, so reassuring. Children loved him and he always spared them a moment. He used to jot down the little stories of the de Valera children. A man who loves children loves all mankind. There was nothing Michael Collins spared himself to bring peace to the unfortunate people of Ireland—not even his own young life.[739]

Seven years later, Winston Churchill would pay homage to his one-time military enemy and political ally. He admired Collins but evidently continued to be ignorant of the ideals that had driven him and that permanently separated the two men:

He was an Irish patriot, true and fearless. His narrow upbringing and his whole life had filled him with hatred for England. His hands had touched directly the springs of terrible deeds. We hunted him for his life, and he had slipped half a dozen times through steel claws. But now he had no hatred of England.[740]

Shane Leslie wrote the following lines:

What is that curling flower of wonder
As white as snow, as red as blood?
When Death goes by in flame and thunder
And rips the beauty from the bud.

They left his blossom white and slender
Beneath Glasnevin's shaking sod;
His spirit passed like sunset splendour
Unto the dead Fianna's God.

Good luck be with you, Collins,
Or stay or go you far away;
Or stay you with the folk of fairy,
Or come with ghosts another day.

Brendan Behan's mother, Kathleen, nicknamed Michael Collins her 'Laughing Boy'. She and her first husband had both served in the Rising. In 1935, when he was twelve years old, Brendan wrote a lament for the 'Laughing Boy'.

> 'Twas on an August morning, all in the dawning hours,
> I went to take the warming air, all in the Mouth of Flowers,
> And there I saw a maiden, and mournful was her cry,
> 'Ah what will mend my broken heart, I've lost my Laughing Boy.
>
> So strong, so wild and brave he was, I'll mourn his loss too sore,
> When thinking that I'll hear the laugh or springing step no more.
> Ah, cure the times and sad the loss my heart to crucify,
> That an Irish son with a rebel gun shot down my Laughing Boy.
>
> Oh had he died by Pearse's side or in the GPO,
> Killed by an English bullet from the rifle of the foe,
> Or forcibly fed with Ashe lay dead in the dungeons of Mountjoy,
> I'd have cried with pride for the way he died, my own dear Laughing Boy.
>
> My princely love, can ageless love do more than tell to you,
> Go raibh maith agat for all you tried to do,
> For all you did, and would have done, my enemies to destroy,
> I'll mourn your name and praise your fame, forever, my Laughing Boy.'[741]

Appendix VI

Addresses outside Dublin

Annamoe, Co. Wicklow: Home of Robert Barton, cousin of Erskine Childers. On 10 November 1922, Childers was spending the night here when Free State soldiers raided the home. In the early morning the troops seized Childers as he drew his small pistol, a present from Michael Collins. He did not fire it, as the ladies present would have been endangered by an exchange of shots—he was always a most chivalrous man. He was charged and tried by military court on 16 November for the offence of possession of an automatic pistol without lawful authority. He was sentenced to death and executed by firing squad at Beggar's Bush Barracks on the morning of Friday 24 November. It was too dark to proceed at the appointed hour, so they had to wait until there was sufficient light. He smoked, chatted and shook hands with the firing party, disclaiming any feeling of ill-will against anyone, and died most bravely.[742] (See Beggar's Bush Barracks, Dublin 4; Bushy Park Road, Dublin 6.)

Ballinamuck, Co. Longford (near Granard): Legga Chapel. On 3 March 1918 Collins made a speech here which was 'calculated to cause disaffection':

> You will not get anything from the British Government unless you approach them with a bullock's tail in one hand and a landlord's head in the other … Do not participate in raids for arms of useless old shotguns and old swords—go where you will find arms that will be of some use to you [RIC barracks], and we call on the Irish Volunteers to defend their arms until death.[743]

This speech led to a warrant for his arrest, sworn out on 11 March 1918, to return him 'to the locality pending his trial at assizes'. He was arrested outside his Bachelor's Walk office on 2 April 1918 and was taken to the DMP's Brunswick Street Station. After he was transported to Longford he was brought before the magistrate, M. Johnson, who 'took depositions and returned the accused for trial at the next assizes for the county. The accused, who was very abusive and insulting, refused to recognise the court or give bail and was remanded to Sligo Gaol.' He was conveyed to Sligo Gaol on 10 April 1918 and released on 20 April. The magistrate granted the adjournment but required bail of £50 and two sureties of £25 each. Michael Doyle of Main Street, Longford, and Michael Cox (a cousin of Brigid Lyons) of Ballymahon Street, Longford, stood surety for Collins.

The official charges, noted as the 'Outrage' on RIC forms, were:

Unlawfully incited to riot.

Unlawfully incited the public to raid for arms.

Unlawfully incited forcible entry.

Unlawfully incited to assault on persons.

Unlawfully incited to steal arms.[744]

A change of venue to the Londonderry Assizes issued on 28 June 1918, with his appearance scheduled for 17 July 1918, but Collins did not appear. A bench warrant was executed on that date. As a consequence of this, his description was inserted in the Dublin Castle newspaper *Hue and Cry* under County Longford. After that, Collins was officially on the run and remained so until the Truce.[745]

Booterstown, Co. Dublin: Kevin O'Higgins's home after the Civil War. He was the nephew of Timothy (T.M.) Healy. O'Higgins was shot just outside his home while walking to Mass on 10 July 1927. Eoin MacNeill was the first to reach him. His killers were Archie Doyle, Timothy Coughlin and Bill Gannon. It was thought that 'in part it was prompted by motives of revenge, in part by an impetus to reactivate the parent body [IRA]. The Civil War was five years away; the country was beginning to enjoy peace. It was time to stir things up again.'[746]

Barnsbury Hall, Islington, London: In November 1909, Collins was sworn in here as a member of the IRB by his fellow post office worker Sam Maguire (a Protestant, originally from Dunmanway) and Pat Bolton. Maguire went on to become the treasurer for the IRB of London.

> Sam Maguire, who was the key man in England for the purchase of arms for the Republican Army Headquarters here, reported daily in person to the office. It was to him that the couriers from the various Republican government departments in Ireland reported. He was at Euston Station every morning to meet the couriers before he went to his own office. He was a Post Office employee and knew Michael Collins very well. It was he who moulded him and initiated him into the whole idea of military republicanism. He was a wonderful man. I don't think he took five minutes of the twenty-four hours for himself. He spent it all working in some way for Ireland. He was from West Cork somewhere near the Skibbereen area. He was a Protestant. Although I worked with him over a period of a couple of years I did not know that. He was transferred to Ireland after the Treaty and worked in the Post Office in the Castle. He was a devotee of Michael Collins and always dealt directly with him.[747]

Now the Anna Scher Theatre.

Brixton Prison, south London: After the murder of his friend Tomás MacCurtain, the lord mayor of Cork, on 20 March 1920, Terence MacSwiney was elected lord mayor. On 12 August 1920 he was arrested in Cork for possession of seditious articles and documents, as well as possessing a cipher key to the British codes. He was tried by summary court martial and sentenced to two years' imprisonment on 16 August. He was imprisoned in Brixton Prison, where he died on 25 October after 74 days on hunger strike.[748]

MacSwiney's ordeal set off riots in Brixton, and also spurred the GHQ staff in Dublin into action—or at least into considering action. Their first idea was to take hostages, to be exchanged for MacSwiney's release. In early September, Collins told Art O'Brien to 'go ahead with finding that place for a hostage'. A week later O'Brien wrote back about the 'apartments'. As MacSwiney's condition worsened, this became an assassination plot: Lloyd George's death in exchange for MacSwiney's. The rest of the cabinet were soon included as well. Gunmen were sent from Dublin and Cork to prepare several elaborate plans; some stayed for months. MacSwiney died on 25 October. When Seán McGrath went to Ireland for his funeral, for 'the first time I saw Michael Collins really upset. He talked then about shooting in England.'[749] Nevertheless, no one was shot. The killings were eventually, quietly, called off, presumably after it was realised that they would be politically counter-productive. These, however, were only the first of a series of Collins's plots over the following months directed at the British government. All followed essentially the same pattern. High-profile targets would be selected, their movements tracked and their kidnapping or murder arranged; all were called off in the end. The proposed victims included Lloyd George (again), his cabinet (again, in a separate plan), MPs of several parties (to be 'arrested' and shot if Sinn Féin TDs were harmed), Basil Thomson, the head of the Special Branch, Field Marshal Henry Wilson, the chief of the Imperial General Staff, and Lord FitzAlan, the lord lieutenant of Ireland. The initiative, the plans and the men usually came from Dublin. Collins was generally aware of or involved in planning these escapades (and was always kept informed by 'his' organisation men in Britain) but never acted alone, contrary to his reputation as 'the man who won the war'. In fact, it was he who was responsible for curbing over-zealous gunmen and for shutting several of the operations down. Cathal Brugha, the minister for defence, on the other hand, was responsible for some of the most bloodthirsty proposals and pursued them ardently and independently, even moving to London to oversee them.

Brompton Road, London: Brompton Oratory: The Church of the Immaculate Heart of Mary. Throughout the autumn of 1921, while he was staying in 15 Cadogan Gardens during the Treaty negotiations, Collins attended daily Mass here. Although he had written anti-clerical articles when he was a young man in London, and he did mock some in the GPO when they asked for a priest, he often wrote of his religion to Kitty Kiernan. On 20 October he reported that he 'got to bed at 3 a.m, but woke at 7.15 for the 8 a.m. Brompton Oratory Mass'. Kitty sent him a relic of the Little Flower (Thérèse of Lisieux was later canonised in 1925), for which he thanked her and vowed: 'I'll pray to her'. Around that time he also started to sign off his letters with 'May God bless my Kit and keep her safe', whereas before his valediction was 'love' or 'Slán leat'. In an undated letter, probably in late October, he mentioned that he had just knelt down and said the Rosary for her. In addition to the Oratory, he sometimes popped into St Mary's Church in Hammersmith Road (probably *en route* to visiting his sister Hannie), especially to light a candle for Kitty. On the morning the Treaty was signed (6 December) Collins finished business at 2.15am. 'To bed about 5,' he wrote, 'and up to go to Mass and didn't (need I say it) forget your candle.' His plans, he added, were 'as yet uncertain. I don't know how things will go now. But with God's help we have brought peace to this land of ours.'[750]

15 Cadogan Gardens, London: Collins used this house during the Treaty negotiations, from 11 October to 6 December 1921. Upon his return here on the morning of 6 December, he wrote his prophetic letter to John O'Kane:

> Think—what have I got for Ireland? Something which she has wanted these past seven hundred years. Will anyone be satisfied with the bargain? Will anyone? I tell you this—early this morning I signed my own death warrant. I thought at the time how odd, how ridiculous—a bullet might just as well have done the job five years ago.[751]

Collins's entourage stayed here, including a security detail: Liam Tobin, Emmet Dalton, Tom Cullen, Joe Dolan, Joe Guilfoyle, Ned Broy and Seán MacBride.

Now an exclusive primary school, Hill House International Junior School.

Cadogan Place at Hammersmith Road: Church of St Mary. Collins occasionally attended Mass here, although he usually attended daily Mass at Brompton Oratory.

Carrick-on-Suir, Co. Tipperary: On 16 March 1922 de Valera spoke here, saying: 'If the Treaty was accepted, the fight for freedom would still go on; and the Irish people, instead of fighting foreign soldiers, would have to fight the Irish soldiers of an Irish government set up by Irish men. They will have to march over the dead bodies of their own brothers. They will have to wade through Irish blood. There are rights which may be maintained by force by an armed minority even against a majority.'[752]

Chancery Lane, London: Sinn Féin headquarters in London.

5 Cromwell Place, South Kensington: Home of Sir John and Lady Hazel Lavery. A neighbour was Winston Churchill, whom Lavery taught to paint. During the Treaty negotiations Collins was a frequent guest, and many of the discussions between Collins and Churchill took place here. Some have claimed that Lady Lavery and Collins had an affair, but others have considered it nothing more than an older woman infatuated with a younger man. After the Treaty was signed, Lady Lavery continued to act as a go-between; since much of her correspondence with Collins was in code, some called her a spy.

Croydon Airfield, England: Croydon was an airport in south London, straddling the boundary between what are now the London boroughs of Croydon and Sutton, and was the main airport for London at the time. During the Treaty negotiations Emmet Dalton was in charge of security for Collins, and he was so concerned that he arranged for an airplane to be ready at the airfield here to fly Collins to Ireland 'at a moment's notice' if necessary. Dalton engaged two flying officers, Jack MacSwiney and Charlie Russell, as pilots. Russell had spent some time in Canada, so he secured a four-passenger Martinsyde Type A-1 Mark II airplane, posing as a representative from the Canadian Forestry Department for the purpose. The plane was never used and became part of the nucleus of the Irish Army Air Corps.[753]

10 Downing Street, London: On 14 July 1921, de Valera went to London to negotiate the terms of the Treaty conference with Lloyd George. He brought with him Arthur Griffith, Austin Stack, Count Plunkett, Robert Barton and Erskine Childers. On the night before they left, Collins argued that he should be included in this delegation, but de Valera refused. It was an acrimonious meeting and left both parties upset. Next day, de Valera had the first of four meetings with Lloyd George at 10 Downing Street.

Lloyd George told his secretary Geoffrey Shakespeare that he 'listened to a very long lecture on the wrongs done to Ireland starting with Cromwell, and when I tried to bring him to the present day, he went back to Cromwell again. It reminded me of a circus round-about when I was a boy.'[754]

From the outset it was de Valera's intent to show as little of his hand as possible. The formal British proposals were delivered to the Irish on 18 July: a 26-county dominion; defence restrictions limiting the size of the Irish army; a prohibition on an Irish navy; insistence on free trade; 'an allowance for the full recognition of the existing powers and privileges of the Parliament of Northern Ireland'. The next day, de Valera indicated that he would accept a dominion but that the British offer was not of unfettered dominion status. He also indicated that Northern Ireland must be represented within the all-Ireland parliament, otherwise the only alternative would be for the 26 counties to be a republic. 'This means war,' replied Lloyd George.

De Valera dismissed the British proposals and called Lloyd George's bluff, as he was not seen to be carrying the British proposals home with him. He wrote to Prime Minister Jan Smuts of the Union of South Africa: 'I was greatly disappointed with the British government's proposals. They seem quite unable to understand the temper of our people, or appear not to have the will to realise the opportunity that is now presented to them.' On 31 July, de Valera asked Smuts to continue to be involved:

My dear General Smuts:–

I received your letter of July 29th, and have had two conversations with Mr Lane. He will tell you that the proposals of the British Government will not be accepted here.

Unless the North East comes in on some reasonable basis no further progress can be made. An Ireland in fragments nobody cares about. A unified Ireland alone can be happy or prosperous.

To the British Commonwealth group and to Britain itself Ireland would readily become friendly, but it is only in freedom that friendship could come. To the principle of national self-determination our people are devotedly attached, for they recognise in it a principle vital to the peace of the world. The Republic is the expression of that principle in their own regard. These then they will not readily abandon, but they are prepared to make great sacrifices in other directions.

The question of procedure and form as distinguished from substance are very important, as I pointed out to you. The British do not seem to realise this at all. Your understanding of the situation is particularly necessary at that end therefore.

I am very glad you are able to remain on for a little time longer. I know how your people are clamouring for you, but the cause you are assisting is a truly great and worthy one.

Very sincerely yours,

Eamon de Valera[755]

(See Treaty debates, Mansion House, Dawson Street, and Earlsfort Terrace Dublin 2.)

On 21 January 1922 James Craig, prime minister of Northern Ireland, met Collins in London in order to resolve the impasse between North and South and to attempt to promote some kind of co-operation between the two governments. Churchill had brought the two together and the meeting went surprisingly well. The result was the first **Craig–Collins Pact**.[756] This agreement contained three main clauses. The first—and the one which was shortly to become the object of much bitter criticism amongst northern nationalists—enshrined Craig's suggested rationalisation of the Boundary Commission. This proposed to exclude the British-appointed chairman, envisaged in the Treaty clause, in favour of mutual agreement between North and South. Secondly, Collins undertook to end the 'Belfast Boycott' in return for a pledge by Craig 'to facilitate in every possible way the return of Catholic workmen—without tests—to the shipyards', subject to the revival of trade. The final clause stipulated that the two governments would endeavour 'to devise a more suitable system than the Council of Ireland' (provided in the 1920 Act) for 'dealing with the problems affecting all-Ireland'. This reflected the Unionist leader's desire to remove the last shadowy link between the two parts of Ireland. The two leaders also agreed that a further meeting would be held shortly in Ireland to discuss the vexed question of political prisoners. The pact's language appeared to recognise that there were now two governments in Ireland. Craig certainly believed this to be the case. Collins did not—or maybe changed his mind—and the agreement fell apart within a few days in a welter of renewed violence. Craig returned to Belfast and met such a wall of opposition over the boundary that he was forced to renege. (See Dame Street, City Hall, Dublin 2.)

In March 1922 another meeting was arranged, and Collins outlined the position of the Provisional Government going into the meeting:

> The Provisional Government have never asked for a meeting, but, true to their consistent desire for peace and harmony in all Ireland, they will now, as hitherto, put no difficulties in the way of such a meeting and will accept the British Government's invitation.
>
> The Provisional Government have been always ready, as the British Ministers well know, to do everything in their power to bring about a peaceful arrangement with Sir James Craig.
>
> On several occasions they have gone far to meet him, and he cannot deny that they have never broken any undertaking that they have given him. Unfortunately Sir James Craig has not been so meticulous in his attitude towards us. He has neither kept his undertakings with us nor done anything to meet us on the several points of controversy.
>
> At this very moment it is no harm to retrace briefly events since the signing of the Pact between Sir James Craig and myself.
>
> This pact was agreed to between us and signed on Saturday 21st January. I undertook by it to get the Belfast Boycott discontinued immediately and Sir James Craig undertook 'to facilitate in every possible way' the return of Catholic workmen who had been expelled from the Belfast shipyards and various other concerns.
>
> It will be remembered that my part of the agreement was carried out at once, and Northern commercial men have been free to enter and sell their wares in any corner of the twenty-six counties since, and I have not heard of one case in which they have been interfered with.

On the other hand, what has Sir James Craig done? It is exactly nine weeks to-day since that agreement was signed, and in all that time not one single expelled Nationalist or Catholic worker has been reinstated in his employment, nor has Sir James Craig, to my knowledge, taken any action whatever or even publicly expressed a wish that his part of the agreement should be honoured.

There are at present 9,000 workers, all citizens of Belfast, who have been driven out of their employment solely because they happen to hold different political and religious views from the 'Sam M'Guffins of the crowd'.

Sir James Craig has not kept his honourable undertaking with me.

On Tuesday last, a Deputation, seven in number, representing the expelled workers, met Sir James Craig, but got nothing from him but a bare statement to the effect that he could not keep his undertaking with me owing to the difference existing from the Boundaries question and the tense feeling created by other causes.

Feeling over the Boundaries question and over the horrible Belfast atrocities, which have revolted the civilized world, is just as keen and just as tense in all parts of Ireland, inside and outside the Six Counties, as it is in the portion of the Six Counties which supports Sir James Craig, but still that did not prevent our part of the agreement being honoured.

If this is the way Sir James Craig intends to honour any obligations he may incur with us, meetings will, I am afraid, serve no good purpose, as he obviously looks upon such agreements as mere scraps of paper.

His accusation that we were promoting trouble in Belfast is an indication of his defined attitude of hostility towards our people and his disregard for the simple truth of the situation. 'Southern Ireland', he declared in a speech in the Belfast Parliament on the 15th instant, 'desires to coerce Ulster citizens and stir up strife here by bombing our citizens and sniping at them, and carrying on their warfare to the best of their ability.' This is, of course, an absolute fabrication, but I must say that I consider it an outrageous statement for any man in Sir James Craig's position to make at any time, but especially at the present tense moment.

Sir Dawson Bates, Sir James Craig's Home Minister, told the Belfast Parliament on the same occasion that as soon as he took up office he ordered their constabulary to refuse to continue the liaison arrangements under the Truce. This was another clear indication of his attitude.

Our position with regard to the North-East corner, as I have stated earlier, has been consistently one of willingness to do all we can to effect peace in that portion of the country and to meet the objections and difficulties of Sir James Craig's party as far as we possibly can. We are always ready to attend every meeting where there is any likelihood of this object being attained, and in this spirit we have accepted the present invitation from the British Government.

But whilst hoping for the best, I can only say that I see no way out of the Northern impasse until Sir James Craig radically alters his present inimical attitude towards the Government of Ireland and towards the helpless minority in Belfast.[757]

On 30 March 1922, a second 'formal' pact was agreed between the British, Northern Ireland and Provisional governments. It reiterated earlier promises made in January but additionally called for a cessation of IRA activity in Northern Ireland, and promised to sort out the border issues through the Boundary Commission. It also made detailed provision for policing by a mixed Catholic/Protestant police force. The pact was essentially a blend of the proposals of the Belfast Catholic businessmen and those of the colonial secretary, with certain amendments. The first clause carried the dramatic headline 'Peace is today declared', while the second contained a pledge by the two Irish governments to co-operate to restore peaceful conditions. The third and most important clause concerned the reorganisation of the police in Belfast. This enshrined the Belfast Catholic suggestion of a scheme of 'mixed Special police' in the city, and provided for the establishment of a Catholic police advisory committee to recommend suitable Catholic recruits. Subsequent clauses provided for non-jury courts and the formation of a joint conciliation committee to prevent outrages. In the sixth clause Collins undertook that IRA activity would cease in the six counties. The seventh provided that the representatives of North and South should meet before the 'Ulster month' began to run to consider the larger issues of Irish unity and the Boundary Commission. This pact, too, was shortly ignored.[758]

Collins wrote to Craig on 27 April, outlining the objections to the performance by the Northern Ireland government, and the second Craig–Collins Pact was at an end:

> The Rt Hon. Sir James Craig,
> Premier, Northern Ireland.
> Your letter of 25th inst. reached this Office late last night. I did not see it until it had already appeared in the Press, consequently I wired you as follows:–
> 'YOUR LETTER ONLY REACHED MY OFFICE LATE LAST NIGHT. CONSIDER PUBLICATION WITHOUT REFERENCE TO ME THE GREATEST WANT OF COURTESY. IN VIEW OF THIS PUBLICATION I PROPOSE HANDING ALL FUTURE COMMUNICATIONS TO THE PRESS AT THE TIME OF DESPATCH.'
> Your letter under acknowledgement so astonishes me by its assertions and general tone that I think it well to set out here my wire of 22nd April, to which, I take it, your letter is a reply:–
> 'ALL HERE ARE AGREED THAT IT IS IMPOSSIBLE TO MAKE ANY

FURTHER PROGRESS UNTIL VITAL CLAUSES OF THE AGREEMENT ARE FULFILLED BY YOU. CONSIDER YOUR ATTITUDE WITH REGARD TO PRISONERS MOST UNSATISFACTORY AND ENTIRELY OUT OF ACCORD WITH LETTER AND SPIRIT OF AGREEMENT. YOUR FAILURE TO AGREE TO INVESTIGATION OF CASES UNDER CLAUSE 5 MOST UNREASONABLE.'

It will be observed that I have raised two main issues in this wire, namely:–

(a) Release of prisoners, and

(b) Failure to agree to investigation under Clause 5.

In your reply you carefully avoid these issues, and I must insist that it is no answer to these assertions to give a long list of vague and indefinite charges, backed up with few dates and little evidence of any kind. You commence your letter by stating that your Government has conscientiously endeavoured to carry out the spirit and the letter of the Agreement. How can you maintain this assertion with regard to the points I make in my wire?

Clause 10 of the Pact states that 'The two Governments shall in cases agreed upon between the signatories arrange for the release of political prisoners in prison for offences before the date hereof'. In pursuance of this Clause I have caused the release of the Specials arrested at Clones, and furnished you, some weeks ago, with a list of 170 persons detained by your Government for purely political causes. So far you have not released one single person on this list.

Clause 5 of the Pact makes provision for a 'Committee to be set up in Belfast of equal numbers, Catholic and Protestant, with an independent chairman, preferably Catholic and Protestant alternating in successive weeks, to hear and investigate complaints as to intimidation, outrages, etc. Such Committee to have access to the heads of the Government. The local press to be approached with a view to inserting only such reports of disturbances etc. as shall have been considered and communicated by this Committee.'

What has your attitude been on this important matter? You have continually and emphatically refused my repeated request to you to get this Committee established and functioning. ...

... Your entire letter has apparently been drafted with a view to keeping attention off of the daily routine of atrocities and murders which continue uninterrupted in the seat of your Government. There is not space here to detail all the abominations that have taken place in Belfast since the signing of our Pact, and I quite understand your desire to draw the attention of civilisation away from them. This much though, I must say—the ink on our Pact was scarcely dry when on the 1st inst. loads of armed Specials, uniformed and ununiformed, in Crossley Tenders and Whippet Cars, invaded during Curfew hours, Stanhope Street and

Arnon Street, where 90% of the inhabitants are Catholics, and entered the houses of many of the Catholics. The result of this armed incursion was that four Catholics, one of them was an old man, and three of whom had fought on the British side in the European War, were tortured and murdered in their beds and in the presence of their wives.

You refer to an alleged 'cowardly ambuscade'. As you appear to be confident as to the identity of the culprits in this case, I trust you will assist the Provisional Government in bringing them to justice.

You make the extraordinary statement that certain Catholics have destroyed Catholic property in your area. Is this statement also intended to assist the big British Press combine which has arranged to do propaganda for you? If not, I trust you will furnish us with particulars of these remarkable Catholics.

... Since the Pact the following awful list of murder, arson, and general crime has been committed in the very centre of your seat of Government:–

From 1st April, 1922 to date:

Catholic[s] killed	24
Catholic[s] wounded	41
Attempted murders	29
No. of (RC) houses burned and looted	75
No. of (RC) families homeless	89
No. of (RC) persons homeless	400
No. of (RC) houses bombed	5
No. of Protestants killed	11
No. of Protestants wounded	34
No. of Protestants' houses looted and burned	11

... This is, you will admit I am sure, an appalling record of crime to happen in the chief city of any Government which calls itself civilised, especially after having entered into an honourable agreement with us in which you undertook to restore ordered conditions in your area.

I would suggest to you that it would be much better for the peace of your area, and the general welfare of our country, if you devoted your energies in co-operating with us in the true spirit of the Agreement, towards establishing civilised conditions in Belfast.

Micheál O Coileáin[759]

Dún Laoghaire, Co. Dublin: Royal Marine Hotel. Collins and Kitty Kiernan were dancing here when Joe O'Reilly came to tell them of the Truce in July 1921.

Sir John and Lady Hazel Lavery stayed here when they came to Ireland so that

John could work on his painting on the subject of the Civil War in August 1922. They were in residence when Collins was killed.

Dungarvan, Co. Waterford: In Dungarvan on 16 March 1922 de Valera said: 'The Treaty ... barred the way to independence with the blood of fellow Irishmen. It was only by Civil War after this that they could get their independence ... If you don't fight today, you will have to fight tomorrow; and I say, when you are in a good fighting position, then fight on.'[760]

Eaton Square, London: Assassination of Field Marshal Sir Henry Wilson. In 1918 Sir Henry Wilson served as chief of the British Imperial General Staff. He continued to hold this position after the war, a time when the British Army was being sharply reduced in size. In July 1919 Wilson accepted promotion to field marshal after Churchill had offered him a choice of either promotion or a peerage.[761]

Throughout the War of Independence, the British were clearly out of touch with the temper of the Irish people, as was evident from some of the ideas proposed in the British cabinet. In 1920 the GOC in Ireland, Gen. Sir Nevil Macready, proposed to take on the IRA with more mobile forces, but Wilson said that Macready's plan was useless. Wilson pressed the British 'to collect the names of Sinn Féiners by districts; proclaim them on church doors all over the country; and shoot them whenever a policeman is murdered; pick 5 by lot and shoot them!'[762]

After Bloody Sunday, Wilson pleaded with Churchill for the imposition of martial law, and that was finally done on 10 December 1920. After retiring from the army in December 1921, he served briefly as a member of parliament, and also as security adviser to the Northern Ireland (Unionist) government.

Wilson, an unrepentant Imperialist and Unionist, thought the Truce and Treaty irresponsible. At the time he was acting as military adviser to the Northern Ireland government, and was a particularly close confidant of James Craig's. The Treaty of 6 December 1922 split the republican movement in Britain as thoroughly as in Ireland, with pro- and anti-Treaty camps rapidly being established on either side of an uncertain middle ground.

Thus was precipitated the assassination of Wilson on 22 June 1922 by Reggie Dunne, O/C of the London IRA, and another London veteran of the British Army, Joseph O'Sullivan.[763] Wilson had been trailed on a journey to unveil a war memorial at Liverpool Street Station, London. After the ceremony Wilson returned home, where O'Sullivan and Dunne shot him as he was walking between the taxi that he had just left and the door of his residence in Eaton Square.[764] Besides Wilson, two policemen and a civilian were wounded whilst both men tried to escape, but they were eventually caught and arrested. O'Sullivan had lost a leg in World War I, so an escape by foot seems incomprehensible. Moreover, the lack of planning was apparent: Dunne and

O'Sullivan had no escape system set up, had to find and buy their own guns only a week before the shooting, and O'Sullivan had gone to work that day and the assassination was carried out on his lunch break.[765]

> Joe went in a straight line while I determined to intercept him [Wilson] from entering the door. Joe deliberately levelled his weapon at four yards' range and fired twice. Wilson made for the door as best he could and actually reached the doorway when I encountered him at a range of seven or eight feet. I fired three shots rapidly, the last one from the hip, as I took a step forward. Wilson was now uttering short cries and in a doubled up position staggered towards the edge of the pavement. At this point Joe fired again and the last I saw of him he [Wilson] had collapsed.[766]

The motive for Wilson's killing is not difficult to imagine. Seán Moylan recalled that Collins had often stated that Wilson was a thorn in his side and had repeatedly made the procurement of arms in Britain much more difficult. Dunne, like most Irish nationalists, was growing more and more outraged by the continuing attacks on Catholics in Northern Ireland and blamed Wilson, in his capacity as military adviser to the Northern Ireland government, for those attacks.[767] Nevertheless, while the motive may be suggested, who was ultimately responsible remains a more elusive question.

It has become accepted (although it was not known publicly at the time) that Collins had ordered his assassination some months previously.[768] British suspicions regarding Collins's involvement were suggested, as documentation mentioning Collins had allegedly been found on the arrested men.[769] Further, Joe Sweeney, the pro-Treaty military leader in County Donegal, recalled that Collins had informed him of his decision to order the shooting of Wilson. In addition, Sweeney stated that Collins seemed very pleased upon hearing the news that the order had been carried out.[770] Conversely, Emmet Dalton, one of Collins's closest confidants at the time, indicated that 'Collins was angry that the London IRA had taken an irresponsible attitude "at this time"'.[771]

Dorothy Macardle wrote that 'popular belief attributed the assassination to the IRB. It was thought Michael Collins ordered it.'[772] Margery Forester agreed:

> There can be little doubt that such an order [for Wilson's assassination] had been given, most probably by Collins, in pre-Treaty days. ... But Collins was not a man who absent-mindedly left execution orders unrevoked. It is infinitely more probable that, far from doing so, he renewed the order to Dunne shortly before it was carried out, when the Belfast pogroms were at their height.[773]

There is no clear and convincing evidence that Dunne and O'Sullivan were the tools of a conspiracy or of Collins in particular. Collins had briefed Dunne only two weeks before the assassination, but the results of that meeting are not known. Tim Pat Coogan, however, quotes the mother of a schoolfriend of his, Gearóid Johnstone, who worked as a courier for Collins when she was a young girl. Peig Ní Bhraonáin was given an assignment to take a dispatch to London in June 1922 by Pat Fleming. She was to meet 'a tall man called Tobin' at Euston Station. Later she thought that she had brought Liam Tobin the instructions to kill Wilson, though she never read the letter.[774] Further to this line of thinking connecting Collins with the assassination, Michael Hopkinson asserts that 'the testimony of many of those who were involved in the events suggests strongly that Collins was directly implicated'.[775]

Calton Younger ambivalently wrote:

[Dunne and O'Sullivan] carried out an ordered execution in exactly the same way that Collins's squad did on many occasions … though whether it was Collins who ordered the killing is still a matter for conjecture; what evidence there is certainly points to it. Even by a process of elimination it is difficult to see who else could have been responsible. At the time, the British Government blamed Rory O'Connor's men … but O'Connor stoutly denied that they had anything to do with it. If they had, they would have admitted it.[776]

Peter Hart, however, claims that the opposite is true:

Collins did not have much control over the IRA any more and would have needed an awfully good reason to arrange such a provocative murder at such a critical time. No such reason has ever been presented. And, since he showed no other signs of madness or bloodlust to give us an irrational explanation, we can acquit him of the charge.[777]

Wilson had been on previous IRA hit-lists (some were and some were not of Collins's devising), but so had many of Britain's military and political élite. His status as a target derived from widespread nationalist rage at the treatment of Catholics in Northern Ireland, whose government he vociferously defended. It has been posited that it was this, and probably also Dunne's deep desire to resolve his political and personal dilemmas through patriotic self-sacrifice, that drove the assassins to seek revolutionary justice.[778]

Ironically, while this is by far the best known and most controversial incident of the British IRA during that time, it might have been an isolated, even desperate, act carried out on the initiative of the killers alone.

At the time the British government, and particularly Churchill, blamed Rory

O'Connor and the IRA/Republicans who were holding the Four Courts and demanded that Collins take the 'necessary steps to take control' of that faction.[779] The British indicated that the Four Courts garrison was to blame and that Collins was not involved at all.[780] The British government was eager for action to be taken against the Four Courts garrison and therefore they readily placed the blame for this event solely on the shoulders of the anti-Treaty militants. Lloyd George wrote to Collins on 22 June and reiterated that unless the Free State government moved on O'Connor and his men in the Four Courts the British would be forced to do so. He wrote that:

> I am desired by His Majesty's Government to inform you that documents have been found upon the murderers of Field-Marshal Sir Henry Wilson which clearly connect the assassins with the Irish Republican Army [...] Other information has reached his Majesty's Government showing that active preparations are on foot among the Irregular elements of the IRA to resume attacks upon the lives and property of British subjects both in England and in Ulster. The ambiguous position of the Irish Republican Army can no longer be ignored by the British Government. Still less can Mr Rory O'Connor be permitted to remain with his followers and his arsenal in open rebellion in the heart of Dublin in possession of the courts of Justice [...] His Majesty's Government cannot consent to a continuance of this state of things, and they feel entitled to ask you formally to bring it to an end forthwith [...] I am to inform you that they regard the continued toleration of this rebellious defiance of the principles of the Treaty as incompatible with its execution. They feel that now you are supported by the declared will of the Irish People in favour of the Treaty, they have a right to expect that the necessary action will be taken by your Government without delay.[781]

(See King's Inns Quay, Four Courts, Dublin 7.)

It is conceivable that Collins was responsible for the assassination, but no solid evidence of this has come forth, with the exception of Joe Sweeney's conversation with Ernie O'Malley and a statement by Joe Dolan that Collins ordered Sam Maguire to carry out the execution and that O'Sullivan and Dunne decided to take the situation into their own hands.[782] Dunne and Maguire had met with both Collins and Rory O'Connor in Dublin just the week before the assassination. But many feel that Maguire was acting on his own or in concert with O'Connor in the Four Courts. Ernest Blythe, however, thought that Collins had no involvement and put the blame on anti-Treaty elements who were out to make trouble for Collins.[783]

In any event, Collins could have wanted to rescue Dunne and O'Sullivan, whether he had any responsibility for the act or not. Collins did, in fact, moot a rescue, but disorganisation and division prevented it from being attempted.[784]

The shooting of Sir Henry Wilson in London on the 22nd June 1922 is an incident around which a lot of speculation and controversy has established itself since then. The shooting, of course, was carried out by Reggie Dunne, who was O/C of the London Irish Volunteers at the time, and Joe O'Sullivan, another of the London Irish Volunteers, but the question of whether they were instructed to carry out this job and, if so, by whom, has given rise to a lot of argument since then, in view of the fact that this incident took place after the signing of the Treaty and the establishment of the Provisional Government.

My own memory of the various incidents surrounding this event is very clear. Though I may forget things that happened yesterday or last week, my memory around that time is very vivid. I knew nothing about the shooting before it occurred and I first learned of it, like everyone else, through the newspaper reports on the day following the shooting. I was then a Staff Captain in the National Army attached to the Military Intelligence Branch at Oriel House. Naturally, we all discussed the shooting, or the report of it that had appeared in the newspapers, but I don't think I spoke to anyone who knew any more about it than I did at the time.

Some time before the trial in London of Dunne and O'Sullivan—I can't remember just how long after the shooting that was, but it was definitely before the trial took place—I was instructed to report to Collins at his office in Portobello Barracks. I got this instruction from Liam Tobin during the daytime, and I reported forthwith to Portobello Barracks where I saw Collins. Collins was a man who wasted no words; he always spoke snappily and to the point. Having mentioned the shooting of Sir Henry Wilson, he immediately came to the point by saying that he wanted to effect a rescue of Dunne and O'Sullivan if at all possible. He said he wanted me to change into civilian attire immediately, report to Sam Maguire in London and there to see what could be done towards effecting a rescue at all costs. The idea was not that I should attempt the rescue immediately but that I should explore the possibilities and report back to Collins without delay. ...

... The rendezvous with Maguire was at Peele's public house in Fetter Lane, which is off Fleet St. That was the usual place where Maguire could be contacted. When I met Maguire, I discussed my mission with him, and I gathered from him that he already knew of the rescue project. He called over another man who was there at the time—Seán Golden, whom I already knew.

The idea we had in mind was that the two prisoners should be rescued while they were being conveyed from the prison to the Court or place of trial, or in course of their return to the prison, whichever happened more conveniently. It was not considered possible to effect a rescue from the prison or from the courthouse, but we did think it might be possible to overpower the escort and rescue the prisoners from the prison van on their way to or from the court. We investigated the route and all possible alternative routes from Wandsworth Prison to the courthouse, and I formed the opinion that a rescue would be feasible. I also got in touch with their solicitor, a Mr McDonald [*sic*], who conveyed the message to me to blow up the prison van sooner than let them hang. I wrote out a report to Collins on the spot, in company with Golden, giving all the details and showing how I thought the job might be done.

Then I came straight back to Dublin and reported to Collins immediately. It was about three days since I had left Dublin.

... but some time afterwards I met Sam Maguire—that was long after the execution of Dunne and O'Sullivan—and we discussed my last visit to him in London and my mission there. He told me that, subsequent to my visit, Tom Cullen had come over to London with apparently the mission from Collins of checking on my report. Whether Tom Cullen reported adversely on the possibility of carrying out the rescue or not, I do not know, but Sam Maguire remarked to me that the job could easily have been done if it had been left to me but that when Cullen came over, he could not see it the way I did and the attempt was consequently abandoned.[785]

J.H. MacDonald, Dunne's and O'Sullivan's solicitor, indicated that Dunne confessed that he had not intended to kill Wilson but rather that the shots were fired without prior arrangement, 'in the heat of the moment'.[786]

O'Sullivan and Dunne were hanged in London on 10 August 1922, and were initially buried in the prison yard at Wandsworth Prison. Both were reinterred in Deansgrange Cemetery, Dublin, in 1967.

Emmet Square, Clonakilty: There is a statue here of Collins in his most familiar speaking pose, with two fingers of his right hand tapping on his left hand. The statue was sculpted by Kevin Holland and dedicated on 22 August 2002, the 80th anniversary of Collins's death. It was unveiled by actor Liam Neeson, who played Collins in the eponymous movie.

Fetter Lane, off Fleet Street, London: The Shamrock Bar. This was Collins's favourite haunt while he lived in London. Like any lad in a big city for the first time, free from the restraints of rural life, he engaged in a period of hard drinking and nights on the town. It was also where he met Sam Maguire.

Frongoch Prison Camp, near Bala, north Wales: Frongoch internment camp in Merionethshire, Wales, was a makeshift place of imprisonment during the First World War. Until 1916 it housed German prisoners of war in an abandoned distillery and crude huts; in the wake of the Rising, however, the German prisoners were moved and it was used as a place of internment for approximately 1,800 Irish prisoners. The camp became fertile ground for the spreading of the revolutionary gospel, with inspired organisers such as Collins giving impromptu lessons in guerrilla tactics. Later the camp became known as the 'University of Revolution' or sometimes 'Sinn Féin University'.

There were two camps, North and South. The South Camp was a disused distillery divided into three parts: the building proper, yards and buildings adjoining, and a big field. The North Camp was a collection of wooden huts and a wired-in field. Outside the barbed wire, the soldiers' quarters were connected to the camps by muddy roads.

Collins was Irish Prisoner 1320 here, and became the leader of Hut No. 10. He smoked 30 cigarettes a day in Frongoch—he gave them up in 1920, after the Tans arrived, saying that he would not be a slave to anything.

Frongoch seemed one long row with warders, and Collins relished the conflict. The most important thing that occurred in Frongoch was the reorganisation of the Irish Republican Brotherhood. Collins played a major part in this, and to the backing of the IRB can be traced his sudden rise from a mere staff captain and ADC to Joe Plunkett in the Rising to his ascendancy within the whole revolutionary movement.

Furry Park, Killester: Home of Crompton and Moya (O'Connor) Llewelyn Davies. When Moya was eleven, her mother and three sisters died of poisoning after eating tainted mussels from a contaminated pool at the rear of their house in Blackrock. James Joyce used the story in *Finnegans Wake*. Her father, James O'Connor, was the centre of an IRB circle in Dublin, and she was a nationalist all her life.

In 1910 she moved to London, where she married Compton Llewelyn Davies, a man thirteen years her senior, and they became friends with Collins's sister Hannie. Collins met her about 1910 in London. The Davies were friends of John and Hazel Lavery and introduced Collins and his sister to them in 1913.

One of Collins's most effective couriers and sources, Moya was imprisoned during the War of Independence. She, Eileen McGrane and Patricia Hoey had been arrested here in March 1921. When one of Collins's offices was raided, papers with her name and address were found, leading to her arrest. The women were taken to Mountjoy Jail and held for two months, though no charges were brought against any of them.

It was said that Compton passed along names and addresses of the Cairo Gang to Collins. In any case, papers found in the raid incriminated him and he was dismissed from his post as solicitor-general at the GPO.

Moya was a very good driver and often used her car to smuggle guns. On 12 February Collins met Leslie Price here. She was one of his most important couriers to Cork. Collins gave her a load of guns, and she and Moya set off for Cork in Moya's car the next day to deliver them to Tom Barry's column. On 24 February Leslie and Moya delivered a smaller consignment of guns in the same way to Liam Lynch outside Mallow. Their next consignment was to Cork on 2 March, and they had to have a tyre puncture fixed by the Auxiliaries on their trip.[787]

Collins often stayed here. He ate dinner here on 17 August 1922 with the Laverys, Sir Horace and Lady Plunkett, Piaras Béaslaí, Christabel Pankhurst, George Bernard Shaw (this was the first occasion on which Shaw met Collins and to which he referred in his letter to Hannie after Collins's death), Joe O'Reilly and others. A man named George Dixon (formerly a marksman with the Connaught Rangers) was apprehended with a rifle. When he claimed that he wanted to kill Collins, he was taken by Collins's guards and shot.[788]

Moya was a fine writer and helped Collins with his book *The path to freedom*. She also ghost-wrote Charles Dalton's book *With the Dublin Brigade*, and Batt O'Connor's *With Michael Collins in the fight for Irish freedom*.

Granard, Co. Longford: Home of the Kiernan family. Catherine Brigid 'Kitty' Kiernan lived here, and Collins met her while staying in the family hotel as he was campaigning in spring 1917. Kitty's was a very comfortable merchant family, with five sisters and one brother. Her parents, Bridget and Peter Kiernan, enjoyed a happy marriage, and life in the Kiernan home was joyous until Kitty reached her teens. In 1907 one of her twin sisters died in her late teens, followed in 1908 by the deaths of both her parents within a couple of months of each other. The family was to be further devastated by the death in 1909 of the remaining twin sister. The Kiernan family owned the Greville Arms Hotel in the town, as well as a grocery shop, a hardware store, a timber and undertaking business and a bar. Around the corner from the hotel they operated a bakery that supplied the town and most of the surrounding countryside. All the family worked in the family enterprises in one capacity or another.

Nothing was too much to ask of the Kiernan family if it was 'for the cause'. Their hotel was an open house, they entertained and they accommodated the crowds on County Longford's great occasions. During the by-election campaigns of May 1917, Collins, his cousin Gearóid O'Sullivan and Harry Boland stayed at the family hotel. Boland was already courting Kitty.

On a later trip to the area, Collins gave the speech at Legga Chapel. (See Ballinamuck, Co. Longford.) For that speech he was arrested when he returned to Dublin.

Collins became besotted with Helen, Kitty's younger sister. When he was taken to jail in Sligo after his arrest, he asked Helen to visit him, which she did. When he found out that she was to marry Paul McGovern, he begged her not to do so. It was said that 'on the night before her wedding, Collins went to her hotel and begged her not to go through with the marriage, and that during the wedding speeches he shredded his handkerchief".[789] His premonitions were correct and McGovern deserted Helen shortly after she became pregnant. (In a quirk of fate, one of her grandsons is Barry McGovern, the actor who played Éamon de Valera in the RTÉ film *The Treaty* in 1992.)

Collins and Boland both stayed in Granard often, and even came to stay in the Kiernan's lakeside home. Kitty had continued her relationship with Harry Boland and he was set to ask her to marry him when de Valera asked him to accompany him to America in June 1919. Boland returned to Ireland in May 1920 and immediately went to Granard. He proposed to her later that year, and asked her to honeymoon in America. Kitty put him off, knowing that she did not want to marry him. By then her affections were split between Boland and Collins. On the day he left for America Harry wrote to her, telling her that he had spent the night before with Collins:

... as I had to catch the 7.35 am [train] I bade him goodbye, only to find him at Kingsbridge as fresh as a daisy to see me off. I need not say to you how much I love him, and I know he has a warm spot in his heart for me, and I feel sure no matter what matter our triangle may work out, he and I shall always be friends.[790]

From then until his death Collins was a frequent visitor to Granard, and the relationship bloomed in Boland's absence. Collins would ask her to come to Dublin, and they often stayed at the Grand Hotel in Greystones, or at the Shelbourne or Gresham in Dublin. She also stayed at Vaughan's Hotel or at his old home, the Munster Hotel in Mountjoy Square. Only when he returned again in late 1921 did Boland realise that things had changed irrevocably between him and Kitty, and with Collins.

On the night of 3 November 1920, eleven lorryloads of military entered Granard, sacked the town and burned the Greville Arms Hotel. All the family were arrested. The others were released overnight but Kitty was held for three days, and Collins was greatly upset. He was particularly angry with Seán MacEoin, who had had RIC District Inspecter Philip Kelleher executed in the hotel on 31 October, which precipitated the raid. After her release, and while the hotel was being rebuilt, Collins invited Kitty to Dublin. It was then that their relationship really blossomed.

Collins and Kitty became engaged on 8 October 1921.[791] On 14 October Kitty wrote: 'you are everything to me and surely you know it'. On 24 October she travelled to London to see Collins and her sister Maud. Boland wrote to her: 'I want to congratulate you. M [Mick] told me of your engagement, and I wish you long life and happiness. Ever yours, H. Boland.'[792] Collins gave her a single-stone engagement ring worth £60.

While the Greville Arms was being rebuilt, the Kiernans stayed in Omard House in Killnaleck, Co. Cavan, and later moved to a large flat over a shop on the New Road back in Granard.[793] It was well into 1922 before the hotel was rebuilt.

On the very day that Collins took over Dublin Castle from the British, 16 January 1922, he wrote to Kitty: '… I am as happy a man as there is in Ireland today'.

Originally 21 June 1922 was to be their wedding day—a double ceremony with Seán MacEoin. That was postponed, however, and Tuesday 22 August was the date that Kitty chose for their wedding, but Collins postponed it until 'later in the year'.

Gearóid O'Sullivan married Maud Kiernan on 10 October 1922. It was to have been a double wedding with Kitty and Michael. Kitty was the bridesmaid, but she was dressed in black.

Kitty married Felix Cronin in 1925. He was a member of the Free State Army and rose to the rank of general. Her first child was named Felix after his father, and her second son was named Michael Collins Cronin. Kitty died in 1945 of Bright's Disease (as did all her siblings), and she is buried in Glasnevin Cemetery. It is said that Gen. Cronin asked that their plot in Glasnevin be as close to Collins's grave as possible.

Greystones, Co. Wicklow: A fashionable resort about twenty miles south of Dublin. De Valera's family lived there while he was in the US.

De Valera was just sitting down to lunch to celebrate his wife Sinéad's birthday on 1 June 1919 when Collins sent a messenger to tell him that the arrangements to smuggle de Valera to the US required his immediate departure.

Between June 1919 and December 1920, while Éamon was in the US, Collins came out here weekly to bring the Dáil president's salary of £25 to Sinéad, and often stayed to play with their children.

Greystones, Co. Wicklow: Grand Hotel. This was where Kitty Kiernan frequently stayed when she came to the Dublin area. She and Collins often met here. Now La Touche.

22 Hans Place, London: During the Treaty negotiations, 22 Hans Place was the headquarters of the Irish Treaty delegation, and the main location for their secretaries and staff. The delegates who stayed here were Arthur Griffith, Charles Gavan Duffy, Éamonn Duggan and Robert Barton. Collins and his security detail stayed at 15 Cadogan Gardens.

In addition to the delegates, the secretaries to the conference stayed here: Erskine Childers, Diarmuid O'Hegarty, John Chartres and Fionan Lynch. There were four typists: Lily O'Brennan, Kathleen McKenna, Ellie Lyons and Alice Lyons. Desmond FitzGerald was the propaganda minister. Also staying in the house as chaperones were the wives of Éamonn Duggan and Fionan Lynch.

On the night the delegates arrived, 11 October 1922, on the pavement in front of the house were the whitewashed words 'Collins the murderer'.

It was at 22 Hans Place, at 11.15pm on 5 December 1921, that the delegates made the historic decision to recommend the treaty to Dáil Éireann. The negotiations finally closed with the signing of the Articles of Agreement at 2.20am on 6 December 1921.

Killarney, Co. Kerry: In a speech in Killarney on 18 March 1922 de Valera was quoted as saying: 'In order to achieve freedom, if our Volunteers continue, and I hope they continue until the goal is reached, if we continue on that movement which was begun when the Volunteers were started and we suppose this Treaty is ratified by your votes, then these men, in order to achieve freedom, will have, I said yesterday, to march over the dead bodies of their own brothers. They will have to wade through Irish blood … The people never have a right to do wrong.'[794]

T. Ryle Dwyer argues that:

From a careful reading of his actual words in Killarney, it is clear that de Valera was not personally threatening civil war. He was saying that such a conflict would almost inevitably ensue if the Treaty was ratified. The press argued that, whether he was foretelling or threatening civil war, it was essentially the same thing, but de Valera disputed this.[795]

King's Cross, London: On 25 April 1914 Collins was enrolled in the 'German' Gymnasium into Company No. 1 of the London Branch of the Irish Volunteers. His cousin, Seán Hurley, enrolled him. P.S. O'Hegarty signed his membership card.

Lincoln Prison, Lincolnshire, England: Following the 'German Plot' arrests in May 1918, Éamon de Valera was imprisoned here. Collins tried to arrange his escape for many months and finally a plan was set in January 1919. (See Mansion House, Dawson Street, 6 Harcourt Street, Dublin 2.) At the very time the First Dáil was meeting in January, Collins and Harry Boland arrived in England to help de Valera to escape. De Valera had asked another prisoner, Seán Milroy, to draw a postcard showing a drunken man with a giant key outside his hall door. The caption read: 'I can't get in'. The reverse side of the postcard depicted the same man in a jail a year later. He was peering through a keyhole and saying: 'I can't get out'. The drawings illustrated the exact measurements of the actual master key and keyhole in the prison doors. De Valera had obtained a wax impression of the key for Milroy to copy. The card was sent out to the relative of another trusted prisoner. From the postcard template, a key was fashioned in Dublin and, in the style of a comic book farce, sent inside a cake to de Valera in jail.

On the night of 3 February, de Valera, Milroy and Seán McGarry unlocked gate after gate with the key until they came to a small door in the outer wall. Collins and Boland, having cut through a perimeter fence, were waiting on the other side of the door with a duplicate key that they inserted from the outside. It snapped in the lock.

This was a moment of despair, but de Valera put his key into the lock from the inside and it pushed out the broken key and opened the door. Boland wrapped his fur coat around de Valera and put his arm on his shoulder to escort the lanky escapee past other 'courting couples' in the area of the prison.

Lisburn, Co. Antrim: Detective Inspector Oswald Ross Swanzy was shot outside a church here on 22 August 1920. Swanzy was one of those responsible for the murder of Thomas MacCurtain, lord mayor of Cork, on 20 March 1920 and one who was indicted for 'wilful murder' by the investigating jury. Collins had him traced to Lisburn and sent a special team to kill him. The man who fired the shots was Seán Culhane, and Dick Mulcahy was also present.[796]

Malahide Road: Winstonville. Collins often stayed overnight here.

6 Minford Gardens, Shepherd's Bush, London: Collins's first home in London when he moved there in 1906. He lived here with his sister Johanna (Hannie) until they moved to Netherwood Road.

Mount Merrion Avenue, Blackrock, Co. Dublin: 'Glenvar': de Valera's office from May 1921, raided by troops of the Worcestershire Regiment on 22 June 1921. He was arrested and taken from Dublin Castle to Portobello Barracks, but was released after one night. (See 112 Newgrange Road, Cabra, Dublin 9.)

5 Netherwood Road, Shepherd's Bush, London: Home of Johanna (Hannie) Collins, Michael's sister. Hannie said of Michael as a child: 'we thought he had been invented for our special edification'. Michael stayed with her here when he moved to London in 1906. He received a small salary of 15/- per week from the post office, and Hannie had to supplement this to feed the 'growing boy'. Like most London Irish, they mixed mainly with their compatriots rather than assimilating into English society and cultural influences. Michael wrote: 'I had Irish friends in London before I arrived, and in the intervening years I had made more friends among Irish residents in London. For the most part we lived our lives apart. We chose to consider ourselves outposts of our nation.' He always said that he hated everything English but he got on very well with English people.

Hannie encouraged his taste for literature, poetry, music and drama, and she tried to get him to go to the theatre when she could afford it.

15 St Helen's Road, Booterstown, Co. Dublin: Home of David Neligan; his DMP badge was No. 46. He left the DMP on 11 May 1920, but at Collins's request returned to become *The spy in the Castle*.[797] He joined the English Secret Service in May 1921 and became Agent No. 68, assigned to the district of Dalkey, Kingstown (Dún Laoghaire) and Blackrock. (See Bannon's Pub, 41 Abbey Street Upper, Dublin 1.) When Neligan joined the Secret Service, he was warmly congratulated by the British major, who shook his hand and said 'Try to join the IRA, my boy, try to join the IRA!' Neligan was so successful in convincing the British that he was on their side that he received pensions from the British as well as the Irish government: an old IRA pension, and pensions from the Irish police, the Irish civil service, the RIC and the British Secret Service.

Count Sevigne (alias Major Geary) was the head of the Secret Service at the time.[798] The oath that Neligan had to take upon being sworn into the Secret Service ended: 'If I fail to keep this Oath in every particular I realize that vengeance will pursue me to the ends of the earth, so help me God'.

Sam's Cross, about three miles from Clonakilty, Co. Cork: Collins's birthplace. There is a memorial to Collins here. **'Woodfield'** was the name given by Collins's mother to the new house she built in 1908.

When Collins returned to Ireland from Frongoch at Christmas 1916, he came back here. He walked the four miles from Clonakilty to find out that his grandmother, Johanna O'Brien, had just passed away. He spent three weeks in the area and was disappointed at the lack of enthusiasm for the Irish nationalist cause. After spending the time 'drinking Clonakilty Wrastler on a Frongoch stomach', he returned to Dublin early in 1917. There he found the nationalist 'spirit' a good deal more pervasive.

The Essex Division, under the command of Major Arthur Emmett Percival, burned the house on 16 April 1921 in reprisal for a recent raid on an RIC barracks at Rosscarbery. The British forced the neighbours to bring straw into the house and then light it. At the same time, Percival ordered all the farm's fowl to be rounded up and placed in one of the outbuildings, which was then burned. When Collins heard of the destruction of Woodfield, he said 'they knew how to hurt me'.

Johnny Collins was not there at the time of the burning, as he was attending a County Council meeting in Cork city. He was captured by the British, however, and imprisoned on Spike Island, where owing to medical neglect he lost the use of his right hand. His wife, Kate, had died in February, leaving eight children, and they were all displaced from the burnt house. Later he married their cousin Nancy O'Brien, who had worked for Michael in the GPO. (See GPO, Sackville Street Upper, Dublin 1.)

In April 1966 a monument to Collins was dedicated; a large boulder with a bronze roundel bearing Collins's profile sculpted by Séamus Murphy is the centrepiece. Tom Barry, who had worked for Collins during the War of Independence and had been very successful in the area, but who had taken the anti-Treaty side, was there at the dedication and said:

Let us leave it that each of us, like I did myself, believed in the correctness of our choice. I concede that those who were on the opposite side believed that their decision was the right one, too.

Woodfield itself has been landscaped as the Michael Collins Memorial Centre, dedicated by President Patrick Hillery on 14 October 1990. There is a bust on the property by sculptor Francis Doyle Jones, donated by the family of Joe McGrath.

Skerries, Co. Dublin: Grand Hotel. Harry Boland, sharing a room with Joe Griffin, was shot here on 30 July 1922 and taken to St Vincent's Hospital, where he died after surgery.[799]

Collins had written to him earlier in July:

Harry—it has come to this! Of all things it has come to this.

It is in my power to arrest and destroy you. This I cannot do.

If you will think over the influence which has dominated you it should change your ideal.

You are walking under false colours. If no word of mine will change your attitude then you are beyond all hope—my hope.[800]

(See Leeson Lane [on St Stephen's Green], St Vincent's Hospital, Dublin 2.)

Soloheadbeg, Co. Tipperary: Soloheadbeg is about two miles outside the town of Tipperary. On 21 January 1919 (the same day as the first meeting of the First Dáil in Dublin) council workers Edward Godfrey and Patrick Flynn, guarded by two armed RIC constables, Patrick MacDonnell and James O'Connell, were carrying gelignite to the local quarry. Volunteers led by Seán Treacy and Dan Breen lay in wait for the convoy and shot dead both constables, who had attempted to ready their rifles. The rebels then rapidly withdrew, taking the gelignite. The four leading officers of the 3rd Tipperary Brigade IRA, Treacy, Breen, Seán Hogan (then only seventeen) and Seámus Robinson, went on the run. Five other Volunteers joined them in the ambush: Tadhg Crowe, Mick McCormack, Paddy O'Dwyer (Hollyford), Michael Ryan (Donohill) and Seán O'Meara (Tipperary), the latter two both cycle scouts.[801]

As a result of this action, south Tipperary was placed under martial law and declared a Special Military Area under the Defence of the Realm Act.

Richard Mulcahy deplored this attack. In his opinion, it was an 'ill judged action with regrettable and unwarranted features'. Collins, however, generally approved this type of action, and thought that the IRA/Volunteers could use all legitimate methods against the 'soldiers and policemen of England'.

Collins had been in touch with many units outside Dublin, all of whom were clamouring for arms. The quality of leadership varied, and some units, rather than obtaining armaments through raids on police stations, relied on Dublin to supply them. (GHQ had prohibited raids on private homes since March 1918.) Some officers who called on Collins to plead their cases wished that they had never made the journey. After a blistering tirade, they would be sent scurrying back to their battalions, resolved to overcome their shortage problem in their own way or in the way he 'suggested'. Nevertheless, Collins did recognise the fact that some units were unable, for reasons other than inertia or ineptitude, to equip themselves adequately, and so he set up secret munitions and bomb-making factories in order to meet demand. Many units, such as the Third Tipperary Brigade in this case, helped themselves.

This 'raid' is generally considered to mark the beginning of the War of Independence.

While Treacy, Breen and Robinson often came to Dublin and were used by Collins, most at GHQ thought them uncontrollable and a kind of nuisance, and did not like their tactics.

Stafford Detention Barracks, Staffordshire, England: After the Rising, Collins arrived here on 1 May 1916 as Irish Prisoner 48F, address 16 Rathdown Road, North Circular Road, Dublin. For the first three weeks all the prisoners were held in solitary confinement.

Thurles, Co. Tipperary: On 17 March 1922 de Valera repeated his earlier bloody imagery and added that if the IRA 'accepted the Treaty and if the Volunteers of the future tried to complete the work the Volunteers of the last four years had been attempting, they would have to complete it, not over the bodies of foreign soldiers, but over the dead bodies of their own countrymen. They would have to wade through, perhaps, the blood of some of the members of the Government, in order to get Irish freedom.'[802]

Upperchurch, Co. Tipperary: The arrival of the Black and Tans (the Tans) in March 1920 changed the entire complexion of the war. These 'irregulars' were established as a section of the Royal Irish Constabulary (RIC) and first appeared in the village of Upperchurch, Co. Tipperary. The British government needed more troops in Ireland to maintain its position, and turned to unemployed demobilised soldiers from World War I. The name came from their uniforms: black tunics and dark tan or khaki trousers, some with civilian hats, but most with the green caps and black leather belts of the RIC. The name was given to them by Christopher O'Sullivan, editor of the *Limerick Echo*, who wrote that they reminded him of a pack of hunting dogs in Limerick: 'Judging by the colour of their cap and trousers, they resembled something one would associate with the Scarteen Hunt'.[803] The Scarteen Black and Tans were well known for their savagery, as were the soldiers.

Collins viewed the Black and Tans and the terror that followed them (and the Auxiliaries) as a sort of mixed blessing. The Auxiliaries were former officers with the RIC rank of 'Temporary Cadets'. They were feared much more than the Tans by the Irish. Clearly such fear drove any doubting nationalists into the arms of Sinn Féin, and Collins took full advantage of that. 'Apart from the loss which these attacks entail, good is done as it makes clear and clearer to people what both sides stand for.'[804]

By November 1920, some 5,498 recruits had been added to the ranks of the RIC: 4,501 Black and Tans and 997 Auxiliaries. Ultimately, there were approximately 12,000 Black and Tans and 1,500 Auxiliaries in Ireland.

Waverly Avenue, Co. Wicklow: Home of Margaret Skinnider. This house was 'behind' Kathleen Clarke's house, and it was to Miss Skinnider's home that Mrs Clarke sent Countess Markievicz when the Clarke home was raided in a search for Markievicz during the War of Independence. The countess stayed here for several months before being captured.

Winthrop Street, Cork, Co. Cork: Wren's Hotel. Sgt Timothy Quinlisk was a former member of the Casement Brigade in Germany before the Rising. Because he had signed up for Casement's Irish Brigade, he had been denied back pay for his period of imprisonment in Germany. He was well educated and spoke French and German fluently. After the war he was discharged from the British army. He lived for a time in Dublin and then in Cork city, and at first Collins helped him out financially. While in Dublin, he stayed at the Munster Hotel in Mountjoy Street.

Always known by Collins and his men by the one name 'Quinlisk', he was a British double agent. Collins and his men suspected him and Collins once gave him £100 to leave the country. Quinlisk, however, came back for more and that sealed his fate. He was an inept spy. Volunteer leaders had quickly placed him under close surveillance and found more than enough reason to execute him. He was told that Collins was here; when he subsequently gave the Cork RIC this information, it was clear that he was a spy. Quinlisk was killed on 19 February 1920 outside Wren's Hotel.

The Cork No. 1 Brigade Council agreed that he should be shot. The execution party from the Second Battalion consisted of Michael Murphy (O/C) and two others. Murphy coldly recalled of the not-quite-dead Quinlisk: 'I then turned him over on the flat of his back and put a bullet through his forehead'.

> I might here state that on the same evening that Quinlisk was executed, following a raid on the mails by some of our lads, one of the letters written by 'Quinn' (as he called himself) … addressed to the County Inspector, RIC, was found. The letter said that Quinlisk 'had information about Michael Collins and would

report again in a few days when the capture of Collins seemed imminent ... The Cork No. 1 Brigade Commandant Seán Hegarty got in touch with GHQ, Dublin, immediately following the identification of 'Quinn' as Quinlisk, and word was received back from Mick Collins that Quinlisk was definitely a spy in the pay of the British.[805]

When Quinlisk's father came from Waterford to claim the body about two weeks later, he had a confrontation with Murphy, who had been informed by the clerk of Cork Poor Law Union of the father's application to the workhouse authorities. At the time of the 1911 census the victim's father, Denis, had been an 'acting sergeant' in the RIC, residing at 10 Cathedral Square in Waterford City.

(See Mountjoy Street, Dublin 1; Harcourt Street, Dublin 2; Appendix II.)

Appendix VII

Documents

IRISH DECLARATION OF INDEPENDENCE,
21 January 1919[806]

First Dáil Éireann

Enacted by the Parliament of the Republic of Ireland

Whereas the Irish People is by right a free people:

And whereas for seven hundred years the Irish People has never ceased to repudiate and has repeatedly protested in arms against foreign usurpation:

And whereas English rule in this country is, and always has been, based upon force and fraud and maintained by military occupation against the declared will of the people:

And whereas the Irish Republic was proclaimed in Dublin on Easter Monday, 1916, by the Irish Republican Army, acting on behalf of the Irish People:

And whereas the Irish People is resolved to secure and maintain its complete independence in order to promote the common weal, to re-establish justice, to provide for future defence, to ensure peace at home and good will with all nations, and to constitute a national policy based upon the people's will with equal right and equal opportunity for every citizen:

And whereas at the threshold of a new era in history the Irish electorate has in the General Election of December, 1918, seized the first occasion to declare by an overwhelming majority its firm allegiance to the Irish Republic:

Now, therefore, we, the elected Representatives of the ancient Irish People in National Parliament assembled, do, in the name of the Irish Nation, ratify the establishment of the Irish Republic and pledge ourselves and our people to make this declaration effective by every means at our command:

We ordain that the elected Representatives of the Irish People alone have power to make laws binding on the people of Ireland, and that the Irish Parliament is the only Parliament to which that people will give its allegiance:

We solemnly declare foreign government in Ireland to be an invasion of our national right which we will never tolerate, and we demand the evacuation of our country by the English Garrison:

We claim for our national independence the recognition and support of every free nation in the world, and we proclaim that independence to be a condition precedent to international peace hereafter:

In the name of the Irish People we humbly commit our destiny to Almighty God Who gave our fathers the courage and determination to persevere through long centuries of a ruthless tyranny, and strong in the justice of the cause which they have handed down to us, we ask His Divine blessing on this the last stage of the struggle we have pledged ourselves to carry through to freedom.

IRISH CONSTITUTION,
21 January 1919[807]

First Dáil Éireann

Article 1
All legislative powers shall be vested in Dáil Éireann, composing of Deputies, elected by the Irish people from the existing Irish Parliamentary constituencies.

Article 2
(a) All executive powers shall be vested in the members, for the time being, of the Ministry.
(b) The Ministry shall consist of a President of the Ministry, elected by Dáil Éireann, and four Executive Officers, viz.:
A Secretary of Finance
A Secretary of Home Affairs
A Secretary of Foreign Affairs
A Secretary of National Defence
each of whom the President shall nominate and have power to dismiss.
(c) Every member of the Ministry shall be a member of Dáil Éireann, and shall at all times be responsible to the Dáil.
(d) At the first meeting of Dáil Éireann after their nomination by the President, the names of the Executive Officers shall be separately submitted to Dáil Éireann for approval.
(e) The appointment of the President shall date from his election, and the appointment of each Executive Officer from the date of the approval by the Dáil of his nomination.
(f) The Ministry or any member thereof may at any time be removed by vote of the Dáil upon motion for that specific purpose, provided that at least seven days' notice in writing of that motion shall have been given.

Article 3

A Chairman elected annually by the Dáil, and in his absence a Deputy Chairman so elected, shall preside at all meetings of Dáil Éireann. Only members of the Dáil shall be eligible for these offices. In case of the absence of the Chairman and Deputy Chairman the Dáil shall fill the vacancies or elect a temporary Chairman.

Article 4

All monies required by the Ministry shall be obtained on vote of the Dáil. The Ministry shall be responsible to the Dáil for all monies so obtained, and shall present properly audited accounts for the expenditure of the same—twice yearly—in the months of May and November. The audit shall be conducted by an Auditor or Auditors appointed by the Dáil. No member of the Dáil shall be eligible for such appointment.

Article 5

This Constitution is provisional and is liable to alteration upon seven days' written notice of motion for that specific purpose.

DÁIL MESSAGE TO THE FREE NATIONS OF THE WORLD, 21 January 1919[808]

To the Nations of the World—Greeting.

The Nation of Ireland having proclaimed her national independence, calls, through her elected representatives in Parliament assembled in the Irish Capital on January 21st, 1919, upon every free nation to support the Irish Republic by recognising Ireland's national status and her right to its vindication at the Peace Congress.

Naturally, the race, the language, the customs and traditions of Ireland are radically distinct from the English. Ireland is one of the most ancient nations in Europe, and she has preserved her national integrity, vigorous and intact, through seven centuries of foreign oppression; she has never relinquished her national rights, and throughout the long era of English usurpation she has in every generation defiantly proclaimed her inalienable right of nationhood down to her last glorious resort to arms in 1916.

Internationally, Ireland is the gateway to the Atlantic; Ireland is the last outpost of Europe towards the West; Ireland is the point upon which great trade routes between East and West converge; her independence is demanded by the Freedom of the Seas; her great harbours must be open to all nations, instead of being the monopoly of England. To-day these harbours are empty and idle solely because English policy is determined to retain Ireland as a barren bulwark for English aggrandisement, and the unique geographical position of this island, far from being a benefit and safeguard to Europe and America, is subjected to the purposes of England's policy of world domination.

Ireland to-day reasserts her historic nationhood the more confidently before the new world emerging from the war, because she believes in freedom and justice as the fundamental principles of international law; because she believes in a frank co-operation between the peoples for equal rights against the vested privileges of ancient tyrannies; because the permanent peace of Europe can never be secured by perpetuating military dominion for the profit of empire but only by establishing the control of government in every land upon the basis of the free will of a free people, and the existing state of war, between Ireland and England, can never be ended until Ireland is definitely evacuated by the armed forces of England.

For these among other reasons, Ireland—resolutely and irrevocably determined at the dawn of the promised era of self-determination and liberty that she will suffer foreign dominion no longer—calls upon every free nation to uphold her national claim to complete independence as an Irish Republic against the arrogant pretensions of England founded in fraud and sustained only by an overwhelming military occupation, and demands to be confronted publicly with England at the Congress of the Nations, that the civilised world having judged between English wrong and Irish right may guarantee to Ireland its permanent support for the maintenance of her national independence.

DÁIL DEMOCRATIC PROGRAMME,
21 January 1919[809]

We declare in the words of the Irish Republican Proclamation the right of the people of Ireland to the ownership of Ireland and to the unfettered control of Irish destinies to be indefeasible, and in the language of our first President, Pádraig Mac Phiarais, we declare that the nation's sovereignty extends not only to all men and women of the nation but to all its material possessions, the nation's soil and all its resources, all the wealth and all the wealth-producing processes within the nation, and with him we re-affirm that all the rights to private property must be subordinated to the public right and welfare.

We declare that we desire our country to be ruled in accordance with the principles of Liberty, Equality and Justice for all, which alone can secure permanence of government in the willing adhesion of the people.

We affirm the duty of every man and woman to give allegiance and service to the commonwealth, and declare it is the duty of the nation to assure that every citizen shall have opportunity to spend his or her strength and faculties in the service of the people. In return for willing service, we, in the name of the Republic, declare the right of every citizen to an adequate share of the produce of the nation's labour.

It shall be the first duty of the government of the Republic to make provision for the physical, mental and spiritual well-being of the children, to secure that no child shall suffer hunger or cold from lack of food or clothing or shelter, but that all shall be provided with the means and faculties requisite for their proper education and training as citizens of a free and Gaelic Ireland.

The Irish Republic fully realises the necessity of abolishing the present odious, degrading, and foreign poor-law system, substituting therefor a sympathetic native scheme for the care of the nation's aged and infirm, who shall no longer be regarded as a burden, but rather entitled to the nation's gratitude and consideration. Likewise it shall be the duty of the Republic to take measures that will safeguard the health of the people and ensure the physical as well as the moral well-being of the nation.

It shall be our duty to promote the development of the nation's resources, to increase the productivity of the soil, to exploit its mineral deposits, peat bogs, and fisheries, its waterways and harbours, in the interest and for the benefit of the Irish people.

It shall be the duty of the Republic to adopt all measures necessary for the re-creation and invigoration of our industries, and to ensure their being developed on the most beneficial and progressive co-operative industrial lines. With the adoption of an extensive Irish consular service trade with foreign nations shall be revived on terms of mutual advantage and good will; while undertaking the organisation of the nation's trade, import and export, it shall be the duty of the Republic to prevent the shipment from Ireland of food and other necessaries until the wants of the Irish people are fully satisfied and provided for.

It shall devolve upon the national government to seek the co-operation of the governments of other countries in determining a standard of social and industrial legislation with a view to general and lasting improvements in the conditions under which the working classes live and labour.

ARTICLES OF AGREEMENT FOR A TREATY BETWEEN GREAT BRITAIN AND IRELAND,
6 December 1921

1. Ireland shall have the same constitutional status in the Community of Nations known as the British Empire as the Dominion of Canada, the Commonwealth of Australia, the Dominion of New Zealand, and the Union of South Africa, with a Parliament having powers to make laws for the peace, order and good government of

Ireland and an Executive responsible to that Parliament, and shall be styled and known as the Irish Free State.

2. Subject to the provisions hereinafter set out the position of the Irish Free State in relation to the Imperial Parliament and Government and otherwise shall be that of the Dominion of Canada, and the law, practice and constitutional usage governing the relationship of the Crown or the representative of the Crown and of the Imperial Parliament to the Dominion of Canada shall govern their relationship to the Irish Free State.

3. The representative of the Crown in Ireland shall be appointed in like manner as the Governor-General of Canada and in accordance with the practice observed in the making of such appointments.

4. The oath to be taken by Members of the Parliament of the Irish Free State shall be in the following form:–

I .... do solemnly swear true faith and allegiance to the Constitution of the Irish Free State as by law established and that I will be faithful to H.M. King George V, his heirs and successors by law, in virtue of the common citizenship of Ireland with Great Britain and her adherence to and membership of the group of nations forming the British Commonwealth of Nations.

5. The Irish Free State shall assume liability for the service of the Public Debt of the United Kingdom as existing as the date hereof and towards the payment of War Pensions as existing at that date in such proportion as may be fair and equitable, having regard to any just claim on the part of Ireland by way of set-off or counter claim, the amount of such sums being determined in default of agreement by the arbitration of one or more independent persons being citizens of the British Empire.

6. Until an arrangement has been made between the British and Irish Governments whereby the Irish Free State undertakes her own coastal defence, the defence by sea of Great Britain and Ireland shall be undertaken by His Majesty's Imperial Forces, but this shall not prevent the construction or maintenance by the Government of the Irish Free State of such vessels as are necessary for the protection of the Revenue or the Fisheries. The foregoing provisions of this article shall be reviewed at a conference of Representatives of the British and Irish governments, to be held at the expiration of five years from the date hereof with a view to the undertaking by Ireland of a share in her own coastal defence.

7. The Government of the Irish Free State shall afford to His Majesty's Imperial Forces
(a) In the time of peace such harbour and other facilities as are indicated in the Annex hereto, or such other facilities as may from time to time be agreed between the British Government and the Government of the Irish Free State; and
(b) In time of war or of strained relations with a Foreign Power such harbour and other facilities as the British Government may require for the purposes of such defence as aforesaid.

8. With a view to securing the observance of the principle of international limitation of armaments, if the Government of the Irish Free State establishes and maintains a military defence force, the establishments thereof shall not exceed in size such proportion of the military establishments maintained in Great Britain as that which the population of Ireland bears to the population of Great Britain.

9. The ports of Great Britain and the Irish Free State shall be freely open to the ships of the other country on payment of the customary port and other dues.

10. The Government of the Irish Free State agrees to pay fair compensation on terms not less favourable than those accorded by the Act of 1920 to judges, officials, members of Police Forces and other Public Servants who are discharged by it or who retire in consequence of the change of government effected in pursuance hereof. Provided that this agreement shall not apply to members of the Auxiliary Police Force or to persons recruited in Great Britain for the Royal Irish Constabulary during the two years next preceding the date hereof. The British Government will assume responsibility for such compensation or pensions as may be payable to any of these excepted persons.

11. Until the expiration of one month from the passing of the Act of Parliament for the ratification of this instrument, the powers of the Parliament and the Government of the Irish Free State shall not be exercisable as respects Northern Ireland, and the provisions of the Government of Ireland Act, 1920, shall, so far as they relate to Northern Ireland, remain of full force and effect, and no election shall be held for the return of members to serve in the Parliament of the Irish Free State for constituencies in Northern Ireland, unless a resolution is passed by both Houses of the Parliament of Northern Ireland in favour of the holding of such elections before the end of the said month.

12. If before the expiration of the said month, an address is presented to His Majesty by both Houses of the Parliament of Northern Ireland to that effect, the powers of the Parliament and the Government of the Irish Free State shall no longer extend to Northern Ireland, and the provisions of the Government of Ireland Act, 1920 (including those relating to the Council of Ireland), shall, so far as they relate to Northern Ireland, continue to be of full force and effect, and this instrument shall have effect subject to the necessary modifications. Provided that if such an address is so presented a Commission consisting of three persons, one to be appointed by the Government of the Irish Free State, one to be appointed by the Government of Northern Ireland, and one who shall be Chairman to be appointed by the British Government, shall determine in accordance with the wishes of the inhabitants, so far as may be compatible with economic and geographic conditions, the boundaries between Northern Ireland and the rest of Ireland, and for the purposes of the Government of Ireland Act, 1920, and of this instrument, the boundary of Northern Ireland shall be such as may be determined by such Commission.

13. For the purpose of the last foregoing article, the powers of the Parliament of Southern Ireland under the Government of Ireland Act, 1920, to elect members of the Council of Ireland shall after the Parliament of the Irish Free State is constituted be exercised by that Parliament.

14. After the expiration of the said month, if no such address as is mentioned in Article 12 hereof is presented, the Parliament and Government of Northern Ireland shall continue to exercise as respects Northern Ireland the powers conferred on them by the Government of Ireland Act, 1920, but the Parliament and Government of the Irish Free State shall in Northern Ireland have in relation to matters in respect of which the Parliament of Northern Ireland has not the power to make laws under the Act (including matters which under the said Act are within the jurisdiction of the Council of Ireland) the same powers as in the rest of Ireland, subject to such other provisions as may be agreed in manner hereinafter appearing.

15. At any time after the date hereof the Government of Northern Ireland and the provisional Government of Southern Ireland hereinafter constituted may meet for the purpose of discussing the provisions subject to which the last foregoing Article is to operate in the event of no such address as is therein mentioned being presented and those provisions may include:–

(a) Safeguards with regard to patronage in Northern Ireland.

(b) Safeguards with regard to the collection of revenue in Northern Ireland.

(c) Safeguards with regard to import and export duties affecting the trade or industry of Northern Ireland.

(d) Safeguards for minorities in Northern Ireland.

(e) The settlement of the financial relations between Northern Ireland and the Irish Free State.

(f) The establishment and powers of a local militia in Northern Ireland and the relation of the Defence Forces of the Irish Free State and of Northern Ireland respectively, and if at any such meeting provisions are agreed to, the same shall have effect as if they were included amongst the provisions subject to which the powers of the Parliament and the Government of the Irish Free State are to be exercisable in Northern Ireland under Article 14 hereof.

16. Neither the Parliament of the Irish Free State nor the Parliament of Northern Ireland shall make any law so as either directly or indirectly to endow any religion or prohibit or restrict the free exercise thereof or give any preference or impose any disability on account of religious belief or religious status or affect prejudicially the right of any child to attend a school receiving public money without attending the religious instruction at the school or make any discrimination as respects State aid between schools under the management of different religious denominations or divert from any religious denomination or any educational institution any of its property except for public utility purposes and on payment of compensation.

17. By way of provisional arrangement for the administration of Southern Ireland during the interval which must elapse between the date hereof and the constitution of a Parliament and Government of the Irish Free State in accordance therewith, steps shall be taken forthwith for summoning a meeting of members of Parliament elected for constituencies in Southern Ireland since the passing of the Government of Ireland Act, 1920, and for constituting a provisional Government, and the British Government shall take the steps necessary to transfer to such provisional Government the powers and machinery requisite for the discharge of its duties, provided that every member of such provisional Government shall have signified in writing his or her acceptance of this instrument. But this arrangement shall not continue in force beyond the expiration of twelve months from the date hereof.

18. This instrument shall be submitted forthwith by His Majesty's Government for the approval of Parliament and by the Irish signatories to a meeting summoned for the purpose of the members elected to sit in the House of Commons of Southern Ireland and if approved shall be ratified by the necessary legislation.

(Signed)

On behalf of the British Delegation,   On behalf of the Irish Delegation,

D. LLOYD GEORGE	ART Ó GRIOBHTHA
AUSTEN CHAMBERLAIN	MICHEÁL Ó COILEAIN
BIRKENHEAD	RIOBÁRD BARTÚN
WINSTON S. CHURCHILL	E. S. Ó DUGAIN
L. WORTHINGTON-EVANS	SEÓRSA GHABHÁIN UÍ
HAMAR GREENWOOD	DHUBHTHAIGH
GORDON HEWART	
6th December, 1921.	

SPEECH OF MICHAEL COLLINS TO DÁIL ÉIREANN,
19 December 1921[810]

MR MICHAEL COLLINS (MINISTER FOR FINANCE): A Chinn Chomhairle, much has been said in Private Session about the action of the plenipotentiaries in signing at all or in signing without first putting their document before the Cabinet. I want to state as clearly as I can, and as briefly as I can—I cannot promise you to be very brief—what the exact position was.

It has been fully explained how the Delegation returned from London on that momentous Saturday to meet the Cabinet at home. We came back with a document from the British Delegation which we presented to the Cabinet. Certain things happened at that Cabinet Meeting, and the Delegation, on returning, put before the

British Delegation as well as they could their impressions of the decisions—I will not say conclusions—arrived at at that Cabinet Meeting. I do not want unduly to press the word decisions. I want to be fair to everybody. I can only say they were decisions in this way, that we went away with certain impressions in our minds and that we did our best faithfully to transmit these impressions to paper in the memorandum we handed in to the British Delegation.

It was well understood at that Cabinet Meeting that Sir James Craig was receiving a reply from the British Premier on Tuesday morning. Some conclusion as between the British Delegation and ourselves had, therefore, to be come to and handed in to the British Delegation on the Monday night. Now, we went away with a document which none of us would sign. It must have been obvious, that being so, that in the meantime a document arose which we thought we could sign. There was no opportunity of referring it to our people at home. Actually on the Monday night we did arrive at conclusions which we thought we could agree to and we had to say 'Yes' across the table, and I may say that we said 'Yes'. It was later on that same day that the document was signed. But I do not now, and I did not then, regard my word as being anything more important, or a bit less important, than my signature on a document.

Now, I also want to make this clear. The answer which I gave and that signature which I put on that document would be the same in Dublin or in Berlin, or in New York or in Paris. If we had been in Dublin the difference in distance would have made this difference, that we would have been able to consult not only the members of the Cabinet but many members of the Dáil and many good friends.

There has been talk about 'the atmosphere of London' and there has been talk about 'slippery slopes'. Such talk is beside the point. I knew the atmosphere of London of old and I knew many other things about it of old. If the members knew so much about 'slippery slopes' before we went there why did they not speak then? The slopes were surely slippery, but it is easy to be wise afterwards. I submit that such observations are entirely beside the point. And if my signature has been given in error, I stand by it whether it has or not, and I am not going to take refuge behind any kind of subterfuge. I stand up over that signature and I give the same decision at this moment in this assembly [applause].

It has also been suggested that the Delegation broke down before the first bit of English bluff. I would remind the Deputy who used that expression that England put up quite a good bluff for the last five years here and I did not break down before that bluff [applause, and a voice, 'That is the stuff']. And does anybody think that the respect I compelled from them in a few years was in any way lowered during two months of negotiations? That also is beside the point.

The results of our labour are before the Dáil. Reject or accept. The President has suggested that a greater result could have been obtained by more skilful handling.

Perhaps so. But there again the fault is not the delegation's; it rests with the Dáil. It is not afterwards the Dáil should have found out our limitations. Surely the Dáil knew it when they selected us, and our abilities could not have been expected to increase because we were chosen as plenipotentiaries by the Dáil.

The delegates have been blamed for various things. It is scarcely too much to say that they have been blamed for not returning with recognition of the Irish Republic. They are blamed, at any rate, for not having done much better. A Deputy when speaking the other day with reference to Canada suggested that what may apply with safety to Canada would not at all apply to Ireland because of the difference in distance from Great Britain. It seemed to me that he did not regard the delegation as being wholly without responsibility for the geographical propinquity of Ireland to Great Britain. It is further suggested that by the result of their labours the delegation made a resumption of hostilities certain. That again rests with the Dáil; they should have chosen a better delegation, and it was before we went to London that should have been done, not when we returned.

Now, Sir, before I come to the Treaty itself, I must say a word on another vexed question—the question as to whether the terms of reference meant any departure from the absolutely rigid line of the isolated Irish Republic. Let me read to you in full (at the risk of wearying you) the two final communications which passed between Mr Lloyd George and President de Valera.

'*From Lloyd George to de Valera.*' (It is a telegram. In that way the word 'President' was not an omission on my part.)
'GAIRLOCH,
'*Sept. 29th*, 1921.
'His Majesty's Government have given close and earnest consideration to the correspondence which has passed between us since their invitation to you to send delegates to a conference at Inverness. In spite of their sincere desire for peace, and in spite of the more conciliatory tone of your last communication, they cannot enter a conference upon the basis of this correspondence. Notwithstanding your personal assurance to the contrary, which they much appreciate, it might be argued in future that the acceptance of a conference on this basis had involved them in a recognition which no British Government can accord. On this point they must guard themselves against any possible doubt. There is no purpose to be served by any further interchange of explanatory and argumentative communications upon this subject. The position taken up by His Majesty's Government is fundamental to the existence of the British Empire and they cannot alter it. My colleagues and I remain, however, keenly anxious to make in co-operation with your delegates another determined effort to explore every possibility of settlement by personal discussion. The proposals which we

have already made have been taken by the whole world as proof that our endeavours for reconciliation and settlement are no empty form, and we feel that conference, not correspondence, is the most practicable and hopeful way to an understanding such as we ardently desire to achieve. We, therefore, send you herewith a fresh invitation to a conference in London on October 11th where we can meet your delegates as spokesmen of the people whom you represent with a view to ascertaining how the association of Ireland with the community of nations known as the British Empire may best be reconciled with Irish National aspirations.'

'*From de Valera to Lloyd George.*
'30*th Sept.*, 1921.
'We have received your letter of invitation to a Conference in London on October 11th "with a view to ascertaining how the association of Ireland with the community of Nations known as the British Empire may best be reconciled with Irish National aspirations".

'Our respective positions have been stated and are understood, and we agree that conference, not correspondence, is the most practicable and hopeful way to an understanding. We accept the invitation, and our delegates will meet you in London on the date mentioned "to explore every possibility of settlement by personal discussion".'

This question of association was bandied around as far back as August 10th and went on until the final communication. The communication of September 29th from Lloyd George made it clear that they were going into a conference not on the recognition of the Irish Republic, and I say if we all stood on the recognition of the Irish Republic as a prelude to any conference we could very easily have said so, and there would be no conference. What I want to make clear is that it was the acceptance of the invitation that formed the compromise. I was sent there to form that adaptation, to bear the brunt of it. Now as one of the signatories of the document I naturally recommend its acceptance. I do not recommend it for more than it is. Equally I do not recommend it for less than it is. In my opinion it gives us freedom, not the ultimate freedom that all nations desire and develop to, but the freedom to achieve it [applause].

A Deputy has stated that the delegation should introduce this Treaty not, he describes, as bagmen for England, but with an apology for its introduction. I cannot imagine anything more mean, anything more despicable, anything more unmanly than this dishonouring of one's signature. Rightly or wrongly when you make a bargain you cannot alter it, you cannot go back and get sorry for it and say 'I ought to have made a better bargain'. Business cannot be done on those bases. I must make reference to the signing of the Treaty. This Treaty was not signed under personal intimidation. If personal intimidation had been attempted no member of the delegation would have signed it.

At a fateful moment I was called upon to make a decision, and if I were called upon at the present moment for a decision on the same question my decision would be the same. Let there be no mistake and no misunderstanding about that.

I have used the word 'intimidation'. The whole attitude of Britain towards Ireland in the past was an attitude of intimidation, and we, as negotiators, were not in the position of conquerors dictating terms of peace to a vanquished foe. We had not beaten the enemy out of our country by force of arms.

To return to the Treaty, hardly anyone, even those who support it, really understands it, and it is necessary to explain it, and the immense powers and liberties it secures. This is my justification for having signed it, and for recommending it to the nation. Should the Dáil reject it, I am, as I said, no longer responsible. But I am responsible for making the nation fully understand what it gains by accepting it, and what is involved in its rejection. So long as I have made that clear I am perfectly happy and satisfied.

Now we must look facts in the face. For our continued national and spiritual existence two things are necessary—security and freedom. If the Treaty gives us these or helps us to get at these, then I maintain that it satisfies our national aspirations. The history of this nation has not been, as is so often said, the history of a military struggle of 750 years; it has been much more a history of peaceful penetration of 750 years. It has not been a struggle for the ideal of freedom for 750 years symbolised in the name Republic. It has been a story of slow, steady, economic encroach by England. It has been a struggle on our part to prevent that, a struggle against exploitation, a struggle against the cancer that was eating up our lives, and it was only after discovering that, that it was economic penetration, that we discovered that political freedom was necessary in order that that should be stopped. Our aspirations, by whatever term they may be symbolised, had one thing in front all the time, that was to rid the country of the enemy strength.

Now it was not by any form of communication except through their military strength that the English held this country. That is simply a plain fact which, I think, nobody will deny. It wasn't by any forms of government, it wasn't by their judiciary or anything of that kind. These people could not operate except for the military strength that was always there. Now, starting from that, I maintain that the disappearance of that military strength gives us the chief proof that our national liberties are established. And as to what has been said about guarantees of the withdrawal of that military strength, no guarantees, I say, can alter the fact of their withdrawal, because we are a weaker nation, and we shall be a weaker nation for a long time to come. But certain things do give us a certain guarantee. We are defined as having the constitutional status of Canada, Australia, New Zealand, South Africa. If the English do not withdraw the military strength, our association with those places do give us, to some extent, a guarantee that they must withdraw them. I know that it would be finer to stand alone, but if it is necessary to our security, if it is necessary to the development of our own life, and if we find we cannot stand alone, what can we do but enter into some association?

Now I have prepared part of this which I am going to read very carefully. I have said that I am not a constitutional lawyer. I am going to give a constitutional opinion in what I am going to read, and I will back that constitutional opinion against the opinion of any Deputy, lawyer or otherwise, in this Dáil.

[Reading]: The status as defined is the same constitutional status in the 'community of nations known as the British Empire' as Canada, Australia, New Zealand, South Africa. And here let me say that in my judgement it is not a definition of any status that would secure us that status, it is the power to hold and to make secure and to increase what we have gained.

The fact of Canadian and South African independence is something real and solid, and will grow in reality and force as time goes on. Judged by that touchstone, the relations between Ireland and Britain will have a certainty of freedom and equality which cannot be interfered with. England dare not interfere with Canada. Any attempt to interfere with us would be even more difficult in consequence of the reference to the 'constitutional status' of Canada and South Africa.

They are, in effect, introduced as guarantors of our freedom, which makes us stronger than if we stood alone.

In obtaining the 'constitutional status' of Canada, our association with England is based not on the present technical legal position of Canada. It is an old Act, the Canadian Act, and the advances in freedom from it have been considerable. That is the reply to one Deputy who spoke to-day of the real position, the complete freedom equality with Canada has given us. I refer now not to the legal technical status, but to the status they have come to, the status which enables Canada to send an Ambassador to Washington, the status which enables Canada to sign the Treaty of Versailles equally with Great Britain, the status which prevents Great Britain from entering into any foreign alliance without the consent of Canada, the status that gives Canada the right to be consulted before she may go into any war. It is not the definition of that status that will give it to us; it is our power to take it and to keep it, and that is where I differ from the others. I believe in our power to take it and to keep it. I believe in our future civilisation. As I have said already, as a plain Irishman, I believe in my own interpretation against the interpretation of any Englishman. Lloyd George and Churchill have been quoted here against us. I say the quotation of those people is what marks the slave mind. There are people in this assembly who will take their words before they will take my words. That is the slave mind.

The only departure from the Canadian status is the retaining by England of the defences of four harbours, and the holding of some other facilities to be used possibly in time of war. But if England wished to re-invade us she could do so with or without these facilities. And with the 'constitutional status' of Canada we are assured that these facilities could never be used by England for our re-invasion.

If there was no association, if we stood alone, the occupation of the ports might probably be a danger to us. Associated in a free partnership with these other nations it is not a danger, for their association is a guarantee that it won't be used as a jumping-off ground against us. And that same person tells me that we haven't Dominion status because of the occupation of these ports, but that South Africa had even when Simonstown was occupied. I cannot accept that argument.

I am not an apologist for this Treaty. We have got rid of the word 'Empire'. For the first time in an official document the former Empire is styled 'the Community of Nations known as the British Empire'. Common citizenship has been mentioned. Common citizenship is the substitution for the subjection of Ireland. It is an admission by them that they no longer can dominate Ireland. As I have said, the English penetration has not merely been a military penetration. At the present moment the economic penetration goes on. I need only give you a few instances. Every day our Banks become incorporated or allied to British interests, every day our Steamship Companies go into English hands, every day some other business concern in this city is taken over by an English concern and becomes a little oasis of English customs and manners. Nobody notices, but that is the thing that has destroyed our Gaelic civilisation. That is a thing that we are able to stop, not perhaps if we lose the opportunity of stopping it now. That is one of the things that I consider is important, and to the nation's life perhaps more important than the military penetration. And this gives us the opportunity of stopping it. Indeed when we think of the thing from that economic point of view it would be easy to go on with the physical struggle in comparison with it.

Do we think at all of what it means to look forward to the directing of the organisation of the nation? Is it one of the things we are prepared to undertake? If we came back with the recognition of the Irish Republic we would need to start somewhere. Are we simply going to go on keeping ourselves in slavery and subjection, for ever keeping on an impossible fight? Are we never going to stand on our own feet? Now I had an argument based on a comparison of the Treaty with the second document, and part of the argument was to read the clauses of the second document. In deference to what the President has said I shall not at this stage make use of that argument. I don't want to take anything that would look like an unfair advantage. I am not standing for this thing to get advantage over anybody, and whatever else the President will say about me, I think he will admit that.

PRESIDENT DE VALERA: I never said anything but the highest.

MR MICHAEL COLLINS (MINISTER FOR FINANCE): Now I have explained something as to what the Treaty is. I also want to explain to you as one of the signatories what I consider rejection of it means. It has been said that the alternative document does not mean war. Perhaps it does, perhaps it does not. That is not the first part of the argument. I say that rejection of the Treaty is a declaration of war until you have beaten the British Empire, apart from any alternative document. Rejection of the Treaty means your national policy is war. If you do this, if you go on that as a national policy, I for one am satisfied. But I want you to go on it as a national policy and understand what it means. I, as an individual, do not now, no more than ever, shirk war. The Treaty was signed by me, not because they held up the alternative of immediate war. I signed it because I would not be one of those to commit the Irish people to war without the Irish people committing themselves to war. If my constituents send me to represent them in war, I will do my best to represent them in war. Now I was not going to refer to anything that had been said by the speakers of the Coalition side to-day. I do want to say this in regard to the President's remark about Pitt, a remark, it will be admitted, which was not very flattering to us. Well, now, what happened at the time of the Union? Grattan's Parliament was thrown away without reference to the people and against their wishes. Is the Parliament which this Treaty offers us to be similarly treated? Is it to be thrown away without reference to the people and against their wishes?

PRESIDENT DE VALERA: What Parliament?

A VOICE: *[The Free State.]*

MISS MACSWINEY (CORK CITY): Which Parliament?

MR MICHAEL COLLINS (MINISTER FOR FINANCE): I would like you to keep on interrupting, because I was looking at a point here. I am disappointed that I was not interrupted more. In our Private Sessions we have been treated to harangues about principle. Not one Deputy has stated a clear, steadfast, abiding principle on which we can stand. Deputies have talked of principle. At different times I have known different Deputies to hold different principles. How can I say, how can anyone say, that these Deputies may not change their principles again? How can anyone say that anybody— a Deputy or a supporter—who has fought against the Irish Nation on principle may not fight against it again on principle?

I am not impeaching anybody, but I do want to talk straight. I am the representative of an Irish stock; I am the representative equally with any other member of the same stock of people who have suffered through the terror in the past. Our grandfathers have suffered from war, and our fathers or some of our ancestors have died of famine. I don't want a lecture from anybody as to what my principles are to be now. I am just a representative of plain Irish stock whose principles have been burned into them, and we don't want any assurance to the people of this country that we are going to betray them. We are one of themselves. I can state for you a principle which everybody will understand, the principle of 'government by the consent of the governed'. These words have been used by nearly every Deputy at some time or another. Are the Deputies going to be afraid of these words now, supposing the formula happens to go against them? *[PRESIDENT DE VALERA: No, no.]* I have heard Deputies remark that their constituents are in favour of this Treaty. The Deputies have got their powers from their constituents and they are responsible to their constituents. I have stated the principle which is the only firm principle in the whole thing.

Now I have gone into more or less a general survey of the Treaty, apart from one section of it, the section dealing with North-East Ulster. Again I am as anxious to face facts in that case as I am in any other case. We have stated we would not coerce the North-East. We have stated it officially in our correspondence. I stated it publicly in Armagh and nobody has found fault with it. What did we mean? Did we mean we were going to coerce them or we were not going to coerce them? What was the use of talking big phrases about not agreeing to the partition of our country. Surely we recognise that the North-East corner does exist, and surely our intention was that we should take such steps as would sooner or later lead to mutual understanding. The Treaty has made an effort to deal with it, and has made an effort, in my opinion, to deal with it on lines that will lead very rapidly to goodwill, and the entry of the North-East under the Irish Parliament *[applause]*.

I don't say it is an ideal arrangement, but if our policy is, as has been stated, a policy of non-coercion, then let somebody else get a better way out of it.

Now, summing up—and nobody can say that I haven't talked plainly—I say that this Treaty gives us, not recognition of the Irish Republic, but it gives us more recognition on the part of Great Britain and the associated States than we have got from any other nation.

Again I want to speak plainly. America did not recognise the Irish Republic. As things in London were coming to a close I received cablegrams from America. I understand that my name is pretty well known in America, and what I am going to say now will make me unpopular there for the rest of my life, but I am not going to say anything or hide anything for the sake of American popularity. I received a cablegram from San Francisco, saying, 'Stand fast, we will send you a million dollars a month'. Well, my reply to that is, 'Send us half-a-million and send us a thousand men fully equipped'.

I received another cablegram from a branch of the American Association for the Recognition of the Irish Republic and they said to me, 'Don't weaken now, stand with de Valera'. Well, let that branch come over and stand with us both *[applause]*. The question before me was were we going to go on with this fight, without referring it to the Irish people, for the sake of propaganda in America? I was not going to take that responsibility.

And as this may be the last opportunity I shall ever have of speaking publicly to the Dáil, I want to say that there was never an Irishman placed in such a position as I was by reason of these negotiations. I had got a certain name, whether I deserved it or not [Voices: 'You did, well'], and I knew when I was going over there that I was being placed in a position that I could not reconcile, and that I could not in the public mind be reconciled with what they thought I stood for, no matter what we brought back— and if we brought back the recognition of the Republic—but I knew that the English would make a greater effort if I were there than they would if I were not there, and I didn't care if my popularity was sacrificed or not. I should have been unfair to my own country if I did not go there. Members of the Dáil well remember that I protested against being selected.

I want to say another thing. It will be remembered that a certain incident occurred in the South of Ireland, an incident which led to the excommunication of the whole population of that district. At the time I took responsibility for that in our private councils. I take responsibility for it now publicly. I only want to say that I stand for every action as an individual member of the Cabinet, which I suppose I shall be no longer; I stand for every action, no matter how it looked publicly, and I shall always like the men to remember me like that.

In coming to the decision I did I tried to weigh what my own responsibility was. Deputies have spoken about whether dead men would approve of it, and they have spoken of whether children yet unborn will approve of it, but few of them have spoken as to whether the living approve of it. In my own small way I tried to have before my mind what the whole lot of them would think of it. And the proper way for us to look at it is in that way. There is no man here who has more regard for the dead men than I have [hear, hear]. I don't think it is fair to be quoting them against us.

I think the decision ought to be a clear decision on the documents as they are before us—on the Treaty as it is before us. On that we shall be judged, as to whether we have done the right thing in our own conscience or not. Don't let us put the responsibility, the individual responsibility, upon anybody else. Let us take that responsibility ourselves and let us in God's name abide by the decision [applause].

Notes

1   Yeates 2014b.
2   Johnson, Thomas: Witness Statement 1755.
3   Gallagher 1953, 17f.
4   *Evening Telegraph*, 13 April 1920.
5   See Fitzpatrick 2003.
6   Larkin 2006.
7   W.J. (Bill) Stapleton, 'A Volunteer's story', *Irish Independent*, 1916 Golden Jubilee Supplement (April 1966).
8   Younger 1968, 123.
9   Byrne, Vincent: Witness Statement 423.
10   Thornton, Frank: Witness Statement 615.
11   Neligan 1999, 76. Neligan, David: Witness Statement 380.
12   Thornton, Frank: Witness Statement 615.
13   See https://www.youtube.com/watch?v=vV2gzXhz8o8.
14   From the time the Rising prisoners returned from Frongoch the British were tracking them, and the DMP detective notes of 29 May 1917 indicated that 'Collins was the general secretary' here; Stewart 1997, 48, document 7.
15   Clarke 1997, 142.
16   Richard Mulcahy, Notes on Béaslaí's *Michael Collins*, vol. II, 454.
17   O'Kelly, J.J. (Sceilg): Witness Statement 384.
18   Fitzsimmons 2016.
19   Joe Leonard described the attempt, an attack by two men with only one gun—a .38 calibre revolver, which the Squad quickly disdained. 'This wonderful machine got jammed on the first shot, when it became evident that hasty leg movement would be called for and a few blocks away from there would make a wonderful difference.' Leonard, Joseph: Witness Statement 347.
20   Thornton, Frank: Witness Statement 615.
21   Thornton, Frank: Witness Statement 510.
22   Thornton, Frank: Witness Statement 615.
23   MacLysaght 1967, 124.
24   O'Brien, William: Witness Statement 1766.
25   McAleese, Daniel: Witness Statement 1411. He worked in the Custom House.
26   See O'Mahony 2000a; McCann 1938; Traynor 1939.
27   Dwyer 1990, 120.
28   Traynor, Oscar: Witness Statement 340.
29   Daly, Gen. P.: Witness Statement 387. General Daly's Witness Statement lists him as 'Daly'. In other sources he is listed as 'O'Daly' and 'O Dalaigh'. For consistency, he is here named as 'Daly' throughout.
30   O'Shea, Seán: Witness Statement 760.
31   Hales, Donal: Witness Statement 292.
32   Farrington, Annie: Witness Statement 749.
33   O'Reilly, Bridie: Witness Statement 454.
34   Pinkman 1998, 140.
35   Mee, Jeremiah: Witness Statement 379.
36   Murphy, Gregory: Witness Statement 150.
37   From author's correspondence with Constance Cowley, niece of Nance Corcoran.
38   MacWhinney, Linda Kearns: Witness Statement 404.
39   See http://www.historyireland.com/revolutionary-period-1912-23/who-was-ira-ghq-director-of-organisation-in-1921/.
40   Henderson 1945.
41   O'Connor 1996, 127.
42   *Ibid.*, 128.
43   Mulcahy 1970a.
44   Mulcahy 2008.
45   Ernie O'Malley papers, O'Malley notebook, P17b114, UCD.

46 Barry 1981, 182.
47 Oscar Traynor, quoted in Ernie O'Malley papers, UCD.
48 Mulcahy 2008.
49 Deasy 1973, 132.
50 Thornton, Frank: Witness Statement 615.
51 Dolan 2006.
52 Younger 1968, 124.
53 Neligan, David: Witness Statement 380.
54 Sugg 1997b.
55 A. Ó Snodaigh, 'South Longford by-election', *An Phoblacht*, 15 July 1999.
56 Dwyer 2001, 115.
57 On the first count of the votes the election was given to the Irish Parliamentary Party candidate, Patrick McKenna. But another bundle of ballot papers was discovered and McGuinness won by 37 votes.
58 Terry Fagan, North Dublin Inner City Folklore Project, pers. comm.
59 Kennedy, Patrick (Paddy): Witness Statement 499.
60 Stapleton, William J.: Witness Statement 822.
61 Terry Fagan, North Dublin Inner City Folklore Project, pers. comm.
62 Lawless, Sr Eithne: Witness Statement 414.
63 O'Higgins 1925, 40.
64 Daly, Gen. P.: Witness Statement 387. It must be noted that Gen. Daly was the O/C in Kerry during the Civil War and was responsible for one of the most reprehensible revenge killings of that war at Ballyseedy, where he ordered his troops to take nine republican prisoners from jail and tied them to a mine. When the mine detonated, eight of the men were killed; the story only got out because one man was blown far away and survived. Daly headed the subsequent inquiry, which was of course a whitewash. Obviously, Daly did not listen to Collins's lecture on revenge.
65 Kennedy, Patrick: Witness Statement 499.
66 O'Sullivan, Diarmuid: Witness Statement 375.
67 McQuaile, Charles: Witness Statement 276.
68 O'Farrell 1997, 21.
69 Thornton, Frank: Witness Statement 615.
70 Daly, Gen. P.: Witness Statement 387.
71 Wyse-Power, Charles: Witness Statement 420.
72 There has always been confusion over whether the 'signatories' actually affixed their signatures to the paper, but Kathleen Clarke indicated that Tom told her that it was 'signed that night'; Clarke 1997, 69. Michael Molloy, one of the men who printed the Proclamation, said that he carried with him the piece of paper signed by the signatories until he found himself in Richmond Barracks after the surrender, when he chewed it up and spat it out to prevent its discovery. Molloy, Michael: Witness Statement 716. See also M.J. Molloy, 'He helped to print the proclamation', *Evening Herald*, 4 April 1966.
73 See Murphy 1995; Mangran 1935.
74 No. 69 NAI DFA ES Box 33 File 232. Letter to Collins, 29 March 1921.
75 Wyse-Power, Nancy: Witness Statements 541, 587, 732.
76 O'Reilly, Bridie: Witness Statement 454.
77 O'Donoghue 1971b, 106–14.
78 O'Connor, Bridget (Mrs Batt): Witness Statement 330.
79 Dwyer 2001, 168.
80 Ó Broin 1980, 102.
81 O'Connor 1969 [1979], 113.
82 Fanning 1978, 25.
83 Taylor 1970, note on p. 136, quoting Seán Luing.
84 Forester 1989, 140.
85 Mitchell 1995, 239–40.
86 Dwyer 2001, 198.
87 Richard Mulcahy, Notes on Béaslaí's *Michael Collins*, vol. I, 118.
88 O'Kelly, J.J. (Sceilg): Witness Statement 384.
89 O'Connor 1996, 186.
90 Thornton, Frank: Witness Statement 510.

91 Thornton, Frank: Witness Statement 615.
92 O'Connor 1929, 147–8.
93 Younger 1968, 147.
94 See Sheehan 1993.
95 See http://www.ireland.com/focus/easterrising/saturday/.
96 Ryan 1949, 253.
97 Elizabeth O'Farrell always wrote of this as the building in which the leaders met after breakfast on 29 April, and that 'after breakfast, Mr Connolly and the other wounded men were carried through the holes and all the others followed. Mr Connolly was put to bed in a back room in 16 Moore Street. The members of the Provisional Government were in this room for a considerable length of time.' McHugh 1966, 207, 'The account of Miss Elizabeth O'Farrell'; O'Higgins 1925, 84.
98 Miss O'Farrell's account of the scene in 16 Moore Street and her role in the surrender negotiations with the British is most completely given in An t-Éireannach, 12–29 Feabhra 1936, in two chapters of 'Cu Uladh's' Blaidhain na h-Aiserighe, a complete history of the Rising in Irish based on the original statements of the participants and translations of documents, and covering all the Volunteer positions throughout Dublin. Ó Dubhghaill 1966, 266.
99 Dalton, Charles: Witness Statement 434.
100 McGarry, Seán: Witness Statement 368.
101 Traynor, Oscar: Witness Statement 340.
102 O'Malley 1978, 67.
103 Dwyer 2012a, 97.
104 Ceannt, Áine: Witness Statement 264.
105 O'Hegarty 1924 [1998], 38.
106 Harte, Christopher: Witness Statement 2. (His statement was dictated in response to questions and is written in the third person.)
107 Deasy 1973, 81.
108 Noyk, Michael: Witness Statement 707.
109 Lawson, Patrick: Witness Statement 667.
110 Manuscript of Seán Ó Muirthile, Richard Mulcahy papers, UCD.
111 Kline 1993.
112 Staines, Michael: Witness Statements 284, 984.
113 Conlon, Martin: Witness Statement 798.
114 O'Donoghue, Florence: Witness Statement 554.
115 Boylan, Seán: Witness Statements 212, 1715.
116 Younger 1968, 276f.
117 Dwyer 1981, 46.
118 Lynch, Diarmuid: Witness Statement 4.
119 Staines, Michael: Witness Statements 284, 984.
120 Good 1996, 130f.
121 Whelan, William: Witness Statement 369.
122 O'Connor 1969 [1979], 56f.
123 For accounts of these plans, see Pax Murray; Billy Aherne; Denis Brennan; Seán McGrath; Frank Thornton; Denis Kelleher; Liam Tobin: O'Malley papers, P17b188, 100, 107. See also a letter from Florence O'Donoghue to the Sunday Press, 25 January 1959. The best account, by one of the men who went with Brugha from the Dublin IRA, is Good 1996, 130–44. See also Seán McGrath: O'Malley papers, P17b/100, Leo Henderson, P17b/105, and Fintan Murphy, P17b/107.
124 Neligan 1999, 114.
125 Leonard, Joseph: Witness Statement 547.
126 Byrne, Vincent: Witness Statement 423. Byrne did not remember any such meeting. He said that it would be strange for eight to attend a meeting and then only four be told to leave their jobs. He thought at first that the Squad comprised two units of four, with Daly in charge of one unit and McDonnell the other.
127 Slattery, James: Witness Statement 445.
128 Leonard, Joseph: Witness Statement 547.
129 Daly, Gen. P.: Witness Statement 387.
130 Thornton, Frank: Witness Statement 615.
131 Leonard, Joseph: Witness Statement 547.

132 Dalton, Charles: Witness Statement 434.
133 'About April of 1921—some time previous to the burning of the Custom House—a considerable amount of indiscipline crept in amongst the HQ squad and they were inclined to drink rather excessively. Collins was anxious to replace Keogh by Paddy Daly who was a prisoner in Ballykinlar at the time and a teetotaller. He instructed Daly to sign any papers necessary to obtain his release, which he did. When Collins mentioned to Keogh that he intended to put Daly in charge of the squad, Keogh refused to hand over to Daly and the majority of the squad backed Keogh and threatened all kinds of reprisals. In fact, at a meeting in Gardiner St. which was presided over by Oscar Traynor and attended by the squad and members of the ASU and at which I was present, the attitude of the HQ squad was definitely disobedient and they cut up rather rough. This trouble resolved itself at the burning of the Custom House when Keogh and the majority of the squad were arrested; Daly assumed command automatically and the remainder of the squad and the ASU amalgamated and formed what was known as the Dublin Guard. A number of the ASU refused to sign on under Daly'. White, George: Witness Statement 956.
134 Stapleton 1969.
135 Dwyer 2005, 69.
136 Byrne, Vincent: Witness Statement 423.
137 O'Connor 1996, 143.
138 Daly, Gen. P.: Witness Statement 387.
139 See Dalton 1929.
140 Collins 22 Society newsletter, 3 April 2016.
141 The foregoing quotations are from O'Connor 1996, 94f.
142 Dwyer 1990, 24.
143 Traynor, Oscar: Witness Statement 340.
144 Daly, Gen. P.: Witness Statement 387.
145 Leonard, Joseph: Witness Statement 547.
146 *Freeman's Journal*, 3 March 1920.
147 Traynor, Oscar: Witness Statement 340.
148 Lt Col. Andrew J. McCarthy, a member of the St John's Ambulance Brigade, went into the hotel to escort Brugha out, but Brugha refused, saying 'They'll never get me' (quoted in the *Sunday Express*, 18 May 1952). See, in contrast, Ernie O'Malley (1978, 137–8): 'They called on [Brugha] to surrender. He rushed on and fell gravely wounded; later he died. I knew what he must have thought before he rushed out. We had destroyed an effective resistance by the surrender of the Four Courts; the death of a prominent TD and former Minister of Defence was needed to compensate. He had preferred death rather than outlive the dishonour of his comrades. That, to me, was a policy of desperation, and it was unsoldierly. Dying to carry out orders in a job of work was one thing, seeking death was a different idea.'
149 Deasy 1998, 62.
150 Kennedy, Patrick: Witness Statement 499.
151 Doyle, James: Witness Statement 771.
152 Dwyer 2005, 176, 211–12. See Moran 2010.
153 Doyle, James: Witness Statement 771.
154 Farrington, Annie: Witness Statement 749.
155 Deasy 1973, 23.
156 Thornton, Frank: Witness Statement 615.
157 Mernin, Lily: Witness Statement 441.
158 McGarry 2006.
159 Saurin, Frank: Witness Statement 715.
160 See Andrews 1979; 1982.
161 Plunkett, John (Jack): Witness Statements 488, 865.
162 O'Donoghue 1971b, 36–47.
163 Breen 1964, 151f.
164 Plunkett, John (Jack): Witness Statements 488, 865.
165 Tobin, Liam: Witness Statement 1753.
166 *An tÓglach*, 15 August 1918.
167 *Ibid.*, 14 September 1918.
168 Fitzsimmons, Christopher: Witness Statement 581.
169 Stapleton, William J.: Witness Statement 822.

[170] Leonard, Joseph: Witness Statement 547

[171] McCrea, Patrick: Witness Statement 413.

[172] See Moran 2010.

[173] Dwyer 2012a, 243.

[174] Thornton, Frank: Witness Statements 510, 615.

[175] For the IRA/Republican view of Henderson's capture and the follow-on capture of Free State Gen. J.J. O'Connell, see O'Malley 1978, 88f.

[176] Lawless, Sister Eithne: Witness Statement 414.

[177] O'Connor, Bridget (Mrs Batt): Witness Statement 330.

[178] Daithi O'Donoghue, private statement, 26 March 1951.

[179] Gallagher 1953, 230.

[180] See Linklater 1980.

[181] See Mulvihill 1989.

[182] Dwyer 2012a, 82.

[183] McDermott 2001, 156f.

[184] See McDowell 1970.

[185] O'Brien, William: Witness Statement 1766.

[186] Rees 1998, 231.

[187] Murphy, Gregory: Witness Statement 150.

[188] Noyk, Michael: Witness Statement 707.

[189] Michael Noyk, NLI MS 18, 975, p. 12.

[190] Thornton, Brigid Lyons: Witness Statement 259.

[191] Béaslaí 1926a, quoted in Frank Thornton's Witness Statement 615.

[192] Tobin, Liam: Witness Statement 1753.

[193] Thornton, Frank: Witness Statement 615.

[194] *Freeman's Journal*, 19 June 1917; *The Voice of Labour*, 1 May 1919; *New Ireland*, 8 and 15 April 1922.

[195] Countess Markievicz wrote: 'It wasn't talk blocked conscription: it was the astounding fact that the whole male population left at home and most of the women and kids would have died rather than fight for England, and they simply did not dare exterminate a nation' (letter to Eva Gore-Booth, 14 February 1919). Roper 1987, 194–5.

[196] Fitzsimmons, Christopher: Witness Statement 581.

[197] Collins often met with representatives of the IRA from Northern Ireland after the Truce, as he had during the War of Independence. Many of those meetings were held here after he moved his offices to City Hall. Following the killing of Inspector Swanzy on 20 August 1920, riots erupted across Northern Ireland. (See Lisburn, Co. Antrim, Appendix VI.) After that Collins thought that aggressive action in the North provoked an inordinate response against Catholics there. McDermott 2001, 58.

[198] Theodore Roosevelt, 10 April 1899.

[199] *Irish Times*, 4 February 1922.

[200] *Freeman's Journal*, 3 Feburary 1922. For Craig's worries about the possibility of a Boundary Commission changing the border with Northern Ireland see McDermott 2001, 156f.

[201] Dwyer 2012a, 43f.

[202] *Daily Mail*, 30 June 1922. See McDermott 2001, 112, 117.

[203] McDermott 2001, 244.

[204] Thornton, Brigid Lyons: Witness Statement 259.

[205] Daithi O'Donoghue, private statement, 26 March 1951.

[206] O'Connor 1996, 145.

[207] Yeates 2014b.

[208] O'Hegarty, Patrick S.: Witness Statement 26. (The entire statement is handwritten.)

[209] Gallagher 1953, 22–3.

[210] *Hansard*, 24 October 1917. Henry Edward Duke, chief secretary for Ireland 1916–18, estimated that Sinn Féin's membership numbered about 200,000 in October 1917. Dawson 1972 [1920], 118.

[211] Molony, Helena: Witness Statement 391.

[212] Blythe, Ernest: Witness Statement 939.

[213] Macardle 1937 [1965], 915.

[214] *Ibid.*, 232–3.

[215] Johnson, Thomas: Witness Statement 1755.

216 O'Brien, William: Witness Statement 1766.
217 Gallagher 1953, 24–8.
218 Kee 1972, 619.
219 *Ibid.*, 620.
220 Gallagher 1953, 56–62.
221 Collins, letter to Austin Stack, 15 January 1919.
222 Ó Snodaigh 2000a; 2000b; 2000c; 2000e.
223 Johnson, Thomas: Witness Statement 1755.
224 O'Brien, William: Witness Statement 1766.
225 Macardle 1937 [1965], 275–7.
226 Neeson 1968, 68.
227 Mitchell 1974, 107–10. Even after it was amended the Programme was considered 'communistic' by some TDs, including Piaras Béaslaí, Cathal Brugha and Kevin O'Higgins. See Yeates 2012, 298–9.
228 Ó Snodaigh 2000b. Holt (1960, 171) claims that there were 27.
229 *Belfast Newsletter*, 22 January 1919.
230 O'Kelly, Seán T.: Witness Statements 611, 1765.
231 Nunan, Seán: Witness Statement 1744.
232 Ó Snodaigh 2000f.
233 NLI MS 8469.
234 Murphy 1994.
235 Béaslaí 1926b, vol. I, 271.
236 Collins, letter to Sister Celestine, 13 April 1919.
237 Stewart 1997, 164–6, document 89.
238 Gallagher 1953, 68.
239 Macardle 1937 [1965], 986; Hart 2006, 194.
240 See Evans 2012.
241 Fogarty, Most Revd Dr Michael: Witness Statement 271.
242 See Lavelle 1961.
243 *Ibid.*, 70–82. These courts were variously known as 'Dáil courts', 'Republican courts' and 'Sinn Féin/Republican courts' in different sources. For consistency, they are here referred to as 'Dáil/Republican courts'.
244 See Casey 1970; Costello 1990; Maguire 1984; Kotsonouris 1994b. O'Duffy, Seán M.: Witness Statements 313, 618, 619.
245 Bowden 1973.
246 Lord Mounteagle, letter to the *Irish Times*, 15 July 1920.
247 O'Connor 1975 [1981], 150.
248 Kotsonouris 1994b.
249 Davit, Cahir: Witness Statements 993, 1751.
250 Traynor, Oscar: Witness Statement 340.
251 *Irish Times*, 13 September 1919.
252 Mulcahy papers, P7/D/66, UCD.
253 Martin 1963, x.
254 Macardle 1937 [1965], 456.
255 Macready 1924, vol. 2, 602.
256 Mackay 1996, 201.
257 Taylor 1970, 142.
258 Many of the leaders of the IRA outside Dublin were blindsided by the Truce, and most disagreed with it. They thought that the IRA were 'winning' and would soon have a military victory. See Deasy 1998, 11f.; O'Malley 1978, 13: 'We were gaining ground, each day strengthened us and weakened our enemy; then why was it necessary to stop hostilities?'
259 Younger 1968, 166f.
260 Dwyer 2007, 39–41.
261 Cowell 2005, 210–11.
262 O'Kelly, Seán T.: Witness Statements 611, 1765.
263 Gavan Duffy, George: Witness Statement 381.
264 McCartan, Patrick: Witness Statements 99, 100, 766.
265 Bulfin, Éamon: Witness Statement 497.
266 Dwyer 2007, 61.

267 *Ibid.*, 46.
268 Manuscript of Seán Ó Muirthile, Richard Mulcahy papers, UCD.
269 Gaughan 1977, 172.
270 Gallagher 1953, 321.
271 Dwyer 2007, 24.
272 Pakenham 1935 [1972], 266.
273 O'Connor 1929, 171.
274 Kline 1993. See http://oireachtasdebates.oireachtas.ie/debates%20authoring/
debateswebpack.nsf/takes/Dáil1921121900003.
275 *Ibid.*
276 Gallagher 1953, 322.
277 FitzGerald 1935.
278 Younger 1968, 166.
279 Kee 1972, 724.
280 Kline 1993.
281 Diary of Thomas Jones, Lloyd George's personal secretary, 10 November 1921.
282 'The resurrection of Hungary: a parallel for Ireland', *The United Irishman*, 1904.
283 Though all discussion in the Dáil, the newspapers and most books refer to a 'Treaty', the English and Irish delegates did not sign a Treaty. They signed a document entitled 'Articles for Agreement'. The words 'for a Treaty' were added to the English copy, but by that time the Irish copy was being delivered to Ireland. See Pakenham 1935 [1972], 246. For consistency and to conform to other sources, the discussion here and throughout will refer to the 'Treaty'. (See Appendix VII for complete Articles.)
284 Hart 2006, 319.
285 Curran 1980, 130.
286 Neeson 1968, 64.
287 See Colum 1959, 309. 'Griffith expected objections to [the Treaty], but he was reckoning on the President's support.' Desmond FitzGerald had to tell him, in the words he had heard himself from Austin Stack, 'He's dead against it now, anyway'.
288 Many of the IRA felt betrayed as well. 'The officers and men I met seemed dazed. Some had been crying, their eyes were swollen. We awaited the arrest of the delegates. They had no authority to sign without first referring the matter to their Cabinet' (O'Malley 1978, 43).
289 Barton, Robert: Witness Statement 979. Rees 1998, 289.
290 Dwyer 1992, 85.
291 *Irish Independent*, 9 December 1921.
292 O'Connor 1969 [1979], 134.
293 Hopkinson 1988, 25.
294 Packenham 1935 [1972], 266.
295 In the Dáil record, nine pages of the public Dáil debates dealt with partition, and over 300 did not. Of the private debates, only three of 181 pages were devoted to partition.
296 Dáil Éireann, private session, p. 153. Members of the IRA in Northern Ireland were particularly distressed by de Valera's statement that, 'For his part, if the Republic were recognized he would be in favour of giving each party the power to vote itself out …' (McDermott 2001, 107). In McDermott's (2001, 138) opinion, that is the reason why so many republicans in the North sided with Collins rather than de Valera when the split came over the terms of the Treaty.
297 http://oireachtasdebates.oireachtas.ie/debates%20authoring/debateswebpack.nsf/takes/Dáil1921121900003.
298 Dwyer 1981, 114.
299 See Hopkinson 1988, 105f.
300 See Figgis 1922.
301 O'Sheil, Kevin: Witness Statement 1242. Akenson and Fallon 1970.
302 'The IRA and the Treaty', *An Phoblacht*, 17 April 1997.
303 See McDermott 2001, 134f.
304 O'Malley 1978, 65.
305 Deasy 1998, 62.
306 O'Brien, William: Witness Statement 1766.
307 Johnson, Thomas: Witness Statement 1755.
308 Dwyer 2012a, 147.

[309] *Ibid.*, 171.

[310] Gallagher 1979; Towey 1976; Gillis 2011, 37.

[311] Henry 1920, 166.

[312] Regan 1999, 55.

[313] Letter from Thomas Johnson to his son Fred, 5 July 1922 (NLI Archives, Johnson letters, MS 27, 609A).

[314] McGinley, Elizabeth (née Brennan): Witness Statement 860. She was Arthur Griffith's secretary.

[315] Blyth, Ernest: Witness Statement 939.

[316] *Irish Independent*, 15 June 1922.

[317] The *Daily Mail* commented in its editorial: 'After such a speech the Pact can only be described as breaking up' (*Daily Mail*, 16 June 1922).

[318] Deasy 1998, 60.

[319] Neeson 1968, 88–9; Hopkinson 1988, 104f.

[320] Macardle 1937 [1965], 982.

[321] Hopkinson 1988, 110.

[322] Ó Buachalla, Domhnall: Witness Statement 194.

[323] Barry, Tom: Witness Statement 1743. Gillis 2011, 123.

[324] *Irish Volunteer*, 15 May 1915.

[325] O'Hegarty 1924 [1998], 2.

[326] McCarville (McGrane), Eileen: Witness Statement 1752.

[327] Foy 2006, 198.

[328] Hyland, Joseph: Witness Statement 644.

[329] Foran, Peter: Witness Statement 316.

[330] David Neligan (Witness Statement 380) described Hardy: '[James] McNamara and myself knew this man well. He was an Orangeman, with an artificial leg, on the Castle garrison and was an Intelligence Officer in the Auxiliaries and a very hostile killer.'

[331] Art MacEoin, 'Murder in the Castle', *An Phoblacht*, 22 November 2001.

[332] Author's correspondence and documents from Clare Cowley, granddaughter of Molly O'Reilly. See http://mspcsearch.militaryarchives.ie/docs/files//PDF_Pensions/R2/MSP34REF20325 MaryTCorcoran/W34E4055MaryTCorcoran.pdf. See also Fagan 2016, 54f.

[333] See O'Mahoney 2005.

[334] Crozier 1937, 84.

[335] Thornton, Frank: Witness Statement 615.

[336] Byrne, Vincent: Witness Statement 423.

[337] O'Connor 1929, 155.

[338] De Burca and Boyle 2002 [1922], 18.

[339] See http://www.oireachtas.ie/parliament/education/historicaldebatesandspeeches/.

[340] Dáil Éireann, Official Report: Debate on the Treaty between Great Britain and Ireland, 21 December 1921, p. 10506.

[341] Articles of Agreement for a Treaty between Great Britain and Ireland, Article 4.

[342] Macardle 1937 [1965], 579; as recorded by Robert Barton.

[343] Colm Ó Murchada, cabinet notes, 8 December 1922.

[344] Dwyer 2007, 190.

[345] See http://www.oireachtas.ie/parliament/education/historicaldebatesandspeeches/.

[346] Cullen and Luddy 2001, 80.

[347] Diary of Kathleen Lynn, 7 December 1921.

[348] Dáil Éireann, Parliamentary Debates, Vol. 3, 7 January 1922.

[349] O'Connor 1929, 184–5.

[350] De Burca and Boyle 2002 [1922], 78.

[351] *Ibid.*, 79.

[352] Mulcahy 1976.

[353] Gleeson (1962, 134) identifies him as Capt. Fitzgerald.

[354] No. 232 NAI DE 5/19.

[355] O'Reilly, Eily O'Hanrahan: Witness Statements 270, 415.

[356] Daly, Madge: Witness Statements 209, 855.

[357] Heron, Áine: Witness Statement 293.

[358] Patrick Fogarty papers, Allen Library. E/AL/PF/4, 22 January 1917.

[359] Statement of Batt O'Connor, NLI MS 33,914. Gleeson, Joseph: Witness Statement 367.

[360] Nugent, Larry: Witness Statement 907.

361 See Cowell 2005; Griffith and O'Grady 1982.

362 O'Donoghue 1971b, 146–53.

363 Thornton, Brigid Lyons: Witness Statement 259.

364 Cowell 2005, 231.

365 McGarry, Maeve: Witness Statement 826.

366 Molony, Katherine Barry: Witness Statement 731.

367 Thornton, Frank: Witness Statement 510.

368 Saurin, Frank: Witness Statement 715.

369 Thornton, Frank: Witness Statement 615.

370 Dolan, Joseph: Witness Statement 663.

371 See Gallagher 1953, 39–43, for methods used by nationalist publications to 'baffle' Beresford.

372 Not into Dublin Castle, as portrayed in the film *Michael Collins*.

373 Nunan, Seán: Witness Statement 1744.

374 McGuigan 2011.

375 Broy, Éamon: Witness Statements 1280, 1284, 1285.

376 Thornton, Frank: Witness Statement 615.

377 Mulcahy to Broy, Mulcahy papers, P/7b/184.

378 MacAodh 2001a.

379 Slattery, James: Witness Statement 445.

380 See Hart 2002.

381 McGuigan 2011.

382 McGarry 2006.

383 Thornton, Frank: Witness Statement 615.

384 Slattery, James: Witness Statement 445.

385 Dalton, Charles: Witness Statement 434.

386 Nugent, Laurence: Witness Statement 907.

387 Figgis 1924, 195–221; Gallagher 1953, 29–33.

388 Mulcahy 1968.

389 Broy, Éamon: Witness Statement 1280.

390 Ó Snodaigh 1999e.

391 Cosgrave, William: Witness Statements 268, 449.

392 Cusack, Dr Brian: Witness Statement 736.

393 Fahy, Frank: Witness Statement 442. Fahy, Anna: Witness Statement 202.

394 Hayes, Dr Richard: Witness Statements 97, 876.

395 Lyons, George: Witness Statements 11, 104.

396 MacBride, Maud Gonne: Witness Statement 317.

397 MacEntee, Seán: Witness Statement 1052.

398 McCullough, Denis: Witness Statement 914.

399 O'Keeffe, Patrick: Witness Statement 1725.

400 *Irish Independent*, 18, 19, 21 May 1918; *Irish Times*, 18, 19, 21 May 1918.

401 Patrick O'Keeffe, who was chosen as a candidate and was elected from Cork North, maintained that part of the vote against the Treaty was an anti-Collins vote, and that Collins first caused the antagonism because he, Boland and O'Hegarty, all IRB men, had hand-picked the candidates for the 1918 election—and that was resented particularly by those who had aspirations to enter the Dáil in 1919 but who failed to be nominated. Mulcahy 2009, 109.

402 Brennan, Robert: Witness Statements 125, 779, 790.

403 Gallagher 1953, 44–55.

404 Murphy 1994.

405 In March 1918 Lynch was deported to the US because he was an American citizen. He had 'intercepted' a load of pigs to be sent to England for the British army, had them butchered in Dublin and sent the proceeds to their owners—but the pigs never reached England, so the British deported him. He wanted to marry prior to deportation to help with his bride's citizenship, but the British wouldn't authorise it, so he was married in secret in Dundalk Gaol, and his bride accompanied him and his supporters to Amiens Street Station. The following December he was elected to the Dáil in his absence.

406 Lawless, Sr Eithne: Witness Statement 414.

407 Frank Gallagher in *An Phoblacht*, 28 February 1922; Macardle 1937 [1965], 666.

408 *Irish Independent*, 17 March 1922.

409 *Ibid.*, 18 March 1922.

410 *Ibid.*
411 *Ibid.*, 20 March 1922.
412 Dwyer 2006, 144–5.
413 Macardle 1937 [1965], 976.
414 Deasy 1973, 257.
415 Younger 1968, 99.
416 Daly, Gen. P.: Witness Statement 387.
417 Neligan, David: Witness Statement 380.
418 Daly, Gen. P.: Witness Statement 387.
419 Dolan, Joe: Witness Statement 663.
420 Lawless, Sr Eithne: Witness Statement 414.
421 O'Reilly, Bridie: Witness Statement 454.
422 Blythe, Ernest: Witness Statement 939.
423 Gallagher 1953, 89ff.
424 Johnson, Thomas: Witness Statement 1755.
425 Hopkinson 1988, 104.
426 See Figgis 1922.
427 Hayes, Michael: Witness Statement 215.
428 Cosgrave, William: Witness Statements 268, 449. See Meehan 2010.
429 O'Connor 1981, 178.
430 Elaine Byrne, 'Hands that shaped Irish history', *Irish Times*, 29 July 2008.
431 O'Malley 1978, 163.
432 Letter from Collins to Kitty Kiernan, 2 August 1922.
433 Younger 1968, 425.
434 O'Hegarty 1924 [1998], 94–5.
435 Mackay 1996, 275.
436 *Poblacht na hÉireann*, 14 August 1922.
437 *Irish Times*, 15 August 1922.
438 Younger 1968, 128ff.
439 McMahon, Revd J.T.: Witness Statement 362. See also Most Revd Dr Michael Fogarty: Witness Statement 271.
440 Cabinet conclusion 77 (20) 6, of App. III, Conference of Ministers, 24 December 1920.
441 Cope was involved in many discussions of the time, and was often in contact with Collins. He was asked to submit a witness statement concerning his role and how the negotiations evolved. He refused to outline his role or the negotiations but submitted the following letter as his statement: 'It is not possible for this history to be truthful … The IRA must be shown as national heroes, and the British Forces as brutal oppressors. Accordingly the Truce and Treaty will have been brought about by the defeat of the British by the valour of small and ill-equipped groups of irregulars. And so on. What a travesty it will and must be. Read by future generations of Irish children, it will simply perpetuate the long-standing hatred of England and continue the miserable work of self-seeking politicians, who, for their own aggrandizement, have not permitted the Christian virtues of forgiveness and brotherhood to take its place … Ireland has too many histories; she deserves a rest.' Cope, Sir Alfred: Witness Statement 469.
442 Valiulis 1992, 175–6.
443 Coogan and Morrison 1998, 50.
444 Thornton 1975.
445 Gallagher 1953, 83ff.
446 McKenna, Kathleen (née Napoli): Witness Statement 643. McKenna 1970.
447 Mee, RIC Constable Jeremiah: Witness Statement 379. Macardle 1937 [1965], 360. See Gaughan 1975.
448 Marreco 1967, 250.
449 Gallagher 1953, 90–4.
450 Dwyer (2005, 211) correctly identifies the Englishmen and the members of the Squad. An example of the confusion regarding names can be found in Gleeson 1962, 129.
451 Slattery, Jim: Witness Statement 445.
452 Nugent, Laurence: Witness Statement 907.
453 Byrne, Vincent: Witness Statement 423.
454 Saurin, Frank: Witness Statement 715.
455 Tobin, Liam: Witness Statement 1753.

456 Saurin, Frank: Witness Statement 715.
457 Thornton, Frank: Witness Statement 615.
458 Neligan, David: Witness Statement 380.
459 Dwyer 2005, 173. Gleeson (1962, 129) identifies the maid as 'Rosie' and the porter as 'Matt'.
460 Dalton, Charles: Witness Statement 434.
461 Lavan went on the run to the US in 1922 following his involvement in Civil War killings in Kiltimagh, Co. Mayo. He became a wealthy lawyer, was a colourful pillar of the community in Brighton, Michigan, and was a vocal Irish republican his entire life.
462 'Remembering the past: Molly O'Reilly', *An Phoblacht*, 7 October 1999.
463 Author's correspondence with and documents from Clare Cowley, granddaughter of Molly O'Reilly. See http://mspcsearch.militaryarchives.ie/docs/files//PDF_Pensions/R2/ MSP34REF20325MaryTCorcoran/W34E4055MaryTCorcoran.pdf. See also Fagan 2016, 54ff.
464 MacThomais 1965, 37.
465 Saurin, Frank: Witness Statement 715.
466 Akenson and Fallon 1970.
467 Townsend 1978–9.
468 Slattery, James: Witness Statement 445.
469 Tobin, Liam: Witness Statement 1753.
470 IRA/Republicans taken to Oriel House were tortured and abused. For the IRA/Republican view, see O'Malley 1978, 145ff, 155ff and 268ff. O'Malley wrote that the house was 'famous as a knocking shop where prisoners were battered and tortured'.
471 Neligan, David: Witness Statement 380.
472 Browne, Revd Michael: Witness Statement 538.
473 Thornton, Frank: Witness Statement 615.
474 Tobin, Liam: Witness Statement 1753.
475 Dolan, Joe: Witness Statement 663.
476 Saurin, Frank: Witness Statement 715.
477 McGarry 2006.
478 Bell 1967.
479 Traynor, Oscar: Witness Statement 340.
480 Leeson 2003; Foley 2014.
481 Shouldice, Jack: Witness Statement 162.
482 See http://www.irishcentral.com/news/irishvoice/Bloody-Sunday-1920-Black-and-Tans-kill-fourteen.html.
483 Colley, Harry: Witness Statement 1687.
484 Clarke 1997, 71.
485 Griffith, Maud: Witness Statement 205.
486 In some sources the name is spelt Humphries.
487 She is also called Sheila, as cited by Townshend (2013, 47, 73, 85, 419).
488 McCoole 2003, 175.
489 UCDA, Sighle Humphreys Papers, P106/742 and 745.
490 O'Malley 1978, 160ff, 174–5, 180ff.
491 Townshend 2013, 73. See https://www.youtube.com/watch?v=HAxDtQV_J-A.
492 Heron, Áine: Witness Statement 293.
493 O'Connor, Bridget (Mrs Batt): Witness Statement 330.
494 O'Connor 1929, 155–8.
495 *Ibid.*, 178–83.
496 Mannix, Patrick: Witness Statement 502.
497 Plunkett, John (Jack): Witness Statements 488, 865.
498 Ceannt, Áine: Witness Statement 264.
499 Heron, Áine: Witness Statement 293.
500 Molony, Helena: Witness Statement 391.
501 See Buckley 1938.
502 Traynor 1939.
503 Allen 1999; Brady 1974; McNiffe 1997; Fedorowitch 1996.
504 Staines, Michael: Witness Statement 284.
505 T. Ryle Dwyer, 'Every lost life in war deserves some respect', *Irish Examiner*, 5 April 2016.
506 Dwyer 2012a, 163; Lowe (n.d.).
507 See Comerford 1986.

[508] Dalton, Charles: Witness Statement 434.

[509] M. Ryan 2007, 88.

[510] O'Donovan, Julia: Witness Statement 475.

[511] Vinnie Byrne and Seán Doyle were incorrectly identified as among the Volunteers involved, according to *An Phoblacht* of 20 November 1997. They were at 38 Mount Street Upper. Sgt Patrick Mannix of the DMP stated, however, that Smith was an agent: 'The owner of the house named Smith, who was a Secret Service Agent, was also shot'. Mannix, Patrick: Witness Statement 502.

[512] Woods, Mary: Witness Statement 624.

[513] *Ibid.*; O'Malley papers, UCD P17a/150.

[514] Daly, Una: Witness Statement 610.

[515] Dolan, Joe: Witness Statement 663.

[516] Stapleton, William: Witness Statement 822.

[517] Daly, Gen. P.: Witness Statement 387.

[518] O'Malley 1978, 193ff.

[519] Duggan 1995.

[520] Kee 1972, 743.

[521] Coogan and Morrison 1998, 52.

[522] Hopkinson 1988, 164–5, 172.

[523] Daly, Una: Witness Statement 610. She was Liam Mellows's secretary.

[524] O'Kelly, Seán T.: Witness Statement 611.

[525] O'Donovan, Julia: Witness Statement 475.

[526] Beaumont, Mrs Seán (Maureen McGavock): Witness Statement 385.

[527] Smyth 1997.

[528] Lynn, Dr Kathleen: Witness Statement 357.

[529] See Mulholland 2002.

[530] Molony, Helena: Witness Statement 391.

[531] Brennan, Robert: Witness Statements 125, 779, 790.

[532] Mulcahy 1976.

[533] Ceannt, Áine: Witness Statement 264.

[534] Ginnell, Alice: Witness Statement 982.

[535] Molony, Helena: Witness Statement 391.

[536] Minutes of Conference of Women Delegates, 1 August 1917: Sheehy-Skeffington Papers, MS 21,194, National Library of Ireland.

[537] Sinn Féin Convention Report, MS 21,523, National Library of Ireland.

[538] McDonnell, Daniel: Witness Statement 486.

[539] O'Connor 1996, 184.

[540] Dolan, Joe: Witness Statements 663, 900.

[541] Aherne, Maurice: Witness Statement 483. He was usually assigned to the Dublin Bridewell.

[542] O'Donovan, Julia: Witness Statement 475.

[543] O'Byrne, Máire: Witness Statement 1029.

[544] Matthews 2010, 7ff.

[545] Nunan 1967.

[546] Matthews 2010, 15.

[547] Agnew, Arthur: Witness Statement 152.

[548] Gleeson, Joseph: Witness Statement 367.

[549] Good, Joe: Witness Statement 388.

[549] Robinson, Séamus: Witness Statements 156, 1721, 1722.

[550] Bracken, Peadar: Witness Statements 12, 361.

[551] Daly, Denis: Witness Statement 110. He worked in London for the British post office and joined the IRB in 1913; he was great friends with Michael Collins in London.

[553] Dillon 2007, 226.

[554] Soughley, Michael T.: Witness Statement 189.

[555] Broy, Éamon: Witness Statement 1284. Author's personal interview with Áine Broy.

[556] Taylor 1970, 236.

[557] Richard Mulcahy, Notes on Béaslaí's *Michael Collins*, vol. II, p. 73.

[558] Sinn Féin Publicity Department, 9 July 1922, Sinn Féin Papers, National Library of Ireland.

[559] *Irish Times*, 8 July 1922.

[560] Coady 1966.

561 For the most detailed description of the conditions at the North Dublin Union see Buckley 1938, *passim*, but especially pp 59–61; Macardle 1923.

562 Foley, Michael: Witness Statement 539.

563 Broy, Éamon: Witness Statements 1280, 1284, 1285.

564 Seán Cronin, *Kevin Barry* (pamphlet, 1965); *Irish Independent*, 13 and 15 October 2001; *Irish Times*, 7 September and 15 October 2001; *An Phoblacht*, 17 October 2001.

565 Hopkinson 1993b.

566 Daly, Gen. P.: Witness Statement 387.

567 O'Connor, Bridget (Mrs Batt): Witness Statement 330.

568 *Irish Independent*, 28 September 1917; Macardle 1937 [1965], 228.

569 Joseph Lawless served under Ashe in the 5th Battalion at Ashbourne in the Rising and described Ashe thus: 'He was an artist, with an artist's love of the beautiful, and a poetic outlook on life. I would say that his mind was free from any special inhibitions or complexes; his fervent patriotism and deeply religious feelings combining in his love of God and his fellow man. He thought deeply and would only pursue a course when he was satisfied of its righteousness, but, having once decided his course of action, he threw his whole heart into the pursuit.' Lawless, Joseph: Witness Statement 1043.

570 Nugent, Larry: Witness Statement 907.

571 Barton, Robert: Witness Statement 979.

572 O'Donoghue 1971b, 50.

573 *Ibid.*, 51–3.

574 Gallagher 1928, 88.

575 Hansard: HC Deb. 12 April 1920, vol. 127, cc1486–94.

576 Traynor, Oscar: Witness Statement 340.

577 Dwyer 2005, 211–12. See Moran 2010.

578 Donnelly, Simon: Witness Statements 113, 433, 481.

579 Dalton, Charles: Witness Statement 434.

580 Cowell 2005, 188–9.

581 Leonard, Joseph: Witness Statement 547.

582 McCrea, Patrick: Witness Statement 413.

583 Stapleton, William: Witness Statement 822.

584 Daly, Gen. P.: Witness Statement 387.

585 O'Donoghue 1971b, 146–53.

586 For a complete list see McCoole 2003, 218ff.

587 O'Donnell, Mrs Bernard: Witness Statement 750.

588 Kearns 1922, 54–7.

589 O'Keeffe, Patrick: Witness Statement 1725.

590 O'Malley 1978, 195–8.

591 White 1948 [1986], 131.

592 Hopkinson 1988, 191.

593 Coogan 1966, 52.

594 *Irish Times*, 9 December 1922; Coogan and Morrison 1998, 237.

595 Coogan and Morrison 1998, 234.

596 Mullane, Brigid (Bridie): Witness Statement 485.

597 For a complete list see McCoole 2003, 218ff.

598 O'Donel, Geraldine: Witness Statement 861.

599 Jerome Reilly, 'Mater nuns supported Rising, RIC files claim', *Irish Independent*, 2 April 2006.

600 Author's correspondence with and documents from Clare Cowley, granddaughter of Molly O'Reilly. See http://mspcsearch.militaryarchives.ie/docs/files//PDF_Pensions/R2/MSP34REF20325MaryTCorcoran/W34E4055MaryTCorcoran.pdf. See Fagan 2016, 54ff.

601 McCrea, Pat: Witness Statement 413.

602 O'Malley 1978, 80.

603 Since the passing of the Treaty by the Dáil, Collins had been trying to supply IRA units in the North with weapons. He was also behind a scheme to pay teachers who would teach an IRA-inspired curriculum. Many of his activities seemed to be counterproductive and exacerbated the pograms in the North. One of the incidents was the so-called 'Clones Affair', when several Ulster Special Constables were killed in a gun battle at the railway station in Clones. For information on the battle and its resulting killings in the North see Dwyer 2012b; see also Lynch 2004. Lynch posits: 'The Clones affray also illustrates the shadowy and confused role of

Michael Collins, who, stuck in his cocoon of conspiracy, continued in his deluded belief that an aggressive IRA policy could achieve similar results to those of the War of Independence. His failure to understand the Northern situation meant that his policy was at best a failure and at worst counterproductive, doing little else but confirming unionist prejudices and highlighting the Northern Catholic minority's vulnerability. The Clones affray signalled neither the end nor the beginning of a new phase in North–South relations: it was a tragic accident that never should have happened.'

604 McDermott 2001, 161.

605 Letter from Rory O'Connor from Mountjoy Jail, 15 September 1922 (UCD Archives, Aiken papers, P104/1253(1)). For information on British O/C Gen. Macready's transfer of weapons to Collins and the Free State both prior to the attack on the Four Courts and after it was attacked see Gillis 2011, 63ff.

606 Hopkinson 1988, 115ff; Younger 1968, 322ff.

607 For a discussion of the shells used in the bombardment and the mining of the Four Courts by the IRA, resulting in the destruction of hundreds of years' worth of documents in the Records Office, see Gillis 2011, 124ff.

608 Diary of J.F. Homan, given to Frank Saurin in 1922 and lodged in the National Library of Ireland.

609 For the intent of the garrison in mining the Records Office, see O'Malley 1978, 103ff.

610 Ibid., 123.

611 Harling, Seán: Witness Statement 935.

612 Figgis 1924, 15–21.

613 Figgis 1922.

614 O'Malley 1936 [1979], 71.

615 'Shot in a taxi-cab', Freeman's Journal, 20 November 1924; Irish Times, 20 November 1924.

616 O'Reilly, Bridie: Witness Statement 454.

617 Deasy 1973, 81.

618 Ryan, Dr James M.: Witness Statement 70.

619 Breen, Daniel: Witness Statements 1739, 1763.

620 Stewart 1997, document 1, p. 39.

621 Gillis 2011, 126.

622 Mernin, Lily: Witness Statement 441.

623 Ryan 1996, 70.

624 McGarry 2006.

625 O'Shea, Seán: Witness Statement 760.

626 Leonard, Joseph: Witness Statement 54.

627 Good, Joe: Witness Statement 388.

628 Neligan (1999, 72) names him Bernard Hugh Mulloy; Hart (2006, 238ff) names him 'Patrick' Molloy.

629 Tobin, Liam: Witness Statement 1753.

630 Thornton, Frank: Witness Statement 615.

631 Mernin, Lily: Witness Statement 441.

632 McDonnell, Michael: Witness Statement 225.

633 Ryan 1996, 70.

634 Thornton, Frank: Witness Statement 615.

635 McGarry 2006.

636 O'Callaghan, Margaret: Witness Statement 747.

637 O'Reilly, Bridie: Witness Statement 454. She was O'Sullivan's secretary and refers to the owner as 'Miss Gleeson'.

638 Dwyer 2005, 211–12; O'Malley 1936 [1979], 252ff, 272.

639 See Moran 2010.

640 MacBride, Maud Gonne: Witness Statement 317.

641 Macardle, Dorothy: Witness Statement 457.

642 Kate O'Callaghan was the widow of the lord mayor of Limerick, Michael O'Callaghan, who was murdered by the Black and Tans and who died in her arms in their home on 22 February 1921. She movingly tells her story in 'A curfew night in Limerick' (Fitzgerald 1924, 147–50). O'Callaghan, Cait: Witness Statement 688.

643 For a complete list see McCoole 2003, 218ff.

644 Barry 1981, 183.

[645] Curran, Revd M.J.: Witness Statement 687.
[646] Nugent, Larry: Witness Statement 907.
[647] Slattery, James: Witness Statement 445.
[648] P.J. Little, 'A 1916 document', *Capuchin Annual* (1942). Smith, Eugene: Witness Statement 334. Plunkett, Grace Gifford: Witness Statement 257.
[649] Broy, Éamon: Witness Statement 1280. Murphy, Gregory: Witness Statement 150.
[650] Good, Joe: Witness Statement 388.
[651] Desmond Ryan, 'Seán Treacy', in 'The Active Service Unit', *Dublin Brigade Review* (1951), 75.
[652] Breen, Daniel: Witness Statements 1739, 1763.
[653] O'Malley 1978, 153ff.
[654] Osborne 2003, 101.
[655] Margaret M. Pearse, 'St Enda's', *Capuchin Annual* (1942); St Enda's School papers, UCD Library; http://www.rte.ie/radio1/doconone/documentary-podcast-this-man-had-kept-a-school-bilingual-padraig-pearse-education.html.
[656] *Evening Herald*, 6 November 1965.
[657] Doherty and Keogh 1998, 90.
[658] Breen, Daniel: Witness Statements 1739, 1763.
[659] Byrne, Vincent: Witness Statement 423.
[660] Leonard, Joseph: Witness Statement 547.
[661] McDonnell, Michael: Witness Statement 225.
[662] Slattery, Jim: Witness Statement 445.
[663] Sugg 1999; Breen 1964, 81ff.
[664] Daly, Gen. P.: Witness Statement 387.
[665] Lord French, letter to Lord Londonderry, 3 January 1920.
[666] Daly, Madge: Witness Statements 209, 855.
[667] Lawless, Sister Eithne: Witness Statement 414.
[668] Lynn, Dr Kathleen: Witness Statement 357.
[669] Thornton, Dr Brigid Lyons: Witness Statement 259.
[670] McKenna, Kathleen Napoli: Witness Statement 643.
[671] Mernin, Lily: Witness Statement 441.
[672] Wyse-Power, Nancy: Witness Statements 541, 587, 732.
[673] Carey and de Burca 2003.
[674] *The Times*, 10 November 1920.
[675] See Bowden 1972; 1973; Dolan 2006; Crozier 1937, 95ff; O'Meara 1995.
[676] There is no mention of a 'Cairo Gang' in the reports and records of 1919–22. The term first appears in Rex Taylor's *Michael Collins* (1958 [1970]): 'In Cairo sixteen officers were chosen for a special task … The Cairo group travelled under assumed names and arrived in Dublin singly on different dates. They were in plain clothes and posing as commercial travellers … rented flats in Pembroke Street and Mount Street.' McDowell (1997) wrote: 'They were not to go near the Castle but to report to Colonel Ormonde Winter daily at either the Cairo café or Kidd's restaurant; they called themselves the Cairo group—the Squad called them the "Cairo gang".' The agents did frequent the Cairo Café (59 Grafton St., five doors from the corner of South King St.) and Kidd's Buffet (Kidd's was where the Berni Inn was until the 1980s in Nassau St. and where Lillie's Bordello is now at the bottom of Grafton St.) or the Porterhouse pub at 46 Nassau St. and the Squad did call them the 'Cairo Gang', but the origin of the name is unclear.
[677] Gleeson 1962, 101–23.
[678] Mernin, Lily: Witness Statement 441.
[679] Béaslaí 1926b, vol. I, p. 448.
[680] Richard Mulcahy, Notes on Piaras Béaslaí's *Michael Collins*, Mulcahy papers, UCD.
[681] Dolan 2006.
[682] Taylor 1958 [1970], 104.
[683] Daly, Gen. P.: Witness Statement 387. See Moran 2010.
[684] Forester 1989, 170.
[685] Thornton, Frank: Witness Statement 615.
[686] Neligan, David: Witness Statement 380.
[687] Gleeson 1962, 181.
[688] *Ibid.*, 191.
[689] McCrea, Pat: Witness Statement 413.

690 See Foley 2014.
691 Carey and de Burca 2003.
692 Dwyer 2005, 190.
693 Crozier 1937, 78.
694 Richard Mulcahy, Notes on Béaslaí's *Michael Collins*, vol. II, p. 51.
695 Crozier 1937, 84.
696 Carey and de Burca 2003.
697 Front-page notice in both the *Irish Times* and the *Irish Independent*, 23 August 1922.
698 Liam Deasy disagreed that any meetings between Collins and anti-Treaty forces were contemplated or attempted. Collins was travelling in full military convoy: 'As such there could be no question of any intention on his part, as was suggested elsewhere, of meeting us [anti-Treaty IRA] for discussions' (Deasy 1998, 81).
699 Malone 2000, 93.
700 Dalton's longest account appeared in the *Freeman's Journal* on 22 August 1923, exactly one year after the ambush.
701 Collins's notebook, 21 August 1922. Quoted in the *Sunday Independent*, 10 May 1964.
702 On 15 February 1964 O'Donoghue met with six men who were in Béal na mBláth at one time or another that day: Liam Deasy, Tom Kelleher, Jim Hurley, Dan Holland, Pete Kearney and Tom Crofts. His notes of the meeting are in the National Library, MS 31, 305.
703 Dwyer 2001, 357.
704 See http://www.rte.ie/archives/2015/0821/722718-michael-collins/.
705 Private Michael Corry, the driver of Collins's Leyland Thomas car, said that there were *two* Crossley tenders with ten men in each, and a *third* tender with 'ropes, saws, picks, food, etc.'. He also said that Collins's wound was in 'the left ear lobe'. In his statement, Capt. Seán O'Connell also said that 'there was a bad wound near his left ear'. Timmie Kelleher, who acted as a guide for the convoy early in the day, said that the convoy consisted of *two* Crossley tenders with eight men each. There is even disagreement on the colour of Collins's car: most agree that it was some shade of pale yellow, but some claim that it was silver, some that it was blue and some a metallic silver grey. Further, some name the pub owned by Jeremiah Collins as the 'Five Alls', when it is known to be the 'Four Alls'.
706 Meda Ryan interview with Emmet Dalton, 2 April 1974.
707 Meda Ryan interview with Jeremiah Collins, 16 December 1973.
708 Meda Ryan interview with Emmet Dalton, 2 April 1974.
709 Griffith and O'Grady 1982, 293–4.
710 Meda Ryan interview on 16 January 1975 with Con Slattery, who was with Hales's pro-Treaty forces on the day of the ambush.
711 Florence O'Donoghue papers, MS 31, 305, National Library of Ireland. Collins met O'Donoghue on Monday 21 August in Macroom.
712 Meda Ryan interview with Tim Kelleher, 19 April 1974.
713 There is no consensus as to who or even how many were in the ambush party during the day or at the time of the shooting. Early in the day, the party set the ambush with the cart across the road, laid a mine and waited all day for the column's return, but then dismantled the mine and were in the process of moving the cart when Collins's party came upon them. It has been said that there were many more IRA/Republicans in the ambush party during the day, but by the time the convoy arrived it is thought that there were only four members left in the ambush party, with three other groups of two or three men 'passing through', including Liam Deasy and his deputy, Tom Crofts, who walked through about 7.00pm. See Deasy 1998, 76ff; Ryan 1989, 192; Twohig 1990, 16.
714 Hopkinson 1988, 176ff; Younger 1968, 443ff.
715 Emmet Dalton, statement to the *Freeman's Journal*, 22 August 1923.
716 Interview by Cathal O'Shannon with Emmet Dalton (Twohig 1990, 60); *Shadow of Béal na mBláth*, https://www.youtube.com/watch?v=k6Yv7zriFTw.
717 Ryan 1989, 125 (throughout the book Ryan names him as Sonny 'Neill'); Twohig 1990, 284; Coogan 1992, 418; Mackay 1996, 289. However, see also Twohig 1990, 106, 158.
718 In contrast, Feehan (1991, 129ff, 133) writes that 'It was certainly *not* Sonny O'Neill' (emphasis added), but he declines to name anyone in particular. Coogan (1992, 420) also includes an interview by Fr Aiden O'Driscoll with ambush survivor Tom Foley on 2 September 1989, in which Foley said '[Sonny O'Neill] … had left the ambush position an hour before it'.
719 See http://www.militaryarchives.ie/, Denis 'Sonny' O'Neill. Under laws enacted between 1924

and 1949, people who were involved in military service or intelligence work between 1916 and 1923 were able to claim a pension from the state, while dependants of deceased fighters could also claim benefits. To prove their claim, however, they had to give precise and detailed accounts of their actions and provide corroborative evidence from other witnesses. Some documents relating to the Collins ambush somehow survived a government order of 1932 specifying that files relating to 1922 and 1923, the period of the Civil War, be destroyed by burning in case their contents led to reprisals. See Phelan 2014. Unlike many intelligence files from the period, which were destroyed in 1932, O'Neill's remained intact. He was described as having a 'very downcast appearance, hardly ever smiles, never looks a person in the face when speaking', though, significantly, he was also a 'first-class shot'. Another file describes him as a very unscrupulous individual and a most aggressive enemy of the present government. See McGreevey and Collins 2014.

[720] Twohig 1990, 258: interview with Jim Kearney on 22 September 1988. Feehan (1991, 130–2) wrote that Jim Kearney was not a member of the ambush party at any time.

[721] Ryan 1989, 144.

[722] *Ibid.*, 138–9. Ahern was a Volunteer who was involved in the killings of RIC officers Swanzy and Smyth, and apparently did not mention this to Ryan. See Witness Statements of Seán Culhane (746), Stephen Foley (1669) and Col. Thomas Fox (369). Feehan (1991, 95) gives a contrary account of the treatment that Collins's body received at the hospital.

[723] *The Cork Examiner*, 24 August 1922.

[724] Ryan 1989, 138–9; Feehan 1991, 95.

[725] Feehan 1991, 95.

[726] Ryan 1989, 117. Younger (1968, 444) and O'Farrell (1997, 166) identify the vessel as the SS *Innisfallen*.

[727] Linge 1998.

[728] Deasy 1998, 75ff.

[729] Mackay 1996, 286.

[730] *Irish Times*, 24 August 1922.

[731] Ryan 1989, x.

[732] *West London Observer*, 25 August 1922.

[733] O'Connor 1929, 190–2.

[734] Fogarty, Most Revd Dr Michael: Witness Statement 271.

[735] *Irish Independent*, 29 August 1922.

[736] *Daily Chronicle*, 23 August 1922; *Evening Press*, 23 August 1922.

[737] *Daily Telegraph*, 23 August 1922.

[738] *London Daily Sketch*, 24 August 1922.

[739] Cowell 2005, 251–2.

[740] Kline 1993.

[741] Behan would later incorporate the poem into his 1958 play *The hostage*, which depicts the events leading up to the planned execution of an eighteen-year-old IRA member in a Belfast jail.

[742] Duggan 1995.

[743] Stewart 1997, document 28, pp 80–3. Notes taken by Sgt M. Casey, RIC files, Public Records Office, London.

[744] Stewart 1997, document 72, p. 141.

[745] Collins papers, National Library of Ireland.

[746] For a personal account of the men involved see Coogan 1966, 261ff.

[747] McGinley, Elizabeth (née Brennan): Witness Statement 860. She was Arthur Griffith's secretary.

[748] See Costello 1995.

[749] Hart 2000.

[750] Kenny 2007.

[751] Costello 1997, 79. 'John O'Kane' is thought to be a pseudonym for one of Collins's friends, perhaps a London friend, but his exact identity remains unknown. No one of that name is listed in the London business or residential directories of the period. According to Rex Taylor (1958 [1970]), John O'Kane was an Irish businessman from County Galway who lived in Hampstead and at whose home 'Collins was made welcome ... Mostly, whenever he found it impossible to see O'Kane personally, he sent a note or letter and it is chiefly from these documents that the real position of Collins, and the burden he bore, are to be seen.' In an appendix on his sources Taylor states that of the four people who gave him source material he

could only divulge the name of Eithne O'Kane, niece of John O'Kane. His identity remains a mystery, as does Collins's reason for writing to him.

752 *Irish Independent*, 17 March 1922. Of his speeches quoted here, de Valera later claimed that he was misunderstood, that he was merely warning of war rather than encouraging it, and that the *Irish Independent* misinterpreted his words on each occasion. On 23 March he wrote to the *Irish Independent* that attempts to characterise his utterances as incitements to Civil War were 'villainous' (*Irish Independent*, 23 March 1922). However, the *London Times* also quoted his speeches and editorialised: 'Mr de Valera's wild speeches in the South of Ireland have shocked the whole country. They indicate a rapid change in his attitude for some little time ago he was protesting that the will of the electors must be respected'. Hopkinson 1988, 71; Younger 1968, 250.

753 Dalton, Emmet: Witness Statement 641.

754 Dwyer 2007, 32.

755 See http://www.difp.ie/docs/1921/Anglo-Irish-Treaty/145.htm.

756 Hopkinson 1988, 81ff; Younger 1972, 133ff.

757 No. 256, NAI DT S1801A; http://www.difp.ie/docs/1922/Northern-Ireland/256.htm.

758 Boyle 1977; Hopkinson 1990. For Craig's worries about the possibility of a Boundary Commission changing the border with Northern Ireland see McDermott 2001, 156ff.

759 No. 278, NAI DT S1801A; http://www.difp.ie/docs/1922/Northern-Ireland/278.htm.

760 *Irish Independent*, 18 March 1922; Coogan 1995, 310.

761 See Ash 1968; Callwell 1927; Hart 1992.

762 Diary of Thomas Jones, 31 May 1920. He was Lloyd George's personal secretary.

763 Hart 1992.

764 See http://www.nickelinthemachine.com/2008/10/knightsbridge-michael-collins-and-the-murder-of-field-marshall-sir-henry-wilson/.

765 Statements of A.A. Wilson and Ernest John Jordan, Lloyd George Papers, F/97/1/30.

766 Dunne's report, smuggled out of prison, published in the *Sunday Press*, 14 August 1955; Hart 2003, 194.

767 Dunne's prison letters (NLI, MS 2653); statement of Robert Dunne (Reggie's father), Lloyd George Papers, F/97/1/30. Collins was greatly affected by attacks on Catholics in the North, and was engaged in many schemes which he thought would give them relief. Others have written, however, that Collins's efforts were counterproductive. Lynch (2004) posits: 'The Clones affray also illustrates the shadowy and confused role of Michael Collins, who, stuck in his cocoon of conspiracy, continued in his deluded belief that an aggressive IRA policy could achieve similar results to those of the War of Independence. His failure to understand the Northern situation meant that his policy was at best a failure and at worst counterproductive, doing little else but confirming unionist prejudices and highlighting the Northern Catholic minority's vulnerability.'

768 McDermott 2001, 191.

769 The papers found on Dunne were determined to be irrelevant to the assassination. The Special Branch's investigation determined that the two men acted on their own. Conclusions of a Conference (CAB 23/30, c. 36 [22], and appendix 3).

770 Hopkinson 1988, 112ff. See Griffith and O'Grady 1982, 281. See also notes of conversations with Sweeney in 1962 and 1964, Mulcahy papers (P7D/43).

771 Ryan 1989, 20.

772 Macardle 1937 [1965], 737.

773 Forester 1989, 316.

774 Coogan 1992, 372ff.

775 Hopkinson 1988, 112ff.

776 Younger 1972, 148ff; he does not explain why 'If they had, they would have admitted it'.

777 Hart 2006, 397. See also Hart 1992; 2003, 194–220.

778 In the 1950s a campaign to rehabilitate Dunne and O'Sullivan and to show that they acted on Collins's orders gained momentum. See O'Sullivan and Lee 1958.

779 O'Connor was the IRA director of engineering and had been put in charge of operations in Britain in late 1920. See O'Connor's own account, 'Reorganising Britain', in the Mulcahy papers, P7/A/24. It was O'Connor, not Collins, who dealt with Dunne and O'Sullivan in 1920 and 1921.

780 Conclusions of a Conference of Ministers, 22 and 23 June 1922 (PRO, CAB 23/30, c.36 [22] and c.38 [22]). For the position of IRA/Republicans in the Four Courts, see O'Malley 1978,

84ff.

781 Letter from Lloyd George to Michael Collins, 22 June 1922 (TNA, Cabinet Office papers, CAB 21/255).

782 See the courtroom statement of Reginald Dunne, Art O'Brien papers (NLI, MS 8442). Taylor 1961, 167–71.

783 *Irish Independent*, 23 June 1922.

784 Hart 2000.

785 Dolan, Joseph: Witness Statement 900.

786 Taylor 1961, 182–4.

787 Ryan 1996 [2007], 81.

788 Collins 2005.

789 O'Connor 1969 [1979], 41.

790 Letter from Harry Boland to Kitty Kiernan, 10 January 1922.

791 Some reports say that it was Christmas. It appears that it was not announced until a few weeks after the event.

792 Letter from Harry Boland to Kitty Kiernan, 10 January 1922.

793 Ryan 1996 [2007], 73.

794 *Irish Independent*, 20 March 1922; Coogan 1995, 311.

795 Dwyer 2001, 346.

796 McDermott 2001, 50ff.

797 Neligan 1999, 68ff.

798 Neligan, David: Witness Statement 380.

799 O'Malley 1978, 149.

800 Letter from Collins to Harry Boland, 28 July 1922, in Taylor 1958 [1970], 94.

801 *Freeman's Journal*, 23 January 1919; Aengus Ó Snodaigh, 'Gearing up for war: Soloheadbeg 1919', *An Phoblacht*, 21 January 1999; Kee 1972, 632.

802 *Irish Independent*, 18 March 1922; Coogan 1995, 310.

803 'This day, 25 March, Feast of the Annunciation, 1920, marked the arrival of the first Black and Tan in Limerick, *en route* to Newcastle West. To the late Christopher O'Sullivan, a local journalist/editor/proprietor of the old *Limerick Echo*, goes the credit of having given the new police force their colourful name, due to their manner of dress: a black tunic, as worn by the Royal Irish Constabulary, and khaki or tan trousers of the British soldier.' *Limerick Leader*, 25 March 1980; Bennett 1964 [2001].

804 Letter from Collins to Donal Hales, 13 August 1920.

805 Murphy, Michael: Witness Statement 1547.

806 Dáil Éireann, *Minutes of the Proceedings of the First Parliament of the Republic of Ireland*, 21 January 1919.

807 Dáil Éireann, *Minutes of the Proceedings of the First Parliament of the Republic of Ireland*, 21 January 1919.

808 Dáil Éireann, *Minutes of the Proceedings of the First Parliament of the Republic of Ireland*, 21 January 1919.

809 Dáil Éireann, *Minutes of the Proceedings of the First Parliament of the Republic of Ireland*, 21 January 1919.

810 See http://oireachtasdebates.oireachtas.ie/debates%20authoring/debateswebpack.nsf/takes/Dáil1921121900003.

Bibliography

PRIMARY SOURCES

Archive, Michael Collins Centre, Castleview, Clonakilty.

Kevin Barry papers, University College Library.

Ernest Blythe papers, University College Library.

British Parliamentary Archive papers, 'The Irish Uprising, 1914–1921'.

Cathal Brugha papers, University College Library.

Máire Ni Shuibhne Brugha papers, University College Library.

Clann na Poblachta Party papers, University College Library.

Michael Collins papers, National Library of Ireland.

Michael Collins papers, document reference CO 904/196, Public Records Office, Kew, London.

Michael Collins (b. 1925) papers (MSS 40,420–40,433), National Library of Ireland.

Cumann na nGaedheal Party papers, University College Library.

Dáil Éireann:
> Correspondence Relating to Peace Negotiations, June–September 1921.
> Minutes of the Proceedings of the First and Second Parliaments of Ireland, 1919–21.
> Minutes of the Treaty Debates, 1921–2.

Department of the Taoiseach.

Department of Foreign Affairs, Documents on Irish Foreign Policy: *The Anglo-Irish Treaty, December 1920–December 1921*, edited by C. Crowe, R. Fanning, M. Kennedy, D. Keogh and E. O'Halpin. National Archives.

Éamon de Valera papers, University College Dublin.

Frank Gallagher papers, National Library of Ireland.

Arthur Griffith papers, National Library of Ireland.

T.M. Healy papers, University College Library.

Sighle Humphreys papers, University College Library.

Irish Republican Brotherhood papers, University College Library.

Irish Volunteers papers, University College Library.

Lt Gen. Sir Hugh Jeudwine papers, Imperial War Museum, Box 72/82/2.

Seán Lemass papers, University College Library.

Patrick McCartan papers, National Library of Ireland.

Denis McCullough papers, University College Library.

Seán MacEntee papers, University College Library.

General Seán MacEoin papers, University College Library.

Eoin MacNeill papers, National Library of Ireland.

Macready Committee Report, Cabinet Paper 1317, 19 May 1919, 'Formation of a special force for service in Ireland', British Public Record Office, WO32/9517.

Mary MacSwiney papers, University College Library.

Terence MacSwiney papers, University College Library.

Military Archives of Ireland, Cathal Brugha Barracks, Dublin:
> 'British Over-sea Commitments, 1919, 1920, 1921', Liaison Papers 1921–1922, Box 4.
> Frank Thornton papers.

Bureau of Military History Witness Statements:
> Aghlas (Ashe), Nora: Statement 645. Aherne, Maurice: Statement 483. Archer, Liam: Statement 819. Barton, Robert C.: Statement 979. Béaslaí, Piaras: Statements 261, 675. Beaumont, Seán: Statement 709. Blythe, Ernest: Statement 939. Brennan, Robert: Statements 125, 779, 790. Browne, Revd Michael: Statement 538. Browne, Msgr Patrick: Statement 729. Broy, Éamon: Statements 1280, 1284, 1285. Byrne, Bernard C.: Statement 631. Byrne, Christopher:

1744. O'Brien, Liam: Statement 323. Ó Buachalla, Domhnall: Statement 194. O'Callaghan, Margaret: Statement 747. Ó Ceallaigh, Padraig: Statement 376. O'Connor, Bridget (Mrs Batt): Statement 330. O'Donel, Geraldine: Statement 861. O'Donnell, Mrs Bernard (née Eithne Coyle): Statement 750. O'Donoghue, Daithi: Statement 548. O'Donoghue, Florence: Statement 554. O'Donoghue, Very Revd Thomas: Statement 1666. O'Donovan, Julia: Statement 475. O'Duffy, Seán M.: Statements 313, 618, 619. O'Flanagan, Michael: Statements 800, 908. O'Hegarty, P. S.: Statement 26. O'Hegarty, Seán: Statement 54. O'Keeffe, Patrick (Paudeen): Statement 1725. O'Keeffe, Seán: Statement 188. O'Kelly, J. J. (Sceilg): Statements 384, 427. O'Kelly, Kathleen (née Murphy): Statement 180. O'Kelly, Seán T.: Statements 611, 1765. O'Mara, M. A.: Statement 690. O'Mullane, Brigid (Bridie): Statement 485. Ó Rahilly, Áine: Statement 333. O'Reilly (Ó Reilly), Bridie: Statement 454. O'Reilly, Eily (née O'Hanrahan): Statements 270, 415. O'Reilly, Michael W.: Statement 886. O'Shea, Seán: Statement 760. O'Sullivan, Dermot: Statement 508. O'Sullivan, Diarmuid: Statement 375. Plunkett, Grace Gifford: Statement 257. Price, Gen. Éamon: Statement 995. Reynolds, Molly: Statement 195. Robinson, Séamus: Statements 156, 1721, 1722. Ryan, Desmond: Statements 724, 725. Ryan, Dr James: Statement 70. Ryan, Mairin (née Cregan): Statement 416. Saurin, Charles: Statement 288. Saurin, Frank: Statement 715. Sheehan, Patrick: Statement 490. Shouldice, Jack (John F.): Statements 162, 679. Slater, Thomas (Tom): Statement 263. Slattery, James (Jim): Statement 445. Smith (Smyth), Eugene: Statement 334. Stack, Una: Statements 214, 418. Staines, Michael: Statements 284, 943, 944. Stapleton, William James (Bill): Statement 822. Thornton, Dr Brigid (née Lyons):

Statement 259. Thornton, Frank: Statements 510, 615. Thornton, Nora: Statement 655. Traynor, Oscar: Statement 340. White, George: Statement 956. Woods, Mary (née Flannery): Statement 624. Wyse-Power, Charles: Statement 420. Wyse-Power, Nancy: Statements 541, 587, 732.

Kathleen Barry Moloney papers, University College Library.

General Richard Mulcahy papers, University College Dublin.

North Dublin Inner City Folklore Project, Amiens Street, Dublin.

Michael Noyk papers, National Library of Ireland.

Batt O'Connor papers, University College Library.

Rory O'Connor papers, University College Library.

Florence O'Donoghue papers, National Library of Ireland.

Diarmuid O'Hegarty papers, University College Library.

Seán T. O'Kelly papers, National Library of Ireland.

Ernie O'Malley papers, University College Library.

Lt Gen. A.E. Percival papers, 'Guerilla Warfare in Ireland, 1919–1921', Imperial War Museum, Folder 411, pp 19–23.

Count George Noble Plunkett papers, National Library of Ireland.

'Record of the Rebellion in Ireland in 1920–1921 and the Part Played by the Army in Dealing with it', Imperial War Museum, Box 78/82/2.

'Report on the Intelligence Branch of the Chief of Police from May 1920 to July 1921', Col. Ormonde de l'Epee Winter, Public Records Office, WO 35/214.

'Report on Bloody Sunday', File WO 35/38, Public Records Office.

Royal Commission on the Rebellion in Ireland, Report (1916), Cd. 8279, Minutes of Evidence, Cd. 8311.

Desmond Ryan papers, University College Library.

Dr James Ryan papers, University College Library.

St Enda's School papers, University College Library.

Sinn Féin Party papers, University College Library.

Austin Stack papers, National Library of Ireland.

Gen. Sir E.P. Strickland papers, 'The Irish Rebellion in the 6th Divisional Area: From after the 1916 Rebellion to December 1921'. Imperial War Museum, P. 362, pp 97–8.

Trinity College Library, Manuscript Department:

R. Erskine Childers papers.

Fogarty, M., Letter on the Death of Thomas Ashe from the Bishop of Killaloe, 30 September 1914.

Plunkett, G.N., 'Letter to the People of North Roscommon upon Election to Office', 17 March 1917 (Manuscript 2074).

Sir Henry Wilson papers, Imperial War Museum, DS/MISC/80, HHW/2/2B.

Winter, Ormonde, 'A Report of the Intelligence Branch of the Chief Police Commissioner, 1921'. PRO.

SECONDARY SOURCES

Aalen, F.H.A. and Whelan, K. 1992 *Dublin city and county from prehistory to the present.* Dublin.

Aan de Wiel, J. 2003 *The Catholic Church in Ireland 1914–1918.* Dublin.

Abbott, R. 2000 *Police casualties in Ireland, 1919–1922.* Cork.

Acland, F. 1920 *A report of a fortnight's tour in Ireland* (pamphlet).

Acland, F. 1921 The Sinn Féin fellowships. *Westminster Gazette,* 29 April 1921.

Adams, R.J.Q. and Poirier, S. 1978 *The conscription controversy in Great Britain, 1900–1918.* Basingstoke.

Adas, M. 1979 *Prophets of rebellion.* Chapel Hill, NC.

Ainsworth, J. 2000 British security policy in Ireland, 1920–1921: a desperate attempt by the Crown to maintain Anglo-Irish unity by force. Unpublished paper delivered at the 11th Irish-Australian Conference, Murdoch University, Perth, 25–30 April 2000. (Available as an eprint at eprints.qut.edu.au.)

Aitken, W.M. (Lord Beaverbrook) 1963 *The decline and fall of Lloyd George.* London and New York.

Akenson, D.H. and Fallon, J.F. 1970 The Irish Civil War and the drafting of the Free State Constitution. *Éire-Ireland* 5.

Alderman, C.L. 1972 *The wearing of the green: the Irish rebellion, 1916–1921.* New York.

Alexander, Y. and O'Day, A. (eds) 1986 *Ireland's terrorist dilemma.* Dordrecht.

Allen, G. 1999 *The Garda Síochána.* Dublin.

Ambrose, J. 2007 *Dan Breen and the IRA.* Cork.

Andrew, C. and Dilks, D. (eds) 1984 *The missing dimension. Governments and intelligence communities in the twentieth century.* London.

Andrews, C.S. 1979 *Dublin made me.* Cork.

Andrews, C.S. 1982 *Man of no property.* Cork.

Anon. 1917 *Arthur Griffith: a study of the founder of Sinn Féin.* Dublin.

Anon. 2002 Death and funeral of Mrs M.A. Collins, Woodfield, Clonakilty. *West Cork People,* Commemorative Edition, 22 August 2002.

Arthur, Sir G. 1932 *General Sir John Maxwell.* London.

Ash, B. 1968 *The last dictator: a biography of Field Marshal Sir Henry Wilson.* London.

Asquith, Lady C. 1968 *Diaries, 1915–1918.* London.

Asquith, H.H. (Earl of Oxford and Asquith) 1920 *The Paisley Policy.* London.

Augusteijn, J. 1996 *From public defiance to guerrilla warfare.* Dublin.

Augusteijn, J. (ed.) 2002 *The Irish Revolution.* Basingstoke.

Baker, J. 1988 *My stand for freedom: autobiography of an Irish Republican soldier.* Westport.

Ballinger, W.A. 1969 *The men that God made mad.* New York.

Bambury, C. 1986 *Ireland's permanent revolution.* London.

Barry, M. 2014 *The green divide. An illustrated history of the Irish Civil War.* Dublin.

Barry, T. 1974 *The reality of the Anglo-Irish war 1920–21 in West Cork: refutations, corrections and comments on Liam Deasy's* Towards Ireland Free. Dublin.

Barry, T. 1981 *Guerilla days in Ireland: a personal account of the Anglo-Irish war.* Dublin.

Bartlett, T. and Jeffrey, K. (eds) 1996 *A military history of Ireland.* Cambridge.

Béaslaí, P. (n.d., *c.* 1922) *With the IRA in the fight for freedom: the red path of glory.* The Kerryman.

Béaslaí, P. 1922 A comrade's tribute: the message of a hero's death. *An Saorstat,* 29 August 1922.

Béaslaí, P. 1926a *How it was done—IRA intelligence: Dublin's fighting story.* Dublin.

Béaslaí, P. 1926b *Michael Collins and the making of a new Ireland* (2 vols). London.

Béaslaí, P. 1937 *Michael Collins.* Dublin.

Béaslaí, P. 1953 The National Army is founded. *Irish Independent,* 5 January 1953.

Beckett, J.C. 1963 *The making of modern Ireland, 1603–1923.* New York.

Beckett, J.C. 1973 *A short history of Ireland.* London.

Beckett, J.C. 1976 *The Anglo-Irish tradition.* Ithaca, NY.

Bell, J.B. 1967 The Thompson submachine gun in Ireland. *Irish Sword* 8 (31).

Bell, J.B. 1991 *The gun in politics: an analysis of Irish political conflict, 1916–1986.* New Brunswick, NJ.

Bell, J.B. 1997 *The secret army: the IRA.* Dublin.

Bennett, D. 1991 *The encyclopaedia of Dublin.* Dublin.

Bennett, R. 1964 *The Black and Tans* (reprinted 2001). London.

Bew, P. 2007 *Ireland: the politics of enmity, 1789–2006.* Oxford.

Boland, K. 1977 *Up Dev.* Dublin.

Borgonovo, J. (ed.) 2006a *Florence and Josephine O'Donoghue's War of Independence: a destiny that shapes our ends.* Cork.

Borgonovo, J. 2006b *Spies, informers and the Anti-Sinn Féin Society.* Dublin.

Bowden, T. 1972 Bloody Sunday, a reappraisal. *European Studies Review* 2 (1).

Bowden, T. 1973 The Irish underground and the War of Independence 1919–1921. *Journal of Contemporary History* 8 (2).

Bowden, T. 1976 The IRA and the changing tactics of terrorism. *Political Quarterly* 47.

Bowers, C.G. 2009 *Ireland's orators. A history of Ireland's fight for freedom.* Biographical Center for Research, New York.

Bowman, J. 1979 De Valera on Ulster, 1919–1920: what he told America. *Irish Studies in International Affairs* 1.

Bowman, J. 1980 Sinn Féin's perspective of the Ulster Question: autumn, 1921. *The Crane Bag* 4 (2).

Bowman, J. 1982 *De Valera and the Ulster Question, 1917–1973.* Oxford.

Bowman, T. 2008 *Carson's Army: the Ulster Volunteer Force 1910–1922.* Manchester.

Boyce, D.G. 1972 *Englishmen and Irish troubles: British public opinion and the making of Irish policy, 1918–1922.* London. (Reprinted Aldershot, 1994.)

Boyce, D.G. and O'Day, A. (eds) 2006 *The Ulster crisis.* Basingstoke.

Boyle, K. 1977 The Tallents Report on the Craig–Collins pact of 30 March 1922. *The Irish Jurist* 12.

Brady, C. 1974 *Guardians of the peace.* Dublin.

Brady, C. (ed.) 1994 *Interpreting Irish history: the debate on historical revisionism.* Dublin.

Brady, E. 1924 *Ireland's Secret Service in England.* Dublin.

Brasier, A. and Kelly, J. 2000 *Harry Boland, a man divided.* Dublin.

Breen, D. 1964 *My fight for Irish freedom.* Dublin.

Brennan, R. 1950 *Allegiance.* Dublin.

Brennan-Whitmore, W.J. 1917 *With the Irish in Frongoch.* Dublin.

Brewer, J.D. 1990 *The Royal Irish Constabulary: an oral history.* Belfast.

Briollay, S. (writing under the pseudonym of Roger Chauvire) 1922 *Ireland in rebellion.* Dublin.

Briscoe, R. 1958 *For the life of me.* London.

Broderick, M. 2001 *Wild Irish women.* Dublin.

Bromage, M.C. 1956 *De Valera and the march of a nation.* New York.

Bromage, M.C. 1964 *Churchill and Ireland.* Notre Dame, IN.

Brophy, K. 2001 Barry and comrades are laid to rest with honour and dignity. *Irish Independent,* 15 October 2001.

Browne, C. (n.d.) *The story of the 7th. A concise history of the 7th Battalion Cork No. 1 Brigade IRA from 1915–1921.*

Brugha, M. MacSwiney 2005 *History's daughter.* Dublin.

Buckland, P. 1972 *Irish Unionism, the Anglo-Irish and the new Ireland.* Dublin.

Buckland, P. 1973 *Irish Unionism, Ulster Unionism and the origins of Northern Ireland.* Dublin.

Buckland, P. 1980 *James Craig.* Dublin.

Buckley, M. 1938 *The jangle of the keys.* Dublin.

Bull, P. 1996 *Land, politics and nationalism.* Dublin.

Butler, D. and Freeman, J. 1961 *British political facts, 1900–1960.* New York.

Butler, E. 1971 *Barry's flying column: the story of the IRA's Cork No. 3 Brigade, 1919–1921.* London.

Callanan, F. 1996 *T.M. Healy.* Cork.

Callwell, Major Gen. Sir C.E. 1927 *Field Marshal Sir Henry Wilson.* London.

Campbell, C. 1994 *Emergency law in Ireland, 1918–1925.* Oxford.

Canning, P. 1985 *British policy towards Ireland, 1921–1941.* Oxford.

Carey, T. 2001 *Hanged for Ireland.* Dublin.

Carey, T. and de Burca, M. 2003 Bloody Sunday 1920: new evidence. *History Ireland* 11 (2).

Carroll, F.M. 1978 *American opinion and the Irish question, 1910–1923.* Dublin.

Carroll, F.M. (ed.) 1985 *The American Commission on Irish Independence 1919. The diary, correspondence and report.* Dublin.

Carty, J. 1951 *Ireland—from the Great Famine to the Treaty of 1921.* Dublin.

Casey, J. 1970 Republican courts in Ireland, 1919–1922. *Irish Jurist* 5.

Casey, J. 1974 The genesis of the Dáil courts. *Irish Jurist* 9.

Chamberlain, A. 1935 *Down the years.* London.

Chartres, J. (writing under the pseudonym of Edward Seaton) 1922 The bloody English. *Irish Press* (Philadelphia), 7 January–15 April 1922.

Chartres, J. (writing under the pseudonym of Fear Faire) 1927 The English peril. *The Nation,* 26 March, 2 April and 9 April 1927.

Chesterton, G.K. (n.d.) *What are reprisals?* (pamphlet).

Chevasse, M. 1961 *Terence MacSwiney.* Dublin and London.

Childers, R.E. 1911 *The framework of Home Rule.* London.

Childers, R.E. 1920 Military rule in Ireland. *Daily News,* March–May 1920.

Chorley, K. 1943 *Armies and the art of revolution.* London.

Chubb, B. 1982 *The government and politics of Ireland.* Stanford.

Churchill, W.S. 1931 *The world crisis, 1911–1918.* London.

Clarke, K. 1997 *Revolutionary woman: my fight for Ireland's freedom* (ed. Helen Litton). Dublin.

Clerkin, P. 2001 *Dublin street names.* Dublin.

Clifford, B. 1993 *The Irish Civil War: the conflict that formed the state.* Aubane.

Clifford, B. 1997 *War, insurrection and election in Ireland, 1914–21.* Belfast.

Coady, S. 1966 Remembering St John's Convent. *Capuchin Annual* (1966).

Coalter, M. 2006 *Rebel with a cause. Dan Breen and the IRA.* Cork.

Coates, T. (ed.) 2000 *The Irish uprising, 1914–1921: papers from the British Parliamentary Archive.* London.

Cockerill, Brig. Gen. Sir G. 1944 *What fools we were.* London.

Coleman, M. 2003 *County Longford and the Irish revolution.* Dublin.

Coleman, S. 2007 The day we decided to sit down and fight. *Sunday Tribune,* 12 August 2007.

Collier, B. 1961 *Brass hat: a biography of Field Marshal Sir Henry Wilson*. London.

Collins, L. 2005 Michael Collins had a stalker. *Irish Independent*, 9 October 2005.

Collins, M. 1996 [1922] *The path to freedom* (ed. T.P. Coogan). Cork.

Collins, P. (ed.) 1994 *Nationalism and Unionism: conflict in Ireland, 1885–1921*. Belfast.

Collins, T. 1986 *The Irish hunger strike*. Dublin.

Collis, M. 1968 *Somerville and Ross: a biography*. London.

Colum, P. 1959 *Arthur Griffith*. Dublin.

Colvin, I.D. 1934 *Life of Lord Carson*, Vols II and III. London. (See Marjoribanks 1932 for Vol. I.)

Comerford, M. 1969 *The First Dáil, January 21st 1919*. Dublin.

Comerford, M. 1986 Women in struggle. In P. McGlynn (ed.), *Éire Amach na Casca* (pamphlet). Dublin.

Comerford, R.V. 2003 *Ireland*. London.

Conlon, L. 1969 *Cumann na mBan and the women of Ireland, 1913–1972*. Kilkenny.

Connell, J.E.A. Jr 2016 *Dublin Rising 1916*. Dublin.

Connolly, C. 1996 *The illustrated life of Michael Collins*. Boulder, CO.

Connolly, J. 1910 *Labour in Irish history* (reprinted 1983). Dublin.

Connolly, J. 1915 *The re-conquest of Ireland*. Dublin.

Connolly, L. 2002 *The Irish women's movement*. New York (Dublin, 2003).

Connolly, N. (O'Brien) 1975 *Portrait of a rebel father*. Dublin and London.

Connolly, N. (O'Brien) 1981 *We shall rise again*. London.

Conway, An t-Athair C. 1990–2 The Third Tipperary Brigade (1921–1923). *Tipperary Historical Journal* (1990), 9–26; (1991), 35–49; (1992), 23–30.

Coogan, T.P. 1966 *Ireland since the Rising*. London.

Coogan, T.P. 1992 *Michael Collins, the man who made Ireland*. London.

Coogan, T.P. 1995 *De Valera: long fellow, long shadow*. London.

Coogan, T.P. 2000 *The IRA* (rev. edn).
London.

Coogan, T.P. 2002 Collins' place in history stands the test of time. *Irish Independent*, 22 August 2002.

Coogan, T.P. 2016 *The Twelve Apostles: Michael Collins, the Squad and Ireland's fight for freedom*. London.

Coogan, T.P. and Morrison, G. 1998 *The Irish Civil War*. London.

Cooke, P. 1986 *Scéal Scoil Éanna*. Dublin.

Cooper, D. 1953 *Old men forget*. London.

Corkery, D. 1920a *The hounds of Banba*. Dublin.

Corkery, D. 1920b Terence MacSwiney. *Studies: The Irish Jesuit Quarterly Review* (December 1920).

Costello, F. 1990 The Republican courts and the decline of British rule in Ireland. *Éire-Ireland* **25** (3).

Costello, F. 1995 *Enduring the most: the life and death of Terence MacSwiney*. Dingle.

Costello, F. (ed.) 1997 *Michael Collins in his own words*. Dublin.

Costello, F. 2003 *The Irish revolution and its aftermath, 1916–1923*. Dublin.

Costigan, G. 1968 The Anglo-Irish conflict, 1919–1921: a war of independence or systematized murder? *University Review* **5** (1).

Cottrell, P. 2006 *The Anglo-Irish War: the Troubles of 1913–1922*. Oxford.

Counahan, G. 1970 The people backed the movement, 1920. *Capuchin Annual* (1970).

Cowell, J. 1980 *Where they lived in Ireland*. Dublin.

Cowell, J. 1996 *Dublin's famous people and where they lived*. Dublin.

Cowell, J. 2005 *A noontide blazing. Brigid Lyons Thornton: rebel, soldier, doctor*. Dublin.

Coxhead, E. 1965 *Daughters of Erin*. London.

Coyle, E. 1933 The history of Cumann na mBan. *An Phoblacht*, 8 April 1933.

Creel, G. 1919 *Ireland's fight for freedom*. New York.

Cronin, S. 1971 *The story of Kevin Barry*. Cork.

Cronin, S. 1972 *Ideology of the IRA*. Ann Arbor, MI.

Cronin, S. 1980a *Frank Ryan: the search for the republic*. Dublin.

Cronin, S. 1980b *Irish nationalism: its roots and ideology*. Dublin.

Cronin, S. 1987 *Washington's Irish policy, 1916–1986. Independence, partition, neutrality*. Tralee.

Crosbie, J. 2001 Executed men finally to receive a proper burial. *Irish Times*, 7 September 2001.

Crowley, T. 2015 *In search of Michael Collins*. Castleview, Clonakilty.

Crozier, Gen. F.P. 1930 *A brass hat in no man's land*. London.

Crozier, Gen. F.P. 1931 *A word to Ghandi: the lesson of Ireland*. London.

Crozier, Gen. F.P. 1932 *Ireland forever*. London and Toronto.

Crozier, Gen. F.P. 1937 *The men I killed*. London.

Cullen, M. and Luddy, M. 2001 *Female activists, Irish women and the change, 1900–1960*. Dublin.

Curran, C.P. 1966 Griffith, MacNeill and Pearse. *Studies: the Irish Jesuit Quarterly Review* (Spring 1966).

Curran, J. 1972 Lloyd George and the Irish settlement, 1921–1922. *Éire-Ireland* 7.

Curran, J. 1975 The decline and fall of the IRB. *Éire-Ireland* 10 (1).

Curran, J.M. 1980 *The birth of the Irish Free State, 1921–1923*. University of Alabama.

Curtin, N. 1994 *The revolution in Ireland, 1879–1923*. Oxford.

Curtis, L. 1924 The Irish Boundary Question. *The Round Table* 57 (December 1924).

Curtis, L. 1991 *Ireland* (with introduction 'The Anglo-Irish Treaty and the lost world of imperial Ireland' by P. Walsh) (pamphlet). Belfast.

Curtis, L. 1994 *The cause of Ireland: from the United Irishmen to partition*. Belfast.

Czira, S.G. 1974 *The years flew by*. Dublin.

Dalton, C. 1929 *With the Dublin Brigade*. London.

Darling, W. 1952 *So it looks to me*. London.

David, E. (ed.) 1977 *Inside Asquith's cabinet. From the diaries of Charles Hothouse*. London.

Davis, R.P. 1974 *Arthur Griffith and non-violent Sinn Féin*. Dublin.

Davis, R. 1976 Arthur Griffith. *Dublin Historical Society* (1976).

Davis, R. 1977 The advocacy of passive resistance in Ireland, 1916–1922. *Anglo-Irish Studies* 3.

Davis, R. 2008 The IRB: a natural outcome of Young Irelandism? *History Ireland* 16 (6).

Davis, T. 1994 The Irish Civil War and the 'International Proposition' of 1922–1923. *Eire-Ireland* (Summer 1994).

Davitt, C. 1968 The civil jurisdiction of the courts of justice in the Irish Republic. *Irish Jurist* 3.

Dawson, R. 1972 [1920] *Red terror and green*. London.

Deasy, L. 1973 *Towards Ireland free: the West Cork Brigade in the War of Independence, 1917–1921*. Dublin.

Deasy, L. 1998 *Brother against brother*. Cork.

De Blacam, A. 1918 *Towards the republic*. Dublin.

De Breadun, D. 2008 Free State account of controversial Kerry IRA deaths in 1923 contradicted by Garda report. *Irish Times*, 31 December 2008.

De Burca, P. and Boyle, J. 2002 [1922] *Free State or Republic?* Dublin.

Desmond, S. 1923 *The drama of Sinn Féin*. London.

Dillon, G. 1960 The Irish Republican Brotherhood. *University Review* 2 (9).

Dillon, G.P. 2007 *All in the blood*. Dublin.

Diner, H. 1983 *Erin's daughters in America*. Baltimore.

Doherty, G. and Keogh, D. (eds) 1998 *Michael Collins and the making of the Irish state*. Cork.

Doherty, G. and Keogh, D. 2003 *De Valera's Ireland*. Cork.

Dolan, A. 2006 Killing and Bloody Sunday, November 1920. *Historical Journal* 49 (3).

Donnelly, B. (ed.) 1994 The National Army enters Cork, August 1922: a diary account by Mr Frank Bewitt. *Irish Archives* (Autumn 1994).

Donnelly, M. 1994 *The last post: Glasnevin Cemetery*. Dublin.

Dowling, M. 1997 'The Ireland that I would have': de Valera and the creation of the Irish national image. *History Ireland* 5 (2).

Doyle, J., Clarke, F., Connaughton, E. and Somerville, O. 2002 *An introduction to the Bureau of Military History, 1913–1921*. Dublin.

Duff, D. 1934 *Sword for hire*. London.

Duff, D. 1940 *The rough with the smooth*. London.

Duggan, G.C. (writing under the pseudonym of 'Periscope') 1922 The last days of Dublin Castle. *Blackwood's Magazine* 212.

Duggan, J. 1995 Poltergeist pistol. *History Ireland* 3.

Dwane, D.T. 1922 *The early life of Éamon de Valera*. Dublin.

Dwyer, T.R. 1980 *Éamon de Valera*. Dublin.

Dwyer, T.R. 1981 *Michael Collins and the Treaty: his differences with de Valera*. Dublin.

Dwyer, T.R. 1982a *De Valera's darkest hour, 1919–1932*. Dublin.

Dwyer, T.R. 1982b The key to ending partition that Michael Collins couldn't turn. *Sunday Independent*, 22 August 1982.

Dwyer, T.R. 1990 *Michael Collins: the man who won the war*. Cork.

Dwyer, T.R. 1992 *De Valera: the man and the myths*. Swords.

Dwyer, T.R. 2001 *Tans, terror and troubles: Kerry's real fighting story, 1913–1923*. Cork.

Dwyer, T.R. 2005 *The Squad and the intelligence operations of Michael Collins*. Cork.

Dwyer, T.R. 2006 *Big Fellow, Long Fellow: a joint biography of Collins and de Valera*. Cork.

Dwyer, T.R. 2007 *I signed my death warrant: Michael Collins and the Treaty*. Cork.

Dwyer, T.R. 2012a *Michael Collins and the Civil War* (2nd edn). Cork.

Dwyer, T.R. 2012b Sectarian violence spreads across the North. *Irish Examiner*, 2 July 2012.

Dwyer, T.R. 2015 The biographer who unwittingly made Michael Collins gay. *Irish Examiner*, 25 June 2015.

Ebenezer, L. 2006 *Fron-Goch and the birth of the IRA*. Llanrwst.

Edwards, O.D. 1987 *Éamon de Valera*. Cardiff.

Eichacker, J.M. 2002 *Irish republican women in America*. Dublin.

English, R. 1998 *Ernie O'Malley: IRA intellectual*. Oxford.

English, R. 2003 *Armed struggle: a history of the IRA*. London.

English, R. and O'Malley, C. (eds) 1991 *Prisoners: the Civil War letters of Ernie O'Malley*. Dublin.

Ervine, St J. 1949 *Craigavon, Ulsterman*. London.

Evans, G. 2012 The raising of the first Dáil Éireann loan and the British responses to it, 1919–1921. Unpublished Ph.D thesis, National University of Ireland, Maynooth.

Fagan, T. (ed.) 2016 *Rebels and heroes: hidden stories from Dublin's northside*. Dublin.

Fallon, C. 1986 *Soul of fire: a biography of Mary MacSwiney*. Dublin.

Fallon, C. 1987 Civil War hungerstrikes: women and men. *Éire* 22.

Falls, C. 1923 Irish Free State's first year. *Literary Digest* 74 (3 February 1923).

Falls, C. 1967 Maxwell, 1916, and Britain at war. In F.X. Martin (ed.), *Leaders and men of the Easter Rising, Dublin 1916*. London.

Fanning, R. 1978 *The Irish Department of Finance, 1922–58*. Dublin.

Fanning, R. 2013 *Fatal path*. London.

Fanning, R., Kennedy, M., Keogh, D. and O'Halpin, E. 1998 *Documents on Irish foreign policy, 1919–1922*. Dublin.

Farragher, S.P. 1984 *Dev and his Alma Mater*. Dublin.

Farrell, B. 1971a *The founding of Dáil Éireann*. Dublin.

Farrell, B. 1971b *Chairman or chief? The role of the taoiseach in Irish government*. Dublin.

Farrell, B. 1983 *Seán Lemass*. Dublin.

Farrell, B. (ed.) 1994 *The creation of the Dáil*. Dublin.

Farrell, M. 1976 *Northern Ireland: the Orange state*. London.

Fedorowitch, K. 1996 The problems of disbandment: the Royal Irish Constabulary and imperial migration,

1919–29. *Irish Historical Studies* **30** (117).

Feehan, J.M. 1991 *The shooting of Michael Collins: murder or accident?* Cork.

Feeney, B. 2002 *Sinn Féin, a hundred turbulent years.* Dublin.

Feeney, T. 2008 *Seán MacEntee: a political life.* Dublin.

Ferriter, D. 2007 *Judging Dev: a reassessment of the life and legacy of Éamon de Valera.* Dublin.

Ferriter, D. 2014a *A nation not a rabble.* Dublin.

Ferriter, D. 2014b Michael Collins was no trail-blazing feminist. *Irish Times*, 29 August 2014.

Figgis, D. 1917 *A chronicle of jails.* Dublin.

Figgis, D. 1922 *The Irish constitution explained.* Dublin.

Figgis, D. (writing under the pseudonym of Michael Ireland) 1923 *The return of the hero.* London.

Figgis, D. 1924 *Recollections of the Irish war.* London.

Finch, B.-A. 2003 Birth pangs of a new nation: Senator Thomas Westropp Bennett and the Irish Free State. *History Ireland* **11** (4).

Fingall, Countess E. 1991 [1937] *Seventy years young.* Dublin.

FitzGerald, D. 1935 Mr Packenham on the Anglo-Irish Treaty. *Studies: The Irish Jesuit Quarterly Review* **24**.

FitzGerald, D. 1939 *Prelude to statescraft.* London.

Fitzgerald, G. 2003 *Reflections on the Irish state* (ed. F. Fitzgerald). Dublin.

Fitzgerald, W. (ed.) 1924 *The voice of Ireland.* Dublin and London.

Fitzgibbon, C. 1973 *The life and times of Éamon de Valera.* New York.

Fitzpatrick, D. 1977 *Politics and Irish life, 1913–1921: provincial experience of war and revolution.* Dublin.

Fitzpatrick, D. 1978 The geography of Irish nationalism: 1910–1922. *Past and Present* **78**.

Fitzpatrick, D. (ed.) 1990 *Revolution: Ireland, 1917–1923.* Dublin.

Fitzpatrick, D. 1998 *The two Irelands.* Oxford.

Fitzpatrick, D. 2002 'Decidedly a personality': de Valera's performance as a convict, 1916–1917. *History Ireland* **10** (2).

Fitzpatrick, D. 2003 *Harry Boland's Irish revolution.* Cork.

Fitzsimmons, F. 2016 The Irish National Aid and Volunteers' Dependants' Fund. *History Ireland* **24** (3).

Flynn, B. 2002 *Pawns in the game: Irish hunger strikes 1912–1991.* Cork.

Foley, C. 1992 *Legion of the rearguard: the IRA and the modern Irish state.* London.

Foley, M. 2014 *The bloodied field.* Dublin.

Follis, B.A. 1995 *A state under siege: the establishment of Northern Ireland.* Oxford.

Forester, M. 1989 *Michael Collins: the lost leader.* Dublin.

Foster, G.M. 2015 *The Irish Civil War and society: politics, class and conflict.* London.

Foster, R. 1986 We are all revisionists now. *Irish Review* **1**.

Foster, R.F. 1988 *Modern Ireland, 1600–1972.* London.

Foster, R.F. 1992 *The Oxford history of Ireland.* Oxford.

Fox, R.M. 1927 Ireland, retrospect and prospect. *Nineteenth Century* **102**.

Fox, R.M. 1935 *Rebel Irishwomen.* Dublin and Cork.

Fox, R.M. 1938 *Green banners: the story of the Irish struggle.* London.

Foy, M.T. 2006 *Michael Collins' intelligence war.* Stroud (Dublin, 2007).

Fraser, T.G. and Jeffrey, K. (eds) 1993 *Men, women and war.* Dublin.

Freeman, P.A. 1963 The career of Michael Collins with special reference to the Treaty of 1921. Unpublished thesis, Bristol University.

French, Hon. E.G.F. 1931 *The life of Field Marshal Sir John French.* London.

Gallagher, F. 1928 *Days of fear: a diary of a hunger strike.* London.

Gallagher, F. 1930 Literature of the conflict. *Irish Book Lover* **18**.

Gallagher, F. (writing under the pseudonym of David Hogan) 1953 *The four glorious years.* Dublin.

Gallagher, F. 1957 *The indivisible island: the*

story of the partition of Ireland. London.

Gallagher, F. 1965 The Anglo-Irish Treaty (ed. and Introduction by T.P. O'Neill). London.

Gallagher, M. 1979 The Pact Election of 1922. Irish Historical Studies 21.

Gallen, L. 2002 Donegal women in the Civil War. An Phoblacht, 31 January 2002.

Gardiner, A.G. 1920 Stop the terror. Daily News, 6 November 1920.

Garvin, T. (ed.) 1988 The revolution in Ireland. Basingstoke.

Garvin, T. 1996 1922: the birth of Irish democracy. Dublin.

Gaughan, J.A. (ed.) 1975 Memoirs of Constable J. Mee, RIC. Dublin.

Gaughan, J.A. 1977 Austin Stack: portrait of a separatist. Dublin.

Gibbon, M. 1968 Inglorious soldier. London.

Gillis, L. 2011 The fall of Dublin. Cork.

Gilmore, G. (n.d.) The relevance of James Connolly in Ireland today. Dublin.

Girvin, K. 2007 Seán O'Hegarty: Officer Commanding First Cork Brigade, IRA. Cork.

Gleeson, J. 1962 Bloody Sunday. London.

Gogarty, O. St J. 1937 As I was going down Sackville Street. New York.

Golding, G.M. 1982 George Gavan Duffy, 1882–1951. Dublin.

Gonne, M. 1943 The real case against partition. Capuchin Annual (1943).

Good, J. 1996 Enchanted by dreams: the journal of a revolutionary (ed. M. Good). Tralee.

Good, J.W. 1922 Partition in practice. Studies 11.

Gough, Gen. H. 1921 The situation in Ireland. Review of Reviews 63.

Greaves, C.D. 1987 [1971] Liam Mellows and the Irish revolution. London.

Griffith, A. 1904 The resurrection of Hungary: a parallel for Ireland (pamphlet). Dublin.

Griffith, K. 1972 Hang up your brightest colours. Dublin.

Griffith, K. and O'Grady, T. 1982 Ireland's unfinished revolution: an oral history. [Originally published as Curious journey: an oral history of Ireland's unfinished revolution.] London.

Grinnell, L. 1918 D.O.R.A. at Westminster. Dublin.

Gunther, J. 1936 Inside de Valera. Harper's Magazine (August 1936).

Gwynn, D. 1928 The Irish Free State. London.

Gwynn, D. 1933 De Valera. London.

Gwynn, D. 1950 The history of partition, 1912–1925. Dublin.

Gwynn, S. 1922a Ireland's constitution. The Nation, 26 July 1922.

Gwynn, S. 1922b Dáil Éireann and the Irish constitution. Fortnightly Review 113.

Gwynn, S. 1924 Free Ireland in evolution. Living Age, 3 May 1924.

Gwynn, S. 1932 Shift in Irish leadership. Current History 36.

Hallinan, C.T. 1922 Ireland's role in the British Empire. New Republic 29 (9 February 1922).

Hally, Col. P.J. 1967 The Easter 1916 Rising in Dublin: the military aspects. Irish Sword 8 (30).

Hammond, B. 1977 Soldier of the rearguard. Fermoy.

Hammond, J.L. 1921a A tragedy of errors. The Nation, 8 January 1921.

Hammond, J.L. 1921b The terror in action. The Nation, 30 April 1921.

Harkness, D.W. 1969 The restless dominion: the Irish Free State and the British Commonwealth of Nations, 1921–1931. London (New York, 1970).

Harkness, D.W. 1970 Mr de Valera's Dominion: Irish relations with Britain and the Commonwealth, 1932–1938. Journal of Commonwealth Political Studies 8 (3).

Harrington, N. 1992 The Kerry landing, August 1922. Dublin.

Harrison, H. 1932 The neutrality of Ireland. London.

Harrison, H. 1939 Ulster and the British Empire. London.

Hart, P. 1992 Michael Collins and the assassination of Sir Henry Wilson. Irish Historical Studies (November 1992).

Hart, P. 1997 The geography of revolution in Ireland, 1917–1923. Past and Present 155.

Hart, P. 1999 *The IRA and its enemies: violence and community in Cork, 1916–1923*. Oxford.

Hart, P. 2000 Operations abroad: the IRA in Britain, 1919–1923. *English Historical Review* 115 (460).

Hart, P. (ed.) 2002 *British Intelligence in Ireland, 1920–21: the final reports*. Cork.

Hart, P. 2003 *The IRA at war, 1916–1923*. Oxford.

Hart, P. 2005 Peter Hart and his enemies. *History Ireland* 13 (4).

Hart, P. 2006 *Mick: the real Michael Collins*. London.

Hartley, S. 1987 *The Irish question as a problem in British foreign policy, 1914–1918*. London.

Hartline, M.C. and Kaulbach, M.M. 1996 Michael Collins and Bloody Sunday: the intelligence war between the British and Irish intelligence services. *CIA Historical Review Program*, 2 July 1996 (approved for release 1994).

Harvey, A.D. 1992 Who were the Auxiliaries? *Historical Journal* 35 (3).

Haverty, A. 1988 *Countess Markievicz: an independent life*. London.

Hawkins, F.M.A. 1970 Defence and the role of Erskine Childers in the Treaty negotiations of 1921. *Irish Historical Studies* 11.

Hayes, M. 1958 Dáil Éireann and the Irish Civil War. *Studies: The Irish Jesuit Quarterly Review* 1.

Henderson, F. 1945 Irish leaders of our time: Richard McKee. *An Cosantóir* 5.

Henry, R.M. 1920 *The evolution of Sinn Féin*. Dublin.

Hepburn, A.C. 1998 *Ireland, 1905–1925, Vol. II*. Newtownards.

Herlihy, J. 1997 *The Royal Irish Constabulary*. Dublin.

Herlihy, J. 1999 *The Royal Irish Constabulary: a complete alphabetical list of officers and men, 1816–1922*. Dublin.

Herlihy, J. 2001 *The Dublin Metropolitan Police: a complete alphabetical list of officers and men, 1836–1925*. Dublin.

Hezlet, Sir A. 1973 *The B-Specials: a history of the Ulster Special Constabulary*. London.

Hittle, B.E. 2011 *Michael Collins and the Anglo-Irish War: Britain's counter-insurgency failure*. Chicago.

Hobson, B. 1931 The origin of Óglaigh na hÉireann. *An tÓglach* (June 1931).

Holt, E. 1960 *Protest in arms: the Irish Troubles, 1916–1923*. London.

Hopkinson, M. 1988 *Green against green: a history of the Irish Civil War*. Dublin.

Hopkinson, M.A. 1990 The Craig–Collins pacts of 1922: two attempted reforms of the Northern Ireland government. *Irish Historical Studies* 27 (106).

Hopkinson, M. 1993a President Woodrow Wilson and the Irish Question. *Studia Hibernica* 27.

Hopkinson, M. 1993b Review article: Biography of the revolutionary period: Michael Collins and Kevin Barry. *Irish Historical Studies* 28 (111).

Hopkinson, M. 2004 *The Irish War of Independence*. Dublin.

Horgan, J.J. 1997 *Lemass*. Dublin.

Hyde, H.M. 1953 *Carson*. London.

Irish Free State Official Handbook, *Saorstát Éireann* (Dublin, 1932).

Jackson, A. 1993 *Sir Edward Carson*. Dublin.

Jackson, A. 1999 *Ireland: 1798–1998*. Oxford.

Jenkins, R. 1964 *Asquith*. London.

Jones, T. 1951 *Lloyd George*. London.

Jones, T. 1971 *Whitehall Diary, Vol. III. Ireland, 1918–1925*. Oxford.

Jordan, A.J. 2007 *W.T. Cosgrave: founder of modern Ireland*. Westport.

Kautt, W.H. 1999 *The Anglo-Irish War, 1916–1921*. Westport CT and London.

Kavanagh, S. 1969 The Irish Volunteers' intelligence organisation. *Capuchin Annual* (1969).

Kearney, R. 1980 The IRA's strategy of failure. *The Crane Bag* (1980).

Kearns, K. 1994 *Dublin tenement life: an oral history*. Dublin.

Kearns, K. 1997 *Dublin street life and lore*. Dublin.

Kearns, L. 1922 *In times of peril* (ed. A.P. Smithson). Dublin.

Kearns, M. 2001 Mary (98) recalls her vigil the day Kevin Barry was hanged. *Irish*

Independent, 13 October 2001.

Keatinge, P. 1978 *A place among the nations.* Dublin.

Kee, R. 1972 *The green flag* (combining three separate volumes entitled *The most distressful country*, *The bold Fenian men* and *Ourselves alone*). London.

Kee, R. 1981 *Ireland: a history.* London.

Kelly, J. 1980 We were framed. *Hibernia*, 31 July 1980.

Kelly, M. 2008 Nationalism's pilot light? *History Ireland* 16 (6).

Kenna, G.B. 1922 *Facts and figures of the Belfast pogrom.* Dublin.

Kenny, M. 2007 Michael Collins's religious faith. *Studies* 96 (384).

Keogh, D. 1987 The Treaty split and the Paris-Irish Race Convention. *Études Irlandaises* 12.

Keogh, D. 2005 *Twentieth-century Ireland: revolution and state-building.* Dublin.

The Kerryman 1947a *Dublin's fighting story, 1916–1921, told by the men who made it.* Tralee.

The Kerryman 1947b *Kerry's fighting story, 1916–1921.* Tralee.

The Kerryman 1948 *Limerick's fighting story, 1916–1921.* Tralee.

The Kerryman 1961 *Rebel Cork's fighting story, 1916–1921.* Tralee.

The Kerryman 1971 *Sworn to be free: the complete book of IRA jailbreaks, 1918–1921.* Tralee.

Kissane, B. 2005 *Politics of the Irish Civil War.* Oxford.

Kline, B. 1993 Churchill and Collins 1919–1922: admirers or adversaries? *History Ireland* 1 (3).

Knirk, J. 1997 *Ghosts and realities: female TDs and the Treaty debate.* New Jersey.

Knirk, J. 2006 *Women of the Dáil.* Dublin.

Kohn, L. 1932 *The constitution of the Irish Free State.* London.

Kostick, C. 1996 *Revolution in Ireland: popular militancy, 1917 to 1923.* London.

Kotsonouris, M. 1994a *Retreat from revolution: the Dáil courts, 1920–1924.* Dublin.

Kotsonouris, M. 1994b Revolutionary justice: the Dáil Éireann courts. *History*

Ireland 2 (3).

Kotsonouris, M. 2000 The George Gavan Duffy Papers. *History Ireland* 8 (4).

Laffan, M. 1970 The Sinn Féin Party. *Capuchin Annual* (1970).

Laffan, M. 1971 The unification of Sinn Féin in 1917. *Irish Historical Studies* 17.

Laffan, M. 1983 *The partition of Ireland, 1911–1925.* Dundalk.

Laffan, M. 1999 *The resurrection of Ireland: the Sinn Féin Party, 1916–1923.* Cambridge.

Larkin, F.M. 2006 A great daily organ: The *Freeman's Journal*, 1763–1924. *History Ireland* 14 (3).

Lavelle, P. 1961 *James O'Mara: a staunch Sinn Féiner.* Dublin.

Lavery, B. 2001 Irish rebury 10 republicans hanged by British in 1920s. *New York Times*, 15 October 2001.

Lavery, Sir J. 1940 *The life of a painter.* Boston.

Lawlor, S. 1980 Ireland from Truce to Treaty, war or peace? July to October 1921. *Irish Historical Studies* 22.

Lawson, Lt Gen. Sir H. 1921 *A report on the Irish situation* (pamphlet). London.

Lawson, Lt Gen. Sir H. (n.d.) *A second report on the situation* (pamphlet). London.

Lee, J.J. 2001 De Valera's use of words: three case-studies. *Radharc* 2.

Lee, J. and Ó Tuathaigh, G. 1982 *The age of de Valera.* Dublin.

Leeson, D. 2003 Death in the afternoon: the Croke Park Massacre, 21 November 1920. *Canadian Journal of History* 38 (1).

Leiberson, G. (ed.) 1966 *The Irish uprising, 1916–1922.* New York.

Lenihan, E. 1991 *Defiant Irish women.* Cork.

Linge, J. 1998 The Royal Navy and the Irish Civil War. *Irish Historical Studies* 31 (121).

Linklater, A. 1980 *An unhusbanded life: Charlotte Despard, suffragette, socialist, and Sinn Féiner.* London.

Lowe, W.J. (n.d.) *Disbandment and after: the old RIC in the new Free State.*

Luddy, M. 1995 *Hanna Sheehy Skeffington.* Dundalk.

Luddy, M. and Murphy, C. 1990 *Women*

surviving: studies in Irish women's history in the 19th and 20th centuries. Dublin.

Lynch, D. 1957 *The IRB and the 1916 insurrection* (ed. F. O'Donoghue). Cork.

Lynch, R. 2004 The Clones affray, 1922: massacre or invasion? *History Ireland* 12 (3).

MacAodh, S. 2001a IRA wipe out 'G' Division. *An Phoblacht*, 6 September 2001.

MacAodh, S. 2001b Terence MacSwiney. *An Phoblacht*, 25 October 2001.

MacAodh, S. 2001c Murder in the Castle. *An Phoblacht*, 22 November 2001.

Macardle, D. 1923 Military Prison, North Dublin Union, 1 May 1923. *Éire-Ireland*, 26 May 1923.

Macardle, D. 1924 *Tragedies of Kerry, 1922– 1923* (reprinted 1998). Dublin.

Macardle, D. 1937 *The Irish Republic* (reprinted 1965). New York.

MacAtasney, G. 2005 *Seán MacDiarmada, the mind of the revolution*. Dublin.

McCann, J. 1938 Burning of the Custom House. *The Kerryman*, 17 March 1938.

McCartan, P. 1932 *With de Valera in America*. Dublin.

McCartan, P. (ed.) 1964–5 Extracts from the papers of Dr Patrick McCartan. *Clogher Record* (1964 and 1965).

McCarthy, J.R. 2006 *Kevin O'Higgins*. Dublin.

McCarthy, P.J. 1989 The RAF and Ireland, 1920–1922. *Irish Sword* 17.

McColgan, J. 1980 Partition and the Irish administration, 1920–1922. *Administration* 28.

McColgan, J. 1997 Implementing the 1921 Treaty, Lionel Curtis and the constitutional procedure. *Irish Historical Studies* 20 (79).

McConnell, J. and McGarry, F. 2008 Difficulties and opportunities: making sense of the Fenians. *History Ireland* 16 (6).

McCoole, S. 1996 *Hazel: a life of Lady Lavery*. Dublin.

McCoole, S. 1997 *Guns and chiffon*. Dublin.

McCoole, S. 2003 *No ordinary women: Irish female activists in the revolutionary years.*

Dublin.

Macready, Gen. Sir N. 1924 *Annals of an active life* (2 vols). London.

McDermott, J. 2001 *Northern divisions: the Old IRA and the Belfast pogroms, 1920– 1922.* Belfast.

MacDonnacha, M. 2002a Civil War executions begin. *An Phoblacht*, 28 November 2002.

MacDonnacha, M. 2002b Partitionist states established. *An Phoblacht*, 5 December 2002.

MacDonnacha, M. 2002c The Civil War— 80th anniversary—Part 3. *An Phoblacht*, 12 December 2002.

MacDonnacha, M. 2002d The Civil War— 80th Anniversary—Part 4. *An Phoblacht*, 19 December 2002.

McDonnell, K.K. 1972 *There is a bridge at Bandon*. Cork.

McDonnell, V. 2008 *Michael Collins: most wanted man*. Cork.

McDowell, R.B. 1970 *The Irish convention of 1917–1918*. London.

MacDowell, V. 1997 *Michael Collins and the Irish Republican Brotherhood*. Dublin.

Mac Eoin, A. 2001 Terence MacSwiney. *An Phoblacht*, 25 October 2001.

MacEoin, U. (ed.) 1980 *Survivors*. Dublin.

McGarry, F. 2006 Keeping an eye on the usual suspects: Dublin Castle's 'Personality Files', 1899–1921. *History Ireland* 14 (6).

McGee, O. 2005 *The IRB: the Irish Republican Brotherhood from the Land League to Sinn Féin*. Dublin.

MacGiolla, C. (ed.) 1966 *Intelligence notes 1913–1916 preserved in the State Paper Office*. Dublin.

McGreevey, R. and Collins, S. 2014 Gunman believed to have killed Michael Collins was granted a military pension. *Irish Times*, 3 October 2014.

McGuigan, J. 2011 Michael Collins on file? *History Ireland* 19 (4).

McHugh, R. (ed.) 1966 *Dublin, 1916*. London.

McInerney, M. 1967 James Ryan. *Irish Times*, 15–17 March 1967.

McInerney, M. 1968 Gerald Boland's story.

Irish Times, 8–19 October 1968.

McInerney, M. 1974 Seán MacEntee. *Irish Times*, 22–25 July 1974.

Mackay, J. 1996 *Michael Collins: a life.* Edinburgh.

McKeane, I. 1995 Michael Collins and the media: then and now. *History Ireland* 3 (3).

McKenna, K. 1970 The Irish Bulletin. *Capuchin Annual* (1970).

McKillen, B. 1982 Irish feminism and national separatism. *Éire-Ireland* 17.

McLaughlin, T. 2006 The aftermath. *An Cosantóir* (April/May 2006).

MacLysaght, E. 1967 Larkin, Connolly and the Labour Movement. In F.X. Martin (ed.), *Leaders and men of the Easter Rising, Dublin 1916.* London.

McMahon, Msgr J.T. 1970 *The cream of their race: Irish truce negotiations, December 1920–January 1921* (pamphlet). Ennis.

MacManus, M.J. 1944 *Éamon de Valera.* Dublin.

McManus, R. 2002 *Dublin 1910–1940: shaping the city and suburbs.* Dublin.

McNiffe, L. 1997 *A history of the Garda Síochána.* Dublin.

Macready, Gen. Sir N. 1925–42 *Annals of an active life* (2 vols). London.

McRedmond, L. (ed.) 1992 *Ireland: the revolutionary years. Photographs from the Cashman Collection, Ireland, 1910–1930.* Dublin.

MacSwiney, T. 1921 *Principles of freedom* (reprinted 1936). Dublin.

MacThomais, É. 1965 *Down Dublin streets, 1916.* Dublin.

McVeigh, J. 1998 Constance Markievicz: aiming for the stars. *An Phoblacht*, 17 September 1998.

Maguire, C.A. 1984 The Republican courts. *Capuchin Annual* (1984).

Maher, J. 1998 *Harry Boland, a biography.* Cork.

Malone, J. 1996 *Blood on the flag: an autobiography of a freedom fighter* (trans. P.J. Twohig). Ballincollig.

Malone, T. 2000 *Alias Seán Forde.* Danesfort.

Malouf, M. 2002 With Dev in America:

Sinn Féin and recognition politics, 1919–21. *Interventions: International Journal of Postcolonial Studies* 4 (1).

Mangran, H.C. 1935 John Chartres. *Irish Independent*, 25 October 1935.

Mansergh, N. 1991 *The unresolved question: the Anglo-Irish settlement and its undoing, 1912–1972.* New Haven.

Marjoribanks, E. 1932 *Life of Lord Carson*, Vol. I. London. (See Colvin 1934 for Vols II and III.)

Markievicz, Countess C. 1918 *A call to the women of Ireland.* Dublin.

Markievicz, Countess C. 1926 Cumann na mBan. *Cumann na mBan* 11 (10).

Marreco, A. 1967 *The rebel countess: the life and times of Constance Markievicz.* London.

Martin, F.X. (ed.) 1963 *The Irish Volunteers.* Dublin.

Martin, F.X. (ed.) 1967 *Leaders and men of the Easter Rising.* London.

Matthews, A. 2010 *The Kimmage Garrison, 1916: making billy-can bombs at Larkfield.* Dublin.

Maume, P. 2001 From deference to citizenship: Irish republicanism, 1870–1923. *The Republic* 2.

Maye, B. 1997 *Arthur Griffith.* Dublin.

Meehan, C. 2010 *The Cosgrave Party. A history of Cumann na nGaedheal, 1923–1933.* Dublin.

Middlemas, K. (ed.) 1971 *Tom Jones Whitehall Diary.* London.

Mills, M. 1969 Seán Lemass looks back. *Irish Press*, 20 January–6 February 1969.

Mitchell, A. 1974 *Labour in Irish politics.* Dublin.

Mitchell, A. 1995 *Revolutionary government in Ireland: Dáil Éireann, 1919–1922.* Dublin.

Mitchell, D. 1966 *Women on the warpath.* London.

Moran, M. 2010 *Executed for Ireland: the Patrick Moran story.* Cork.

Morgan, E. 1998 Ireland's lost action hero: Michael Collins, a secret history of Irish masculinity. *New Hibernia Review* 2 (1).

Moylan, S. 2003 *Seán Moylan: in his own words.* Millstreet.

Moynihan, M. (ed.) 1980 *The speeches and*

statements by Éamon de Valera, 1917–1973.
Dublin.

Mulcahy, Gen. R. 1968 Conscription and the General Headquarters staff. *Capuchin Annual* (1968).

Mulcahy, Gen. R. 1970a Chief of Staff, 1919. *Capuchin Annual* (1970).

Mulcahy, Gen. R. 1970b The development of the Irish Volunteers, 1916–1922. *An Cosantóir* 40.

Mulcahy, R. 1976 Michael Collins and the making of a new Ireland. A paper read to the Irish Historical Society, 10 February 1976. *Studies* (Autumn 1976).

Mulcahy, R. 1999 *Richard Mulcahy (1886–1971): a family memoir.* Dublin.

Mulcahy, R. 2003 The Mulcahy tapes and papers. *History Ireland* 8 (1).

Mulcahy, R. 2008 Mulcahy and Collins—a conjunction of opposites. *History Ireland* 13 (2).

Mulcahy, R. 2009 *My father, the general, and the military history of the revolution.* Dublin.

Mulholland, M. 2002 *The politics and relationships of Kathleen Lynn.* Dublin.

Mulvihill, M. 1989 *Charlotte Despard.* London.

Murdoch, R. 1971 Robert Barton. *Sunday Press*, 26 September–3 October 1971.

Murphy, B. 1994 The First Dáil Éireann. *History Ireland* 2 (1).

Murphy, B.P. 1995 *John Chartres: mystery man of the Treaty.* Dublin.

Murphy, B.P. 2006 *The origin and organisation of British propaganda in Ireland, 1920.* Dublin.

Murphy, Major H.L. 1946 Countess Markievicz. *An Cosantóir* (June 1946).

Myles, W. 1960 The Irish Christian Brothers. In Irish Christian Brothers, *St Mary's, Clonmel, Centenary Record, 1860–1960.*

Nankivell, J.M. and Loch, S. 1922 *Ireland in turmoil.* London.

Neeson, E. 1966 *The Civil War in Ireland.* Cork.

Neeson, E. 1968 *The life and death of Michael Collins.* Cork.

Neeson, E. 1998 *Birth of a republic.* Dublin.

Neligan, D. 1999 *The spy in the castle.*
London.

Nelson, J. 1997 *Michael Collins: the final days.* Dublin.

Nevinson, H. 1921 The Anglo-Irish War. *Contemporary Review* 667.

Newsinger, J. 1978 I bring not peace but a sword: the religious motif in the Irish War of Independence. *Journal of Modern History* 13.

Ni Chumnaill, E. 1933 The history of Cumann na mBan. *An Phoblacht*, 8 April 1933.

Ni Dheirg, I. 1978 *The story of Michael Collins.* Cork.

Nic Shiubhlaigh, M. 1955 *The splendid years* (as told to Edward Kenny). Dublin.

Nolan, D. (ed.) 1946 *With the IRA in the fight for freedom.* Tralee.

Norman, D. 1988 *Terrible beauty: a life of Constance Markievicz.* London.

Norris, D. 2012 *A kick against the pricks.* Dublin.

Novak, R. 2008 Keepers of important secrets: the Ladies Committee of the IRB. *History Ireland* 16 (6).

Nunan, E. 1967 The Kimmage Garrison. *An tÓglach* (Winter 1967).

Nunan, S. 1970 President de Valera's mission to the USA, 1919–20. *Capuchin Annual* (1970).

O'Beirne-Ranelagh, J. 1976 The IRB from Treaty to 1924. *Irish Historical Studies* 20 (77).

O'Brien, G. 1993 The record of the first Dáil debates. *Irish Historical Studies* 28 (111).

Ó Broin, L. 1980 *Michael Collins.* Dublin.

Ó Broin, L. 1983 *In great haste: letters of Michael Collins and Kitty Kiernan.* Dublin.

Ó Broin, L. 1989 *W.E. Wylie and the Irish revolution, 1916–1921.* Dublin.

O'Carroll, J.P. and Murphy, J.A. (eds) 1983 *De Valera and his times.* Cork.

Ó Ceallaigh, S.T. 1961 Memoirs. *Irish Press*, 3 July–9 August 1961.

Ó Ceallaigh, S.T. 1963 The founding of the Irish Volunteers. *Capuchin Annual* (1963).

Ó Ceallaigh, S.T. 1973 *Seán T.* Dublin.

O'Ceirin, K. and O'Ceirin, C. 1996 *Women of Ireland.* Galway.

O'Connor, B. 1929 *With Michael Collins in the fight for independence.* London.

O'Connor, F. 1969 *The Big Fellow* (reprinted 1979). London.

O'Connor, U. 1981 [1975] *A terrible beauty is born: the Irish Troubles, 1912–1922.* London.

O'Connor, U. 1996 *Michael Collins and the Troubles.* New York.

O'Doherty, L. 1970 Dublin, 1920. *Capuchin Annual* (1970).

O'Donnell, J. 1990–1 Recollections based on the diary of an Irish Volunteer. *Cathair na Mart: Journal of the Westport Historical Society* **10** (1) (1990); **11** (1991).

O'Donoghue, F. 1954 *No other law* (reprinted 1986). Dublin.

O'Donoghue, F. 1963 Guerrilla warfare in Ireland. *An Cosantóir* **23**.

O'Donoghue, F. 1967 The reorganisation of the Volunteers. *Capuchin Annual* (1967).

O'Donoghue, F. 1971a *Tomás MacCurtain, soldier and patriot.* Tralee.

O'Donoghue, F. (ed.) 1971b *IRA jailbreaks 1918–1921.* Cork.

O'Donovan, D. 1989 *Kevin Barry and his time.* Glendale.

Ó Dubhghaill, M. 1966 *Insurrection fires at Eastertide.* Cork.

Ó Duigneain, P. 1991 Linda Kearns—the Sligo nurse in the 1916 Rising. *Sligo Champion,* 5 April 1991.

Ó Duigneain, P. 2002 *Linda Kearns.* Manorhamilton.

Ó hEochaidh, É. (n.d.) *Liam Mellows* (booklet).

O'Faolain, S. 1933 *The life of de Valera.* Dublin.

O'Faolain, S. 1934 *Constance Markievicz.* London.

O'Faolain, S. 1939 *De Valera.* London.

O'Farrell, B. 1971 *The founding of Dáil Éireann.* Dublin.

O'Farrell, P. 1981 *The Seán MacEoin story.* Dublin.

O'Farrell, P. 1983 *The Ernie O'Malley story.* Dublin.

O'Farrell, P. 1993 *Seán MacEoin: the blacksmith of Ballinalee.* Mullingar.

O'Farrell, P. 1997 *Who's who in the Irish War of Independence and Civil War.* Dublin.

O'Farrell, P. 1978 *Memoirs of Irish Volunteer activity, 1917–1924.* New York.

O'Hegarty, P.S. 1919 *Sinn Féin: an illumination.* Dublin and London.

O'Hegarty, P.S. 1924 *The victory of Sinn Féin* (reprinted 1998). Dublin.

O'Higgins, B. 1925 *The soldier's story of Easter Week.* Dublin.

O'Higgins, K. 1922 *Civil War and the events that led to it.* Dublin.

Ó Luing, S. 1970 *I die in a good cause: a study of Thomas Ashe, idealist and revolutionary.* Tralee.

O'Mahony, S. 1987 *Frongoch, university of revolution* (reprinted 1995). Killiney.

O'Mahony, S. 2000a *The burning of the Custom House in Dublin, 1921.* Dublin.

O'Mahony, S. 2000b *Three murders in Dublin Castle* (pamphlet). Dublin.

O'Mahony, S. 2001 *The first hunger strike— Thomas Ashe, 1917.* Dublin.

O'Mahony, S. 2005 *Three murders in Dublin Castle, 1920.* Dublin.

O'Malley, C.K.H. 1989 Ernie O'Malley autobiographical letter. *Cathair na Mart: Journal of the Westport Historical Society* **9** (1).

O'Malley, C. 2010 *The men will talk to me.* Cork.

O'Malley, C.H.K. and Dolan, A. (eds) 2007 *No surrender here! The Civil War papers of Ernie O'Malley.* Dublin.

O'Malley, E. 1936 *On another man's wound* (reprinted 1979). Dublin.

O'Malley, E. 1939 *An army without banners: adventures of an Irish Volunteer.* Dublin.

O'Malley, E. 1978 *The singing flame.* Dublin.

O'Malley, E. 1982 *Raids and rallies.* Dublin.

O'Meara, M. 1995 *Bloody Sunday, 1920– 1995: a commemorative booklet.* Dublin.

O'Neill, M. 2000 *Grace Gifford Plunkett and Irish freedom: tragic bride of 1916.* Dublin.

Ó Neill, T. and Ó Fiannachta, P. 1968–70 *De Valera* (2 vols). Dublin.

Ó Rahilly, A. 1991 The Civil War: a teenager's recollections 70 years on. *Tipperary Historical Review* (1991).

Ó Rahilly, The 1915 The history of the Irish Volunteers. *Gaelic American,* 2

January 1915.

Ó Riain, S. 1969 Dáil Éireann, 1919. *Capuchin Annual* (1969).

O'Rourke, P. 1999 Remembering the past: Fitzgerald, Murphy and MacSwiney. *An Phoblacht*, 2 November 1999.

Ó Ruairc, L. 2004 Did the Black and Tans run from the rifles of the IRA? *History Ireland* 12 (2).

Ó Snodaigh, A. 1997a General amnesty—1917. *An Phoblacht*, 13 June 1997.

Ó Snodaigh, A. 1997b Sir Henry Wilson executed. *An Phoblacht*, 19 June 1997.

Ó Snodaigh, A. 1999a Electoral success—the first step. *An Phoblacht*, 17 June 1999.

Ó Snodaigh, A. 1999b The Mansion House 'Irish Assembly'. *An Phoblacht*, 8 July 1999.

Ó Snodaigh, A. 1999c Unbroken and unbowed—the POWs return home. *An Phoblacht*, 22 July 1999.

Ó Snodaigh, A. 1999d Sinn Féin and Sinn Féin. *An Phoblacht*, 30 September 1999.

Ó Snodaigh, A. 1999e Usk jail death, 1918. *An Phoblacht*, 2 December 1999.

Ó Snodaigh, A. 2000a The Declaration of Independence. *An Phoblacht*, 13 January 2000.

Ó Snodaigh, A. 2000b An Chead Dáil Éireann opens. *An Phoblacht*, 20 January 2000.

Ó Snodaigh, A. 2000c Ireland's independence declared. *An Phoblacht*, 27 January 2000.

Ó Snodaigh, A. 2000d An Address to Free Nations. *An Phoblacht*, 3 February 2000.

Ó Snodaigh, A. 2000e The democratic programme. *An Phoblacht*, 9 March 2000.

Ó Snodaigh, A. 2000f The first cabinet. *An Phoblacht*, 16 March 2000.

Ó Snodaigh, A. 2000g Press coverage for First Dáil. *An Phoblacht*, 30 March 2000.

Ó Snodaigh, A. 2000h Remembering the past: the 1917 IRA Convention. *An Phoblacht*, 27 April 2000.

O'Sullivan, M. 1994 *Seán Lemass*. Dublin.

O'Sullivan, N. 2007 *Every dark hour: a history of Kilmainham Gaol*. Dublin.

O'Sullivan, P. and Lee, F. 1958 The execution of Field Marshal Sir Henry

Wilson: the facts. *Sunday Press*, 10 August 1958.

Osborne, C. 2003 *Michael Collins, himself.* Douglas, Co. Cork.

Osborne, C. 2007 *The Michael Collins album: a life in pictures.* Cork.

Packenham, F. (Lord Longford) 1935 *Peace by ordeal* (reprinted 1972). London.

Packenham, F. (Lord Longford) and O'Neill, T.P. 1970 *Éamon de Valera: a biography.* Dublin.

Packenham, T. 1969 *The year of liberty.* London.

Pearse, P.H. 1922 *Collected works of Patrick H. Pearse: plays, stories, and poems* (5th edn). Dublin.

Phelan, S. 2014 Michael Collins's 'killer' met him twice. *Irish Independent*, 2 October 2014.

Phoenix, E. 1994 *Northern nationalism: nationalist politics, partition and the Catholic minority in Northern Ireland, 1890–1940.* Belfast.

Pinkman, J.A. 1998 *In the legion of the vanguard* (ed. F.E. Maguire). Dublin.

Rees, R. 1998 *Ireland, 1905–25. Volume I. Text and historiography.* Newtownards.

Regan, J. 1995 Looking at Mick again—demilitarising Michael Collins. *History Ireland* 3 (3).

Regan, J. 1999 *The Irish counter-revolution, 1921–1936.* Dublin.

Ring, J. 1996 *Erskine Childers.* London.

Robins, J. 1993 *Custom House people.* Dublin.

Roper, E. (ed.) 1987 *Prison letters of Countess Markievicz.* London.

Ryan, A. 2006 *Comrades: inside the War of Independence.* Dublin.

Ryan, D. 1934 *Remembering Sion.* London.

Ryan, D. 1936 *Unique dictator: a study of Éamon de Valera.* London.

Ryan, D. 1949 *The Rising: the complete story of Easter Week.* Dublin.

Ryan, D. 1968 *Michael Collins: the invisible army.* Tralee.

Ryan, L. and Ward, M. (eds) 2004 *Irish women and nationalism: soldiers, new women and wicked hags.* Dublin.

Ryan, L. and Ward, M. (eds) 2007 *Irish*

women and the vote. Dublin.

Ryan, M. 1982 *The Tom Barry story*. Dublin.

Ryan, M. 1989 *The day Michael Collins was shot*. Dublin.

Ryan, M. 1996 *Michael Collins and the women in his life*. Dublin. (Republished as *Michael Collins and the women who spied for Ireland* (Cork, 2007).)

Ryan, M. 2003 *Tom Barry: IRA freedom fighter*. Cork.

Ryan, M. 2005a *The real chief: the story of Liam Lynch*. Dublin.

Ryan, M. 2005b Tom Barry and the Kilmichael ambush. *History Ireland* 13 (5).

Ryan, M. 2007 *Michael Collins and the women who spied for Ireland*. Cork.

Ryan, M. 2011 The Commander-in-Chief's cap badge? *History Ireland* 19 (5).

Ryan, R. 1985 The man who stood next to Collins's killer. *Cork Examiner*, 5 November 1985.

Shaw, Revd F. 1972 The canon of Irish history: a challenge. *Studies: The Irish Jesuit Quarterly Review* (Summer 1972).

Sheehan, T. 1990 *Mrs Lindsay, lady hostage*. Dripsey.

Sheehan, T. 1993 *Execute hostage Compton-Smith*. Dripsey.

Sheehan, W. 2007 *Fighting for Dublin: the British battle for Dublin, 1919–1921*. Cork.

Sigerson, S.M. 2013 *The assassination of Michael Collins*. CreateSpace Independent Publishing.

Simon, Sir J.A. 1921 Irish reprisals: Auxiliary Division's record. *London Times*, 25 April 1921.

Sinead, J. 2007 *The IRA in Kerry: 1916–1921*. Cork.

Sinn Féin: a century of struggle (Dublin, 2005).

Smith, N.C. 2007 *Dorothy Macardle: a life*. Dublin.

Smyth, H.P. 1997 Kathleen Lynn, MD, FRCSI (1874–1955). *Dublin Historical Record* 30.

Stapleton, W.J. (Bill) 1969 Michael Collins's Squad. *Capuchin Annual* (1969).

Stephens, J. 1922 *Arthur Griffith, journalist and statesman*. Dublin.

Stewart, A.T.Q. 1981 *Edward Carson*. Dublin.

Stewart, A.T.Q. (ed.) 1997 *Michael Collins: the secret file*. Belfast.

Street, Major C.J.C. (writing under the pseudonym of 'I.O.') 1922a *The administration of Ireland, 1920*. London.

Street, Major C.J.C. 1922b *Ireland in 1921*. London.

Stubbs, J.O. 1990 The Unionists and Ireland, 1914–1918. *Historical Journal* 33.

Sturgis, M. 1999 *The last days of Dublin Castle: the Mark Sturgis diaries* (ed. Michael Hopkinson). Dublin.

Sugg, W. 1997a British Intelligence wiped out. *An Phoblacht*, 20 November 1997.

Sugg, W. 1997b Bloody Sunday. *An Phoblacht*, 27 November 1997.

Sugg, W. 1997c State executions. *An Phoblacht*, 11 December 1997.

Sugg, W. 1998 Death of Liam Lynch. *An Phoblacht*, 30 April 1998.

Sugg, W. 1999 Christmas Week ambush. *An Phoblacht*, 16 December 1999.

Taillon, R. 1996 *When history was made: the women of 1916*. Belfast.

Talbot, H. 1923 *Michael Collins' own story*. London.

Tallant, N. 2004 Dev tricked public into investing in *Irish Press*, file reveals. *Irish Independent*, 31 October 2004.

Tansill, C.C. 1957 *America and the fight for Irish freedom, 1866–1922*. New York.

Taylor, A.J.P. (ed.) 1971 *Lloyd George: twelve essays*. London.

Taylor, R. 1958 [1970] *Michael Collins*. London.

Taylor, R. 1961 *Assassination: the death of Sir Henry Wilson and the tragedy of Ireland*. London.

Thornton, Cmdt B.L. 1975 Women and the Army. *An Cosantóir* (November 1975).

Tierney, M. 1964 Eoin MacNeill: a biographical study. *Saint Patrick* (1964).

Toby, T. 1997 *Exemplary violence used in British colonial policy: one explanation for General John Maxwell's violent reaction to the Easter Rising of 1916*. Boston MA.

Towey, T. 1976 The reaction of the British government to the 1922 Collins/de

Valera pact. *Irish Historical Studies* 22 (65).

Townshend, C. 1975 *The British campaign in Ireland, 1919–1921.* Oxford.

Townsend, C. 1978–9 The Irish railway strike of 1920—industrial action and civil resistance in the struggle for independence. *Irish Historical Studies* 21.

Townshend, C. 1979a Bloody Sunday: Michael Collins speaks. *European Studies Review* 9.

Townshend, C. 1979b The Irish Republican Army and the development of guerrilla warfare, 1916–1921. *English Historical Review* 94.

Townshend, C. 1979c Martial law: legal and administrative problems of civil emergency in Britain and the Empire, 1800–1940. *Historical Journal* 25.

Townshend, C. 1983 *Political violence in Ireland: government and resistance since 1848.* Oxford.

Townshend, C. 1989 Military force and civil authority in the United Kingdom, 1914–1921. *Journal of British Studies* 28.

Townshend, C. 1998 The meaning of Irish freedom: constitutionalism in the Free State. *Transactions of the Royal Historical Society* (6th ser.) 8.

Townshend, C. 2013 *The Republic: the fight for Irish independence.* London.

Travers, P. 1988 *Settlements and divisions: Ireland, 1870–1922.* Dublin.

Travers, P. 1994 *Éamon de Valera.* Dublin.

Traynor, O. 1939 The burning of the Custom House—Dublin's fighting story. *The Kerryman* (1939).

Twohig, P.J. 1990 *The dark secret of Bealnablath: the Michael Collins story.* Ballincollig.

Twohig, P.J. 1994 *Green tears for Hecuba.* Cork.

Urquart, D. 2000 *Women in Ulster politics, 1890–1940.* Dublin.

Urquart, D. 2001 *Irish women's history reader.* Dublin.

Valiulis, M.G. 1992 *Portrait of a revolutionary: General Richard Mulcahy and the founding of the Irish Free State.* Blackrock.

Van Voris, J. 1967 *Constance de Markievicz: in the cause of Ireland.* Amherst MA.

Vane, Sir F. 1929 *Agin the government.* London.

Walsh, M. 2008 *The news from Ireland: foreign correspondents and the Irish revolution.* Dublin.

Walsh, O. 2002 *Ireland's independence, 1880–1923.* London.

Ward, A. 1974 Lloyd George and the 1918 Irish conscription crisis. *Historical Journal* 17.

Ward, M. 1983 *Unmanageable revolutionaries: women and Irish nationalism.* Dingle.

Ward, M. 1990 *Maud Gonne.* California.

Ward, M. 1996 The League of Women Delegates and Sinn Féin, 1917. *History Ireland* 4 (3).

Ward, M. 1997 *Hanna Sheehy Skeffington: a life.* Cork.

Ward, M. (ed.) 1995 *In their own voice* (reprinted 2001). Dublin.

Wells, W.B. 1917 *An Irish apologia: some thoughts on Anglo-Irish relations and the war.* Dublin.

Wells, W.B. 1919 *John Redmond: a biography.* London.

Wells, W.B. and Marlowe, N. 1916 *A history of the Irish rebellion of 1916.* Dublin.

White, T. deVere 1948 *Kevin O'Higgins* (reprinted 1986). London and Tralee.

Whyte, J.H. 1980 *Church and state in modern Ireland: 1922–1979.* Dublin.

Wilkinson, B. 1974 *The zeal of the convert: the life of Erskine Childers.* Washington DC.

Williams, A.F.B. 1921 A truce in Ireland. *Manchester Guardian*, 9 December 1921.

Williams, D.T. (ed.) 1966 *The Irish struggle, 1916–1921.* London.

Williams, D.T. (ed.) 1973 *Secret societies in Ireland.* Dublin.

Winter, O. 1955 *Winter's tale.* London.

Woodcock, C. 1921 *Experiences of an officer's wife in Ireland.* London.

Wright, F. 1988 *Northern Ireland: a comparative analysis.* Dublin.

Yeates, P. 2012 *A city in wartime, 1914–1918.* Dublin.

Yeates, P. 2014a *A city in turmoil, 1919–1921.* Dublin.

Yeates, P. 2014b Michael Collins's 'Secret

Service Unit' in the Trade Union movement. *History Ireland* **19** (3).

Yeates, P. 2015 *A city in civil war, 1921–1924.* Dublin.

Yeates, P. 2016 'Oh God, what did I do to deserve this?' The life and death of Detective Sergeant John Barton. *History Ireland* **24** (5).

Yeates, P. and Wren, J. 1989 *Michael Collins.* Dublin.

Younger, C. 1968 *Ireland's civil war.* London.

Younger, C. 1972 *A state of disunion.* London.

Younger, C. 1981 *Arthur Griffith.* Dublin.

INTERNET RESOURCES

Bloody Sunday, initial press reports: http://www.gaa.ie/centenary/bloody-sunday-archive/1920-initial-press-report-bloody-sunday/.

Department of the Taoiseach: http://www.taoiseach.gov.ie/index.asp?locID=383&docID=511.

Great Irish Journeys: Michael Collins: https://youtu.be/0qb1c5NXtwA.

Hang up your brightest colours: https://www.youtube.com/watch?v=jwNJ3aFZg44.

Hidden History: The Intelligence War in Dublin: https://www.youtube.com/watch?v=Q5eL4cL9Zt8&feature=em-subs_digest.

List of members of the Irish Republican Army: http://en.wikipedia.org/wiki/List_of_members_of_the_Irish_Republican_Army.

Michael Collins and the Intelligence War: http://www.generalmichaelcollins.com/life-times/rebellion/intelligence-war/.

Michael Collins, Ireland's Greatest: https://www.youtube.com/watch?v=vV2gzXhz8o8.

Michael Collins's Last Day: https://www.youtube.com/watch?v=0qb1c5NXtwA.

National Library of Ireland: http://www.nli.ie/1916/.

Ned Broy: The greatest spy of Ireland's freedom struggle: https://youtu.be/E1IEl7NarLw.

Shadow of Béal na mBláth: https://www.youtube.com/watch?v=k6Yv7zriFTw.

Index